PROGRESSIVE

Complete Learn To Play RHYTHM GUITAR Manual

by

Peter Gelling

CONTENTS

CONTENTS CONTINUED

CONTENTS CONTINUED

CONTENTS CONTINUED

For information about other books in this series, contact:

LTP Publishing Pty Ltd.
Email: info@learntoplaymusic.com
or visit our web page at:
www.learntoplaymusic.com

INTRODUCTION

Progressive COMPLETE LEARN TO PLAY RHYTHM GUITAR MANUAL is the ultimate Rhythm guitar manual. It assumes you have no prior knowledge of music or playing the Guitar, and will take you **from beginner to professional level**. In the course of the book you will learn **all the essential techniques of rhythm guitar in all styles of music**, along with how to read traditional music notation, guitar TAB, and rhythm notation. By the end of the book you will be ready to play in a band in any style, and will be ready for any musical situation.

The book is divided into sections, the first covering the basics of left and right hand technique, basic rhythms and chords, picking and music reading. The later sections deal with using the whole fretboard, using more advanced rhythms, chords and techniques, and playing in all keys in a variety of styles including Rock, Funk, Blues and Jazz. The accompanying CDs contain all the examples in the book so you can play along with them.

There is also a special section on tuning, an index of all chord types and a glossary of musical terms. Through the book you will have learned about many chord types and musical styles, so you may wish to learn more about some of them.

- To learn more about chords and their uses, see
  Complete Learn to Play Guitar Chords Manual.
- To learn more about lead guitar and improvising, see
  Complete Learn to Play Lead Guitar Manual.
- To learn more about Rock guitar and its related styles, see
  Complete Learn to Play Rock Guitar Manual.
- To learn more about Blues guitar and its related styles, see
  Complete Learn to Play Blues Guitar Manual.
- To learn more about fingerpicking with the right hand, see
  Complete Learn to Play Fingerpicking Guitar Manual.
- To learn more about Classical guitar, see
  Complete Learn to Play Classical Guitar Manual.
- To learn more about Jazz guitar, see
  Complete Learn to Play Jazz Guitar Manual.

All guitarists should know all of the information contained in this book.
The best and fastest way to learn is to use this book in conjunction with:

1. Buying sheet music and song books of your favourite recording artists and learning to play their songs.
2. Practicing and playing with other musicians. You will be surprised how good a basic drums/bass/guitar combination can sound even when playing easy music.
3. Learning by listening to your favourite CDs.

Also in the early stages it is helpful to have the guidance of an experienced teacher. This will also help you keep to a schedule and obtain weekly goals.

For more books and recordings by the author, check out **www.bentnotes.com**

USING THE COMPACT DISCS

This book comes with **two compact discs** which demonstrate almost all the examples in this book. The book shows you where to put your fingers and what technique to use and the recording lets you hear how each example should sound. Practice the examples slowly at first, gradually increasing tempo. Once you are confident you can play the example evenly without stopping the beat, try playing along with the recording. You will hear a drum beat at the beginning of each example, to lead you into the example and to help you keep time. To play along with the CD your guitar must be in tune with it (see page 232). If you have tuned using an electronic tuner (see below) your guitar will already be in tune with the CD. A small diagram of a compact disc with a number as shown below indicates a recorded example.

CD 2 **23.0** ← CD Track Number

ELECTRONIC TUNER

The easiest and most accurate way to tune your guitar is by using an **electronic tuner**. An electronic tuner allows you to tune each string individually to the tuner, by indicating whether the notes are sharp (too high) or flat (too low). If you have an electric guitar you can plug it directly in to the tuner. If you have an acoustic guitar, the tuner will have an inbuilt microphone. There are several types of electronic guitar tuners but most are relatively inexpensive and simple to operate. Tuning using other methods is difficult for beginning guitarists and it takes many months to master, so we recommend you purchase an electronic tuner, particularly if you do not have a guitar teacher or a friend who can tune it for you. Also if your guitar is way out of tune you can always take it to your local music store so they can tune it for you. Once a guitar has been tuned correctly it should only need minor adjustments before each practice session.

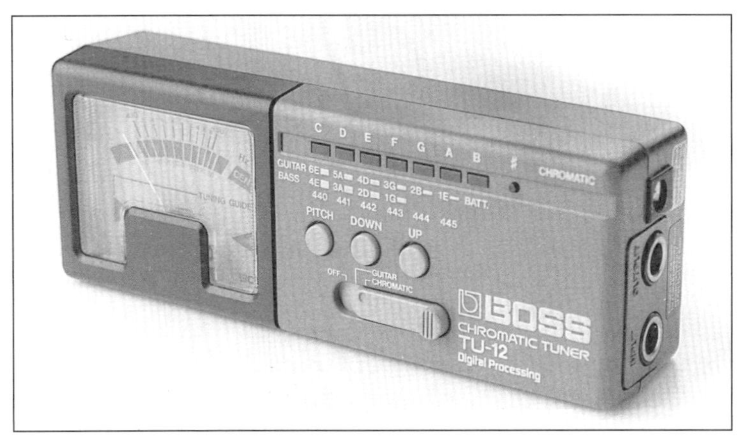

Electronic Tuner

TUNING YOUR GUITAR

Before you commence each lesson or practice session you will need to tune your guitar. If your guitar is out of tune everything you play will sound incorrect even though you are holding the correct notes. On the accompanying CD the **first track** contains the **six strings of the guitar**. For a complete description of how to tune your guitar, see page 232.

1. 6th String
E Note (Thickest string)

5th String
A Note

4th String
D Note

3rd String
G Note

2nd String
B Note

1st String
E Note (Thinnest string)

ACOUSTIC GUITARS

Classical Guitar
(Nylon Strings)

The **classical guitar** has nylon strings and a wider neck than the other types of guitar. It is most commonly used for playing Classical, Flamenco and Fingerstyles. Generally it is much cheaper than other types of guitar and is recommended for beginning guitarists.

Steel String Acoustic

The **steel string acoustic** has steel strings and is most commonly played by strumming or fingerpicking groups of notes called chords. This is the type of acoustic guitar you will hear in most modern styles of music e.g. Top 40 Rock and Pop music.

ELECTRIC GUITARS

Electric guitars have **pick-ups** (a type of inbuilt microphone) and need to be played into an **amplifier** (amp) to be heard.

The **solid body electric** is commonly used in Metal, Rock, Blues and Pop Music. Famous solid body guitars are the **Gibson Les Paul** and the **Fender Stratocaster**.

The **hollow body electric** (semi acoustic) is most commonly used in Jazz and Blues music.

Acoustic guitars can be amplified by using a microphone placed near the sound hole or by placing a portable pick-up on the body of the guitar e.g. for performances at large venues where the acoustic guitar needs amplification to be heard.

ELECTRIC GUITARS

Solid Body Electric

Hollow Body Electric
(semi acoustic)

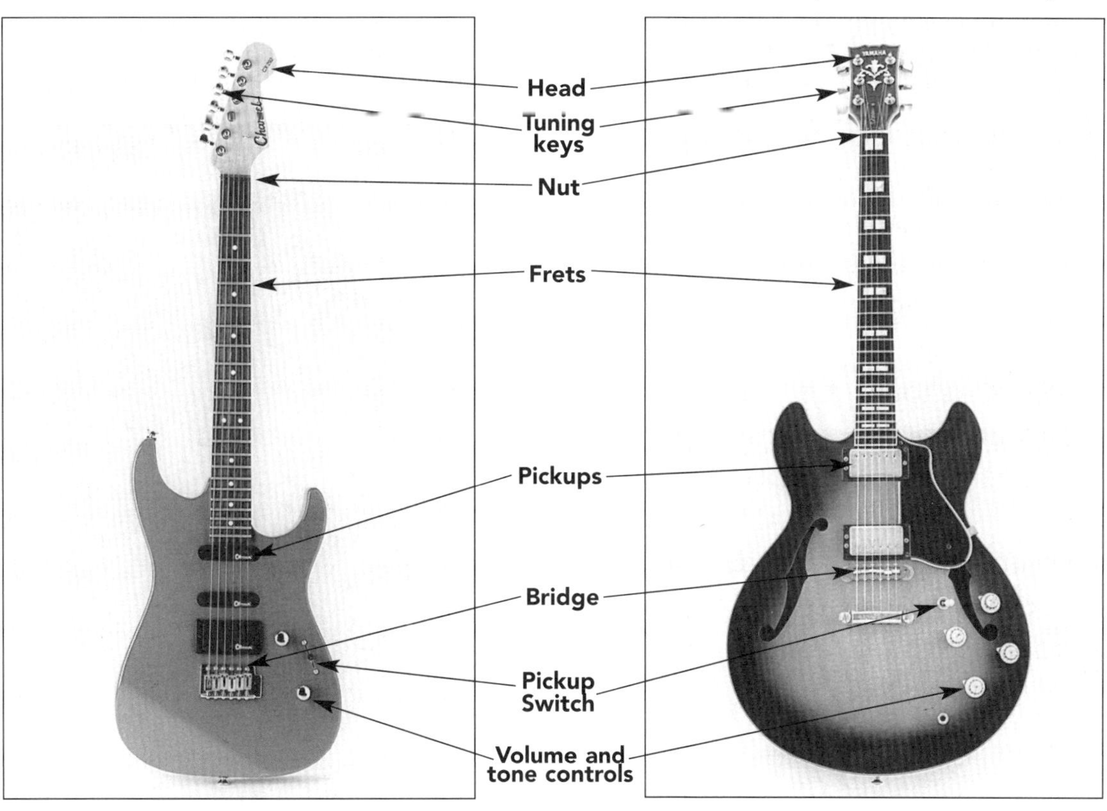

AMPLIFIERS

Combo
(combined amp and speaker)

Stack
(separate amp head and speaker)

STRINGS

It is important to have the correct set of strings fitted to your guitar, especially if you are a beginner. Until you build enough strength in your hands to fret the chords cleanly, light gauge or low tension strings are recommended. A reputable music store which sells guitar strings should be able to assist with this. Do not put steel strings on a classical guitar or it will damage the neck of the guitar. It is important to change your strings regularly, as old strings go out of tune easily and are more difficult to keep in tune.

HOW TO HOLD THE GUITAR

SITTING

1. Sit up straight on the front part of the chair as shown in the photo below.

2. Raise your right leg by crossing it over your left leg or by placing your right foot on a footstool (as shown in the photo below). Then place your guitar on your right leg.

3. The guitar should be close to your body in an upright position with the neck pointing slightly upwards.

The main aim is to be comfortable and have easy access to the guitar fretboard. A music stand will also be helpful.

STANDING

Use a wide guitar strap and adjust it to a comfortable length.

USING THE PICK

The right hand is used to play the strings by plucking them with a pick. A pick is a piece of plastic shaped like a triangle.

Hold the pick lightly between your **thumb and first finger**, as shown in the following photo.

Use the tip of the pick to play the string.

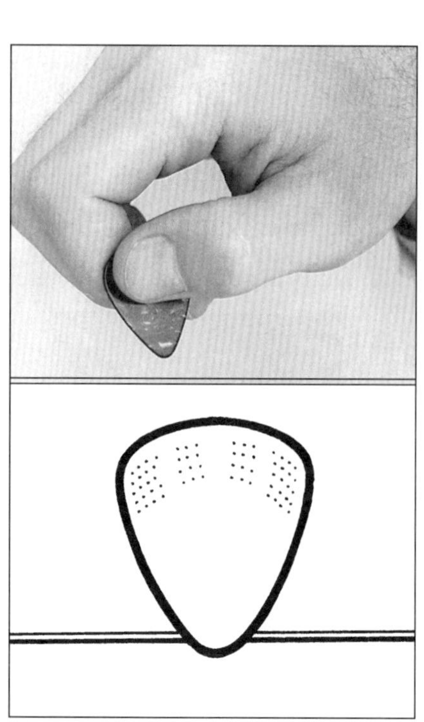

The correct position for your right arm is shown in the photos below. Notice that your forearm rests on the upper edge of the guitar, just below the elbow. Be careful not to have your elbow hanging over the face of the guitar, or your right hand too far along the fretboard. Also when you are playing single notes, support your right hand by placing the second and third fingers on the body of the guitar.

If you are playing an **acoustic** guitar, pick the strings over the sound hole as this makes the best sound.

If you are playing an **electric** guitar, pick the strings between the pick-ups.

ACOUSTIC

ELECTRIC

If you are strumming a chord, do not support your right hand with your fingers on the body of the guitar but still rest your forearm on the upper edge of the guitar.

LEFT HAND POSITION

The left hand fingers are numbered as such:

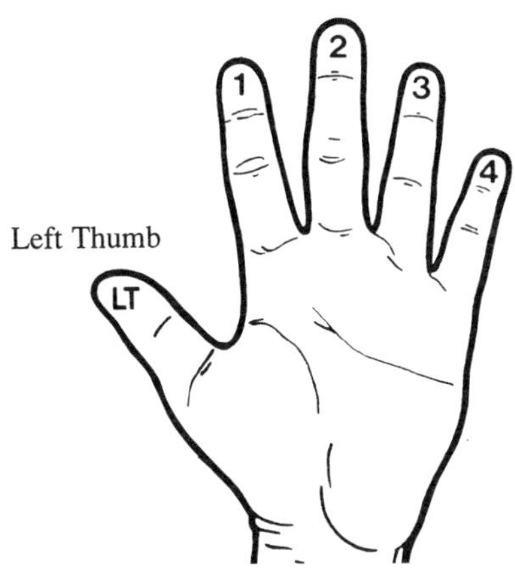

LEFT HAND PLACEMENT

Your fingers should be **ON THEIR TIPS** and placed just **BEHIND** the frets (not on top of them).

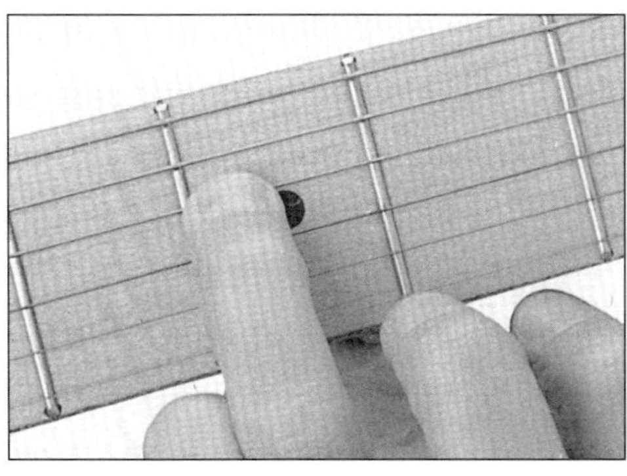

Be careful not to allow the thumb to hang too far over the top of the neck (Photo A), or to let it run parallel along the back of the neck (Photo B).

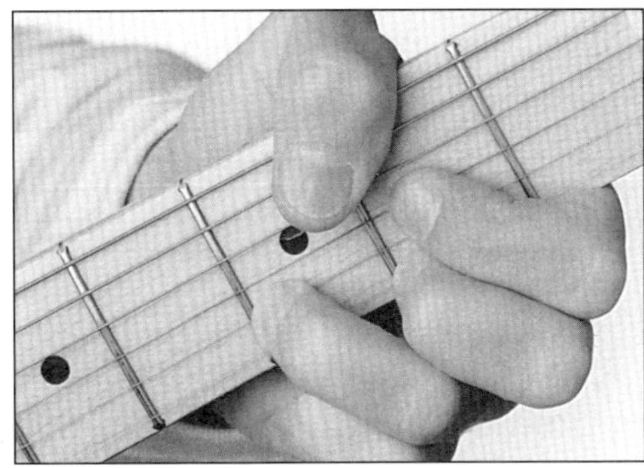

Photo A: INCORRECT

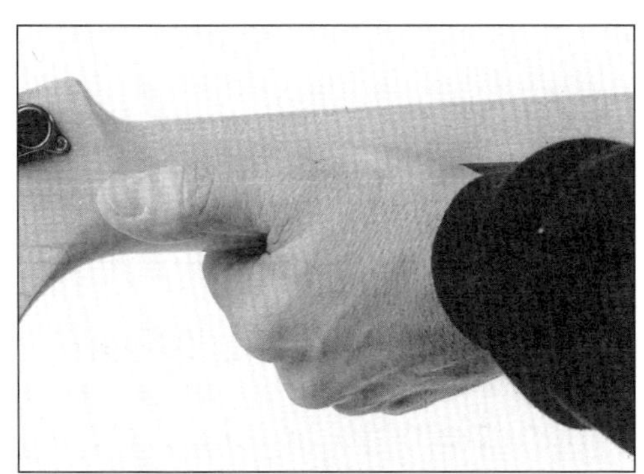

Photo B: INCORRECT

THE RUDIMENTS OF MUSIC

The musical alphabet consists of 7 letters: **A B C D E F G**

Music is written on a **staff**, which consists of 5 parallel lines between which there are 4 spaces.

MUSIC STAFF

The treble or 'G' clef is placed at the beginning of each staff line.

Treble or 'G' clef ⟶

This clef indicates the position of the note G. (It is an old fashioned method of writing the letter G, with the centre of the clef being written on the second staff line.)

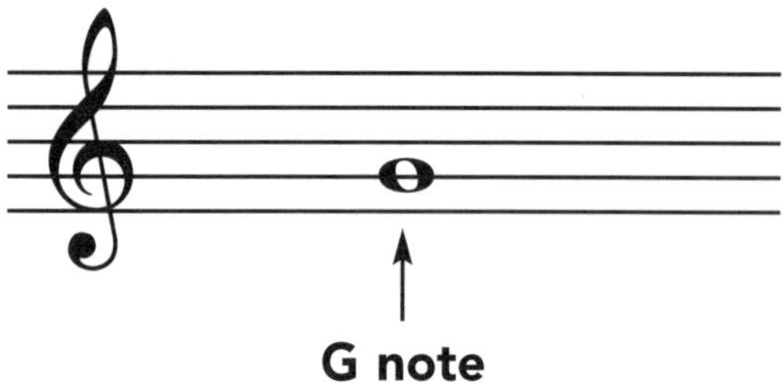

The other lines and spaces on the staff are named as such:

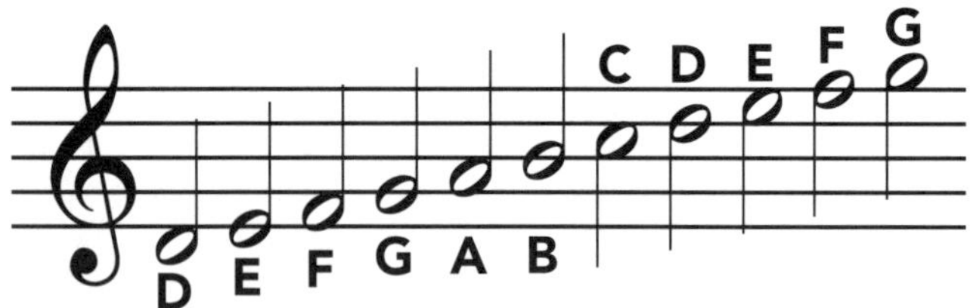

Extra notes can be added by the use of short lines, called **leger lines**.

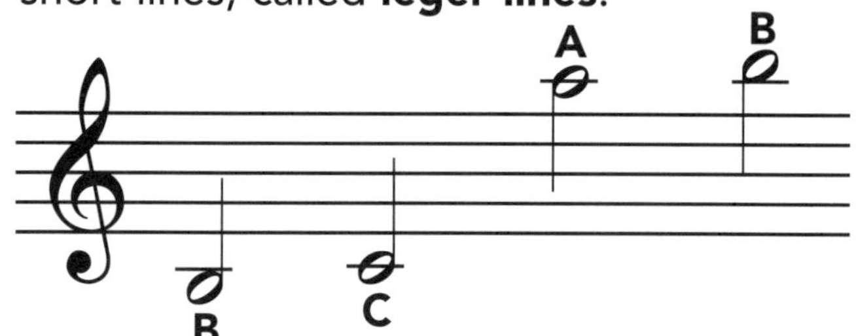

When a note is placed on the staff its head indicates its position, e.g.:

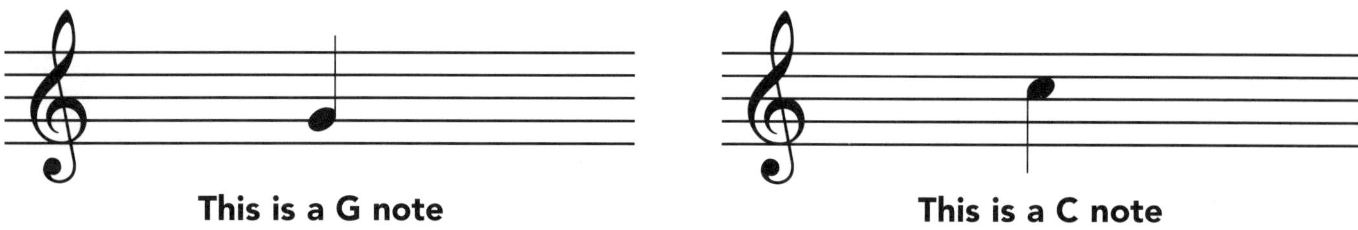

This is a G note **This is a C note**

When the note head is below the middle staff line the stem points upward and when the head is above the middle line the stem points downward. A note placed on the middle line (**B**) can have its stem pointing either up or down.

Bar lines are drawn across the staff, which divides the music into sections called **bars** or **measures**. A **double bar line** signifies either the end of the music, or the end of an important section of it.

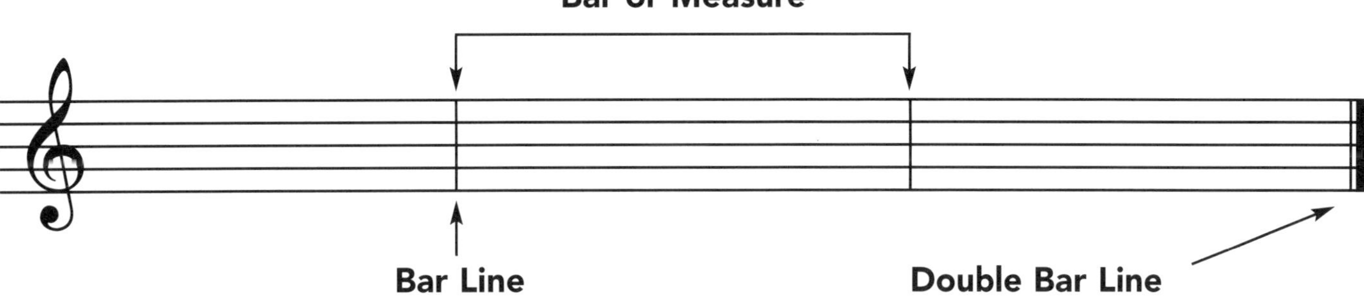

TIME SIGNATURES

At the beginning of each piece of music, after the treble clef, is the **time signature**.

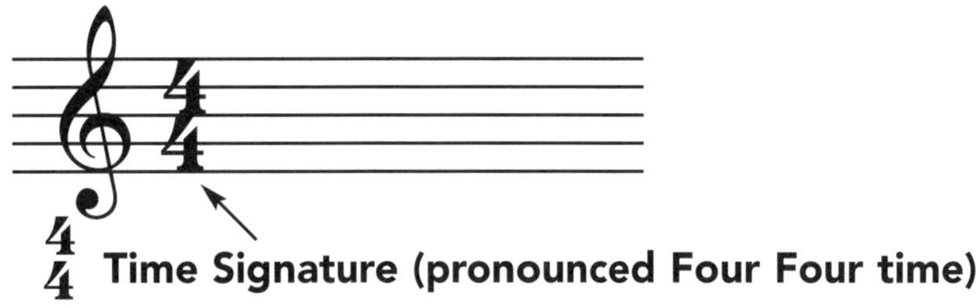

The time signature indicates the number of beats per bar (the top number) and the type of note receiving one beat (the bottom number). For example:

4 – this indicates 4 beats per bar.

4 – this indicates that each beat is worth a quarter note (crotchet).

Thus in $\frac{4}{4}$ time there must be the equivalent of 4 quarter note beats per bar, e.g.

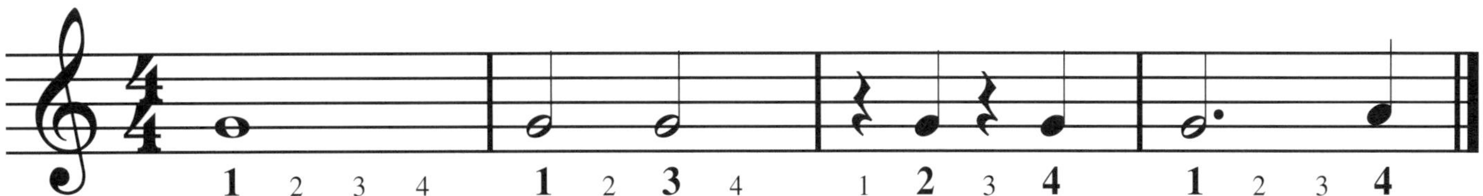

$\frac{4}{4}$ is the most common time signature and is sometimes represented by this symbol called **common time**.

The next most common time signature is is Three Four Time written $\frac{3}{4}$.

$\frac{3}{4}$ indicates 3 quarter note beats per bar, e.g.

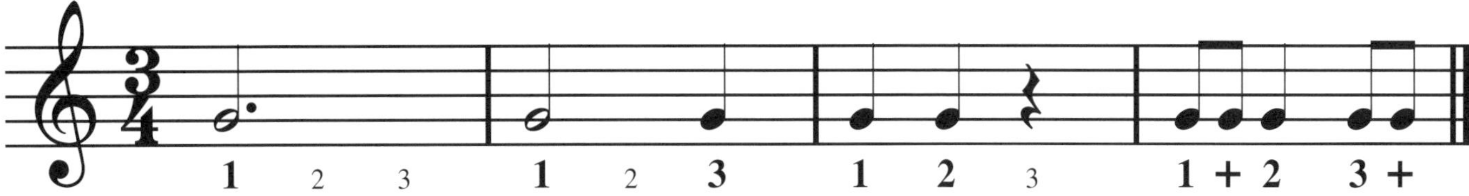

NOTE VALUES

The table below sets out the most common notes used in music and their respective time values (i.e. length of time held). For each note value there is an equivalent rest, which indicates a period of silence.

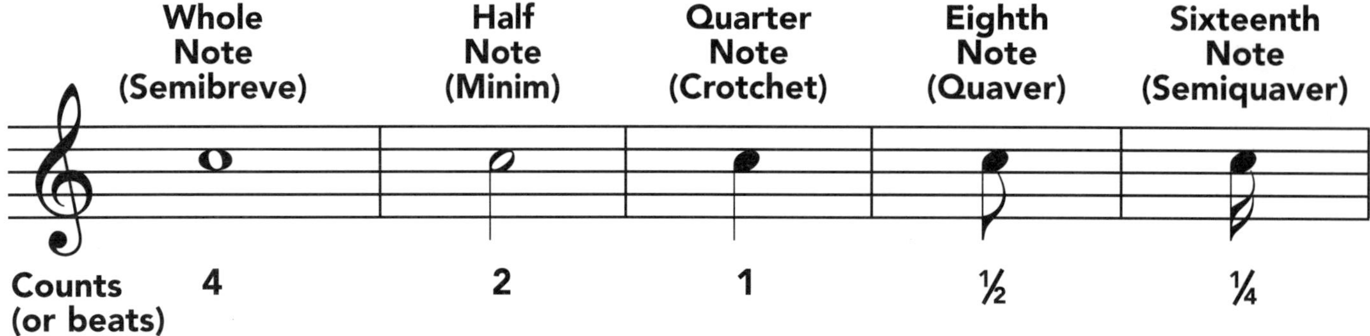

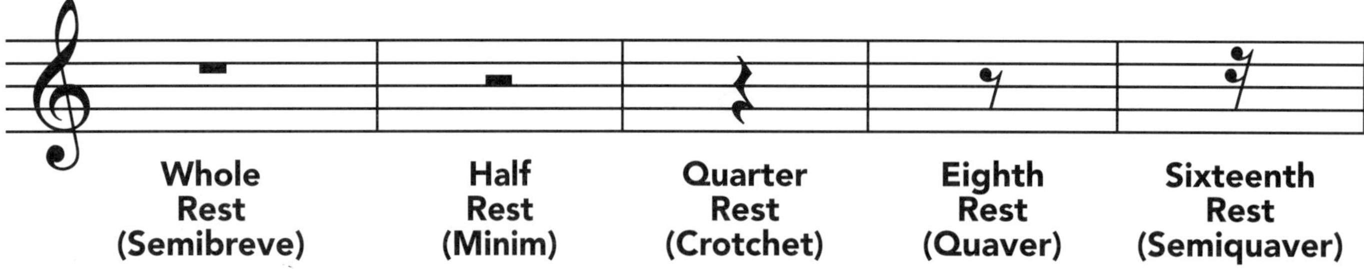

If a **dot** is placed after a note it increases the value of that note by half, e.g.

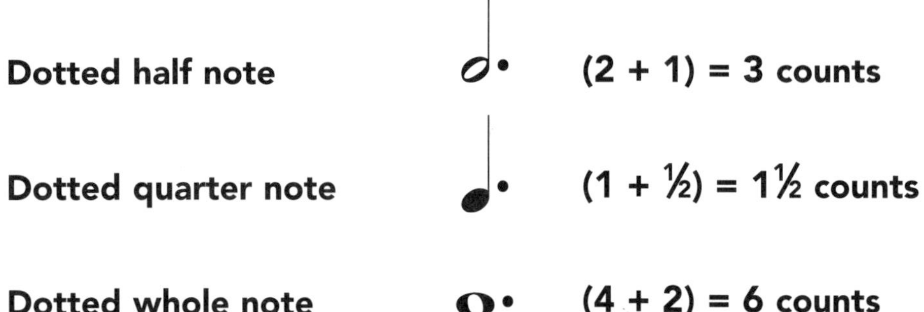

The timing of basic note values, rhythms and rests can also be illustrated in the following table.

NOTES, RHYTHMS AND RESTS

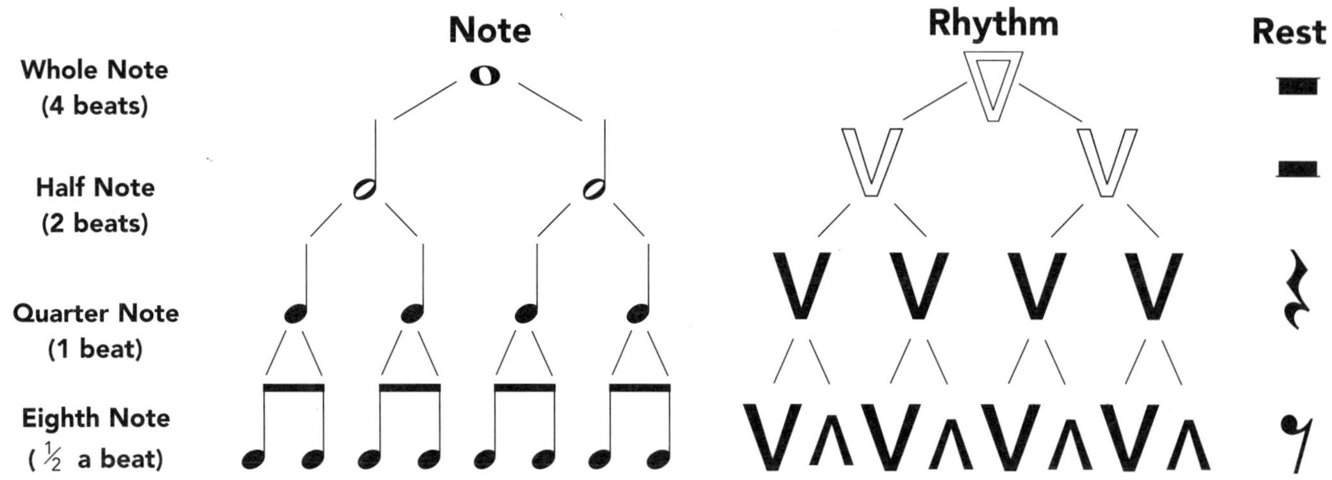

CHORD DIAGRAMS

Chords are learnt with the help of a **chord diagram**. This will show you exactly where to place your left hand fingers in order to play a particular chord. A chord diagram is a grid of horizontal and vertical lines representing the strings and frets of the guitar as shown below.

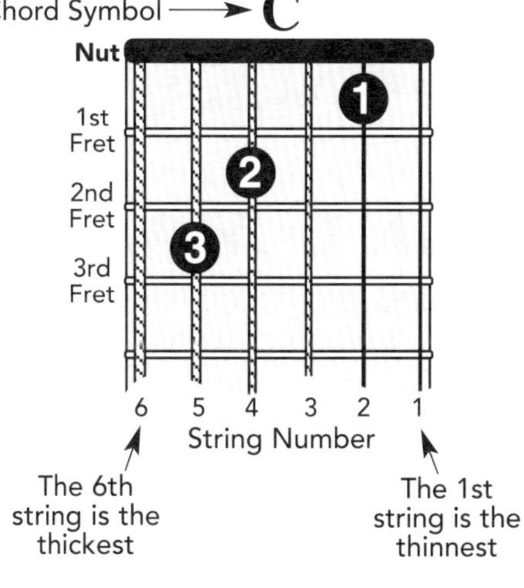

LEFT HAND FINGERING

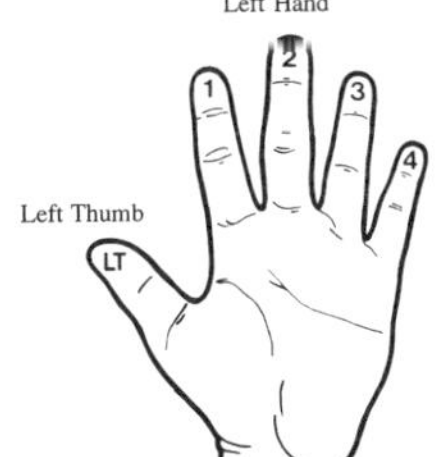

❶ Index Finger ❸ Ring Finger
❷ Middle Finger ❹ Little Finger

The **black dots** show you where to place your left hand fingers.The **white number** tells you which finger to place on the string just before the fret. If there is no dot on a string, you play it as an open (not fretted) string.
The other chord diagram symbols used in this book are summarized with the following two chord shapes.

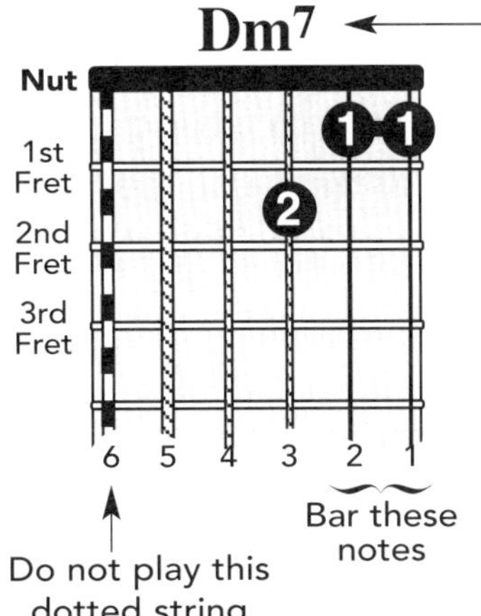

Chord symbol for D minor seventh chord.

A **dotted** string indicates that string is not to be strummed. A small **bar** connecting two black dots indicates they are held down by the same finger. This is called **barring.**

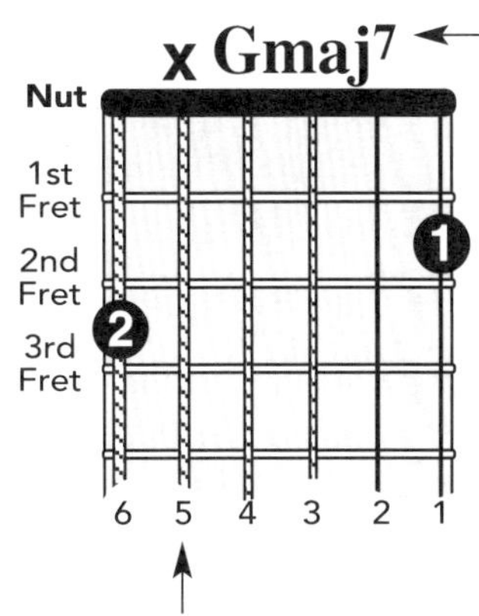

Chord symbol for G major seventh chord.

Dampen this string with the **second finger** by lightly touching it.

An **X** on the string indicates that string is to **dampened** by another finger lightly touching it. The string is still strummed as a part of the chord but it is not heard.

RHYTHM SYMBOLS

This is a **half note strum.**
It lasts for **two** beats.
There are **two** half note strums in one bar of $\frac{4}{4}$ time.

These are a pair of **eighth note strums.**Each strum lasts for **half a beat**. There are **eight** eighth note strums in one bar of $\frac{4}{4}$ time. Play the larger downward strum louder.

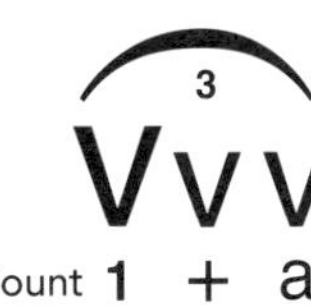

This is a group of three **eighth note triplet strums.** Each strum in the group lasts for **one third** of a beat. There are **twelve** eighth note triplet strums in one bar of $\frac{4}{4}$ time. Play the larger downward strum louder.

This is a **quarter note strum**. It lasts for **one** beat. There are **four** quarter note strums in one bar of $\frac{4}{4}$ time.

These Strums are a group of **sixteenth note strums.** Each strum lasts for **one quarter** of a beat. There are **sixteen** sixteenth note strums in one bar of $\frac{4}{4}$ time. Play the larger downward strum louder.

A broken strum symbol indicates that the strings are not to be strummed.

LESSON ONE

THE C MAJOR CHORD

A **chord** is a group of three or more notes played together. Chords are used to accompany a singer, or an instrumentalist who is playing the melody of a song. The first chord you will learn is the **C major chord**, usually just called the **C chord**. The **C major** chord is indicated by the letter **C**. This is called the **chord symbol**.

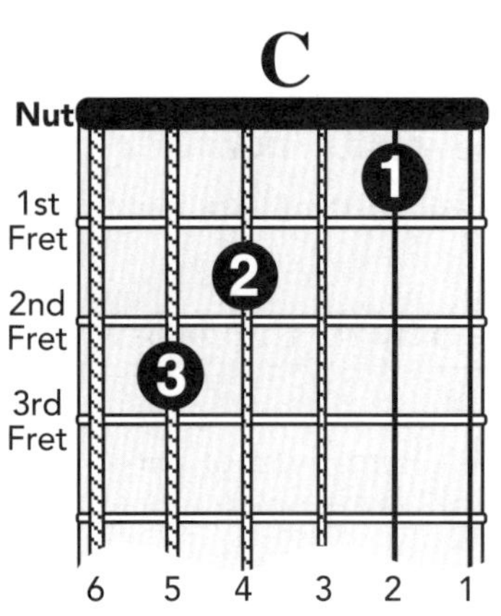

C Major Chord

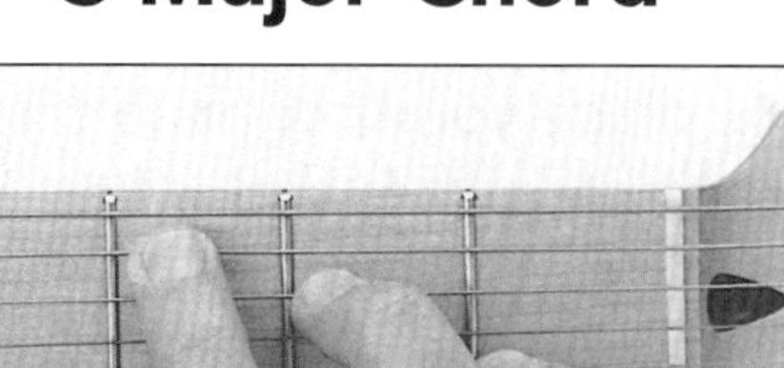

Chord Symbol

To play the **C** chord, place the **first** finger of your left hand just behind the **first** fret of the **second** string, the **second** finger just behind the **second** fret of the **fourth** string and your **third** finger just behind the **third** fret of the **fifth** string.

STRUMMING

Play **all six** strings with the pick at the same time, using a **downward** motion. This is called a **strum.** Hold the pick lightly and strum from the wrist. Keep your wrist relaxed. If any notes buzz or sound deadened you may have to press harder with the left hand fingers and make sure that your fingers are just behind the fret (not too far back).

Count: 1

This is the symbol for a downward **quarter note strum**.
It lasts for **one beat**.
There are **four** quarter note strums in one bar of $\frac{4}{4}$ time.

Count: 1 2 3 4

This is a **whole note strum**.
It lasts for **four beats**.
There is **one** whole note strum in one bar of $\frac{4}{4}$ time.

In the following example there are four bars of the **C major** chord played in $\frac{4}{4}$ time. The chord symbol is written above the staff and is placed at the beginning of each bar. Play the chord with four quarter note strums in each bar. The two dots at the end of bar 4 are a repeat sign, telling you to play the piece again from the start. To make the example sound finished always end with a whole note strum ∇ of the first chord.

CD 1 **2.0**

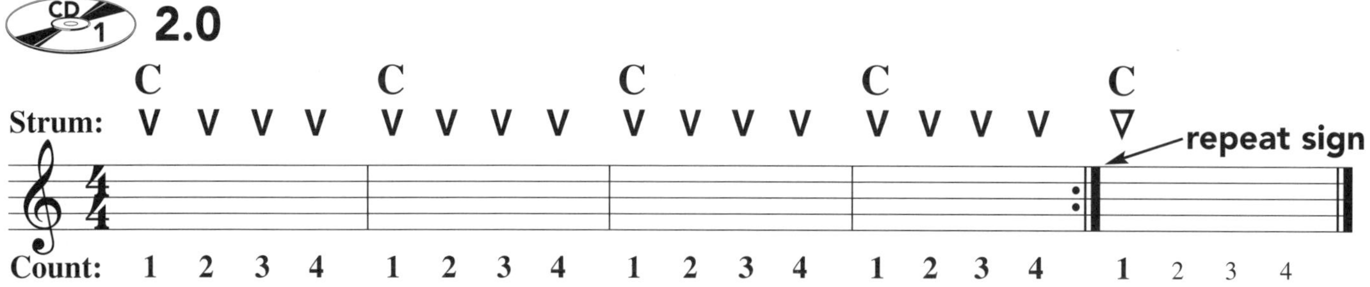

THE SEVENTH CHORD

Another type of common chord is the **dominant seventh** chord. It is usually referred to as the **seventh** chord. The chord symbol for the seventh chord is the number **7** written after the alphabetical letter. The symbol for the **D seventh** chord is **D7**.

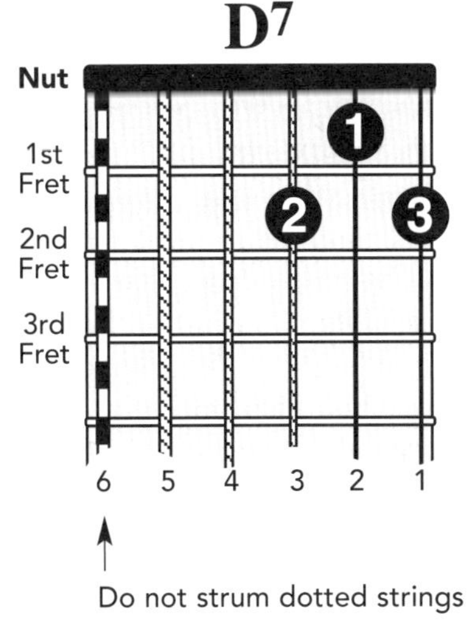

Do not strum dotted strings

D Seventh Chord

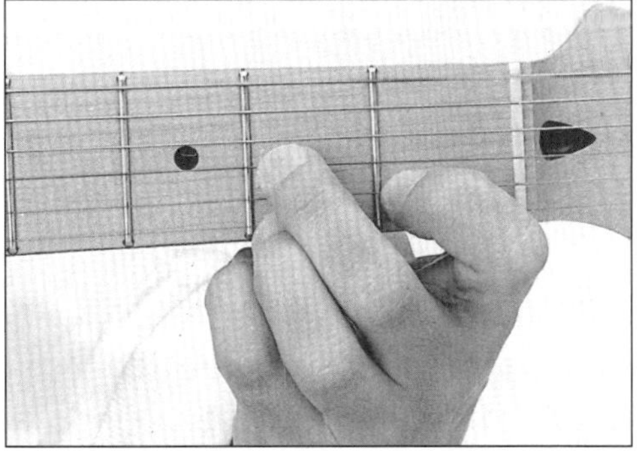

Chord Symbol

D^7

To play the **D7** chord, use the first **three** fingers of your left hand as shown in the diagram, but strum only **five** strings. Do not strum the **6th** string (as indicated by the dotted line).

THE HALF NOTE STRUM

Count: 1 2

This is a **half note strum**.
It lasts for **two** beats.
There are **two** half note strums in one bar of $\frac{4}{4}$ time.

 **2.1**

The example below contains four bars of the **D7** chord. Play two half note strums in each bar. The **bold** numbers tell you to strum the chord, the **smaller** numbers indicate to hold it until the next strum.

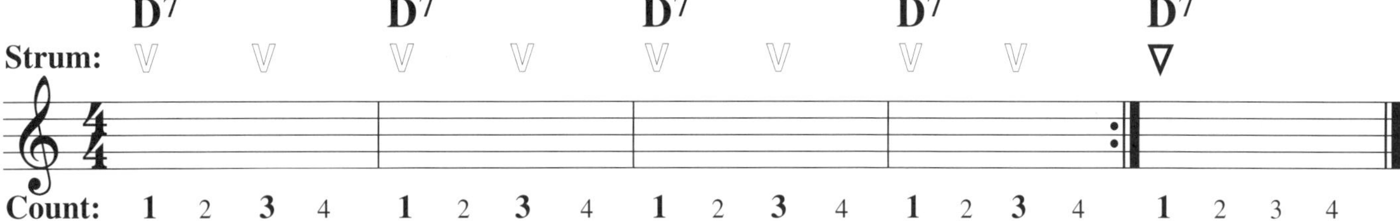

CHORD PROGRESSIONS

The following example is called a **chord progression**, meaning **a series of chord changes** (in this case – between **C** and **D7**). Chord progressions are common in all styles of music, and the more you know, the more songs you will be able to play.

2.2

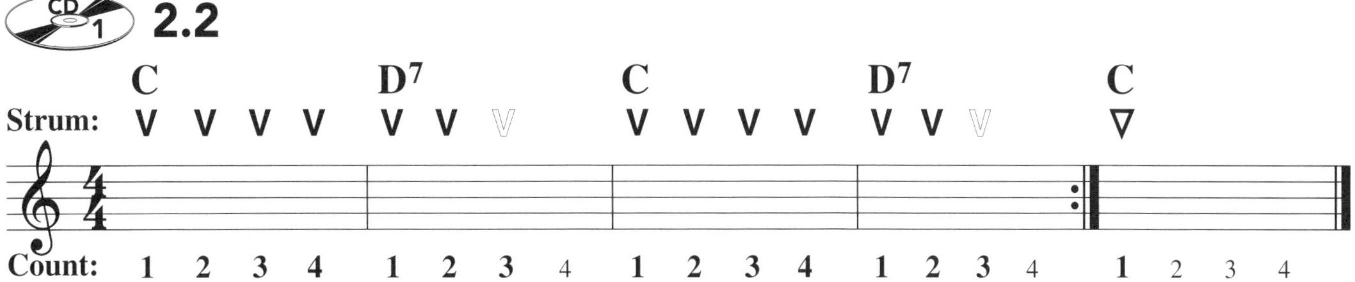

PIVOT FINGER

When changing between the **C** and **D7** chords, do not move your first finger as it is common to both chords. The first finger acts as a **pivot** around which the other fingers move. This will make the chord changes easier.

G7

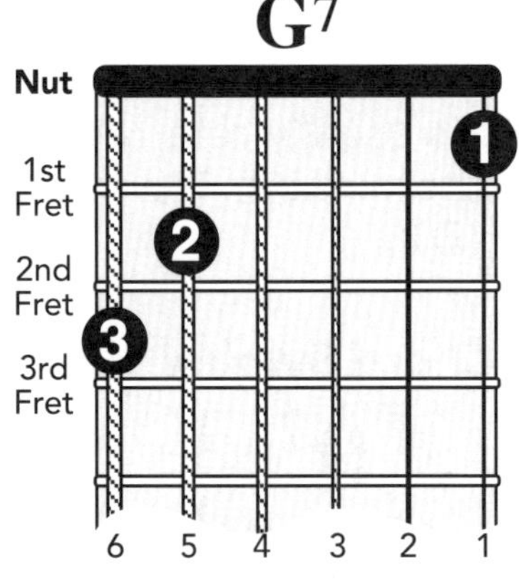

G Seventh Chord

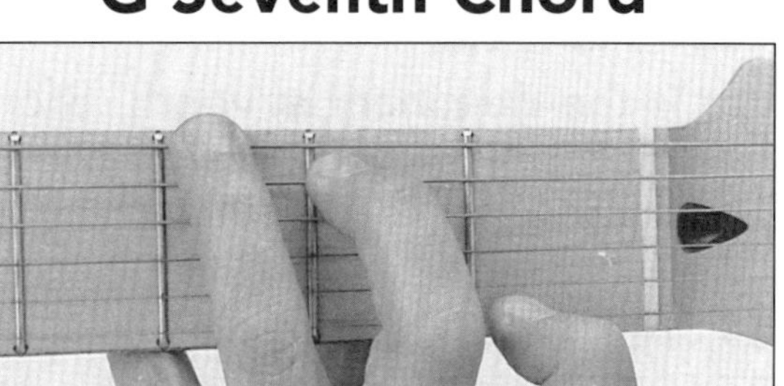

Chord Symbol

G7

To play the **G7** chord, place the **first, second** and **third** fingers of your left hand as shown in the diagram. Strum all **six** strings.

3.0

The following chord progression contains the three chords you have learnt so far. Remember to use the pivot finger when changing between **C** and **D7**.

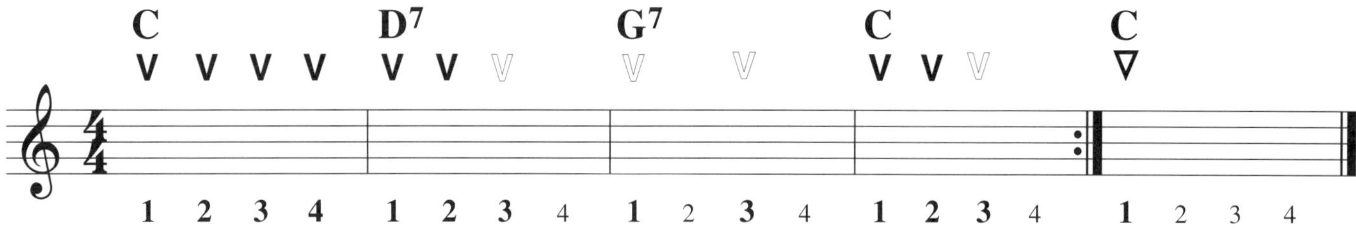

3.1

The following chord progression contains two chords in each bar. Each chord receives two beats.

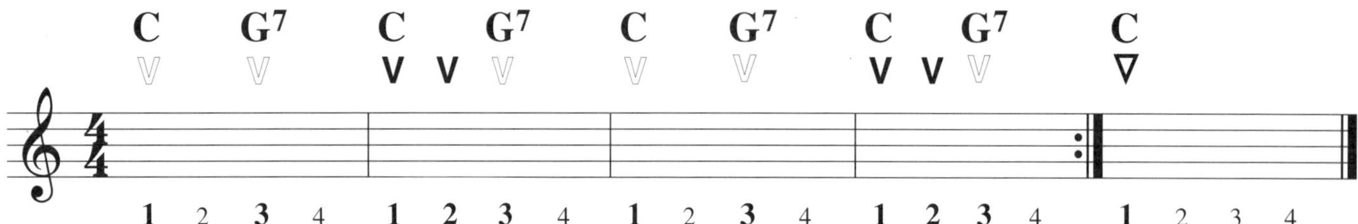

RHYTHM PATTERNS

Instead of writing the strumming above each bar of music, it is easier to write it as a **rhythm pattern**. This indicates which strumming pattern to use in each bar throughout the song. The rhythm pattern above the following example shows four strums per bar, each strum having the value of a quarter note.

Rhythm Pattern

V	V	V	V
1	2	3	4

3.2

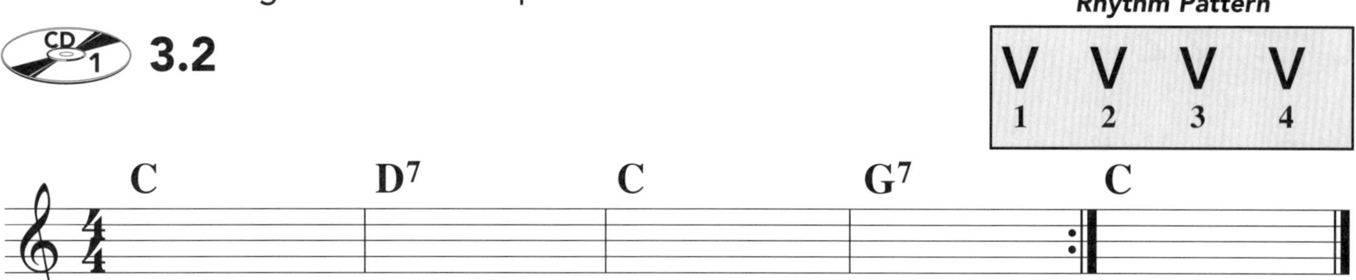

OPEN CHORD SHAPES

All the chord shapes you are learning here are examples of **open chords** – meaning they contain open strings (i.e. no finger is placed on the fret). Later in the book, you will learn other chord types (e.g. bar chords) which do not contain open strings.

LESSON TWO

A

Nut

1st Fret

2nd Fret

3rd Fret

6 5 4 3 2 1

A Major Chord

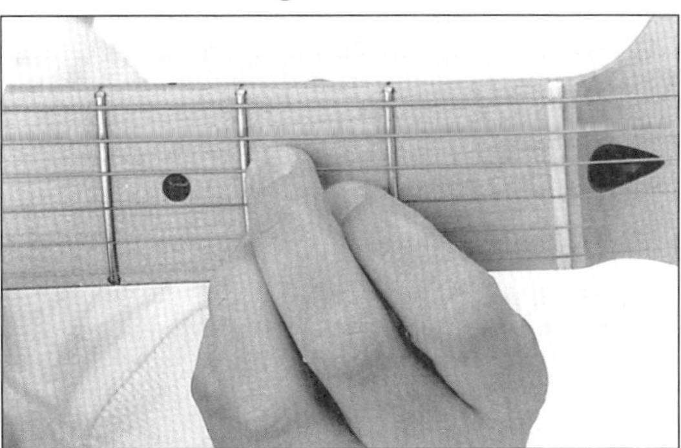

Chord Symbol

A

To play the **A** chord, place the **first, second** and **third** fingers of your left hand as shown in the diagram. Strum all **six** strings.

4.0

When changing between **C** and **A** use your second finger as a **pivot**.

Rhythm Pattern

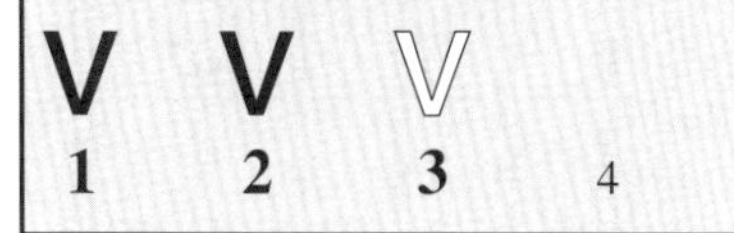

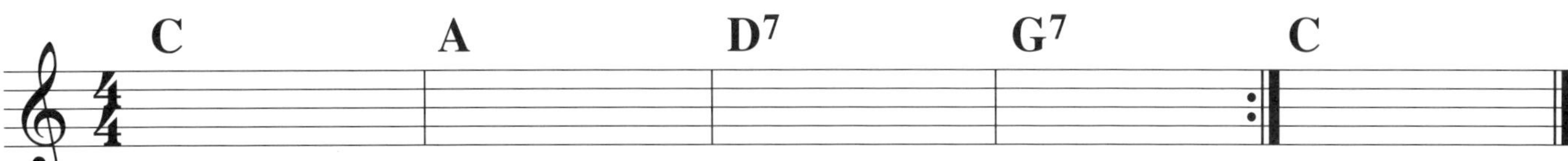

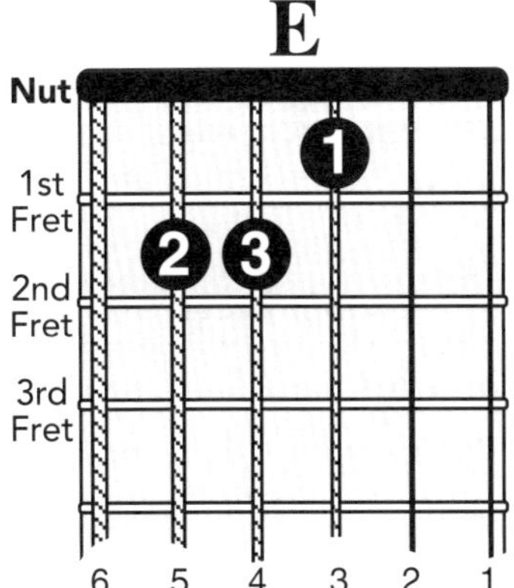

E Major Chord

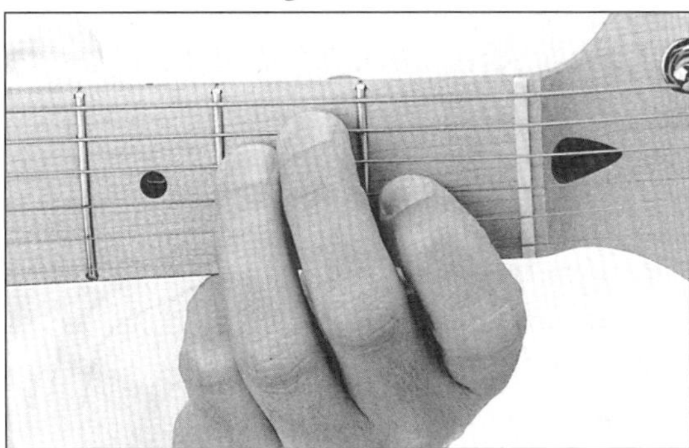

Chord Symbol

To play the **E** chord, place the **first, second** and **third** fingers of your left hand as shown in the diagram. Strum all **six** strings.

SLIDE FINGER

When changing from **E** to **A**, do not lift your first finger off the third string, but slide it down to the second fret. Only touch the string very lightly as you slide along it. The use of the slide finger will make changing between E and A chords easier. Practice the change until it is comfortable and then play the following chord progression using the two bar rhythm pattern as shown.

Rhythm Pattern

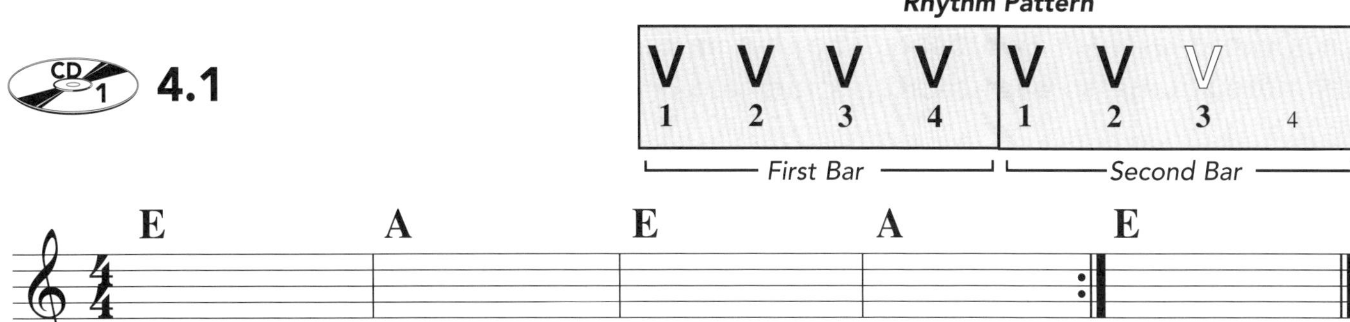

The following chord progression uses the same two bar rhythm pattern as in the previous example but some bars contain two chords, each receiving two beats.

4.2

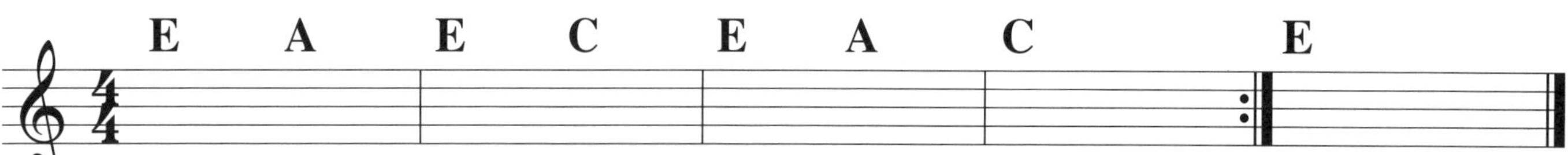

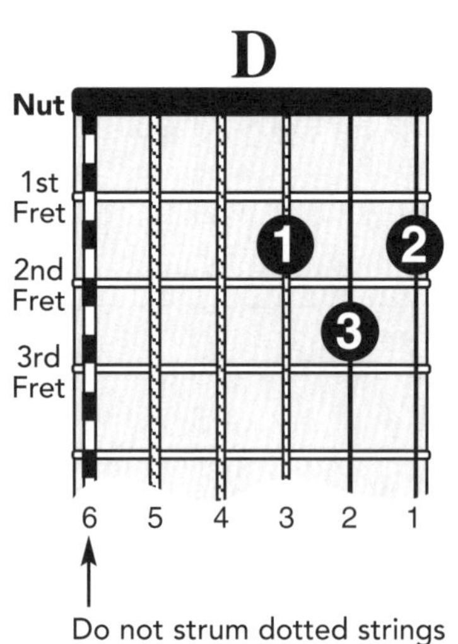

D Major Chord

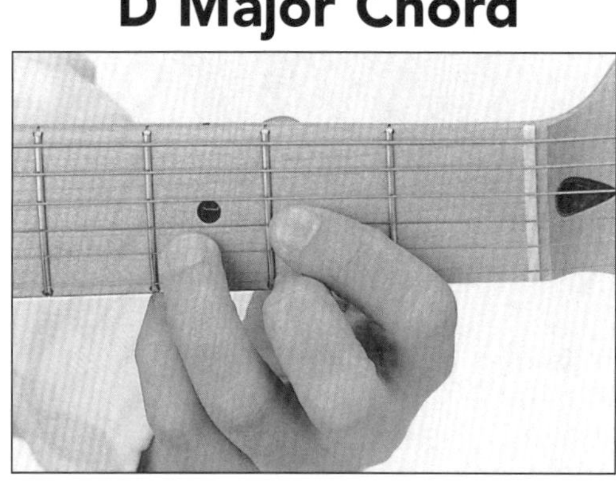

Chord Symbol

To play the **D** chord, place the **first, second** and **third** fingers of your **left** hand as shown in the diagram, but strum only **five** strings. Do not strum the **6th** string (as indicated by the dotted line).

When changing between **E** and **A**, or **E** and **D**, **slide** your **first** finger along the **third** string (only lightly touching it). When changing between the **A** and **D** chords, use your **first** finger as a **pivot** and slide your **third** finger along the second string. The first finger remains in contact with the third string throughout each of the following chord progressions.

5.0

Rhythm Pattern

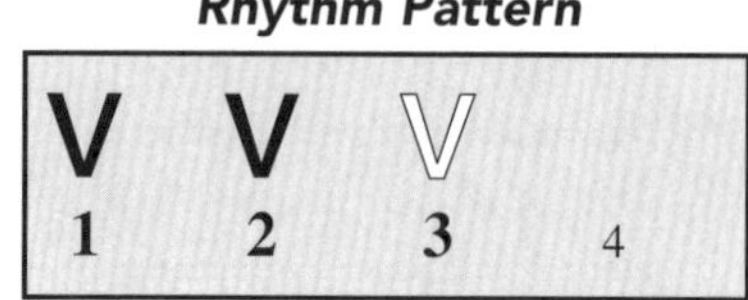

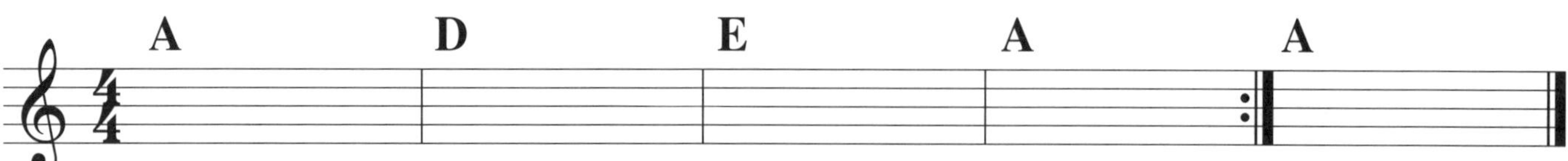

5.1

In this chord progression there are two chords in each bar. Each chord lasts for **two** beats. The rhythm pattern has two half note strums, so each chord is strummed once.

Rhythm Pattern

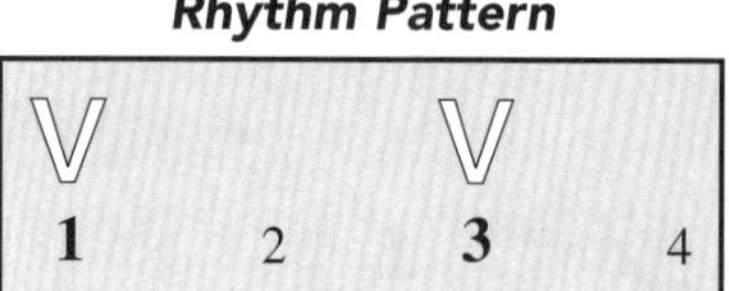

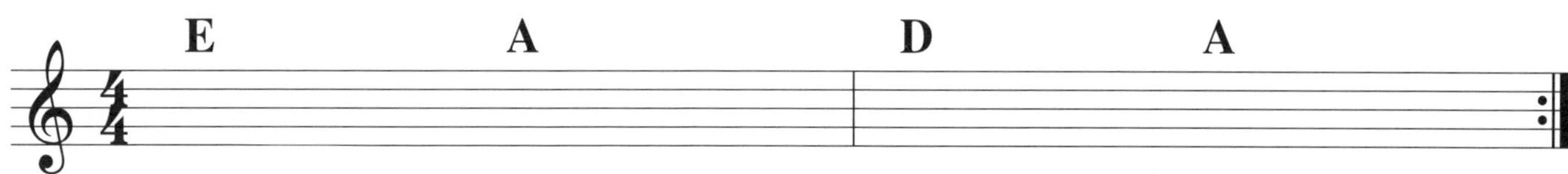

Always look for slide and pivot fingers to make your chord changes smoother, faster and easier.

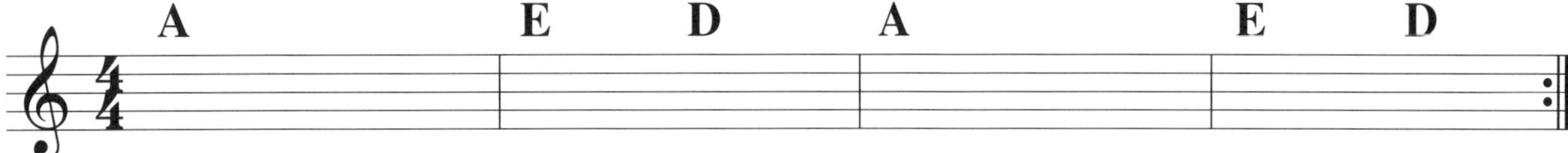

12 BAR BLUES

12 Bar Blues is a pattern of chords which repeats every 12 bars. There are hundreds of songs based on this chord progression, i.e. they contain basically the same chords in the same order. 12 bar blues is commonly used in Rock music and is the basis of Blues music.

Some well known songs which use this 12 bar chord pattern are:

- Original Batman TV Theme
- Rock Around the Clock - Bill Haley
- Johnny B Goode - Chuck Berry
- Blue Suede Shoes - Elvis Presley
- In the Mood - Glenn Miller
- Surfin' USA - The Beach Boys
- The Jack - ACDC
- Ice Cream Man - Van Halen
- Killing Floor - Jimi Hendrix
- Give Me One Reason - Tracy Chapman
- Why Didn't You Call Me? - Macy Gray
- Oh Pretty Woman - Gary Moore

The following 12 bar Blues is in the **key of A major**. When a song is said to be in the key of **A major**, it means that the most important chord (and usually the first chord) is the **A** chord.

This pattern of chords will probably sound familiar to you. Instead of writing a chord symbol above each bar of music it is common to only write a chord symbol when the chord changes, e.g. the first four bars of this Blues are all **A** chords, played according to the rhythm pattern. To help keep time **accent** (play louder) the first strum of every bar. End this 12 bar Blues by strumming an **A** chord.

5.3 12 Bar Blues in A

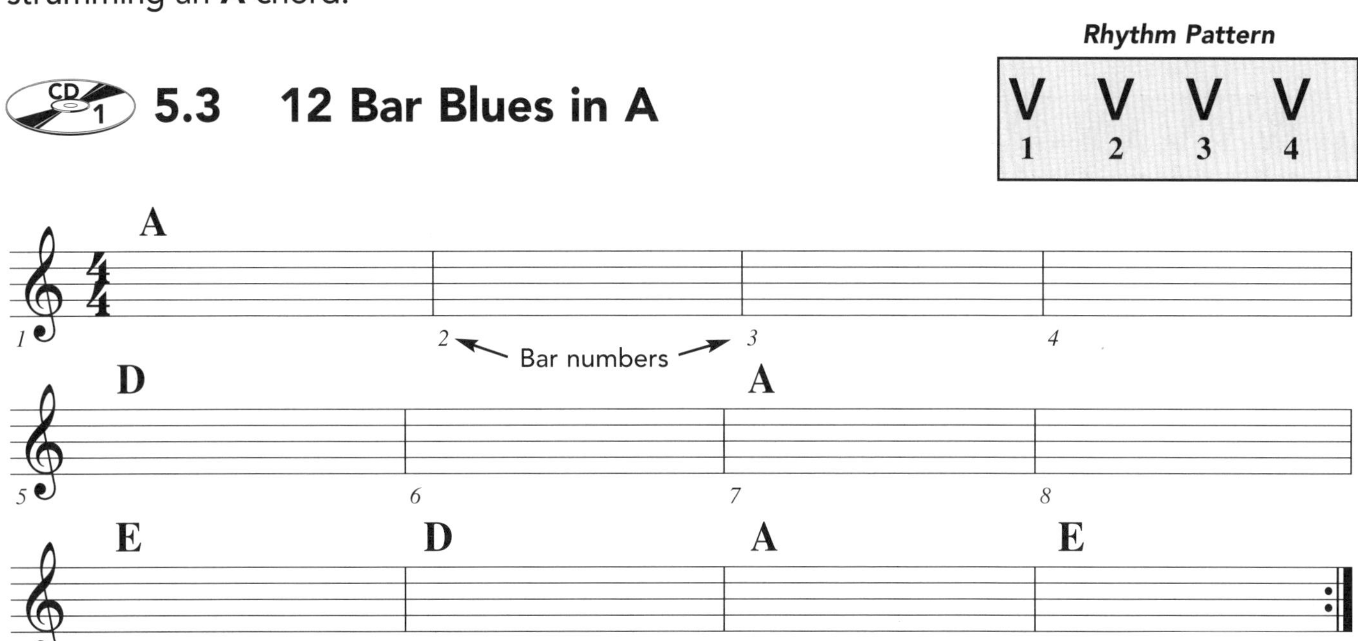

LESSON THREE

EIGHTH NOTE RHYTHMS

All the rhythm patterns you have played so far use a downward strum (**V**), on the first, second, third and fourth beat. To make rhythm patterns more interesting, **up strums** can also be used. An **eighth note rhythm** uses a combination of a down and an up strum within one beat. The downstrum "on the beat" is played louder than the upstrum which is "off the beat".

An **up strum** is indicated by a **Λ**, and is played on the "**and**" section of the count. To play an up strum start the strum at the **first** string (the thinnest) and strum all six strings.

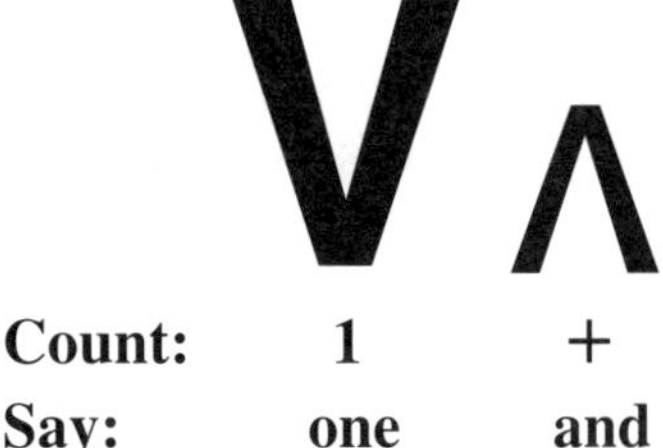

There are **two** eighth note strums per beat. There are **8** eighth note strums in one bar of music in $\frac{4}{4}$ time.
The downstrum "on the beat" is played louder than the upstrum which is "off the beat" (the '+' section of the count).

EIGHTH NOTE RHYTHM PATTERNS

Here are some **eighth note rhythm patterns** in $\frac{4}{4}$ time. Practice them while holding an **E** chord and then apply these patterns to the chord progressions in Lessons One and Two. Any of these patterns can be used on any chord progression in $\frac{4}{4}$ time.

6.

1. V V Λ V V
1 2 + 3 4

2. V V V Λ V
1 2 3 + 4

3. V V Λ V Λ V Λ
1 + 2 + 3 + 4 +

4. V V Λ V Λ V
1 2 + 3 + 4

5. V Λ V Λ V Λ V Λ
1 + 2 + 3 + 4 +

6. V Λ V Λ V V Λ
1 + 2 + 3 4 +

7. V Λ V V V
1 + 2 3 4

8. V Λ V Λ V V
1 + 2 + 3 4

9. V Λ V Λ V Λ V
1 + 2 + 3 + 4

10. V V V V Λ
1 2 3 4 +

11. V Λ V V Λ V
1 + 2 3 + 4

12. V V Λ V V Λ
1 2 + 3 4 +

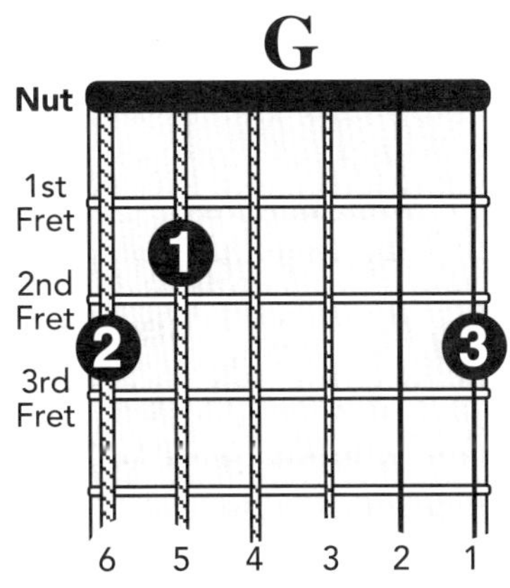

G Major Chord

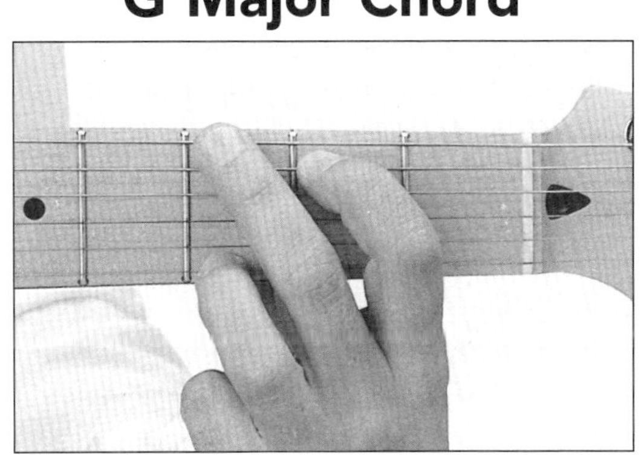

Chord Symbol

G

To play the **G** chord, place the **first, second** and **third** fingers of your left hand as shown in the diagram. Strum all **six** strings.

The following chord progression contains a G chord and uses eighth note rhythm pattern 1. When changing between the **A** and **C** chords use your **second** finger as a **pivot**. When changing between **D7** and **G**, **slide** your **third** finger along the **first** string.

Rhythm Pattern

V	V	∧	V	V
1	2	+	3	4

CD 1 **7.0**

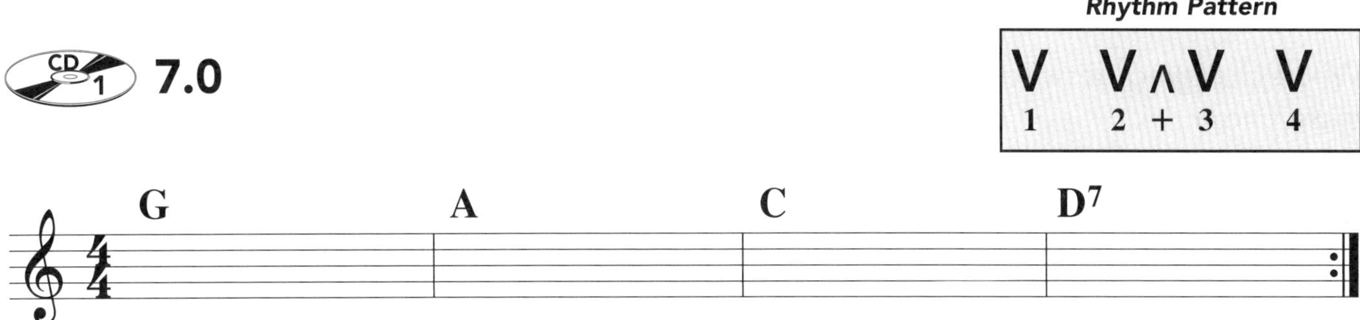

Practice new chord changes using a basic rhythm pattern first. Once you are confident with the progression, then use the eighth note rhythm pattern. You can apply any rhythm pattern to a chord progression. This one uses eighth note rhythm pattern **5**.
When changing between **D** and **A** use your **first** finger as a **pivot**. Use your **second** finger as a **pivot** when changing between **A** and **C** chords.

Rhythm Pattern

V	V	V	∧	V
1	2	3	+	4

CD 1 **7.1**

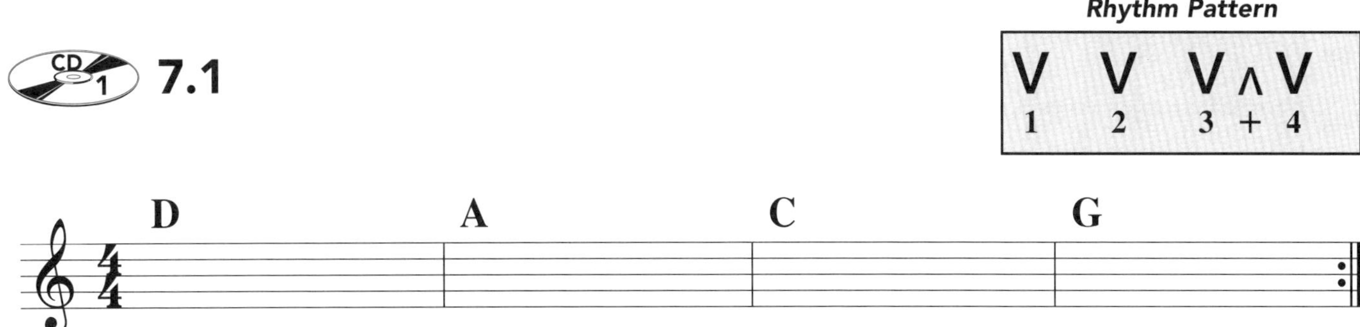

This chord progression uses eighth note rhythm pattern **2**. Use your **second** finger as a **pivot** when changing between **A** and **C** chords.

Rhythm Pattern

V	V	∧	V	∧	V
1	2	+	3	+	4

CD 1 **7.2**

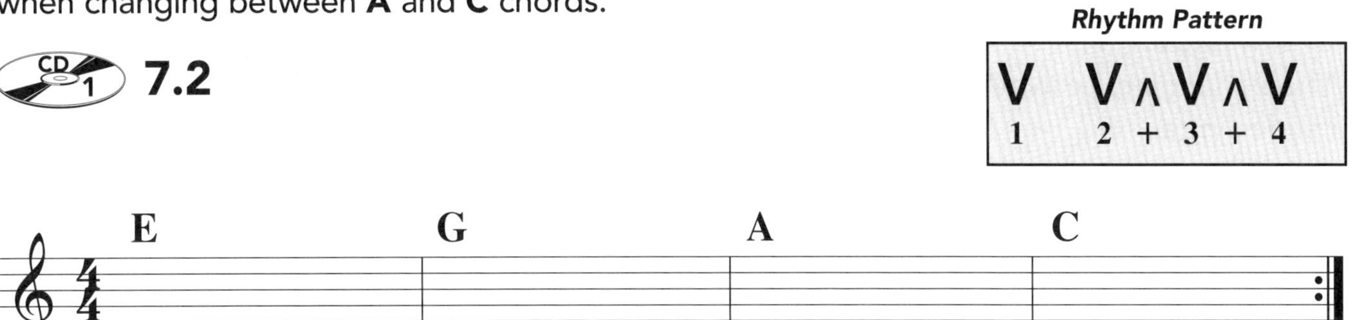

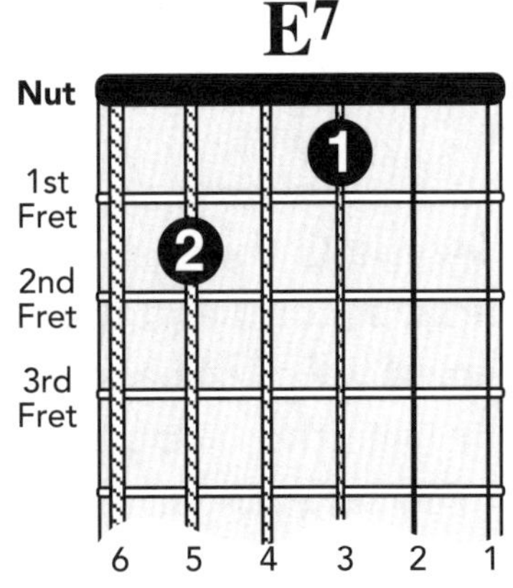

E Seventh Chord

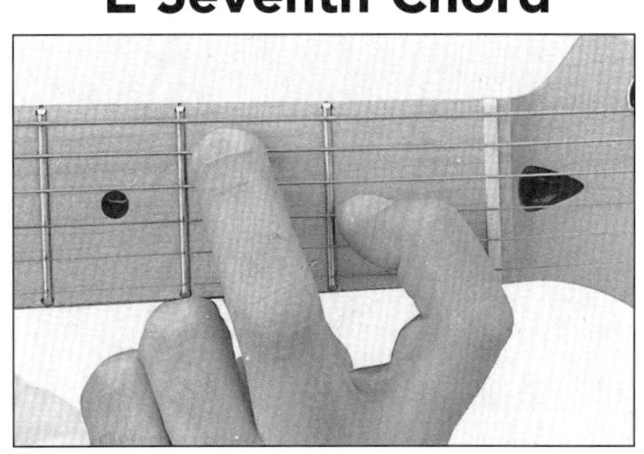

Chord Symbol

E7

To play the **E7** chord, use the **first** and **second** fingers of your left hand as shown in the diagram, and strum all **six** strings. The **E7** chord shape is just the **E** chord shape with the **third** finger lifted off.

8.0

The following chord progression contains an **E7** chord and uses eighth note rhythm pattern **1**.

Rhythm Pattern

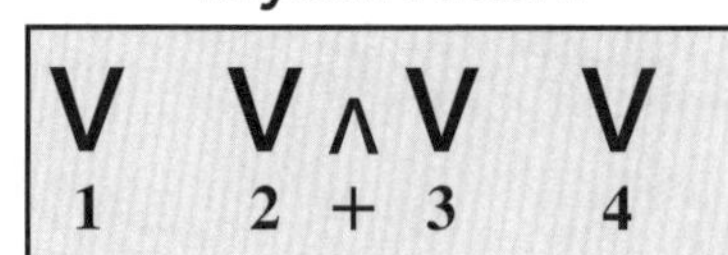

When changing between **D** and **E7** use your **first** finger as a **slide** finger.
When changing between **A** and **D** use your **first** finger as a **pivot**.

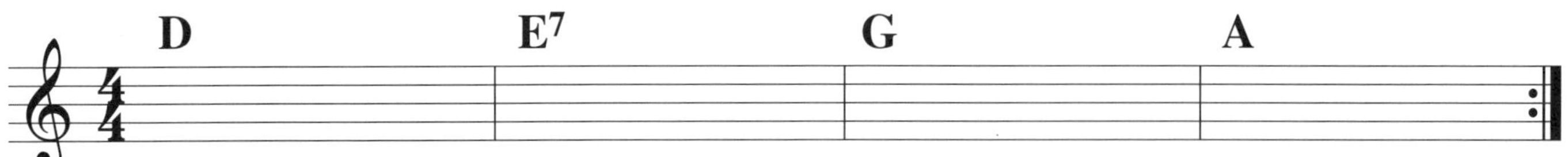

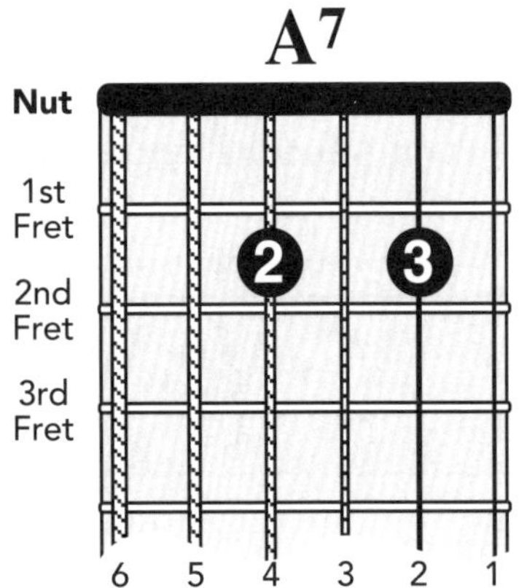

A Seventh Chord

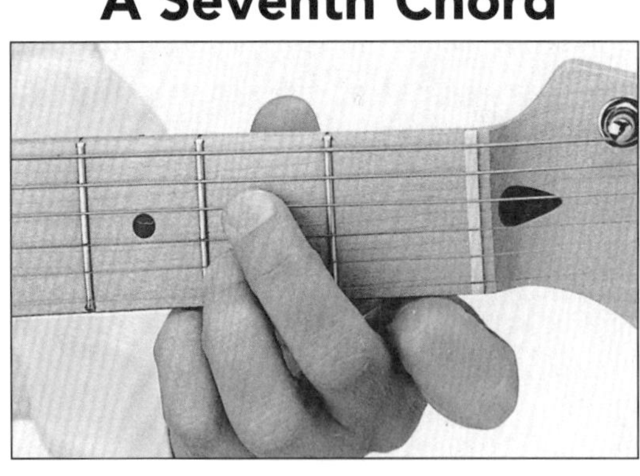

Chord Symbol

A7

To play the **A7** chord, use the **second** and **third** fingers of your left hand as shown in the diagram, and strum all **six** strings. The **A7** chord shape is just an **A** chord shape with the **first** finger lifted off.

8.1

Rhythm Pattern

V ∧ V ∧ V V
1 + 2 + 3 4

This progression contains an **A7** chord and uses eighth note rhythm pattern **7**.
When changing between **D7** and **G** use your **third** finger as a **slide** finger.

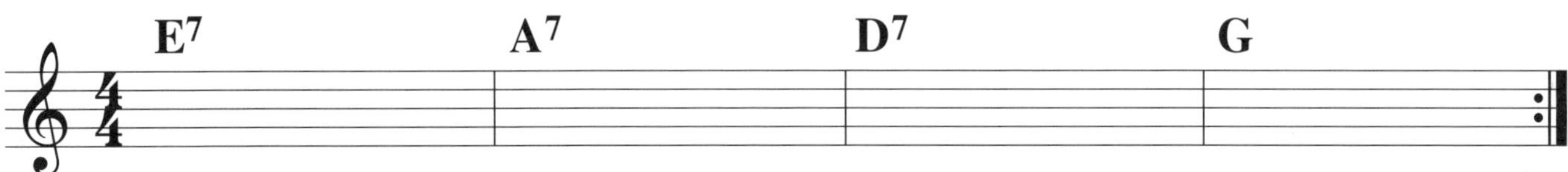

LESSON FOUR

MINOR CHORDS

There are three main types of chords: **Major**, **Seventh**, and **Minor**. The chord symbol for the **minor** chord is a small '**m**' placed after the letter name. Here are some commonly used minor chord shapes.

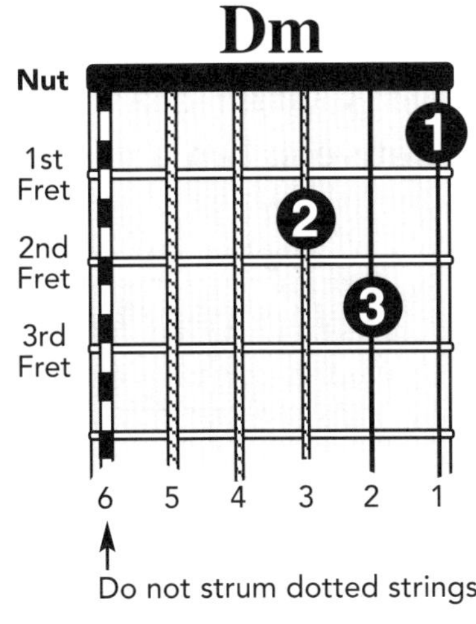

D Minor Chord

Chord Symbol

Dm

To play the **Dm** chord, use the **first**, **second** and **third** fingers of your left hand as shown in the diagram. Strum only **five** strings.

9.0

In the following progression use a **pivot** finger when changing from **C** to **A7** and **Dm** to **G7**. Use a **slide** finger between **A7** and **Dm**.

Rhythm Pattern

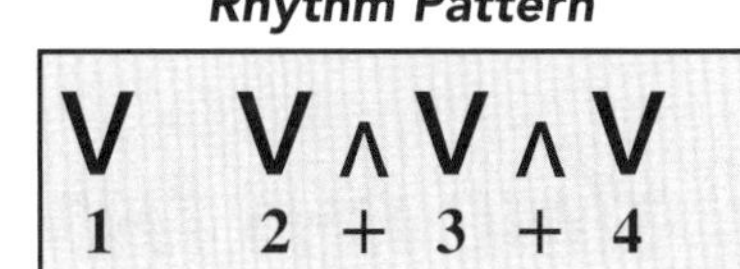

A Minor Chord

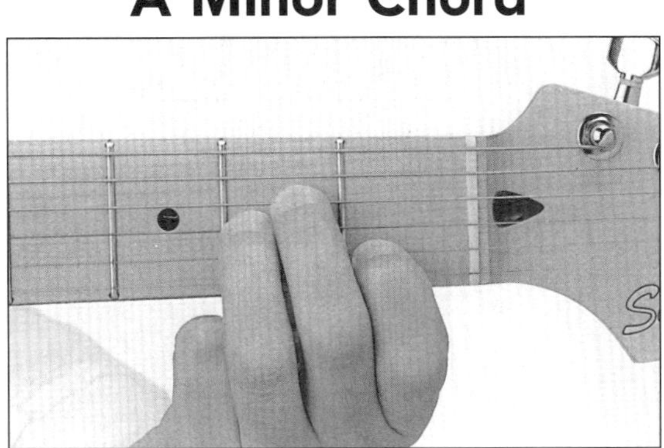

Chord Symbol

Am

To play the **Am** chord, use the **first**, **second** and **third** fingers of your left hand as shown in the diagram. Strum all **six** strings.

Rhythm Pattern

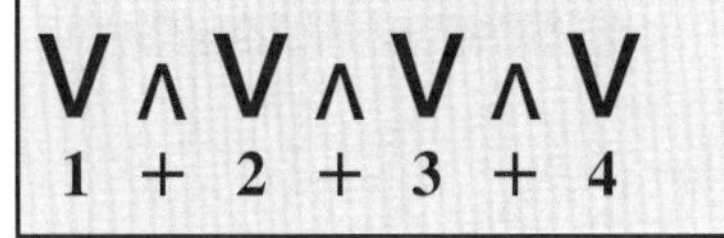

CD 1 **9.1**

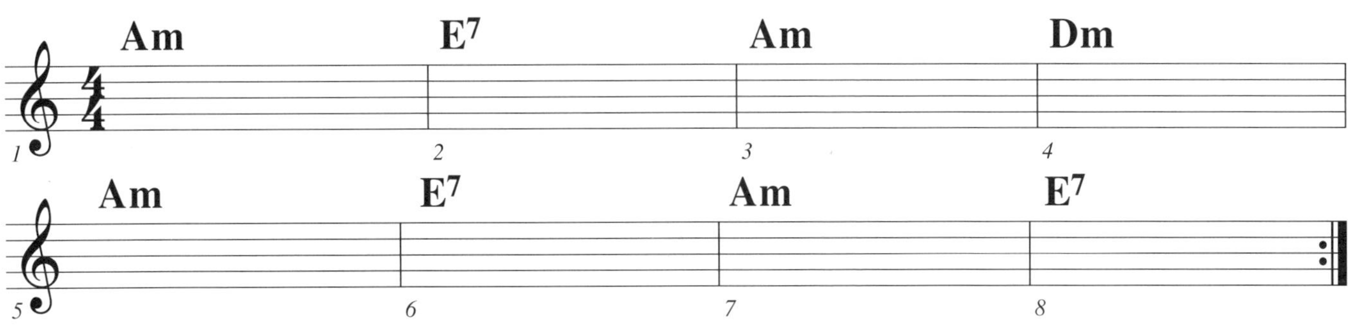

THE THREE FOUR TIME SIGNATURE

$\frac{3}{4}$ This is the **three four time signature**. It indicates that there are **three** beats in each bar. Three four time is also known as waltz time. There are three quarter notes in one bar of $\frac{3}{4}$ time.

The following chord progression is in $\frac{3}{4}$ time. To help keep time, **accent** (play louder) the first strum in each bar. Use your **first** and **second** fingers as **pivots** when changing between **C** and **Am**. Use your **first** finger as a **pivot** when changing between **Dm** and **G7**.

10.0

Rhythm Pattern

V V V
1 2 3

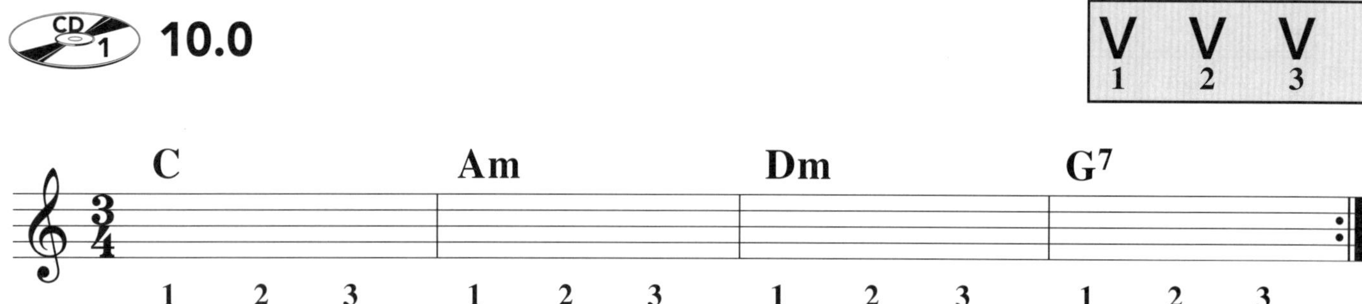

$\frac{3}{4}$ TIME RHYTHM PATTERNS

Practice the following $\frac{3}{4}$ **time rhythm patterns** holding a **C** chord shape. Apply any of these patterns to the above chord progression.

10.1

1. V V ∧ V — 1 2 + 3

2. V ∧ V V — 1 + 2 3

3. V V V ∧ — 1 2 3 +

4. V ∧ V ∧ V — 1 + 2 + 3

5. V V ∧ V ∧ — 1 2 + 3 +

6. V ∧ V ∧ V ∧ — 1 + 2 + 3 +

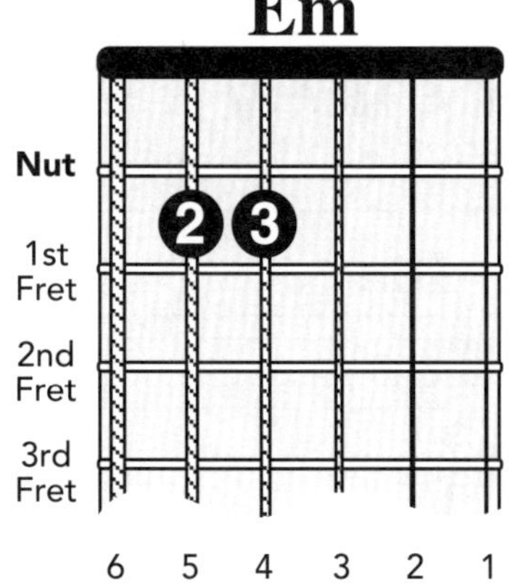

E Minor Chord

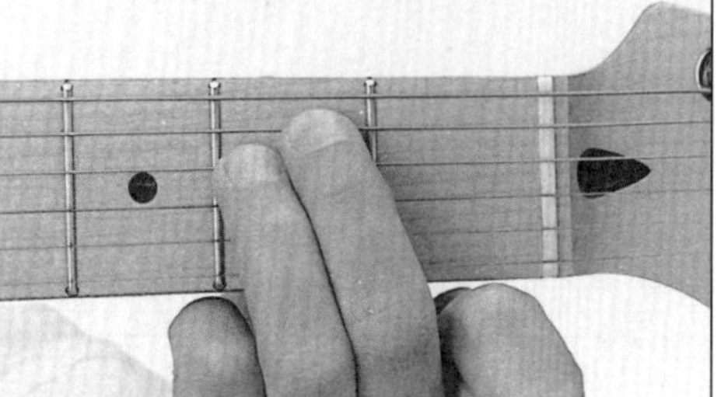

Chord Symbol

Em

To play the **Em** chord, use the **second** and **third** fingers of your left hand as shown in the diagram. Strum all **six** strings. The **Em** chord shape is just the **E** chord shape with the **first** finger lifted off.

The following chord progression is in $\frac{3}{4}$ time and uses three minor chords. Use your **first** finger as a **pivot** when changing between **Dm** and **G7**. Use your **second** finger as a **pivot** when changing between **G7** and **Em**.

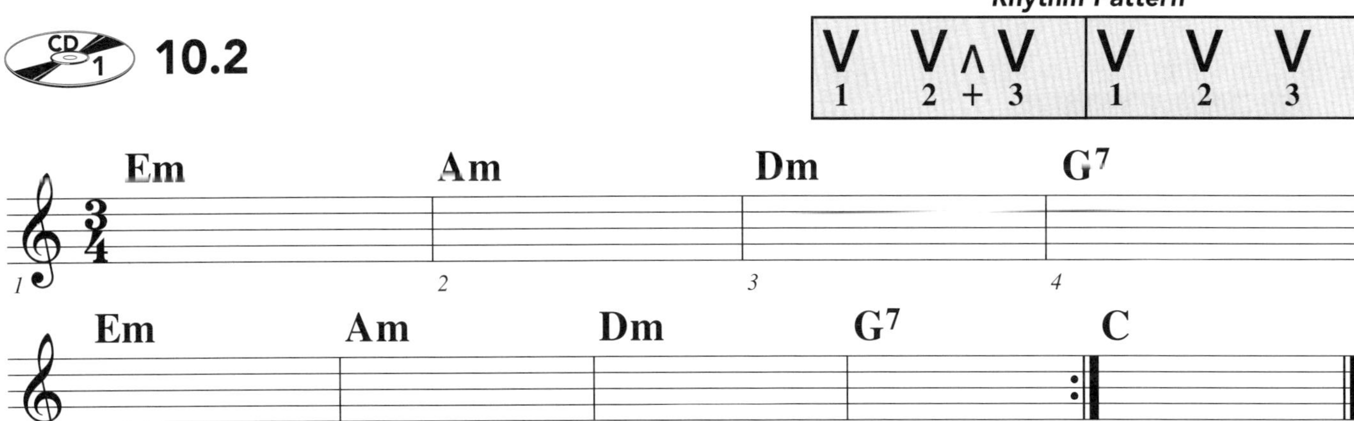

BASS NOTE RHYTHM PATTERNS

Bass notes are the notes on the **6th, 5th and 4th strings**. Instead of strumming the complete chord for every beat, try picking the bass note of the chord on the first beat and then strum the first three or four strings of the chord on the 2nd and 3rd beats. Play the following bass note rhythm holding a **G** chord shape.

Base Note Rhythm Pattern

♩	V	V
1	2	3

Pick the lowest note of the chord that has the same letter name as the chord. This is called the **root note**.

When playing a **G** chord, pick the **6th** string note (G note).
When playing an **Em** chord, pick the **6th** string note (E note).
When playing an **Am** chord, pick the **5th** string note (A note).
When playing a **D7** chord, pick the **4th** string note (D note).

Practice this rhythm technique on each chord separately at first Remember to hold the full chord shape with your left hand even though you are not playing all the strings.

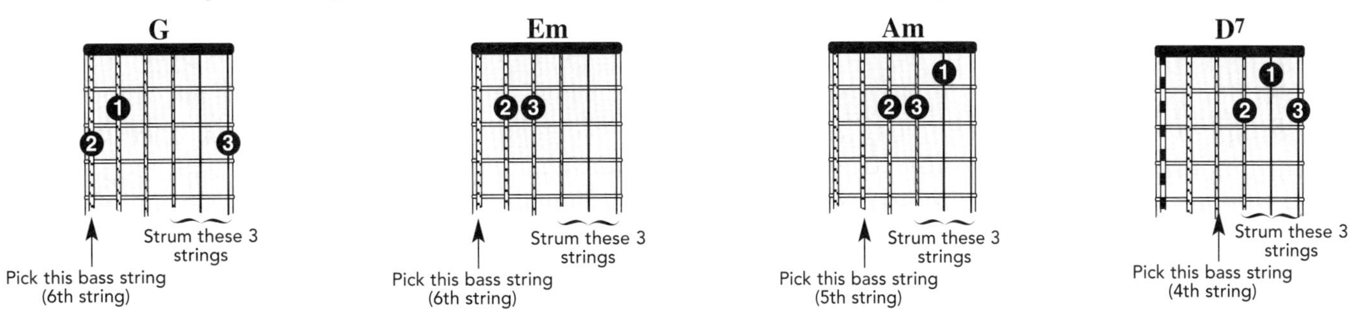

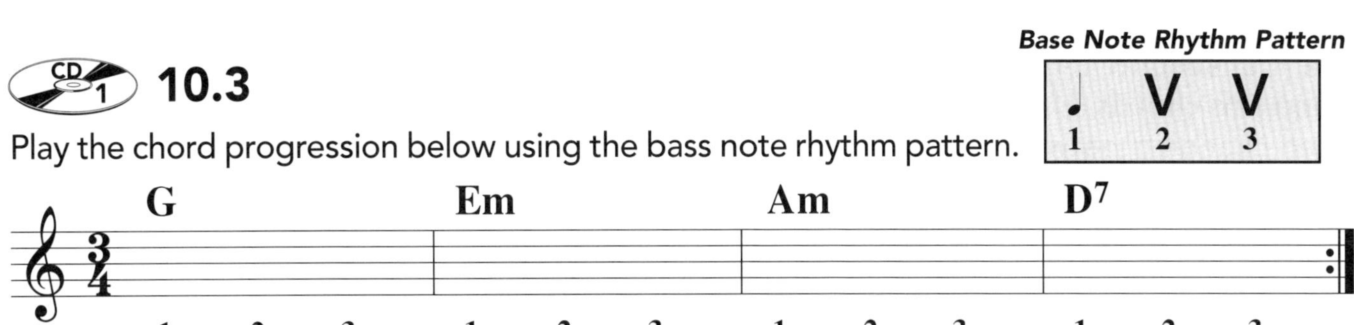

Play the chord progression below using the bass note rhythm pattern.

LESSON FIVE

F

Nut
1st Fret
2nd Fret
3rd Fret
6 5 4 3 2 1

F Major Chord

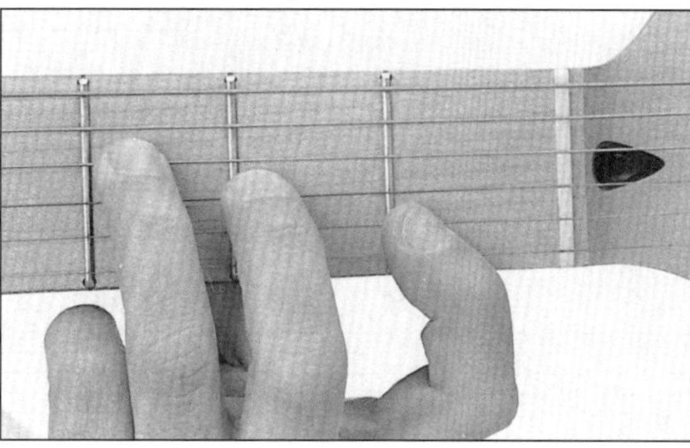

Chord Symbol

F

To play the **F** chord, use the **first**, **second** and **third** fingers of your left hand as shown in the diagram. Strum only **five** strings. The **first** finger **bars** across the first two strings. This is quite difficult at first. The **F** chord is easier to play if you position your **third** and **second** fingers before positioning your first finger.

11.0

Remember that you can use any rhythm pattern you like on any chord progression as long as they have the same time signature e.g. $\frac{4}{4}$ time.

Rhythm Pattern

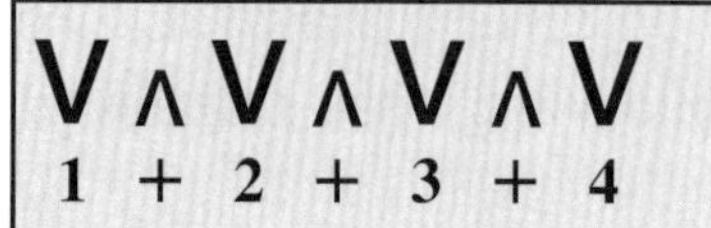

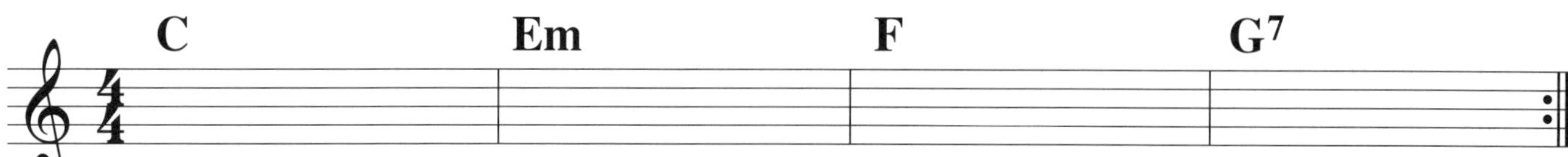

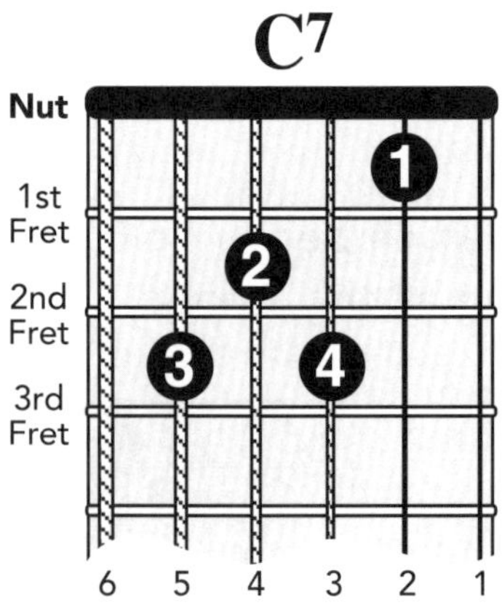

C Seventh Chord

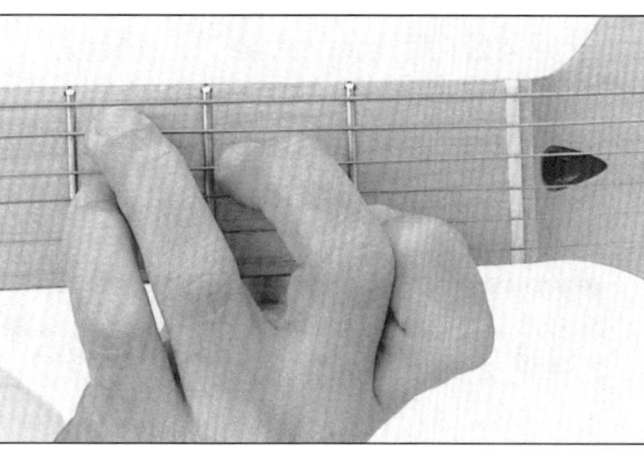

Chord Symbol

To play the **C7** chord, use the **four** fingers of your left hand as shown in the diagram, and strum all **six** strings. The **C7** chord is a **C** chord with an added **B♭** note played by the fourth finger.

11.1

Use your **second** finger as a **pivot** when changing between the **F** and **Dm chords**. Use your **first** and **second** fingers as **pivots** when changing between **Am** and **C7**.

Rhythm Pattern

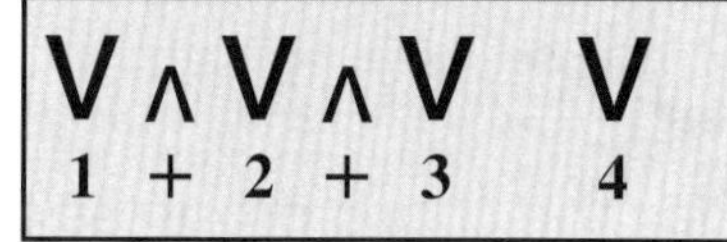

F Dm Am C7

TURNAROUND PROGRESSIONS

In Lesson 2 you were introduced to the 12 Bar Blues chord progression. Another common chord progression is called the **turnaround**. Like 12 Bar Blues, it is the basis of many songs, and will probably sound familiar. Unlike 12 Bar Blues, where the progression occurs over a fixed number of bars, the Turnaround progression may vary in length as in the examples below, however the chord sequence remains the same. Some of the biggest hits of all time are based on the turnaround progression. Every year since the beginning of Rock music there have been hit songs based on Turnaround progressions.

Stand by Me - John Lennon
I Will Always Love You - Whitney Housten
Return to Sender - Elvis Presley
All I Have to do is Dream - Everly Brothers
Always Look on the Bright Side of Life - Monty Python
The Young Ones - The Young Ones
Bizarre Love Triangle - New Order
Everlasting Love - U2
Last Kiss - Pearl Jam

11.2 Turnaround in G Major

Rhythm Pattern

V V V ∧ V
1 2 3 + 4

G | Em | C | D7 :|

ALTERNATIVE CHORD FINGERINGS

Em

To make the chord changes in the above progression easier, play the **Em** chord with your **first** and **second** fingers. This allows the use of **pivot** fingers between **G** to **Em** and **Em** to **C**. A pivot can also be used between **C** and **D7** and a **slide** finger between **G** and **D7.** Alternative fingering for any chord shape can be used to make chord progressions easier to play.

11.3 Turnaround in C Major

Rhythm Pattern

V V V V
1 2 3 4

In this turnaround there are two chords in each bar. Use your **first** and **second** fingers as **pivots** when changing between **C** and **Am.**

C Am | F G7 | C Am | F G7 :|

Notice the similarity in sound in the Turnaround progressions above. They are the **same** progression but in two different keys.

LESSON SIX

Bm

Nut

1st Fret

2nd Fret

3rd Fret

6 5 4 3 2 1

B Minor Chord

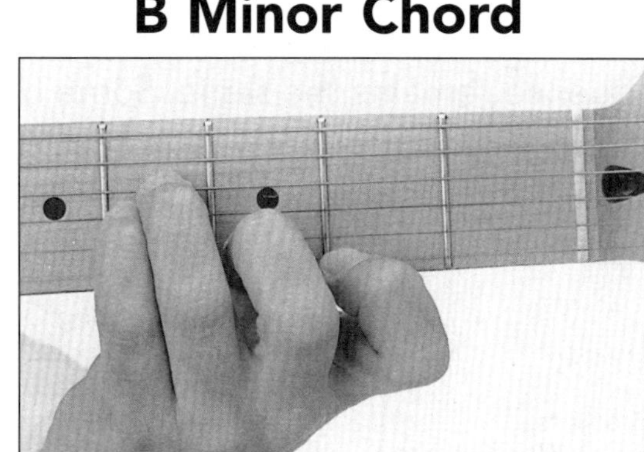

Chord Symbol

Bm

To play the **Bm** chord, use the **first**, **second**, **third** and **fourth** fingers of your left hand as shown in the diagram. Strum only **four** strings.

The following progression is a turnaround in the key of D major. It contains the Bm chord and there are two chords per bar each receiving two counts. Notice the similarity in the sound of the progression to the other turnarounds in this lesson.

12.0

Rhythm Pattern

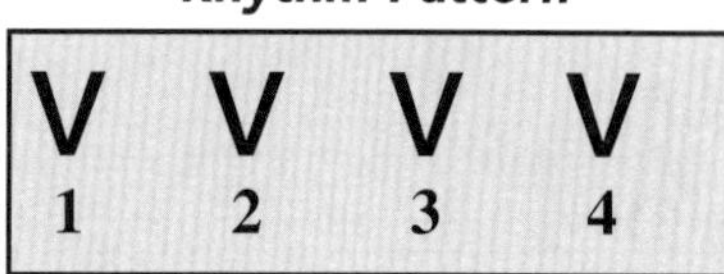

The following turnaround is in the key of **G major**. Each chord is played for two bars.

12.1

Rhythm Pattern

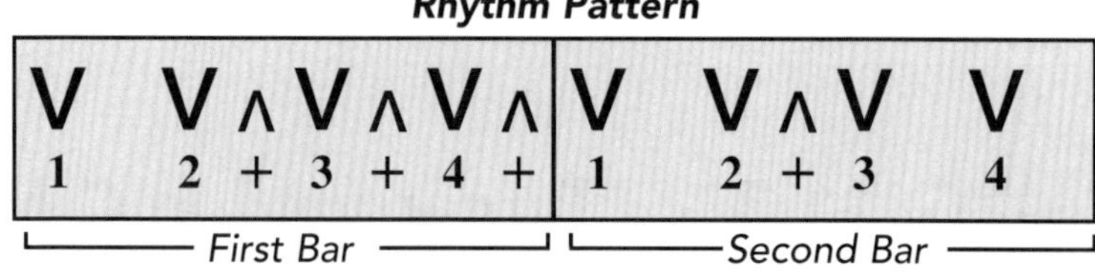

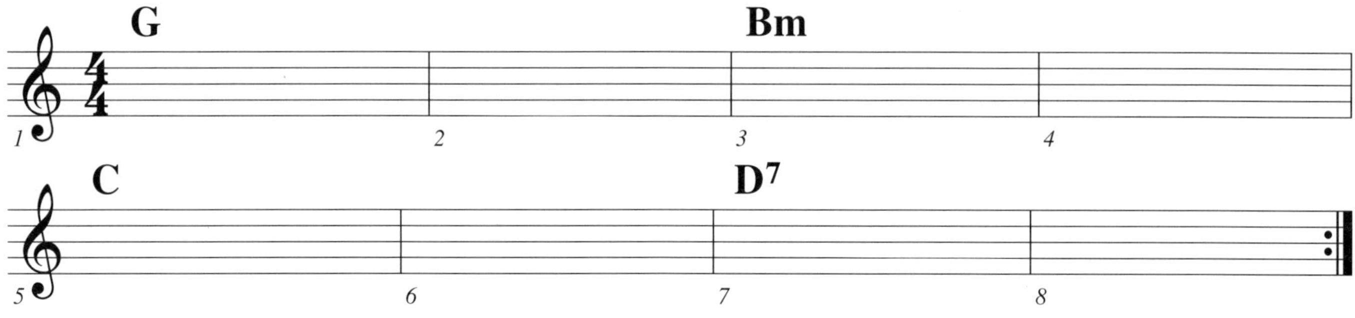

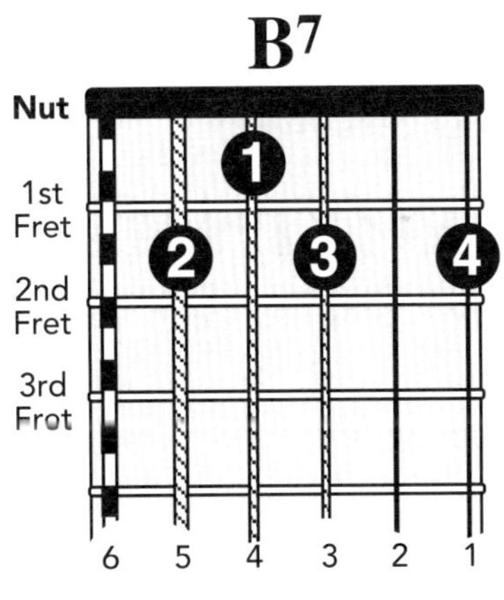

B Seventh Chord

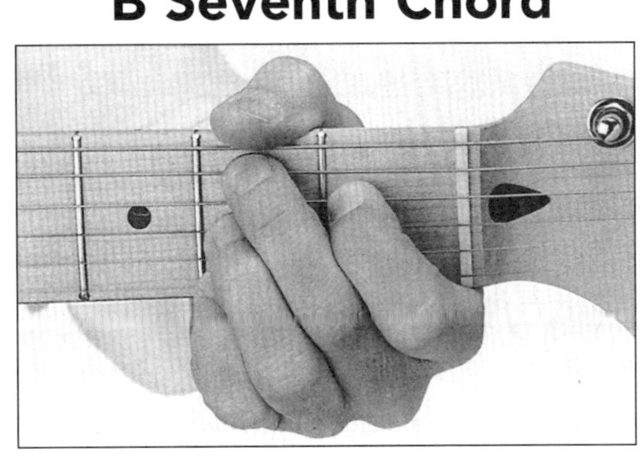

Chord Symbol

B7

To play the **B7** chord, use all **four** fingers of your left hand as shown in the diagram. Strum only **five** strings.

Some guitarists deaden the 6th string by lightly touching it with the left hand thumb which reaches over the top of the neck. The 6th string can then be strummed but it won't sound. This technique can apply to any chord where the 6th string note is not a part of that chord shape.

13.0

Rhythm Pattern

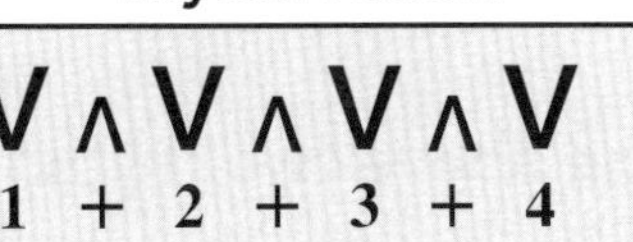

13.1

Rhythm Pattern

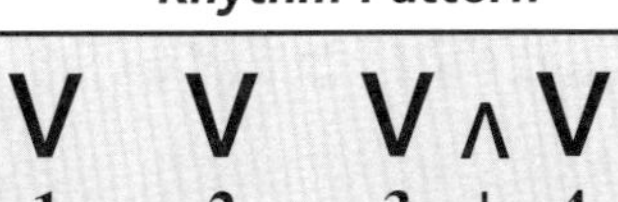

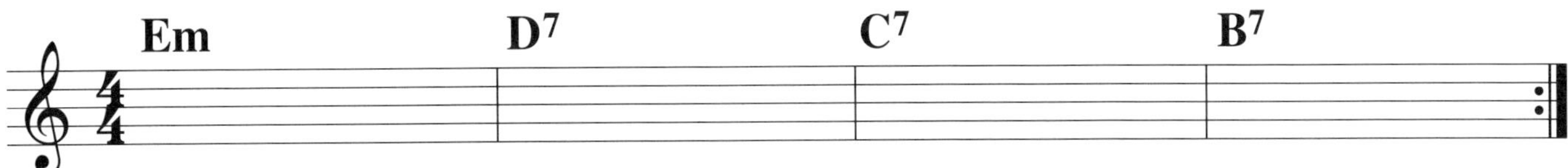

13.2

Rhythm Pattern

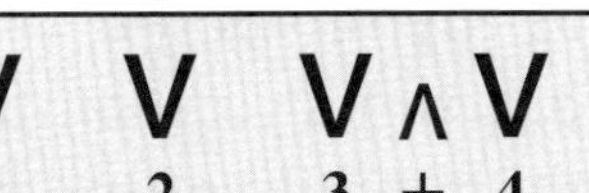

The following progression contains both **B7** and **Bm**.

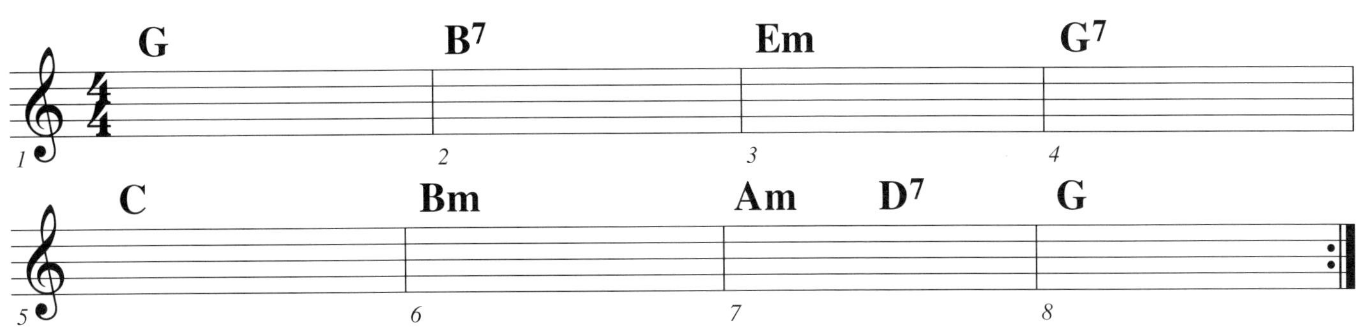

LESSON SEVEN

SILENT STRUMS AND CONTINUOUS RHYTHMS

The basic $\frac{4}{4}$ rhythm pattern learnt in Lesson 1 consisted of four down strums i.e.

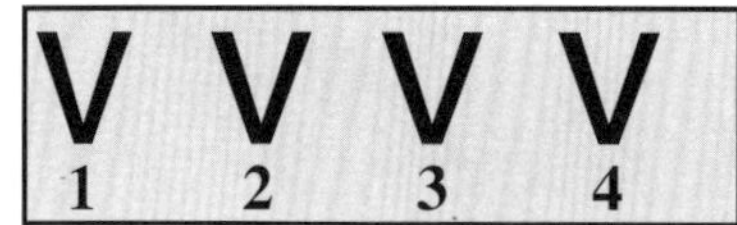

Watch your right hand as you play this pattern again. You will notice that your hand actually moves **up and down in a continuous motion**, but it only makes contact with the strings on the **down** strum (**V**). The silent upward motion can be represented by a broken upward strum (∧) indicating a silent upward strum.

So the basic rhythm **could** be written as:

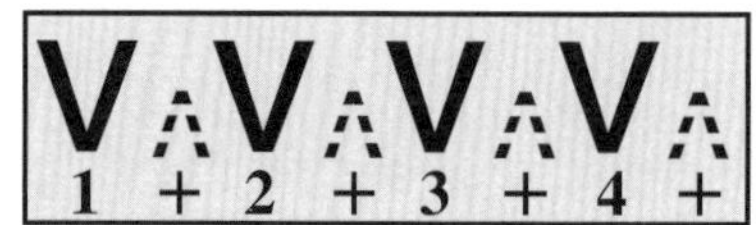

The above two rhythm patterns sound exactly the same.

When you play eighth note rhythms, (see Lesson 3) you will see that your right hand also moves up and down in a continuous motion sometimes making contact with the string and sometimes not. Some very useful and interesting rhythm patterns can result by incorporating eighth note rhythms with **silent down strums**.

SILENT STRUM SYMBOLS

When an **upward** strum is made without contacting the strings it can be represented by: ∧

When a **downward** strum is made without contacting the strings it can be represented by V

14.0

Try the following rhythm holding a **C** chord.

1.

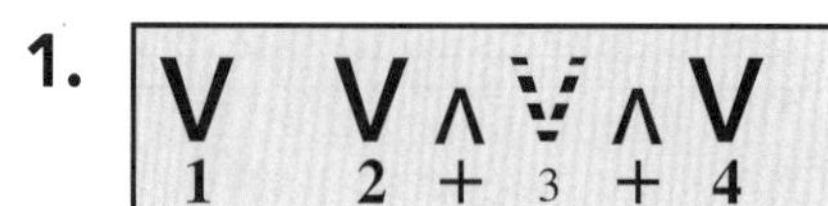

This rhythm is the same as **eighth note rhythm pattern 2** in Lesson Three, except that the down strum on the third beat does not make contact with the strings. Practice this rhythm until you perfect it. You can apply it to any chord progression you like. This is a very important rhythm and will be the basis of many other rhythms.
Apply this rhythm pattern to the following chord progression. Use **pivot** and **slide** fingers where possible to make the chord changes easier.

14.1

Rhythm Pattern

1.

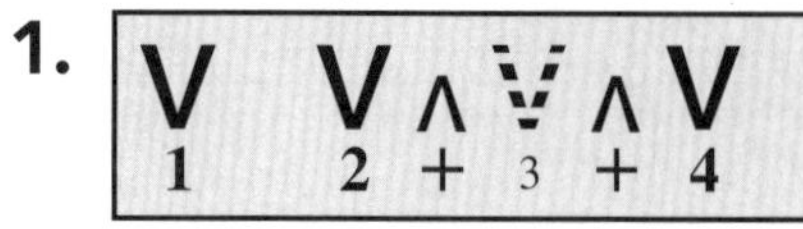

C | Am | Dm | G7

Try a variation of this rhythm pattern on the following turnaround progression in the key of **G**. To make the chord changes easier use the alternative Em fingering on page 29.

14.2

2.
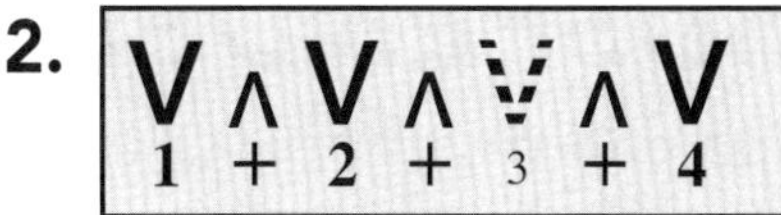

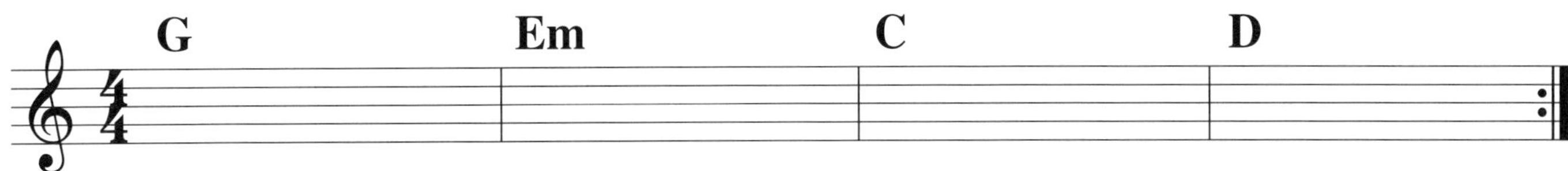

Variation 3 has a silent **down** strum on the 2nd and 3rd beat. Apply it to the progression below.

14.3

3.
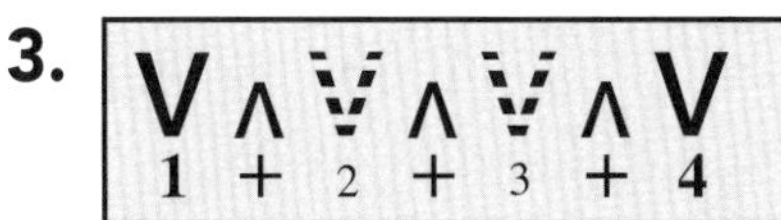

When changing between **C** and **A7** use your **second** finger as a pivot.

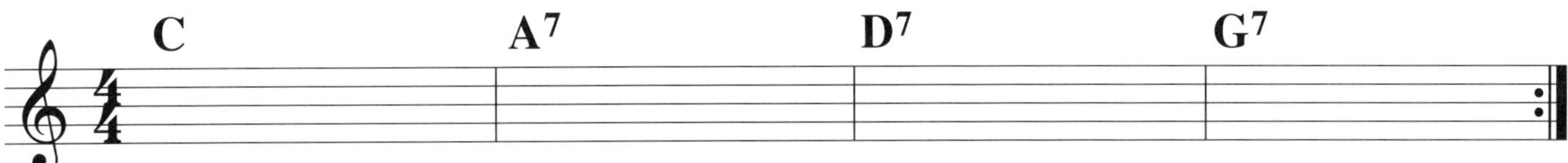

RHYTHM VARIATIONS

Try the following rhythm variations and make up your own. Apply these rhythms to any chord progression you like. A **G chord** is used on the recording. All these variations are in 4/4 time, but the same principle can be applied to 3/4 time. Also note that in all these rhythms your **right** hand moves up and down in a **continuous motion**. These rhythm patterns can sound "off the beat". This is called **syncopation**.

15.

4.
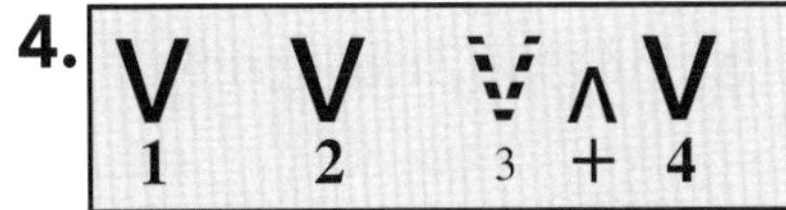

5.
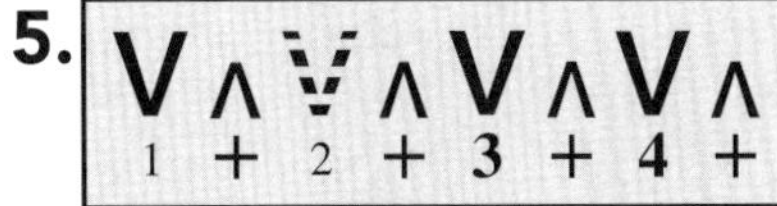

6.
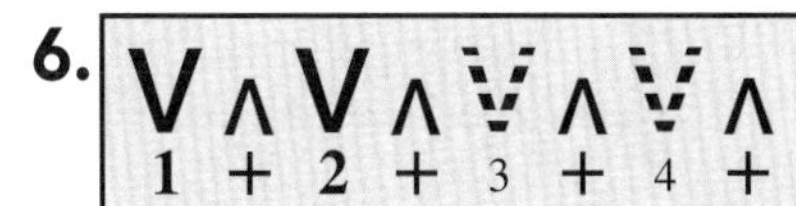

7.
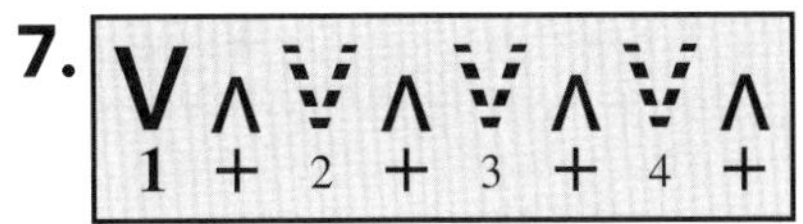

8.
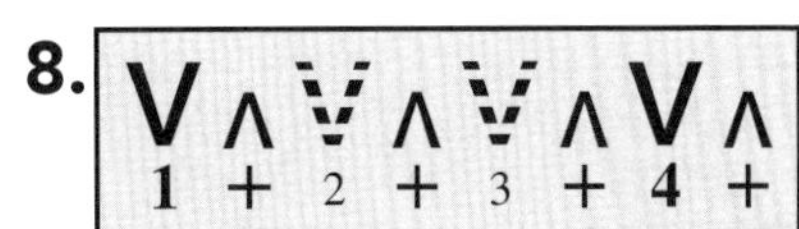

9.
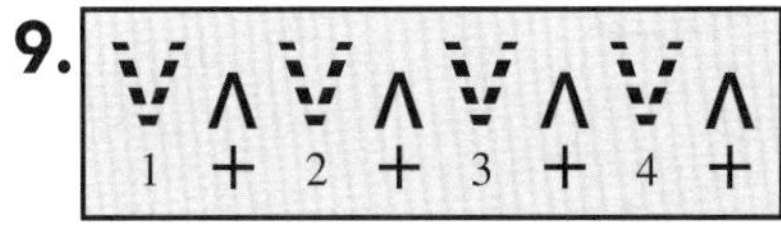

LESSON EIGHT

SUSPENDED CHORDS

The chord symbol for a suspended chord is the major chord symbol plus the word **sus** (or sometimes **sus4**).Suspended chords are often used to add interest to a progression if there is a long section of music containing only one chord.

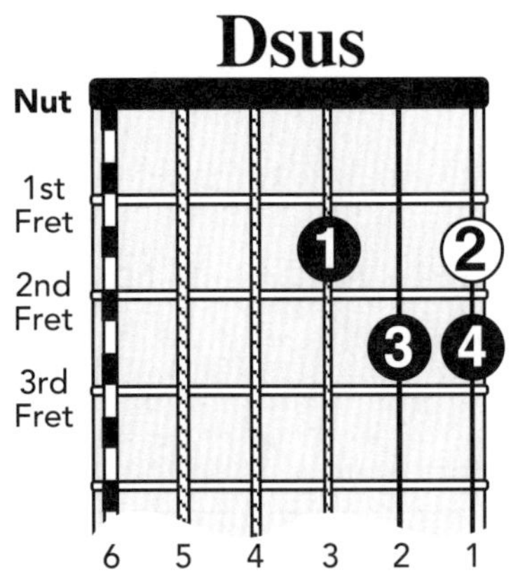

D suspended

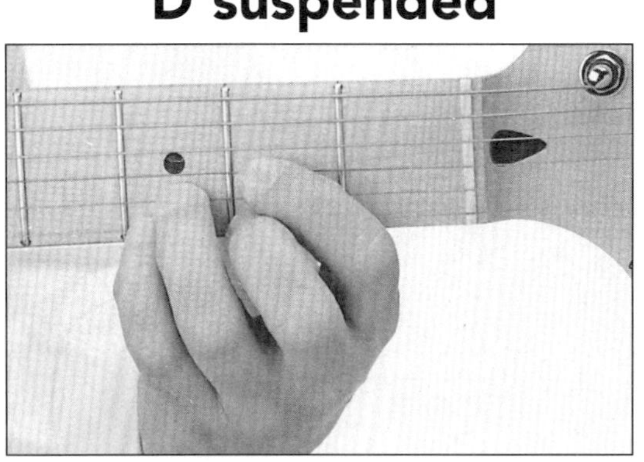

Chord Symbol

Dsus

Hold a **D major** chord shape then place your **fourth** finger on the **third** fret of the **1st** string.

The **open circle** on the chord diagram indicates that you hold the major chord shape and add the suspended note with your **fourth** finger. Suspended chords are usually played just before or just after the major chord, so it is easier to change between them if the major chord shape is held in position.

16.0

Rhythm Pattern

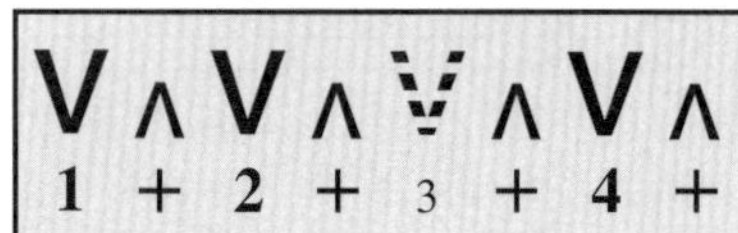

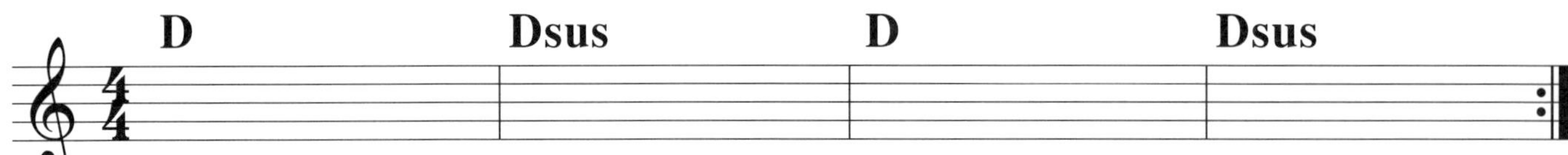

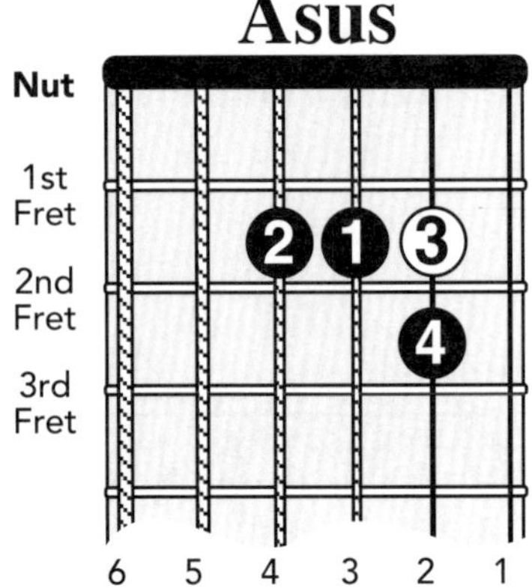

A suspended

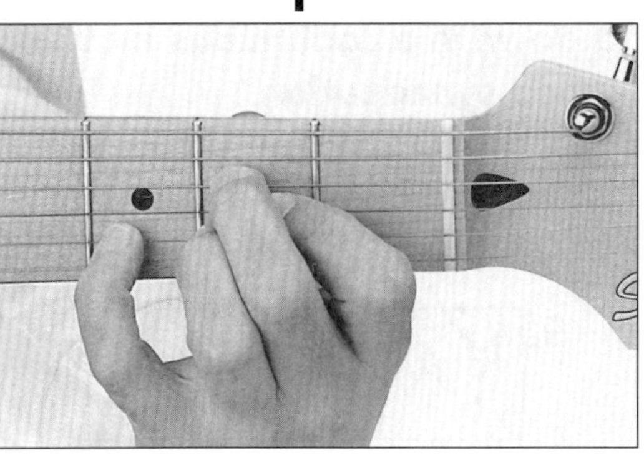

Chord Symbol

Asus

Hold an **A major** chord shape then place your **fourth** finger on the **third** fret of the **2nd** string.

Rhythm Pattern

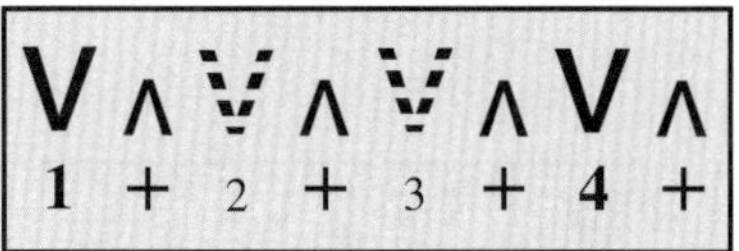

CD 1 **16.1**

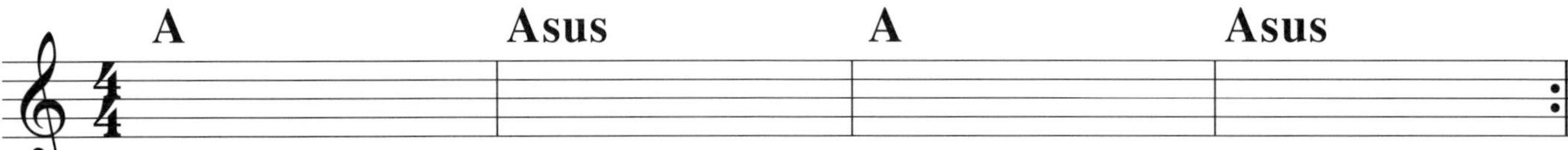

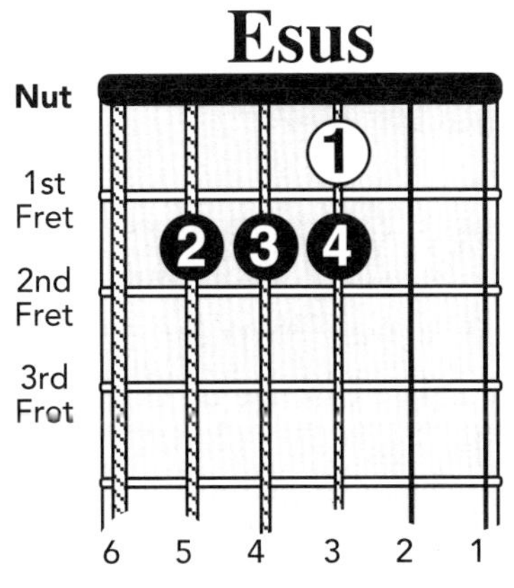

E suspended

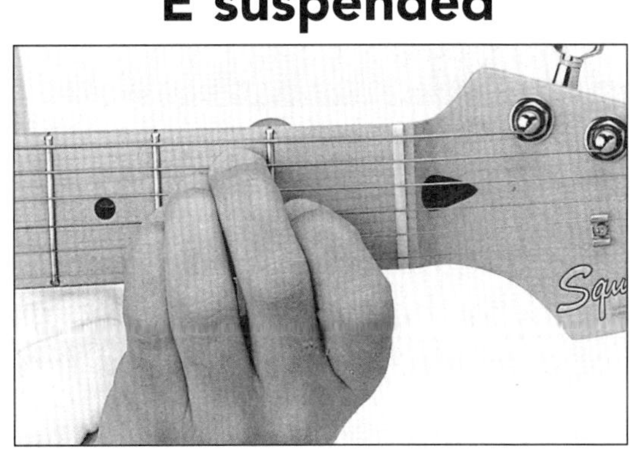

Chord Symbol

Esus

Hold an **E major** chord shape then place your **fourth** finger on the **second** fret of the **3rd** string.

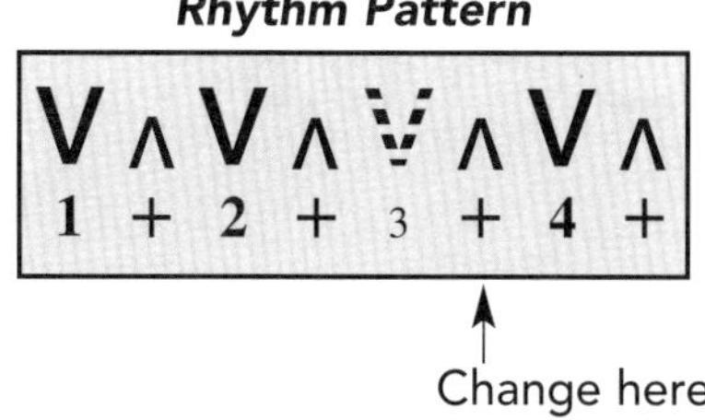

16.2

The following progression is two bars long. Change to the **E sus** chord (i.e. add your fourth finger) on the '**+**' after the 3 count.

E Esus | E Esus :||

The next progression contains all three of the above **sus** chords. Change to the **sus** chord on the '**+**' after the 2 count. Use pivot and slide fingers wherever possible between chord changes.

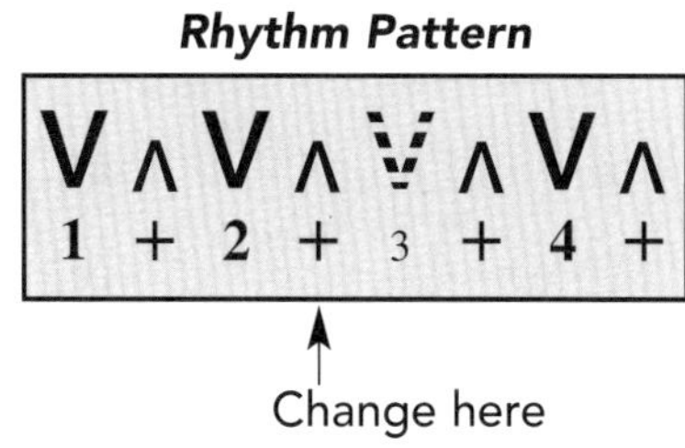

16.3

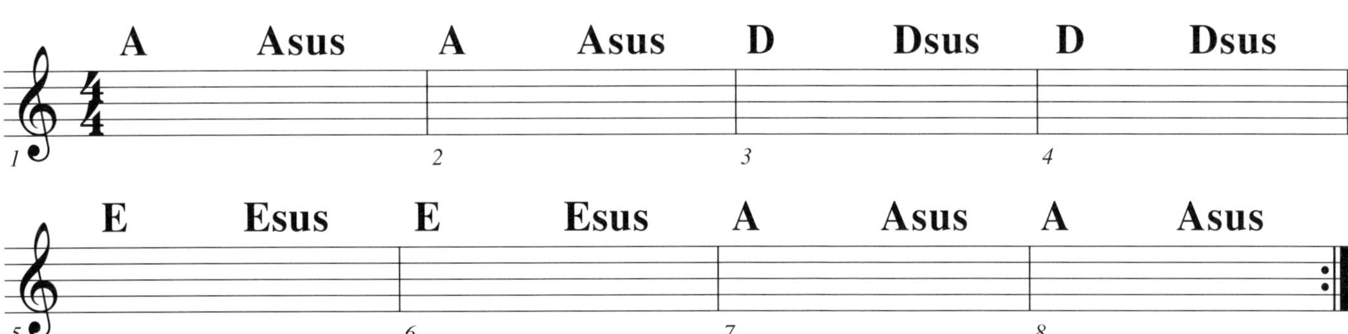

LESSON NINE

BASS NOTE RHYTHM PATTERNS IN $\frac{4}{4}$ TIME

In Lesson 4 you were introduced to bass note rhythm patterns in $\frac{3}{4}$ time. To play a bass note rhythm pattern in $\frac{4}{4}$ time, pick the bass note of the chord on the first beat and strum the first three or four strings of the chord on the 2nd, 3rd and 4th beats.

Play the following bass note rhythm pattern holding a G chord shape.

17.0

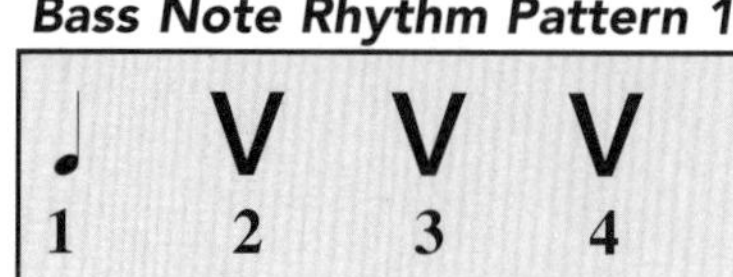

The best bass note to pick is the lowest note of the chord that has the same letter name of the chord. This is called the root note.
When playing a **G** type, pick the **6th** string note (**G note**), eg. G and G7 chords
When playing a **D** type, pick the **4th** string note (**D note**), eg. D, D7 and Dm chords
When playing a **C** type, pick the **5th** string note (**C note**), eg. C and C7 chords
When playing an **A** type, pick the **5th** string note (**A note**), eg. A, A7 and Am
When playing an **E** type, pick the **6th** string note (**E note**), eg. E, E7 and Em chords
When playing a **F** type, pick the **4th** string note (**F note**), eg. F chord

Practice this rhythm technique on each chord separately at first. Remember to hold the full chord shape even though you are not playing all the strings.

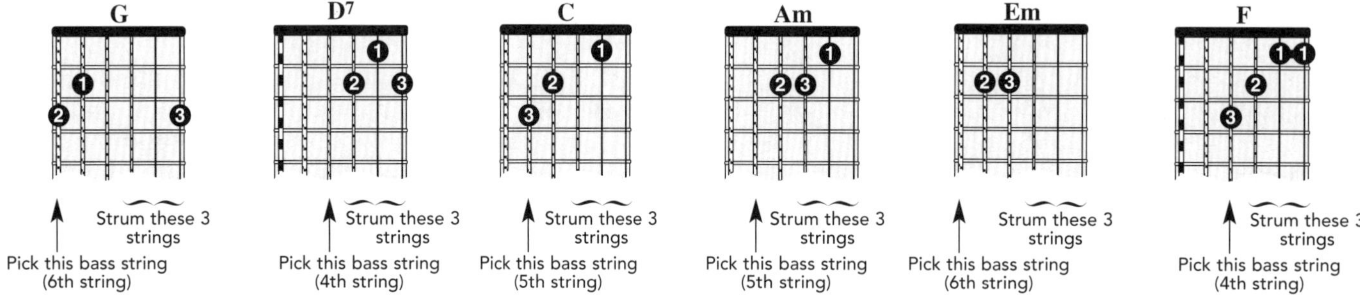

Play the following turnaround progression using bass note rhythm pattern **1**. Play the root note of the first beat of each bar.

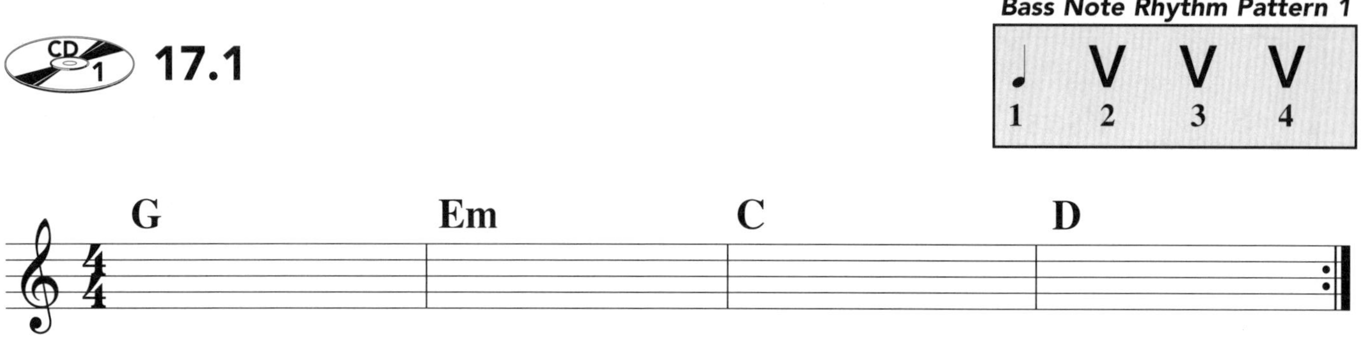

Play the following chord progression using a variation of bass note rhythm pattern 1 which contains **eighth** note strums on the second beat.

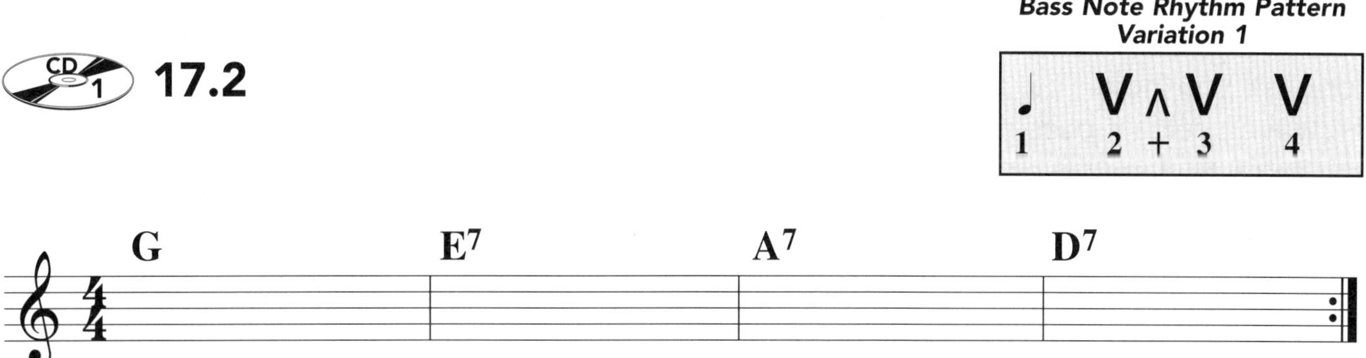

Another variation is to play the bass note on the first and third beats and strum on the second and fourth beats. Play the following bass note strum rhythm pattern, also holding a **G** chord shape. Play the root note of the chord on the first and third beats of the bar.

Bass Note Rhythm Pattern Variation 2

♩ V ♩ V
1 2 3 4

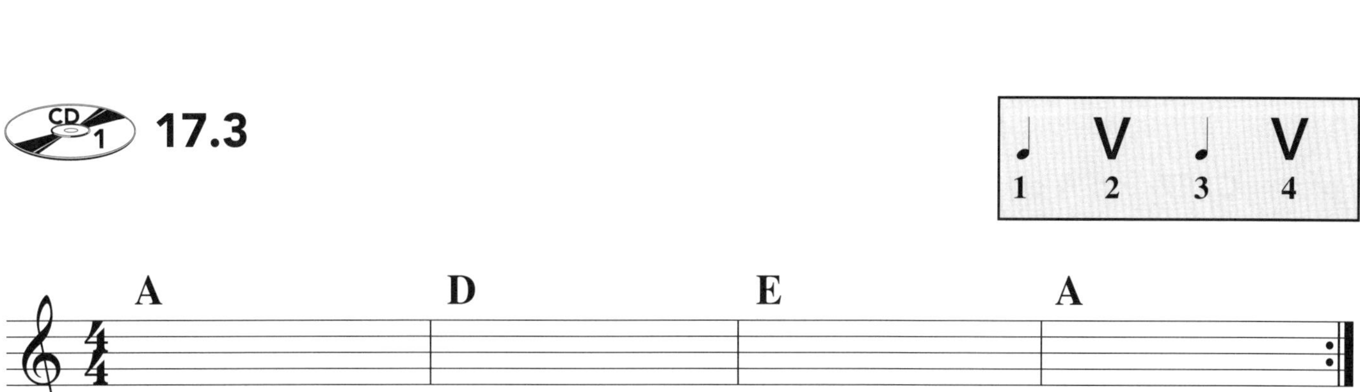

Now apply this variation to the following chord progression which contains two chords in each bar.

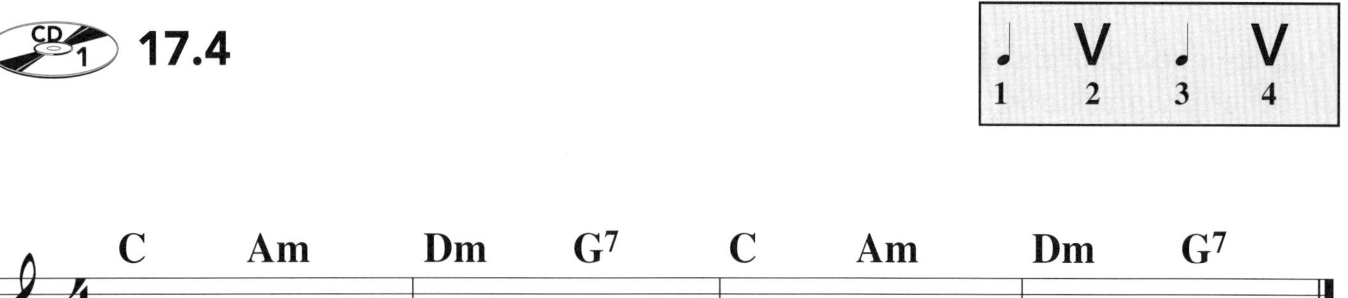

ALTERNATE BASS NOTE PICKING

In the previous examples the same bass note (the root note) is picked on the first and third beats. It is also possible to alternate the bass notes. This is a style commonly used in Country music. You can alternate between any bass notes that are in the chord shapes. As long as you hold the chord shape while picking the bass notes it will sound correct. However, certain bass notes sound better with certain chords. The best notes to use are the ones that sound good to your ear. It is usual to pick the **root note** on the **first beat** followed by a **different bass note** on the **third beat**.

Use alternate bass note picking in the following chord progression. You can also experiment using different bass notes.

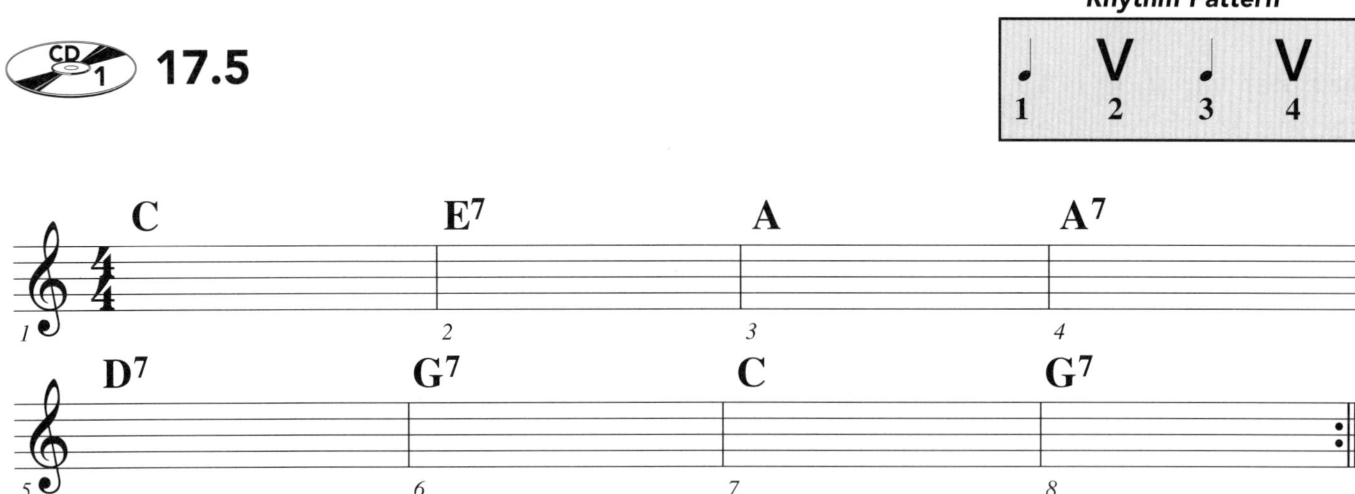

For the **C**, **E7** and **A** chords alternate between the 5th string bass note and the 4th string bass note.

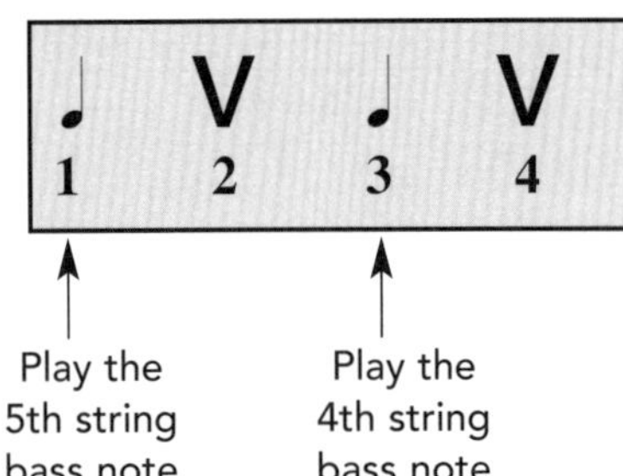

For the **D7** and **A7** chords alternate between the 4th string bass note and the 5th string bass note.

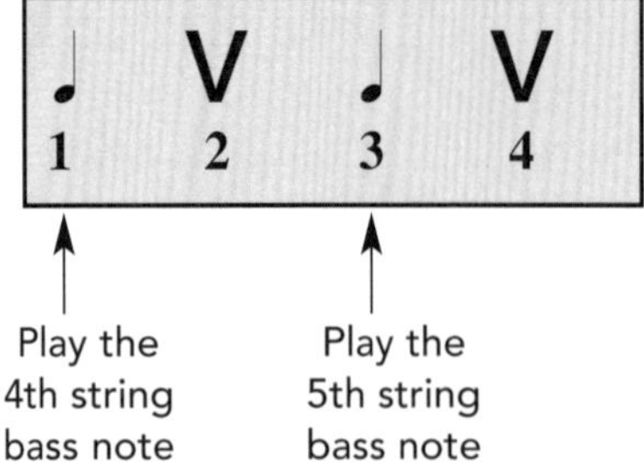

For the **G7** chord alternate between the 6th string bass note and the 4th string bass note.

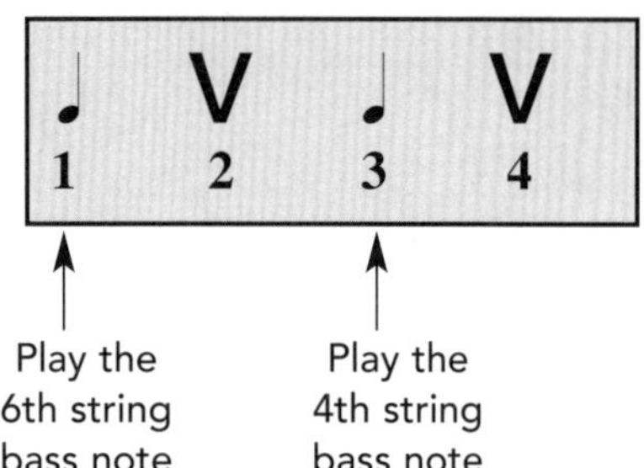

Practice each chord shape separately at first. Then try using alternate bass note picking on other progressions.

LESSON TEN

ALTERNATIVE CHORD SHAPES

There are many different chord shapes that can be used for a particular chord type. Here are some common alternative chord shapes that you should learn. Apply these new shapes to the progressions in this lesson and earlier lessons. Certain chord shapes sound better or are easier to play in some chord progressions than others.

E⁷

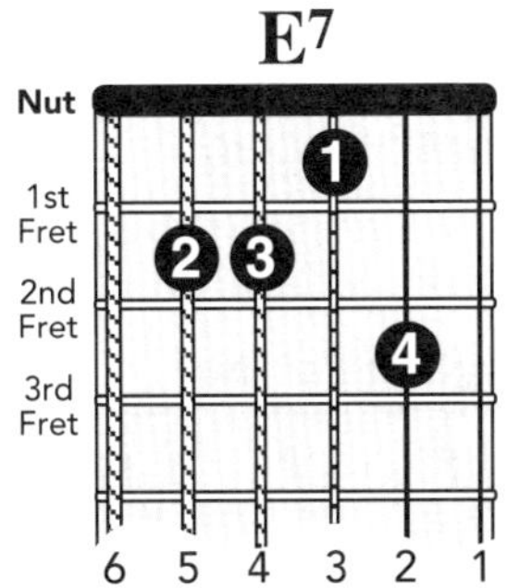

E Seventh

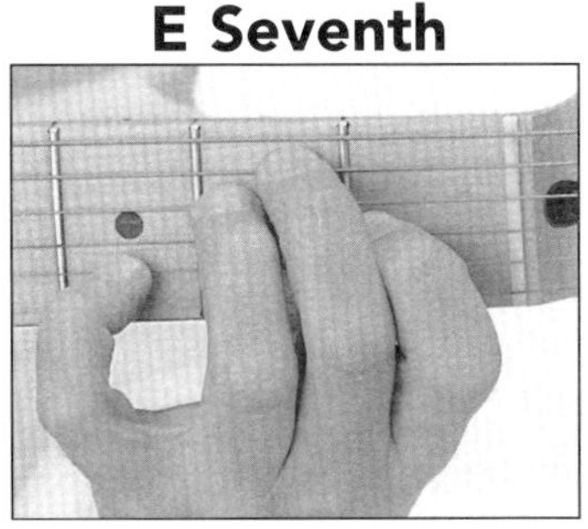

This **E7** shape is an **E** chord with an additional note played by the fourth finger.

A⁷

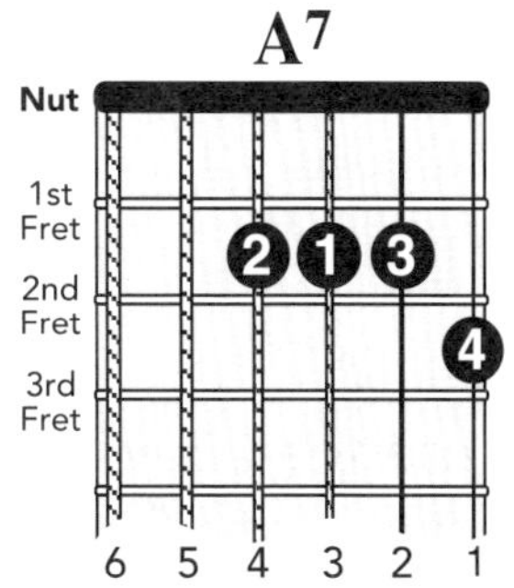

A Seventh

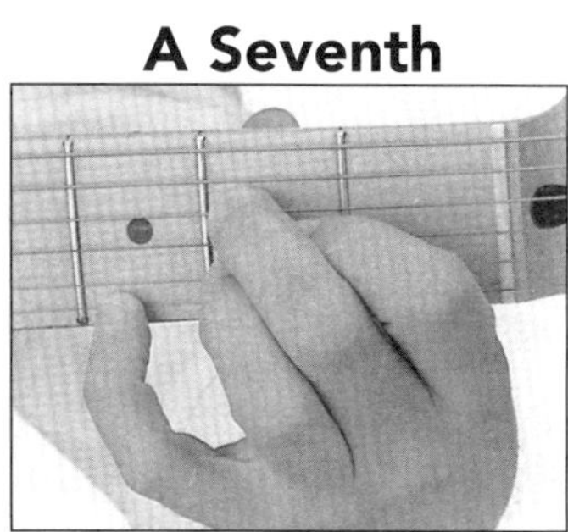

This **A7** shape is an **A** chord with an additional note played by the fourth finger.

18.0

Rhythm Pattern

V	V	V	V
1	2	3	4

E E⁷ A A⁷ D D⁷ G G⁷ C

MAJOR SIXTH CHORDS

Major sixth chords are commonly referred to as **sixth** chords. The chord symbol for the sixth chord is the major chord symbol followed by the number **6**.

E⁶

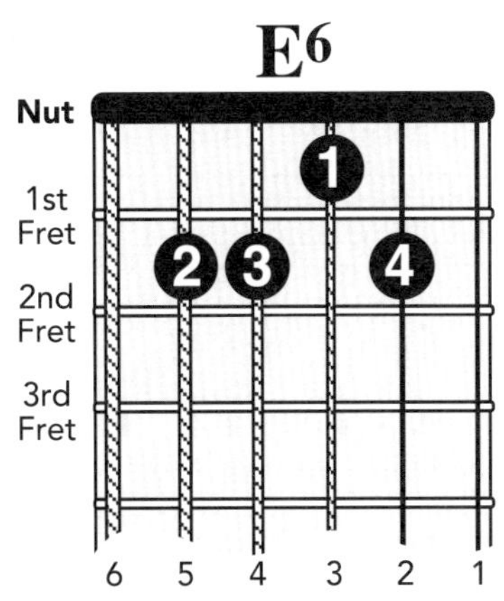

E Sixth Chord

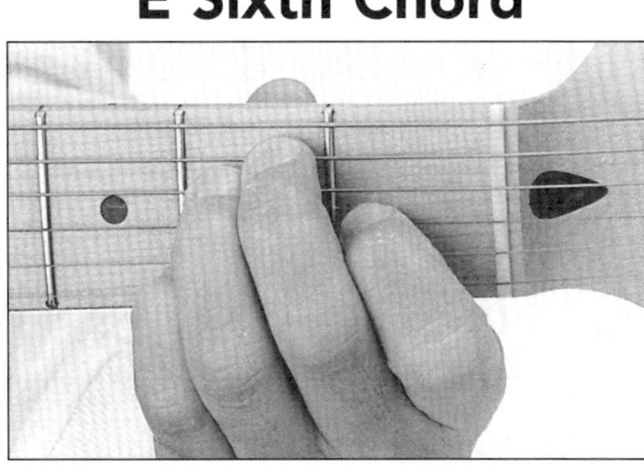

Chord Symbol

E⁶

The **E6** chord shape is an **E** chord with the additional note played by the **fourth** finger.

18.1

In the following chord progression use the alternative **E7** chord shape shown above. Hold the **E** chord shape throughout and move only the **fourth** finger to change chords.

Rhythm Pattern

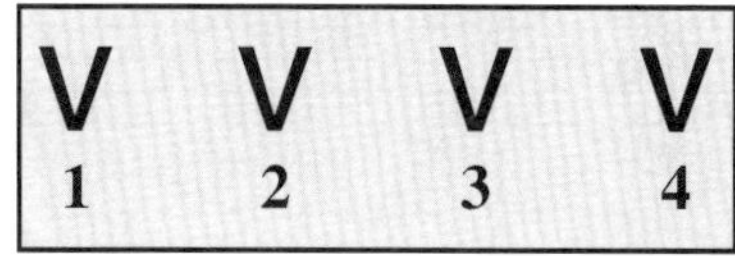

E E⁶ E⁷ E⁶ E E⁶ E⁷ E⁶

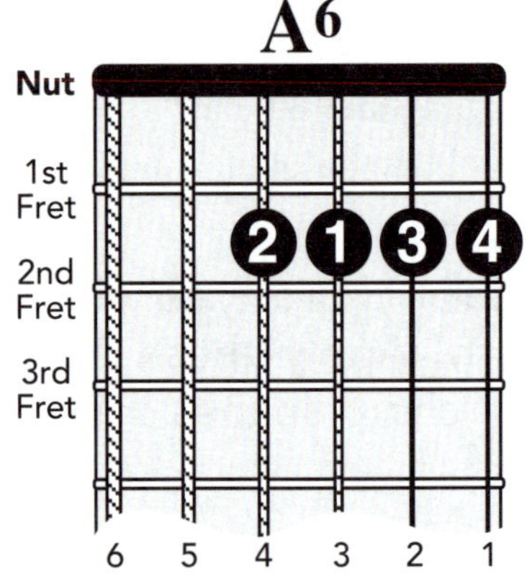

A Sixth Chord

Chord Symbol

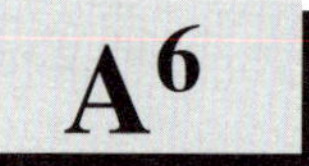

The **A6** chord shape is an **A** chord with the additional note played by the **fourth** finger. Another way of playing this shape is to bar all **four** strings with the **first** finger.

18.2

Rhythm Pattern

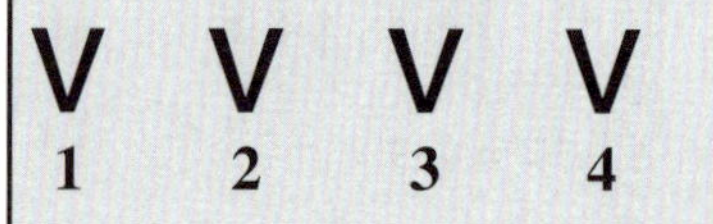

In the progression below use the above fingering for the **A6** chord. For the **A7** chord, just slide the **fourth** finger to the **third** fret of the **1st** string. This will make the chord change easier.

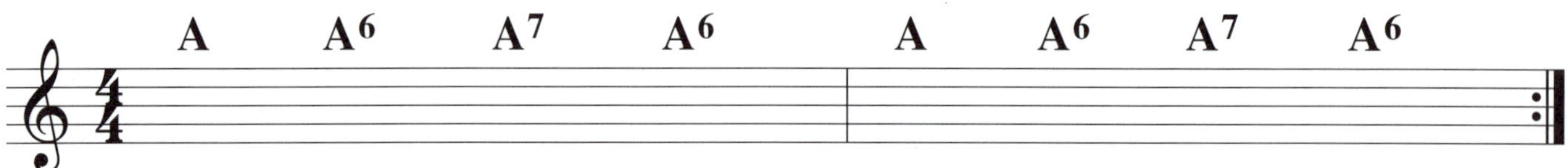

19.

Rhythm Pattern

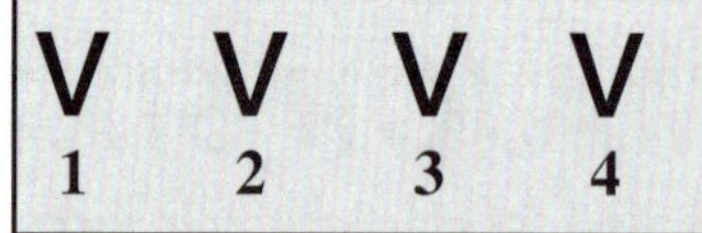

This Blues in **E** uses the previous two progressions. There are four chords in each bar, each receiving one strum, except for bars **9** and **12** where a **B7** chord is played.

LESSON ELEVEN

HOW TO READ MUSIC

Good rhythm guitar players are able to move freely between chords and single notes. To do this well, you need to understand how the notes relate to the chords; and this in turn requires a basic knowledge of music theory. The first step is learning to read music.

There are two methods used to write guitar music: the **traditional music notation** method (using music notes, ♩) and **tablature.** Both are used in this book but you need only use one of them. Most guitarists find tablature easier to read. However, it is important to learn to read traditional music notation as well. Nearly all sheet music is written in traditional notation. Even if you don't read well, you will need a basic knowledge of how rhythms are written.

TABLATURE

Tablature is a method of indicating the position of notes on the fretboard. There are six "tab" lines, each representing one of the six strings of the guitar. Study the following diagram.

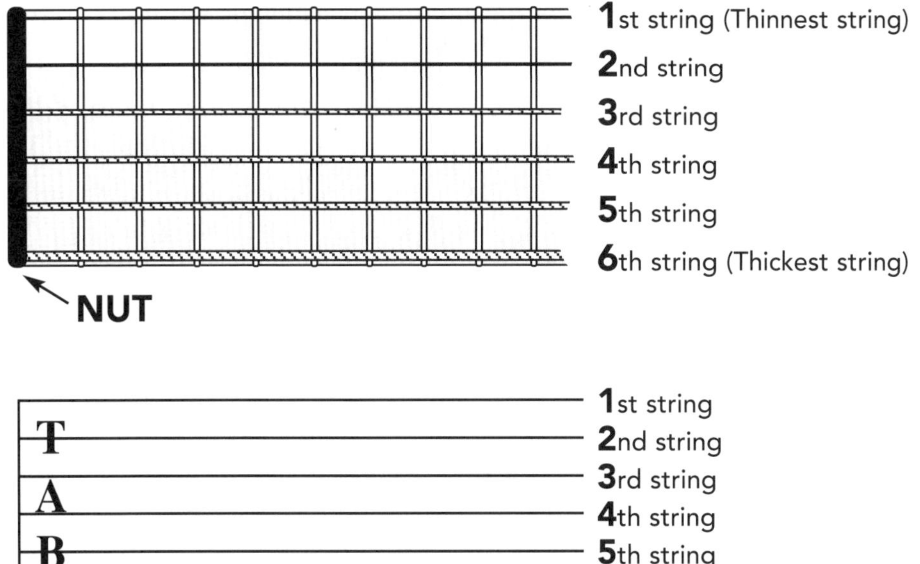

THE LEFT HAND

The left hand fingers are numbered as such:

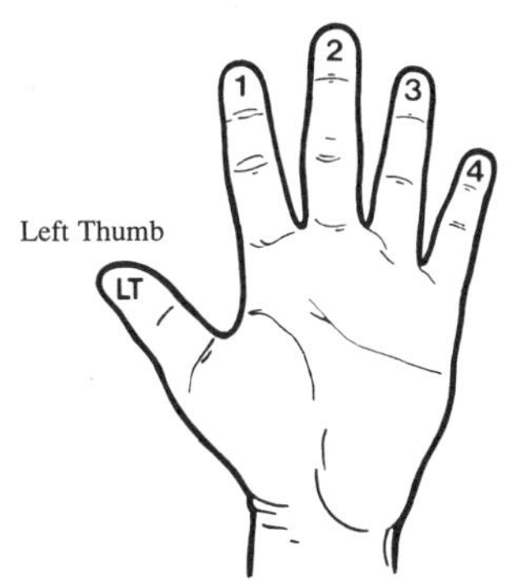

When a number is placed on one of the lines, it indicates the fret location of a note e.g.

T A B 0

This indicates the open (unfretted) 3rd string (a G note).

T A B 3

This indicates the 3rd fret of the 5th string (a C note).

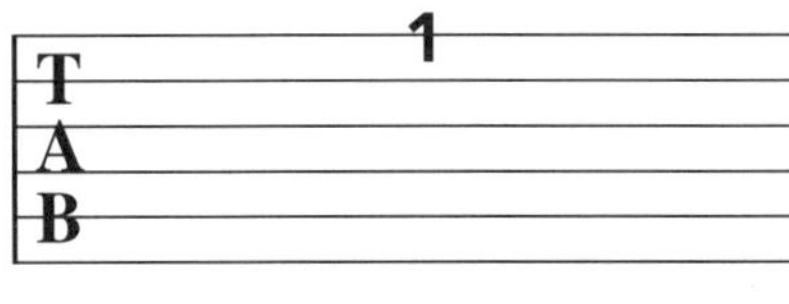

This indicates the 1st fret of the 1st string (an F note).

MUSIC NOTATION

The musical alphabet consists of **7** letters:

A B C D E F G

Music is written on a **STAFF**, which consists of 5 parallel lines. Notes are written on these lines and in the spaces between them.

MUSIC STAFF

THE TREBLE or **'G' CLEF** is placed at the beginning of each staff line.This clef indicates the position of the note G.

The **head** of a note indicates its position, on the staff, e.g.:

When the note head is below the middle staff line the stem points upward and when the head is above the middle line the stem points downward. A note placed on the middle line (**B**) can have its stem pointing either up or down.

LEARNING THE NOTES ON THE STAFF

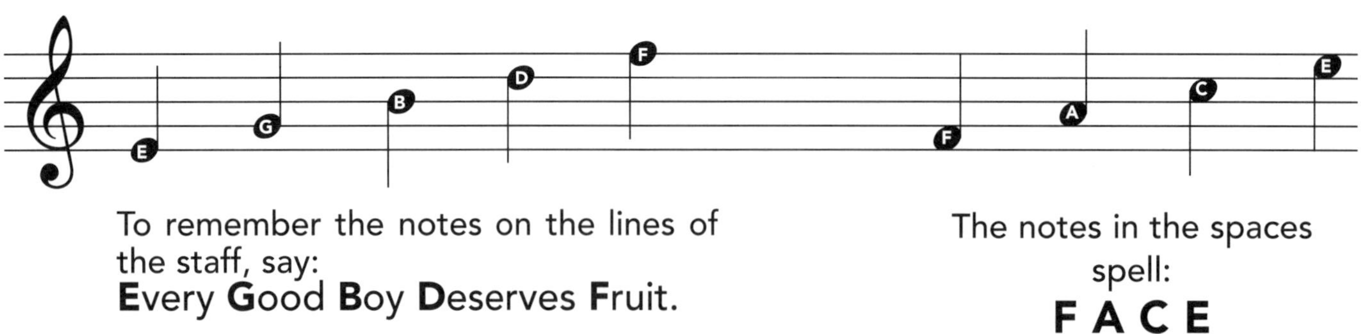

To remember the notes on the lines of the staff, say:
Every **G**ood **B**oy **D**eserves **F**ruit.

The notes in the spaces spell:
F A C E

Extra notes can be added above or below the staff using short lines, called **LEGER LINES**.

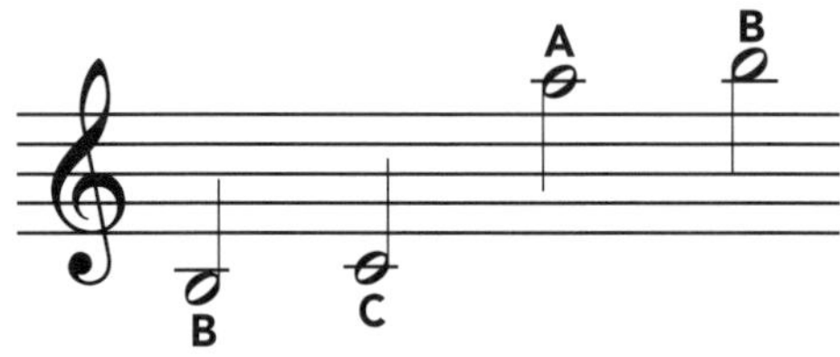

THE QUARTER NOTE

This is a **quarter note**. A quarter note lasts for **one beat**.

THE OPEN STRINGS OF THE GUITAR

The term "**open string**" means a string with no left hand fingers pressed down (unfretted). When correctly tuned, the open strings of the guitar correspond to the notes **E A D G B** and **E** from low to high, as shown below. Notice that the open **4th** string **D** note is in the space below the staff, while the low **A** and **E** notes are on leger lines below the staff. Don't worry if you can't recognize these notes yet, they will all be introduced as the book progresses. An easy way to remember the names of the open strings (from high to low) is to say **E**aster **B**unny **G**ets **D**inner **A**t **E**aster.

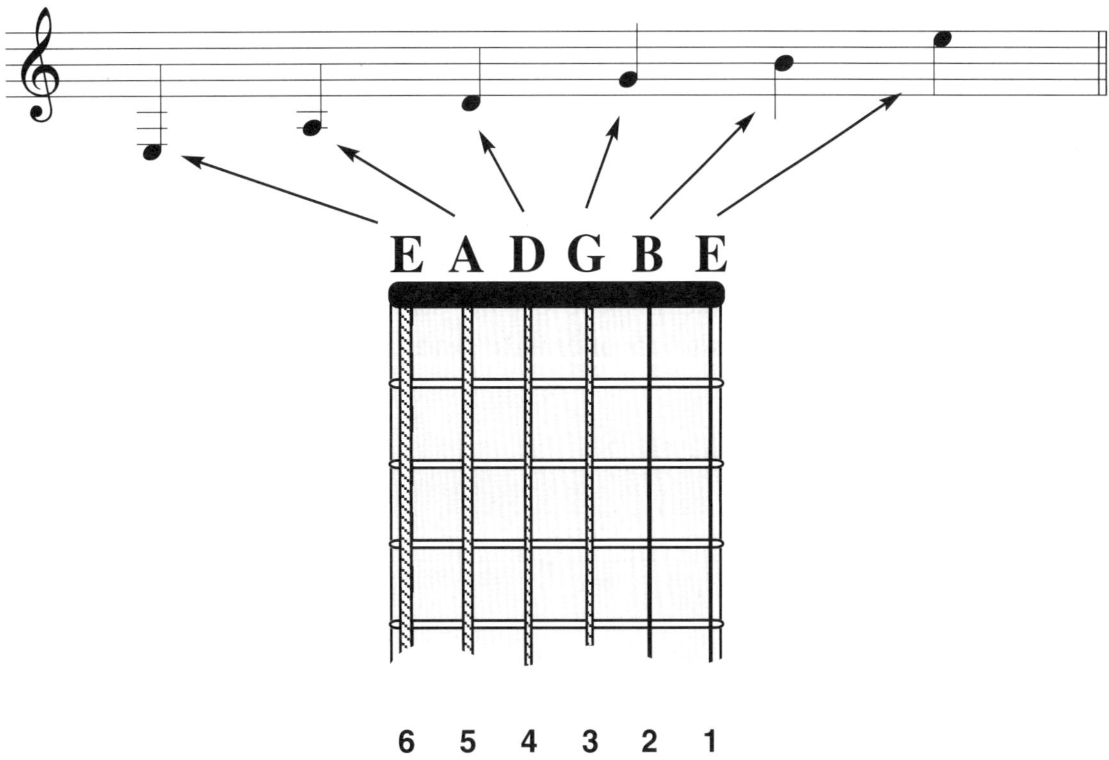

Here is an exercise to help you recognize the notes which represent the open strings of the guitar. Name the notes out loud as you play each one. All the notes here are quarter notes, which last for one beat each. However, don't worry about the timing at this stage; just make sure you are playing the correct notes.

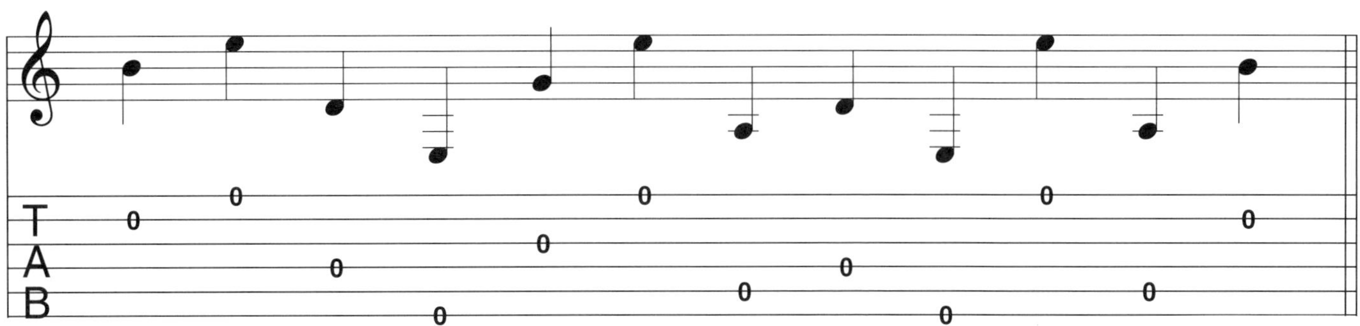

THE OPEN POSITION

The same note can often be played in more than one place on the guitar fretboard. To avoid confusion, the fretboard can be divided into **positions** consisting of groups of **four frets** to go with the **four fingers** of the left hand. The lowest fret of the group of four determines the name of the position. E.g. if the first finger is at the first fret, the other fingers follow naturally at frets 2, 3 and 4. This is described as the **first position**. If all the fingers were moved up one fret (first finger at the 2nd fret) this would be called **second position**, etc. When using the **open strings** as the lowest notes, you are playing in the **open position**. This consists of the open strings and the first three frets; as shown in the photograph below.

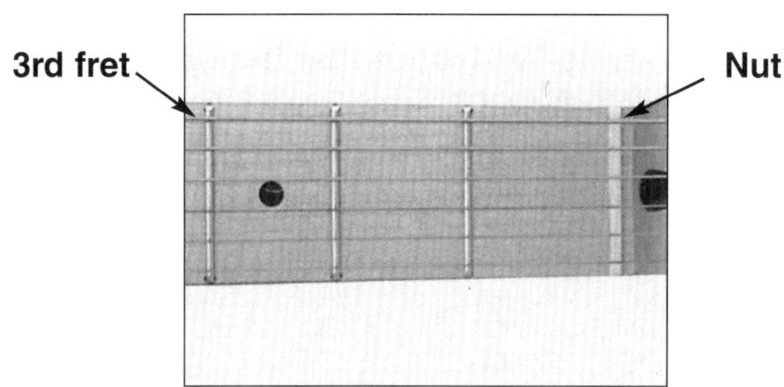

For the following exercise it is important to pay careful attention to the use of the left hand fingers. Do not worry about the note names for now, just follow the TAB. Remember to place the tips of the fingers close to the fretwire to avoid buzzing sounds. It is also important to keep the palm of the hand parallel to the neck, so that the fingers are stretched. This helps develop **independence** of the fingers. All fingers should be equally strong, that is, it should not be easier to play with one finger than the other.

CD 1 **20.**

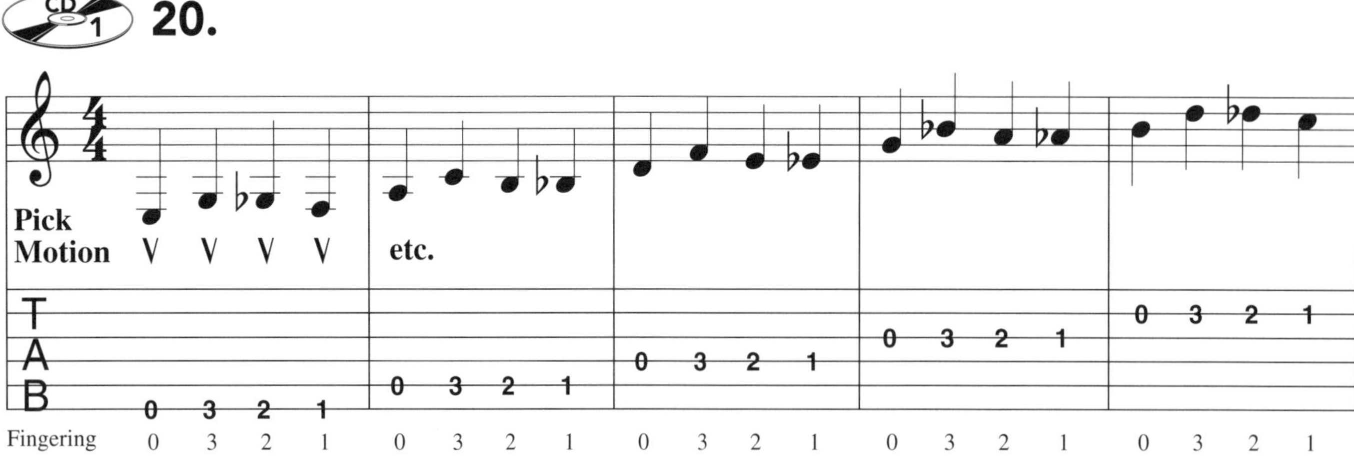

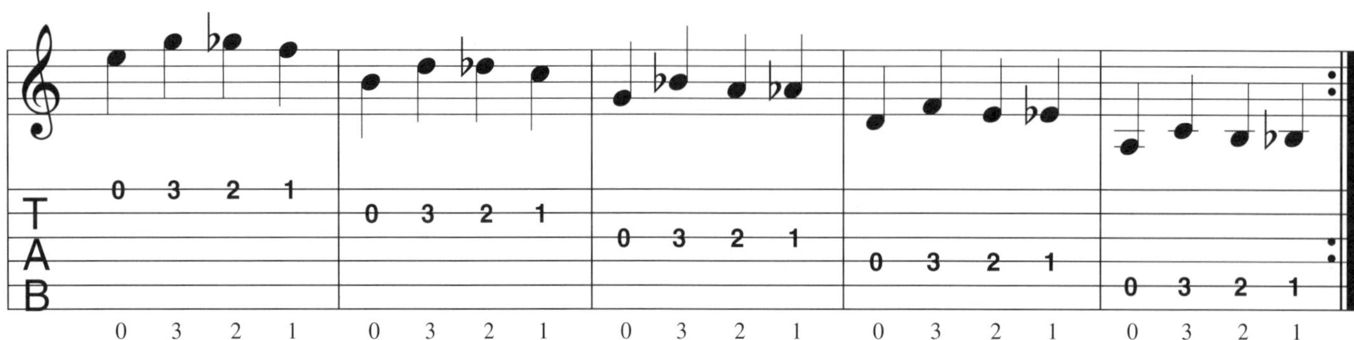

LESSON TWELVE

NOTES ON THE FIRST STRING

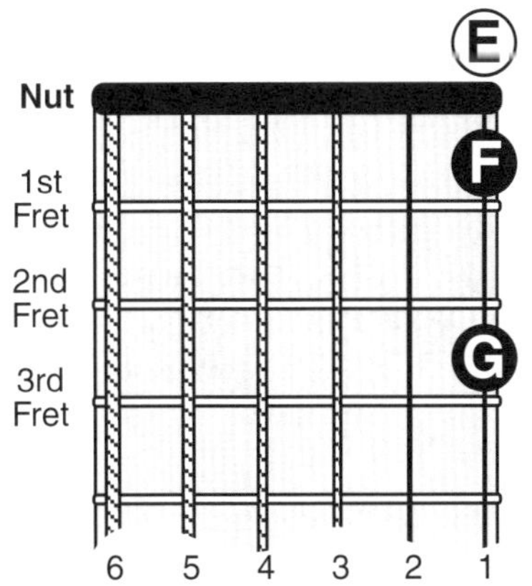

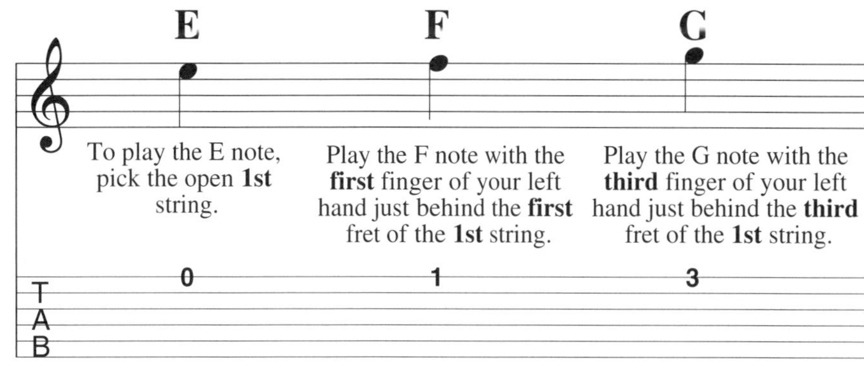

open 1st string

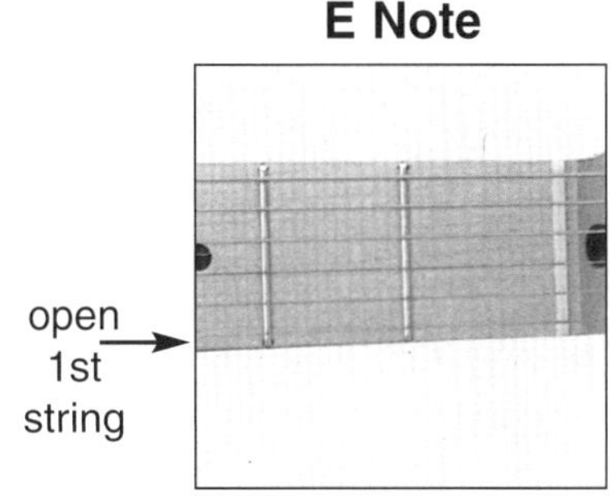

E Note

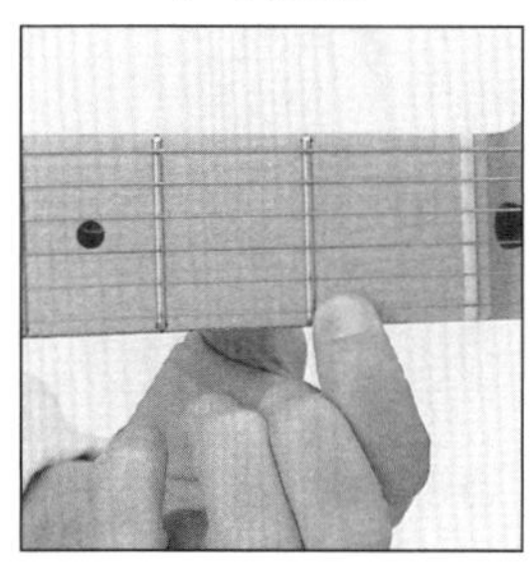

F Note

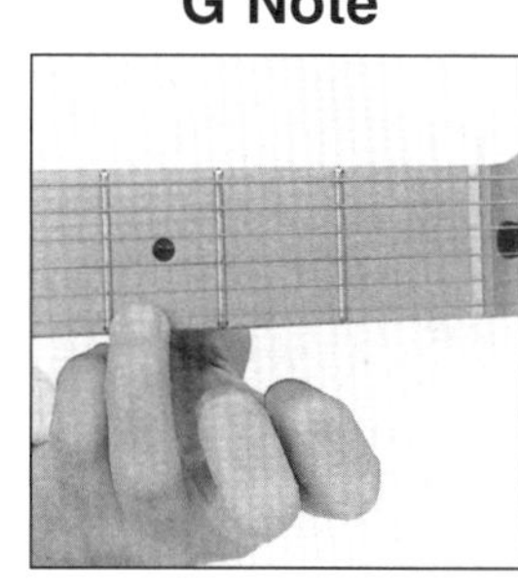

G Note

As a general rule:
Play notes on the **first** fret with your **first** finger.
Play notes on the **second** fret with your **second** finger.
Play notes on the **third** fret with your **third** finger.

The following example uses the notes **E**, **F** and **G** on the first string. As you move from **F** (1st fret) to **G** (3rd fret) leave your first finger on the **F** note. This will create a smoother sound when you return from **G** to **F**. Remember to play on the tips of your fingers and use only downstrokes with the pick. Listen carefully as you play and make sure your notes sound clear and even. To help you develop a good sense of time, **always use a metronome** and tap your foot on each beat. There are two ways to practice this exercise: one is to **name the notes out loud** as you play and the other is to **count** as you play. Use both these methods until the exercise becomes easy.

21.0

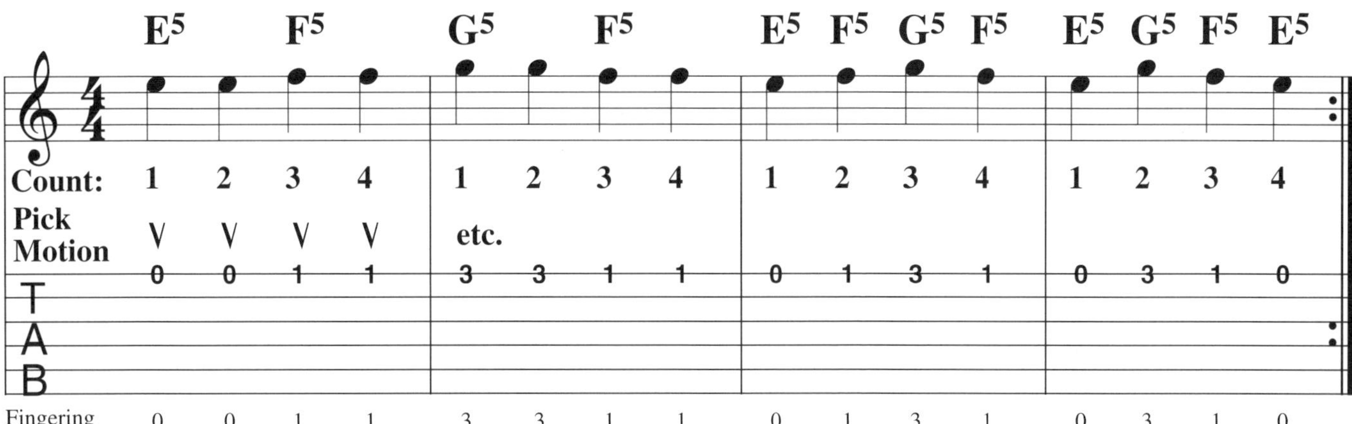

OVERDRIVE AND DISTORTION

One of the most popular sounds in **electric guitar** playing is **distortion**. This is achieved by **overdriving** an amp (turning the pre-amp volume up and the master volume down) or by using a distortion pedal. Pedals have a variety of controls, but usually include **drive** or **distortion** (to control the amount of distortion), **tone** (amount of treble or bass frequencies) and **level** or **output** (overall volume level). These are called **parameters**. They enable you to control and shape the sound to your personal taste. There are many different pedals available and it is best to try out several before buying one.

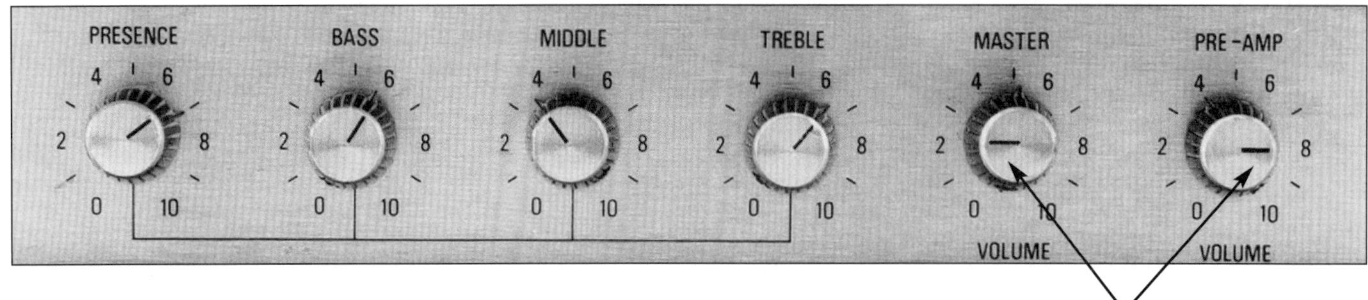

To achieve distortion sounds with an amp, turn your master volume **down** and your pre-amp volume **up**.

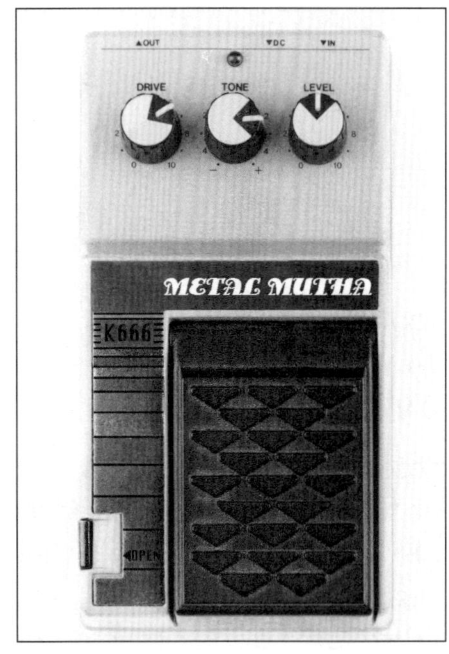

Distortion pedal

21.1

Here is another example using the notes **E**, **F** and **G** on the first string. It has been recorded using an overdrive sound. Set your amp or use a pedal to get an overdrive sound you like and then try playing along with the recording.

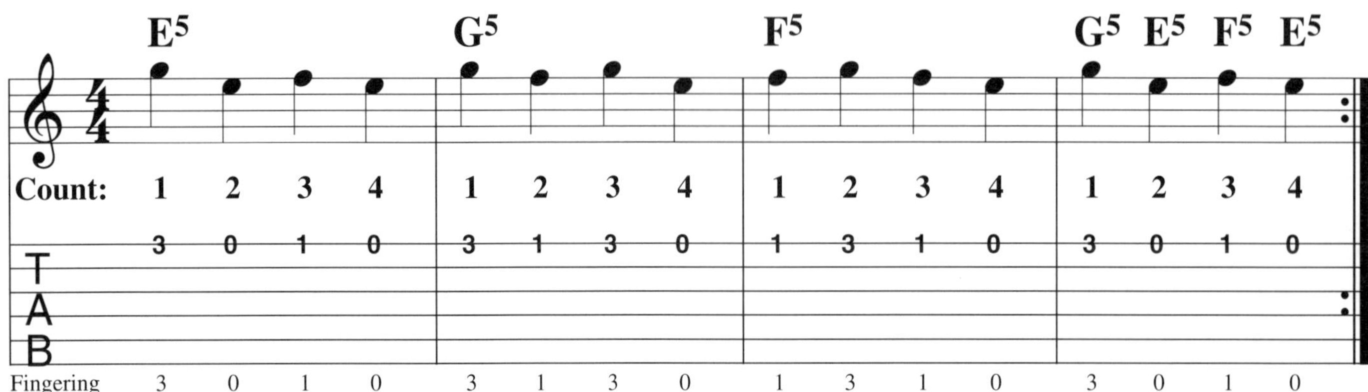

NOTES ON THE SECOND STRING

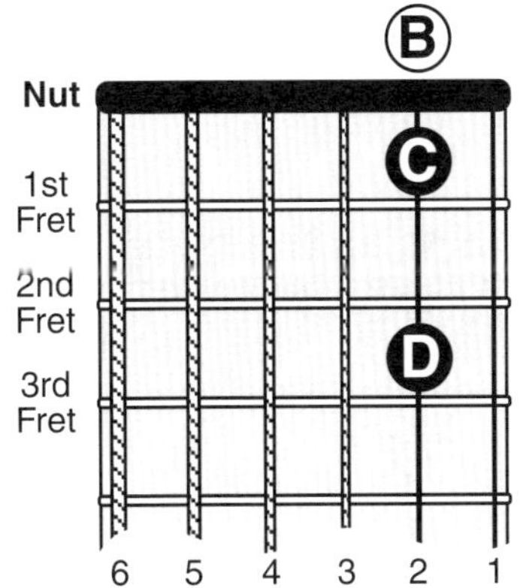

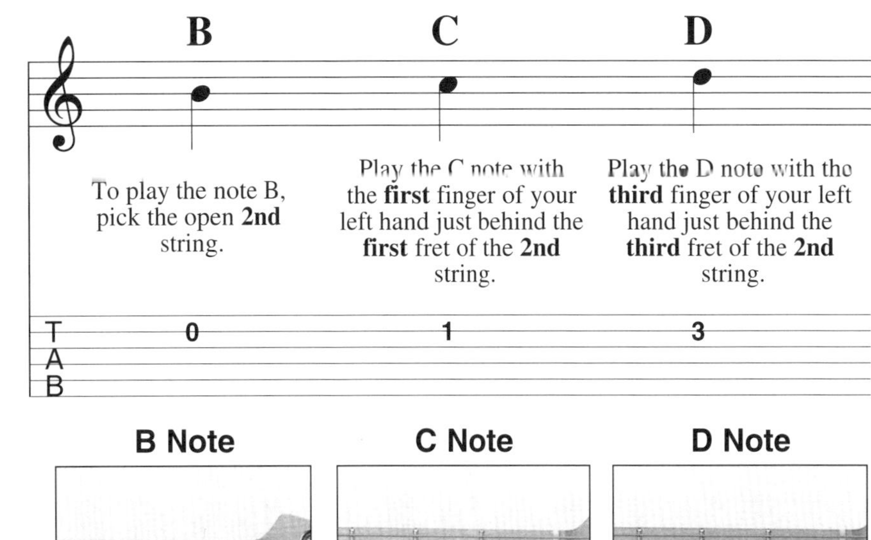

Notes written above the middle line of a staff usually have their stems going down. Notes written below the middle line of the staff usually have their stems going up. The stem for the **B note** can go up or down.

open 2nd string →

B Note **C Note** **D Note**

THE HALF NOTE

One of the ways expression is created in music is by using notes of different values (lengths). Music is like a language, there are short sounds, longer sounds, emphasised sounds and silences. These will all be introduced in the course of the book.

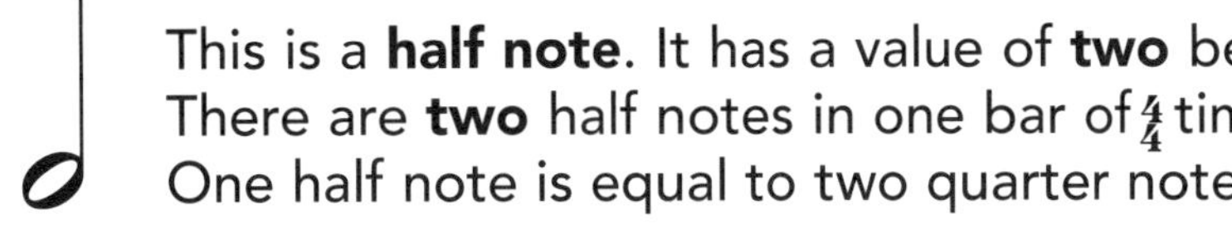

This is a **half note**. It has a value of **two** beats. There are **two** half notes in one bar of $\frac{4}{4}$ time. One half note is equal to two quarter notes.

Count: 1 2

22.0

The following example contains both quarter notes and **half notes**. Remember to count out loud as you play until you can play the example easily and evenly. Once again, it has been recorded using an overdriven sound. You can choose to use either a clean sound or an overdriven sound for any example.

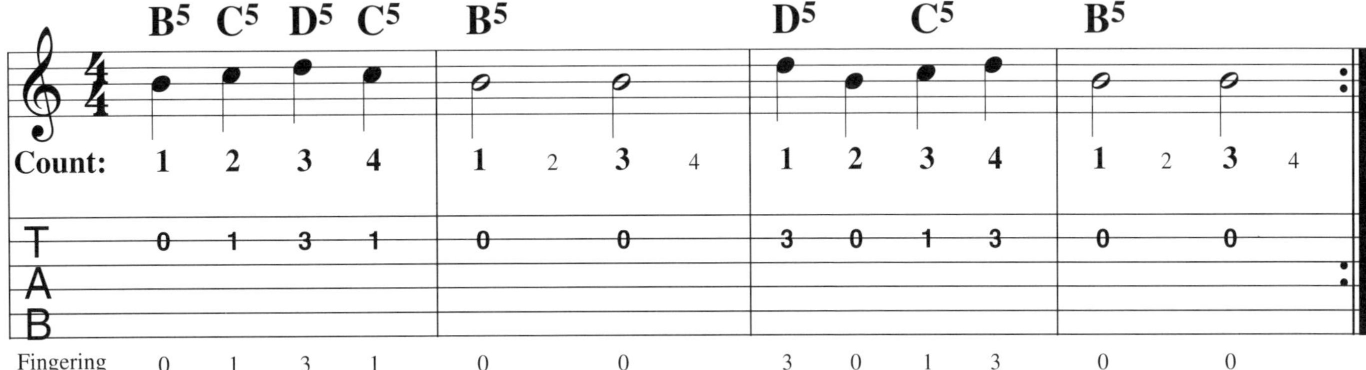

THE WHOLE NOTE

This is a **whole note**.
It lasts for **four** beats.
There is **one** whole note in one bar of $\frac{4}{4}$ time.

Count: 1 2 3 4

22.1

This example uses whole notes, half notes and quarter notes. It contains all the notes you have learnt on both the first and second strings. Remember to practice both naming the notes and counting as you play.

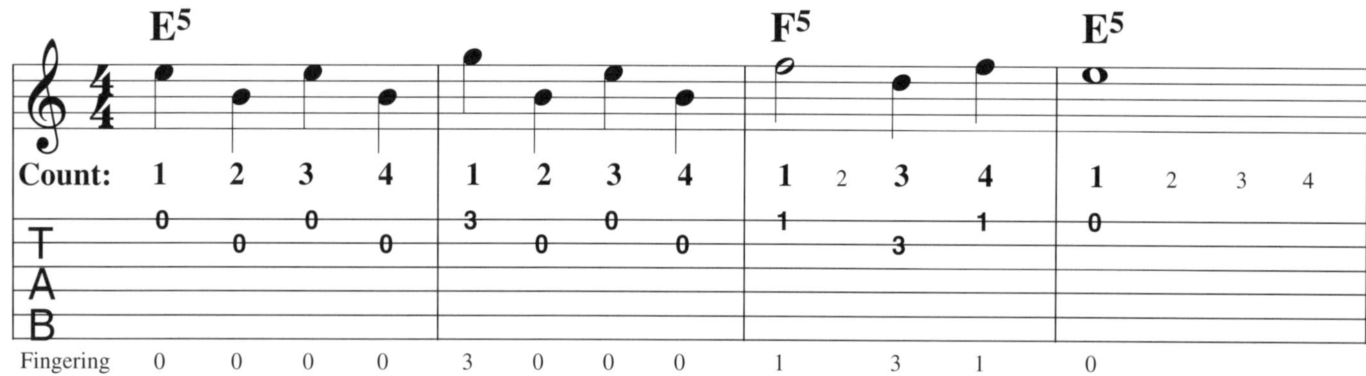

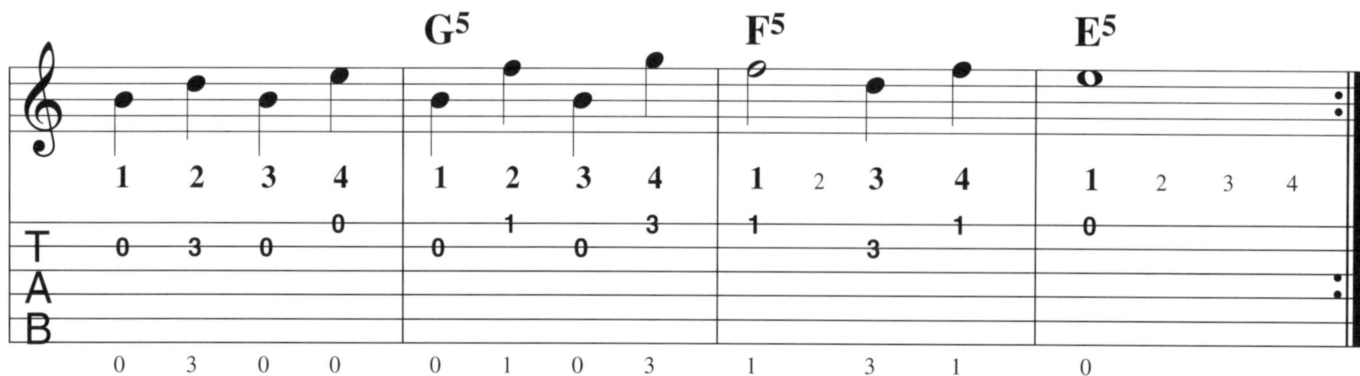

NOTES ON THE THIRD STRING

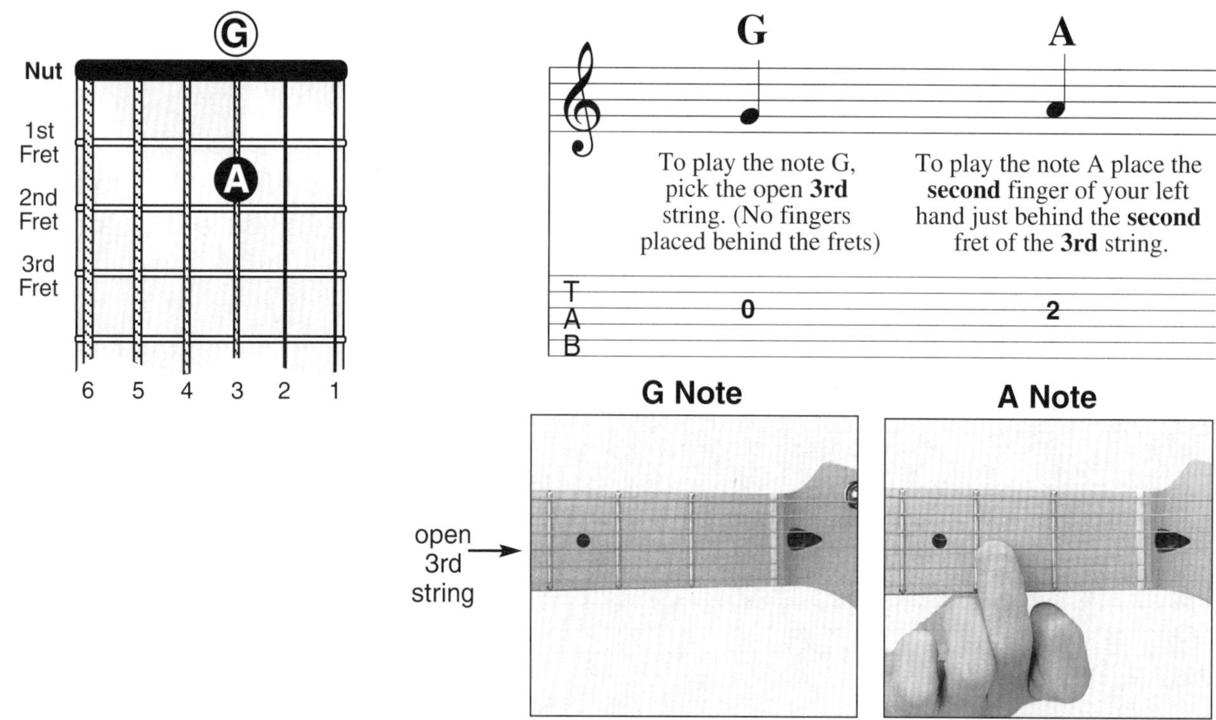

THE OCTAVE

Although there are only seven different letters in the musical alphabet, it is possible to find higher and lower versions of them at various places on the fretboard. The distance between any note and its next higher or lower occurrence is called an **octave** You already know two **G** notes–the open 3rd string and the third fret of the 1st string. These two G notes are an octave apart. The following example makes use of both these G notes.

23.0

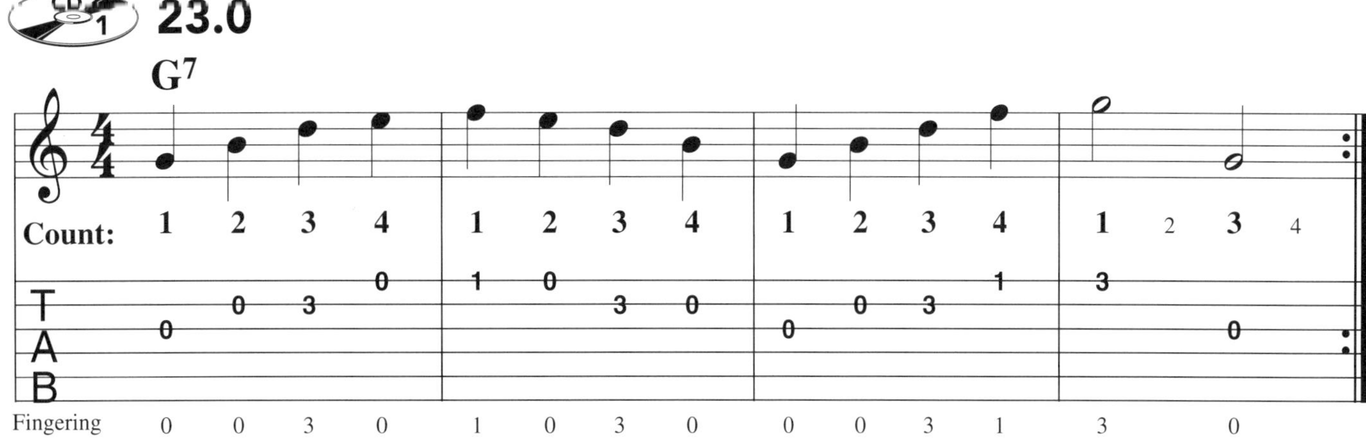

THE DOTTED HALF NOTE

A **dot** written after a note extends its value by **half**.
A dot after a half note tells you to hold it for **three** beats.

Count: 1 2 3

23.1

To finish this lesson, here is an example which makes use of all the notes and note values you have learnt so far. Remember to count as you play and be sure that all your notes are clear and even. Take it slowly at first and gradually work up speed until you can play along with the recording. Experiment with clean sounds and various amounts of overdrive.

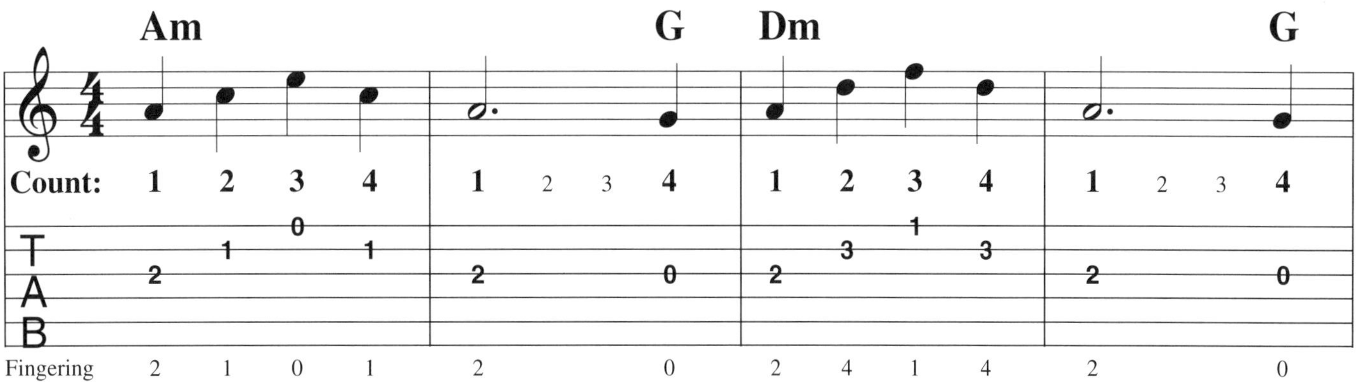

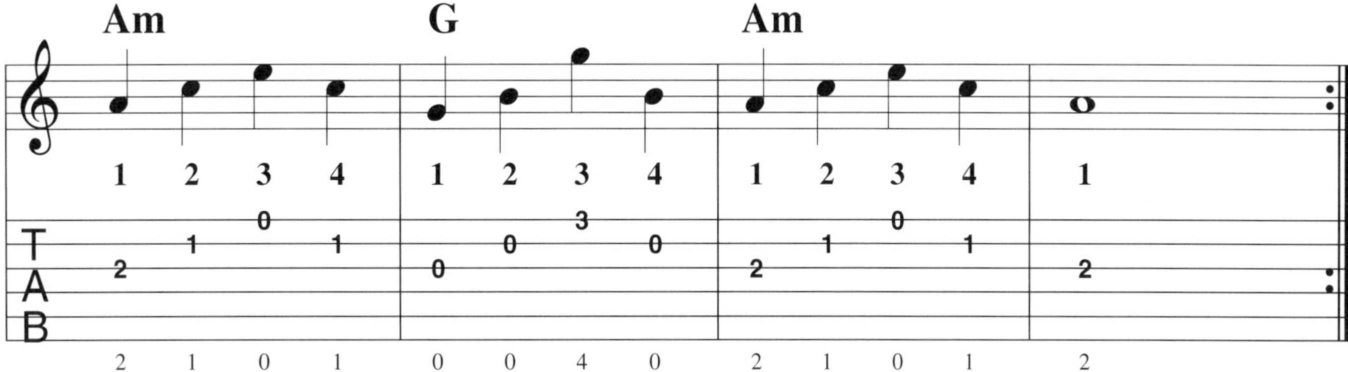

LESSON THIRTEEN

EIGHTH NOTES

In lesson 3 (page 22) you learned about eight note rhythms and alternate strumming. Eight note rhythms are based on eighth notes.

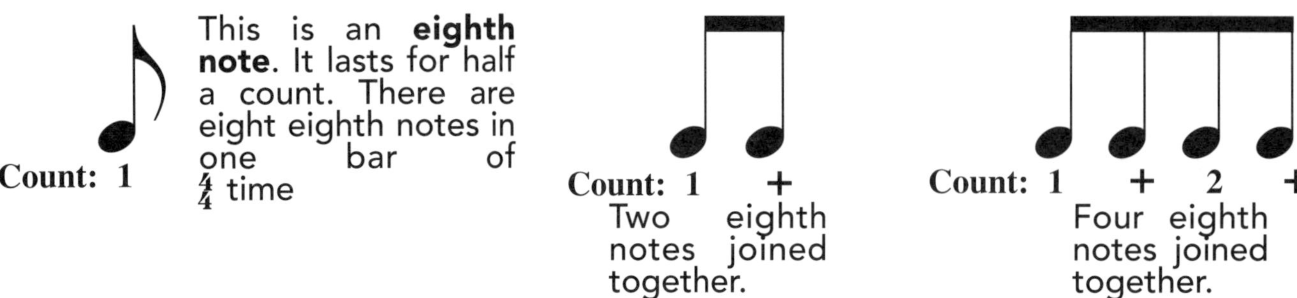

24.0 How to Count Eighth Notes

Count: 1 + 2 + 3 + 4 +
Say: 1 and 2 and 3 and 4 and
TAB: 0 0 0 0 0 0 0 0

ALTERNATE PICKING

You will recall that alternate strumming is used when playing eighth note rhythms. A similar technique is used for picking eighth notes. It involves using a down pick (V) **on** the beat (the number count) and an up pick (Λ) **off** the beat (the 'and' count). This is called **alternate picking**, and is essential for the development of speed and accuracy. Practice example 24.0 using alternate picking until you can do it comfortably and then try the following example, which uses alternate picking for eighth notes and downstrokes for all the quarter and half notes. It is a good idea to practice the first two bars and last two bars separately at first, as the picking is quite different in these two sections.

24.1

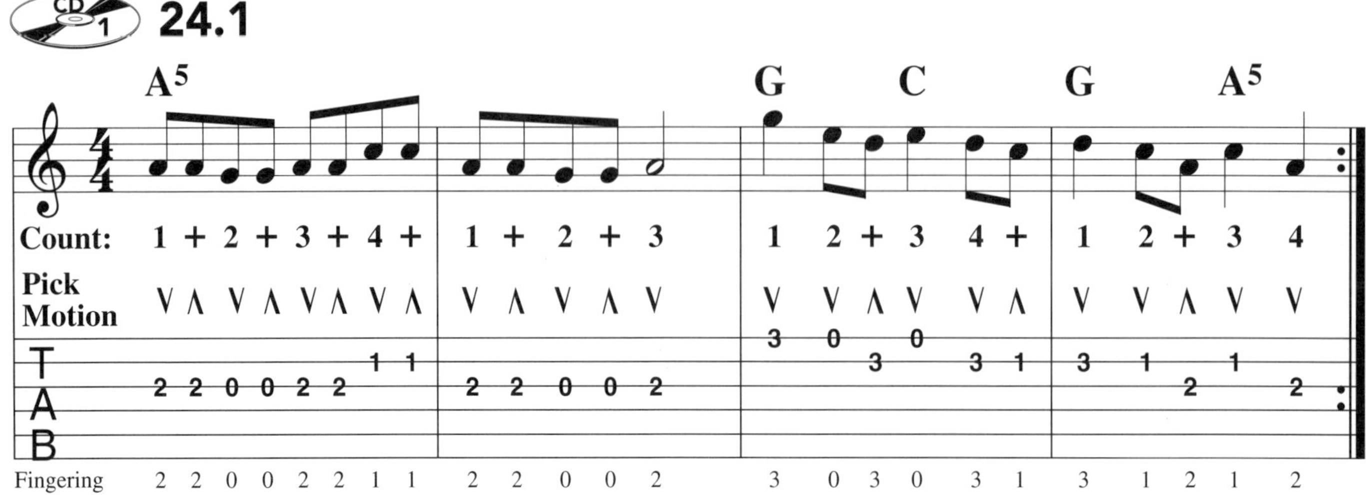

Here are some more examples to help you become comfortable using eighth notes. Remember to use alternate picking and count out loud as you play along with your metronome. Practice each one slowly until you can play it smoothly and evenly. Gradually increase the speed on your metronome until you can play at the same tempo (speed) as the recording.

25.0

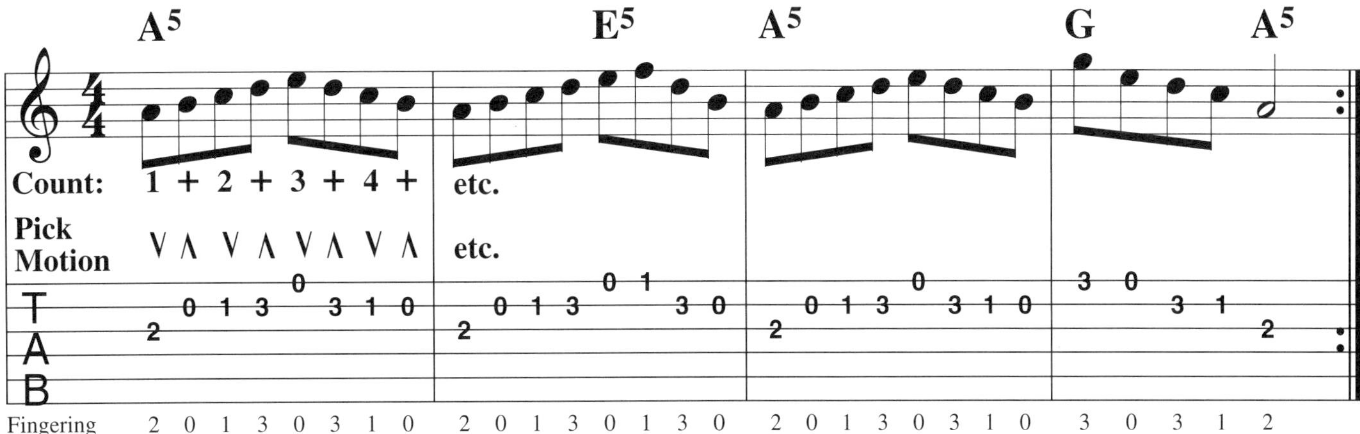

25.1

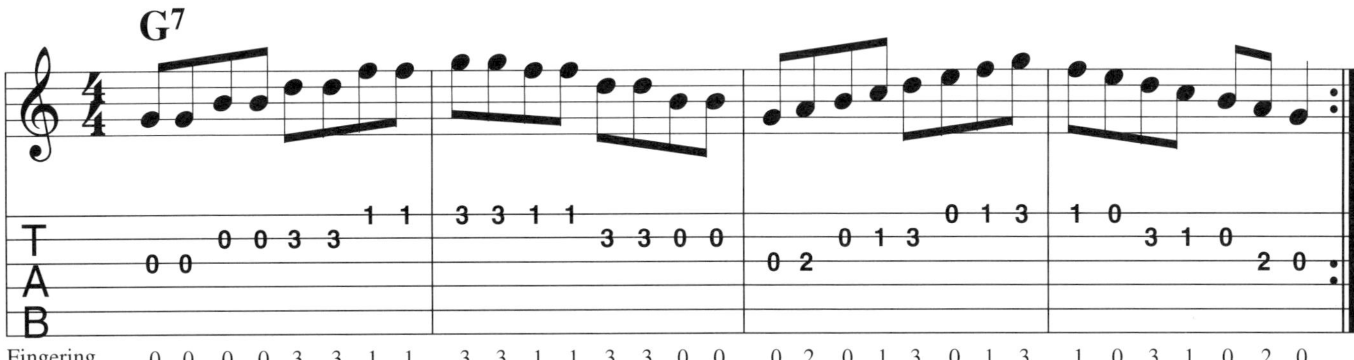

25.2

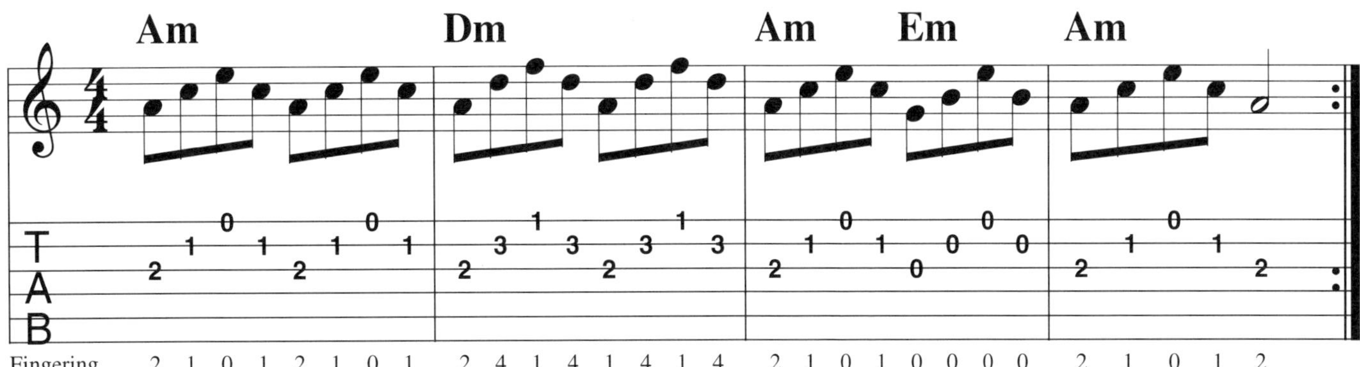

LESSON FOURTEEN

NOTES ON THE FOURTH STRING

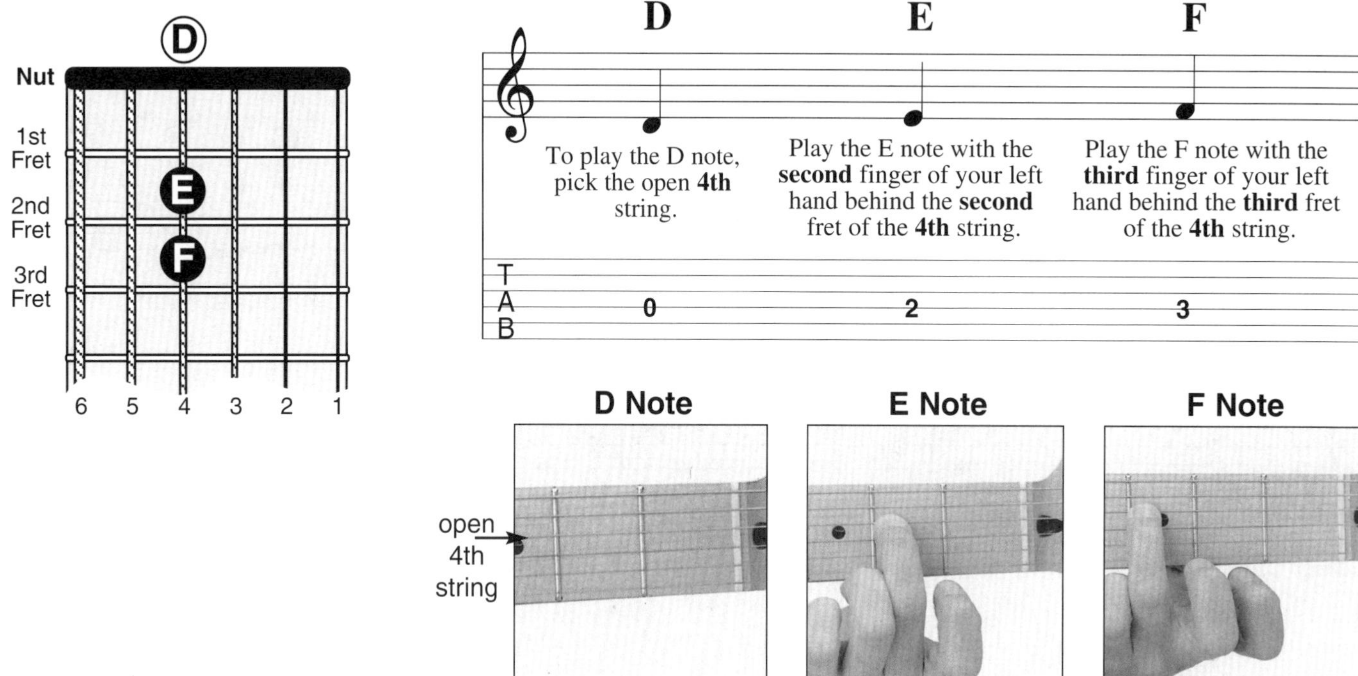

26.

Here is an example which uses the notes **D**, **E** and **F** on the fourth string. As with any new notes, name them out loud as you play until you can do it easily. Notice how the first two bars of this example move between different octaves of the **D** note.

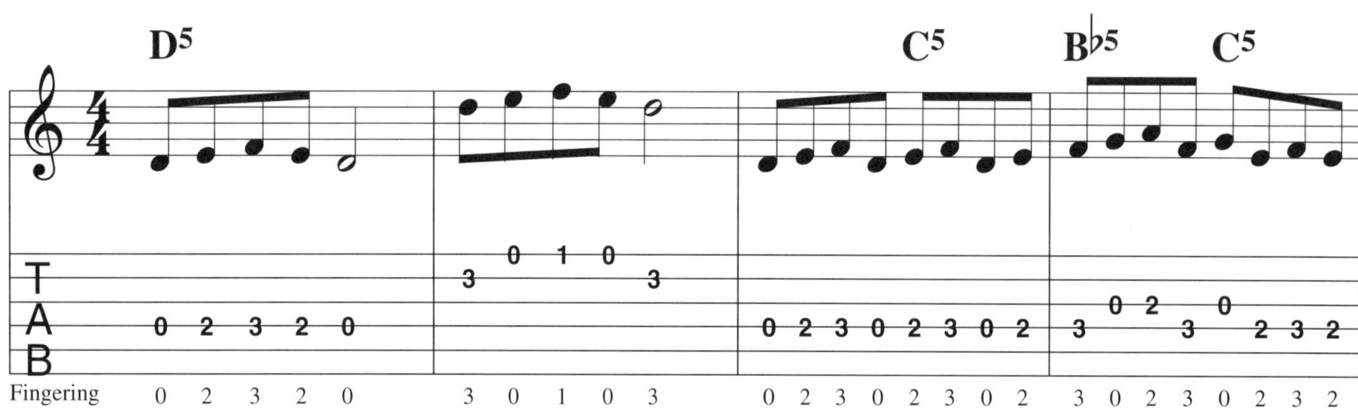

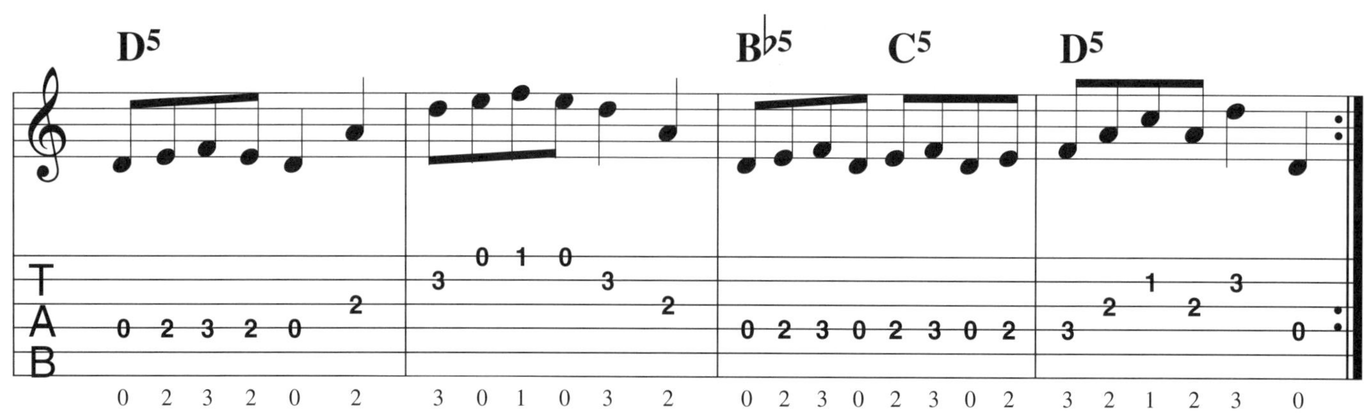

NOTES ON THE FIFTH STRING

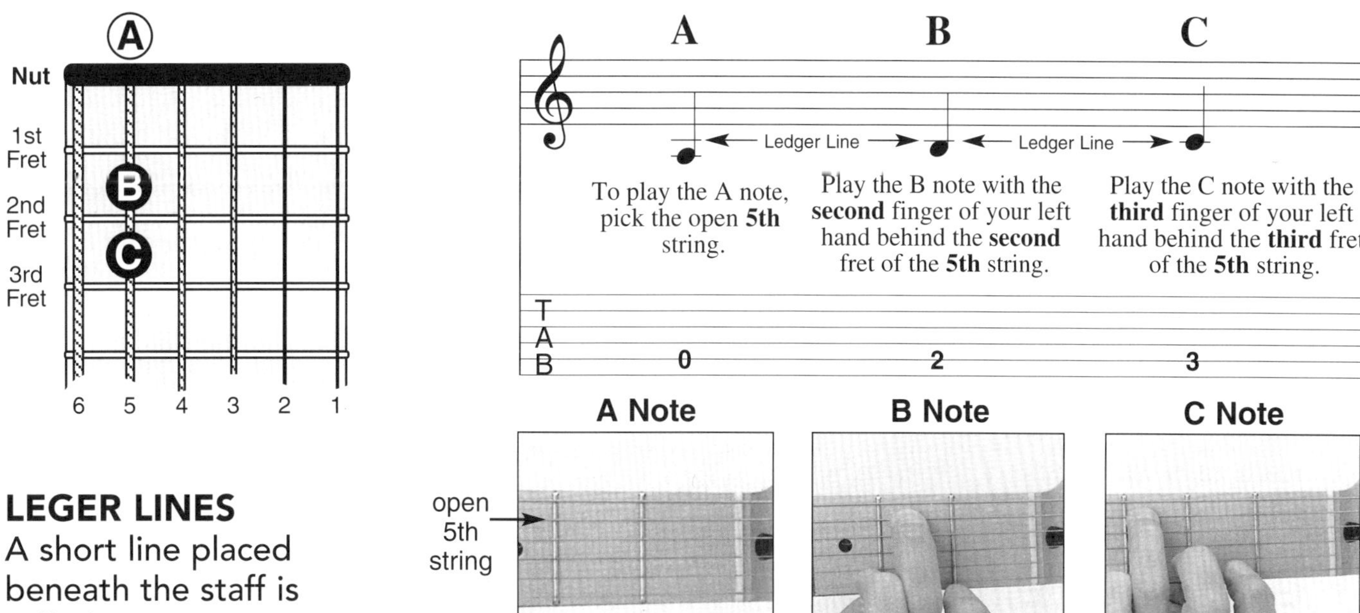

LEGER LINES
A short line placed beneath the staff is called a **Leger Line.**

27.

This example uses the notes **A**, **B** and **C** on the fifth string. It begins the same as the previous example, but moves between different octaves of the **A** note instead of **D**. As before, name the notes out loud until you are comfortable with them. Notice how the low notes alternate with the higher octave of the **A** note in bars 3 and 4. The 2nd finger should remain on the high **A** note throughout these two bars, while the notes **B** and **C** are played by the 1st and 3rd fingers. Take care with the picking in these bars. The low notes are all downstrokes, while the high **A** notes are all upstrokes.

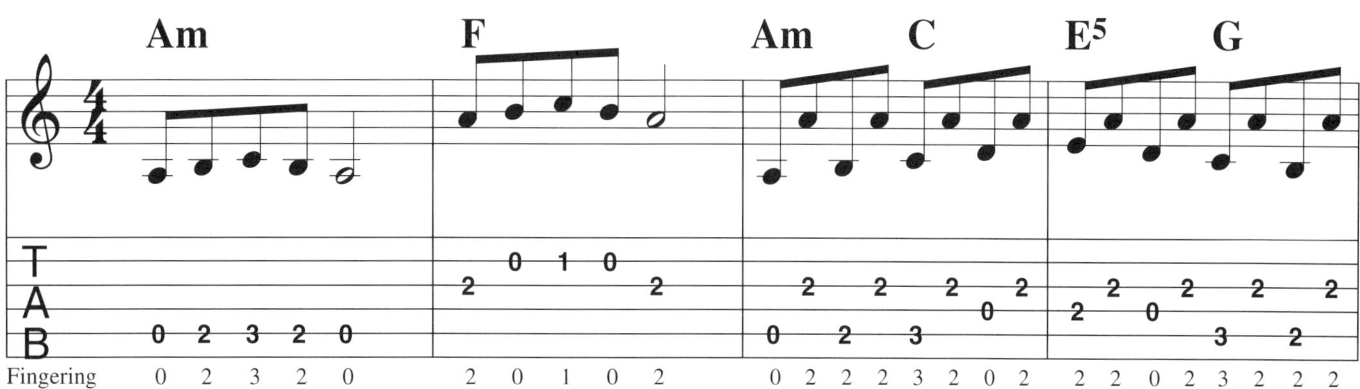

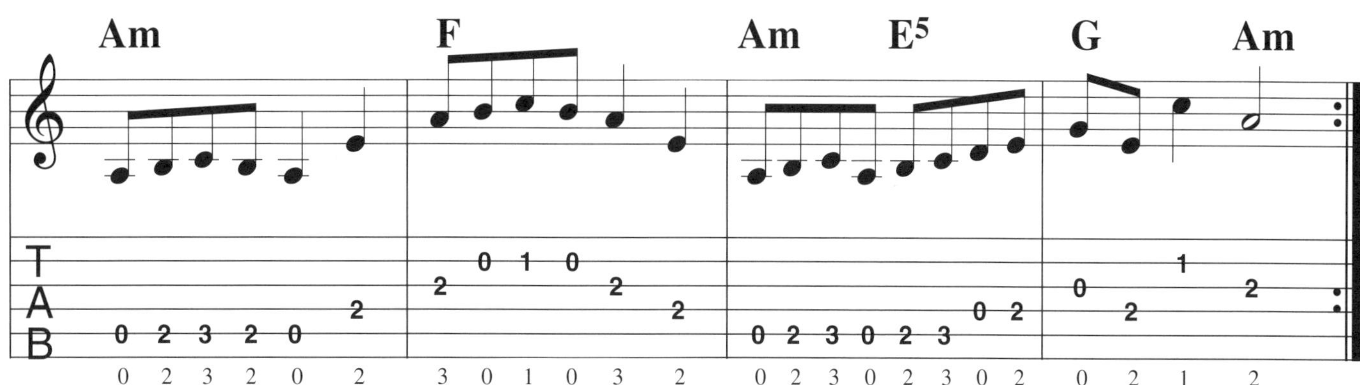

NOTES ON THE SIXTH STRING

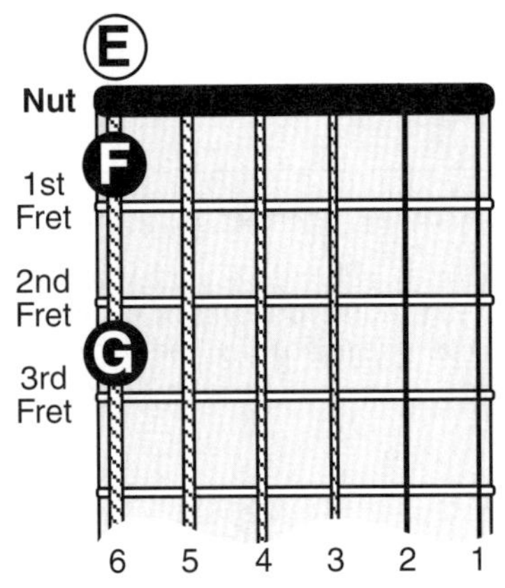

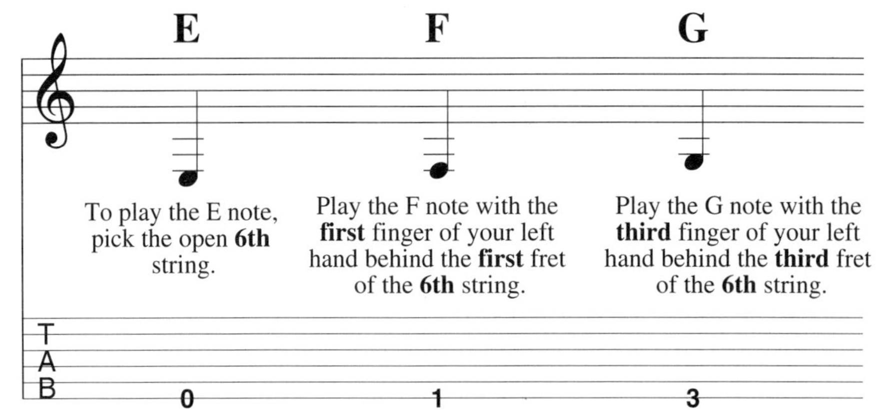

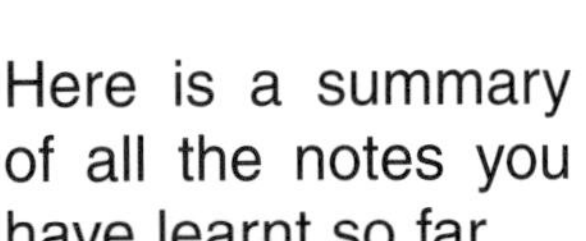
Here is a summary of all the notes you have learnt so far.

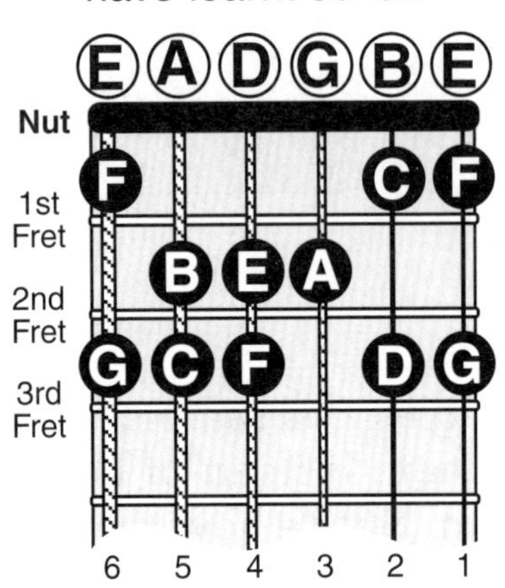

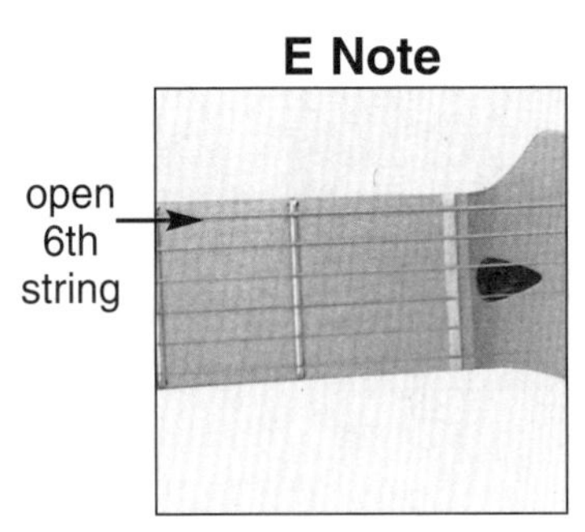

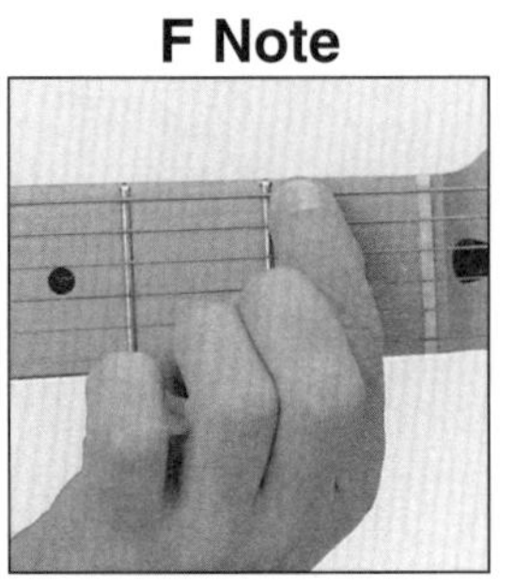

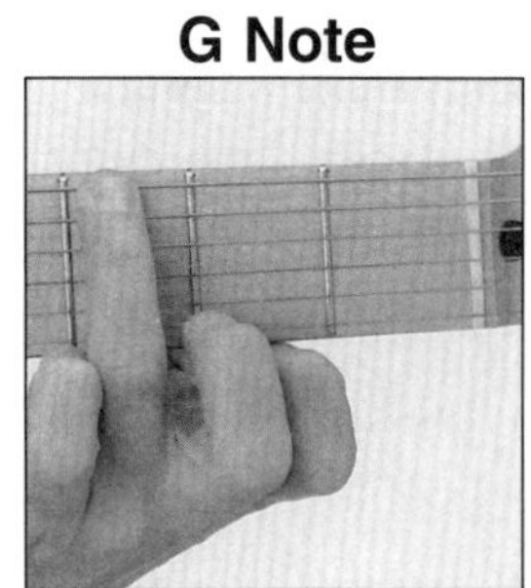

28.

The example below uses these three new notes along with all the other notes you have learnt. Notice that the notes on the sixth string are lower versions of the notes on the first string and require extensive use of leger lines in the written music.

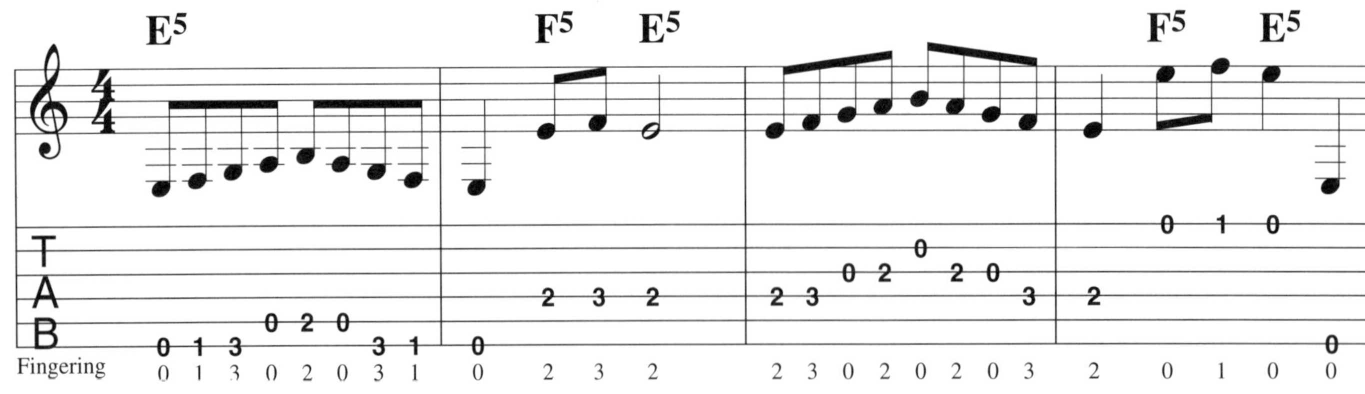

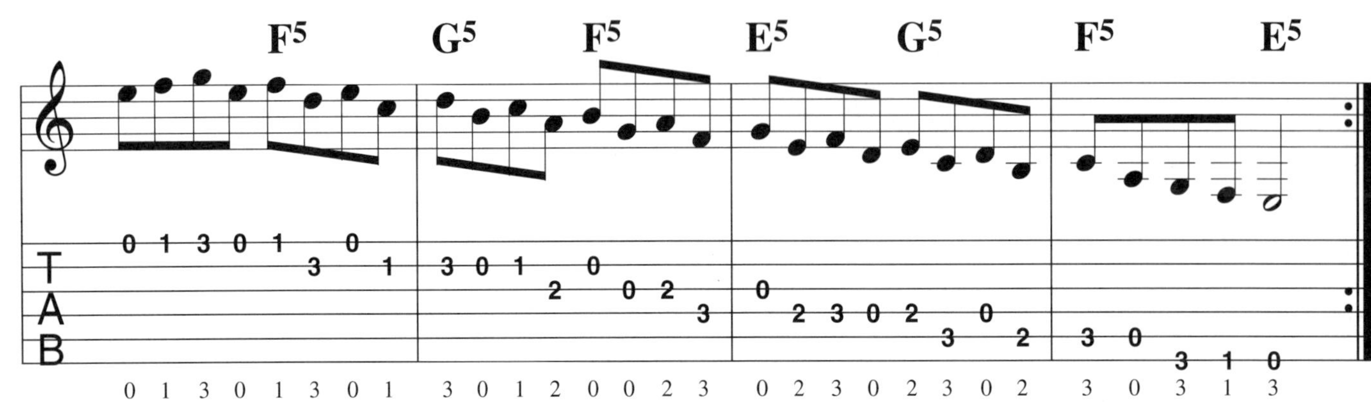

LESSON FIFTEEN

RHYTHM NOTATION

As well as traditional music notation and tablature, guitar music sometimes uses **rhythm notation**. This is similar to traditional notation, except that the notes have a diagonal line instead of a notehead. This tells you that instead of playing individual notes, you will be strumming chords. The names of the chords to be played are written above the notation, as shown in the next few examples.

CD 1 **29.0**

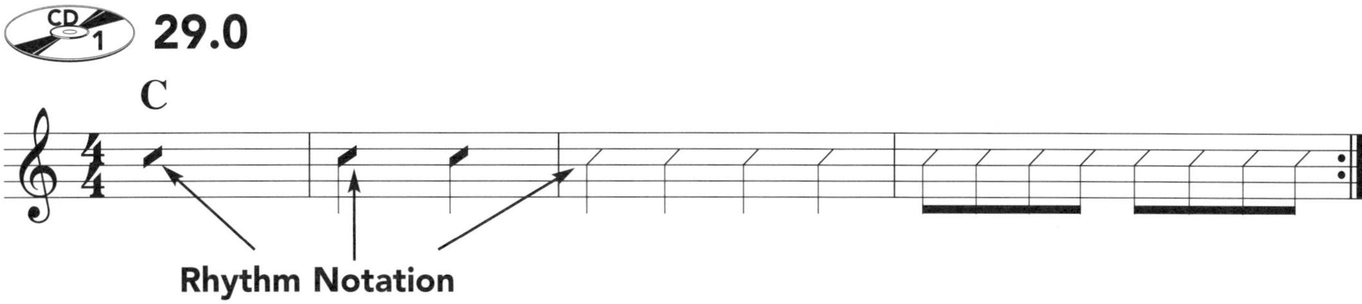

MAJOR CHORD FORMATIONS

Most chord formations are closely related to the **five basic major chord shapes** which are shown below. To remember the 5 shapes, think of the word **CAGED**.

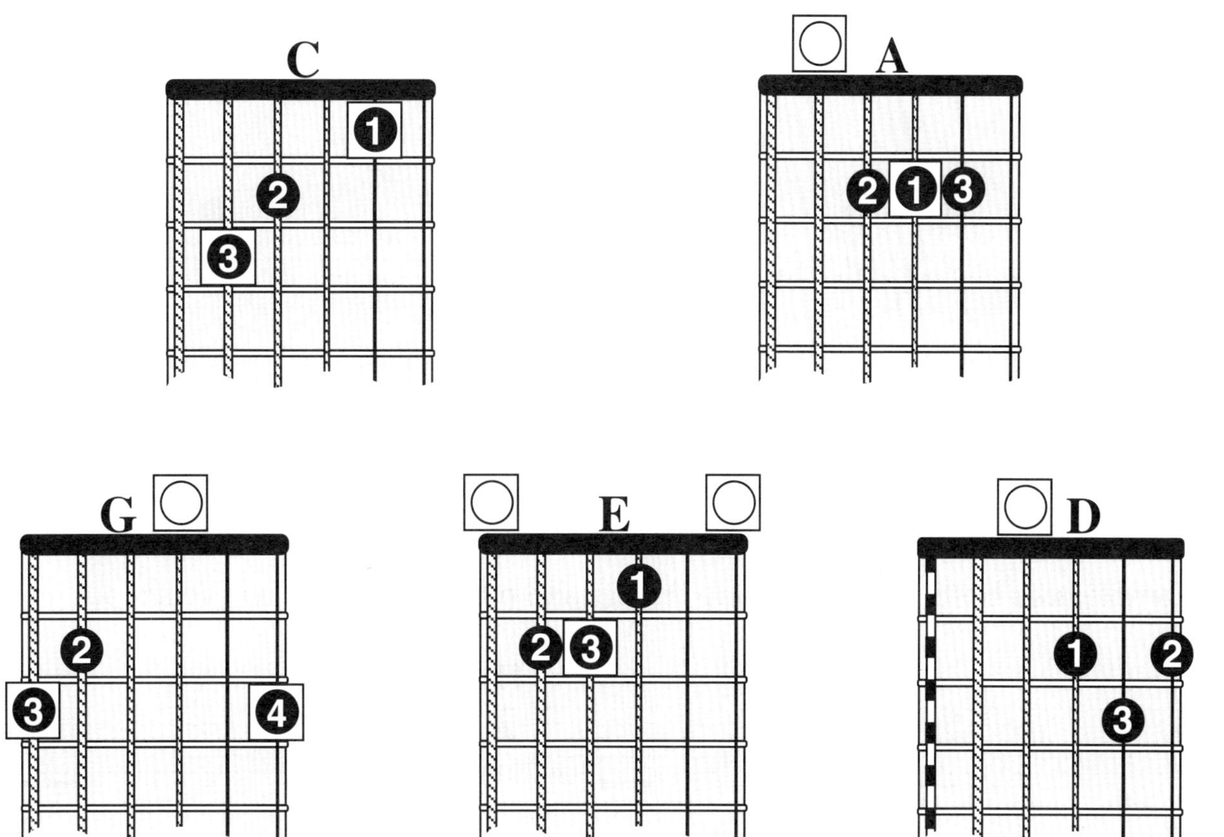

Practice changing between all of these shapes–C to A, C to G, C to E, C to G, A to E, D to G etc. Practice them **slowly with your metronome** until you have them memorized and can instantly move from one chord to any other chord.

Here are some examples to help you get used to rhythm notation. Although you already know these chords, it is worth spending some time on them, as they become particularly important when learning to play chord shapes higher up on the fretboard.

29.1

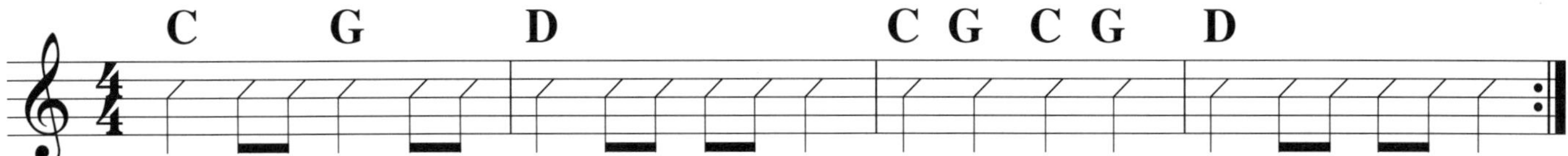

29.2

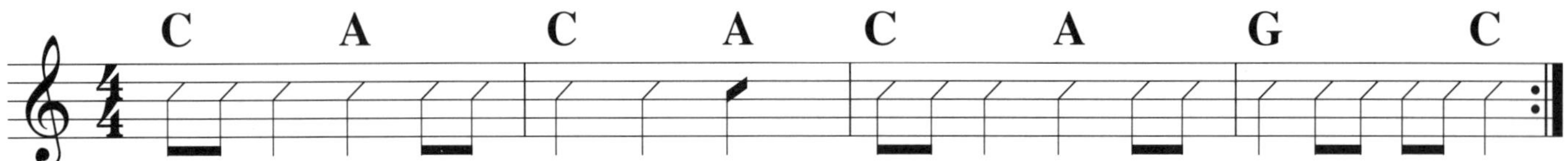

29.3

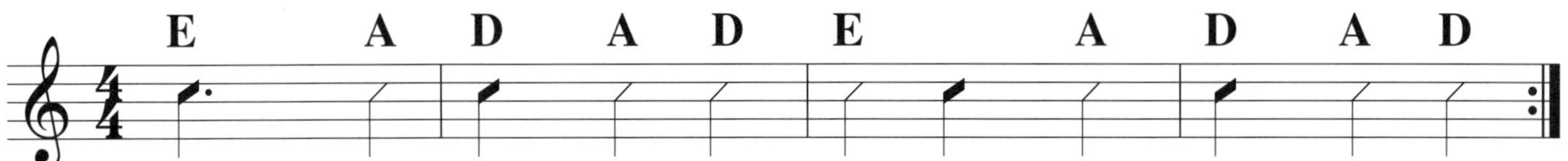

29.4

This example uses both pivot and guide fingers and moves between all five shapes

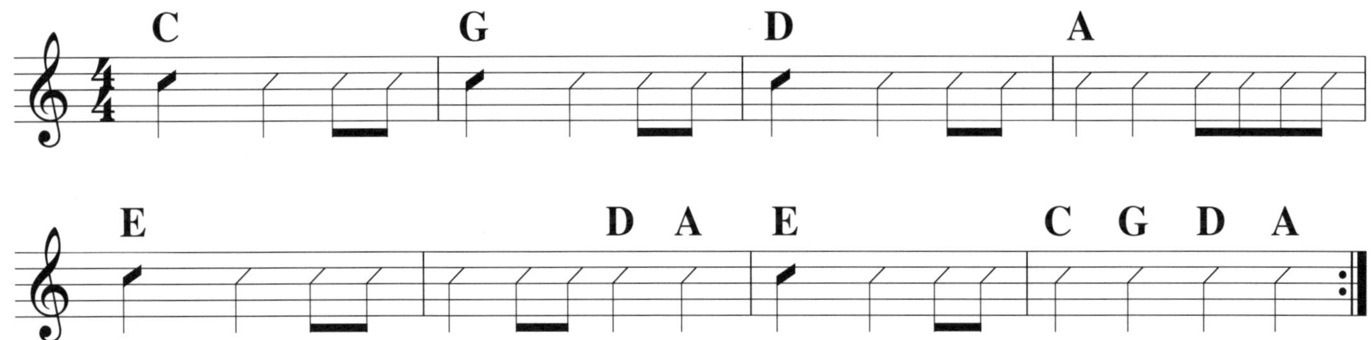

TIES

In traditional notation, a **tie** is a curved line that connects two notes with the **same** position on the staff. A tie indicates that you play the **first** note only, and hold it for the length of both notes. Ties are not necessary in Tab notation where you can just follow the count. Here are some examples demonstrating the use of ties. Count carefully as you play.

30.0

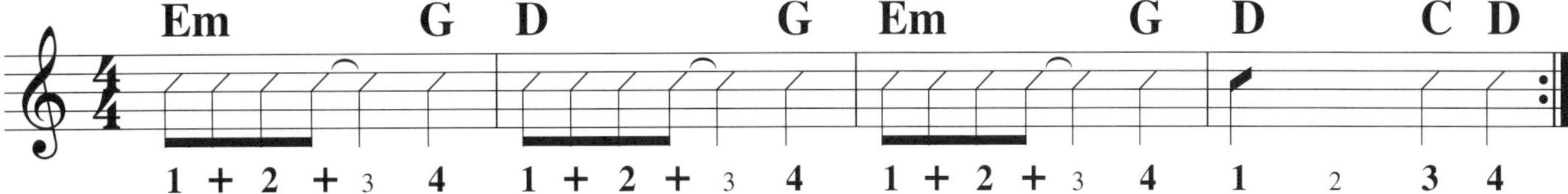

30.1

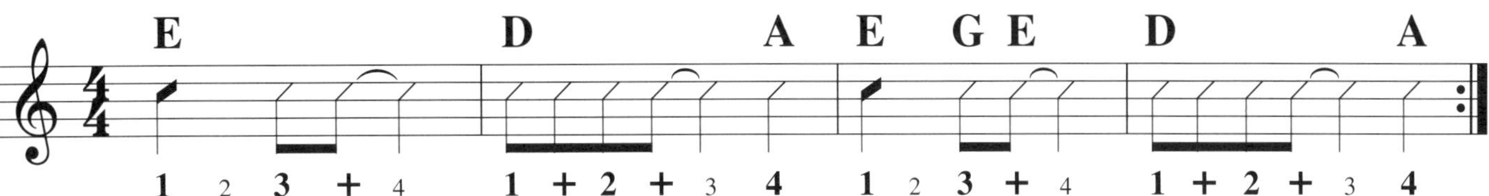

30.2

Now try this 12 bar Blues in the **key of A minor**. Remember to keep your strumming pattern going just above the strings whenever you are not actually strumming a chord.

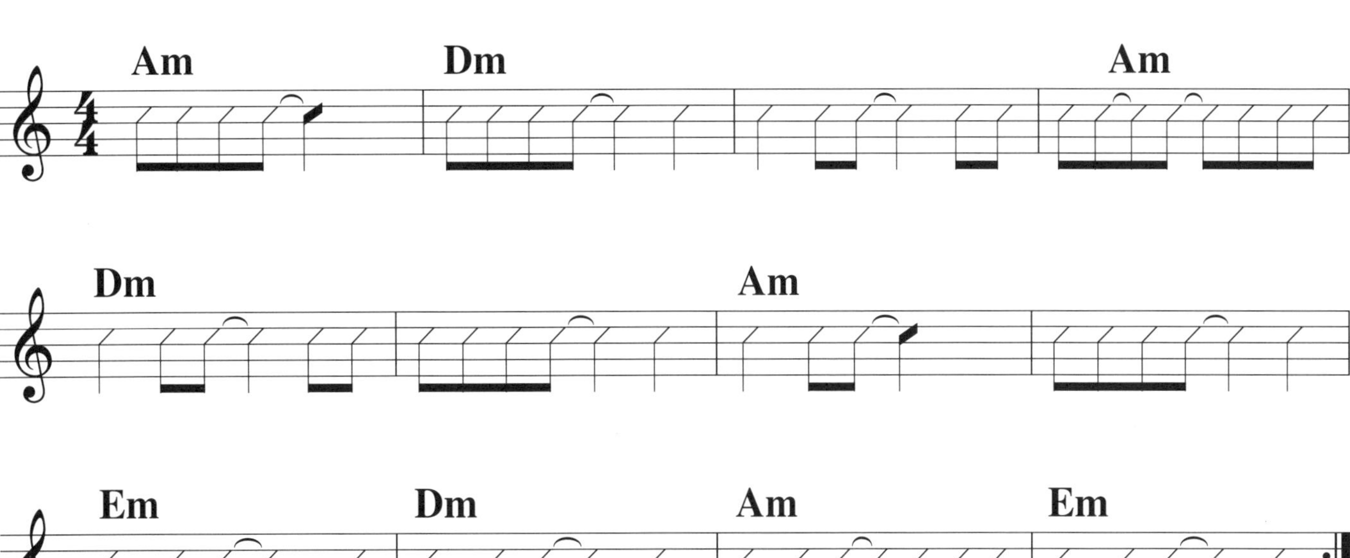

THE LEAD-IN

Sometimes a song does not begin on the first beat of a bar. Any notes which come before the first full bar are called **lead-in notes** (or pick-up notes). When lead-in notes are used, the last bar is also incomplete. The notes in the lead-in and the notes in the last bar add up to one full bar. Here is an example.

31.0

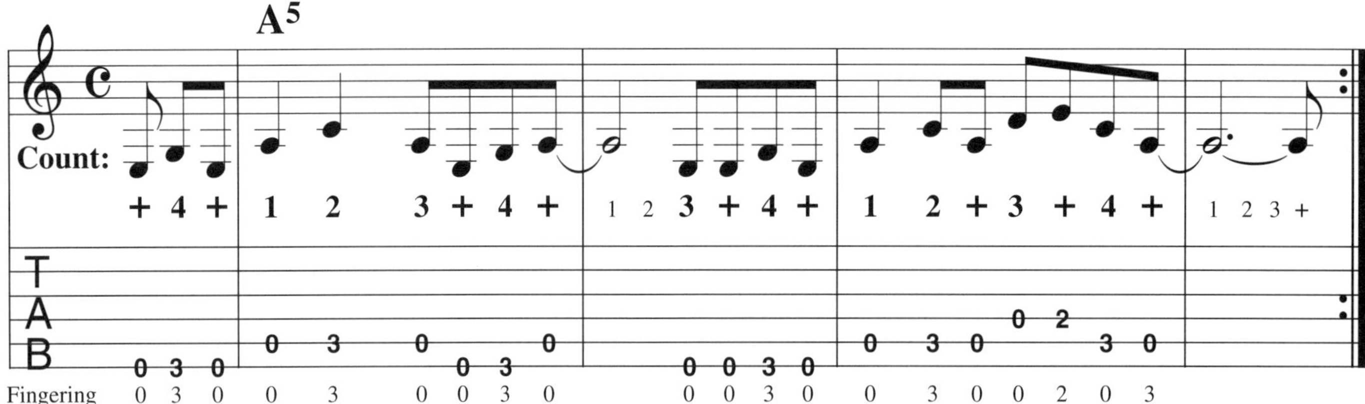

THE DOTTED QUARTER NOTE

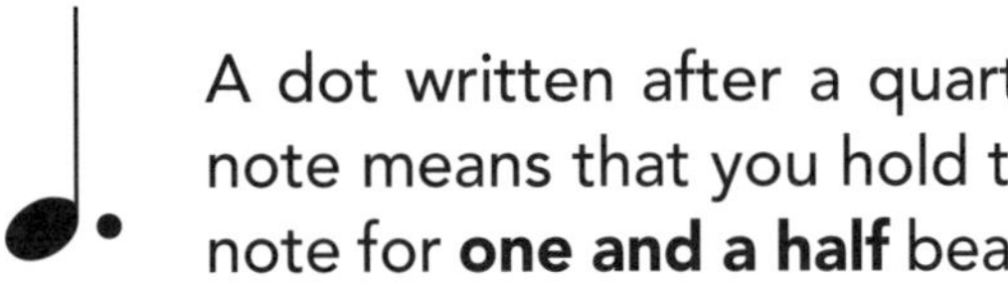

A dot written after a quarter note means that you hold the note for **one and a half** beats.

A dotted quarter note is often followed by an eighth note.

Count 1 2 +

31.1

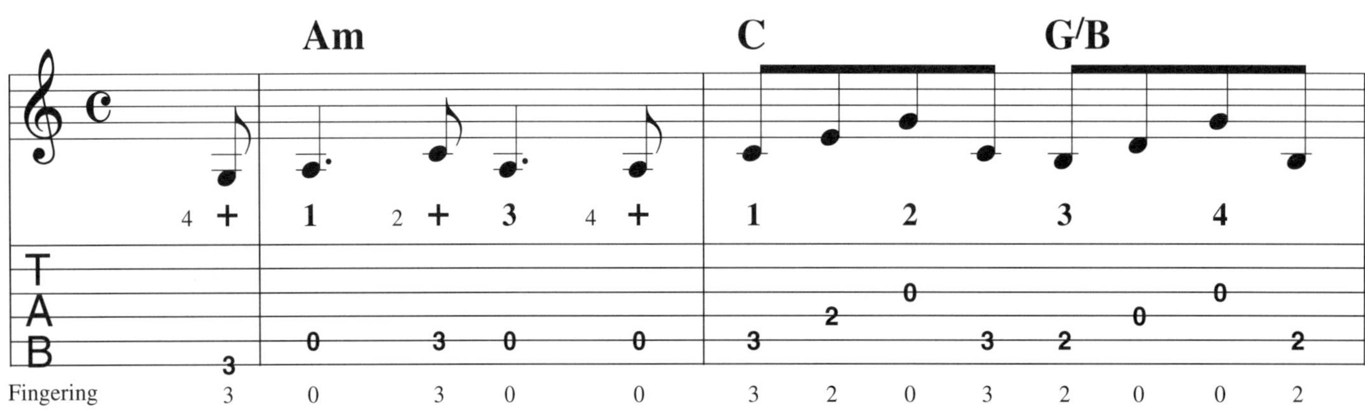

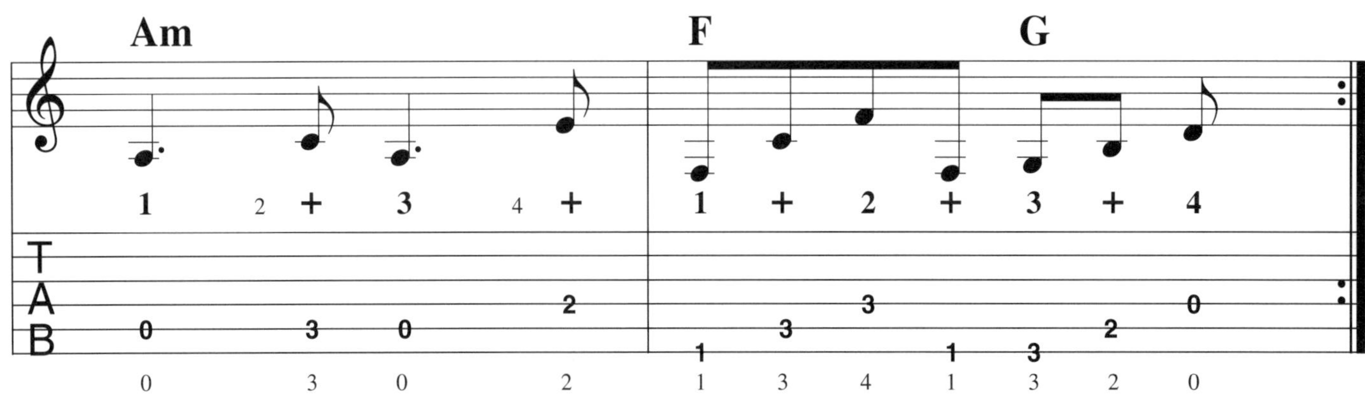

LESSON SIXTEEN

LEARNING ALL THE NOTES

So far you have learnt the open strings of the guitar and all the **natural** notes in the first three frets. However, if you want to be a good musician, it is necessary to learn **all** the notes on the fretboard and also know how to read them. This means learning the notes called **sharps** and **flats** which occur in between some of the natural notes.

TONES AND SEMITONES

A **semitone** is the smallest distance between two notes used in western music. On the guitar, notes which are a semitone apart are **one fret** apart (e.g. the note C on the 3rd fret 5th string is one semitone above the note B at the second fret). This could also be reversed i.e. the note **B** is one semitone (one fret) below the note **C**. Notes which are a **tone** (two semitones) apart, are **two frets** apart. An example of this would be the notes F and G on the sixth string or the first string. Check these on the diagram below and on your guitar.

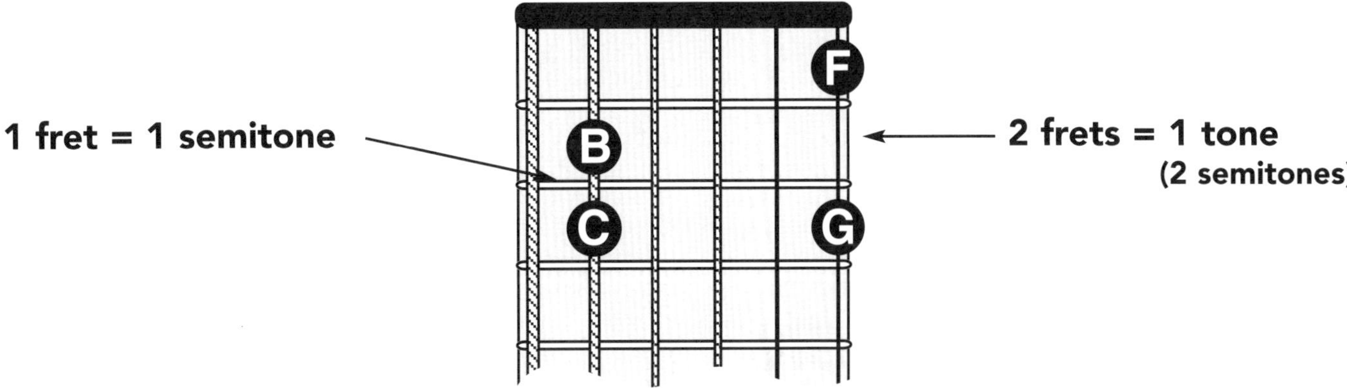

SHARPS

A **sharp sign**(♯) placed **before** a note, raises the pitch of that note by **one semitone (one fret)**. To play a sharp note picture the normal note (the **natural** note) on the fretboard and then place your next finger on the next fret. Try these examples:

C♯	F♯	G♯	C♯
2	2	1	4
2ND STRING 2ND FRET 2ND FINGER	1ST STRING 2ND FRET 2ND FINGER	3RD STRING 1ST FRET 1ST FINGER	5TH STRING 4TH FRET 4TH FINGER

THE CHROMATIC SCALE

Using sharps you can now play five new notes, which occur between the seven natural notes you already know. The following exercise uses all twelve notes which occur within one octave of music. It is an example of a **Chromatic Scale**. Chromatic scales consist entirely of **semitones** (i.e. they move up or down one fret at a time) and the start and finish notes are always the same (this is called the **keynote** or **tonic**). The chromatic scale uses **all twelve notes** used in western music and can begin on **any** note. Note that in example 32.0 there are no sharps between **B** and **C**, or **E** and **F**. This is because they are a semitone apart and there is no room for an extra note between them. Play the exercise slowly and steadily, making sure you use the correct fingering.

32.0

	A	A♯	B	C	C♯	D	D♯	E	F	F♯	G	G♯	A
Fret & Fingering	0	1	2	3	4	0	1	2	3	4	0	1	2
TAB	0	1	2	3	4	0	1	2	3	4	0	1	2

THE NATURAL SIGN

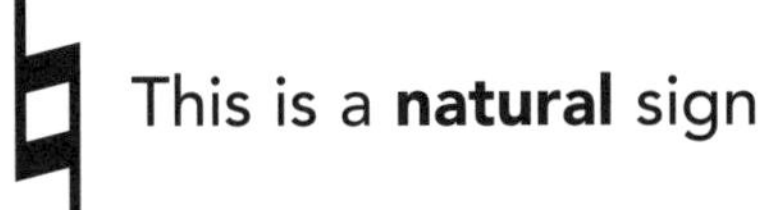

A natural sign cancels the effect of a sharp or flat for the rest of that bar, or until another sharp or flat sign occurs within that bar.

A sharpened note stays sharp until either a **bar line** or a **natural sign** (♮) cancels it as in the following example.

32.1

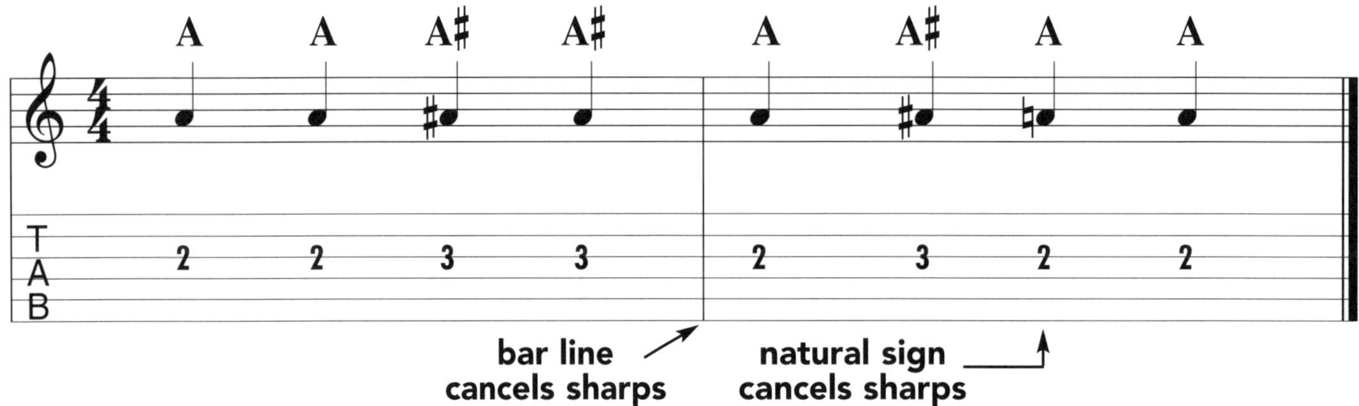

33.

This example makes use of both sharp and natural signs. Play it slowly at first and say the name of each note out loud as you play it.

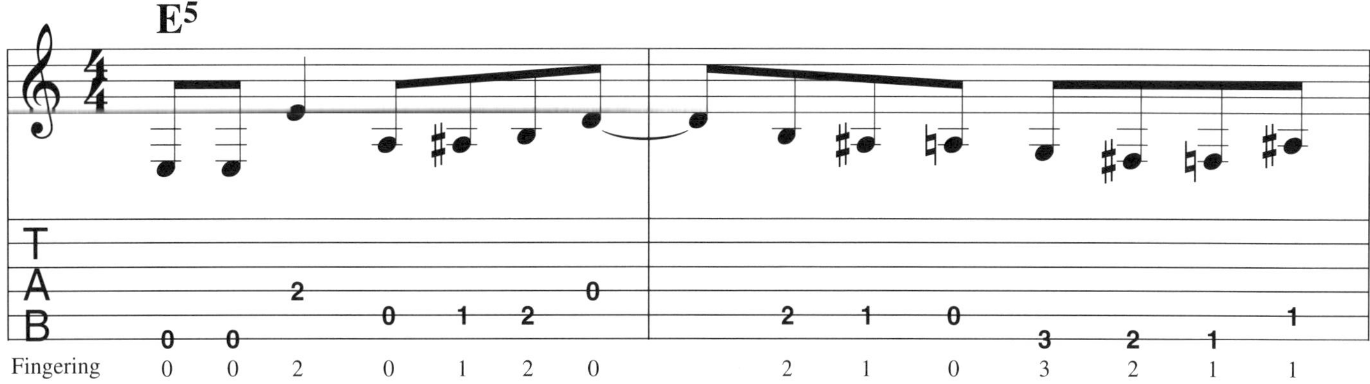

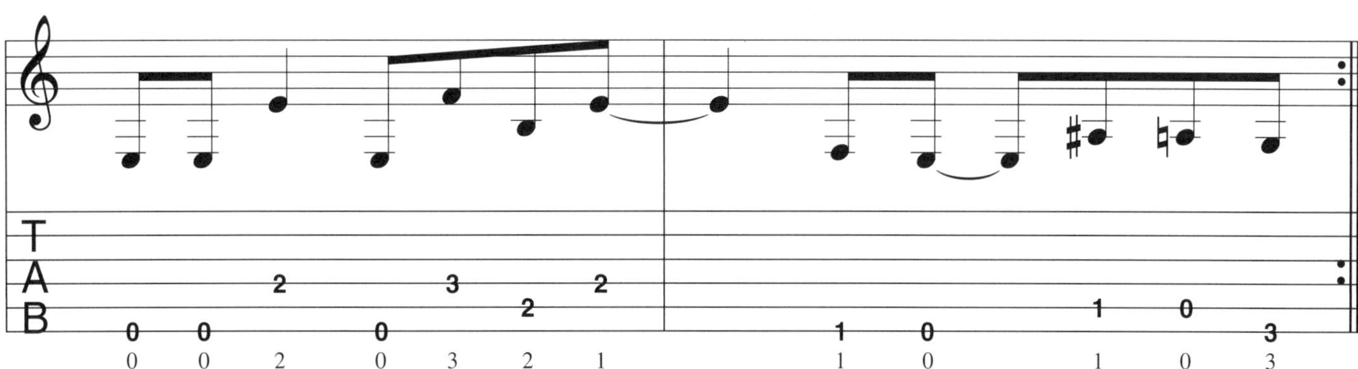

To improve your knowledge of sharps and natural signs, find each of the following notes on the fretboard of your guitar. Write the name of each note above or below the note if necessary.

FLATS

A **Flat** (♭) does the opposite of a sharp. Placed immediately **before** a note, it **lowers** the pitch of that note by one semitone.

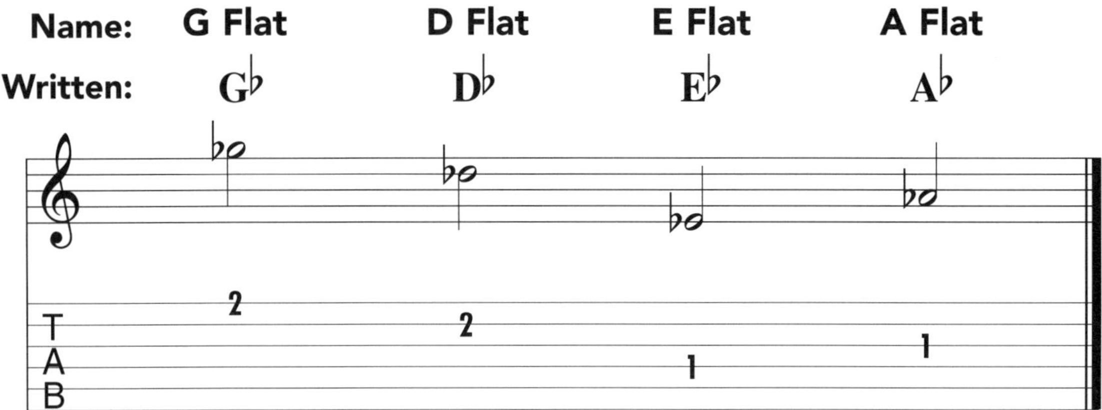

As with sharps, flats are cancelled by a bar line or by a natural sign.

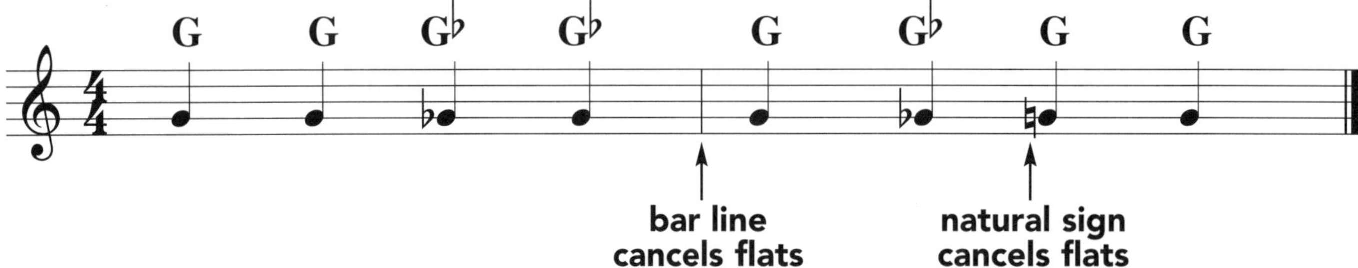

The use of sharps and flats means that the same note can have two different names. For example, F♯ is the same note as G♭ and G♯ is also A♭. These are referred to as **enharmonic** notes. The following diagram outlines all of the notes in the **first position** on the guitar (including both names for the enharmonic notes). The first position consists of the open string notes and the notes on the first **four** frets.

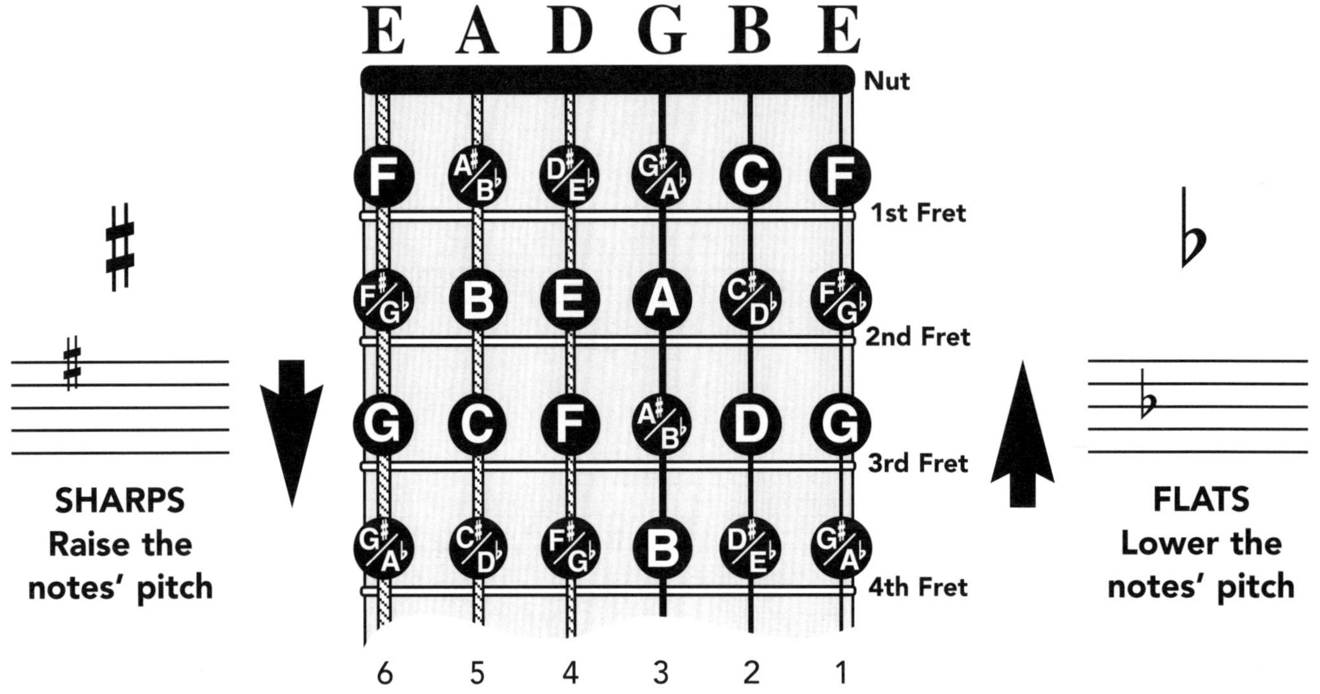

Here is an exercise to improve your knowledge of flats. Once again, write the names above or below the notes and then find them on the guitar.

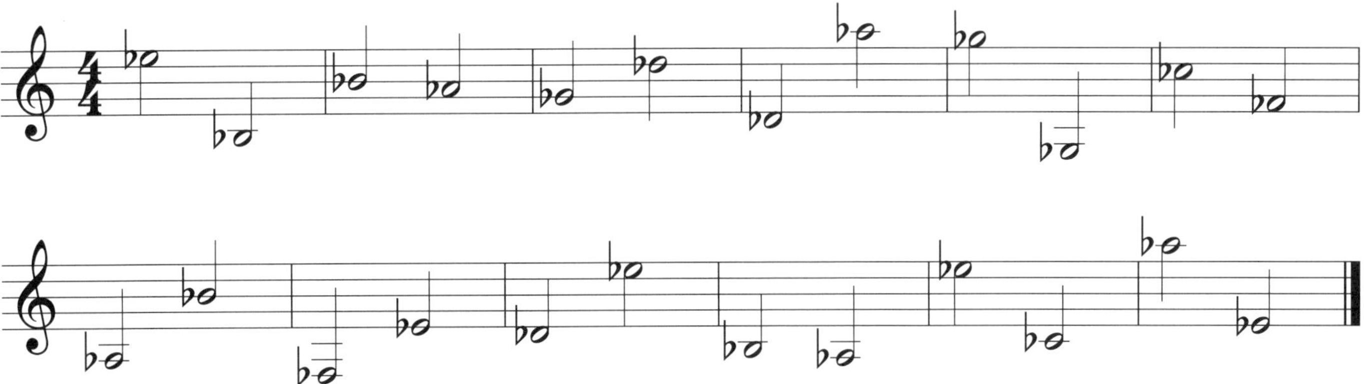

The following example demonstrates two octaves of the **E chromatic scale**. Notice that sharps are used as the scale ascends and flats as it descends. This is common practice when writing chromatic passages in music. As with any example containing new notes, it is important to name the notes out loud as you practice this scale.

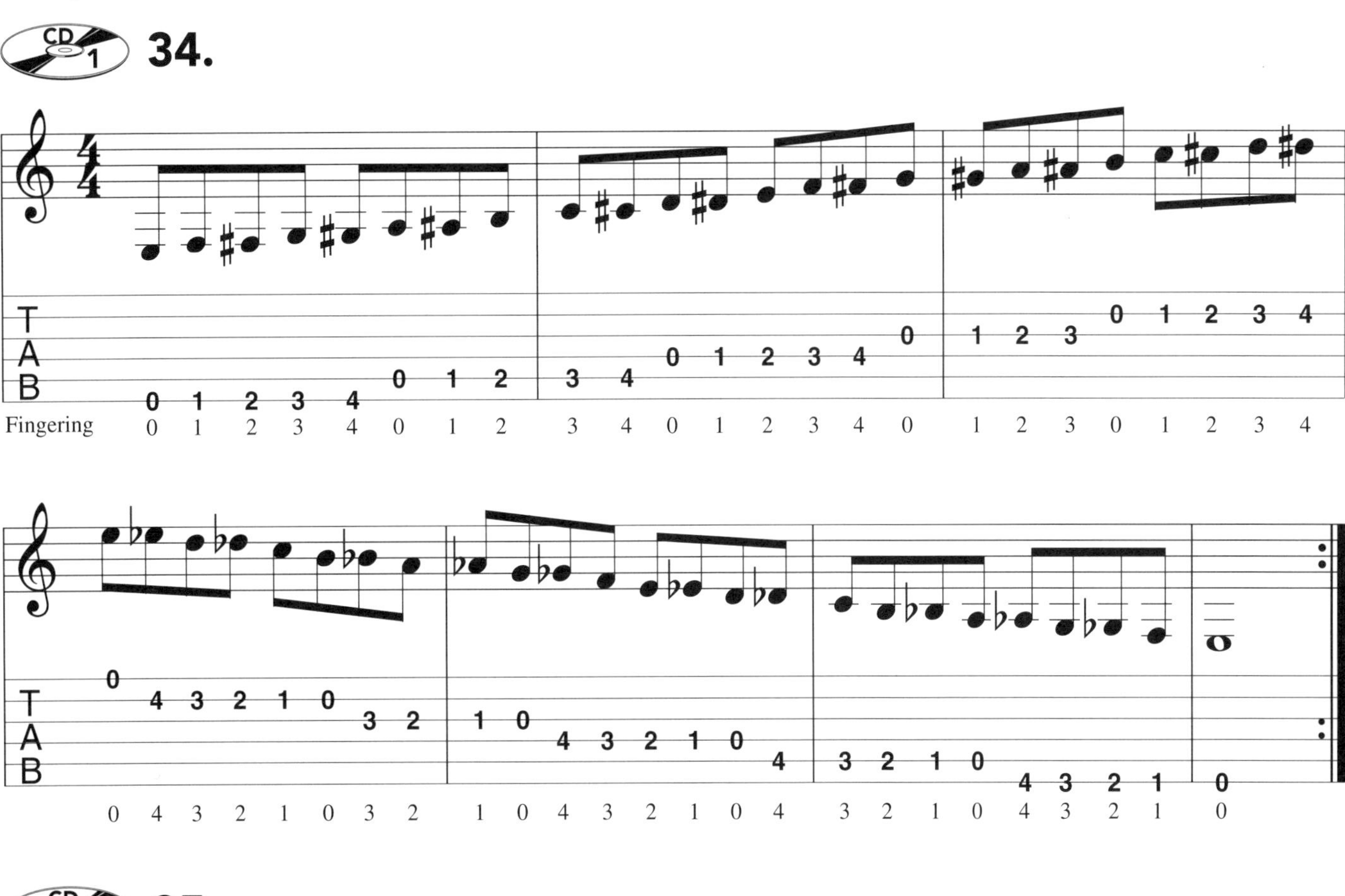

35.

Now play this example which makes use of sharps, flats and naturals.

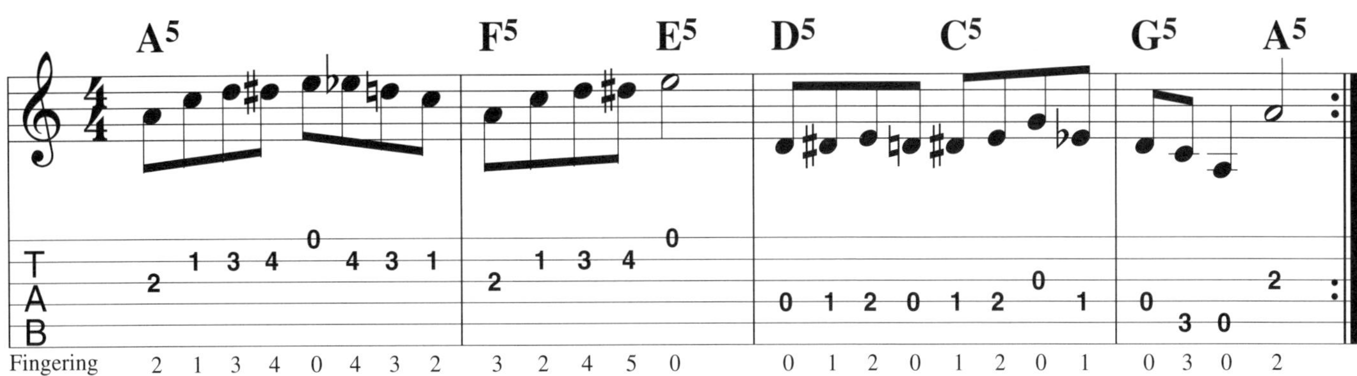

LESSON SEVENTEEN

THE MAJOR SCALE

The **major scale** is a series of **8** notes in alphabetical order that has the familiar sound:

Do Re Mi Fa So La Ti Do

Thus the **C major scale** contains the following notes.

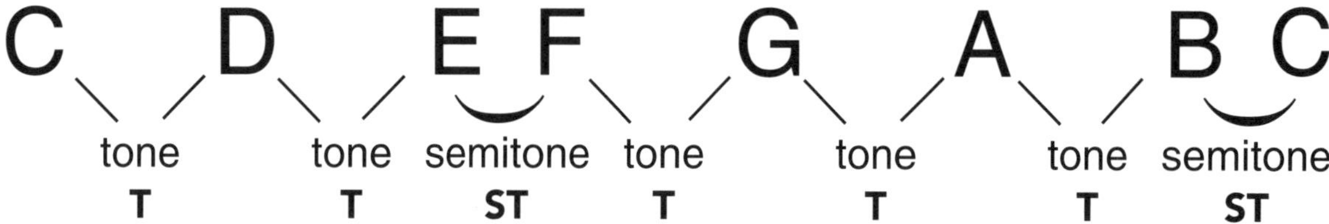

The distance between each note is two frets except for **E F** and **B C** where the distance is only one fret. A distance of two frets is a **tone**, indicated by **T**. A distance of one fret is a **semitone**, indicated by **ST**.
The following example demonstrates one octave of the **C** major scale.

CD 1 **36.**

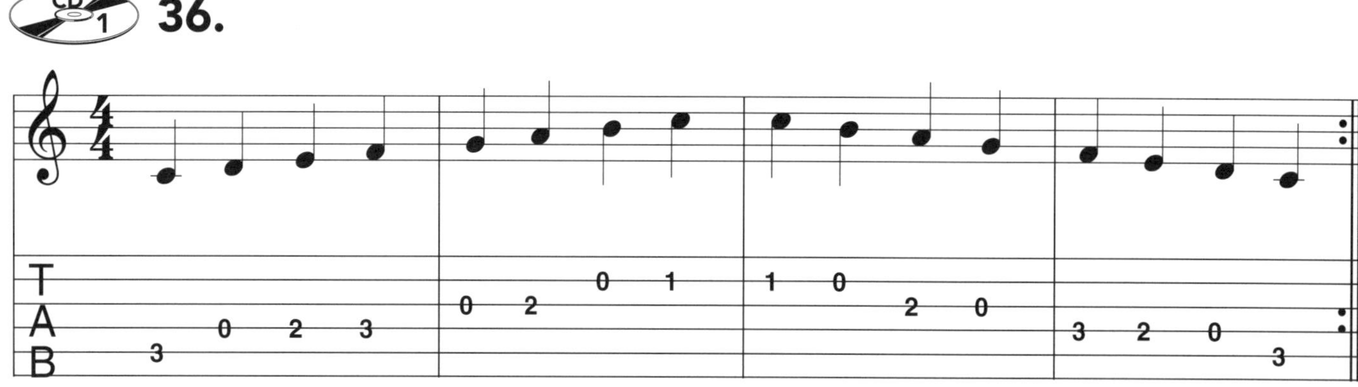

The diagram below shows all the natural notes in the open position. They are all notes of the C major scale, even though the lowest note of the pattern is E and the highest note is G. The key note **C** occurs twice and is indicated with a square around it. This pattern can be described as the full open position fingering of the C major scale. These notes have been used to play thousands of melodies ranging from Classical music to Folk and Country, to Jazz, to classic Rock songs.

C Major Scale in Open Position

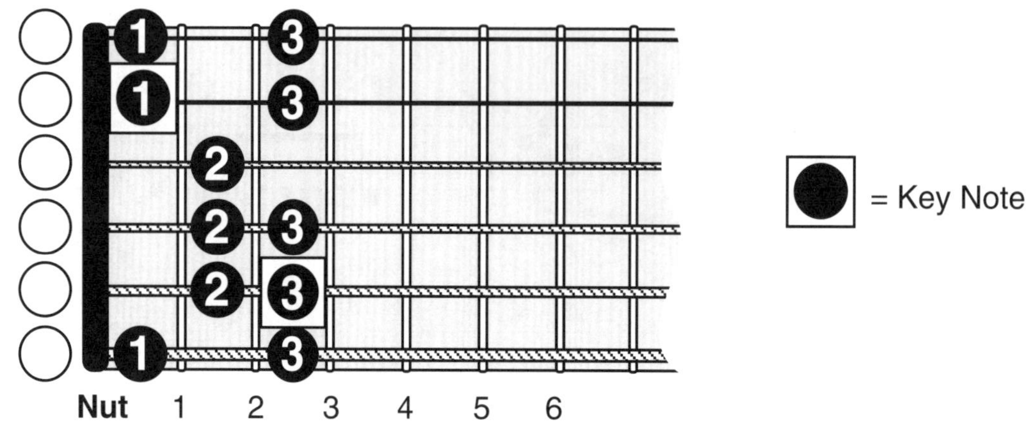

The following example demonstrates a melody created from the C major scale. Once you have memorized the fingering for the scale, experiment with it and create some of your own melodies.

37.

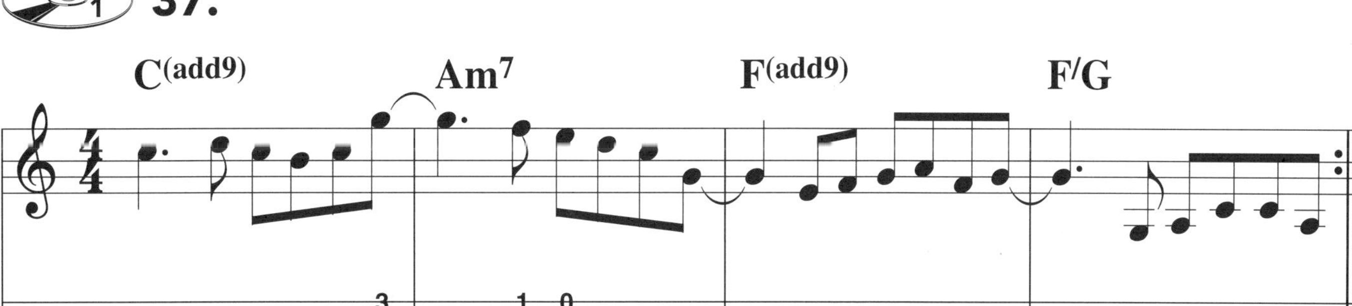

Once you know the pattern of tones and semitones used to create the C major scale, you can build a major scale on any of the twelve notes used in music. It is important to memorize this pattern:

Tone Tone Semitone Tone Tone Tone Semitone

The **semitones** are always found between the **3rd and 4th**, and **7th and 8th degrees** (notes) of the scale. All the other notes are a tone apart.

THE G MAJOR SCALE

To demonstrate how the major scale pattern can start on any note, here is the **G major scale**. Notice that the 7th degree (note) is **F sharp** (**F♯**) instead of F. This is done to maintain the correct pattern of tones and semitones and thus retain the sound of the major scale (**do re mi fa so la ti do**).

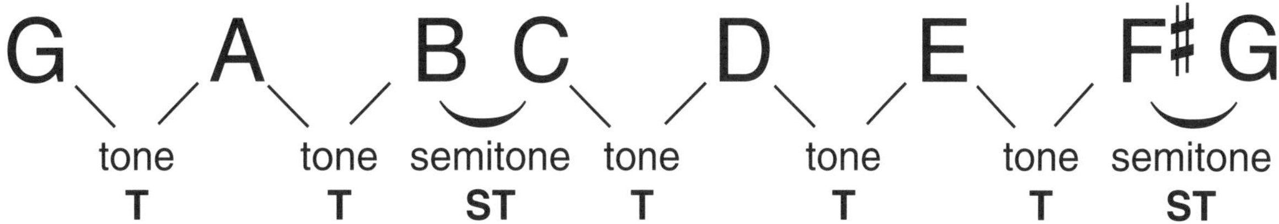

38.

This example shows two octaves of the G Major scale.

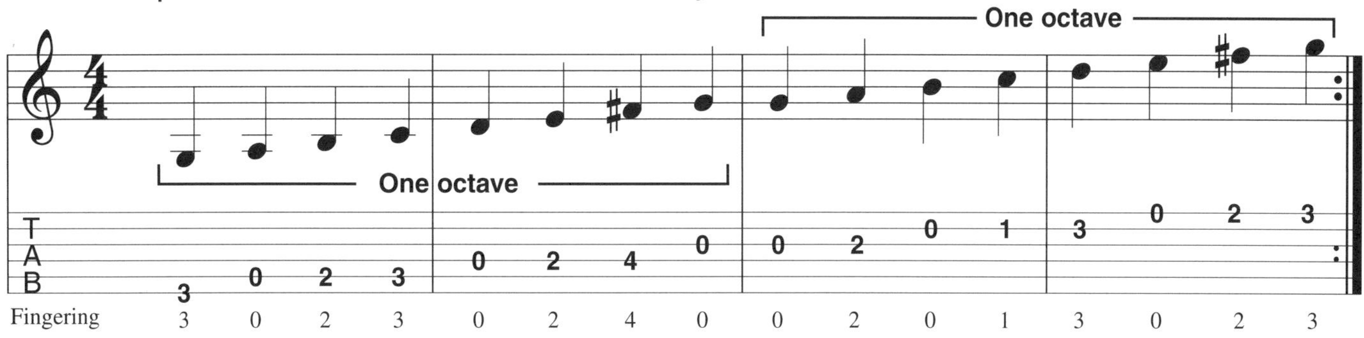

KEYS AND KEY SIGNATURES

The **key** describes the note around which a piece of music is built. When a song consists of notes from a particular scale, it is said to be written in the **key** which has the same notes as that scale. The key signature is written at the start of each line of music, just after the clef.

The number of sharps or flats in any key signature depends on the number of sharps or flats in the corresponding major scale. The major scales and key signatures for the keys of **F** and **G** are shown below. Without sharps and flats, these scales would not contain the correct pattern of tones and semitones which gives the major scale its distinctive sound.

G Major Scale

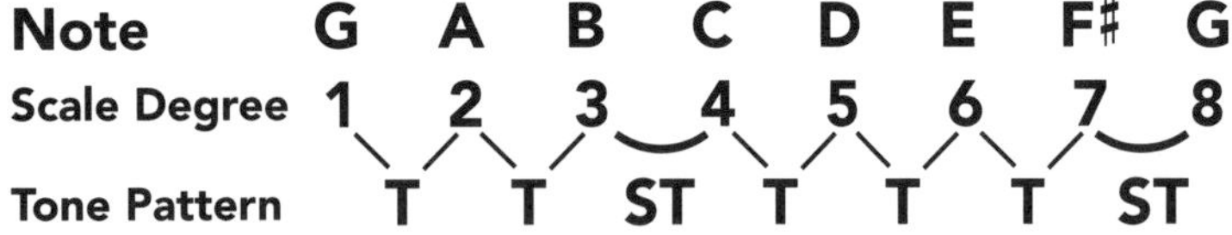

Key Signature of G Major

The **G major** scale contains one sharp, F♯, therefore the key signature for the key of **G major** contains one sharp, F♯.

F Major Scale

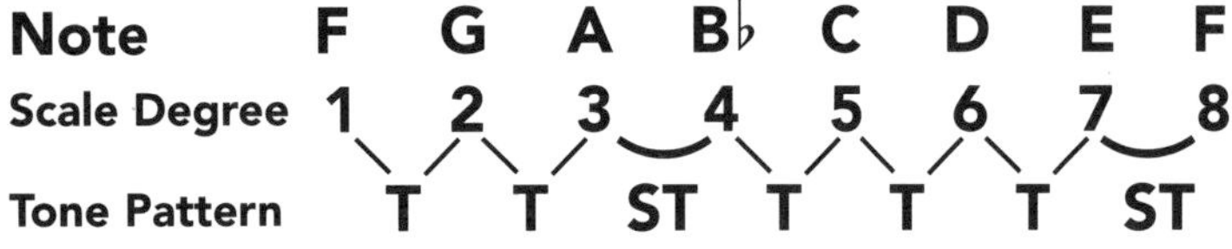

Key Signature of F Major

The **F major** scale contains one flat, B♭, therefore the key signature for the key of **F major** contains one flat, B♭.

Some scales contain sharps while others contain flats because there has to be a separate letter name for each note in the scale. E.g. the G major scale contains F♯ instead of G♭ even though these two notes are identical in sound. If G♭ was used, the scale would contain two notes with the letter name G and no note with the letter name F. In the key of F major, the note B♭ is chosen instead of A♯ for the same reason. If A♯ was used, the scale would contain two notes with the letter name A and no note with the letter name B.

The charts on the following page contain the **key signatures** of all the major scales used in music, along with the number of sharps or flats contained in each key. Because there are 12 notes used in music, this means there are 12 possible starting notes for major scales (including sharps and flats). Note that some of the keys will have sharps or flats in their name, e.g. F♯ major, B♭ major, E♭ major, etc. Keys which contain sharps are called sharp keys and keys which contain flats are called flat keys.

The key signatures for all the major scales that contain sharps are:

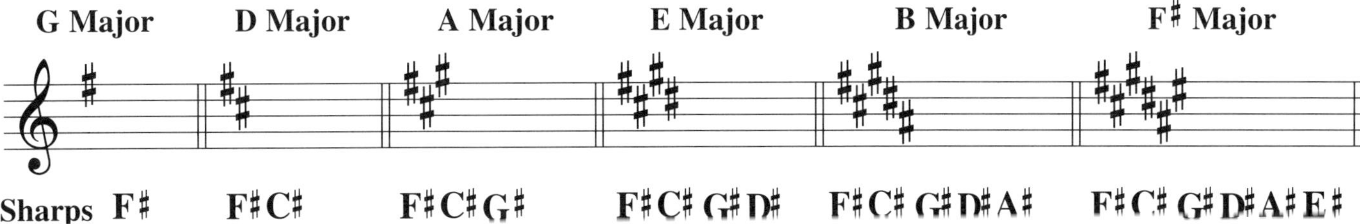

The sharp key signatures are summarised in the table below.

The new sharp ***key*** *is a fifth interval * higher*

Key	Number of Sharps	Sharp Notes
G	1	F♯
D	2	F♯, C♯
A	3	F♯, C♯, G♯
E	4	F♯, C♯, G♯, D♯
B	5	F♯, C♯, G♯, D♯, A♯,
F♯	6	F♯, C♯, G♯, D♯, A♯, E♯

The new sharp ***note*** *is a fifth interval higher*

Written below are the key signatures for all the major scales that contain flats.

The flat key signatures are summarised in the table below.

The new flat ***key*** *is a fourth interval higher*

Key	Number of Flats	Flat Notes
F	1	B♭
B♭	2	B♭, E♭
E♭	3	B♭, E♭, A♭
A♭	4	B♭, E♭, A♭, D♭
D♭	5	B♭, E♭, A♭, D♭, G♭,
G♭	6	B♭, E♭, A♭, D♭, G♭, C♭

The new flat ***note*** *is a fourth interval higher*

* An **interval** is the distance between two notes. Intervals are named by the number of letters they are apart, e.g. C to G is a fifth. Intervals are discussed in detail in the following lesson.

LESSON EIGHTEEN

INTERVALS

An **interval** is the distance between two musical notes. **All melodies and chords are made up of a series of intervals.** Intervals are measured in numbers, and are calculated by counting the number of letter names (**A B C D E F G A**) between and including the notes being measured. Within an octave, intervals are: **Unison** (two notes of the same pitch played or sung together or consecutively), **2nd**, **3rd**, **4th**, **5th**, **6th**, **7th** and **Octave** (two notes an octave apart). Thus **A** to **B** is a **2nd** interval, as is B to C, C to D etc. **A** to **C** is a **3rd** interval, **A** to **D** is a **4th**, **A** to **E** is a **5th**, **A** to **F** is a **6th**, **A** to **G** is a **7th** and **A** to the next **A** is an **octave**.

Intervals may be **melodic** (two notes played consecutively) or **harmonic** (two notes played at the same time). Hence two people singing at the same time are said to be singing in harmony.

INTERVAL QUALITIES

Different intervals have different qualities, as shown below:

Quality	Can be applied to
Perfect	Unisons, 4ths, 5ths and Octaves
Major	2nds, 3rds, 6ths and 7ths
Minor	2nds, 3rds, 6ths and 7ths
Augmented	All intervals
Diminished	All intervals

Interval qualities can be best explained with the aid of a chromatic scale. If you look at the one below, it is easy to see that since **intervals are measured in semitones**, they may begin or end on a sharp or flat rather than a natural note.

A A♯/B♭ B C C♯/D♭ D D♯/E♭ E F F♯/G♭ G G♯/A♭ A

Perfect intervals are **4ths**, **5ths** and **octaves**. If you **widen** a perfect interval by a semitone it becomes **augmented** (added to). E.g. if you add a semitone to the perfect 4th interval **C** to **F**, it becomes the **augmented 4th interval C** to **F♯**. Notice that the letter name remains the same–it is not referred to as C to G♭.

If you **narrow** a perfect interval by a semitone it becomes **diminished** (lessened). E.g. if you lessen the perfect 5th interval **D** to **A** by a semitone, it becomes the **diminished 5th interval D to A♭**. Again, the letter name remains the same–it is not referred to as D to G♯.

Major intervals (2nds, 3rds, 6ths and 7ths) become minor if narrowed by a semitone and **minor** intervals become major if widened by a semitone. A **diminished** interval can be created by narrowing a perfect or minor interval by a semitone. An **augmented** interval can be created by widening a perfect or major interval by a semitone.

INTERVAL DISTANCES

In summary, here is a list of the distances of all common intervals up to an octave, measured in semitones. Each new interval is one semitone further apart than the previous one. Notice that the interval of an octave is exactly twelve semitones. This is because there are twelve different notes in the chromatic scale. Notice also that the interval which has a distance of six semitones can be called either an augmented 4th or a diminished 5th. This interval is also often called a **tritone** (6 semitones = 3 tones).

Minor 2nd - One semitone
Major 2nd - Two semitones
Minor 3rd - Three semitones
Major 3rd - Four semitones
Perfect 4th - Five semitones
Augmented 4th or Diminished 5th - Six semitones
Perfect 5th - Seven semitones
Minor 6th - Eight semitones
Major 6th - Nine semitones
Minor 7th - Ten semitones
Major 7th - Eleven semitones
Perfect Octave - Twelve semitones

The following example demonstrates all of the common intervals ascending within one octave, starting and ending on the note **C**.

39.

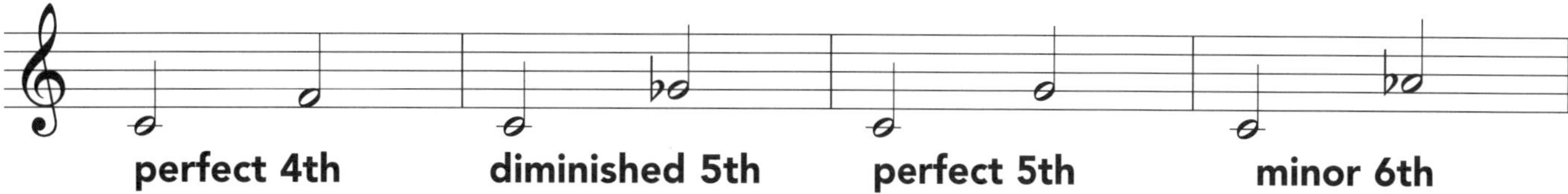

FINDING INTERVALS ON THE FRETBOARD

A good musician can instantly play any interval from any note either harmonically (at the same time) or in ascending or descending order. The diagrams below show the most common ways of playing intervals on the guitar. Learn them one at a time and listen carefully to the sound of each interval as you play it.

Minor 2nd
(One Semitone)

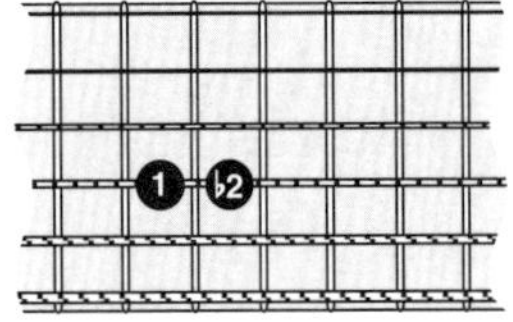

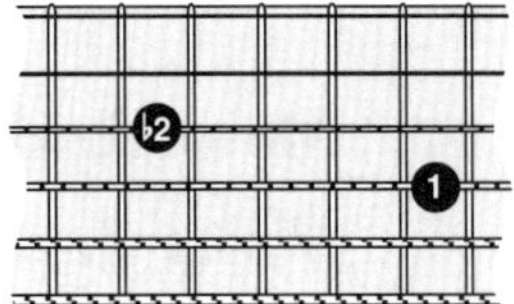

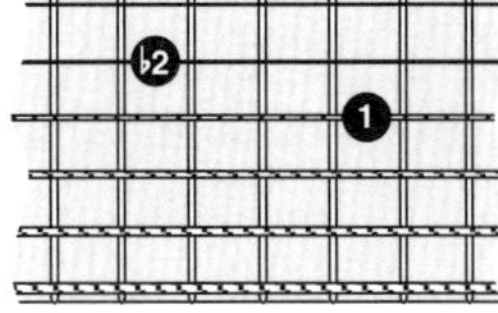

Major 2nd
(Two Semitones)

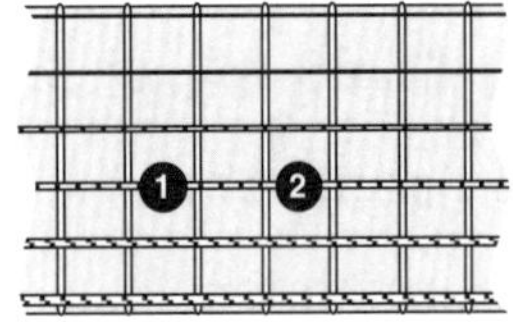

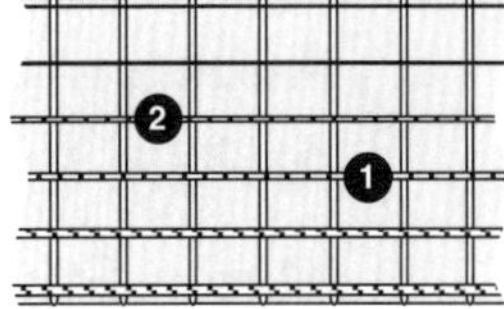

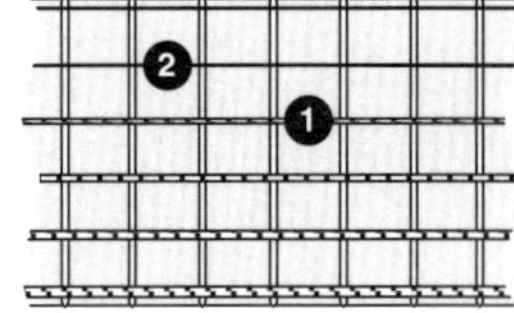

Minor 3rd
(Three Semitones)

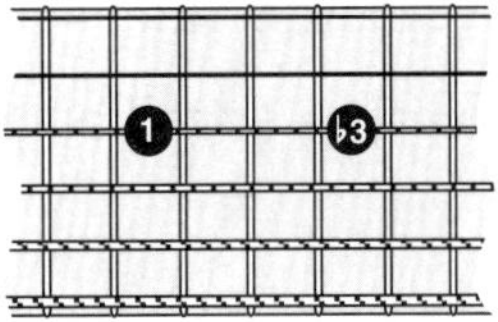

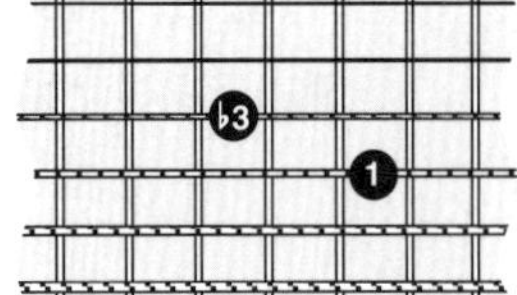

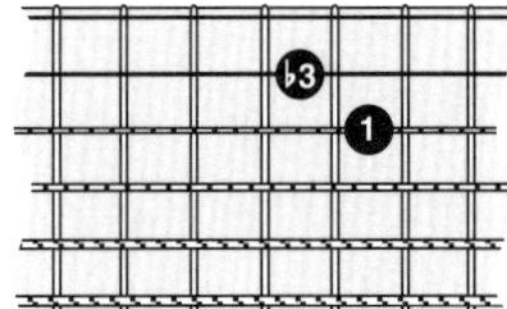

Major 3rd
(Four Semitones)

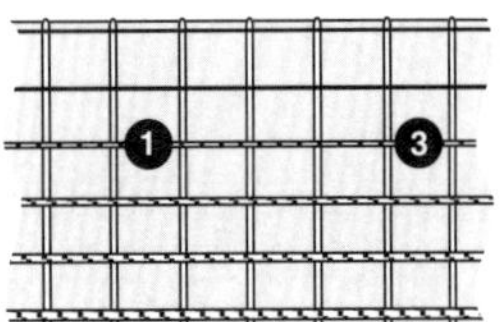

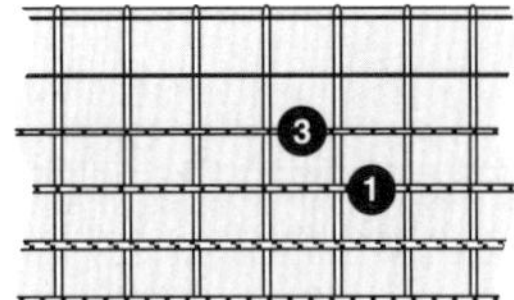

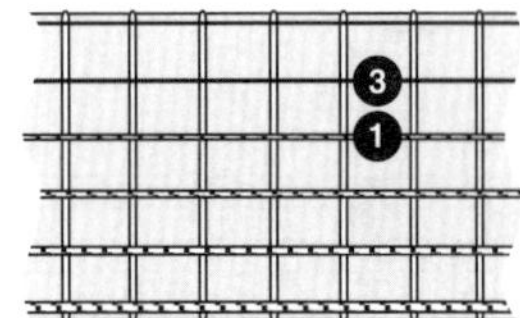

Perfect 4th
(Five Semitones)

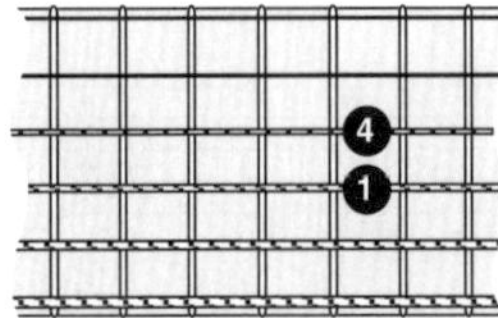

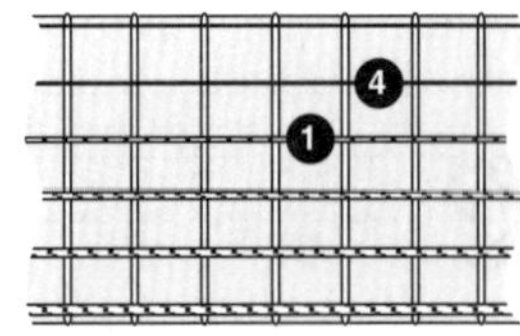

Tritone -Aug 4th or Dim 5th
(Six Semitones)

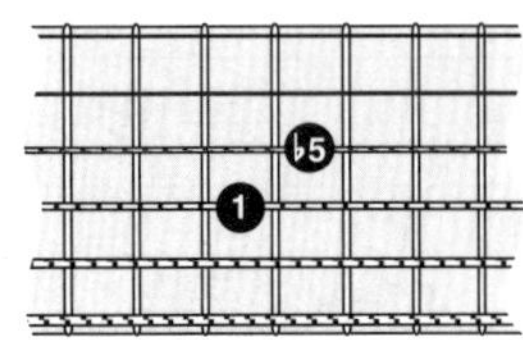

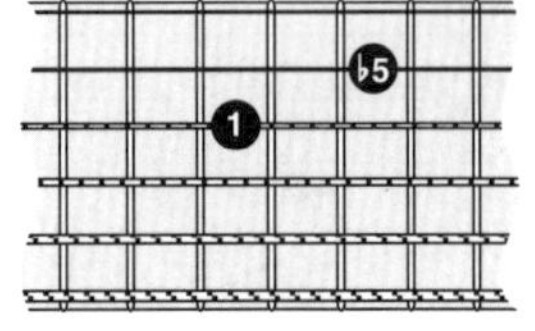

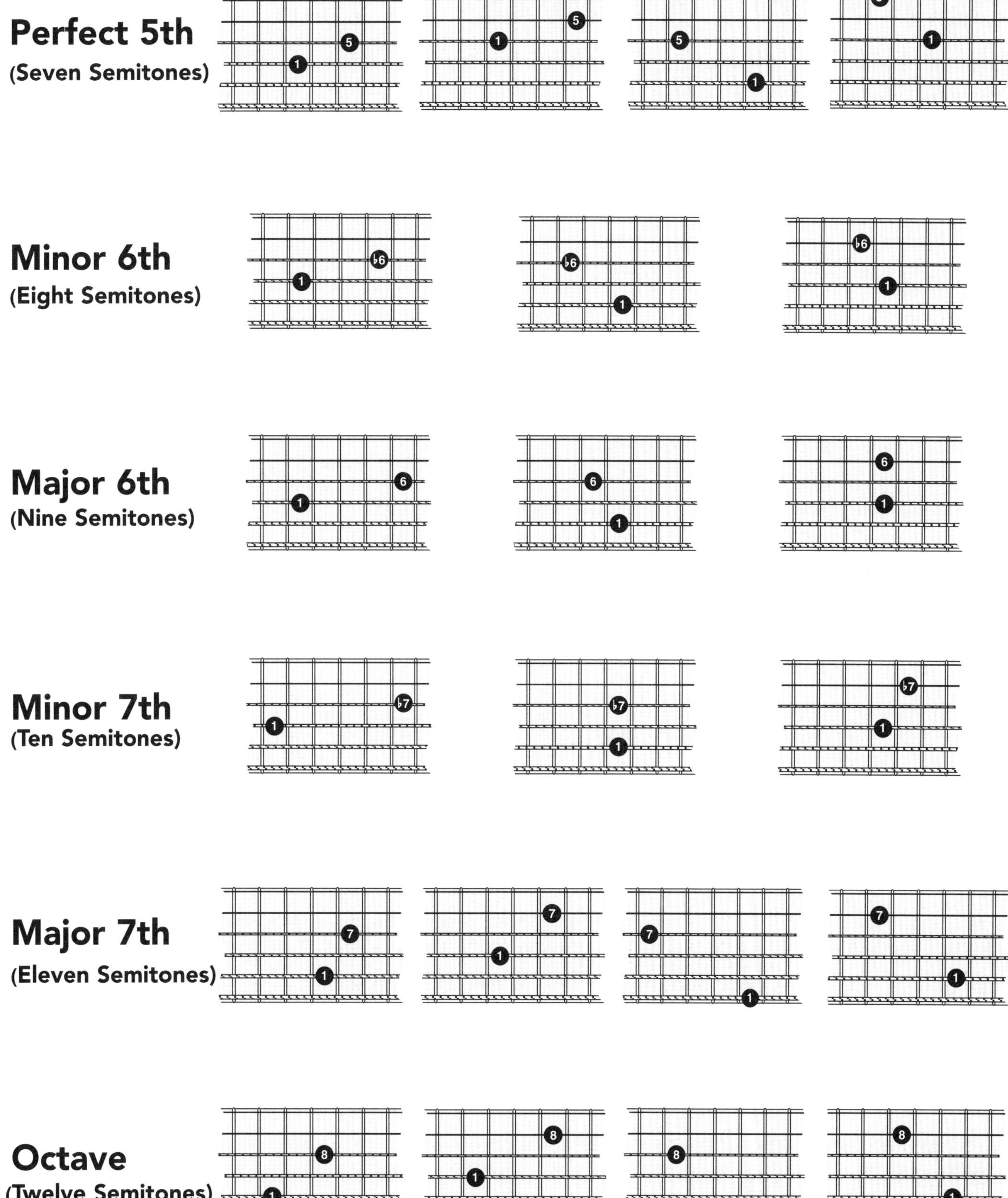

These diagrams show only the most common ways of playing intervals on the guitar, but they are not the only patterns. You should also work on playing every possible interval on each individual string. This is easier than it sounds. All you have to do is work out how many frets apart the interval is: e.g. a perfect 4th is five frets apart, a minor 6th is eight frets apart, etc.

IDENTIFYING INTERVALS BY EAR

Since all melodies are made up of a series of intervals, it is essential to learn to identify intervals by ear and be able to reproduce them at will, both with your voice and on your instrument. If you can sing something accurately, it means you are hearing it accurately. Here are some ways of developing your ability to identify and reproduce intervals. The example used in the first two exercises is a minor 3rd, but it is essential to go through these processes with **all** intervals.

1. Choose an interval you wish to work on (e.g. minor 3rds). Play a starting note (e.g. C) and sing it. Then sing a minor 3rd up from that note (E♭). Hold the note with your voice while you test its accuracy on your instrument. Then choose another starting note and repeat the process. Keep doing this until you are accurate every time. The next step is to sing the interval (in this case a minor 3rd) downwards from your starting note. Again, do this repeatedly until you are accurate every time.

2. Sing the same interval consecutively upwards and then downwards several times. E.g. start on C and sing a minor 3rd up from it (E♭). Then sing a minor 3rd up from E♭ (G♭). Then another minor third up from G♭ (B♭♭ - which is enharmonically the same as A). Then up another minor 3rd (C an octave higher than the starting note). Once you can do this, reverse the process (Start on C and sing a minor 3rd down to A, then another minor 3rd down and then another, etc).

3. Play and sing a starting note (e.g. C) and then think of it as the first degree of the chromatic scale - sing "one". Now sing the flattened second degree of the scale - sing "flat two". This note is a minor 2nd up from your C note (a D♭ note). Then sing the C again ("one"). Then sing the second degree of the scale (a D note - sing "two"). Next, sing your C Note again ("one"). Continue in this manner all the way up the chromatic scale until you reach C an octave above. The entire sequence goes: 1, ♭2, 1, 2, 1, ♭3, 1, 3, 1, 4, 1, ♭5, 1, 5, 1, ♭6, 1, 6, 1, ♭7, 1, 7, 1, 8, 1. As with the previous exercises, once you can do this accurately (check your pitches on your instrument), reverse the process and sing downwards from the top of the scale, working your way down the chromatic scale again. The downward sequence goes 1(8), 7, 1, ♭7, 1, 6, 1, ♭6, 1, 5, 1,♭ 5, 1, 4, 1, 3, 1, ♭3, 1, 2, 1, ♭2, 1, 1, 1(8).

4. As well as hearing intervals melodically (one note at a time), it is important to be able to hear them harmonically (two notes played together). A good way to develop this is to have a friend play random harmonic intervals on either guitar or keyboard while you identify them. Keep your back to your friend while you do this, so that you cannot identify the intervals by sight.

Don't get frustrated if you can't hear intervals accurately at first. Most people have trouble with this. If you work at it regularly for several months, you will see a dramatic improvement in your musical hearing, and you will be able to improvise much more freely, as well as being able to work out parts off CDs more easily.

LESSON NINETEEN

UNDERSTANDING CHORDS

As you learnt in Lesson 1, a **chord** is a group of three or more notes played simultaneously. Different types of chords can be formed by using different combinations of notes. The most basic type of chord contains three different notes and is called a **triad**. The most common triads are **major chords**. All major chords contain three notes taken from the major scale bearing the same letter name as the chord. These three notes are the **1** (first), **3** (third) and **5** (fifth) degrees (notes) of the major scale, so the **chord formula** for the major chord is:

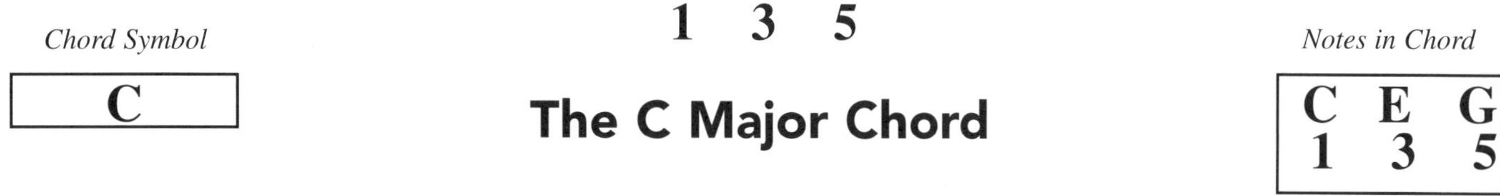

The C major chord is constructed from the C major scale. Using the above chord formula on the C major scale below, you can see that the C major chord contains the notes **C**, **E** and **G**.

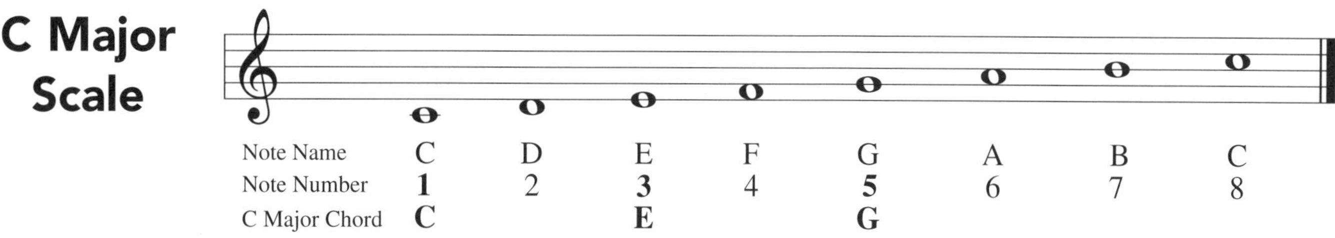

Once you have the correct notes for a C chord they can be arranged in any order. As long as the notes are still C, E and G, you still have a C chord. E.g. a C chord could be played C E G, or E G C, or G C E, or even G E C. These various arrangements of the notes within a chord are called **inversions**. It is also possible to **double** notes within a chord. E.g. the diagram below shows a common way of playing a C major chord on the guitar. It contains two C notes and two E notes. It is still a C major chord because it only contains notes called C, E and G. **Doubling** notes is common when playing chords on the guitar.

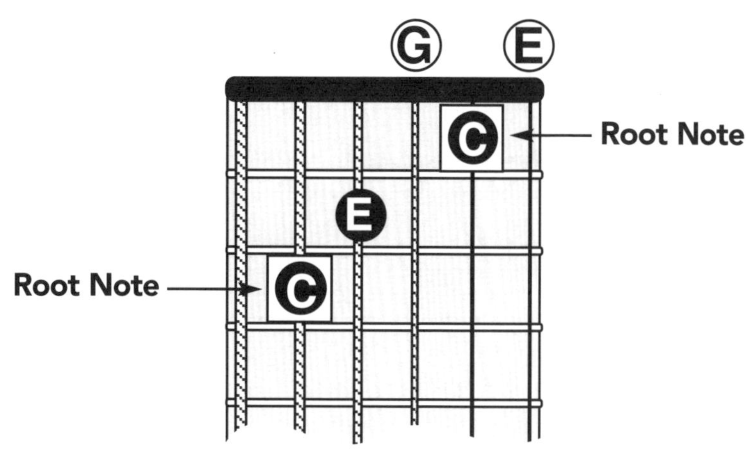

ARPEGGIOS

An **arpeggio** is a chord played one note at a time. The value of arpeggios is that they enable you to play parts which fit chord progressions perfectly, since every note of an arpeggio is a note of the accompanying chord. Written below is a **C major arpeggio** which consists of the notes **C**, **E** and **G**. These are the **root**, **third** and **fifth** of a **C major chord**. To play this arpeggio, simply hold down a C chord shape and pick the notes individually.

CD 1 40 C Major Arpeggio

Here is an example which makes use of arpeggios. Hold down the chord shapes indicated by the chord symbols as much as possible, except when playing notes which are not in the chords (e.g. the B note at the end of bar 2). Take care with your picking and make sure all your notes are clear and even.

41.

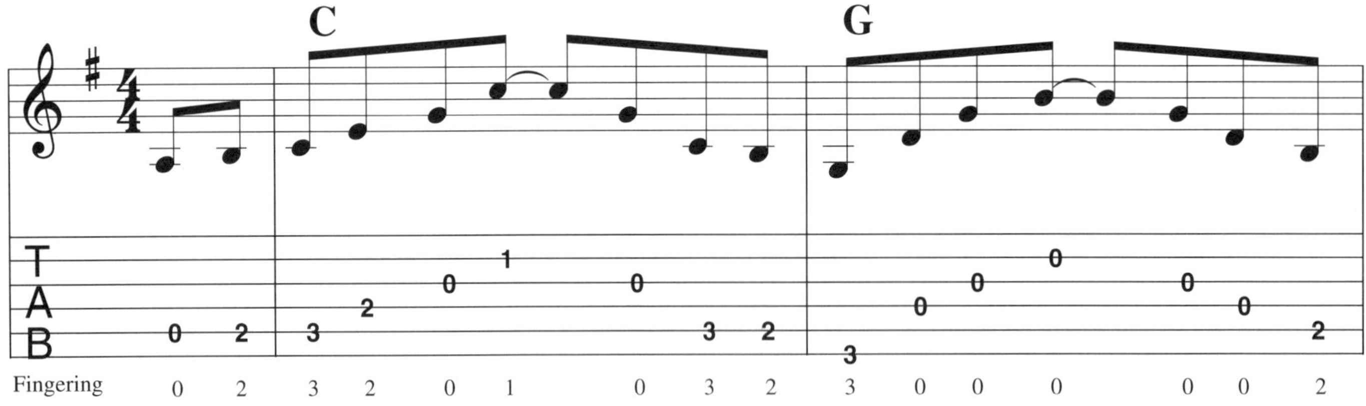

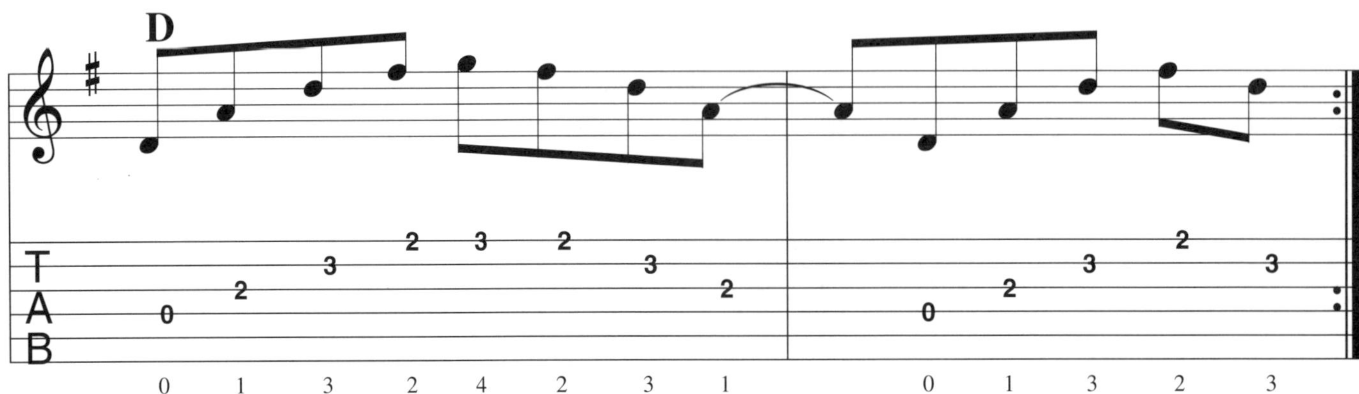

LESSON TWENTY

CHORD CONSTRUCTION–TRIADS

Chords are usually made up of combinations of major and minor third intervals. As mentioned previously, the simplest chords are made up of three notes. These are called **triads**. There are **four** basic types of triads: **major**, **minor**, **augmented** and **diminished**. Examples of each of these are shown below along with the formula for each one.

C Major Chord

Chord Symbol

C

	5	G
Minor Third		
	3	E
Major Third		
	1	C

Notes in Chord

C	E	G
1	3	5

C Minor Chord

Chord Symbol

Cm

	5	G
Major Third		
	♭3	E♭
Minor Third		
	1	C

Notes in Chord

C	E♭	G
1	♭3	5

C Augmented Chord

Chord Symbol

C+

	♯5	G♯
Major Third		
	3	E
Major Third		
	1	C

Notes in Chord

C	E	G♯
1	3	♯5

C Diminished Chord

Chord Symbol

Cdim
or
C°

	♭5	G♭
Minor Third		
	♭3	E♭
Minor Third		
	1	C

Notes in Chord

For every type of chord there is a corresponding arpeggio. Shown below is a **C minor arpeggio** which consists of the notes **C**, **E♭** and **G** which are the **root**, **flattened third** and **fifth** of a **C minor chord**.

42.0 C Minor Arpeggio

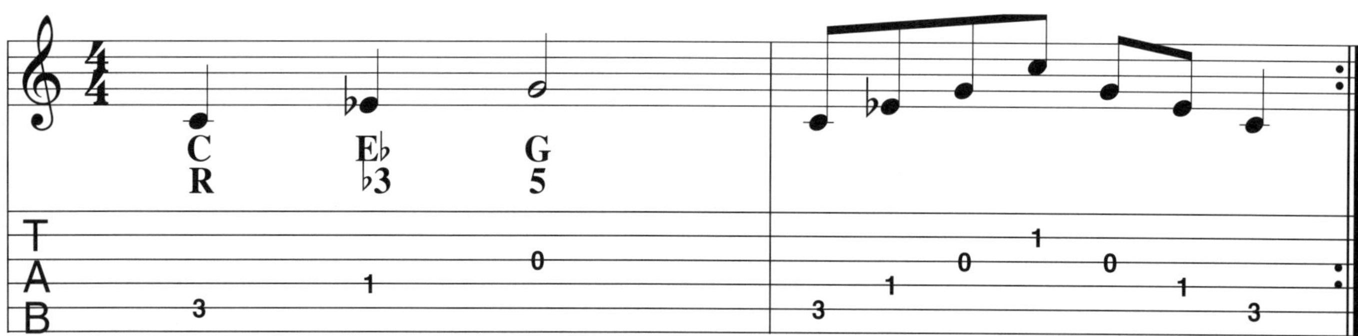

42.1 G Minor Arpeggio

This is a **G minor arpeggio** which consists of the notes **G**, **B♭** and **D**. These are the root, third and fifth of a **G minor chord**.

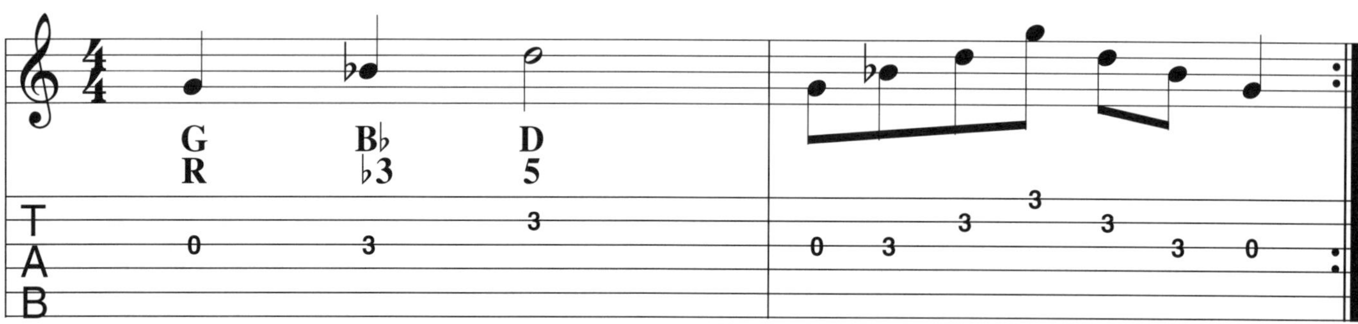

43.

Here is an example which makes use of both major and minor arpeggios.

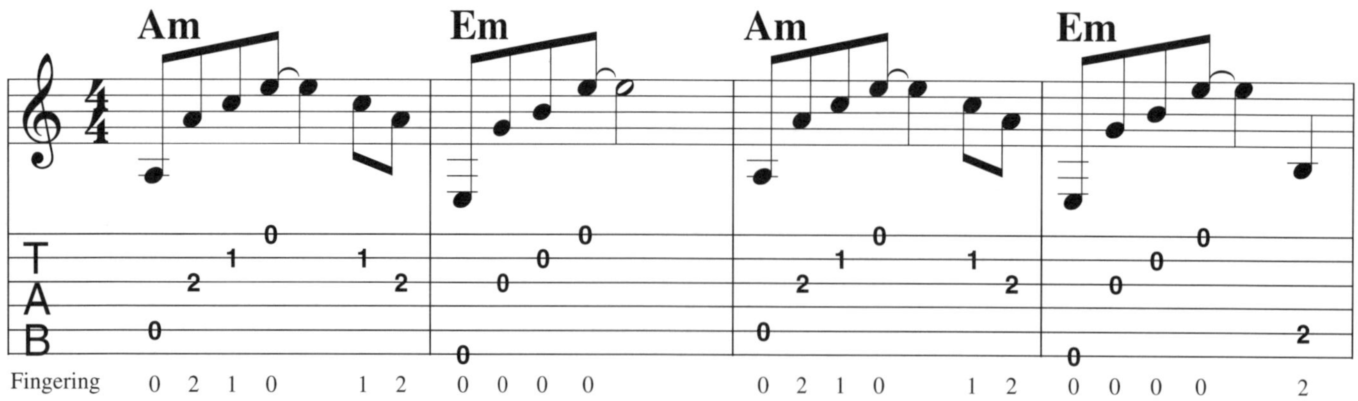

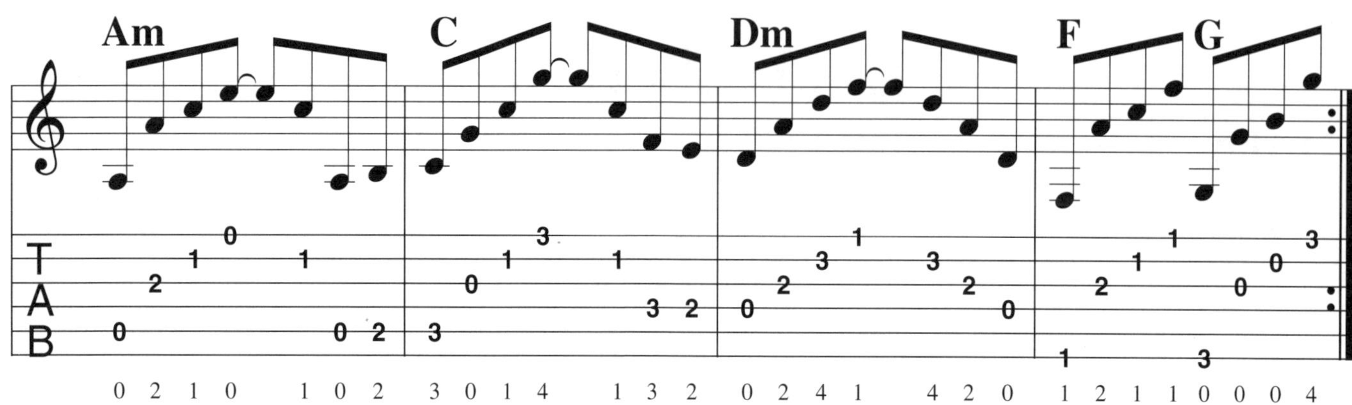

AUGMENTED AND DIMINISHED CHORDS

Augmented and diminished chords are not as common as major or minor chords, but it is still important to learn them. They occur in many pieces of music as a way of creating tension before resolving to either a major or minor chord. Here are some examples demonstrating these chords. Listen to the CD to hear what they sound like.

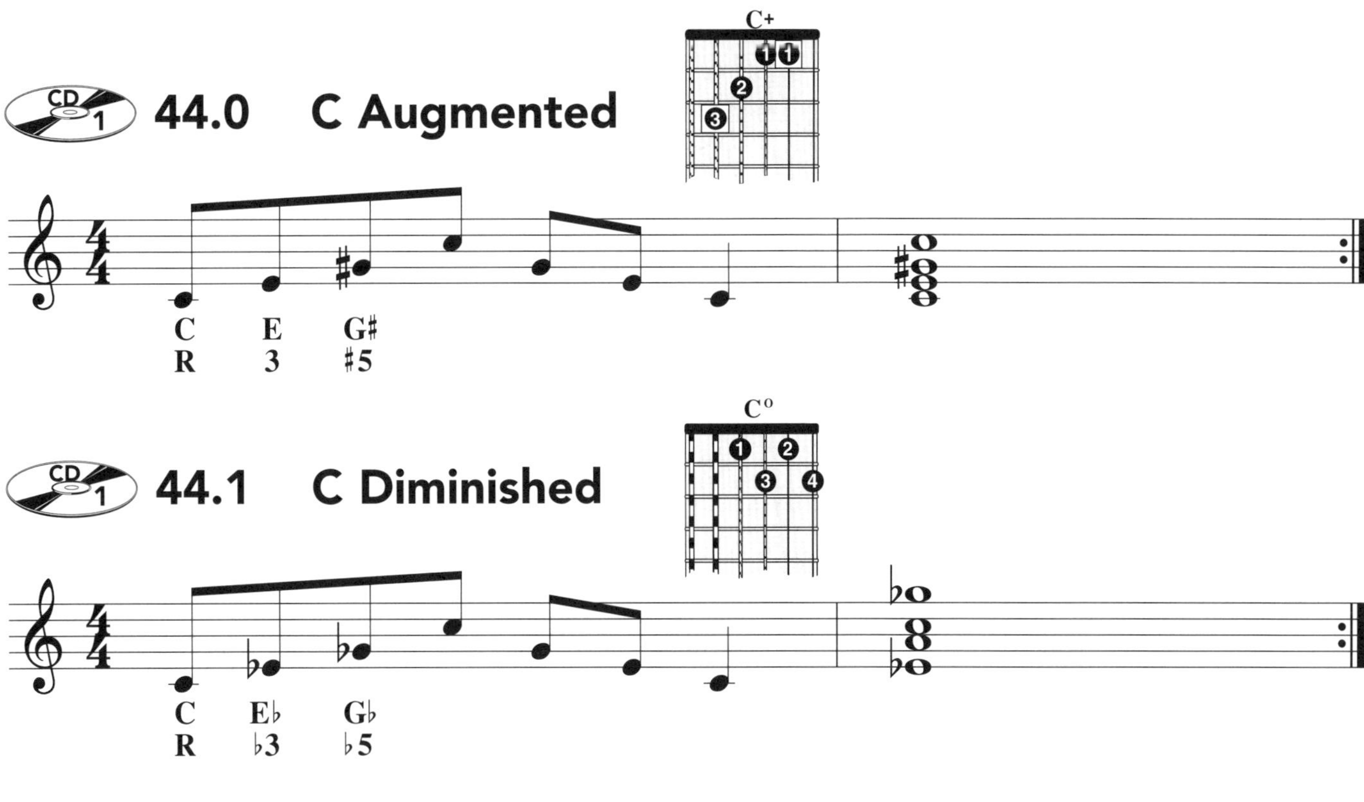

CD 1 45.

Here is an example which uses arpeggios of all four types of triads – **major**, **minor**, **augmented** and **diminished**. Pay careful attention to the fingering.

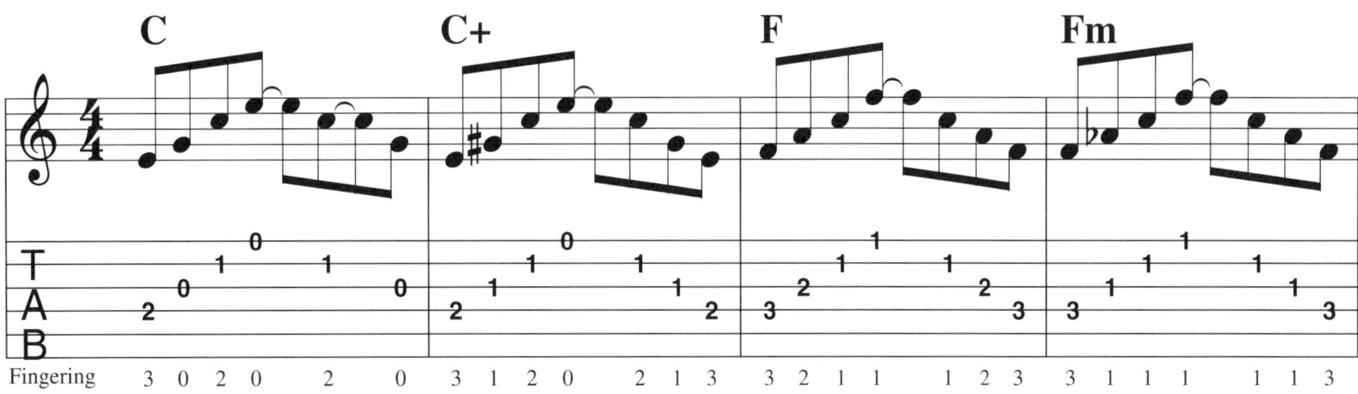

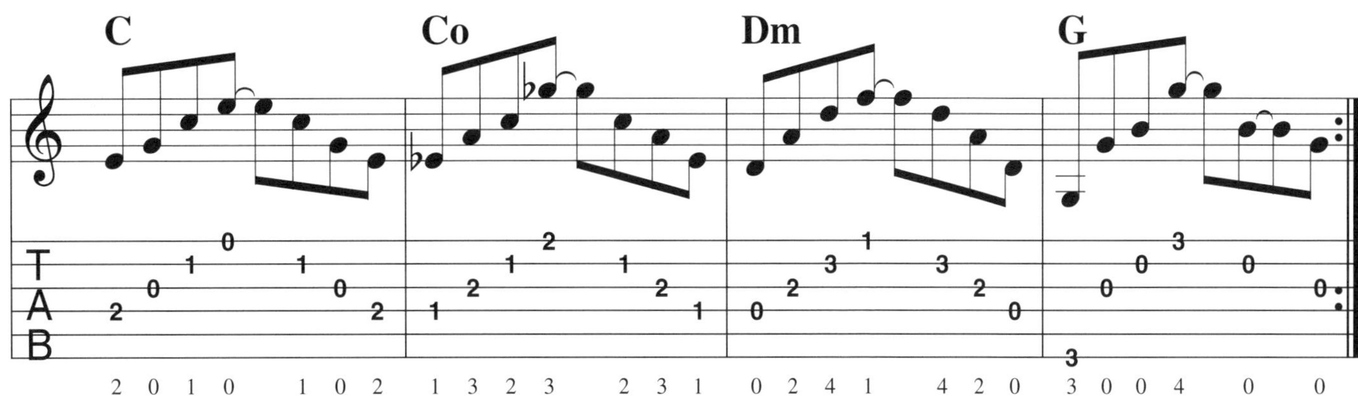

LESSON TWENTY ONE

SCALE TONE CHORDS

In any key it is possible to build chords on each note of a scale. This means that for every major scale there are **seven** possible chords which can be used for creating guitar parts and harmonising melodies. These seven chords are called **scale tone chords**. It is common practice to describe all the chords within a key with **roman numerals**. The example below which demonstrates the seven scale tone triads (three note chords) is in the key of C major.

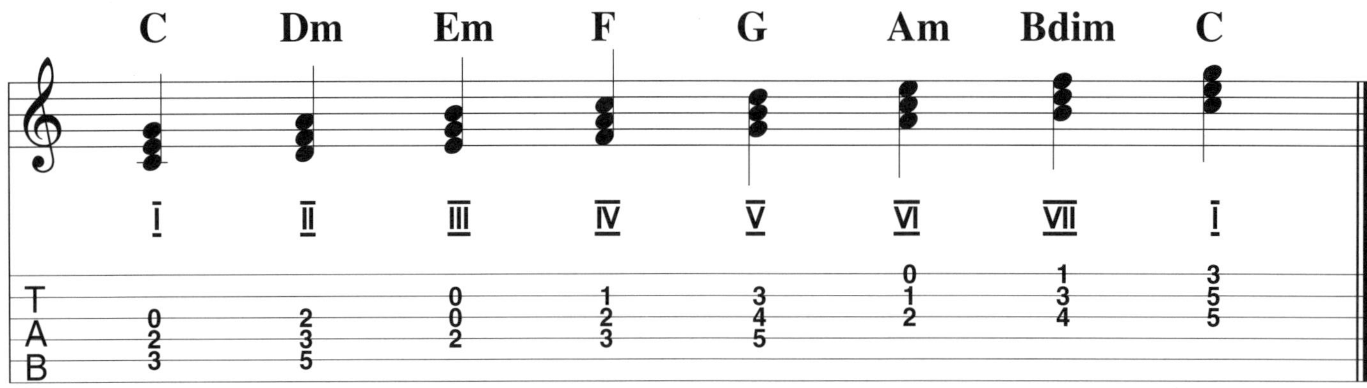

Once you know the notes for any of these chords, you can use any fingering you know to play them. This may involve re-arranging the order of the notes or doubling some of the notes, but as long as the chord shape you are playing contains only the three note names of that particular chord, you are still playing the right chord. The next example demonstrates a common progression in the key of C. This progression would be described as I III IV V III VI II V. The chord shapes used on the recording are shown below.

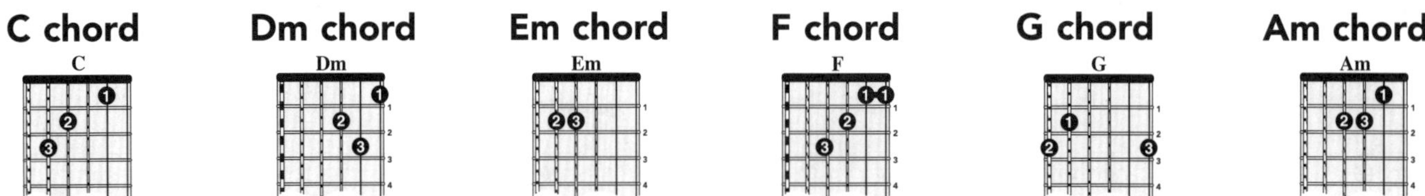

46.0

The rhythm notation indicates that you are strumming chords, but you could also play the chords in this (or any) progression as arpeggios – experiment!

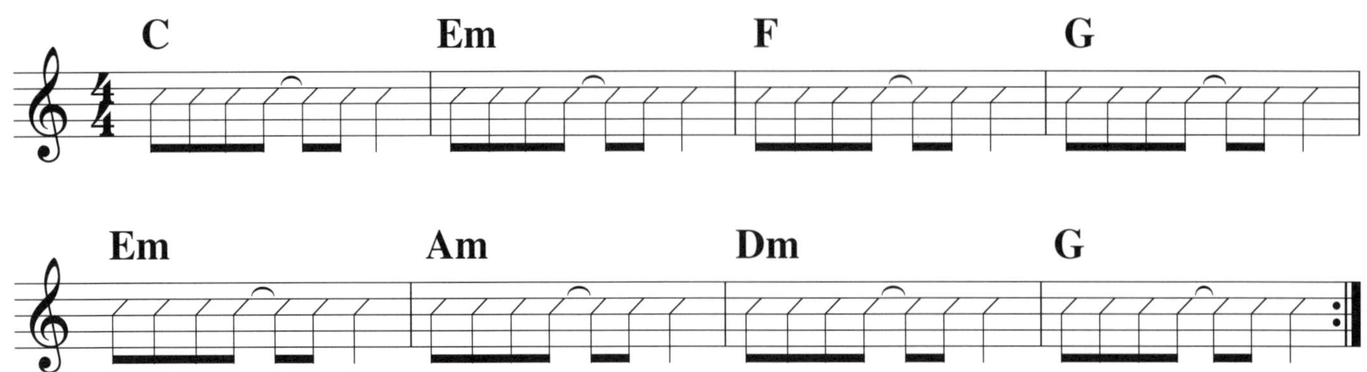

MAJOR KEY TRIAD PATTERN

If you go through all the scale tone chords in the key of C major you come up with the following pattern:

I	**Major**	**(C Major)**
II	**Minor**	**(D Minor)**
III	**Minor**	**(E Minor)**
IV	**Major**	**(F Major)**
V	**Major**	**(G Major)**
VI	**Minor**	**(A Minor)**
VII	**Diminished**	**(B Diminished)**

This pattern remains the same regardless of the key. For **any major key**, Chord I is **always** major, chord II is always minor, chord III is always minor, etc. The only thing that changes from one key to the next is the letter names of the chords. This can be demonstrated by looking at the scale tone triads for the key of **G major** which are shown below.

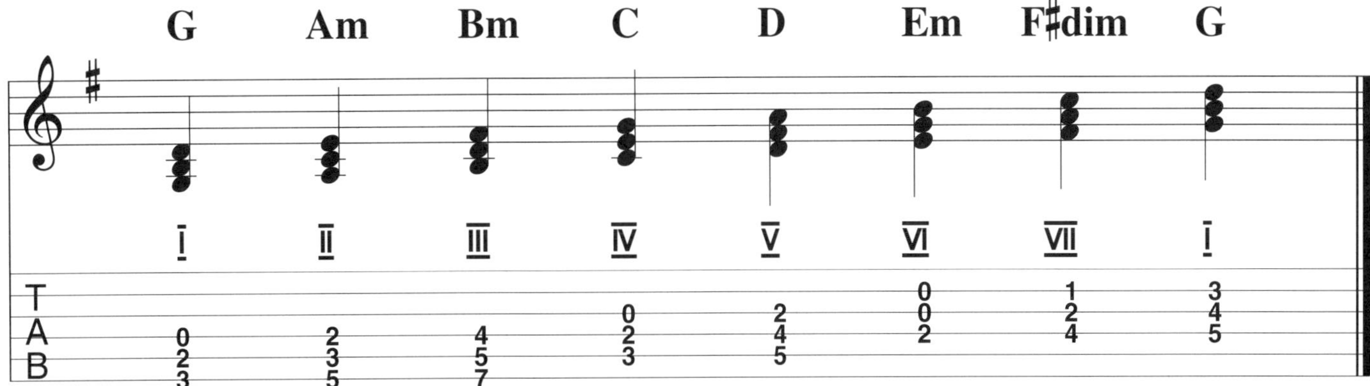

TRANSPOSING

Transposing means changing the key of a piece of music. By simply following the roman numerals and remembering which chords are major, minor, etc, it is easy to transpose chords from one key to another. Here is the progression from example 46.0 **transposed to the key of G**. Write roman numerals under the chords and compare them to example 46.0. Then try transposing other chord progressions you know. Make a habit of transposing every new thing you learn and it will eventually become second nature.

CD 1 **46.1**

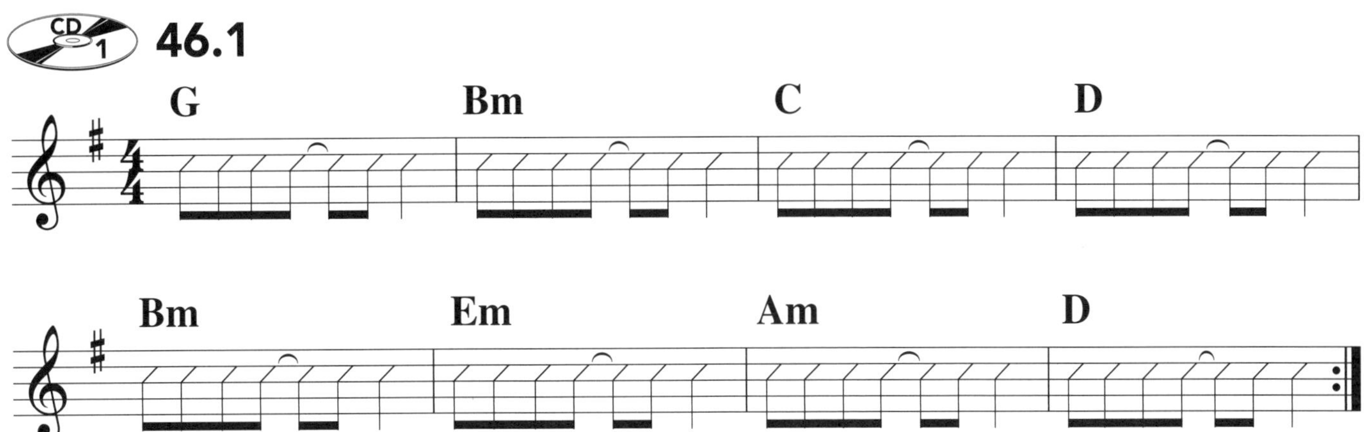

PRIMARY CHORDS

In any key there are some chords which are more commonly used than others. The three most common chords are I, IV and V. These are called the **primary chords**. With these three chords, it is possible to harmonize (accompany with chords) any melody in the key, because between them they contain every note of the scale, as shown below in the key of **C**.

C Major Scale **C D E F G A B C**

	I	IV	V
Primary Triads	G	C	D
	E	A	B
	C	F	G

HARMONIZING MELODIES

To harmonize a melody, you simply play a chord which contains a note from that melody on the **first beat of each bar**. In time, you could also add another chord on the **third** beat of the bar. There is always more than one chord which could be used, but some sound better than others. The more songs you learn and analyze, the easier it becomes to find the right chords to play. If you look at the scale and chords above, you will notice that the notes **C** and **G** appear in more than one of the chords. This means that if you were harmonizing a melody in the **key of C**, you could try both chords wherever one of these notes appear on the first beat of a bar. The following example shows a melody in C major harmonized with chords I, IV and V. Learn it and then transpose it to all the other keys.

CD 1 **47.0**

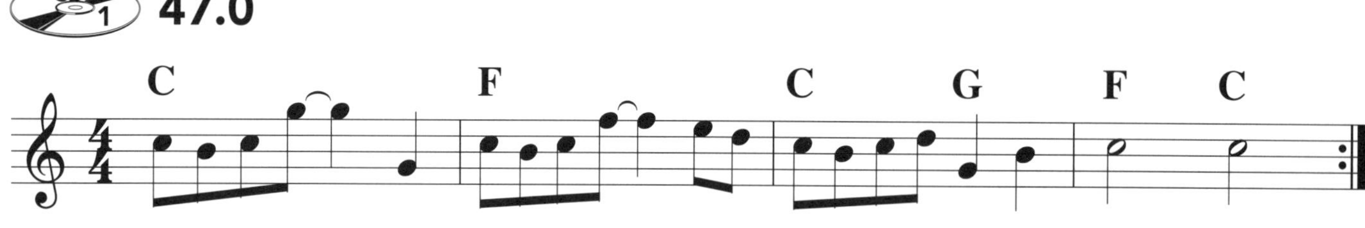

The table below shows the primary chords in all twelve major keys.

PRIMARY TRIADS IN ALL MAJOR KEYS

KEY	I	IV	V	KEY	I	IV	V
C	C	F	G	F	F	B♭	C
G	G	C	D	B♭	B♭	E♭	F
D	D	G	A	E♭	E♭	A♭	B♭
A	A	D	E	A♭	A♭	D♭	E♭
E	E	A	B	D♭	D♭	G♭	A♭
B	B	E	F♯	G♭	G♭	C♭	D♭
F♯	F♯	B	C♯				

Although most melodies can be harmonized using only chords I, IV and V, it is also common to use one or more of the remaining chords (II, III, VI and VII) to create a different feeling. These other chords are called **secondary chords**. As with primary chords, the secondary chord chosen for the harmony in any given bar should contain the melody note which occurs on the first or third beat of that bar (wherever the chord changes). Here is the melody from the previous example harmonized with both primary and secondary chords. Once again, learn it and then transpose both the melody and the chords to all the other keys.

47.1

COMMON PROGRESSIONS

One of the best ways to become familiar with chords in all keys is to take a simple progression and transpose it to all of the keys. This may be slow at first, but the more you do it, the easier it gets. Here are some common progressions to learn and transpose. Remember to practice them in different ways, e.g. as strummed chords and fingerpicked as arpeggios.

I IV V I   I VI IV V   II V I   I VI II V   I IV VII III VI II V

SCALE TONE TRIADS IN ALL KEYS

Scale Note:	I	II	III	IV	V	VI	VII	VIII (I)
Chord Constructed:	major	minor	minor	major	major	minor	dim	major
C Scale	C	Dm	Em	F	G	Am	B°	C
G Scale	G	Am	Bm	C	D	Em	F♯°	G
D Scale	D	Em	F♯m	G	A	Bm	C♯°	D
A Scale	A	Bm	C♯m	D	E	F♯m	G♯°	A
E Scale	E	F♯m	G♯m	A	B	C♯m	D♯°	E
B Scale	B	C♯m	D♯m	E	F♯	G♯m	A♯°	B
F♯ Scale	F♯	G♯m	A♯m	B	C♯	D♯m	E♯° (F°)	F♯
F Scale	F	Gm	Am	B♭	C	Dm	E°	F
B♭ Scale	B♭	Cm	Dm	E♭	F	Gm	A°	B♭
E♭ Scale	E♭	Fm	Gm	A♭	B♭	Cm	D°	E♭
A♭ Scale	A♭	B♭m	Cm	D♭	E♭	Fm	G°	A♭
D♭ Scale	D♭	E♭m	Fm	G♭	A♭	B♭m	C°	D♭
G♭ Scale	G♭	A♭m(G♯m)	B♭m	C♭ (B)	D♭	E♭m	F°	G♭

CHORD SHAPES

Here is a chart of some basic fingerings for major, minor and diminished chords. With the chords shown here you should be able to work out how to play the seven scale tone chords in each of the major keys. Learn the chords outlined by a box first, as these are the easiest and most practical. Although the other shapes are all useful, in many cases bar chords can be used instead. These will be discussed in later lessons. All the boxed chords sound particularly good on acoustic guitars and for fingerpicking. Remember that there is always more than one fingering for a chord, so experiment with doubling notes in these chords or re-arranging the order of the notes.

Major Chords

Chord Symbol

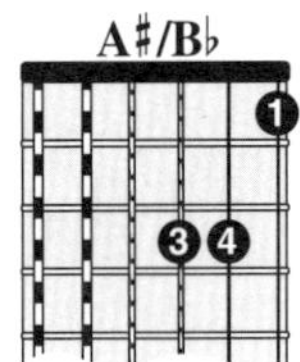

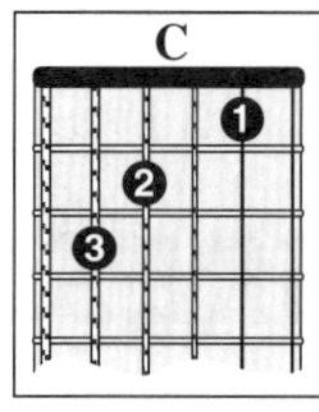

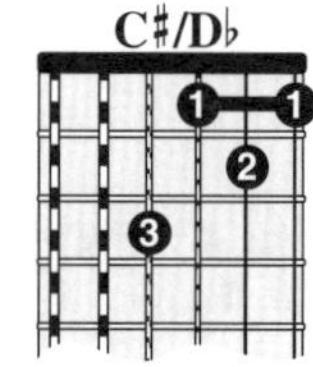

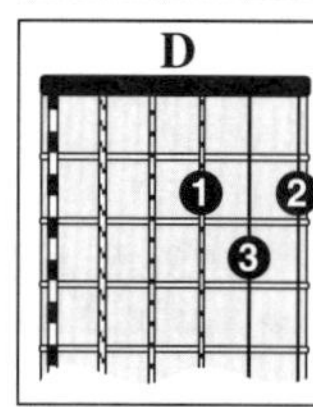

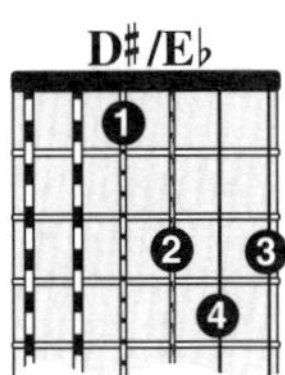

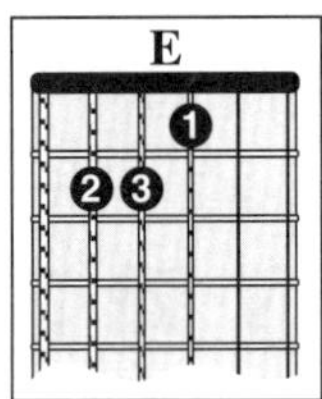

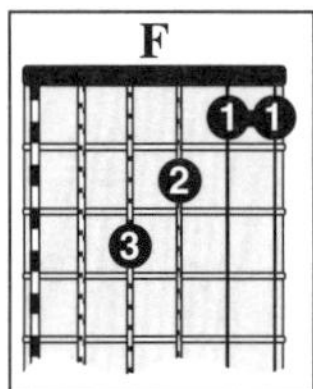

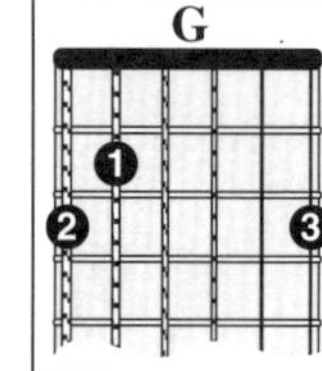

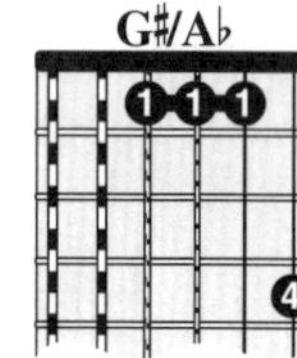

Minor Chords

Chord Symbol

m

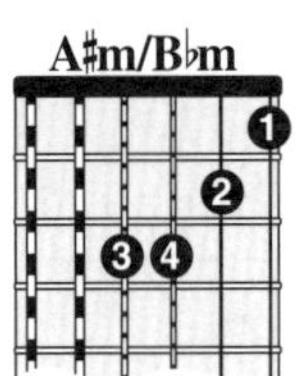

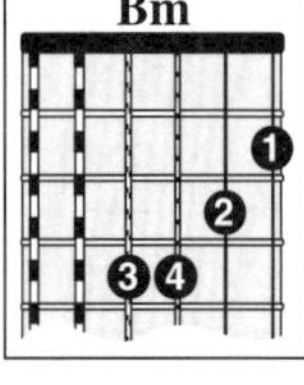

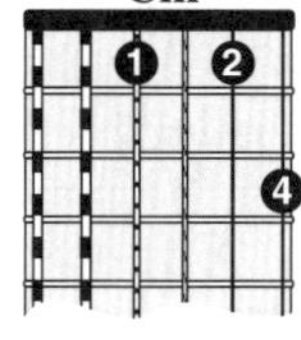

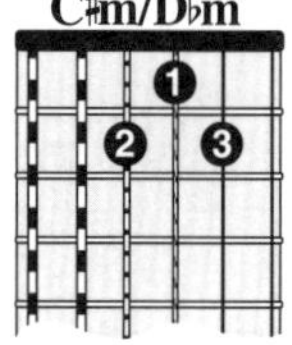

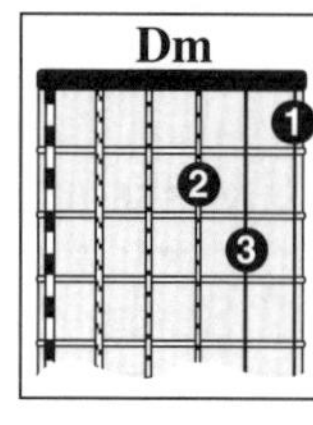

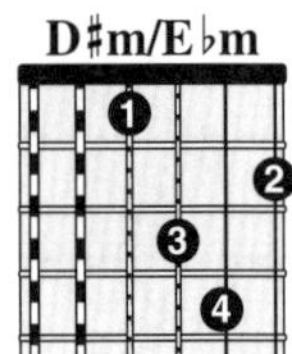

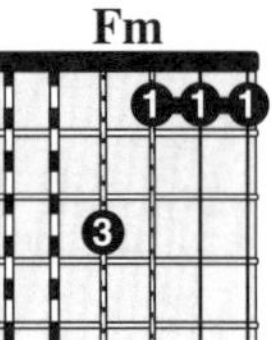

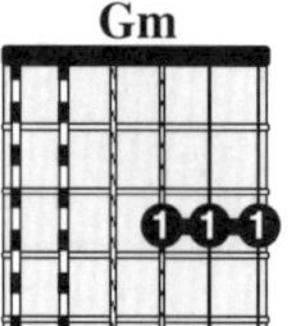

G♯m/A♭m

4th fret

Diminished Chords

Chord Symbol

dim or °

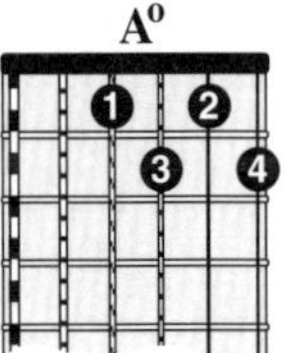

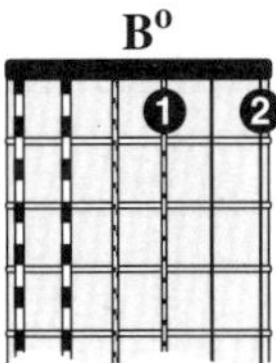

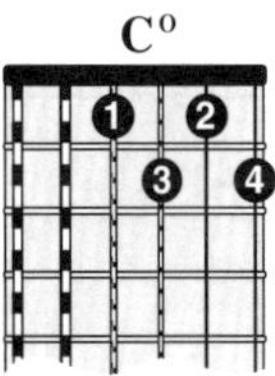

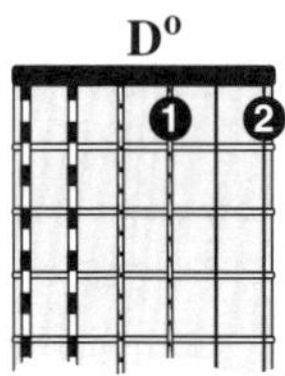

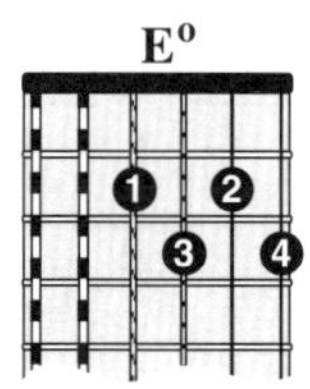

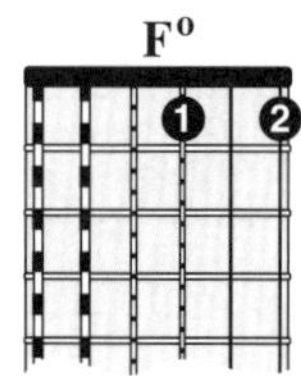

G°

LESSON TWENTY TWO

MINOR SCALES AND KEYS

Apart from major keys, the other basic tonality used in western music is a **minor key**. Minor keys are often said to have a sadder or darker sound than major keys. Songs in a minor key use notes taken from a **minor scale**. There are three types of minor scale – the **natural minor scale**, the **harmonic minor scale** and the **melodic minor scale**. Written below is the **A natural minor** scale.

THE NATURAL MINOR SCALE

The A natural minor contains exactly the same notes as the C major scale. The difference is that it starts and finishes on an **A** note instead of a C note. The A note then becomes the key note. To highlight the difference, the degrees of the scale as they would relate to the A major scale are written under the note names. Notice the **flattened 3rd**, **6th and 7th**.

48.0

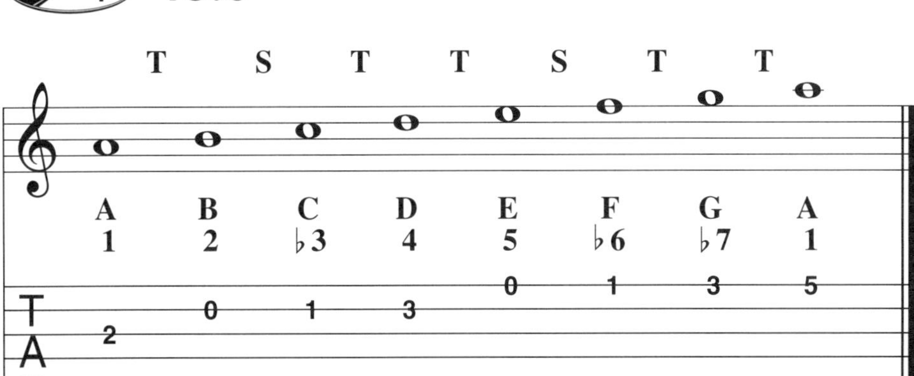

48.1

Here is the full fingering for the **A natural minor** scale in the open position, moving up to the high A at the 5th fret on the first string. Learn it from memory and then play it with your eyes closed, naming the notes out loud, and then naming the scale degrees out loud.

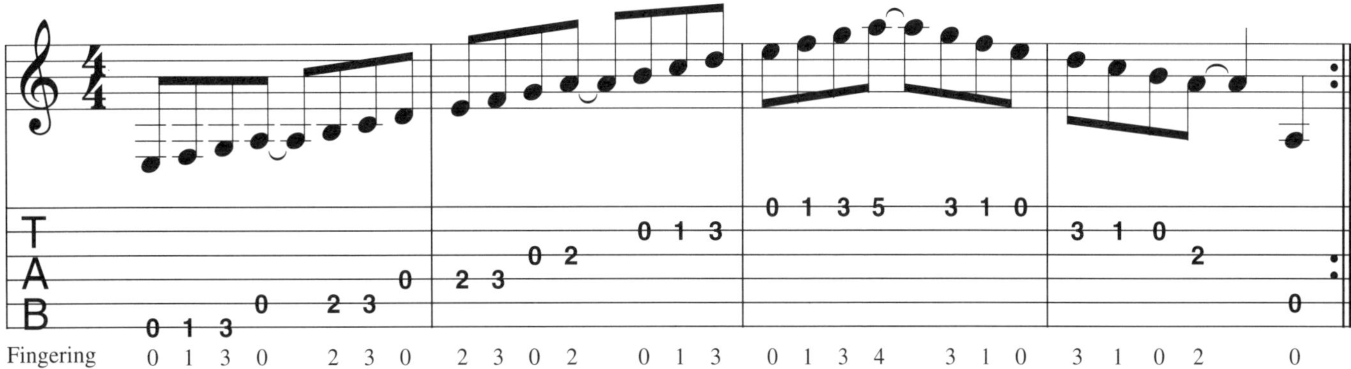

THE HARMONIC MINOR SCALE

The harmonic minor is often described as having an "Eastern" sound. It has a distance of 1½ tones (instead of one) between the **6th** and **7th** degrees. The raised 7th degree is the only difference between the harmonic minor and the natural minor scale.

CD 1 49.0 A Harmonic Minor

CD 1 49.1

Here is the full fingering for the **A harmonic minor** scale in the open position, up to the high A. Remember to play notes at the 4th fret with your 4th finger. As with all scales, learn it from memory and then play it with your eyes closed, naming first the notes out loud, and then naming the scale degrees.

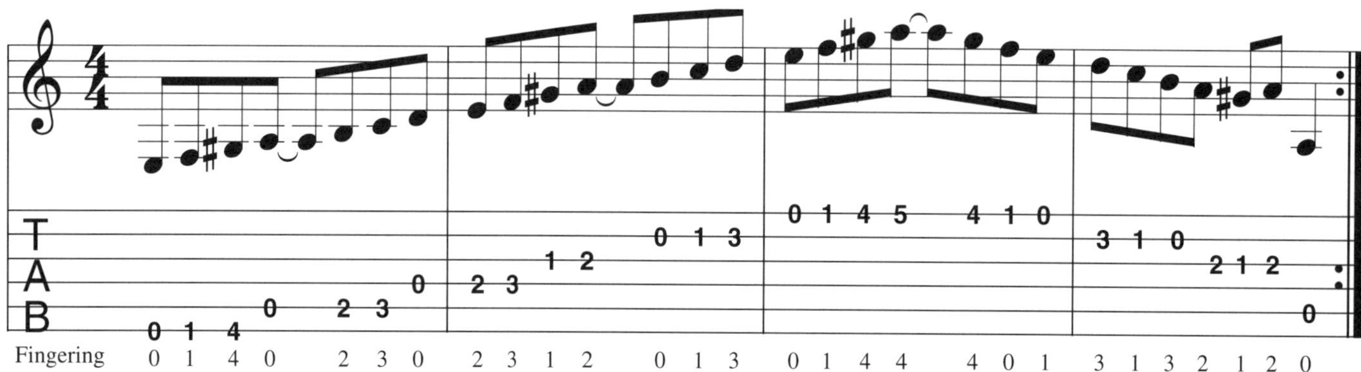

CD 1 49.2

This melody is derived from the A harmonic minor scale. Once you can play it, try transposing it up to the higher octave of the scale.

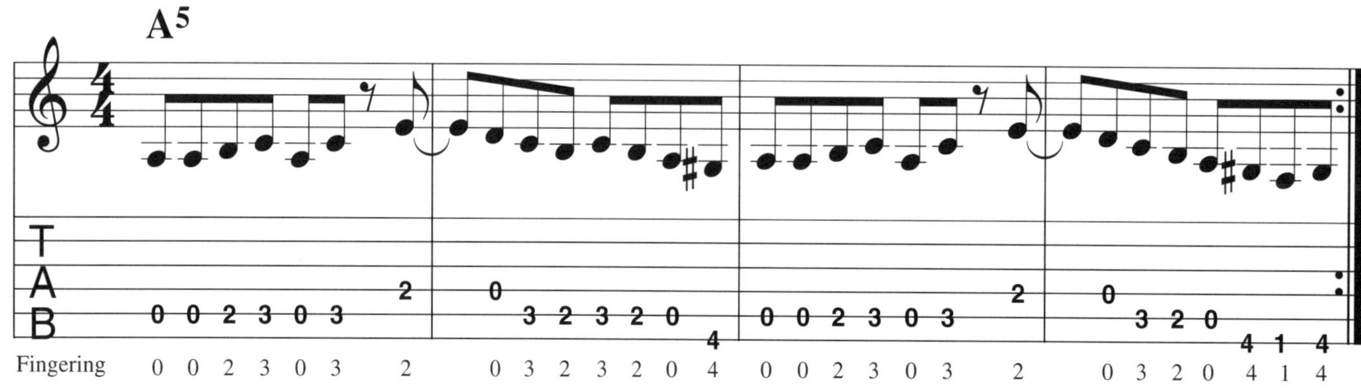

50. Look Sharp

Here is an arpeggio based part in the **key of A minor**, which uses notes from both the natural and harmonic minor scales. Learn it and then try making up your own parts based on the ideas presented here.

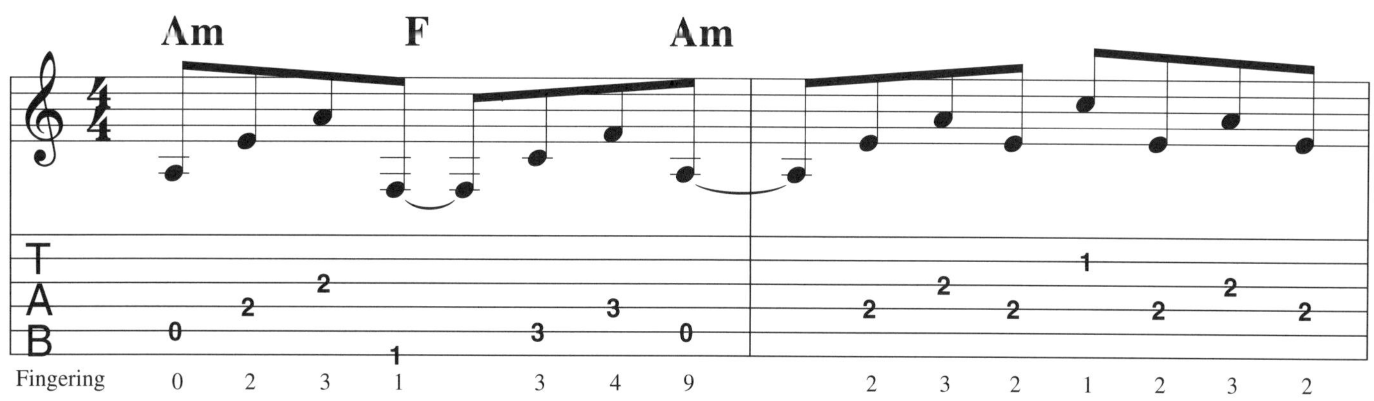

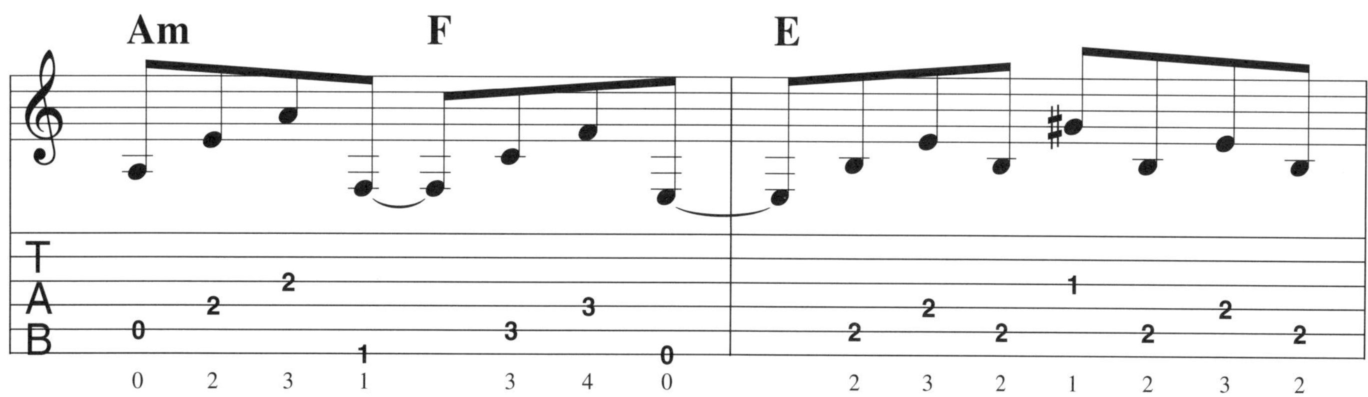

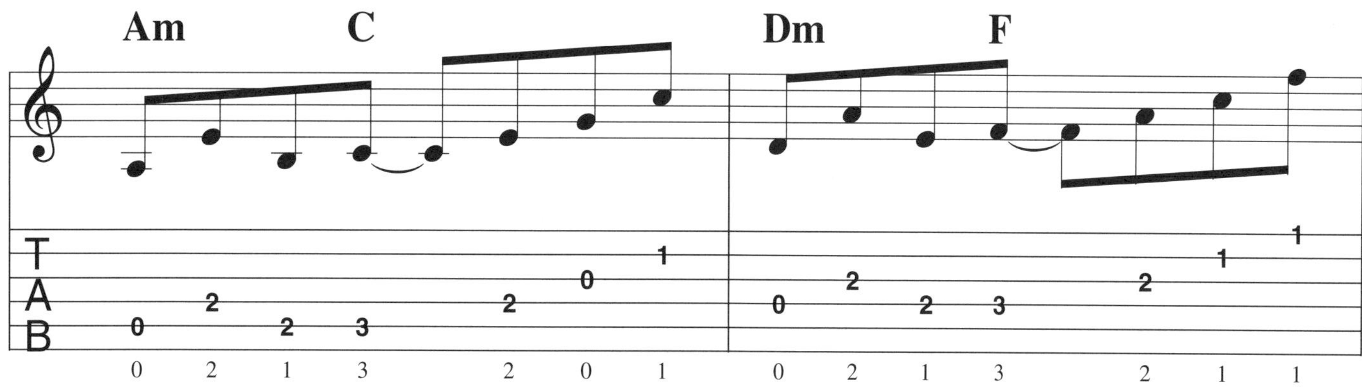

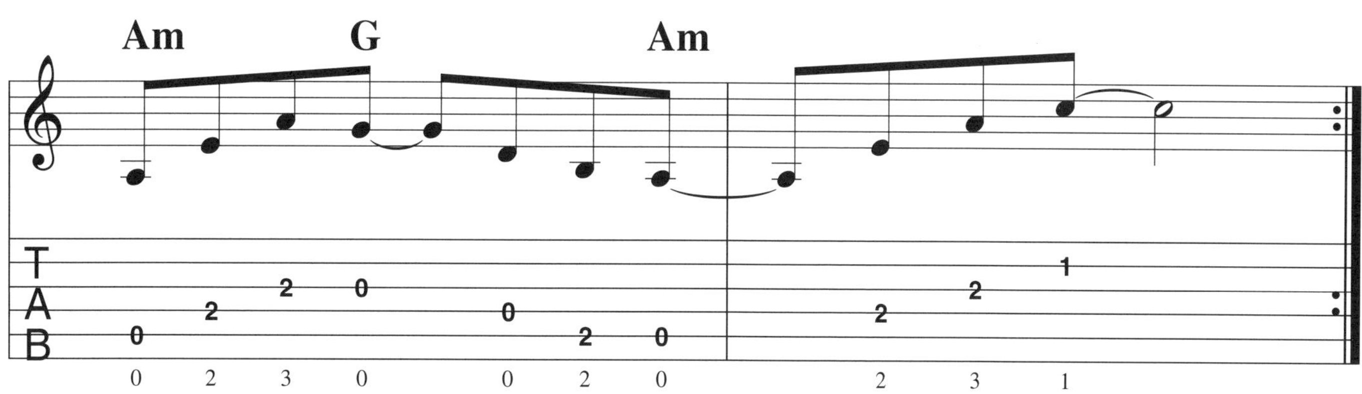

THE MELODIC MINOR SCALE

In Classical music, a **melodic minor** scale has the **6th** and **7th** notes sharpened when ascending and returned to natural when descending. However, in Jazz and other more modern styles, the melodic minor descends the same way it ascends. An easy way to think of the ascending melodic minor is as a major scale with a flattened third degree.

51. A Melodic Minor

TABLE OF MINOR SCALES

This table shows the notes of the **melodic minor** scale in all twelve keys. Remember that the **descending melodic minor is the same as the natural minor**. To work out the notes for the **harmonic minor**, simply **flatten the 6th** degree of the ascending melodic minor.

	T	S	T	T	T	T	S	T	T	S	T	T	S	T	
A MELODIC MINOR*	A	B	C	D	E	F♯	G♯	A	G♮	F♮	E	D	C	B	A
E MELODIC MINOR*	E	F♯	G	A	B	C♯	D♯	E	D♮	C♮	B	A	G	F♯	E
B MELODIC MINOR*	B	C♯	D	E	F♯	G♯	A♯	B	A♮	G♮	F♯	E	D	C♯	B
F♯ MELODIC MINOR*	F♯	G♯	A	B	C♯	D♯	E♯	F♯	E♮	D♮	C♯	B	A	G♯	F♯
C♯ MELODIC MINOR*	C♯	D♯	E	F♯	G♯	A♯	B♯	C♯	B♮	A♮	G♯	F♯	E	D♯	C♯
G♯ MELODIC MINOR	G♯	A♯	B	C♯	D♯	E♯	G	G♯	F♯	E♮	D♯	C♯	B	A♯	G♯
D♯ MELODIC MINOR	D♯	E♯	F♯	G♯	A♯	B♯	D	D♯	C♯	B♮	A♯	G♯	F♯	E♯	D♯
D MELODIC MINOR*	D	E	F	G	A	B♮	C♯	D	C♮	B♭	A	G	F	E	D
G MELODIC MINOR*	G	A	B♭	C	D	E♮	F♯	G	F	E♭	D	C	B♭	A	G
C MELODIC MINOR	C	D	E♭	F	G	A♮	B♮	C	B♭	A♭	G	F	E♭	D	C
F MELODIC MINOR	F	G	A♭	B♭	C	D♮	E♮	F	E♭	D♭	C	B♭	A♭	G	F
B♭ MELODIC MINOR	B♭	C	D♭	E♭	F	G♮	A♮	B	A♭	G♭	F	E♭	D♭	C	B♭
E♭ MELODIC MINOR	E♭	F	G♭	A♭	B♭	C♮	D♮	E♭	D♭	C♭	B♭	A♭	G♭	F♭	E♭
ROMAN NUMERALS	I	II	III	IV	V	VI	VII	VIII	VII	VI	V	IV	III	II	I

LESSON TWENTY THREE

RELATIVE KEYS

If you compare the **A natural minor** scale with the **C major** scale you will notice that they contain the same notes; the only difference is that they start on a different note. Because of this, these two scales are referred to as "relatives", **A minor** is the **relative minor** of **C major** and vice versa.

Major Scale: C Major

Relative Minor Scale: A Natural Minor

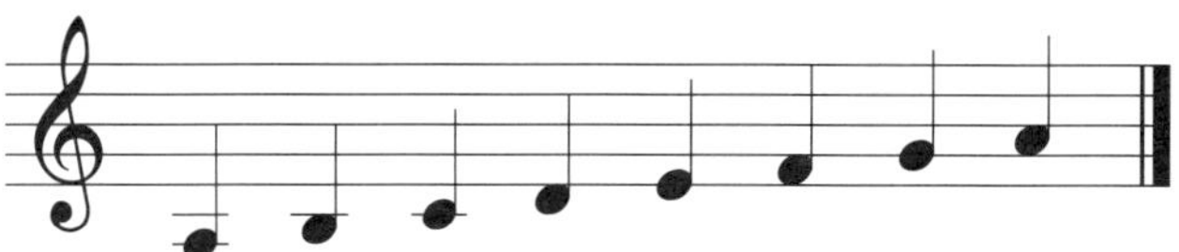

The harmonic and melodic minor scale variations are also relatives of the same major scale, e.g. the **A harmonic** and **A melodic minor** scales are all relatives of **C major**.
For every major scale (and ever major chord) there is a relative minor scale which is based upon the **6th note** of the major scale. This is outlined in the table below.

MAJOR KEY (I)	C	D♭	D	E♭	E	F	F♯	G♭	G	A♭	A	B♭	B
RELATIVE MINOR KEY (VI)	Am	B♭m	Bm	Cm	C♯m	Dm	D♯m	E♭m	Em	Fm	F♯m	Gm	G♯m

Both the major and the relative minor share the same key signature, as illustrated below.

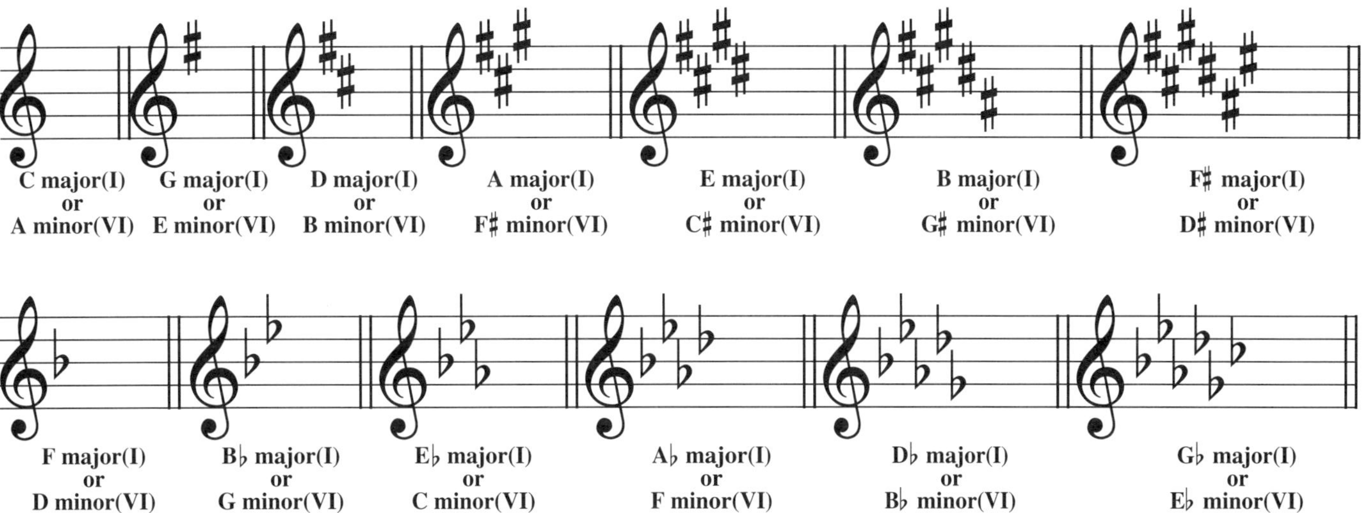

To determine whether a song is in a major key or the relative minor key, look at the last note or chord of the song. Songs often finish on the root note or the root chord which indicates the key. E.g., if the key signature contained one sharp, and the last chord of the song was **Em**, the key would probably be **E minor**, not **G major**. Minor key signatures are always based on the natural minor scale. The sharpened 6th and 7th degrees from the harmonic and melodic minor scales are not indicated in the key signature. This usually means there are **accidentals** (temporary sharps, flats or naturals) in melodies created from these scales.

52. Spiral Staircase

This example alternates between the relative keys of **C major** and **A minor**. The arpeggio style of playing used here is particularly effective when playing a Rock ballad. Notice the chord symbols **G/B** and **C/E**. These are examples of **slash chords**, which are chords with a specific bass note. The first letter is the name of the chord and the second is the bass note. Slash chords are discussed further in the following lesson.

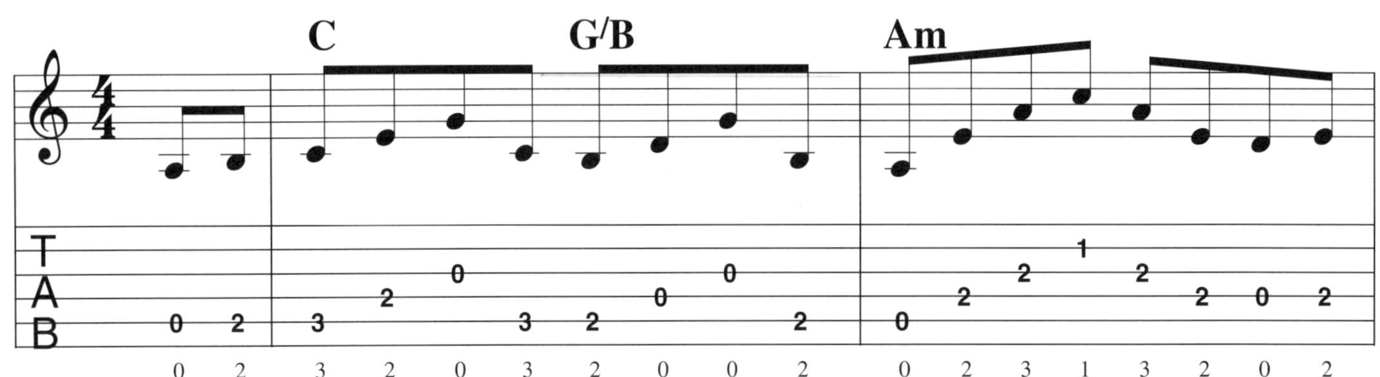

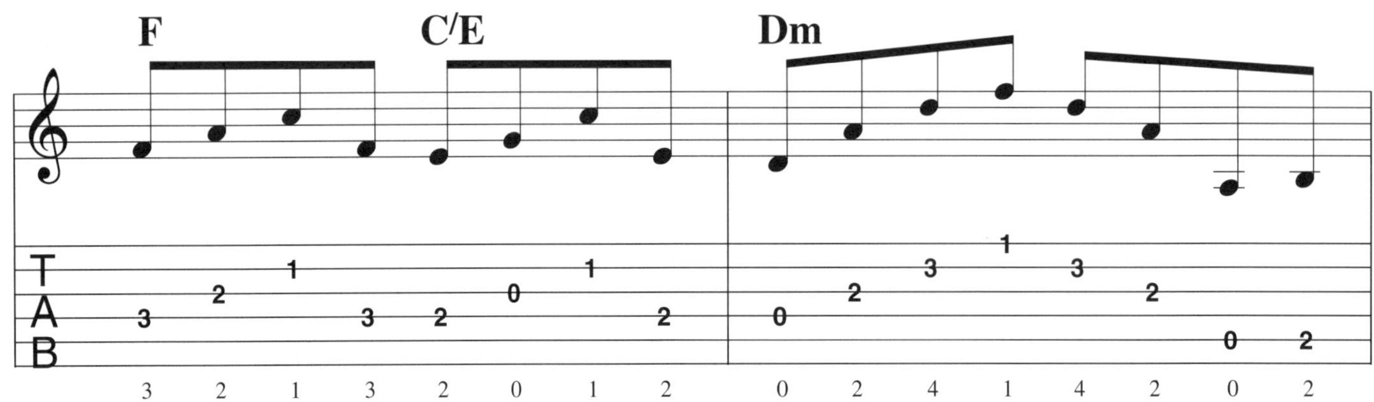

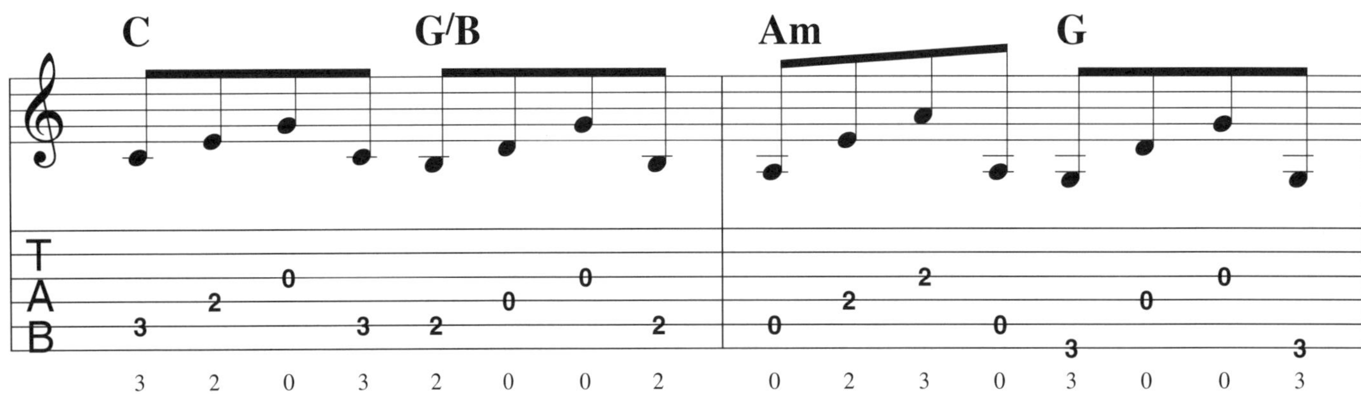

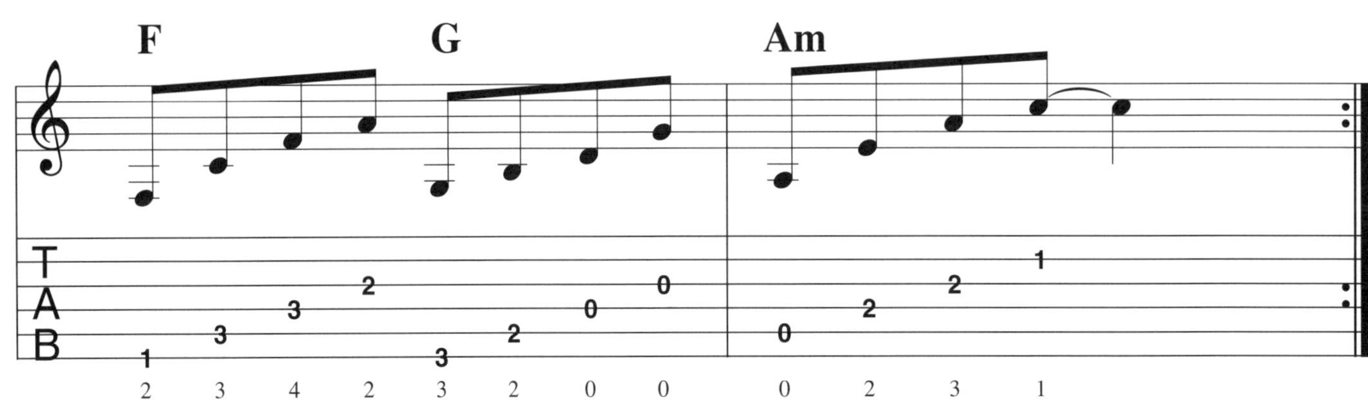

LESSON TWENTY FOUR

MINOR KEY SCALE TONE TRIADS

As you learnt in the previous lesson, to find the relative minor of any major key, you start on the **6th** degree of the major scale. The example below shows the **scale tone triads** for the key of **A minor**, the chords derived from the **natural minor** scale. As you will see, the chords are exactly the same as those contained in the key of C major. The only difference is the starting and finishing point – because the minor scale starts on **A**, A minor will now be chord I instead of VI.

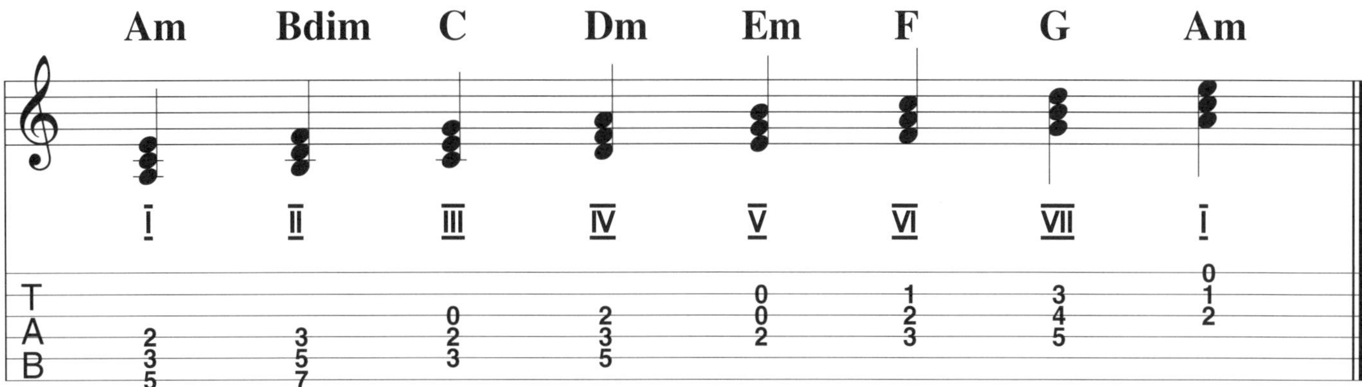

The following progression could be described in two possible ways. All the chords occur in the key of **C major** and also in the key of **A minor**. Because the progression has an obvious minor tonality (sound), musicians would use the second description. Analyze the progression using the roman numerals shown under the chords above, and then experiment with other chord combinations in the key of **A minor**.

53.

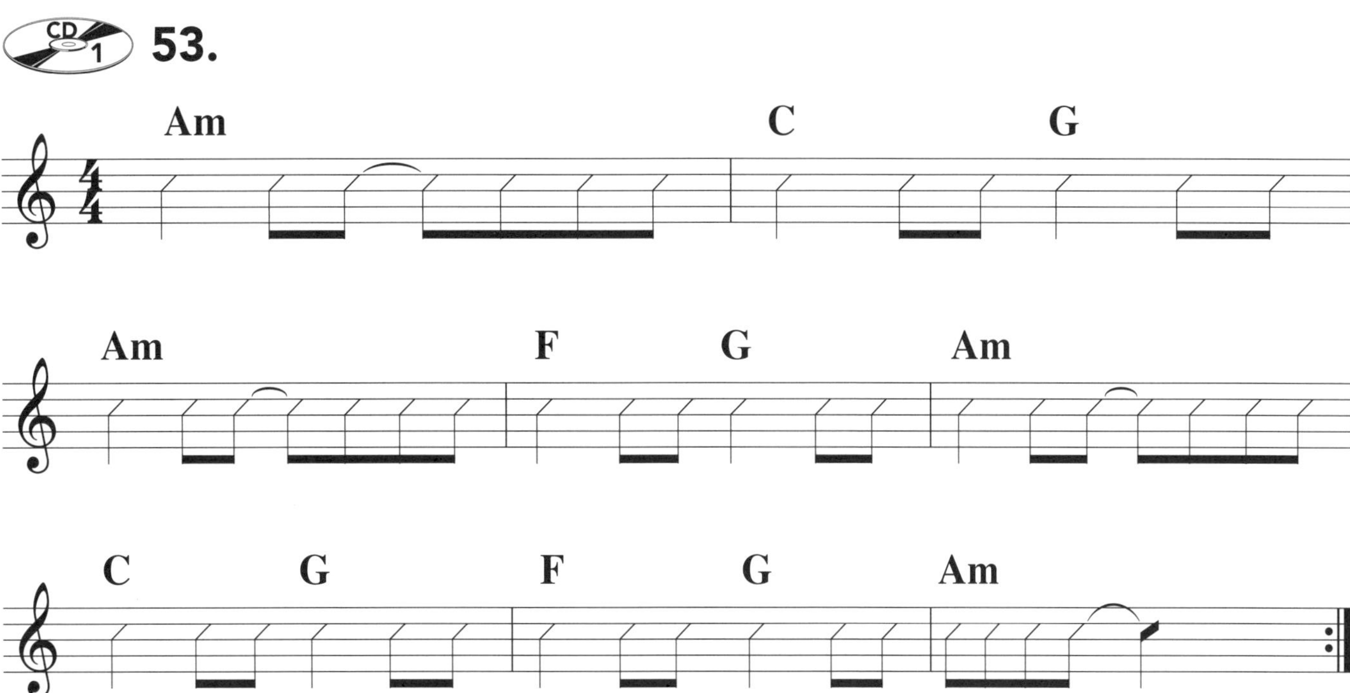

SLASH CHORDS

In the following example, you will notice some divided chord symbols. These symbols indicate a chord with a specific bass note under it. and are called **slash chords**. E.g. in bar 2, the chord symbol **G/B** occurs. This indicates a **G** chord played over a **B** bass note. In bar 4, the symbol **G/D** indicates a **G** chord with a **D** bass note. In bar 5, the symbol **Am/E** indicates an **A minor** chord with an **E** bass note. Slash chords are often used to create smooth, melodic bass lines and the symbols tell you that a note **other than the root** is played as the bass note of the chord.

Slash chords can create many different harmonic effects. Each combination has a specific name and often creates an entirely new chord. Basically you can play **any** chord over any bass note as long as it sounds good. Experiment with playing all the chords you have learnt over various bass notes from the scale of the key you are playing in.

BASS RUNS

Here is the progression from the previous example played as arpeggios. As well as the use of slash chords, notice also the use of **extra bass notes to connect the chords**. These **bass runs** are all notes of the **A natural minor** scale. Experiment with other ways of strumming and picking this progression, and try some bass runs with other progressions you already know. Make a habit of doing this with every new progression you learn. All musicians use the same chords, but good players can create great sounding parts by the way they play the notes within the chords, and the way they connect them.

54.

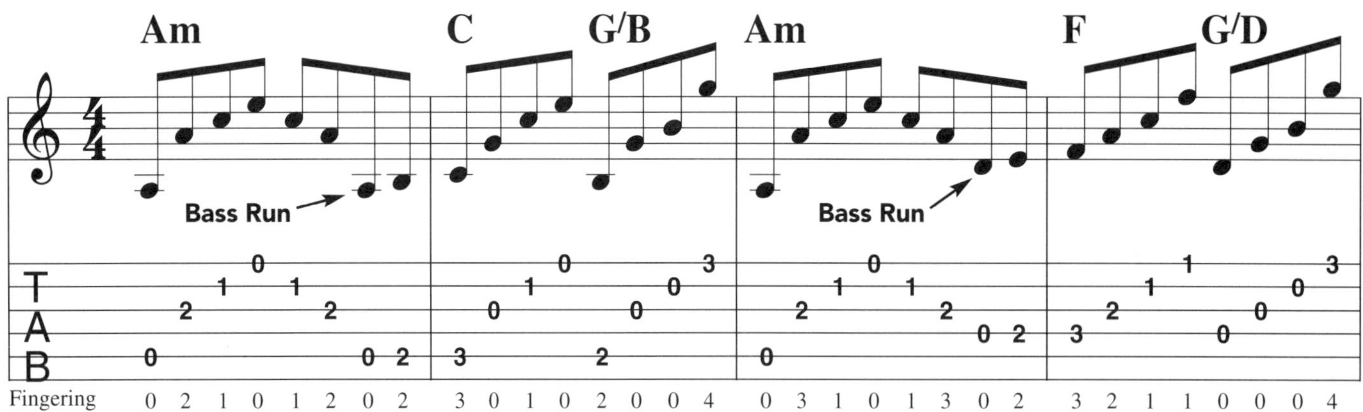

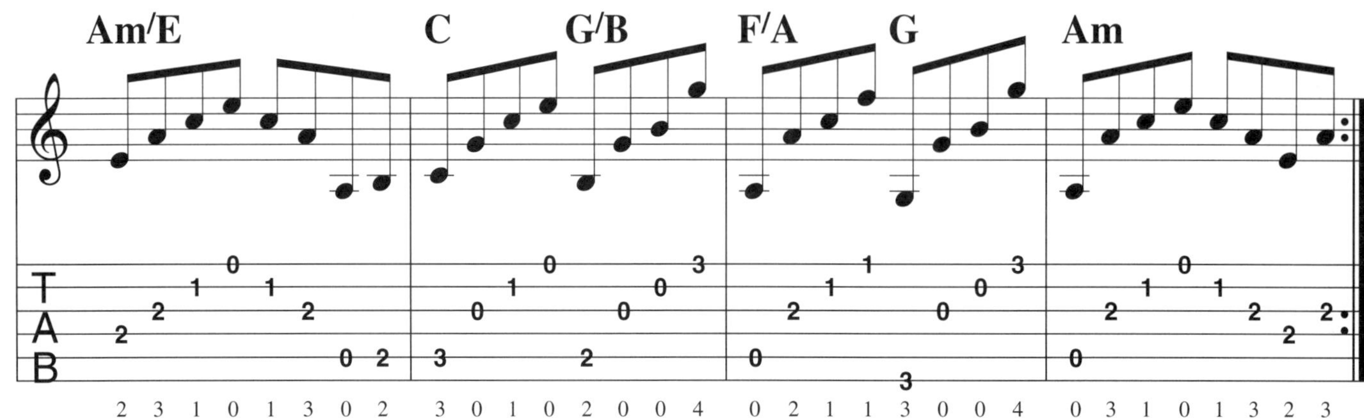

CHORDS IN OTHER MINOR KEYS

Written below are the scale tone chords for the key of **E natural minor** which is the relative minor of G major. Once again, the chords will be the same as those of its relative, but the starting note is E instead of G so **Em** will be chord I.

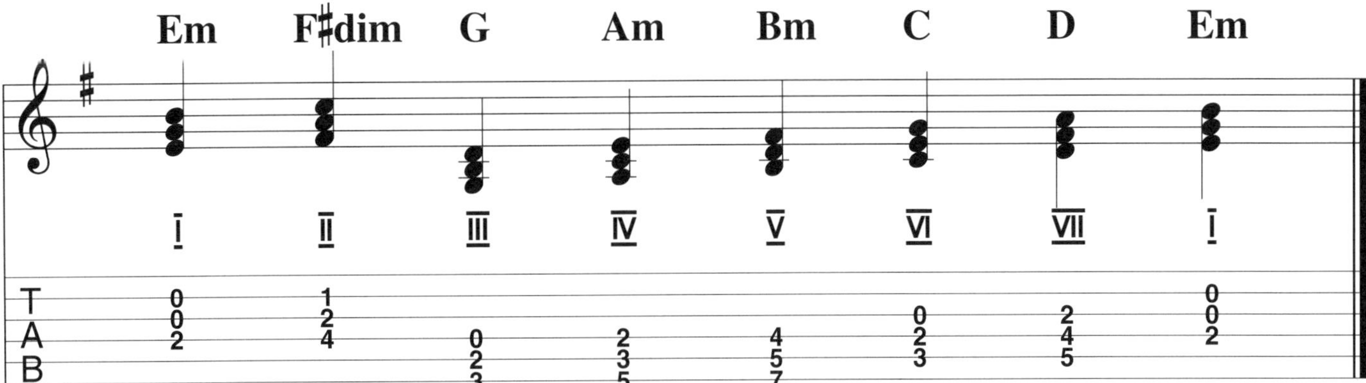

TRANSPOSING IN MINOR KEYS

Like music written in major keys, anything in a minor key can be transposed to other keys. The following example shows the progression from example 53 transposed to the key of **E minor**. Once you have learned the progression in this key, write out the scale tone chords in the remaining eleven minor keys and transpose the progression to those keys as well.

Transposing may seem a bit tedious at first, but it is an essential skill to develop. Any song can be played in any key, and different musicians may choose different keys for the same song. Usually a song will be played in a key that is comfortable for the singer and the musicians have to be able to play it in whatever key that is without wasting too much time working out the chords. The better you are at transposing, the more people you will be able to play with.

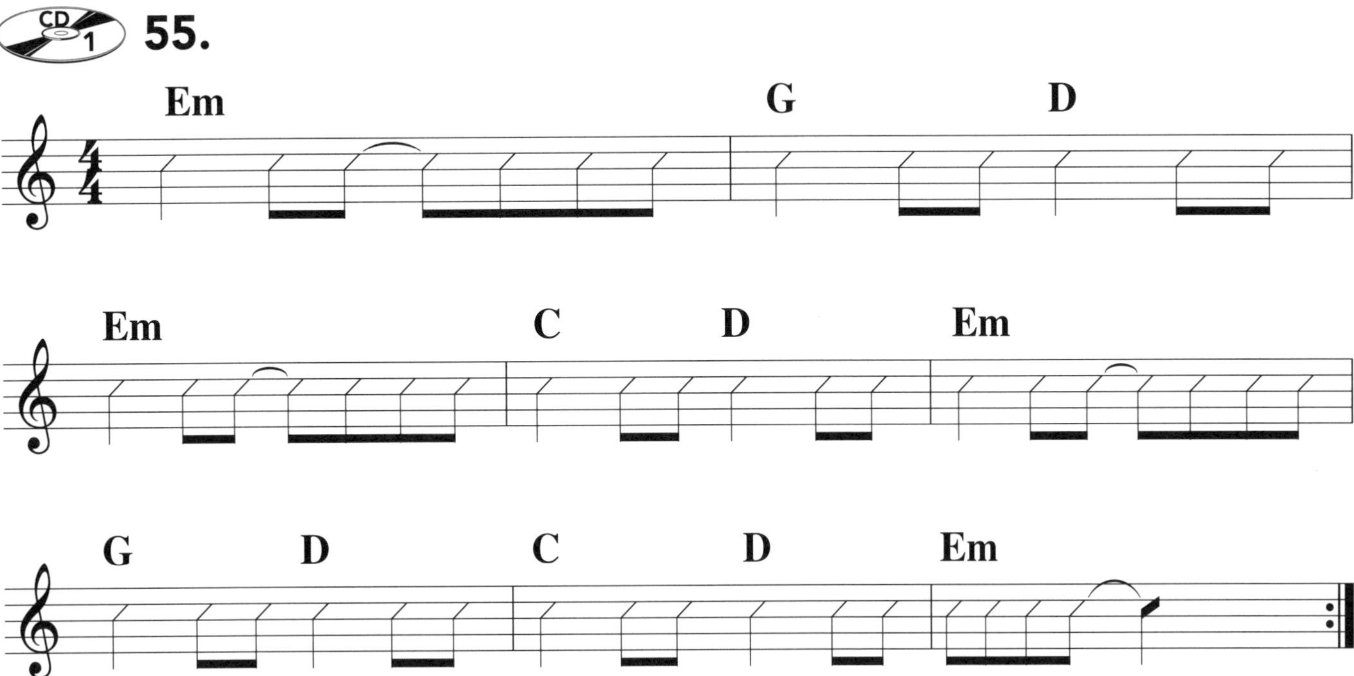

HARMONIC MINOR SCALE TONE CHORDS

Because there are three different minor scales, it is possible to come up with different sets of chords for a minor key by building chords on the notes of each different minor scale. Each variation to the notes of the scale alters the type of chords built on the scale. The letter names of the chords remain the same, but the chord type may change. E.g. shown below are **scale tone chords** derived from the **A harmonic minor scale**. Notice that chord III is now **augmented** instead of major, and also that chord V is **major** instead of minor and chord VII is **diminished** instead of major. These changes are all brought about by the raising of the 7th degree of the scale from **G** to **G♯**.

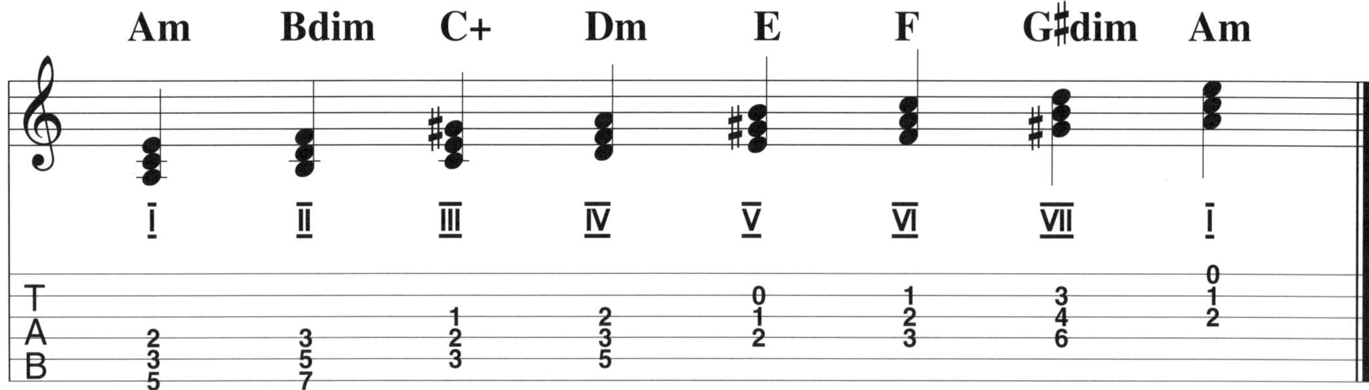

56.

This arpeggio based part uses chords derived from the **A harmonic minor** scale. Experiment with other ways of playing these chords and make up other progressions from them.

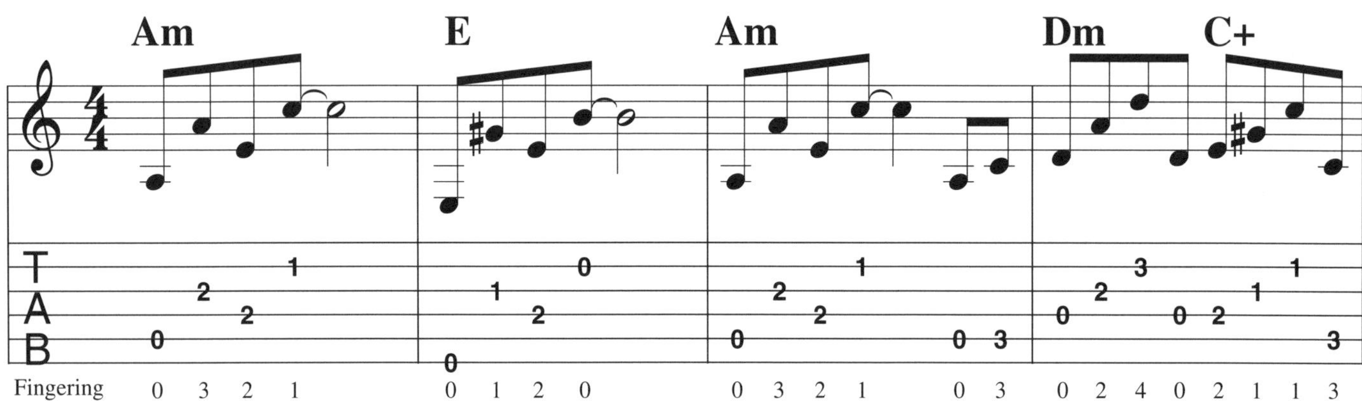

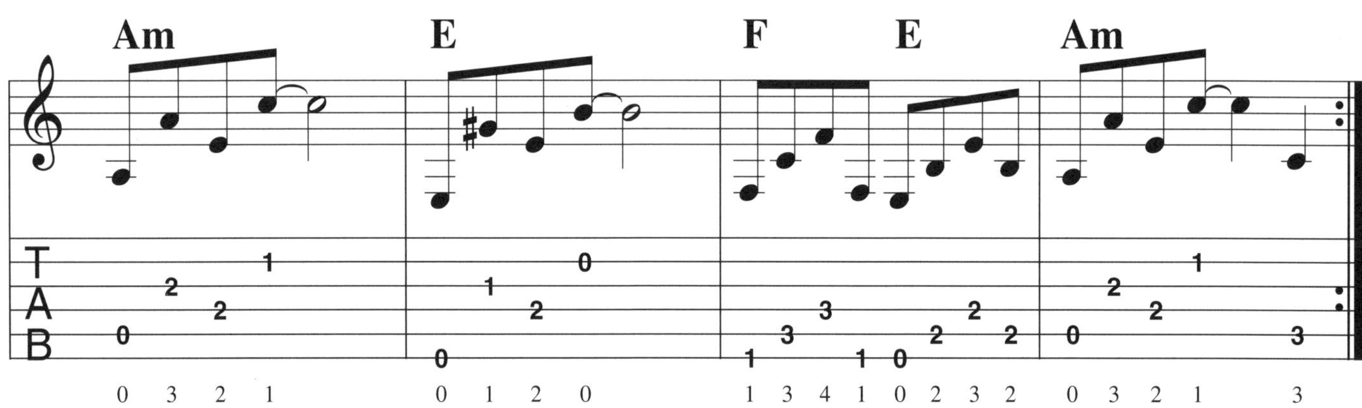

MELODIC MINOR SCALE TONE CHORDS

The scale tone chords derived from the **A melodic minor scale** are shown below. Because of the sharpened 6th degree, there will be more changes to the types of chords derived from this scale. Chord II is now **minor** instead of major, chord IV is **major** instead of minor and chord VI is **diminished** instead of major. These changes are all brought about by the raising of the 6th degree of the scale from **F** to **F♯**.

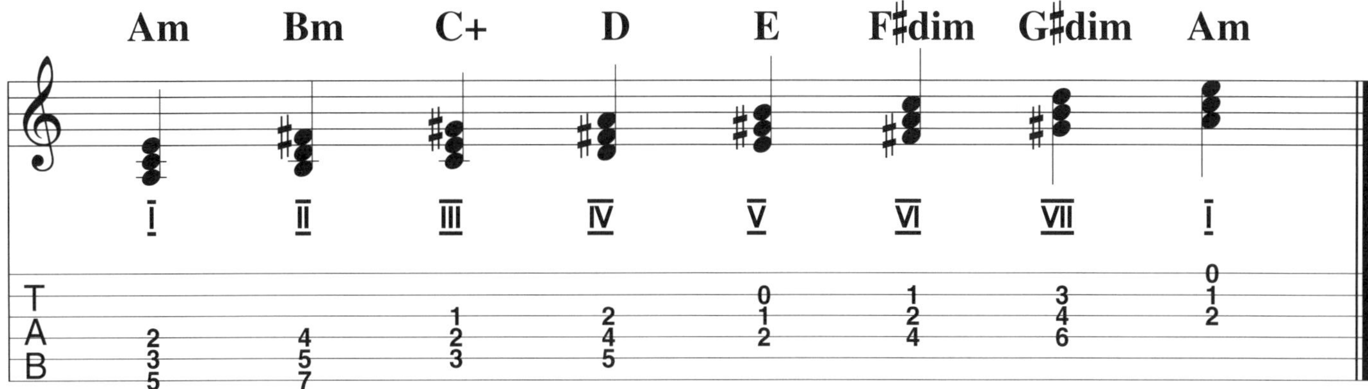

57.

The following example is derived from the **A melodic minor** scale tone chords shown above. It also contains one chromatic note (A♯ or B♭) as part of a repeating bass run.

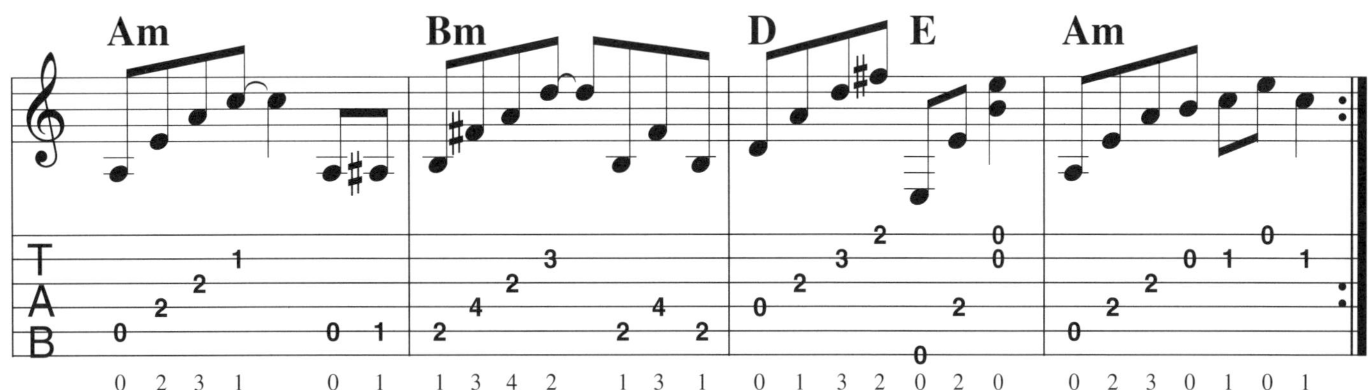

When playing music in minor keys, it is common to use chords from all three types of minor scales. A good example of this is the song "House of the Rising Sun", which is written in $\frac{6}{8}$ **time** and shown below as an arpeggio style accompaniment. Notice the use of bass runs once again. Look through the chords and see which ones come from each type of minor scale. Once you can play it, transpose it to several other keys.

THE SIX EIGHT TIME SIGNATURE

$\frac{6}{8}$

This is the **six eight** time signature.
There are six eighth notes in one bar of $\frac{6}{8}$ time.
The six eighth notes are divided into two groups of three.

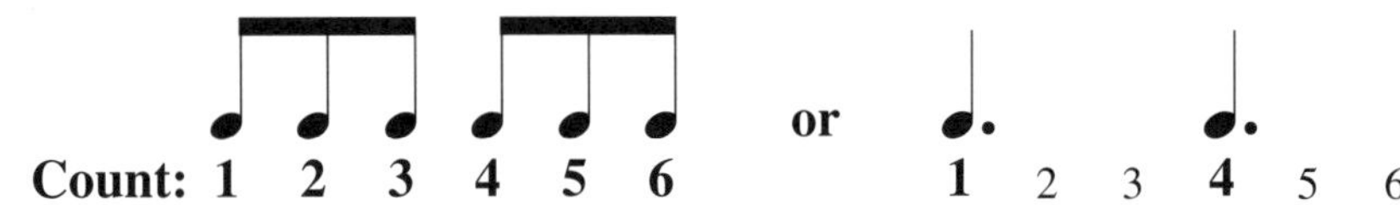

58. House of the Rising Sun

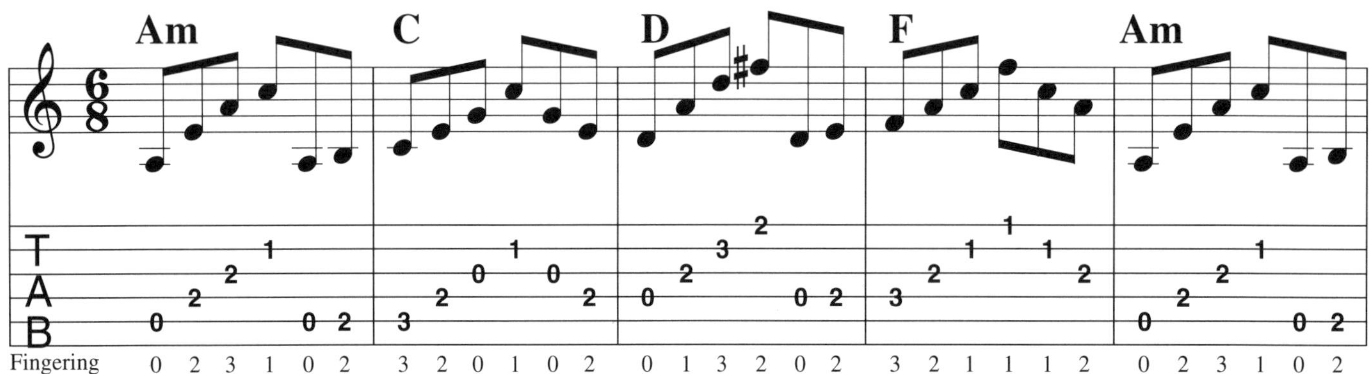

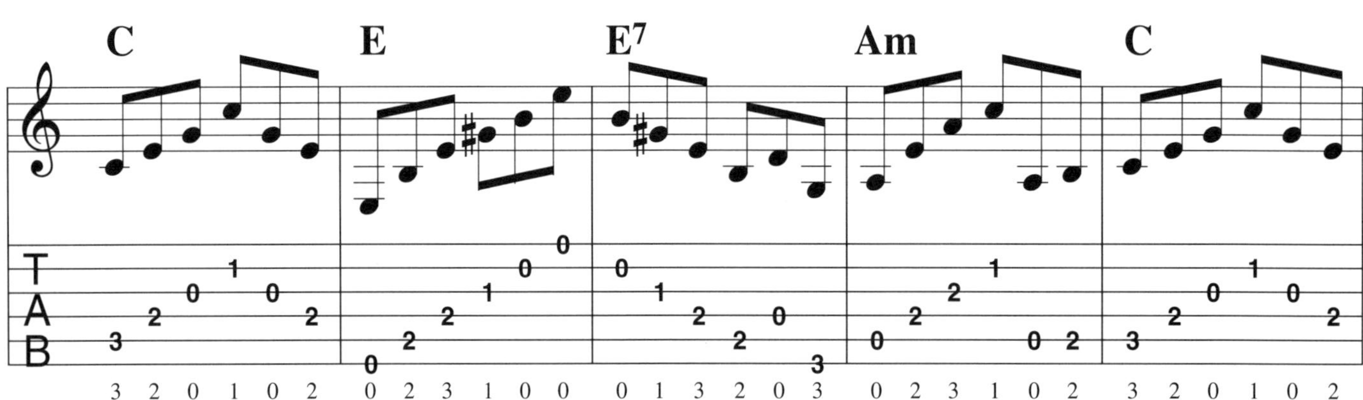

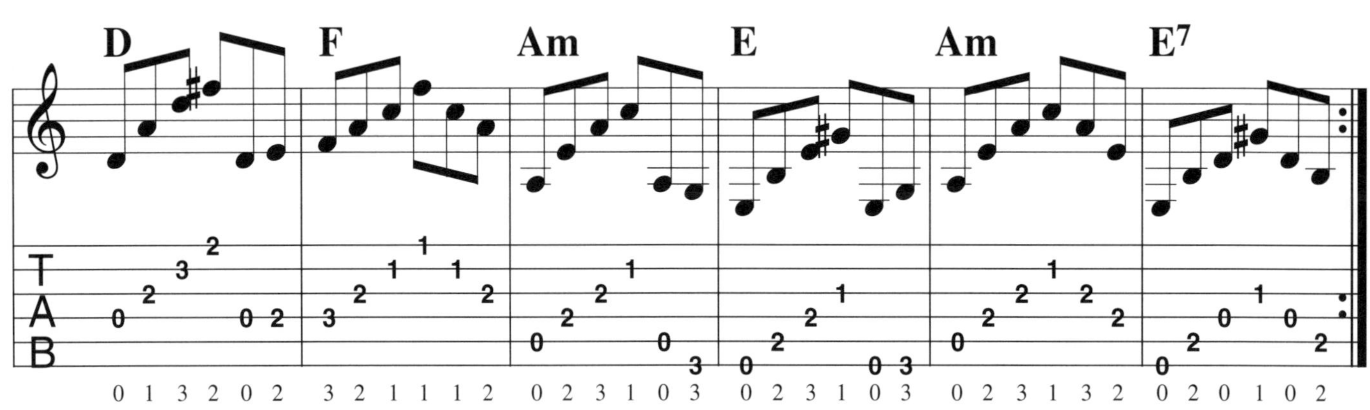

SECTION 2

New Notes, Rhythms and Techniques, Using the Whole Fretboard

LESSON TWENTY FIVE

PLAYING TWO STRINGS TOGETHER

Everything you have played so far has involved either strumming chords or picking one string at a time. However, as a guitar player, it is important to be able to play one, two, three, four, five or six strings together at any given moment, regardless of whether you are playing with a pick or right hand fingers. The example below uses the 1st and 2nd strings together and then the 2nd and 3rd strings together. **All the notes here are played with downstrokes** (even the 8th notes).

CD 1 **59. (All Downstrokes)**

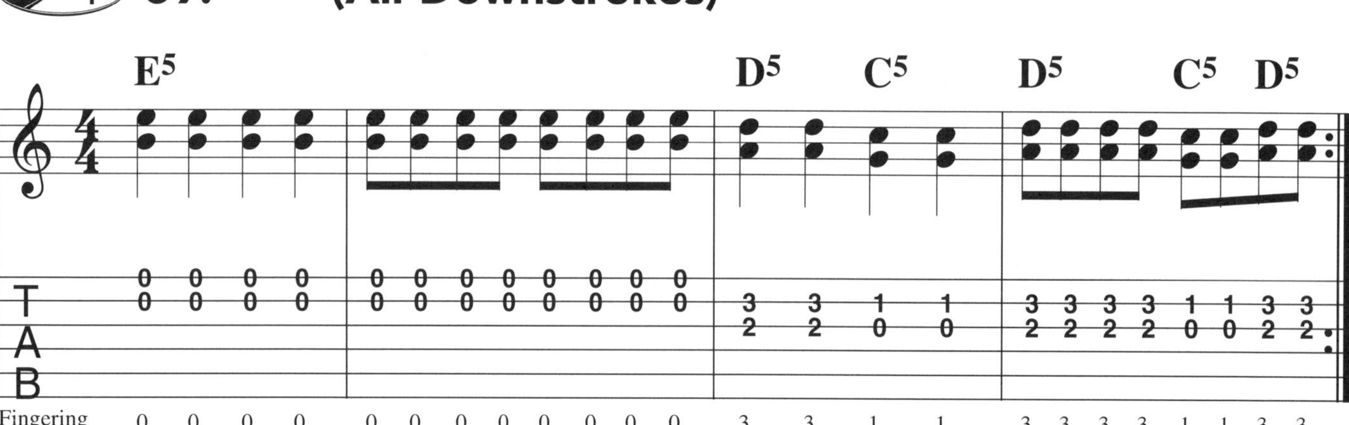

POWER CHORDS

The term "chord" usually applies to three or more notes played together. However, in Rock and several other styles, two notes played together are also often called chords. This especially applies to the formations below which are called **power chords**, or **5th chords**. The **symbol** for these chords consists of a **letter name** and the **number 5** (**E5**, **A5**, **D5**, etc). The **letter name** (which is also the **root note**) refers to the first note of the chord. E.g. the root note of an **A5** chord is **A**. The **5** refers to the other note which is a **5th interval above the root note**.

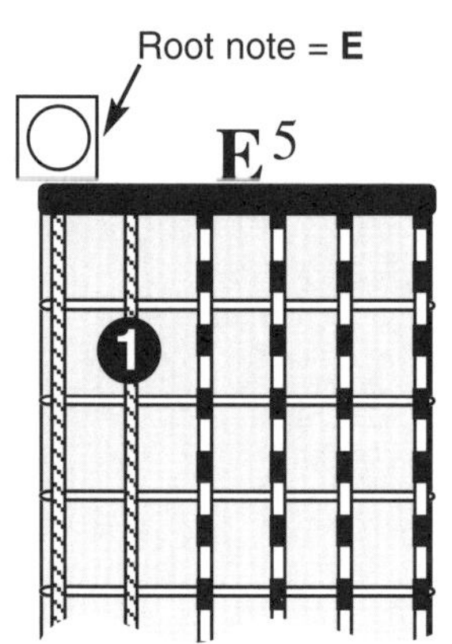

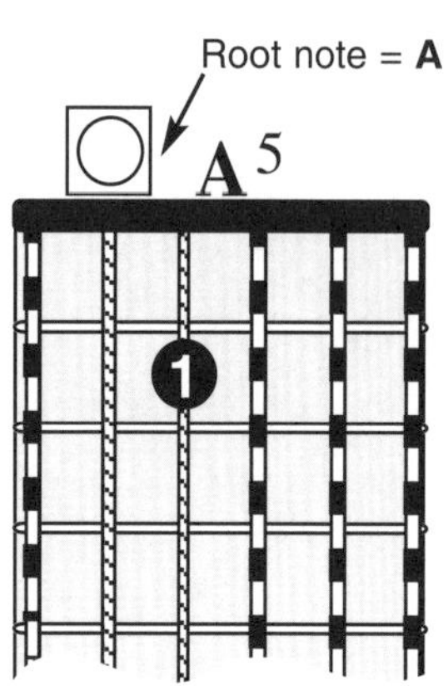

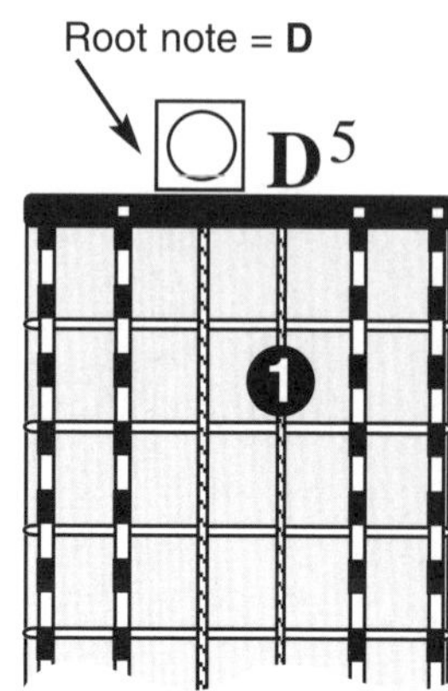

The example below uses the power chord shapes you have just learnt. Notice that the root notes of these chords are simply the open **A**, **D**, and **low E** strings. To change between these chords, all you have to do is move your first finger between the 5th, 3rd and 4th strings. Use all downstrokes with the pick as you play this example.

60.

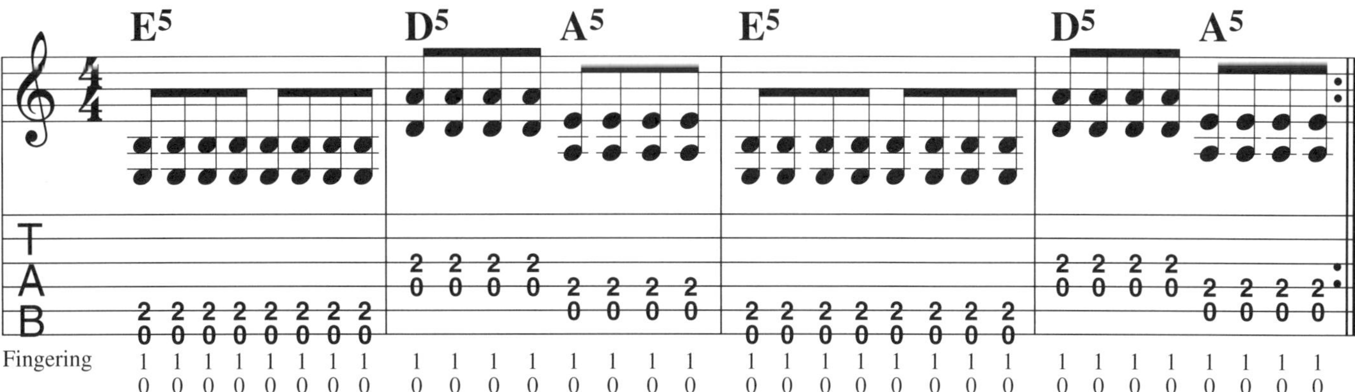

MOVEABLE POWER CHORDS

Power chords can be categorized by the string their root note appears on, thus **E5** is described as a **root 6** chord because it's **root note** is the open **6th string**. **A5** is a **root 5** chord because its root note is the open **5th** string, while **D5** is a **root 4** chord because its root note is the open **4th** string. By using the first finger at the 1st fret and the third finger at the 3rd fret, it is possible to create moveable power chords. This means they can be moved along the strings to create many different power chords. The transition from open power chords to moveable power chords is shown in the diagrams below. The root 5 moveable chord below is called **A♯5** or **B♭5** as it is a **semitone** (one fret) **higher than A** and a semitone **lower** than **B**.

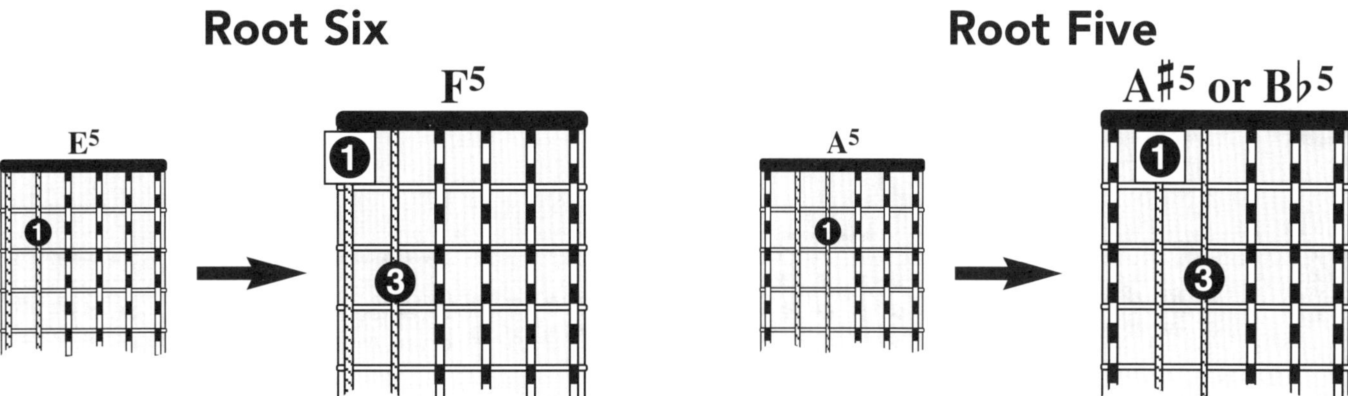

61.

Here is an exercise for changing between open and moveable power chords. The open chords are played here with the open string and 2nd finger.

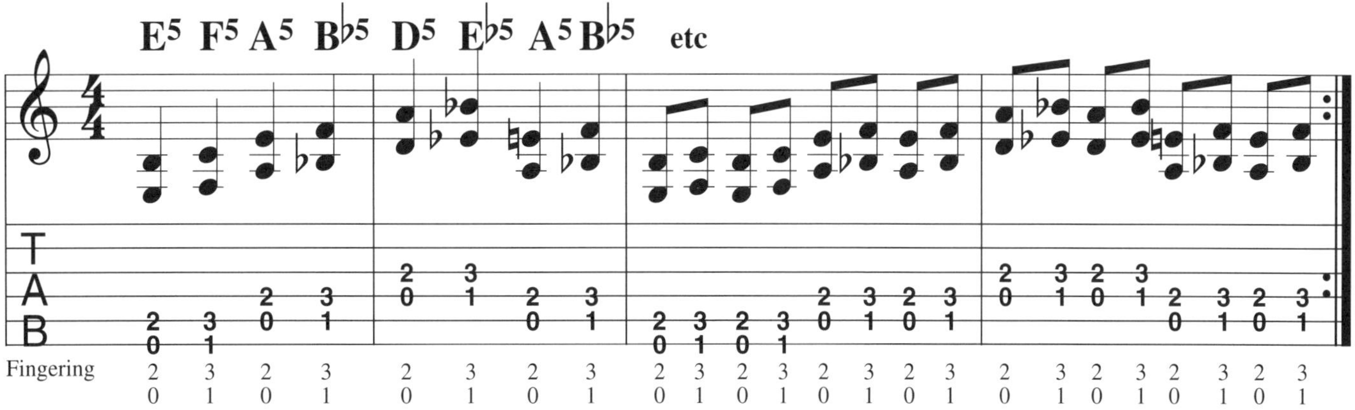

RIGHT HAND DAMPING

When playing power chords, it is common to **damp** the strings slightly with the right hand. This results in a tighter, more chunky sound. Rest the heel of the hand on the strings at the bridge and then pick the strings you want to sound. It may take a bit of practice to get the desired sound; it all depends on the exact position of the right hand and the amount of pressure used on the strings. Here is an example.

62.0 (Played 4 Times)

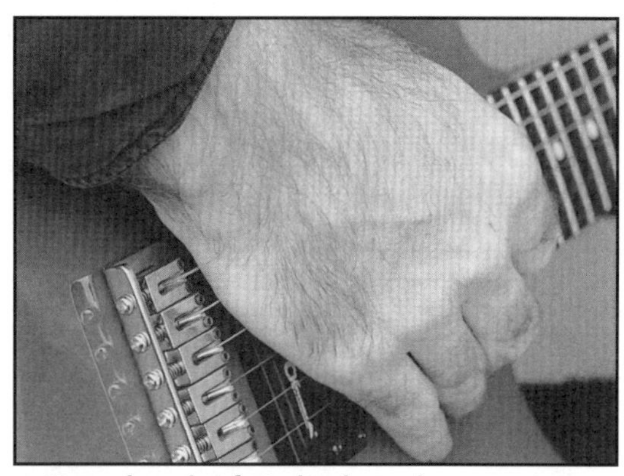

Rest heel of right hand on strings near bridge

A power chord can be formed on **any** root note by selecting the note with the 1st finger and then adding the 3rd finger two frets up on the next (higher) string. Because the formation remains the same regardless of where on the fretboard the chord is played, you don't need to think about the name of the higher note. As long as you know the root note, you can easily find the right chord. The following example uses various root 5 and root 6 power chords built on notes you have already learnt, along with **A5** played as a **root 6** chord at the **5th fret** and **D5** played as a **root 5** chord at the **5th fret**.

62.1

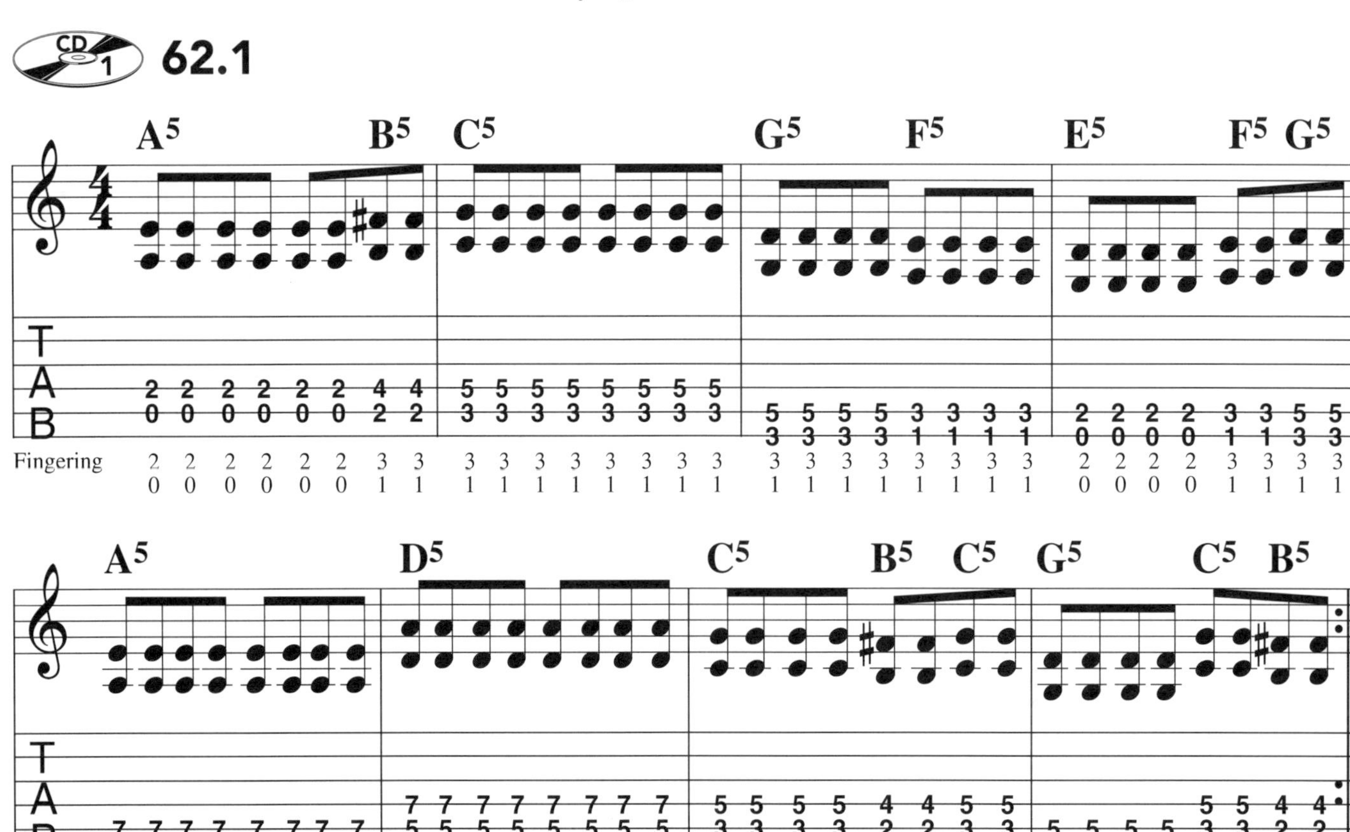

ROCK 'N' ROLL CHORDS

When playing Rock'n'Roll or Blues styles, guitarists commonly use power chords that keep the root note the same, and the other note alternating between the 5th, 6th and flattened 7th degrees. These chords can be referred to as Rock'n'Roll chords, or simply **Rock chords**.

 ROCK CHORD SHAPES

Here are the two–string Rock chord shapes for **A**, **A6** and **A7**. In all three chord shapes only the 5th and 4th strings are strummed. The open 5th string is the root note (**A**).

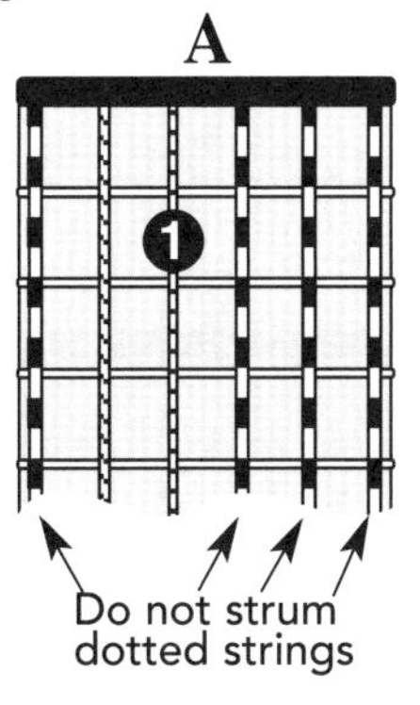

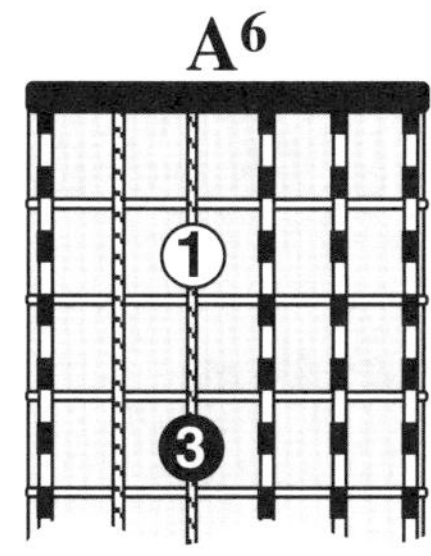

The open circle with the number 1 inside it indicates that you keep your 1st finger in position even though that note is not being played.

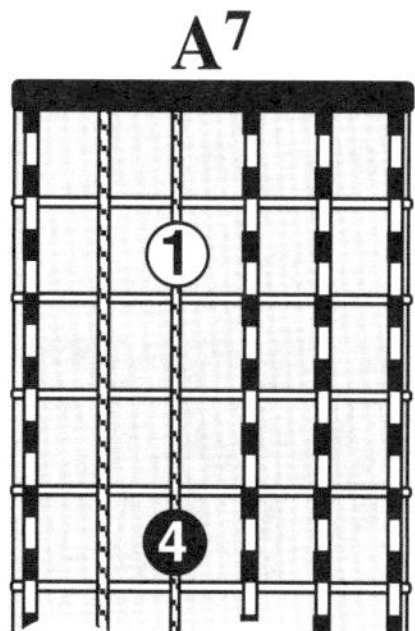

Play the following chord progressions using the above rock chord shapes. Use eighth note strums and only play the 5th and 4th strings. When playing power chords, it is common to use only downstrums, as this achieves the best sound.

63.0

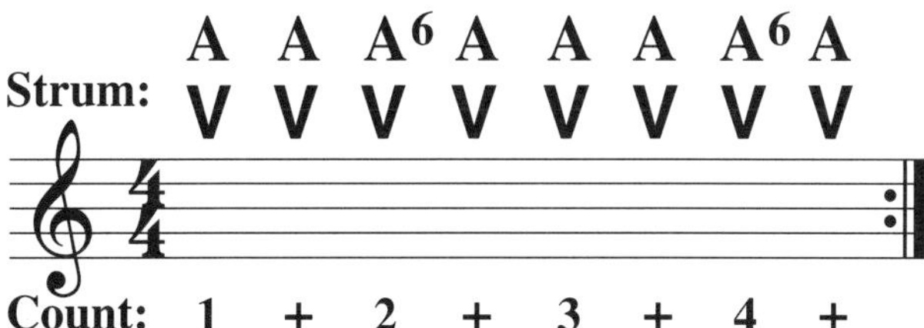

63.1

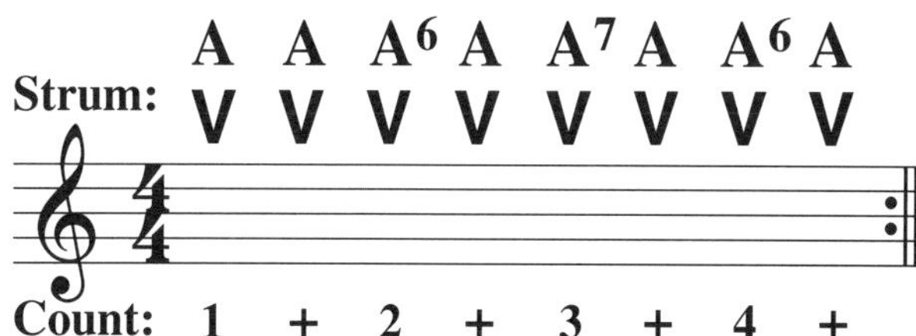

63.2

Here are the previous examples as a two bar pattern.

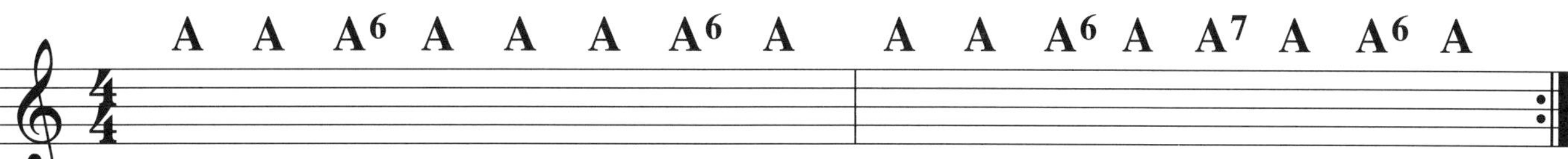

D ROCK CHORD SHAPES

Now learn the two string rock chord shapes for **D**, **D6** and **D7**. Play only the **4th** and **3rd** strings.

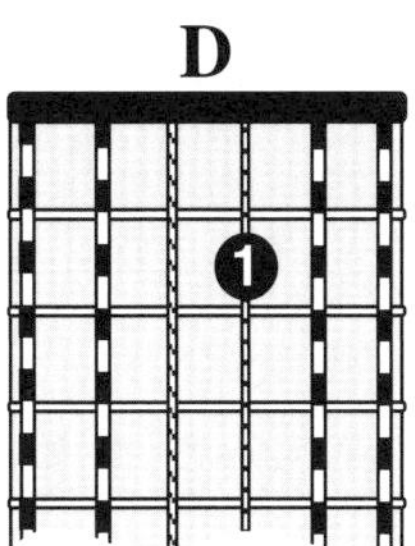

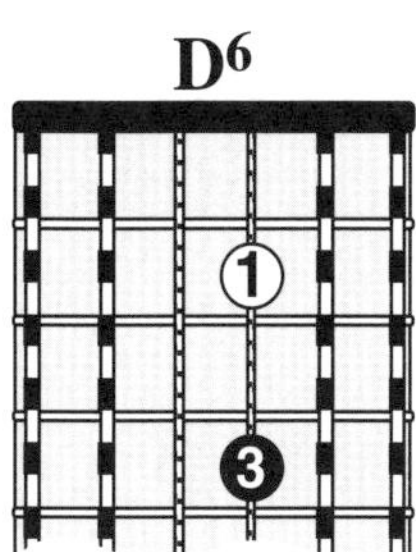

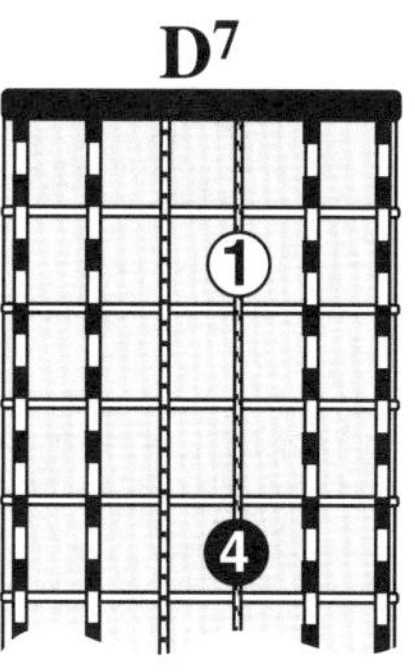

Play the following two bar chord progression using the **D** rock chord shapes. Use only downward eighth note strums playing the 4th and 3rd strings only.

63.3

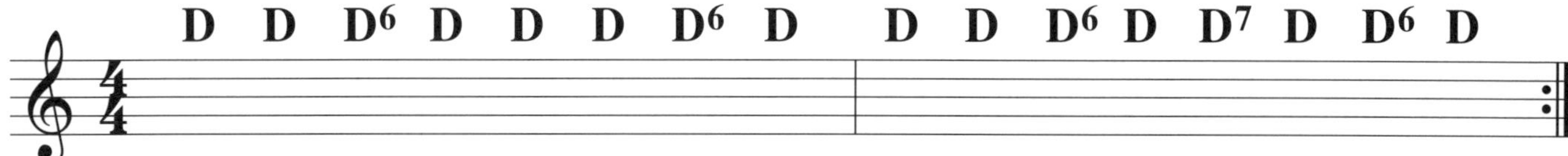

E ROCK CHORD SHAPES

Here are the two string rock chord shapes for **E**, **E6** and **E7**. Play only the **6th** and **5th** strings.

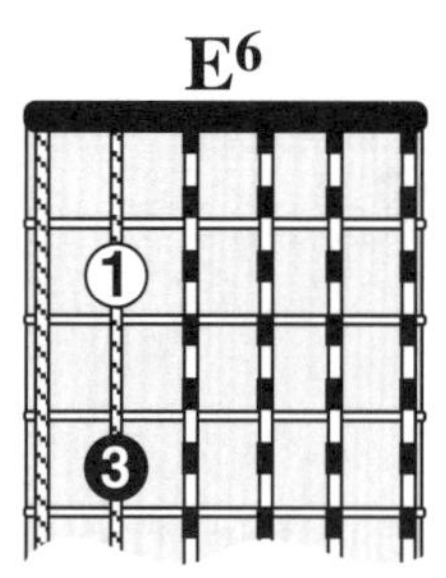

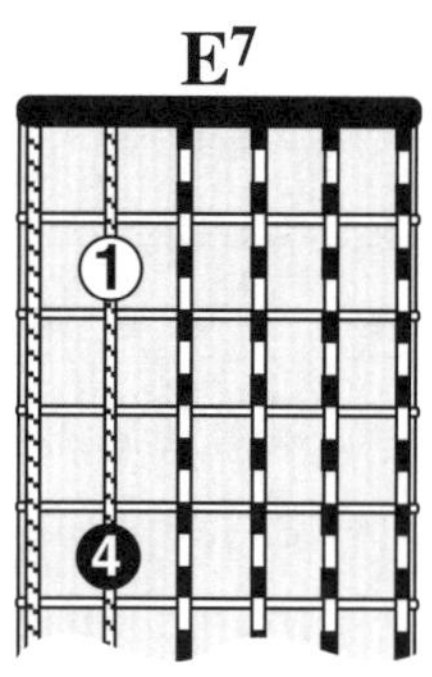

This two bar chord progression uses the above rock chord shapes. Play only downward eighth note strums.

63.4

64. 12 Bar Blues in A

Play the following 12 bar Blues in the key of **A** using rock chords. When there are two bars of a chord, substitute a two bar pattern. For the **A** chord in bars 1 and 2, 3 and 4, 7 and 8, use the two bar pattern in example 63.2. For the **D** chord in bars 5 and 6, use the two bar progression in example 63.3. Try to play this 12 bar Blues from memory. If you hope to play in a band or even jam with your friends, the ability to play songs from memory is an important skill to develop.

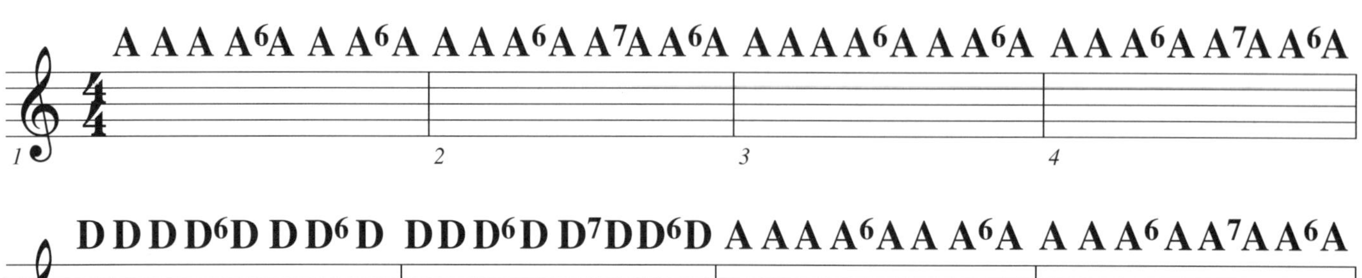

E E E E6 E E E6 E D D D D6 D D D6 D A A A A6 A A A6 A E E E E6 E E E6 E

9 10 11 12

LESSON TWENTY SIX

RESTS

Rests are used to indicate specific periods of silence. A **quarter rest** is worth **one** beat of silence, a **half rest** is worth **two** beats of silence and a **whole rest** is worth a **whole bar** of silence. Small counting numbers are placed under rests. Note that the half rest sits on top of the middle line of the staff, while the whole rest hangs below the fourth line.

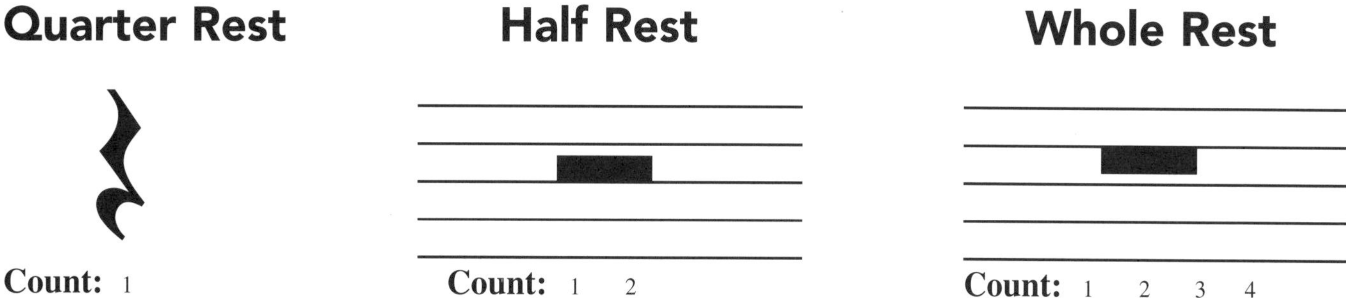

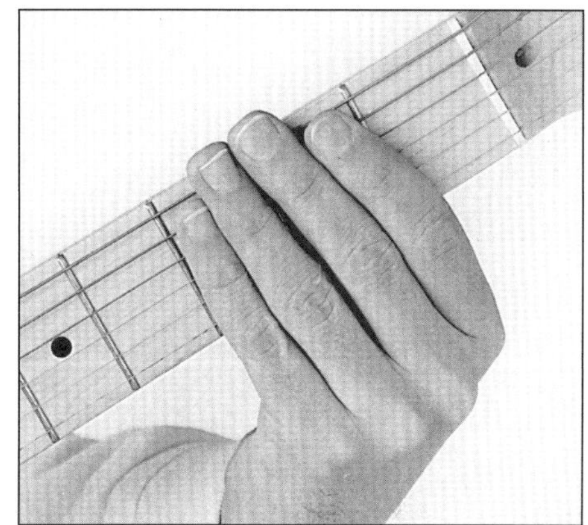

When a rest comes after you have played a note, you must stop the note sounding i.e. stop the strings vibrating. To do this, place your left hand fingers lightly across all the strings. Do not press too hard as this will produce a new note. This **muting** technique is also useful to stop previously played notes sounding at the same time as a new note is played.

65.

Here is an example which uses the three rests shown above. Remember that a rest indicates **silence**. Don't be lazy with the way you mute the strings. Be sure that there are absolutely no sounds still ringing when a rest is indicated. A rest may refer to your part only or the whole band. Notice how the rest in the final bar here leaves room for the drums on the recording. It is also important to count along with your metronome and tap your foot on each beat, regardless of whether a note or a rest appears in the music. This way you will develop a solid and confident sense of time.

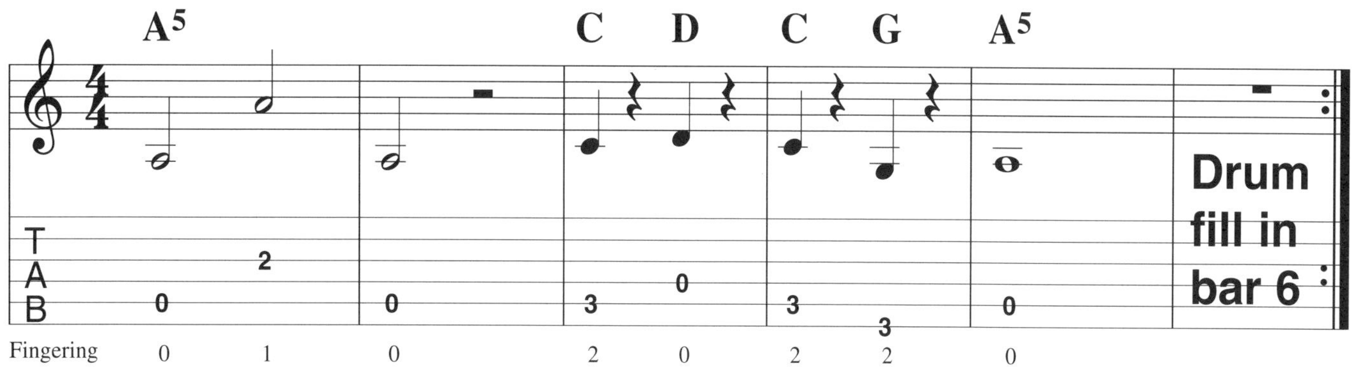

THE EIGHTH REST

This symbol is a **eighth rest.** It indicates **half a beat** of silence.

66.

Try this example which makes use of eighth rests and power chords. Listen to the recording and notice how the rests help drive the rhythm forward. Count carefully at first and be sure to tap your foot only on the beats and not in between.

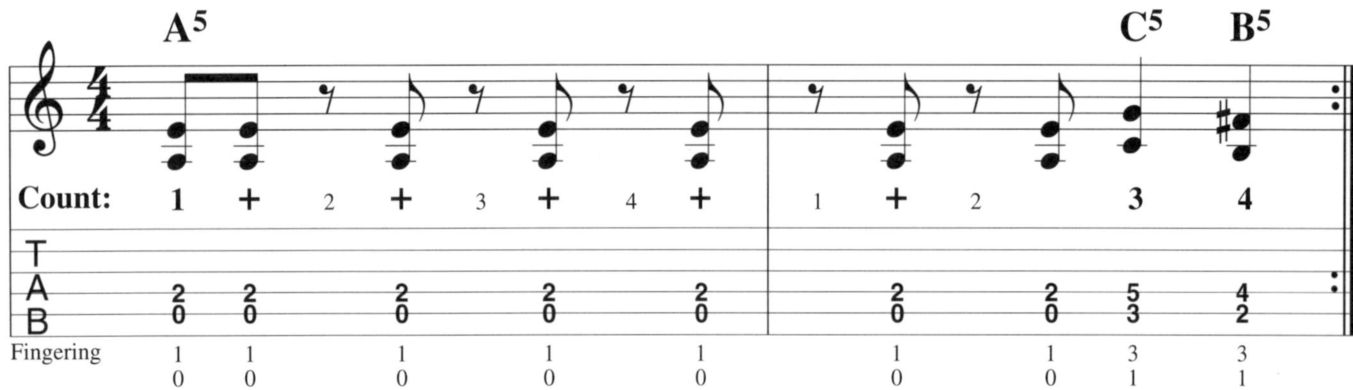

RESTS WITH CHORD PLAYING

A strummed rhythm can often be made more interesting by the use of rests as part of the pattern. When playing chords, rests are often achieved by placing the edge of the right hand over the strings (as shown in the photograph below). Practice this technique with the following example.

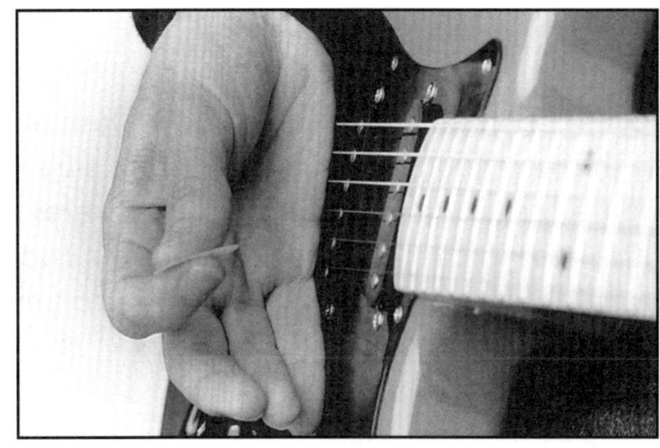

67.

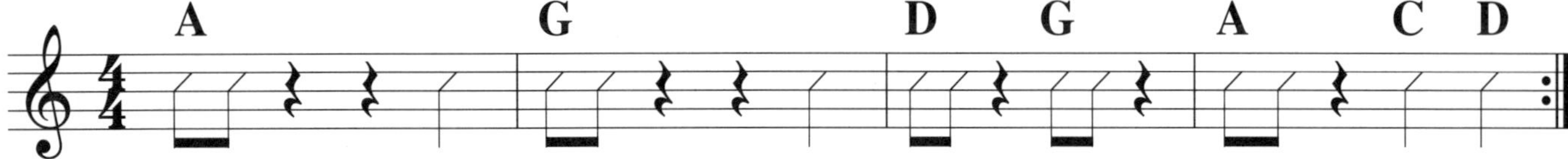

LESSON TWENTY SEVEN

IDENTIFYING RHYTHMS

There is a simple system for identifying any note's position in a bar by naming notes off the beat according to which beat they come directly after. The system works as follows. Within a bar of continuous eighth notes in 4/4 time, there are **eight** possible places where notes could occur. The first beat is called **one** (1), the next eighth note is called the "**and of 1**", then comes beat **two** (**2**), the next eighth note is called the "**and of 2**", then beat **three**, followed by the "**and of 3**", then beat **four**, followed by the "**and of 4**" which is the final eighth note in the bar.

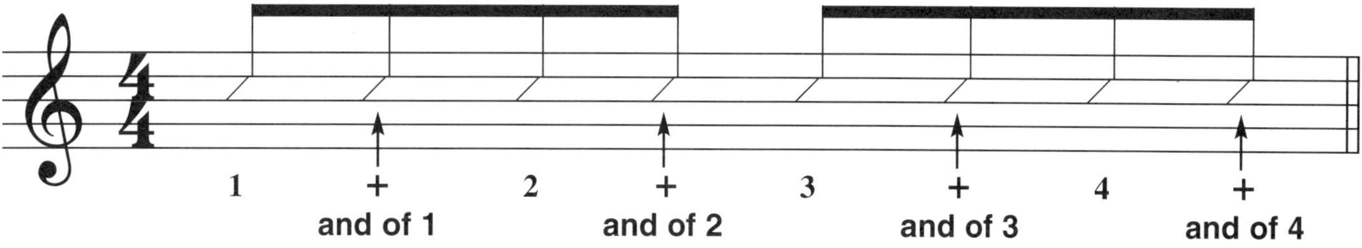

This system is particularly useful if you are having trouble with the timing of a rhythm. You simply identify where the notes occur in relation to each beat and then count them slowly until you have memorized the rhythm.

68.

In the first bar of this example, the notes occur on beat **1, and of two**, **three**, and the **and of 3**. In the second bar, the notes occur on the **and of 1**, the **and of 3** and the **and of 4**. Even though there are many rests here, it is important to keep a constant eighth note strumming motion going in the air just above the strings throughout the example. This is sometimes called **playing air** and is a good way to keep time.

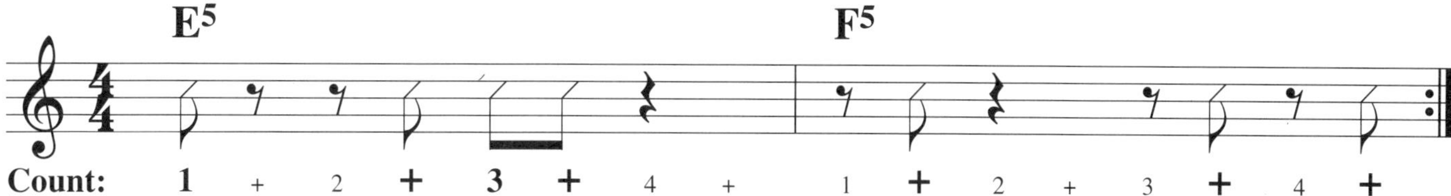

69.

Here is another example which uses eighth rests. Try analyzing it in the manner shown above and then learn it from memory. Remember to count out loud as you play.

PERCUSSIVE STRUMMING

An important rhythm technique used in many styles of music is the **Percussive Strum**. This is achieved by forming a chord shape with the left hand and placing it on the strings, but **without** pressing down on the frets. A percussive strum is indicated by using an **X** in place of a notehead. This technique can be applied to any type of chord. Listen to the following example on the recording to hear what the percussive strum sounds like when applied to Root 5 power chords.

70.0

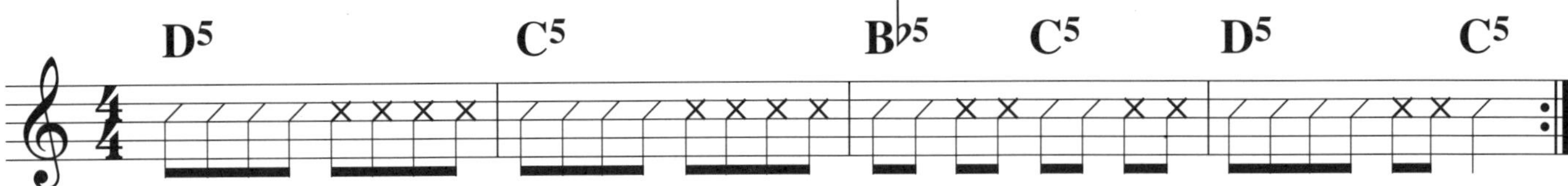

DEVELOPING RHYTHMIC CONTROL

To become a good rhythm player it is essential to have control over where you place notes or chords within the bar, and where you leave spaces. One way to improve this ability is to take each subdivision of the beat (in this case – eighth notes), and practice moving each one to all possible positions within a single beat and then within a bar. To keep the feel of the basic subdivision, use percussive strumming in place of rests. **Remember to use your metronome, count out loud and tap your foot evenly on the beat.**

70.1

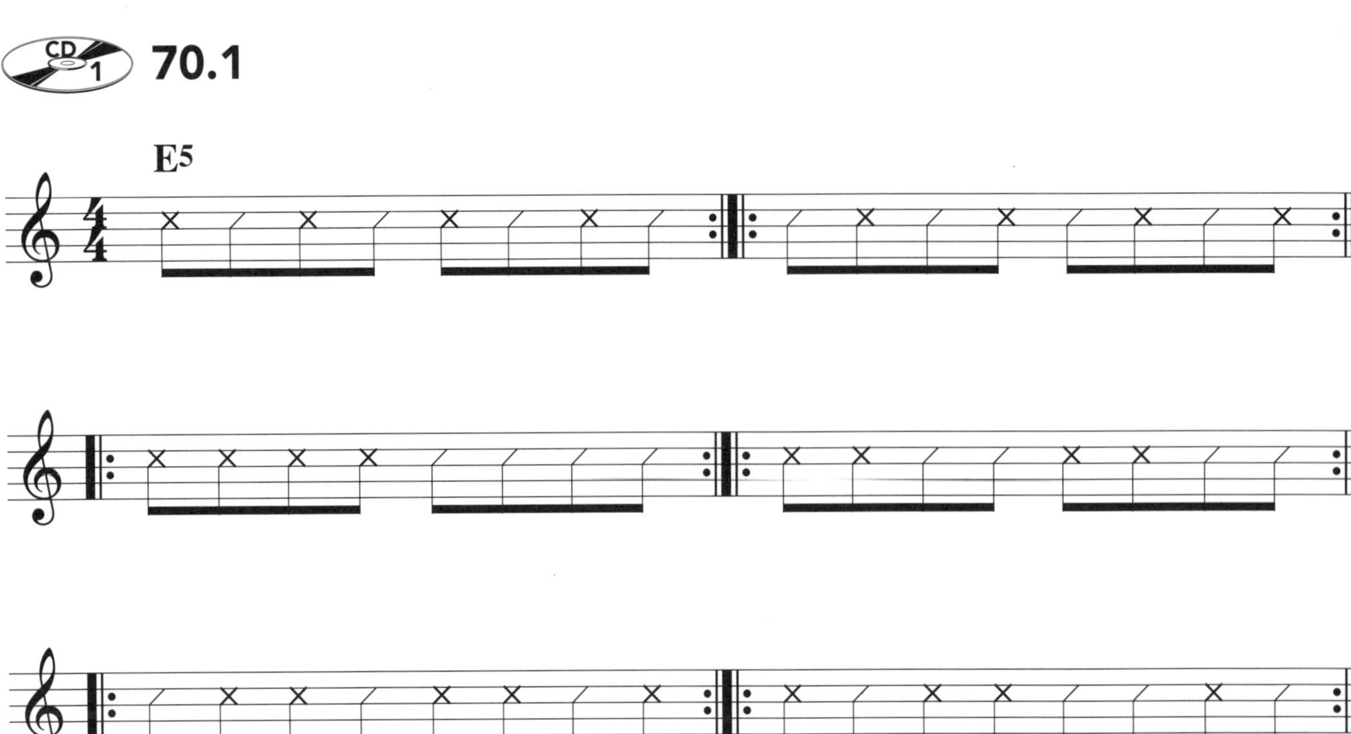

ACCENTS

A simple power chord rhythm can be made to sound 'heavier' by applying an **accent** to some of the strums within the rhythm. An accent is achieved by playing the strum a little louder or stronger. An accent is often shown as a small wedge (>) above or below the note, as shown below.

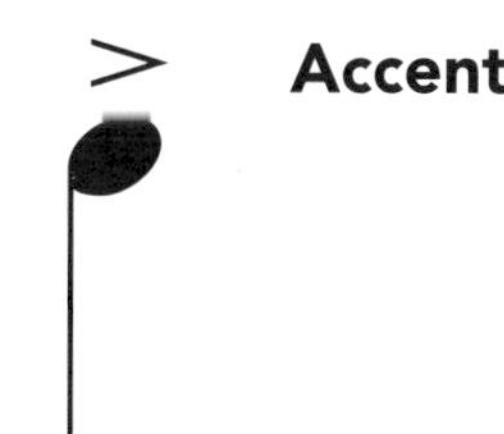

71.0

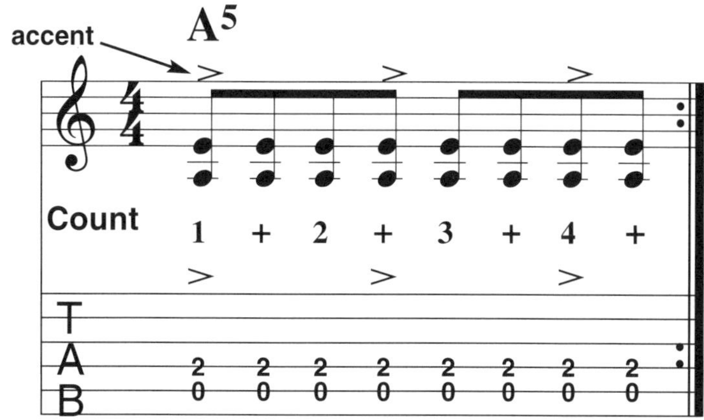

71.1

The following example applies the accent to a simple chord progression that uses the open power chords **A5**, **D5**, and **E5**.

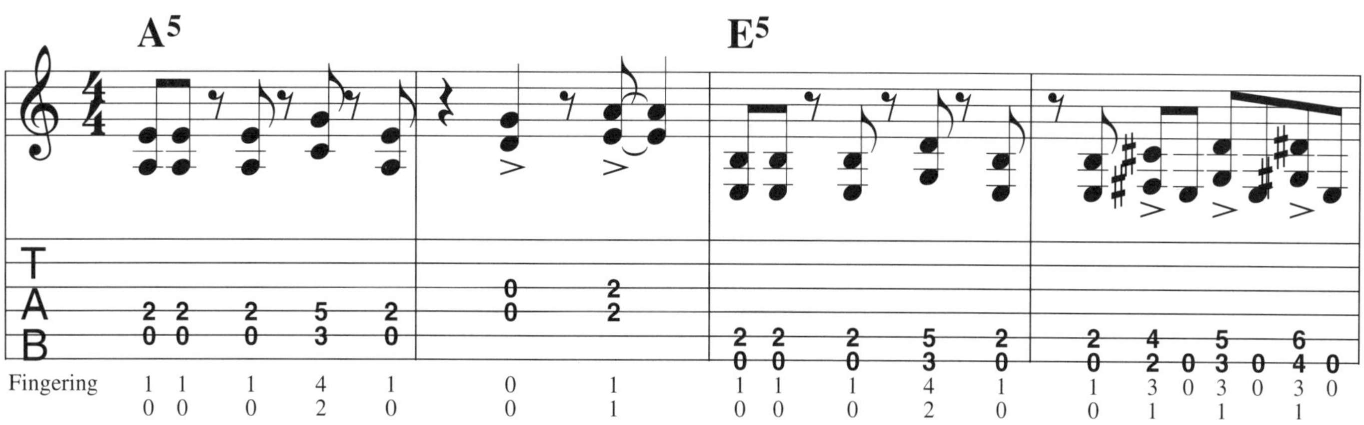

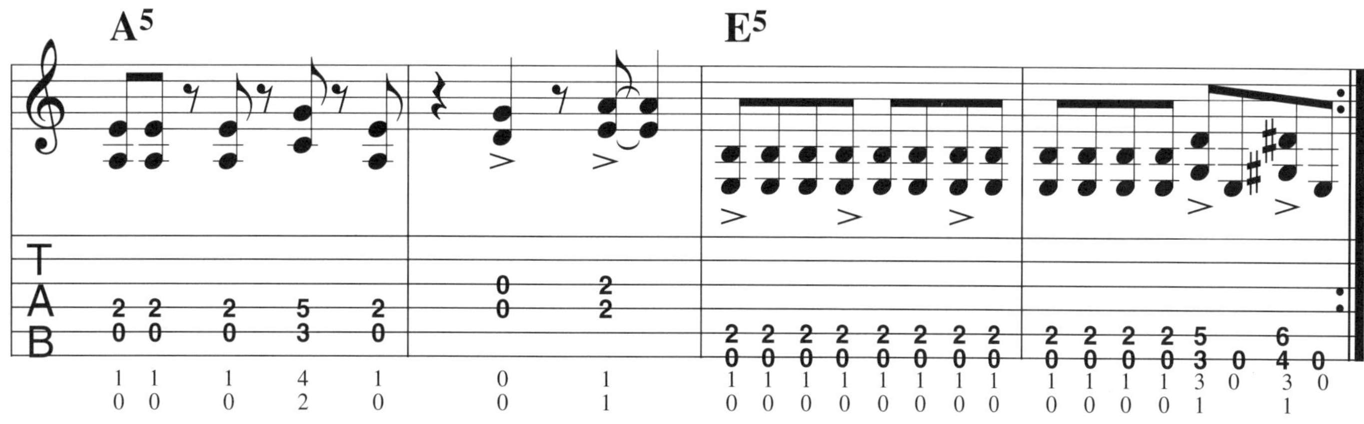

A good way to gain control of accents is to take a systematic approach similar to the earlier percussive strumming exercises; i.e. practice accents on all possible eighth note positions within a bar individually, and then in combinations, as shown below.

72.

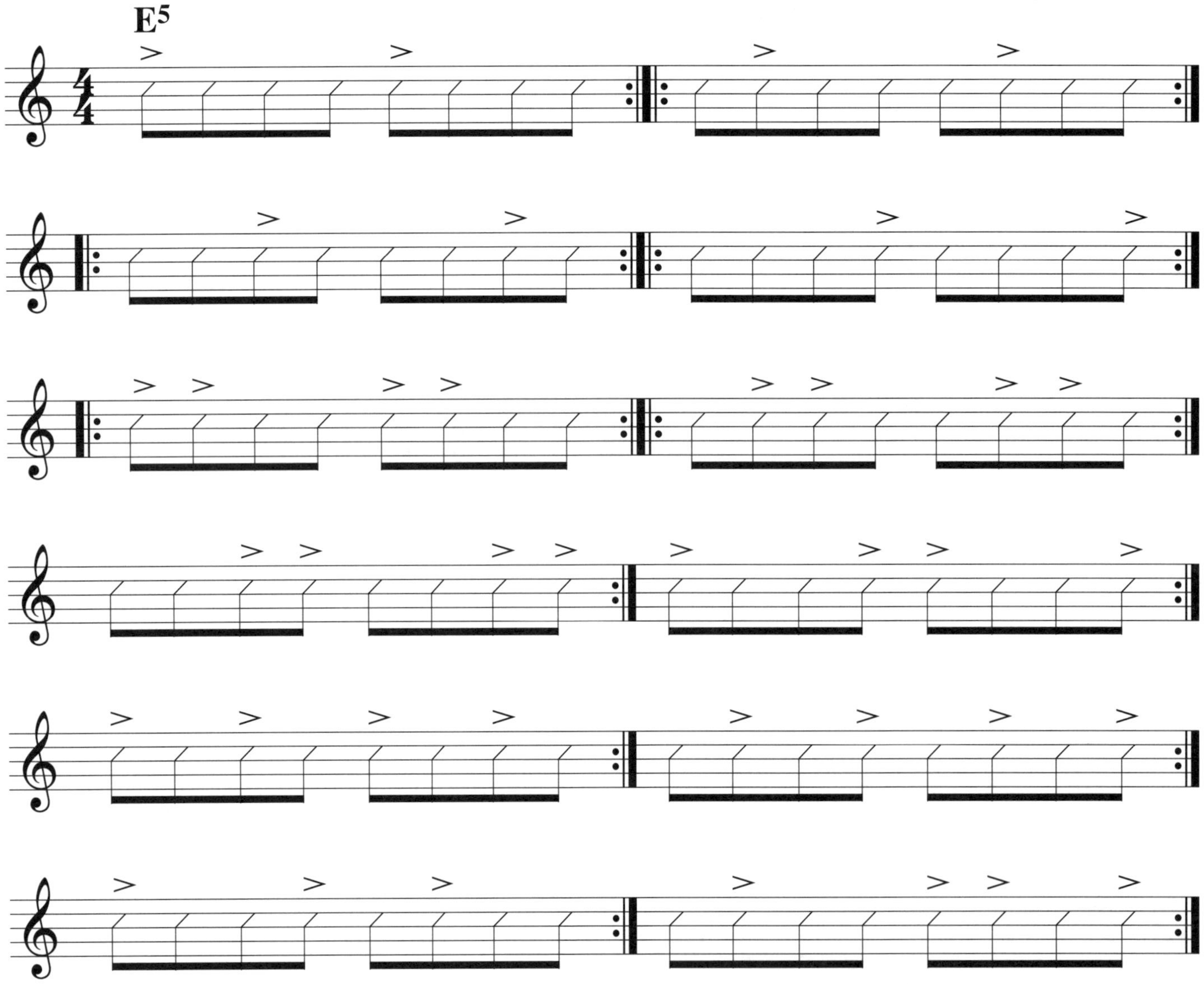

E^5

73.

It is also important to work on using accents with single notes. A good way to do this is to use a simple four finger exercise and play it in eighth notes, first accenting all the notes on the beat, and then all the notes off the beat, as shown here.

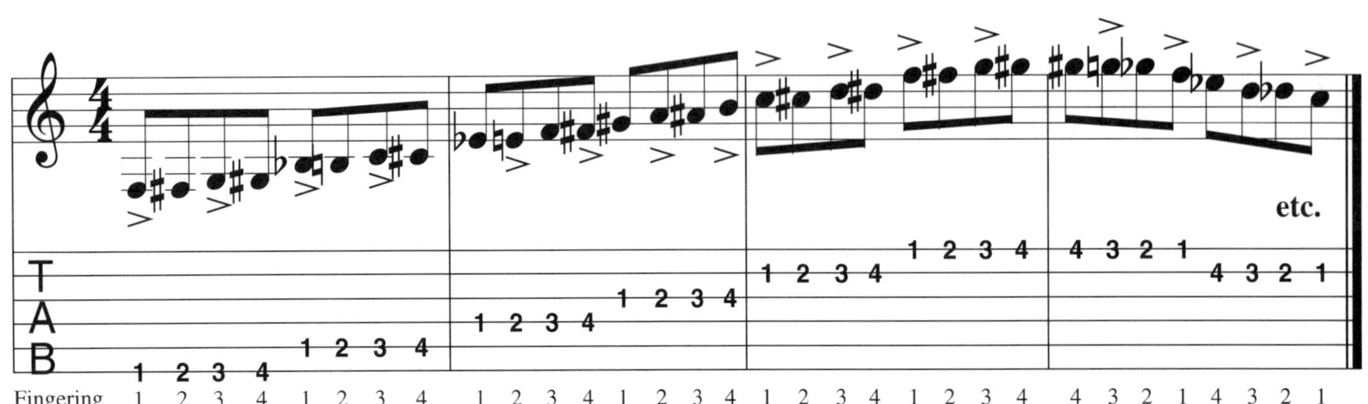

STACCATO

It is not always desirable to leave a chord ringing once it has been played. In rhythm guitar playing it is common to cut the sound of a chord off as soon as it has been played, making the rhythm very crisp. The technique of cutting chords or notes shorter than their written value is called **staccato**. With chords containing open strings, staccato is usually achieved by placing the side of the right hand across all the strings immediately after strumming the chord. Staccato is indicated by placing a **dot** directly above or below the intended note or chord, as shown below.

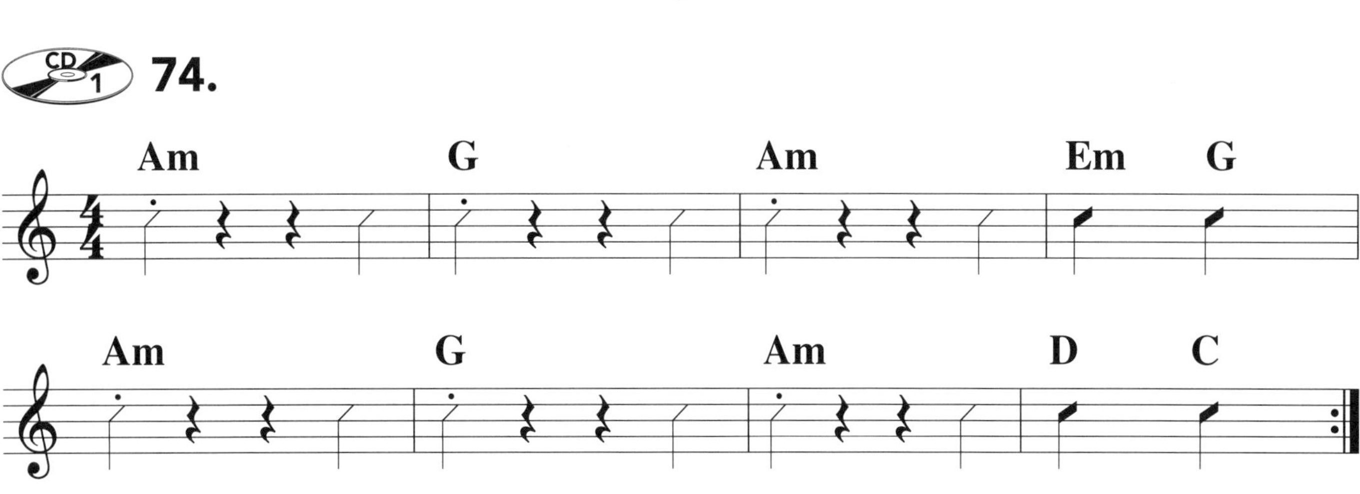

PLAYING TWO STRINGS WITH THE FIRST FINGER

In the following example the first finger plays both the 3rd and 4th strings, as shown in the accompanying photo. Instead of playing on the tip, the last segment of the finger is **flattened** across both strings. This technique is very common in guitar playing and is called **barring** the strings.

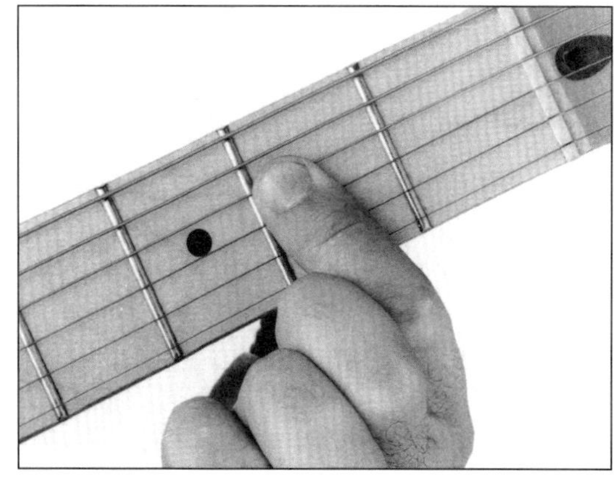

75. (Play 4 times)

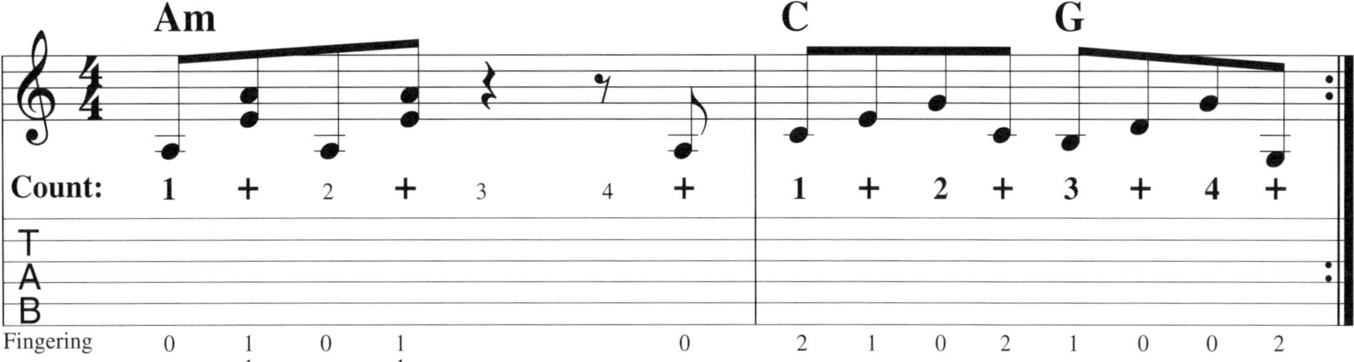

ADD NINE CHORDS

Another useful chord type is the **add nine** (**add9**) chord. These chords are either a major or minor triad with a **9th degree** added. The 9th degree is the same as the second degree of the scale, but an octave higher.

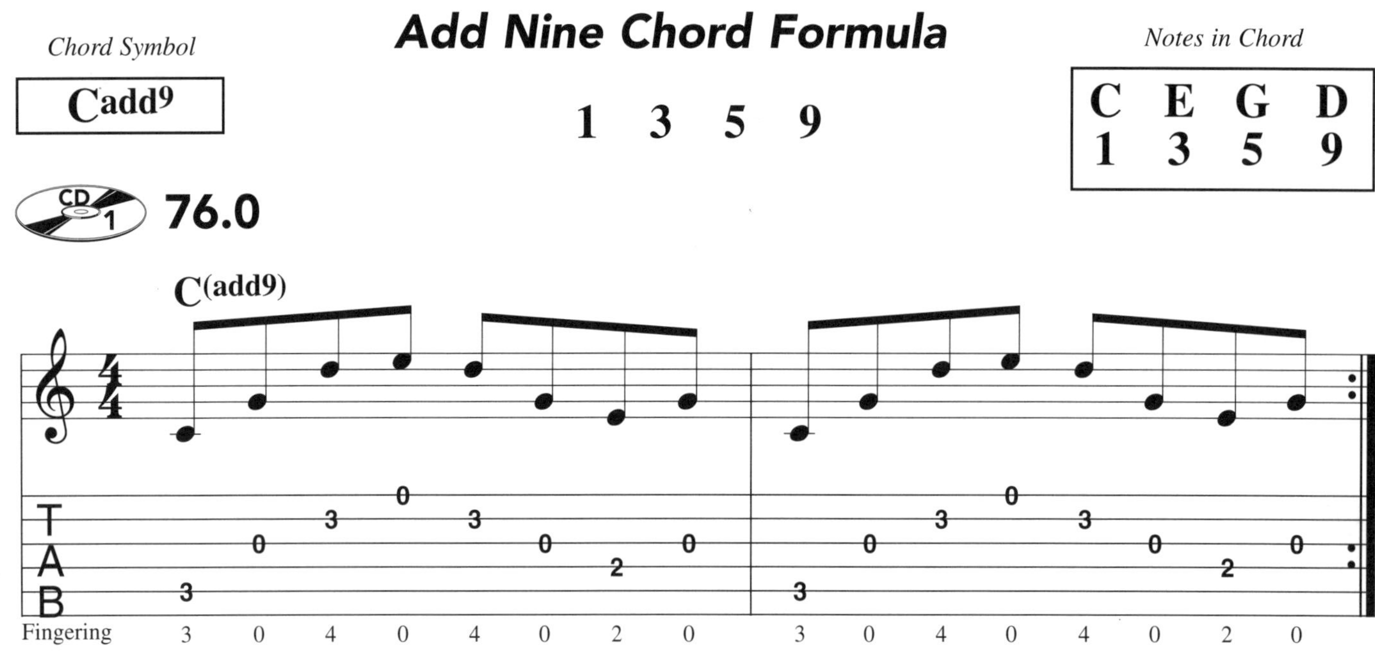

Here are some more **add9** chord shapes. Once you have learnt them, use them to play the examples below.

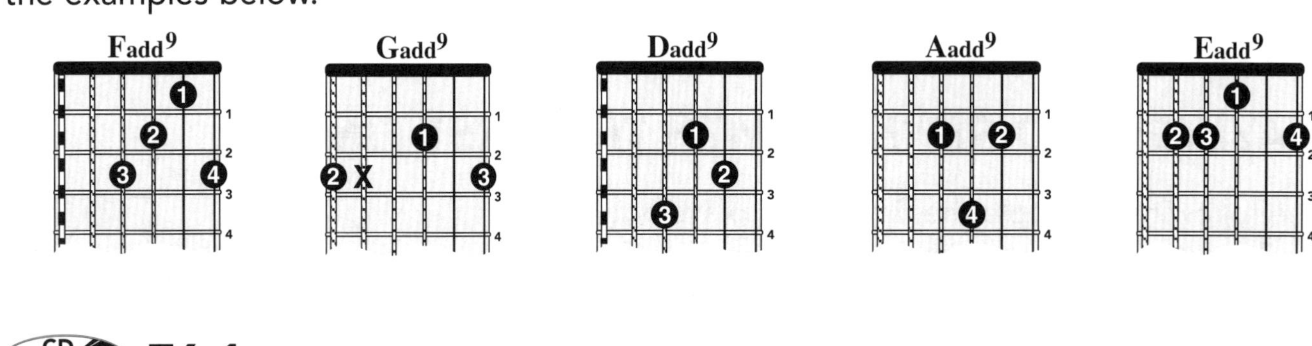

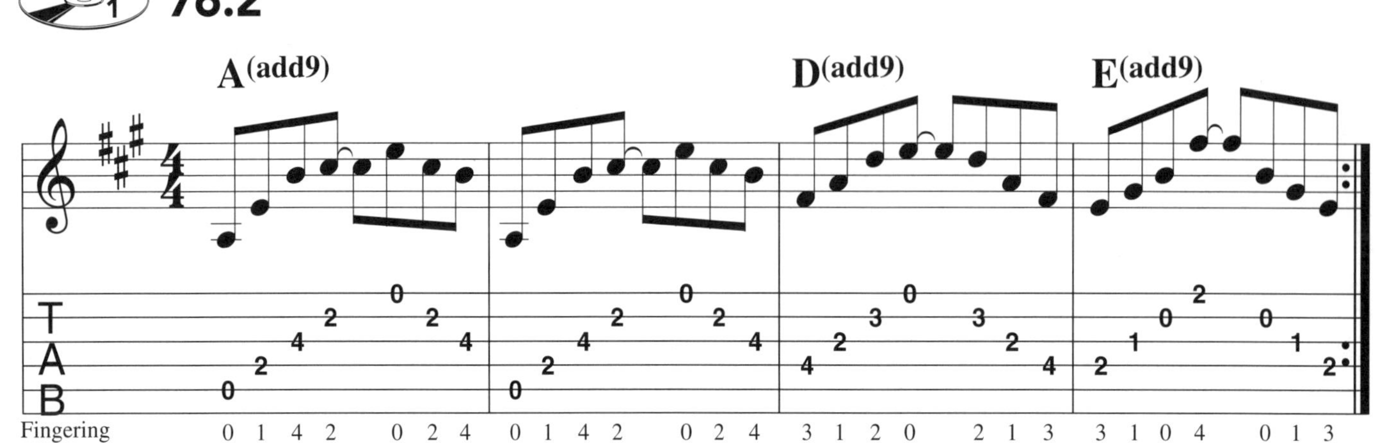

Minor Add Nine Chord Formula

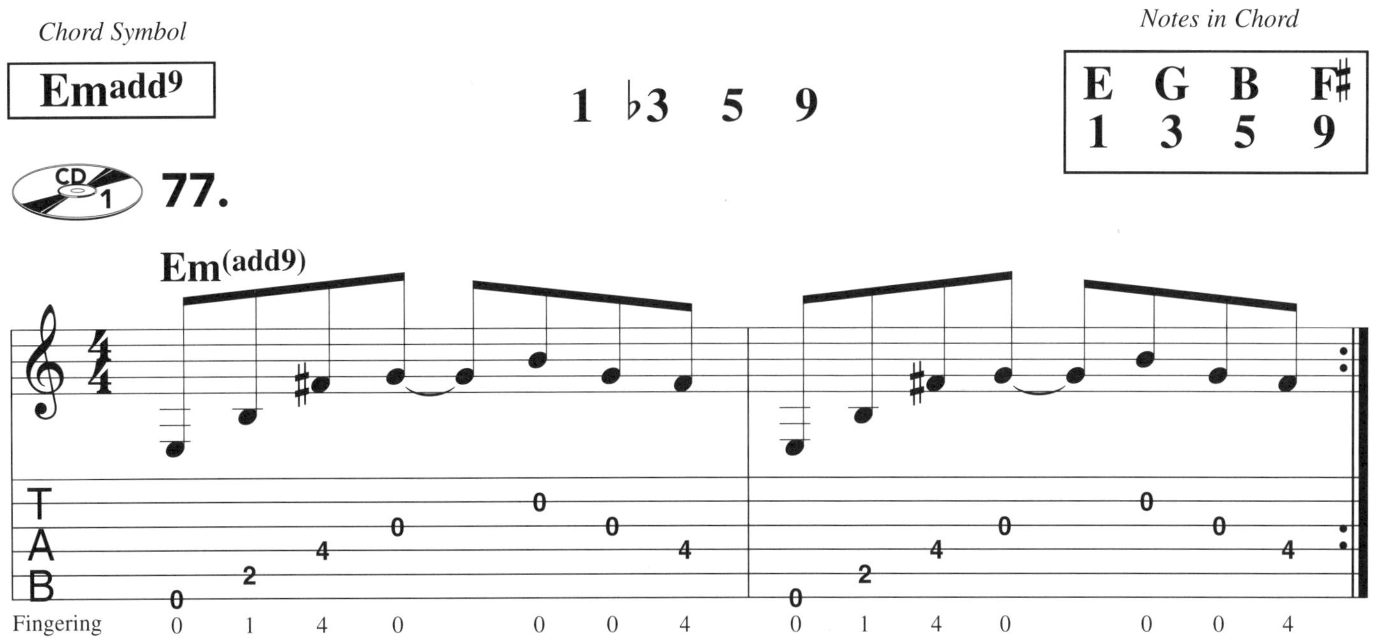

Here are some useful **minor add9** chord shapes. The first two are used in the example below. Experiment with all these chords and substitute them for minor chords in songs.

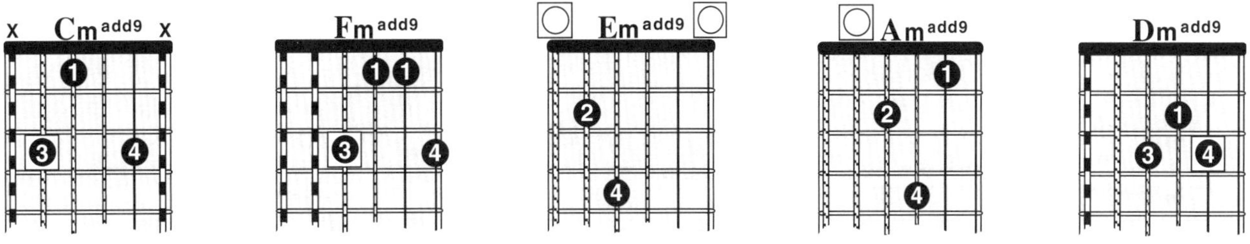

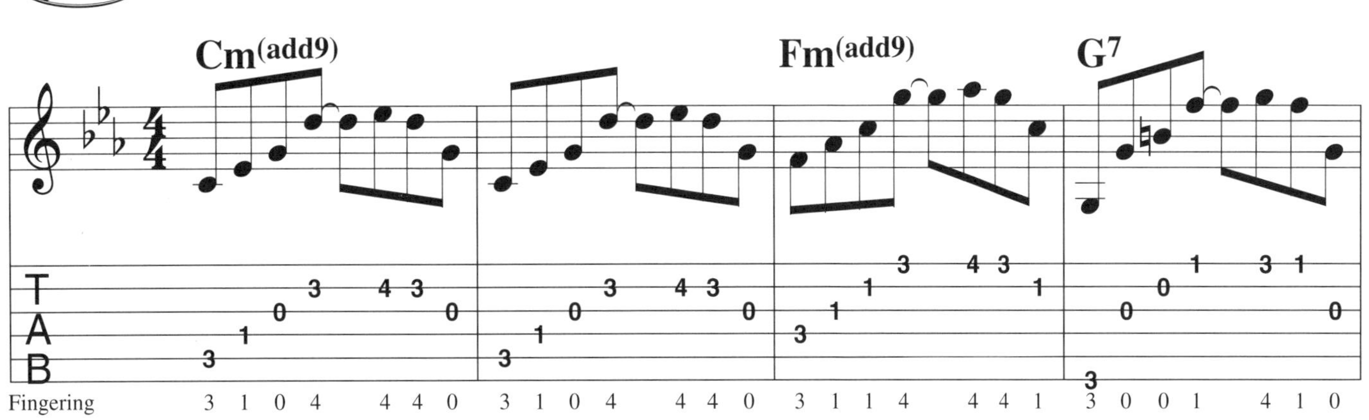

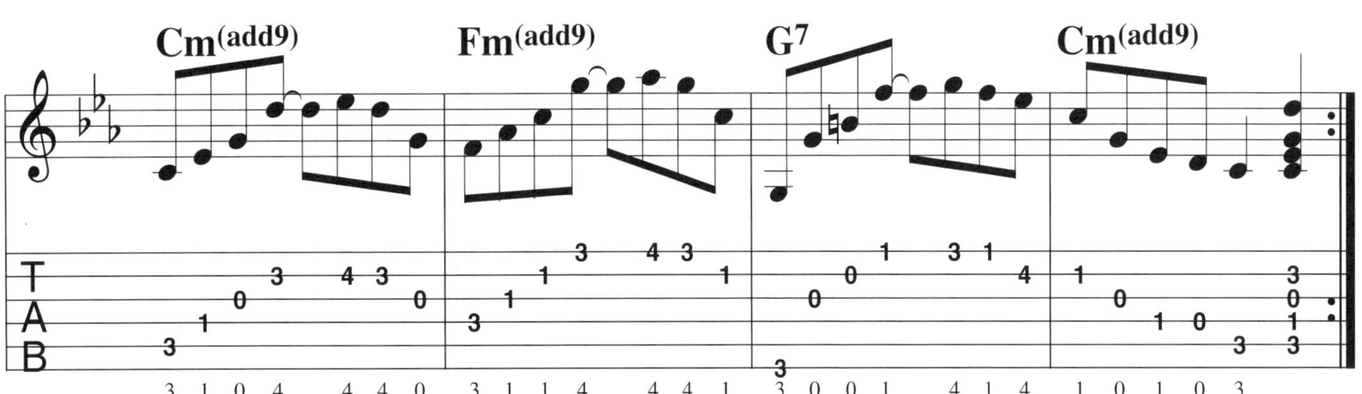

ADDING SCALE TONES TO CHORDS

In this lesson you have learnt two types of add9 chords which are formed by simply adding another scale tone to the existing chord. It is also possible to add other scale tones to chords. You can add any note of the scale of the key you are playing in to any of the chords in that key. Each time you do this, it will change the name of the chord, but knowing all these names is not essential for now. The best thing to do is experiment and memorize the notes and chords which you think sound good together. The example below is in the key of **E minor**. It contains various scale tone additions and substitutions. Learn it and then use the ideas to make up your own progressions.

79. In The Winter Dark

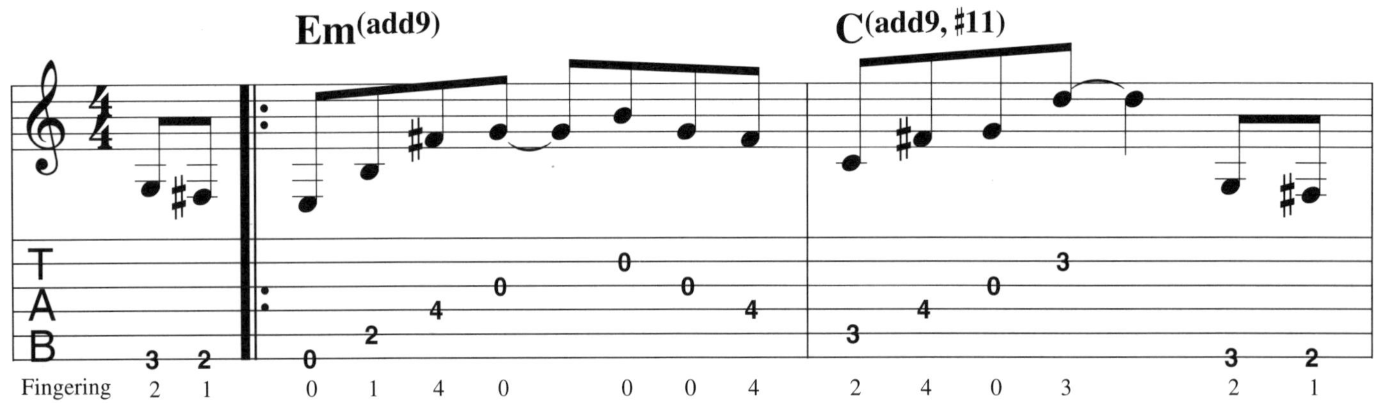

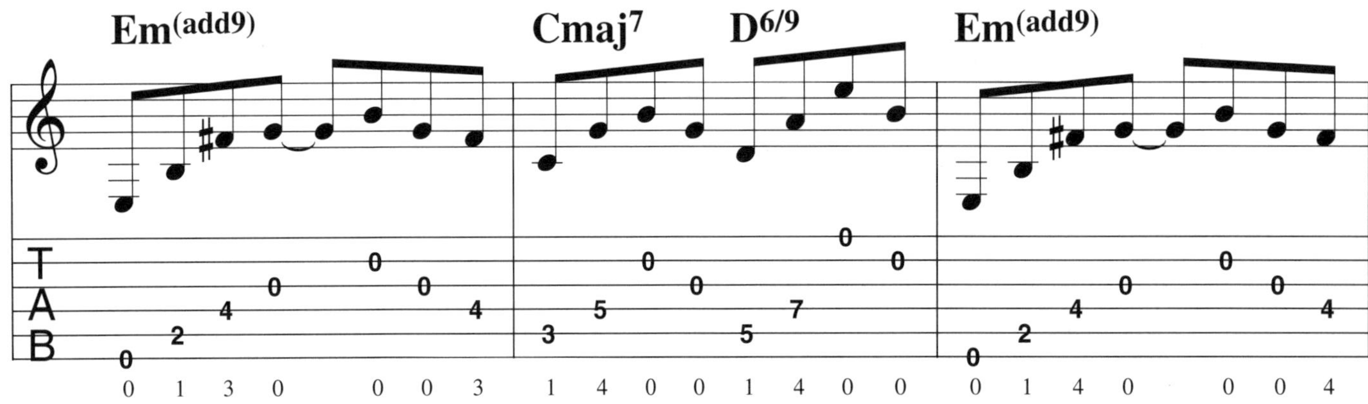

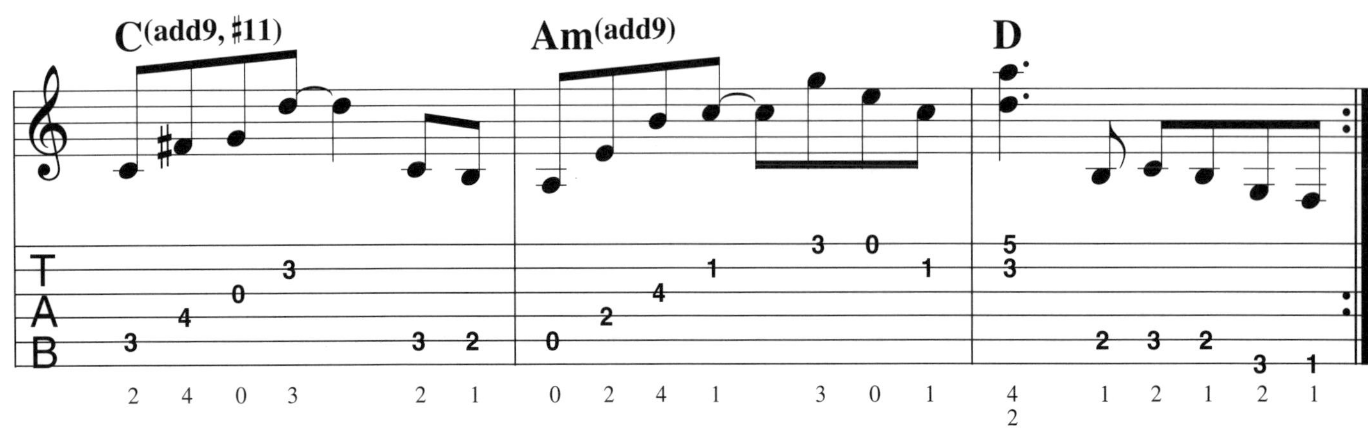

LESSON TWENTY EIGHT

SYNCOPATION

When ties are used to connect eighth notes, an "off the beat" feel is created. This is called **syncopation**. When a chord change is anticipated by half a beat, it is described as giving the rhythm a **push**. These things are demonstrated in the following example.

80.

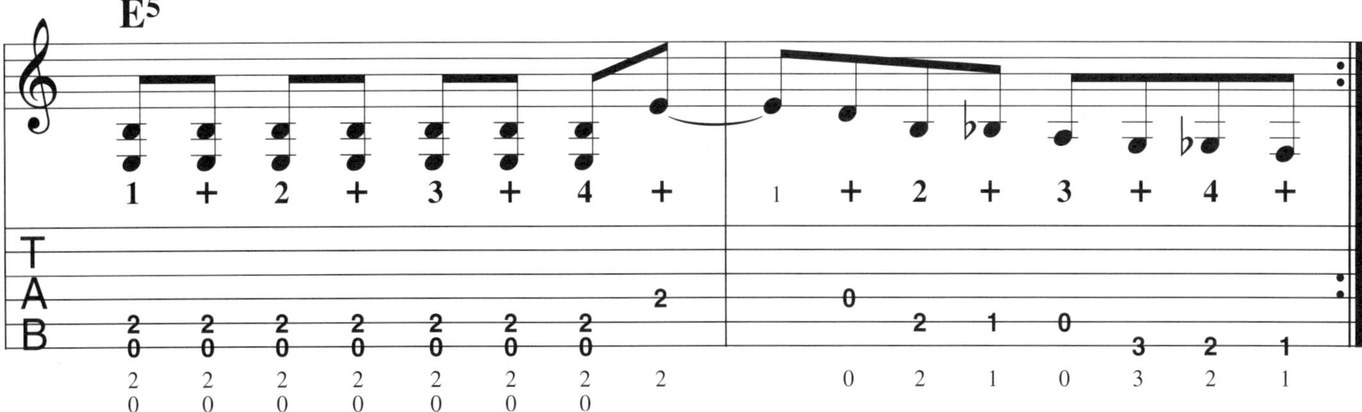

81.

This example uses both rests on the beat and ties on the beat to create syncopation. Notice once again the use of the first finger across the 3rd and 4th strings at the 2nd fret.

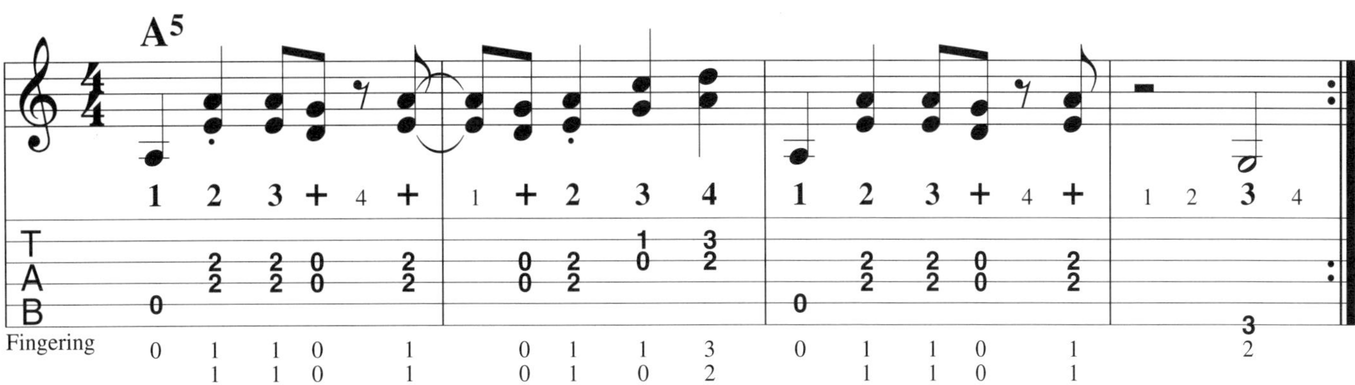

RIFFS

A **riff** is a short pattern of notes (usually one or two bars long) which repeats throughout a verse or section of a song. A riff can also be varied to fit a chord progression. Riffs are common in many styles of music including Rock, Metal, Blues, Jazz and Funk. Many of the examples you have already learnt are riffs. Here are some examples.

82.

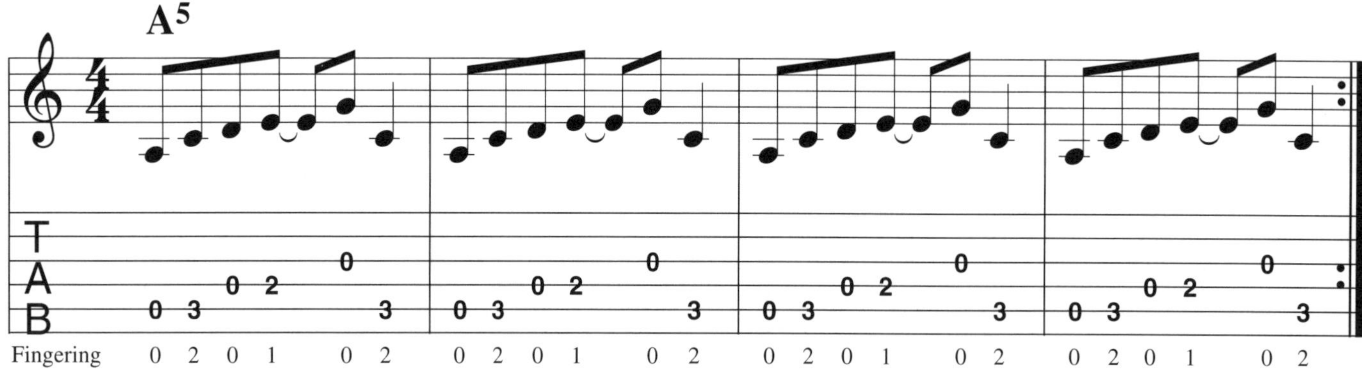

83.

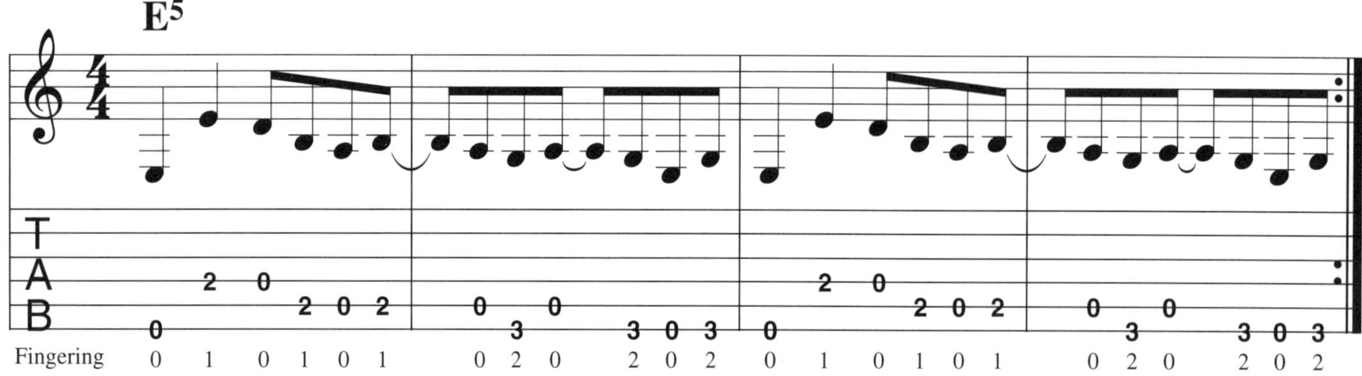

84.

Riffs may be made up of single notes, chords, or a combination of both, as shown in this example.

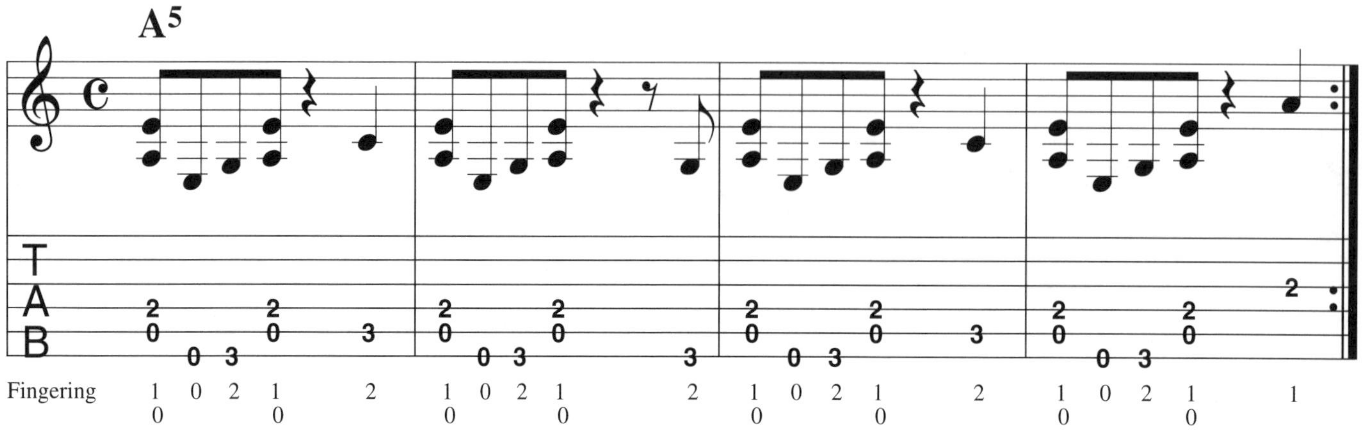

Here are some more riffs. Learn them and then make up some of your own based on the ideas presented here. Don't worry about the notes too much; just experiment until you find something that sounds good and then memorize it.

85.

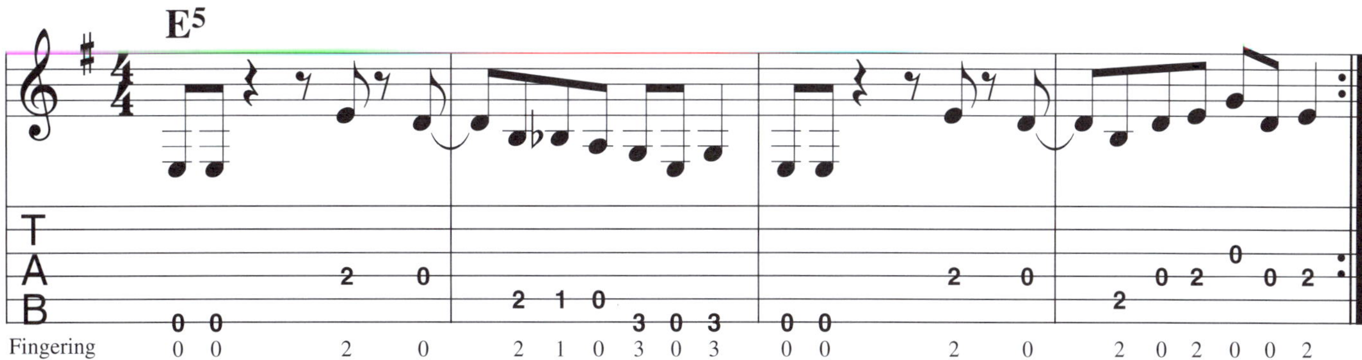

86.

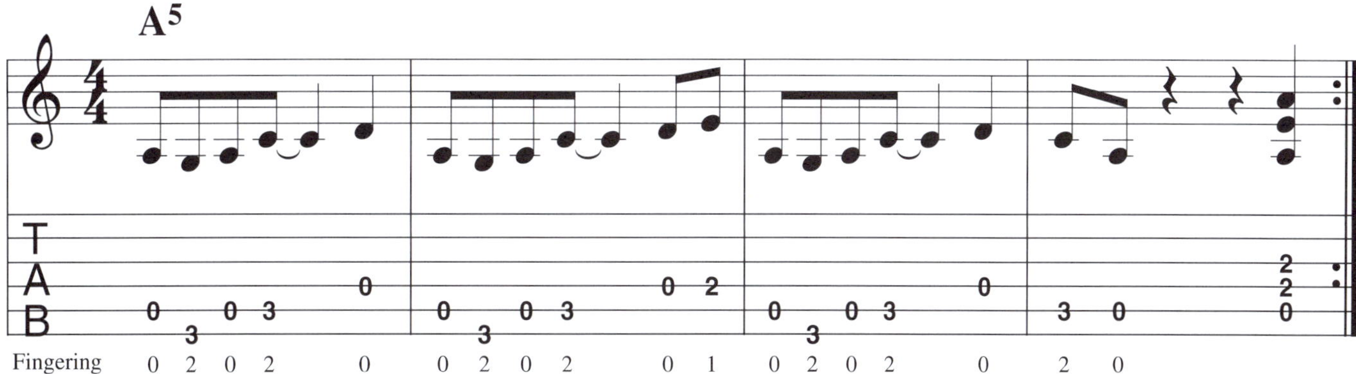

87.

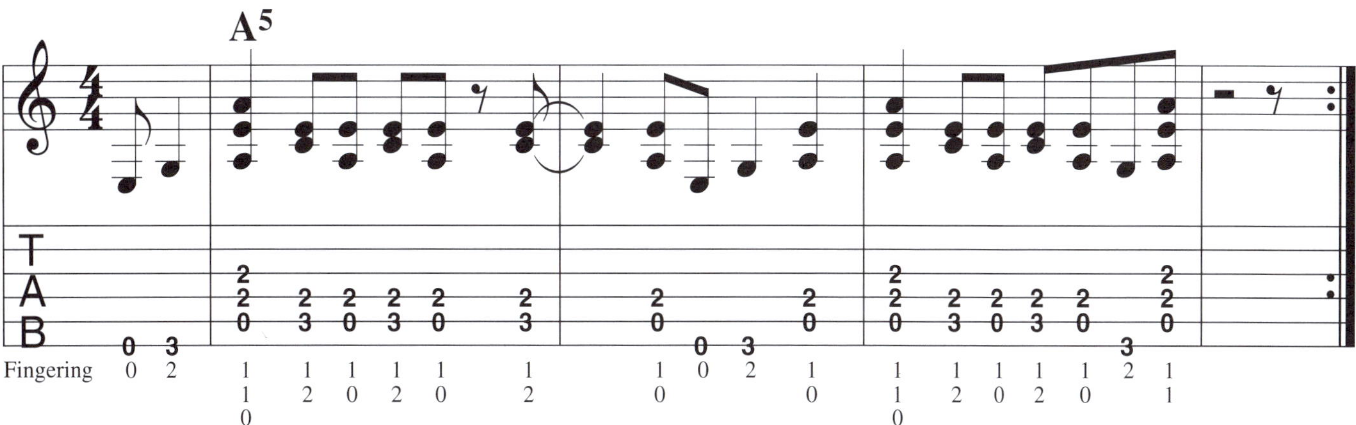

The following 12 bar Blues contains a riff which is altered to fit each new chord as it occurs. As with previous examples, play it slowly at first and gradually increase the tempo.

88. Chasing the Riff

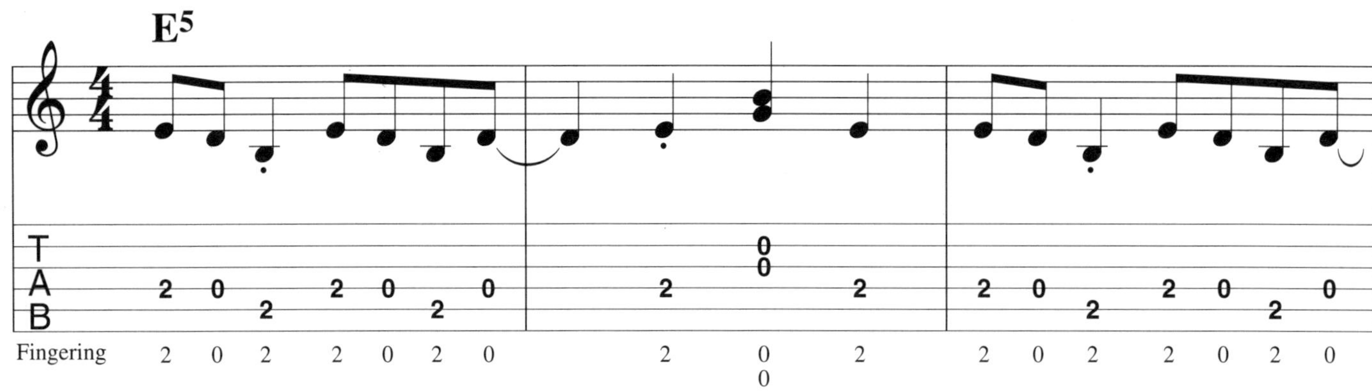

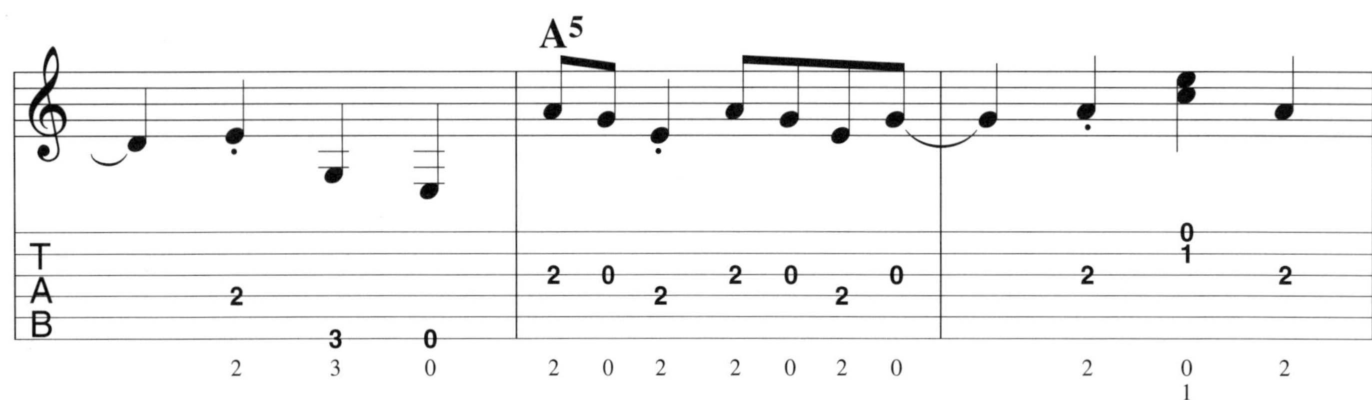

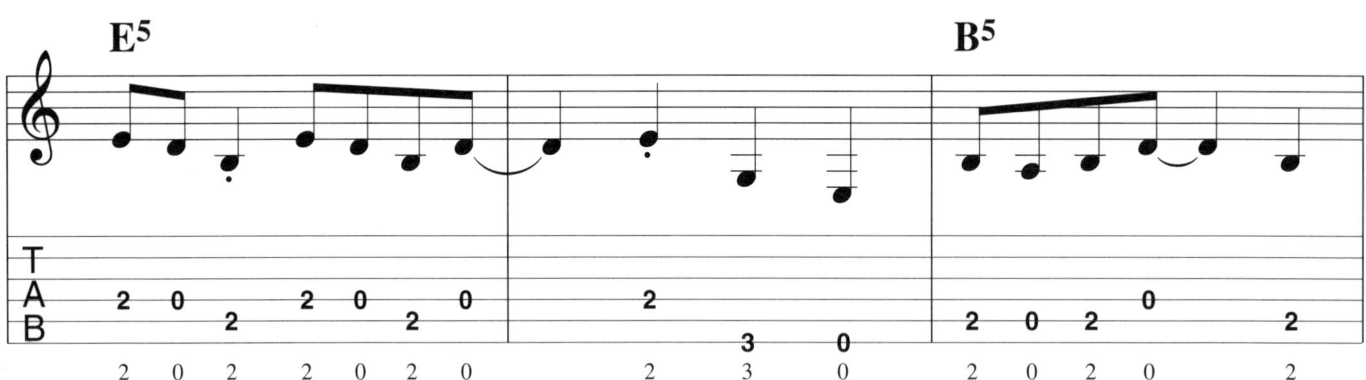

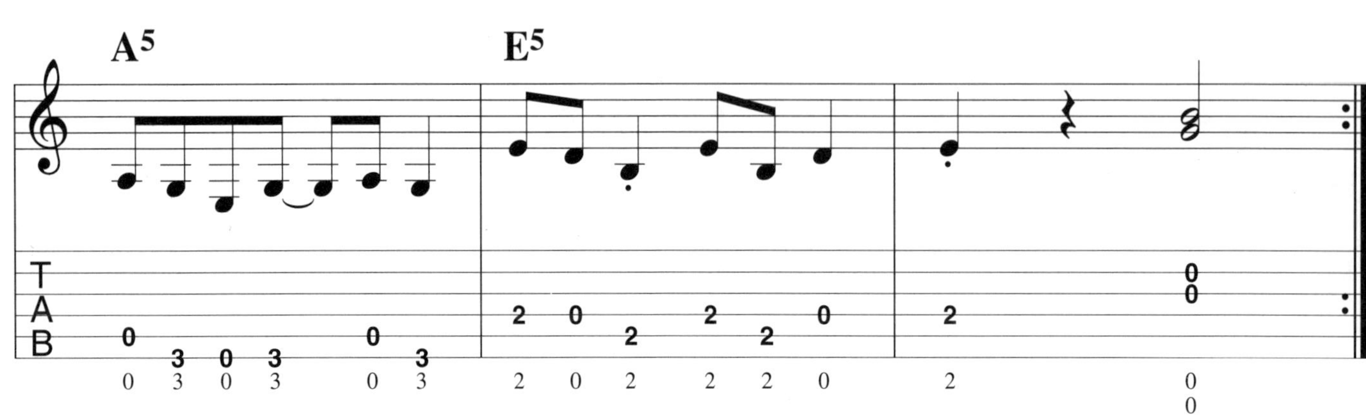

Here is a rhythm part which makes use of power chords, major chords and double note runs. Although this example is in the key of **A**, it is not strictly in a major or minor key, but makes use of elements of both. This is common in Rock. **Whatever sounds good is ultimately the best thing to play**, regardless of what scale, chord or key it comes from. Experiment with all the sounds you have learnt and have fun with them.

89. Rattlesnake Rock

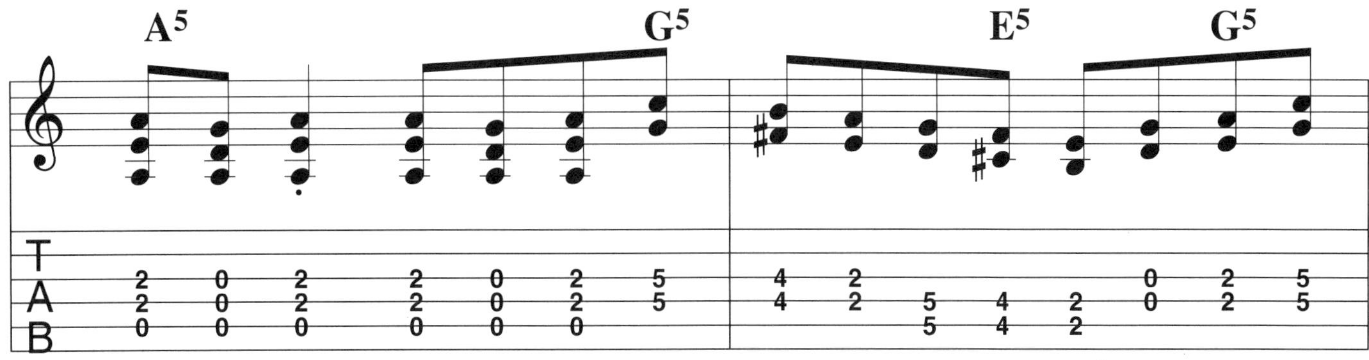

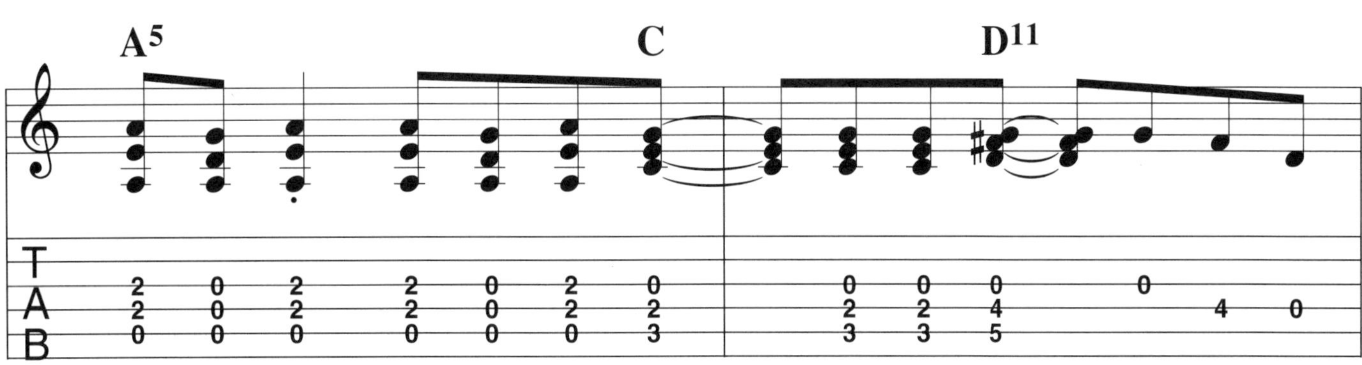

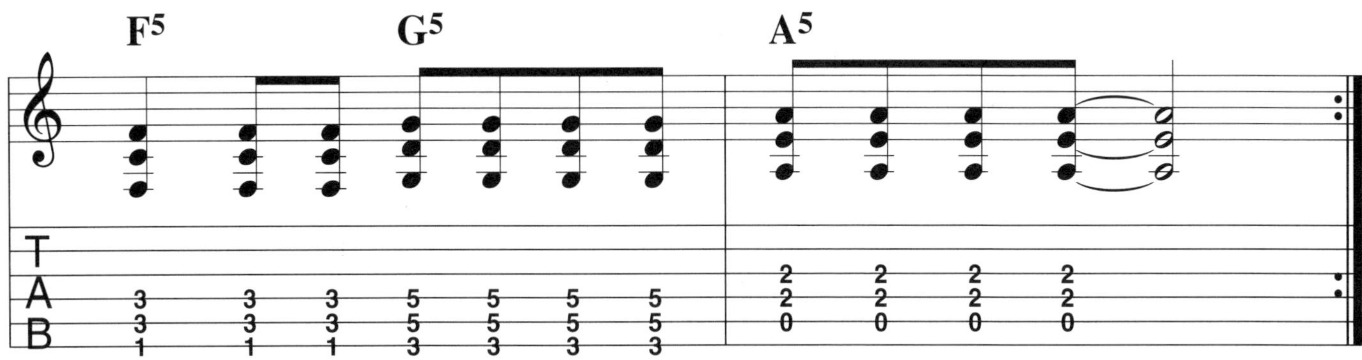

LESSON TWENTY NINE

BAR CHORDS

The term "bar chord" means that the first finger acts as a **bar** (sometimes called a **barre**) across all, or some of the strings. The fact that there are no open strings in a bar chord means it is possible to move the one shape to any position on the fretboard and to play in every key. The term "position" refers to the fret your first finger is at. E.g if your first finger is at the **3rd fret**, you are in the **third position**. If your first finger is at the **8th fret**, you are in the **eighth position**. The diagram and photo below demonstrate an **F major** bar chord (played in the **first position**). Notice that this chord is simply an E chord shape played with the 2nd, 3rd and 4th fingers, with a first finger bar behind it.

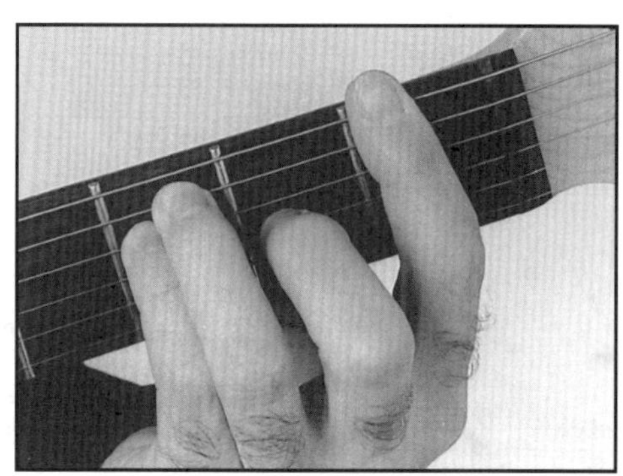

LEFT HAND TECHNIQUE

Bar chords can be difficult to play at first and will require a great deal of practice before they are comfortable to use. Try to keep the first finger of the left hand straight and parallel to the fret. It is also important to keep the other fingers arched and use only the tips of the fingers. The left hand thumb must be kept behind the neck.

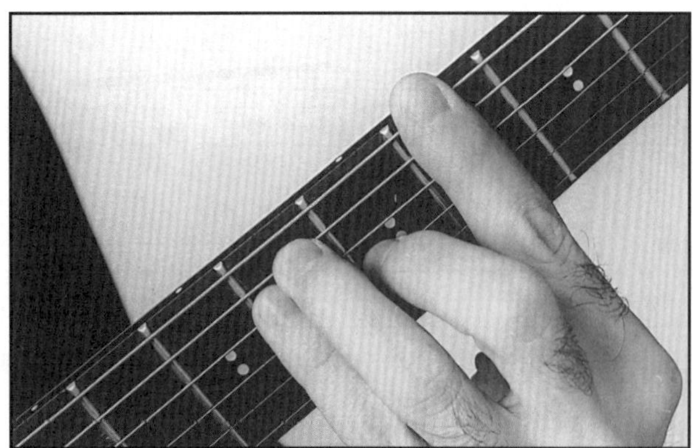

Keep first finger straight.

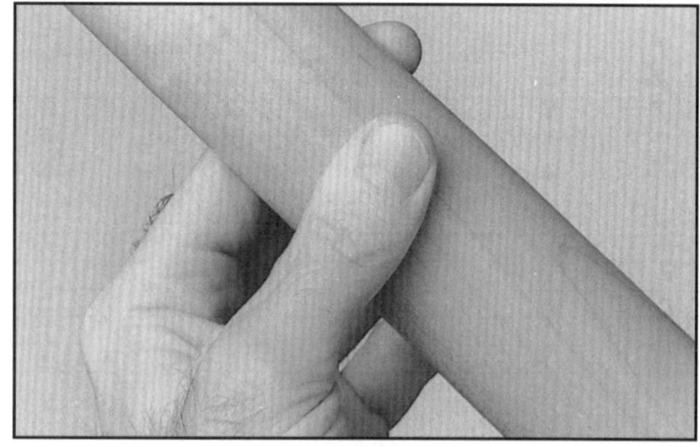

Keep thumb behind neck.

ROOT 6 BAR CHORDS

As with open chords, there are several different types of bar chords, including major, minor and 7th chords. The bar chord shape shown above is referred to as a **root 6** major bar chord because the **root note** (name note) of the chord is on the **6th string**. The root 6 major bar chord can be played at any fret with the name of the chord depending on which note the first finger is fretting on the sixth string. E.g. at the **3rd fret**, this shape would be a **G chord**. At the **5th fret**, it would be an **A chord**, etc.

NOTES ON THE SIXTH STRING

In order to determine exactly where to place your first finger for any particular bar chord, it is essential to know the notes on the sixth string from memory. The diagram below shows the notes on the sixth string up to the 13th fret where the F note repeats an octave higher than the first fret. It is rare to play bar chords any higher than the 12th fret.

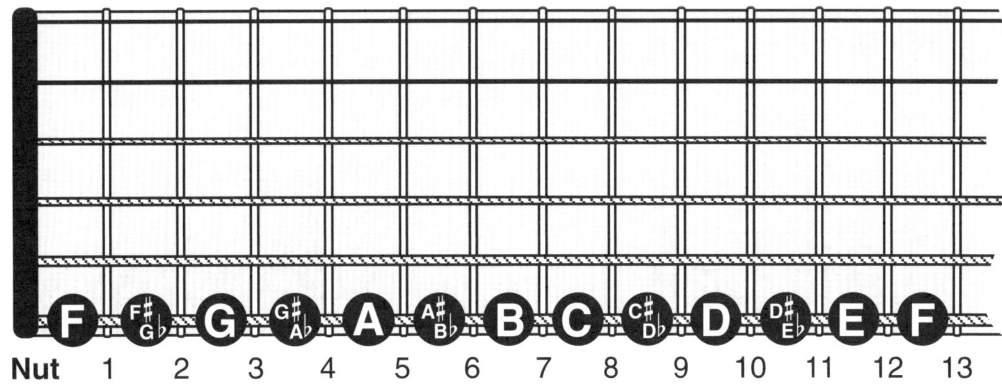

1.0 CD 2 STARTS HERE

Practice playing bar chords at different frets at random until you can instantly name the chord at any fret. Once you can do this, try the following example, which moves the same shape up and down the neck to form all the chords in the progression.

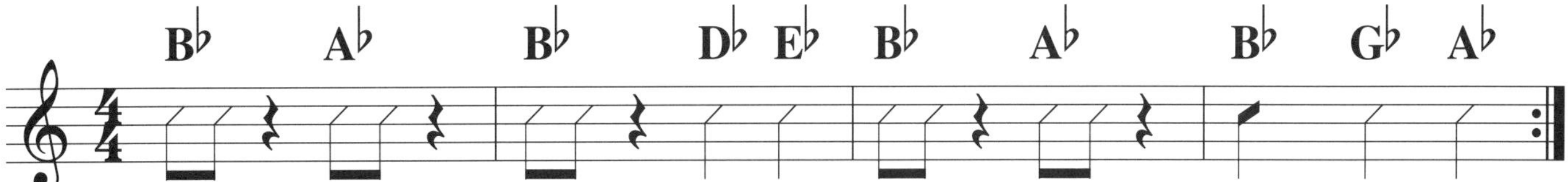

PERCUSSIVE STRUMMING WITH BAR CHORDS

The following example features **percussive strumming** with root 6 bar chords. Wherever percussive strums occur, release the pressure with your left hand, so that the fingers lift up off the fretboard but still remain in contact with the strings. **Keep the bar chord shape** so you are ready to press down again to play the next chord as soon as it occurs.

1.1 (CD2)

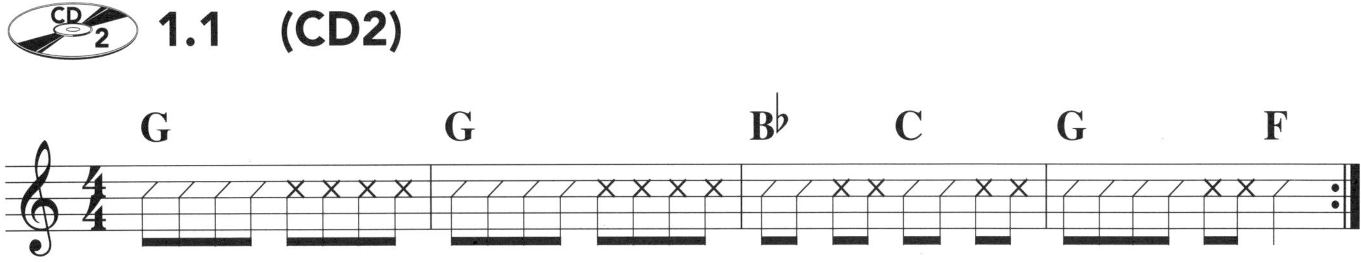

ROOT 5 BAR CHORDS

As the term **root 5** suggests, the root note of these chords can be found on the fifth string, fretted with the first finger bar. Like all bar chords, the same shape can be moved up or down to any position on the fretboard. Below is the basic shape for the root 5 Major bar chord shown in two positions. You will need to have patience with this chord shape, as the combination of the first finger bar and the partial bar with the third finger is particularly difficult at first. Make sure the third finger frets the 4th, 3rd and 2nd strings, but **not** the 1st string.

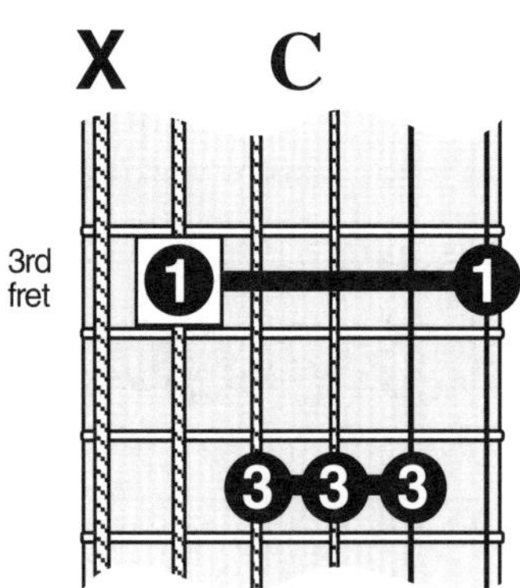

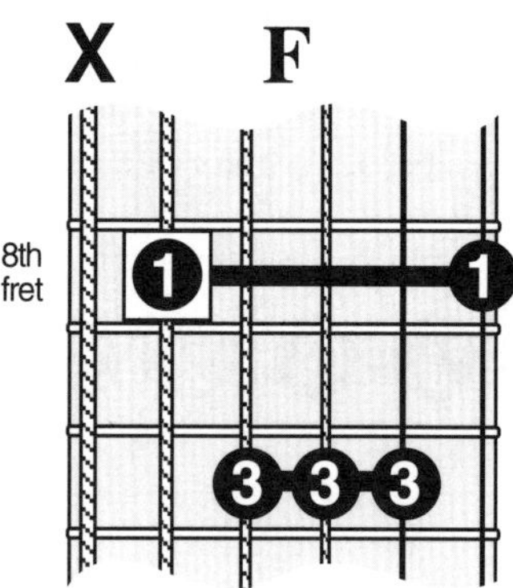

NOTES ON THE FIFTH STRING

To find root 5 bar chords easily, it is essential to know the notes on the 5th string from memory. The diagram below illustrates all notes on the fifth string up to the 13th fret. Try naming a chord and moving to the correct fret. Practice this until you can do it without hesitating or having to think ahead.

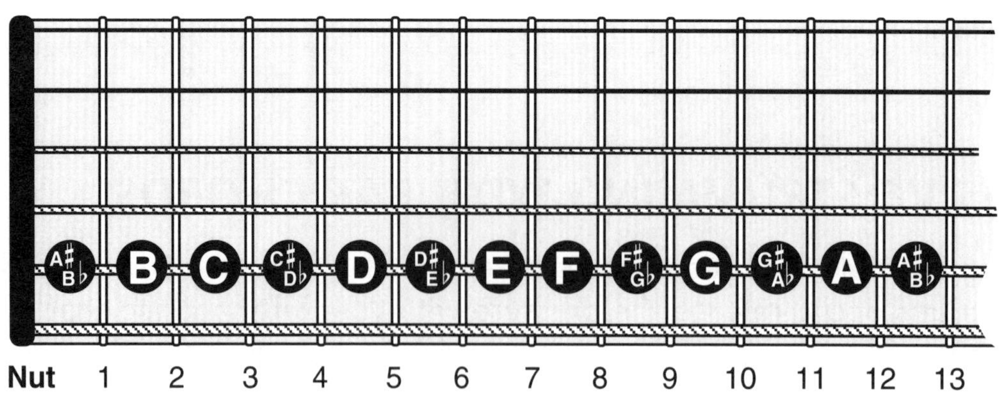

2.0

Here is an example which makes use of root 5 bar chords. Notice once again the use of percussive strumming.

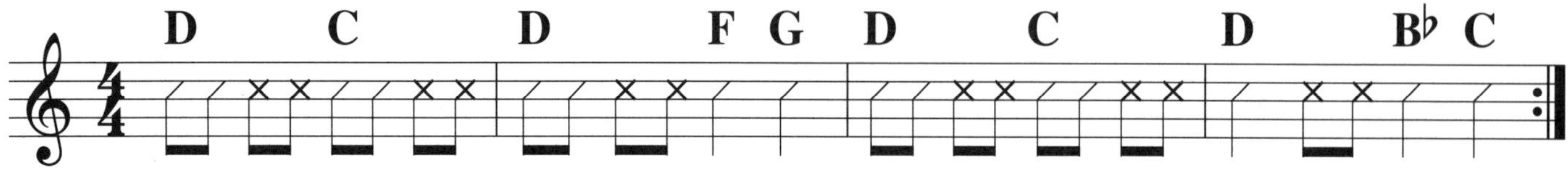

CHANGING BETWEEN SHAPES

Once you know how to play both root 6 and root 5 bar chords, the next step is learning how to combine them. The exercise below will help you gain control of changing between the two major bar chords. The **G** chord is **root 6** while the **C and D** chords are **root 5**. As you play this example, notice that the chords **G, C** and **D** are chords **I**, **IV** and **V** in the **key of G.** You could use these chord shapes to play a 12 bar Blues in the key of G. You could also move the chords to other positions on the fretboard and play a 12 bar Blues in any key. This becomes even easier when you learn the following pattern, which applies to all keys.

If **chord I is root 6,** then **chord IV** will be **root 5 at the same fret,** and **chord V** will be **root 5 two frets higher up the neck.**

2.1

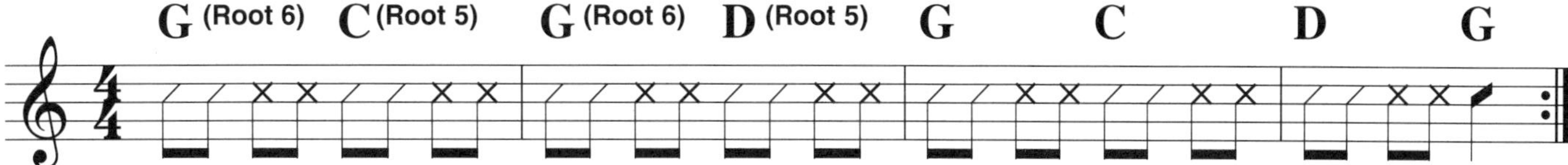

It is also possible to play this progression beginning with a root 5 chord. If **chord I is root 5,** then **chord IV** will be **root 6 two frets lower,** and **chord V** will be **root 6 at the same fret as chord I**. This pattern also applies to **all keys**. Listen to the CD to hear the difference between this example and the previous one.

2.2

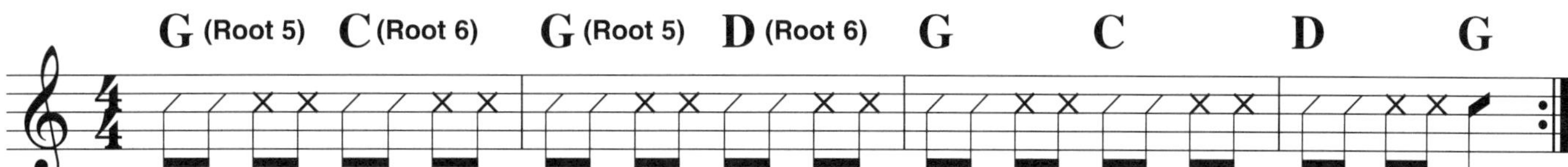

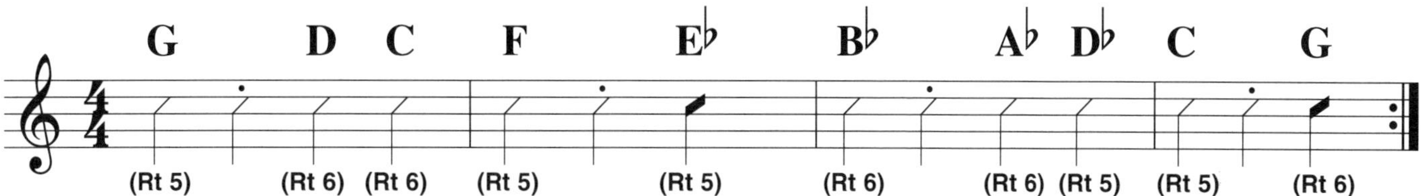

2.3

Here is another example which will give you more practice at changing between root 5 and root 6 bar chords. Notice the use of **staccato** here. As with single notes, staccato with bar chords is achieved by quickly lifting the fingers off the fretboard but not off the strings immediately after strumming the chord.

LESSON THIRTY

LEARNING THE WHOLE FRETBOARD

When using moveable chord shapes, it is important to be able to quickly find the correct fret at which to play each chord, and also to be able to play equally well in all keys. The best way to achieve this is to memorize the names of all the notes on the fretboard. This may seem a daunting task, but it can be done and will be well worth it. More advanced guitar playing requires the use of many different chords, which may take their name from **any** of the six strings, so you need to learn them all equally well.

Notes on the

Here is a fretboard diagram of all the notes on the guitar. Play the notes on each string the open note e.g. the open 6th string is an **E** note and the note on the 12th fret of the

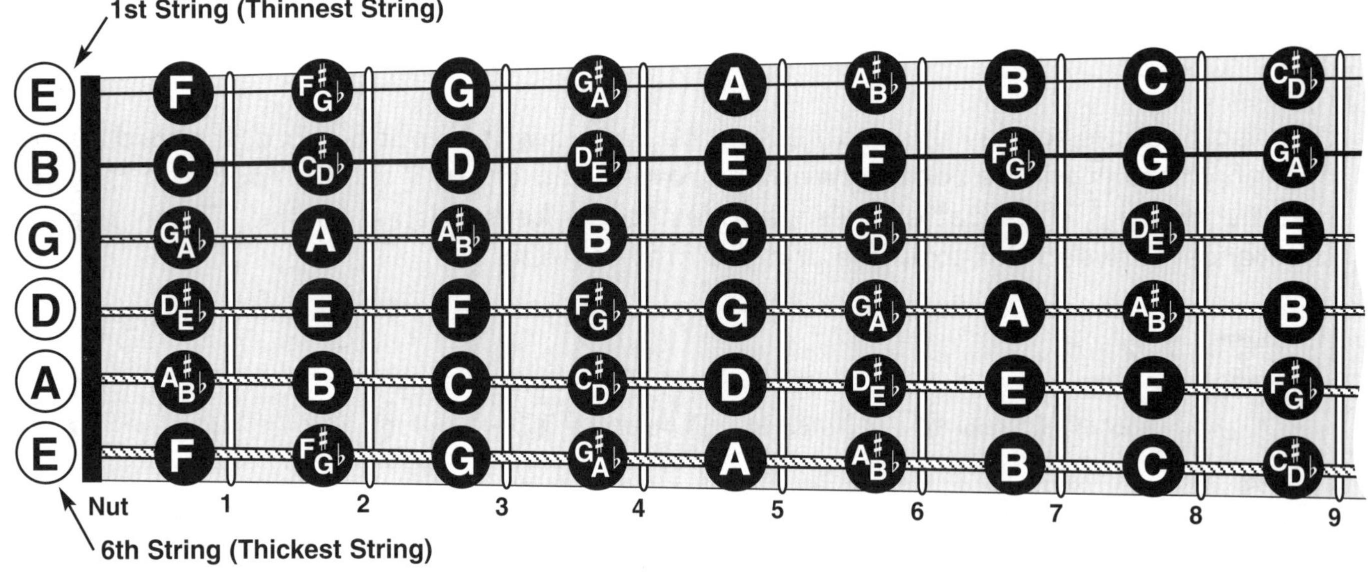

A good way to learn all the notes is to take one string at a time. Call the "in between" notes sharps as you progress up the fretboard and flats as you go back down. The diagram below shows notes on the 4th string only. To practice naming the notes, slide your first finger up one fret at a time and say the name of each note out loud as you go. When you reach the 12th fret where the notes begin to repeat, move back down one fret at a time. You can use any finger to do this exercise, it is the note names that are important, not the fingering.

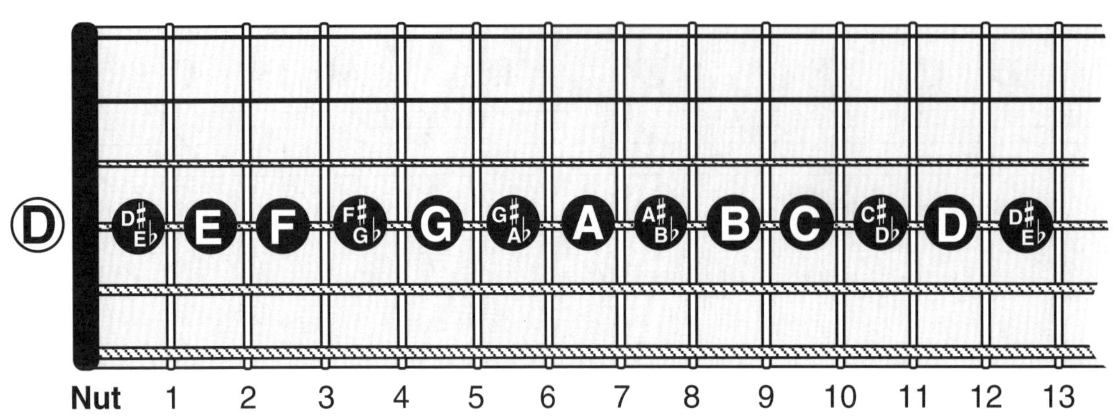

The dots on your guitar are good points of reference. You can use them to help the memorizing process.

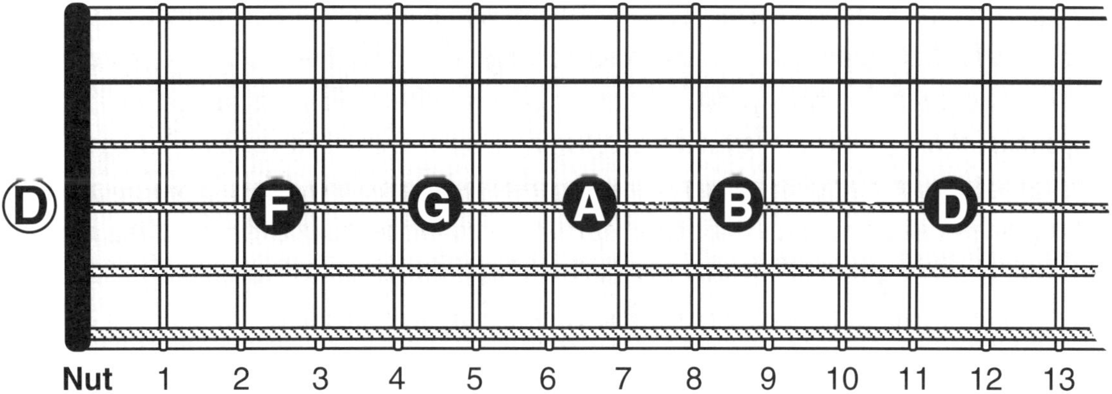

Guitar Fretboard

from the open notes to the 12th fret. The note on the 12th fret is one octave higher than 6th string is also an **E** note, but is one octave higher.

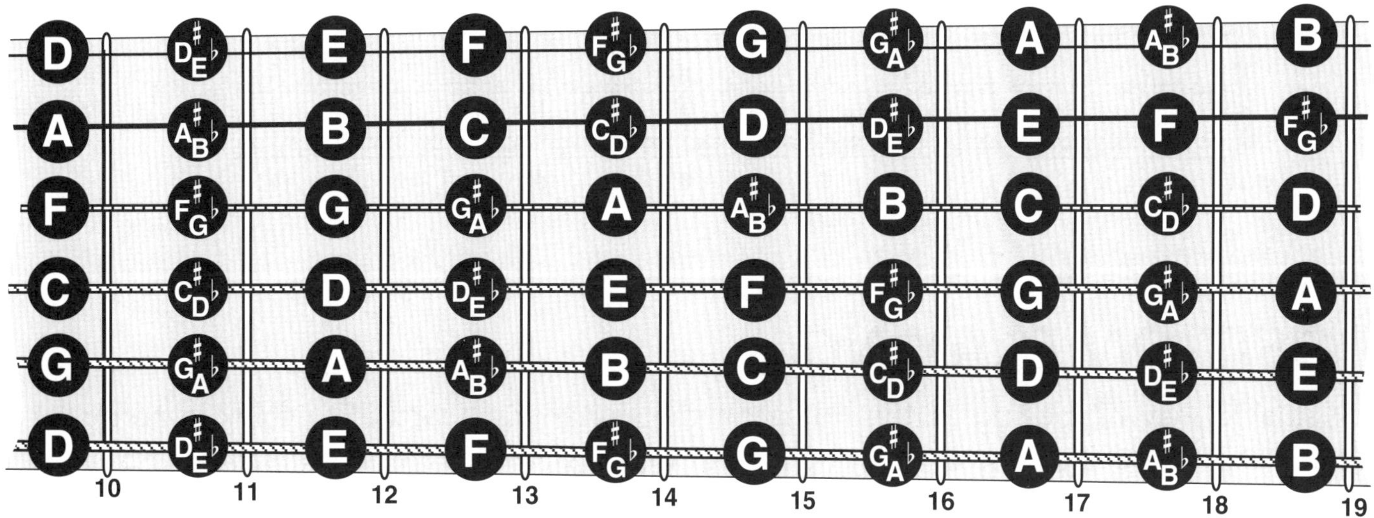

Once you are confident you know the names of the notes along a particular string, pick the name of any note at random and find it on that string as quickly as possible. When this becomes easy, move on to the next string.

Another useful exercise is to find the same note on every string, remembering that a note usually appears twice on each string unless it is at the 11th fret.

Finally, name and play the notes across each fret. Once again use sharps as you go higher in pitch and flats as you go back down.

NOTES IN MORE THAN ONE PLACE

Once you start playing notes all over the fretboard, you quickly realize that you can find the same notes in more than one place. E.g. the **E note** which is the **open first string** can also be found at the **5th fret** on the **second string**, the **9th fret** on the **third string** and the **14th fret** on the **fourth string** (on electric guitars it can also be found at the **19th fret** on the **fifth string**). Once you are comfortable with all the locations of a note, it is easy to play the same melody in many different places on the fretboard. This is valuable when you are improvising or reading music. Practice naming any note and then finding it in as many places on the fretboard as possible. Keep doing this for a few minutes each day, until you are confident you can quickly find all the locations for any note.

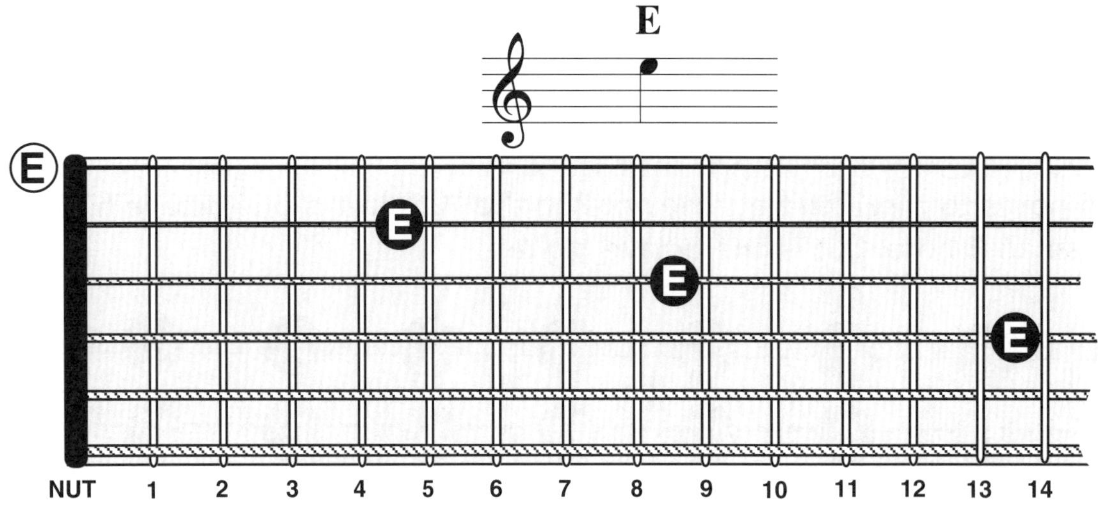

POSITION PLAYING

A valuable way of looking at the notes on the guitar fretboard is to think in terms of **positions**. The position you are playing is determined by which fret the **first finger** of your left hand is at. E.g. if you are playing a melody or chord where your first finger stays at the **first fret**, then you are in the **first position**. If your first finger stays at the **6th fret**, you are in the **6th position**, etc. The example below demonstrates a short phrase played in several different positions, as shown in the tablature. Experiment and find out how many other positions you can use to play this phrase.

CD 2 **3.0**

HIGHER AND LOWER OCTAVES OF NOTES

Another valuable exercise for improving your knowledge of the fretboard is to find all possible octaves of any given note. Remember that an **octave** is the distance between any note and its next repeat at a higher or lower pitch.

An example of this would be the note C♯, which can be found at the **9th and 21st frets** on the **sixth string**, the **4th and 16th frets** on the **fifth string**, the **11th fret** on the **fourth string**, the **6th and 18th frets** on the **third string**, the **2nd and 14th frets** on the **second string**, and the **9th and 21st frets** on the **first string**. These positions are shown in the diagram below. Practice choosing notes at random and finding each one in all possible positions, until you are confident you can instantly find any note in any position.

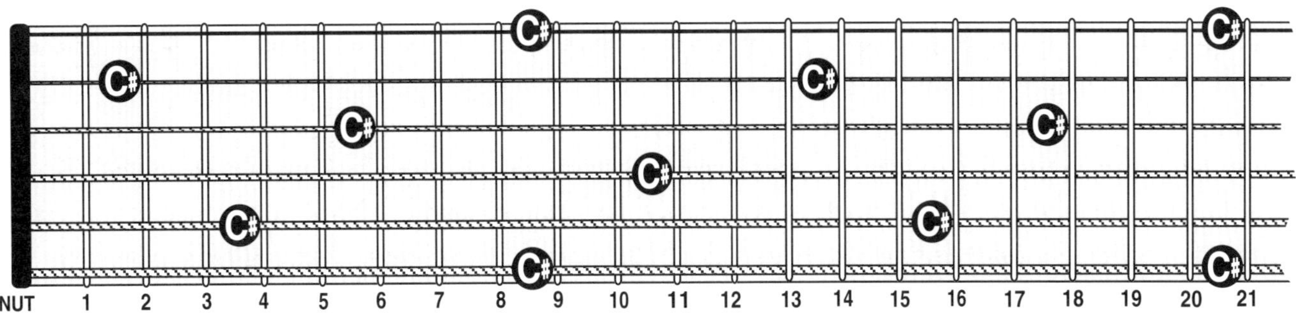

Knowing how to find higher and lower octaves of notes is useful in many ways. You may wish to repeat something you have played but make it sound higher or lower than the first time it was played, or you may play something and think you have the right notes but it sounds too high or too low. Another situation where this is useful is if you are playing call and response with a vocalist or another instrumentalist. You may know which key they are in and what note they are starting on, but you also have to find which octave they are in as well.

The example below shows a phrase played in different positions on the fretboard and also in different octaves.

3.1

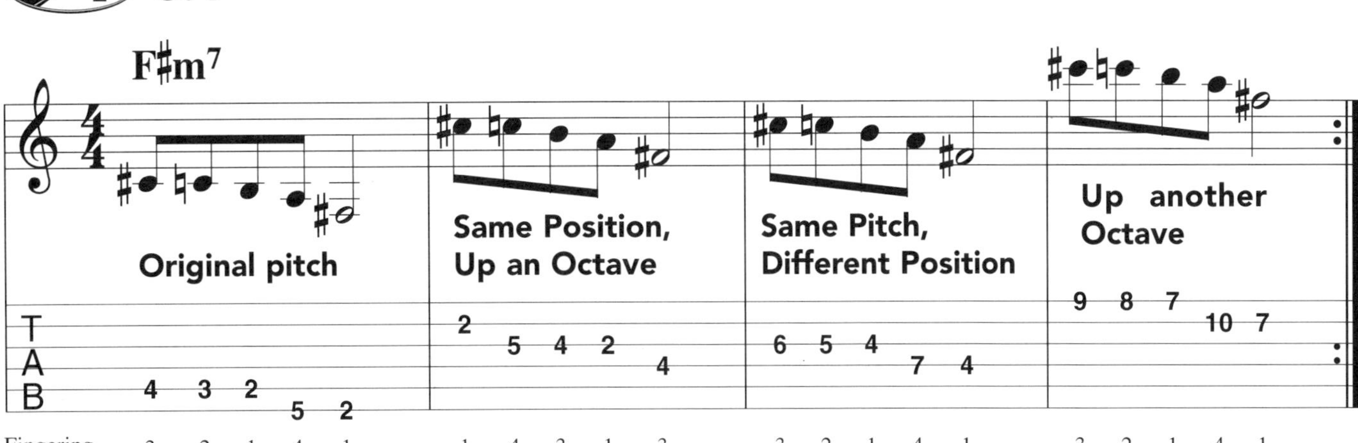

LESSON THIRTY ONE

MOVEABLE CHORD SHAPES IN FIVE FORMS

To become a good guitar player, it is important to have a system for identifying moveable chord shapes all over the fretboard in any key. Most moveable chord formations are closely related to the **five basic major chord shapes** shown below.

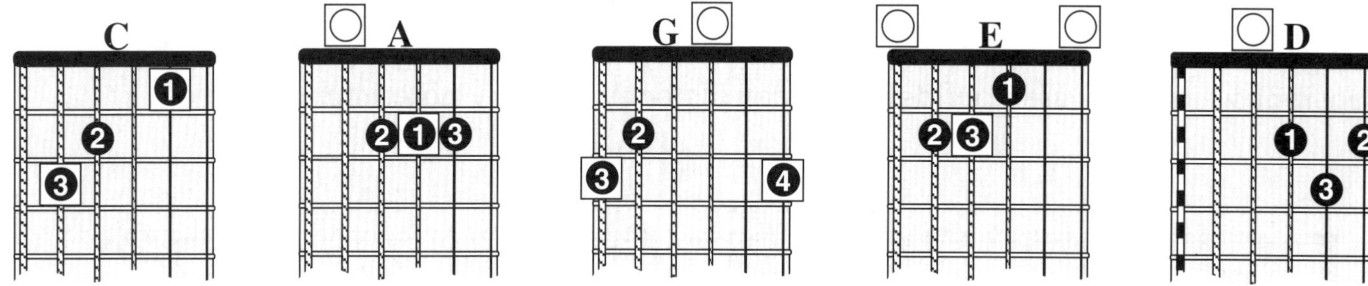

You already know the E form bar chord (root 6) and the A form bar chord (root 5). The C, G and D chords can also be used as the basis for bar chords. There are also many other moveable chord shapes based on these 5 shapes which are useful for Blues playing. The **five basic bar chord forms** are shown below. Notice the order of these forms - **C, A, G, E** and **D.** This order is easy to memorize if you think of the word **caged**.

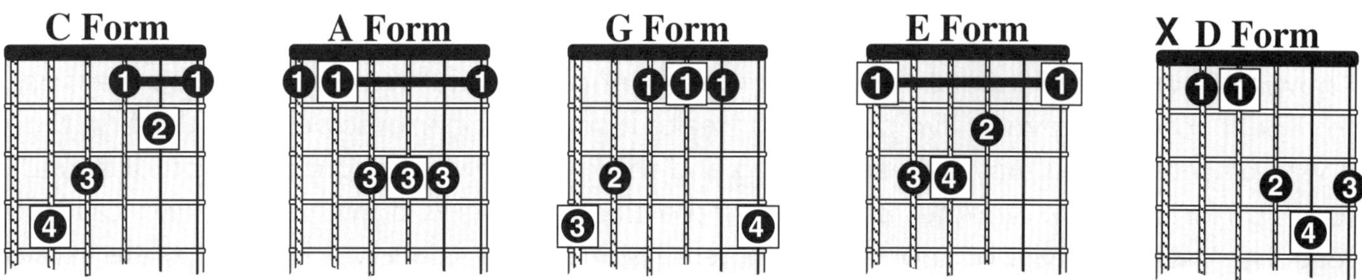

When these five forms (shapes) are placed end to end in the one key, they cover the whole fretboard. E.g. if you start with an **open C chord**, the **A form** bar chord at the **3rd fret** is also a C chord. The **root note** on the **5th string** is shared by both chord forms. The A form chord then connects to a **G form** C chord beginning on the **5th fret**. The **root note** on the **3rd string** is shared by both chord forms. The G form then connects to an **E form** C chord at the **8th fret**. This time there are **two root notes** shared by both forms – one on the **6th string** and one on the **1st string**. The E form then connects to the **D form** at the **10th fret**, this time the shared **root note** is on the **4th string**. To complete the pattern, the D form connects back to the **C form** at the **12th fret**. The shared **root note** between these two forms is on the **2nd string**. This C form is **one octave higher** than the open C form. After this, the whole pattern repeats. The example below demonstrates **all five forms being played as C chords.**

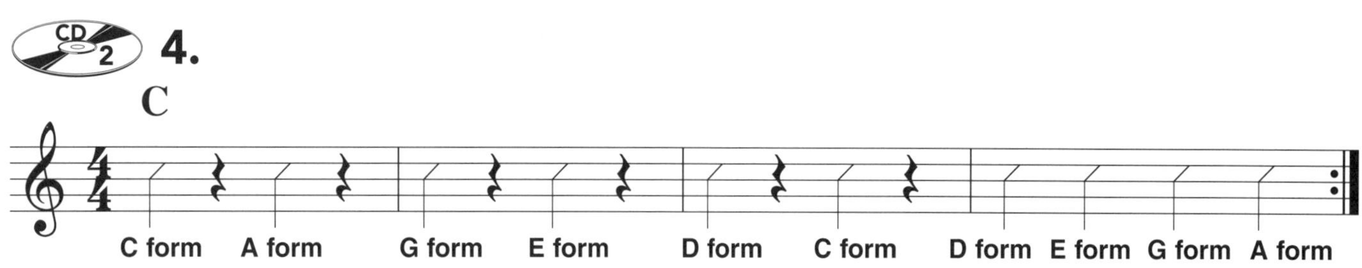

THREE NOTE CHORD VOICINGS

Some of these chord forms are difficult to play, particularly the G form. The most important thing is to be able to **visualize** these shapes, especially the positions of the root notes. Remember that major and minor chords are made up of three different notes. Any more notes in a chord shape are just doublings of those notes. This means it is possible to play just **three notes** from any of these chord forms instead of using the whole shape. Some common examples of **three note voicings** on the top three strings are shown below, along with an example which makes use of them. Once you have learnt them, try transposing them to other keys.

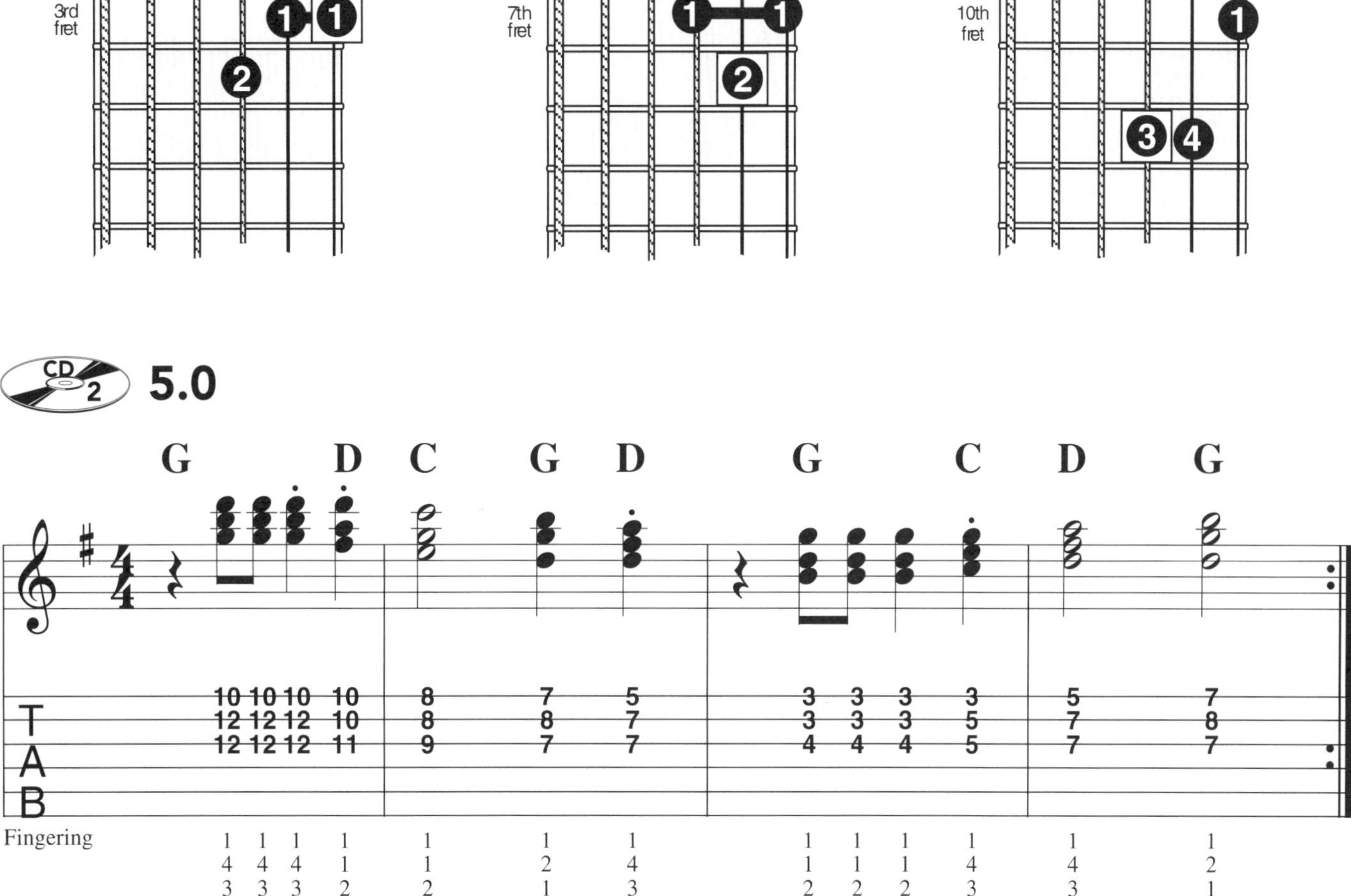

5.1

You should also practice using your chord shapes as arpeggios, as shown here.

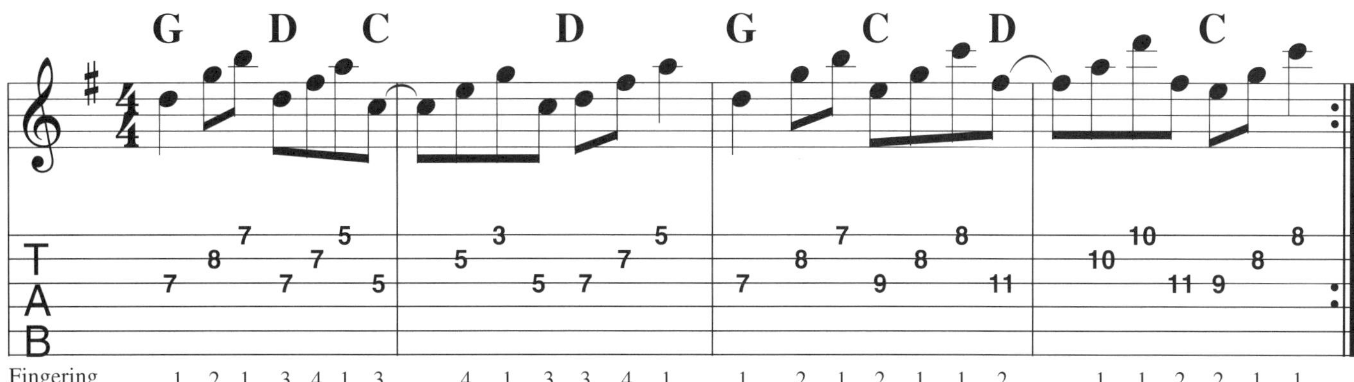

FOUR NOTE CHORD VOICINGS

Here are some useful **four note voicings** of major chords. Memorize the shapes and then transpose them to other keys. This is easy once you know the positions of the root notes.

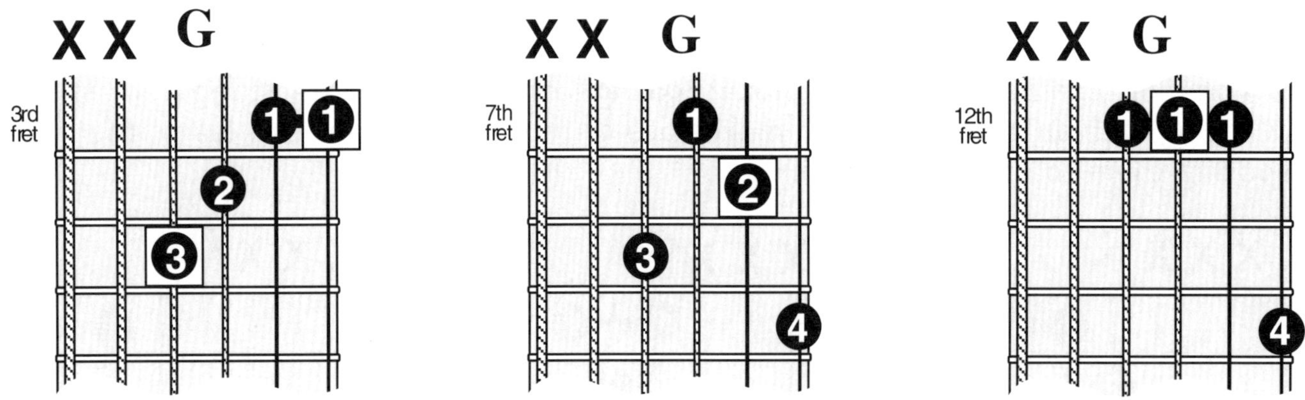

5.2

This example makes use of two of the above four note voicings. Experiment with these chords to come up with your own ideas.

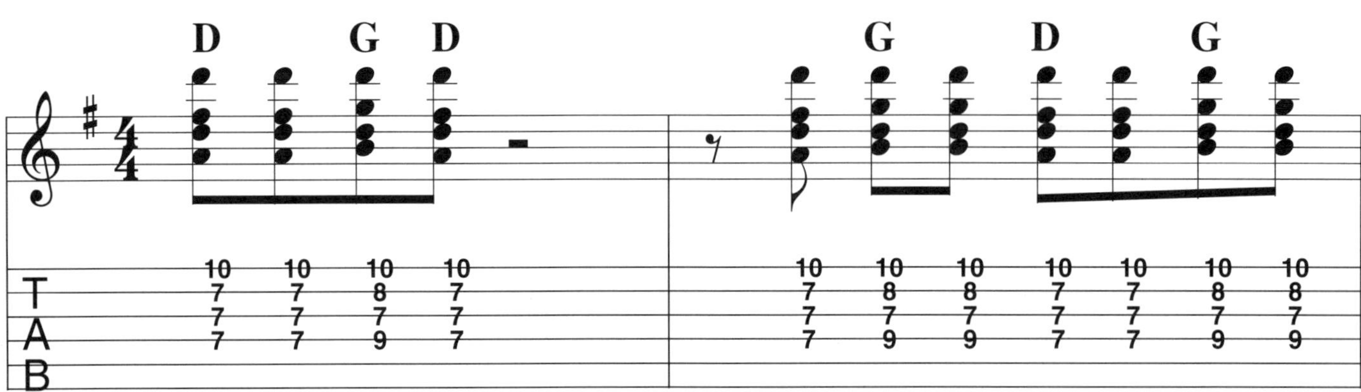

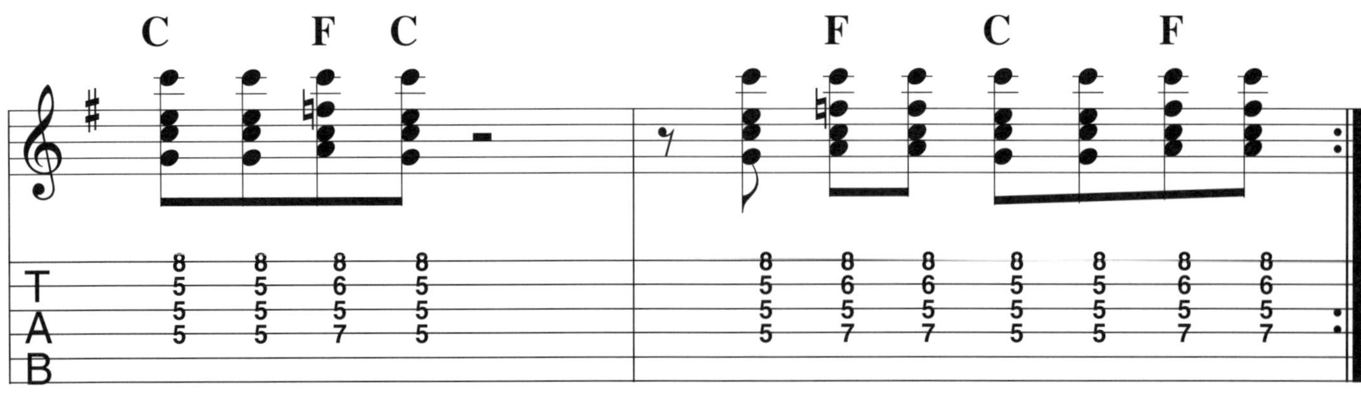

ROOT 4 AND ROOT 3 CHORDS

Just as there are root 6 and root 5 chords, there are also moveable chords which have their root notes on the 4th, 3rd or 2nd strings. Shown below is a D form **root 4** major chord shape, and a progression which uses this shape for all three chords by moving it along the fretboard. This shape is difficult to play at first, so be patient with it.

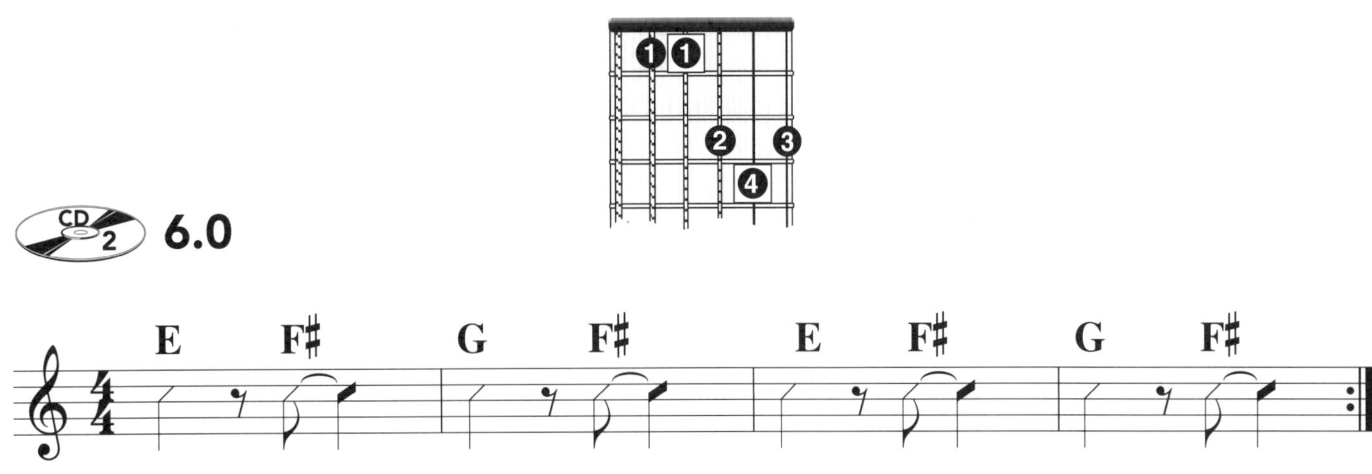

6.1

A power chord can easily be created from the above shape by leaving out the note on the first string. The chord can then be played with two or three notes. Here is an example.

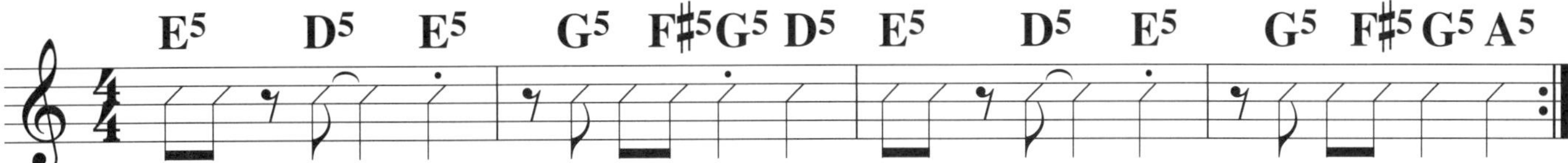

The most common **root 3** chord is a 3 note chord played with either the first finger or the 3rd finger and covering the 2nd, 3rd and 4th strings. Practice alternating between the first and third finger bar as demonstrated in this example.

LESSON THIRTY TWO

MOVEABLE MINOR CHORD SHAPES

Once you know the basic system of moveable major chord shapes (the **C**, **A**, **G**, **E** and **D** forms) it is possible to alter some of the notes to create other chord types, e.g. minor chords. **The positions of the root notes remain the same regardless of the chord type**. Shown below are the five basic forms as open position minor chords.

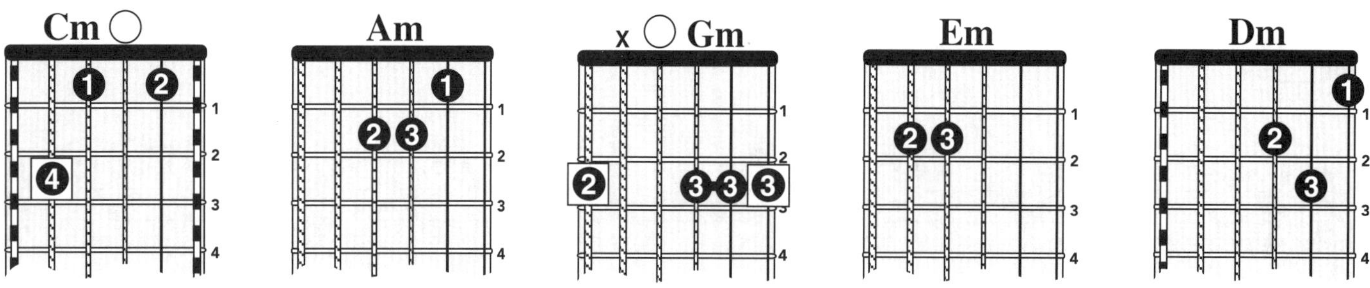

Like major chords, these minor forms can be joined end to end in the same order (CAGED) to cover the whole fretboard. The diagrams below show the five basic forms of moveable minor chords.

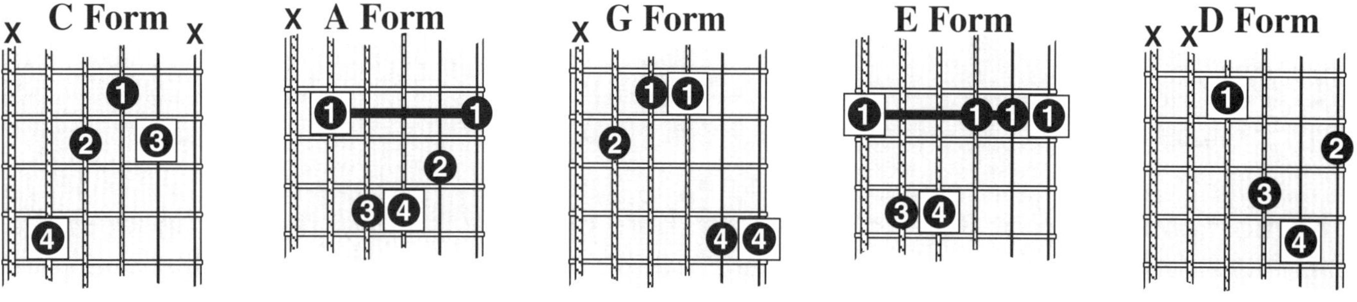

The example below demonstrates **all five forms** being played as **C minor chords.** Practice them slowly and memorize the shapes and positions of the root notes. When you can do this easily, transpose them to other keys.

CD 2 **7.**

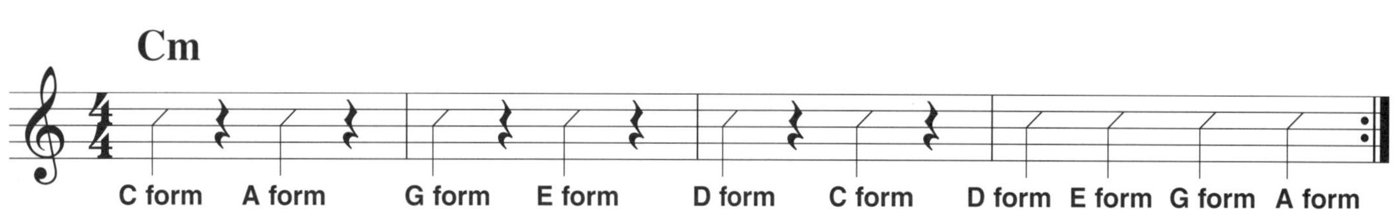

THE HALF BAR

The term **half bar** means the first finger is barring some strings, but not all six. The following example uses an **F minor** chord shape which requires the use of the half bar across three strings. Practice playing it both as a full chord and an arpeggio until you can sound all the notes clearly. Then play the whole example.

THREE AND FOUR NOTE MINOR CHORD VOICINGS

Shown below are some useful three and four note voicings for minor chords followed by some examples which use them along with the major chord shapes you learnt in the previous lesson. Once again, learn them all from memory and then transpose them.

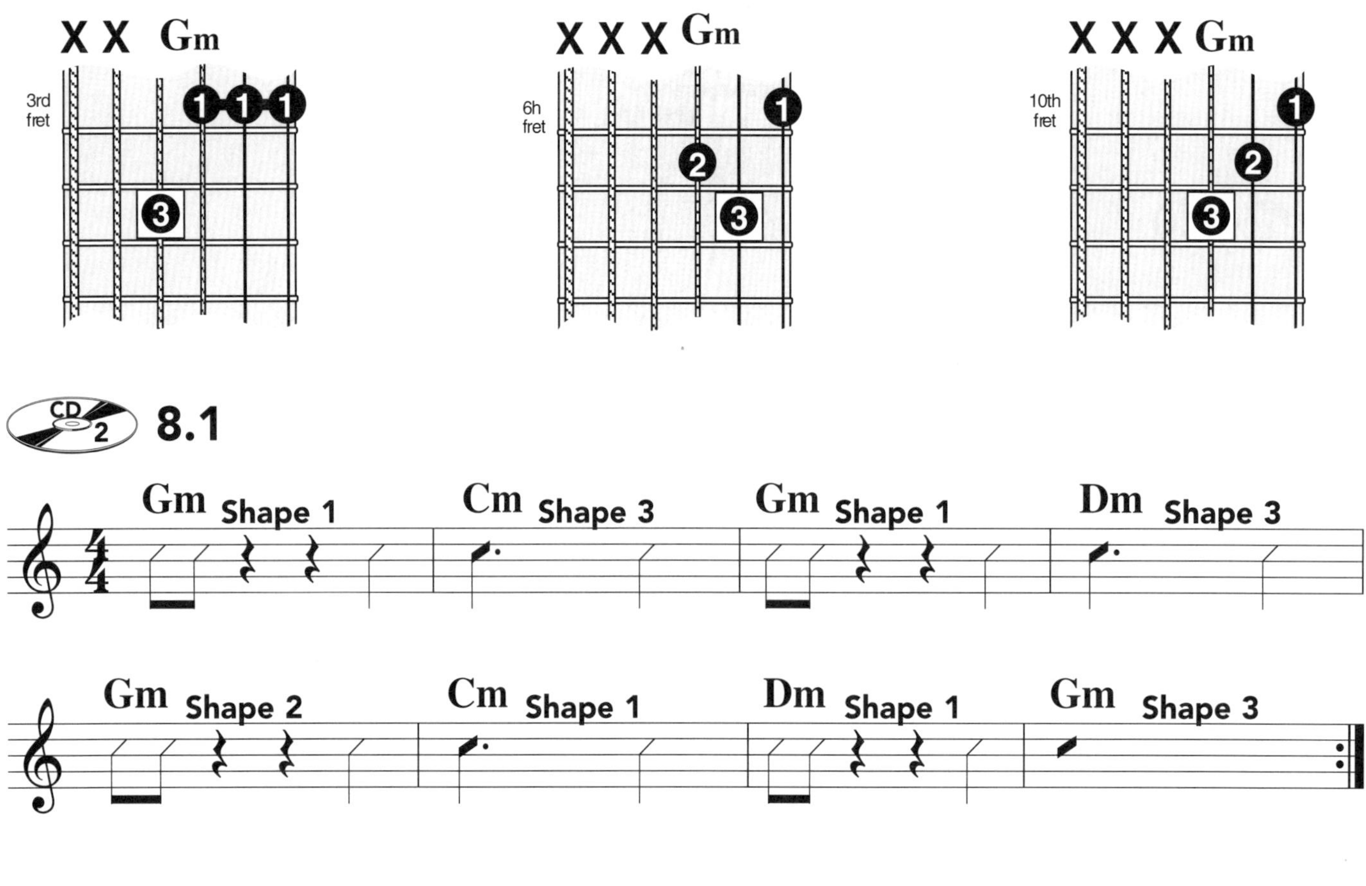

8.2

Hold all three fingers down as you play each group of notes in this example. This will help you to identify each shape and will let all the notes of each chord ring.

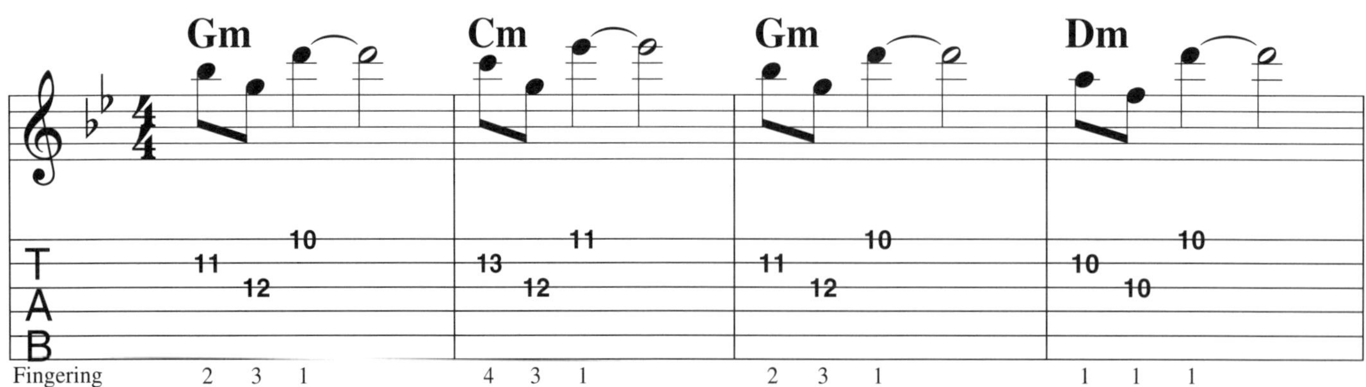

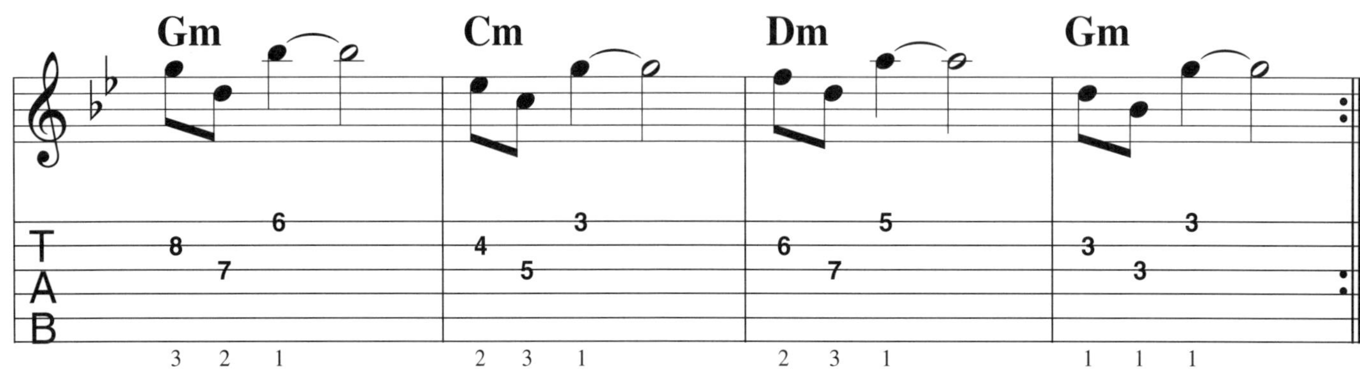

LESSON THIRTY THREE

THE TRIPLET

An eighth note **triplet** is a group of **three** evenly spaced notes played within one beat. Eighth note triplets are indicated by three eighth notes grouped together with the numeral **3** above or below them. Each part of the triplet is worth a third of a beat. Triplets are easy to understand once you have heard them played. Listen to example 9.0 on CD2 to hear the effect of triplets.

CD 2 **9.0**

STRUMMING TRIPLETS

There are several different ways of strumming triplets. Each of them is useful in particular musical situations. The most common way is to use **all downstrokes** of the pick. Try this method with the following example, which contains a **root 6 A7** chord and a **root 5 D7** chord, see lesson 35 .

CD 2 **9.1**

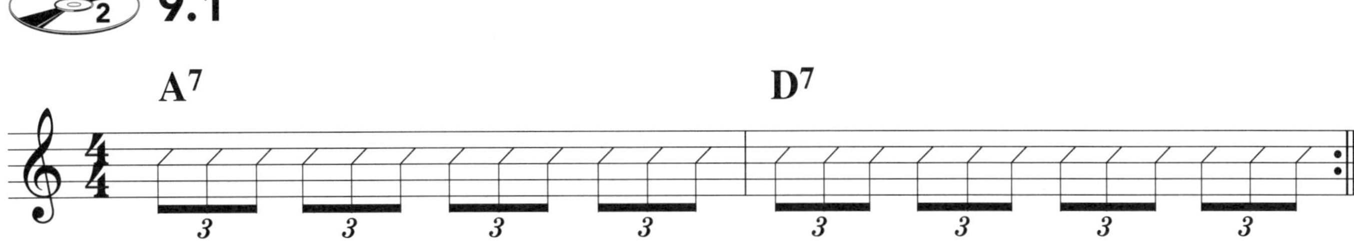

Once you can play this example evenly, try using **alternate strumming**. This means that beats **2** and **4** will begin with an upstroke. To be sure you keep the correct rhythm, count out loud as you play and tap your foot on each beat.

Another useful strumming technique for triplets is to use an upstroke on the middle part of the triplet only, making sure you **begin each new beat with a downstroke**. Once again, tap your foot on each beat and count out loud as you play.

UNDERSTANDING TRIPLET RHYTHMS

In a bar of triplets in $\frac{4}{4}$ time, there are **12** positions for notes within the bar. The first beat is **1**, the middle note of the first triplet is called the "**trip of one**" and the third note of the first triplet is called the "**let of one**". The system then continues through the bar - **2**, **trip of 2**, **let of 2**, etc. It is worth practicing playing notes or chords on each of these positions until you can do them at will. Here are some rhythm exercises using triplets. Count them carefully, as there could be either a note or a rest on any part of each triplet. Remember to practice strumming them all three ways described on the previous page.

CD 2 **10.0**

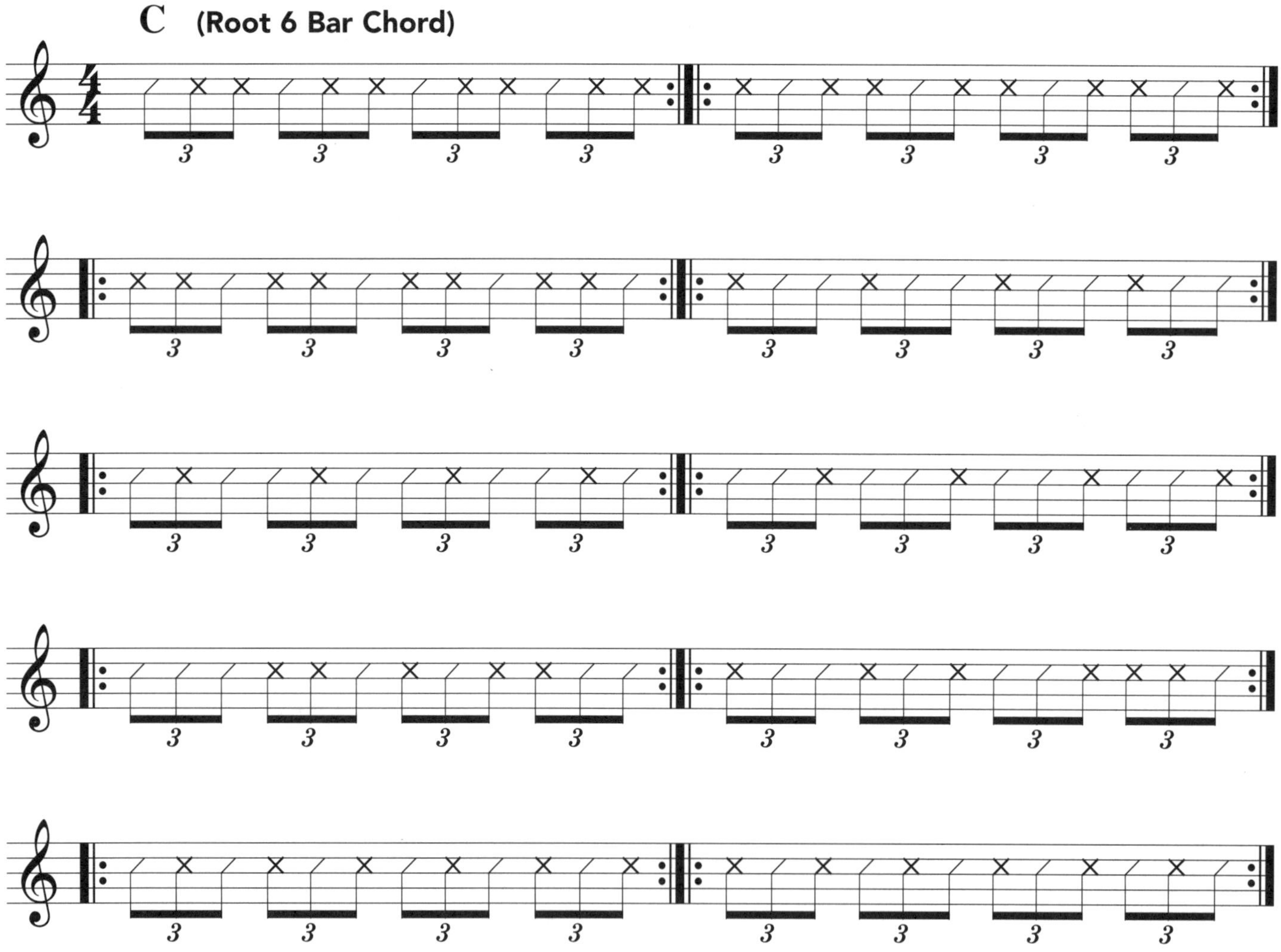

C (Root 6 Bar Chord)

CD 2 **10.1**

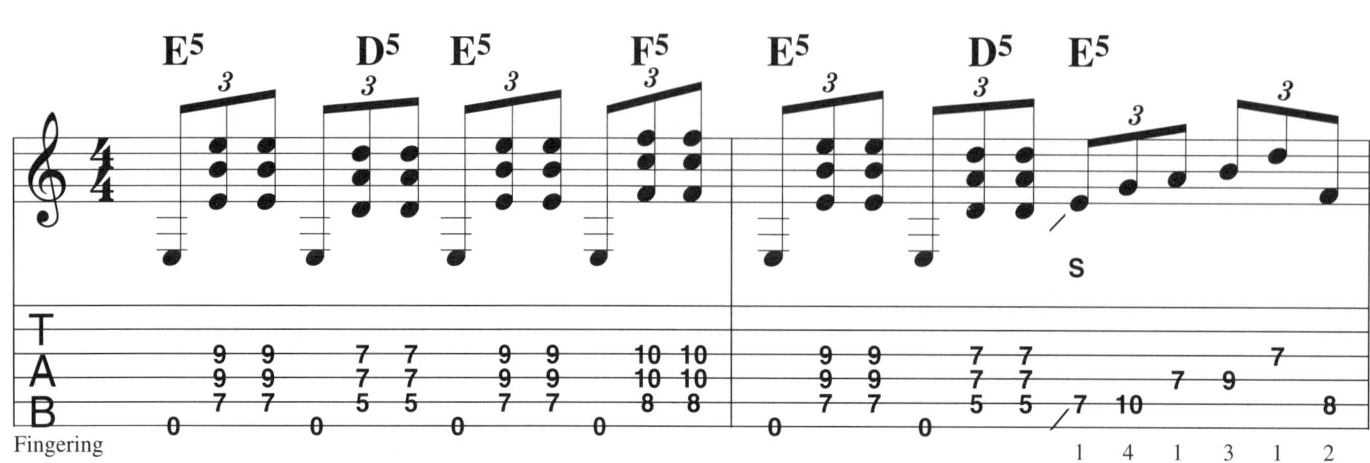

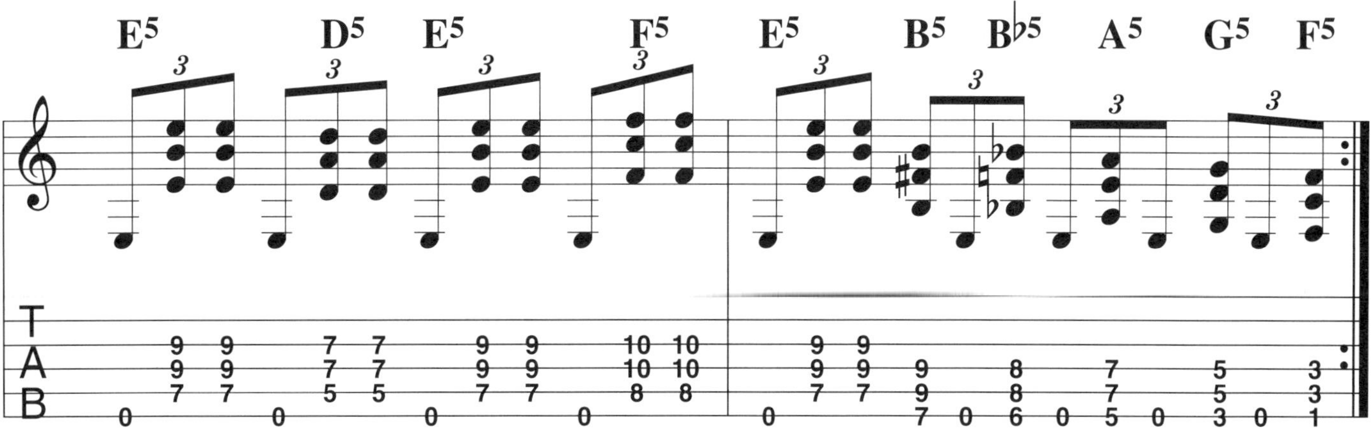

QUARTER NOTE TRIPLETS.

A **quarter note triplet** is three quarter notes played in the time of two. These may be difficult at first. Try working up to them by first using eighth note triplets, Then accent the parts of the beat where the quarter note triplets would fall and finally play the quarter note triplets on their own. Count only the beats in this example and try to feel where the notes fall.

11.0

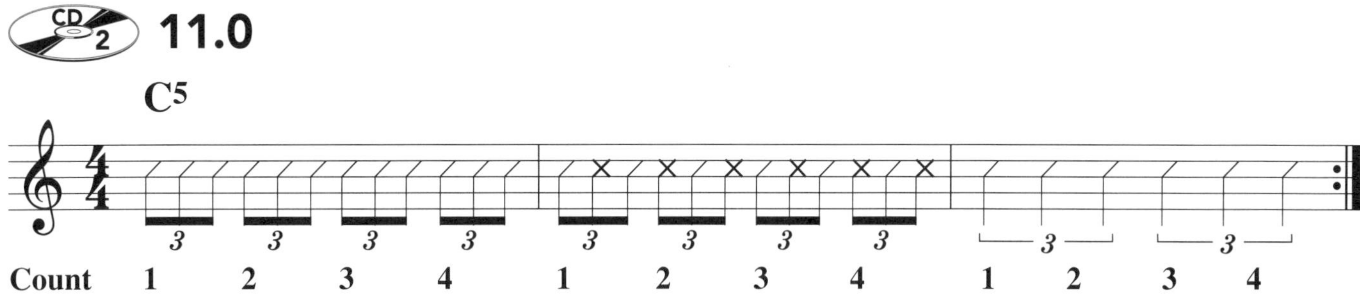

11.1

This example contains both eighth note triplets and quarter note triplets.

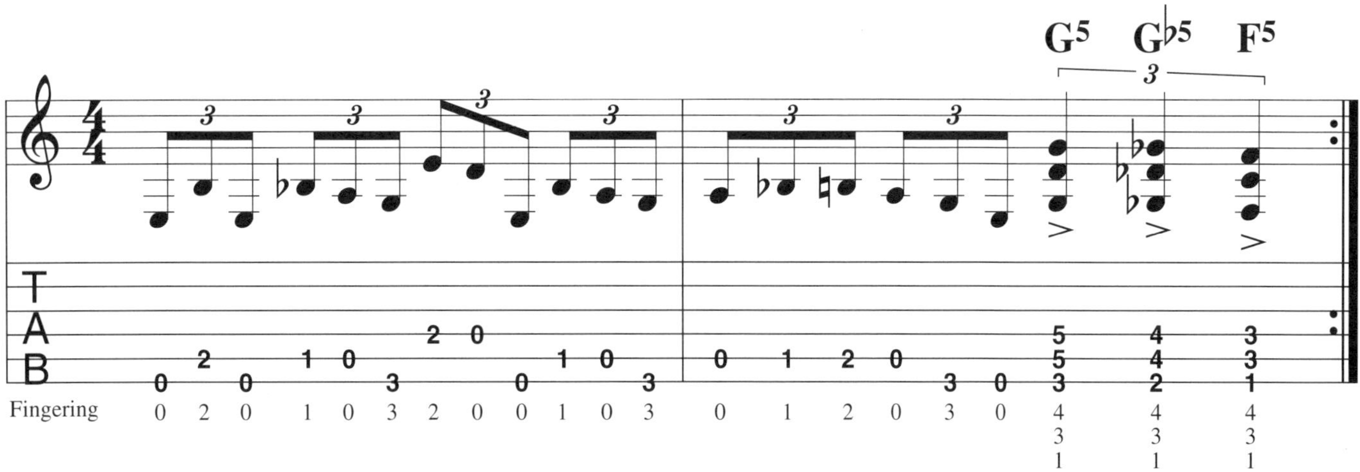

SWING RHYTHMS

A **swing rhythm** can be created by tying the first two notes of the triplet group together.

12.0

12.1

The two eighth note triplets tied together in the example above can be replaced by a quarter note.

To simplify notation, it is common to replace the with ,
and to write at the start of the piece = as illustrated below.

THE SHUFFLE

A **shuffle** is a constant stream of swung eighth notes. It is one of the most common rhythms in Blues and is also used in related styles such as Rock, Jazz, Funk, Gospel and Soul. All the examples on the previous page are shuffles. There is a particular way of playing a shuffle on the guitar which is instantly recognizable. It is played on two adjacent strings like a power chord. The third finger is placed two frets up the neck on the same string as the first finger. The same two strings are played as in the fifth chord. Keep the first finger down even when playing with the third finger. This will result in a smoother, more solid sound. It also helps to use right hand damping with this pattern.

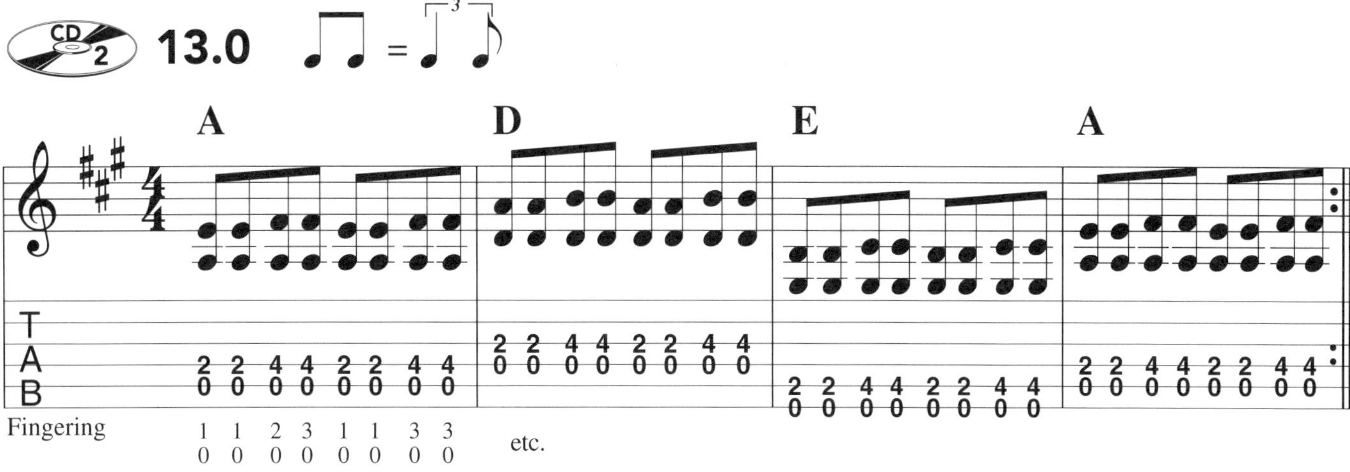

There are many different ways to play a shuffle. Here are some examples. The first one requires the use of the fourth finger at the fifth fret.

CD 2 **13.1**

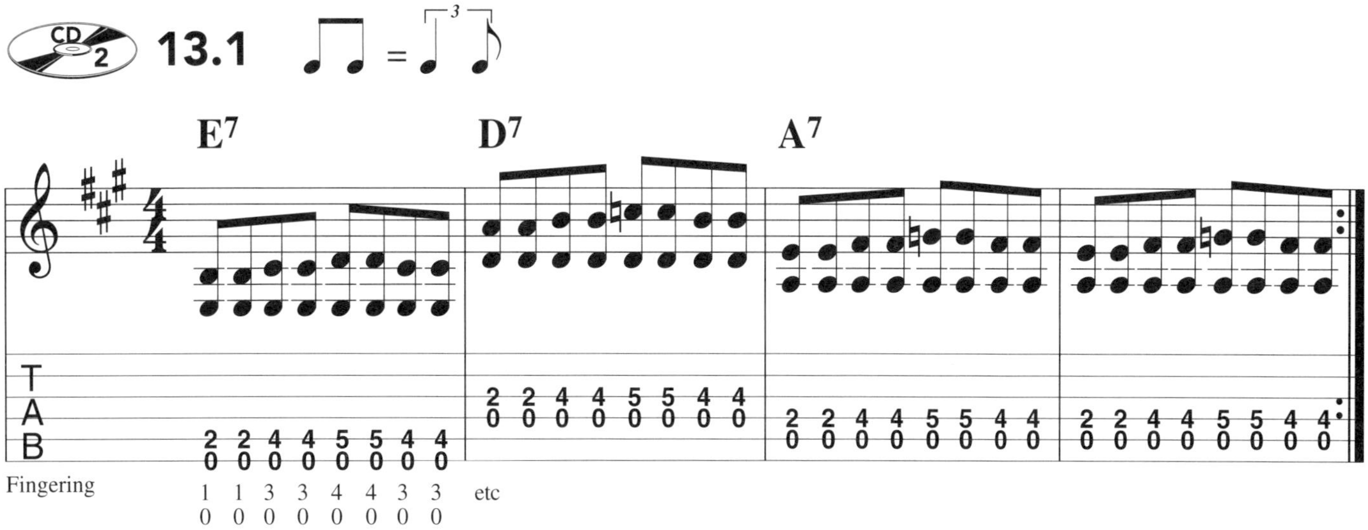

E7 D7 A7

T
A
B

2 2 4 4 5 5 4 4
0 0 0 0 0 0 0 0

Fingering 1 1 3 3 4 4 3 3 / 0 0 0 0 0 0 0 0 etc

CD 2 **13.2**

A7

T
A
B

Fingering 1 1 2 3 4 0 3 1 / 0 0 4 3 1 — 1 1 2 3 4 0 3 1 / 0 0 4 3 1

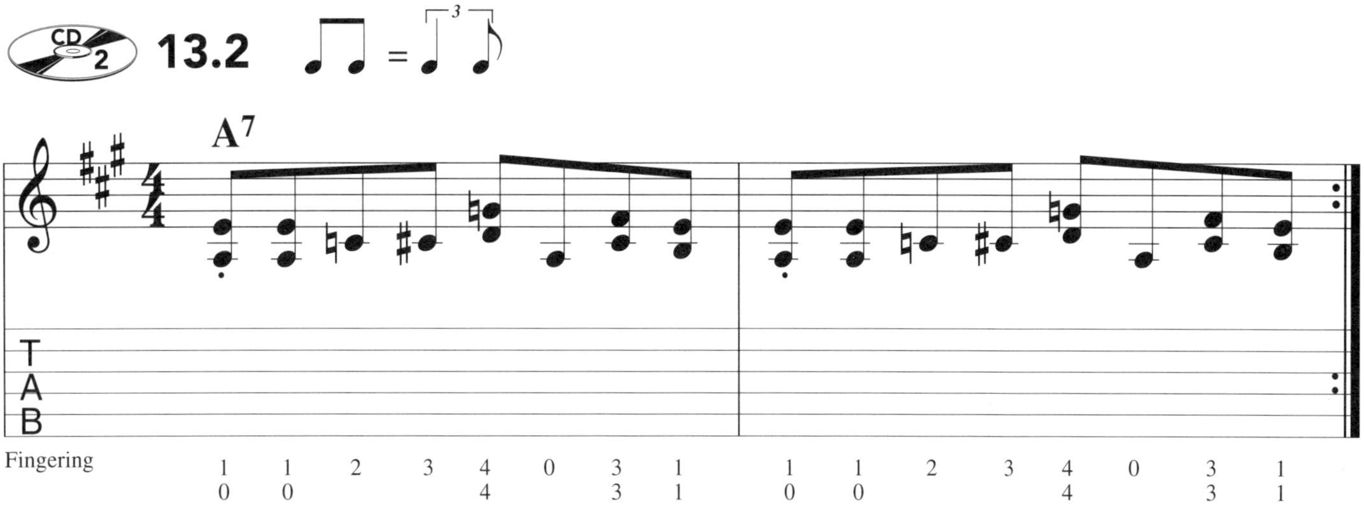

LESSON THIRTY FOUR

MORE ABOUT 12 BAR BLUES

In a basic 12 bar Blues, there are usually three different chords. Each of these relates to one basic **Key.** In Blues, the most common chords are those built on notes **1**, **4** and **5** of the major scale. So in the key of C, these chords would be **C**, **F** and **G**. In the Key of A they would be **A**, **D** and **E**. The example below demonstrates the 12 bar Blues progression played with a **moveable shuffle pattern** in the key of **A**. The first and third fingers remain on the strings, while the fourth finger stretches up two frets on the same string as the third finger. This example is played without right hand damping and uses alternating pick strokes. Listen to the different sound this produces.

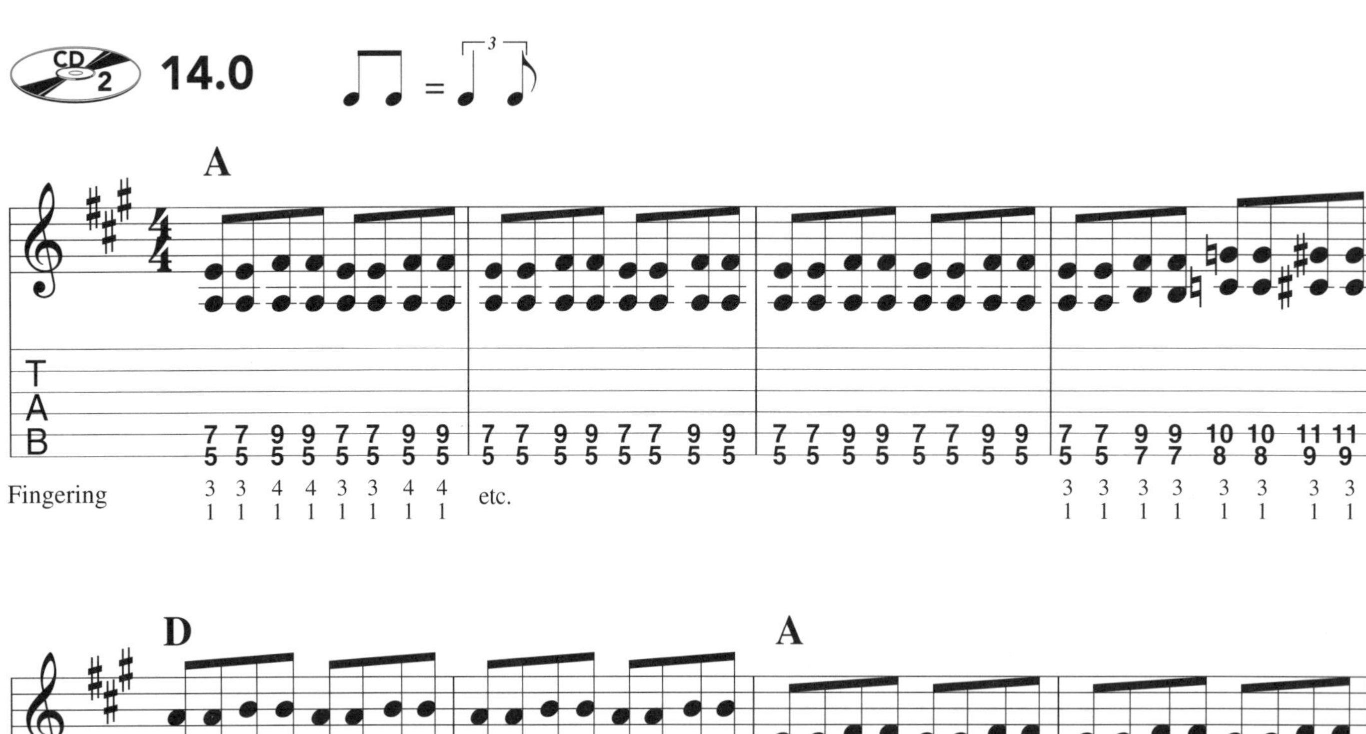

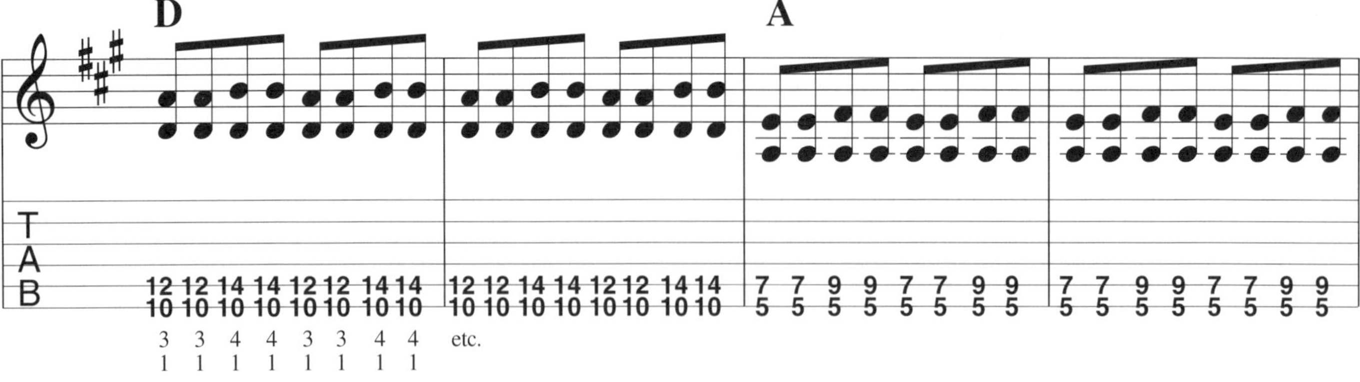

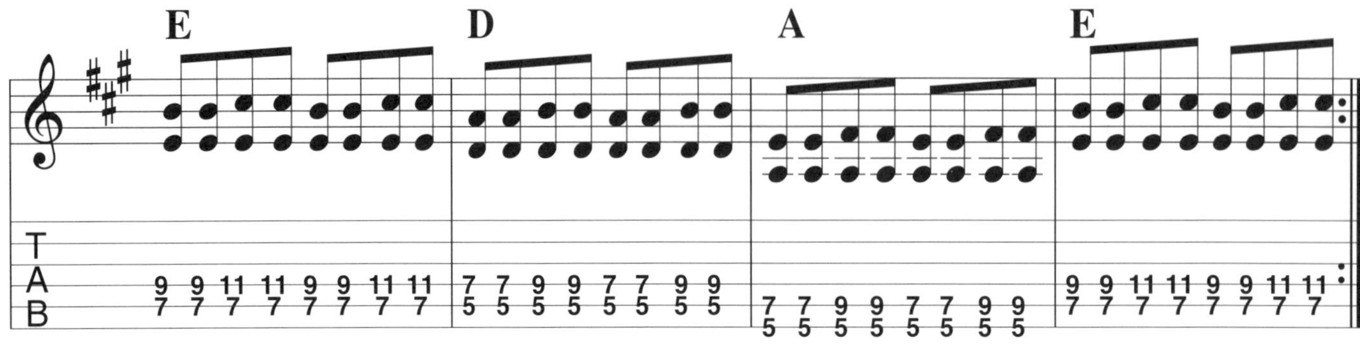

This shuffle pattern can be played in any key simply by moving its root note to the appropriate fret. The following example is in the key of **G** in the **3rd position** (3rd fret).

14.1

The 12 bar Blues progression can also be shown in Roman numerals I, IV and V instead of 1, 4 and 5. The ⁒ symbol is a bar repeat sign. It indicates that this bar is identical to the previous one.

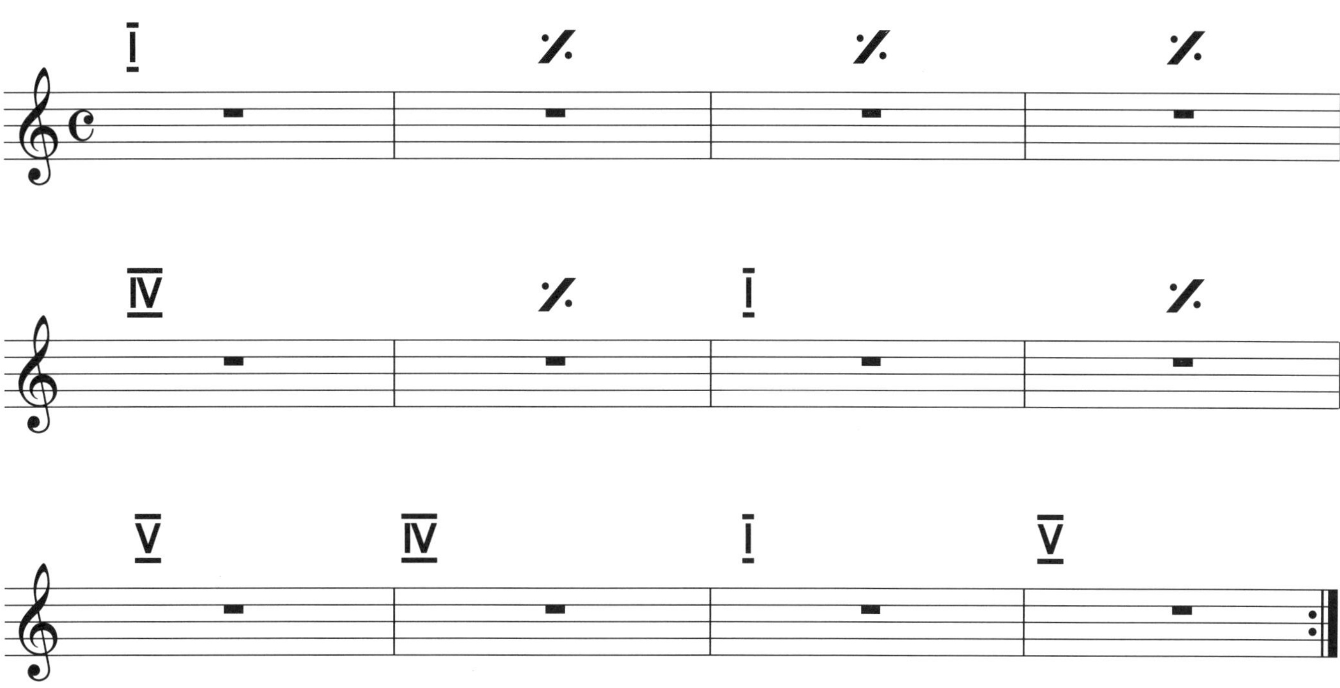

Chords I IV and V in all Keys

This table lists chords I, IV and V in all twelve keys used in music. By using this table, you can play a 12 bar Blues in any key.

KEY	I	IV	V	KEY	I	IV	V
C	C	F	G	F	F	B♭	C
G	G	C	D	B♭	B♭	E♭	F
D	D	G	A	E♭	E♭	A♭	B♭
A	A	D	E	A♭	A♭	D♭	E♭
E	E	A	B	D♭	D♭	G♭	A♭
B	B	E	F♯	G♭	G♭	C♭	D♭
F♯	F♯	B	C♯				

LESSON THIRTY FIVE

SEVENTH CHORDS

Another important chord type is the **Dominant 7th** chord, commonly called a **7th chord**. 7th chords are common in Blues, Rock, Funk, Jazz and many other styles of music. 7th chords can be derived from the major scale by adding the **flattened 7th** degree (note) of the scale to a major chord.

C Major Scale

C	D	E	F	G	A	B	C
1	2	3	4	5	6	7	8

C Chord

C	E	G
1	3	5

C7 Chord

C	E	G	B♭
1	3	5	♭7

Here is a common fingering for a **C7** chord. Practice changing between **F**, **B♭** and **C7** as shown in the following example.

15.0

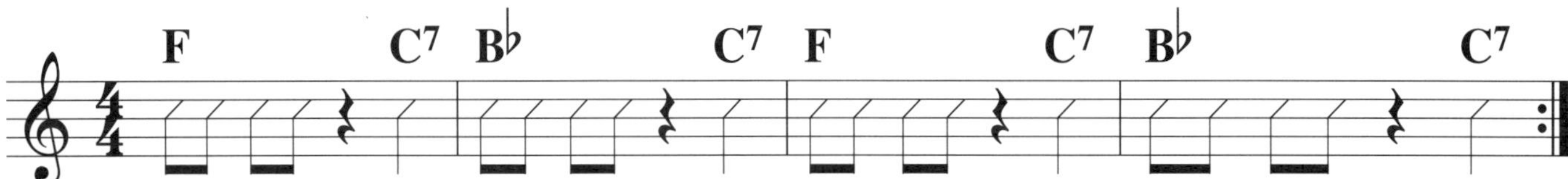

Like major chords, most moveable 7th chord shapes also follow the **five basic open chord forms**, i.e. **C7**, **A7**, **G7**, **E7** and **D7**. Here are the most common shapes for these chords.

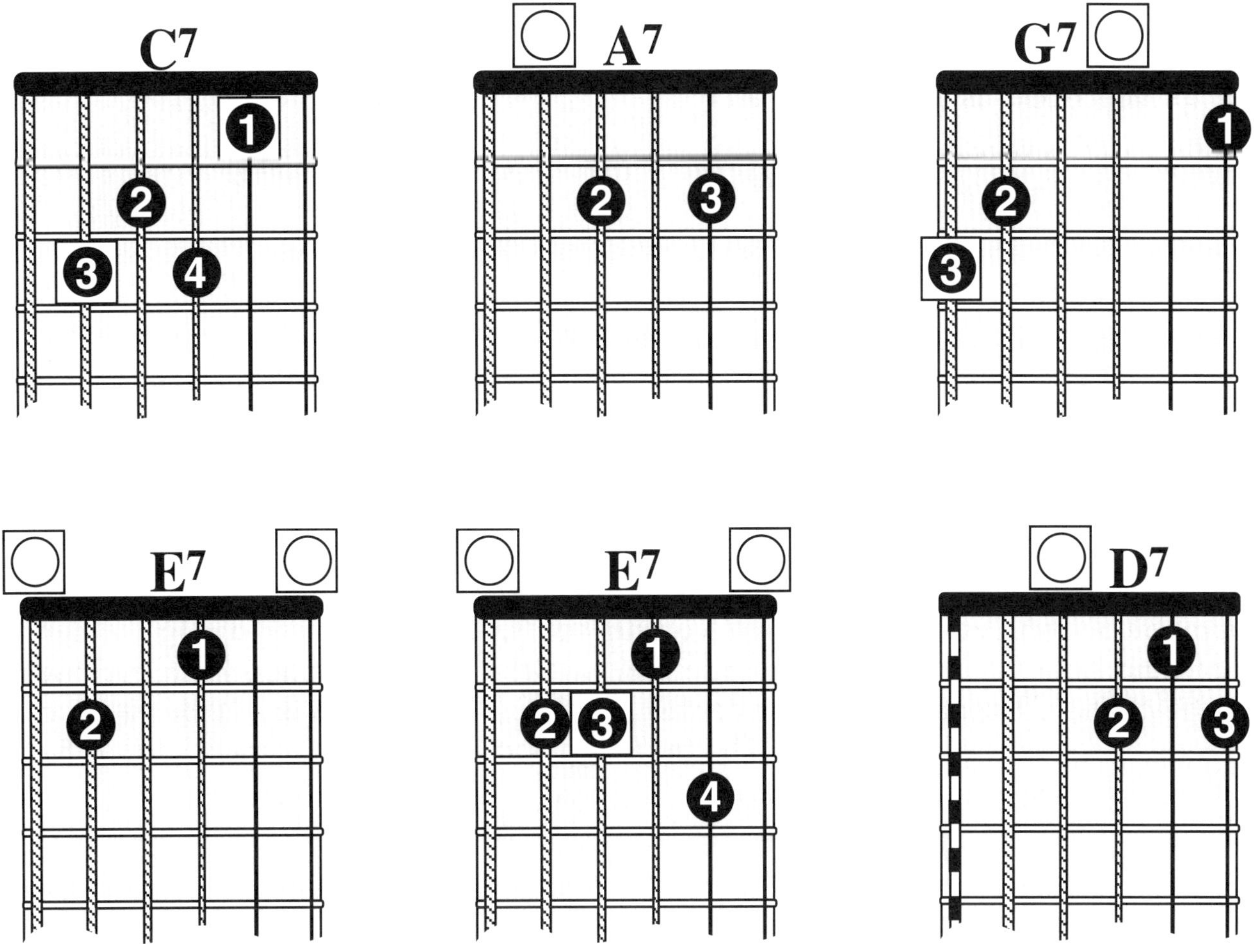

Notice that there are two shapes here for the **E7** chord. It is also possible to find alternative fingerings for the other chords. Once you know which notes make up a particular chord, it is possible to arrange these notes in any order as long as the fingering is practical. The following example should help you become familiar with these basic 7th chord shapes.

CD 2 **15.1**

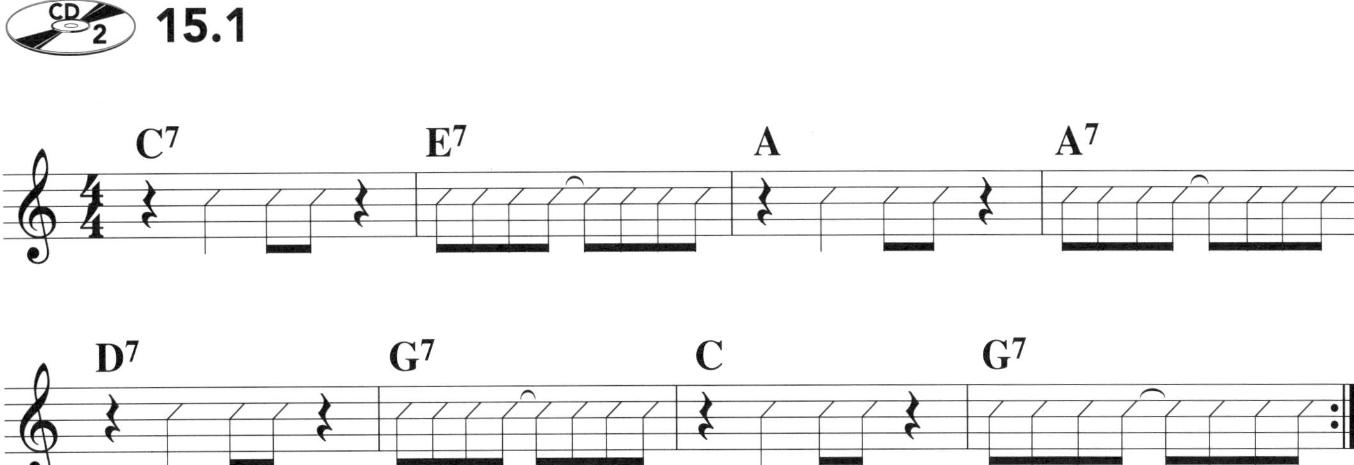

MOVEABLE 7TH CHORD FORMS

Most moveable 7th chord shapes also follow the five basic forms found in chords containing open strings, i.e. **C7**, **A7**, **G7**, **E7** and **D7**. The first position **C7** chord shown below can be described as a **C7 form**. If you damp out the 1st and 6th strings, this form becomes moveable, e.g. if you move it to the **6th fret**, it becomes an **F7** chord which would be described as a **C form** of an **F7**.

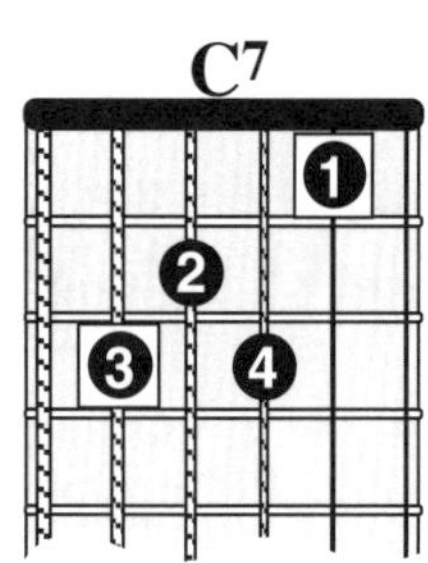

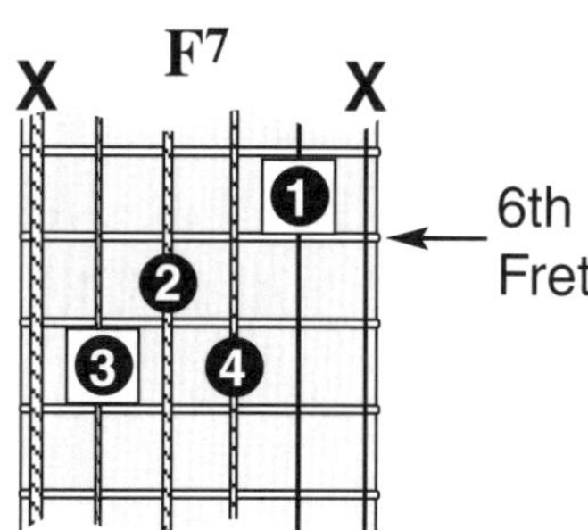

VOICINGS

As with all chords, there is more than one fingering on the guitar for a C7 chord. The diagram below shows an alternative voicing for C7. The term "**voicing**" means the arrangement of notes in a particular fingering, with the notes arranged from the lowest to the highest. The C7 chord will always contain C (1), E (3), G (5) and B♭ (♭7), but it is possible to arrange these notes in any order. The fingering shown below is voiced 3, ♭7, 1, 5.

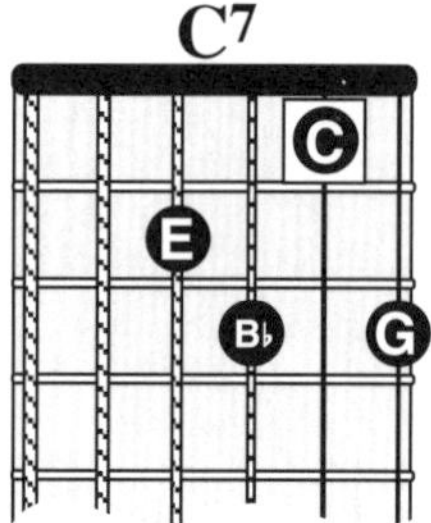

Like the previous C7 shape, this chord is also moveable. The **root note** (**C**) in this voicing is on the **2nd string**, so when moving the chord along the fretboard, whichever note is under your first finger will be the name of the chord. The following example moves between the chords **C7**, **F7** and **G7**.

16.

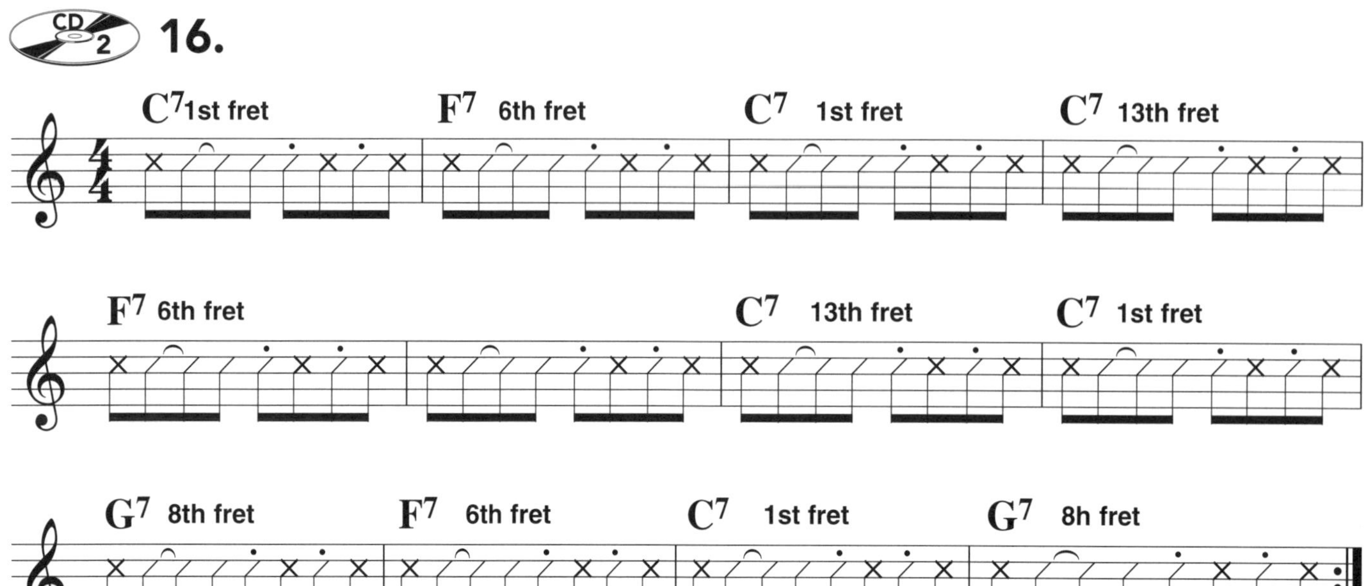

Below are six new moveable 7th chord shapes to go with the two C7 shapes you have already learnt. All these shapes are used in many styles, so be sure to memorize them well.

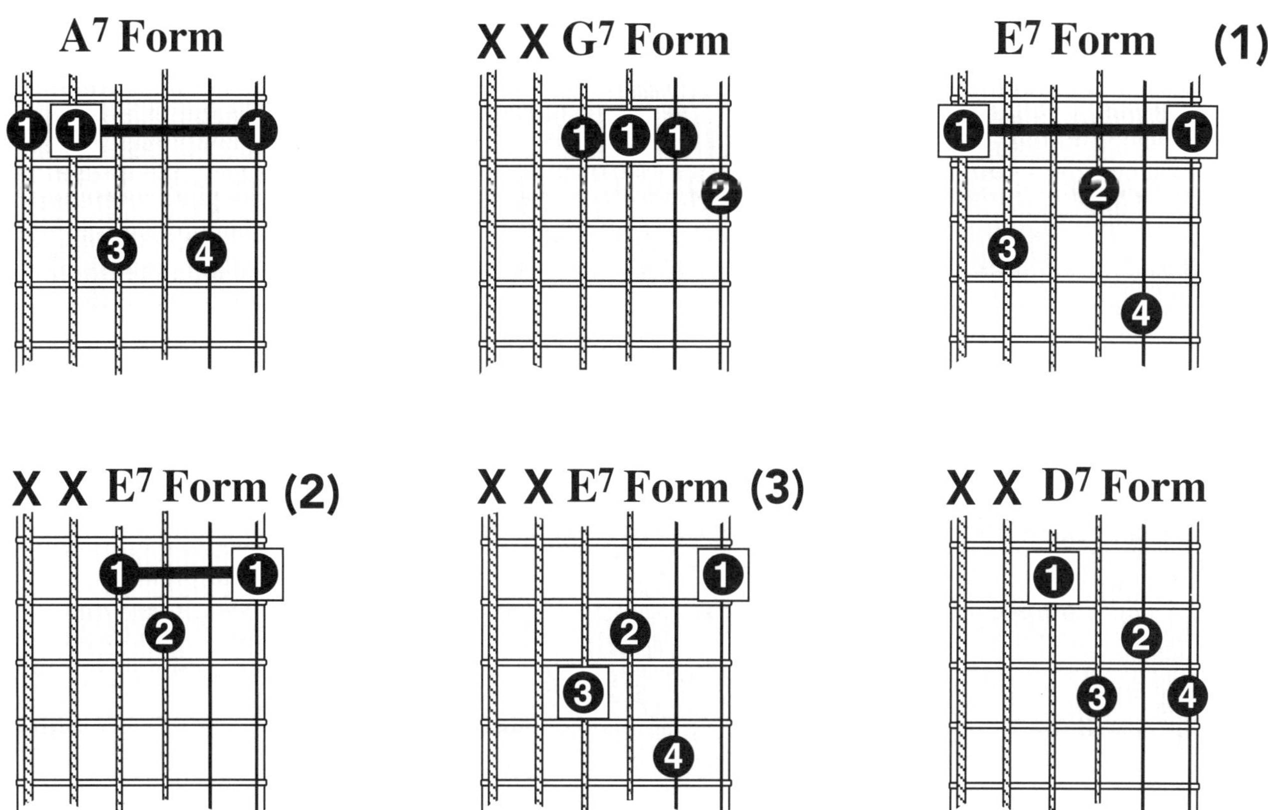

Notice that there are three shapes here for the **E7** chord. It is also possible to find alternative fingerings for the other chords shown here. Once you know which notes make up a particular chord, it is possible to arrange the notes in any order as long as the fingering is practical.

Here are some exercises to help you get comfortable with these 7th chord shapes. The first one uses the **A7 form** moved to a different position on the fretboard for each chord. The **root note** on the **5th string** will tell you which fret to move to for each chord.

17.0

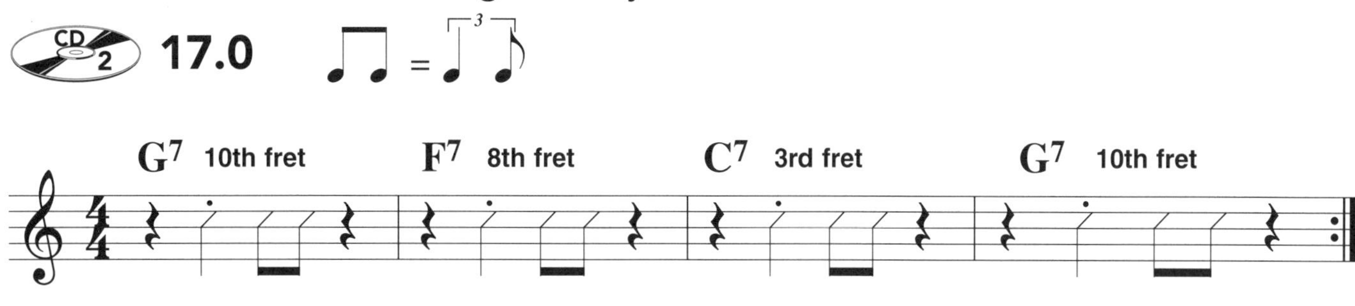

17.1

This one uses a **G7 form** moved between the same chords as the previous example. This time the **root note** is on the **3rd string**.

17.2

This example uses all three variations of the **E7 form**. The **root note** is on the **1st string**.

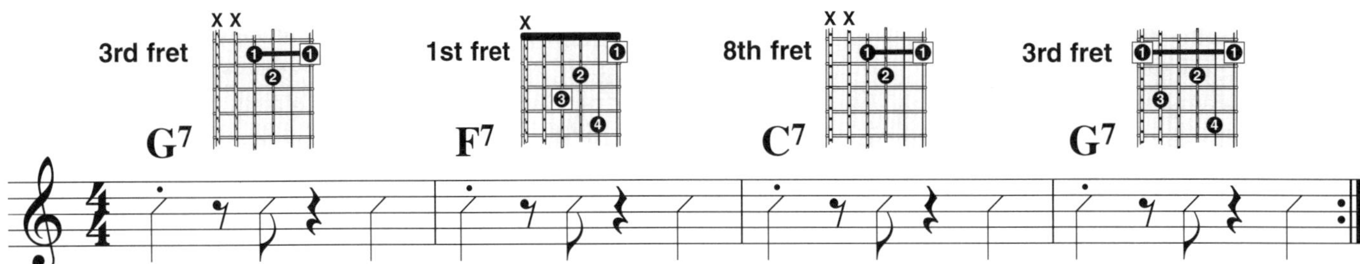

17.3

To complete the five forms, here is one which uses the **D7 form**. The **root note** is on the **4th string**. Take care with the change of rhythm in the final bar.

18.

After learning each of the 7th chord forms, try joining them all up in the one key. This example uses all the moveable 7th chord shapes you have learnt so far. Each of the shapes is played here as a C7 chord.

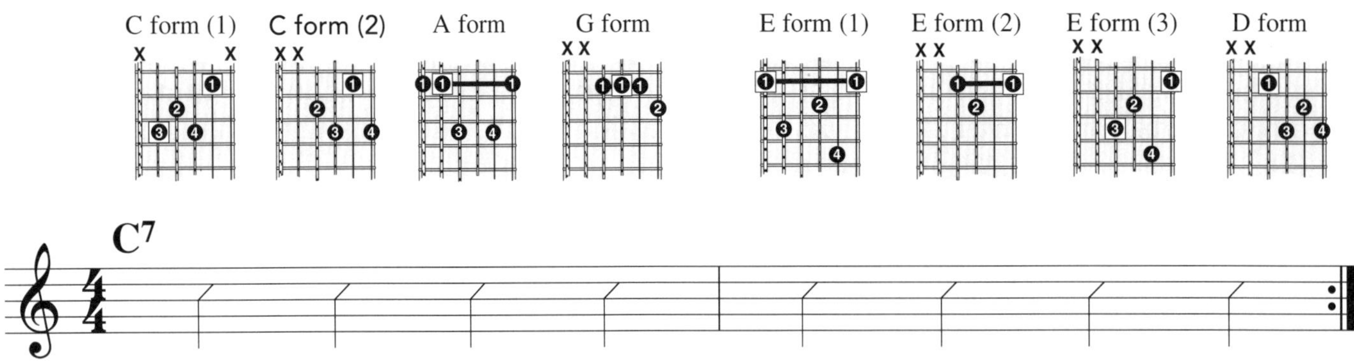

19.

Don't forget to experiment with playing 7th chords as arpeggios, as shown here.

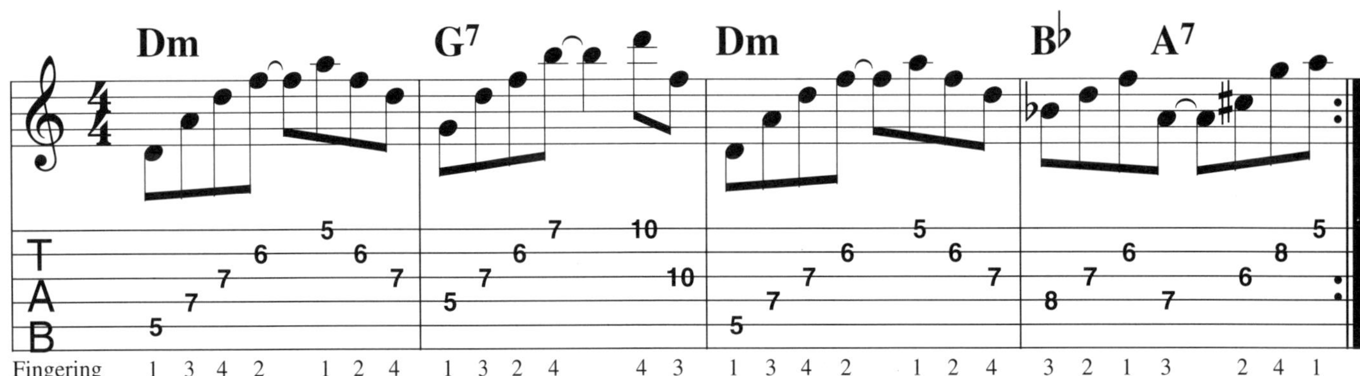

SUPERIMPOSING CHORD FORMS

Once you are comfortable using all these 7th chord shapes, it is a good idea to memorize which forms can be found in the same area of the fretboard as chords I, IV and V in any particular key. E.g if chord I is a **C form** then chord IV can be found as an **E form** at the same fret and chord V can be found as a **G form** one fret down. A good way to learn these patterns is to visualize the forms superimposed on the fretboard. The following example demonstrates these forms in the key of G beginning with a **C form** of a **G7** chord at the **8th fret**.

20.0

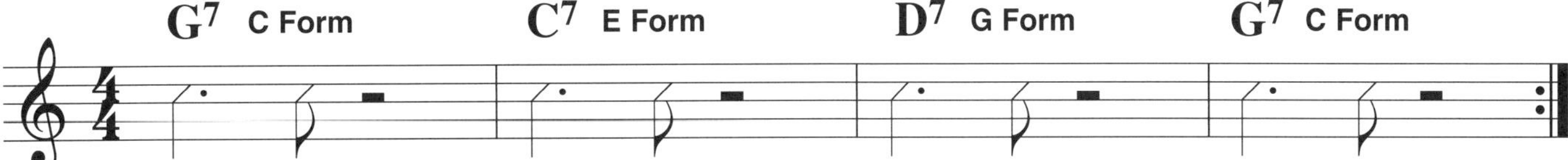

On the right is a summary of chords in positions which are close together on the fretboard. Memorize this summary and then experiment with the chords in all keys. This pattern applies regardless of whether the chord type is major, minor or dominant 7th. The example below uses the pattern in the key of **G minor** beginning with chord I as an **E form** 4 note voicing.

I	IV	V
C Form	E Form	G Form
A Form	D Form	E Form
G Form	C Form	D Form
E Form	A Form	C Form
D Form	G Form	A Form

20.1

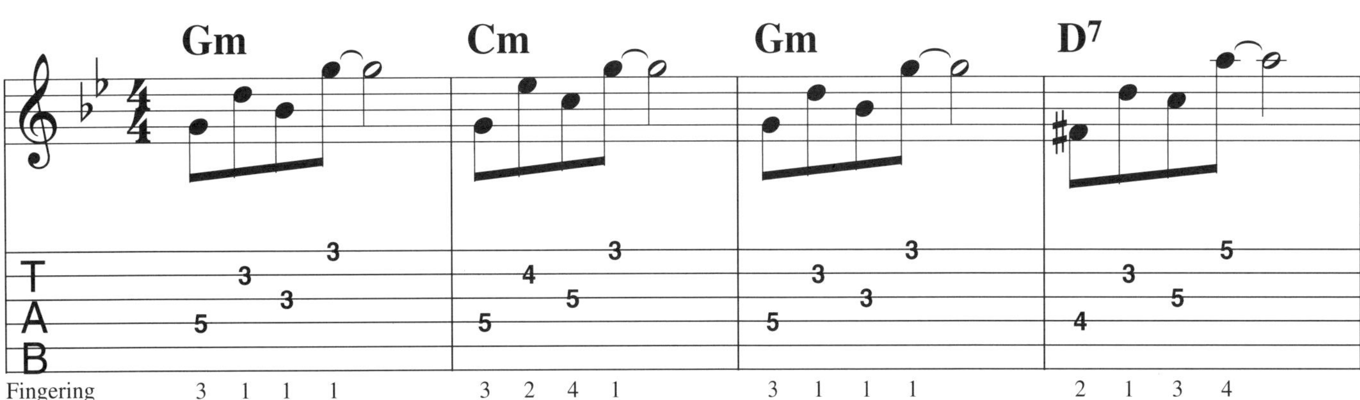

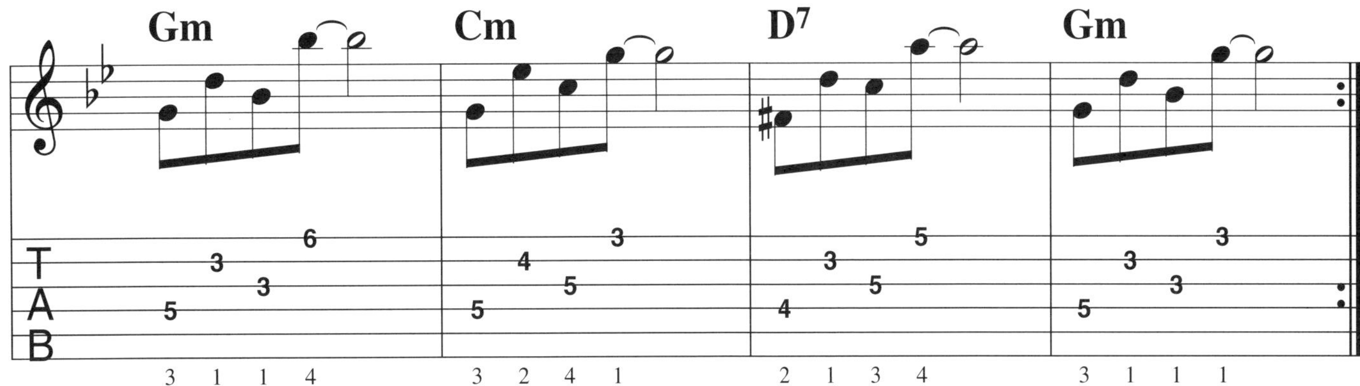

To end this section, here is a 12 bar Blues progression which combines two string shuffle playing with the 7th chord shapes you have learnt. This style of rhythm playing sounds great when you are backing a singer or harmonica player.

CD 2 21. Sonny Boy Blues

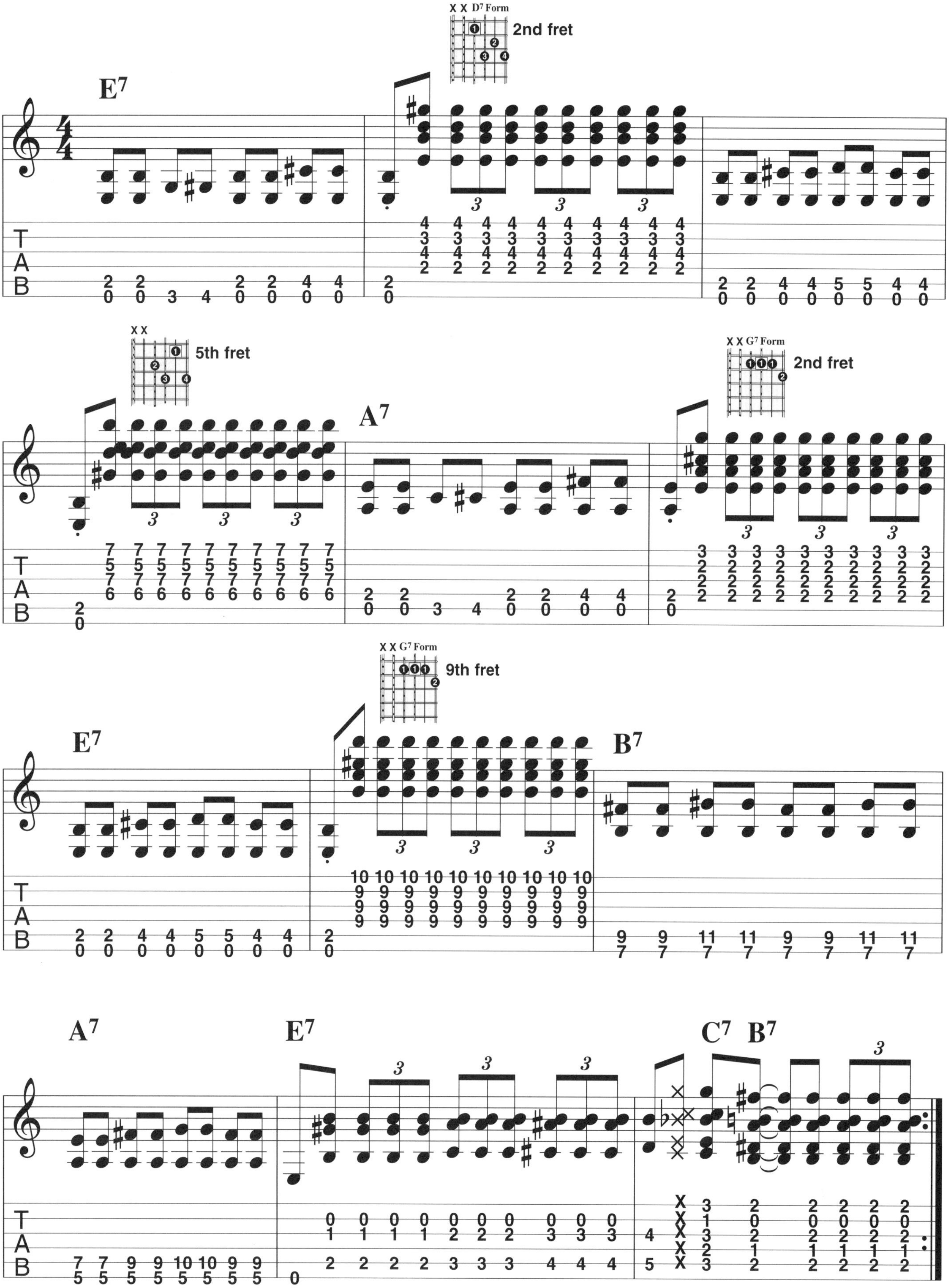

E7

D7 Form 2nd fret

5th fret

A7

G7 Form 2nd fret

E7

G7 Form 9th fret

B7

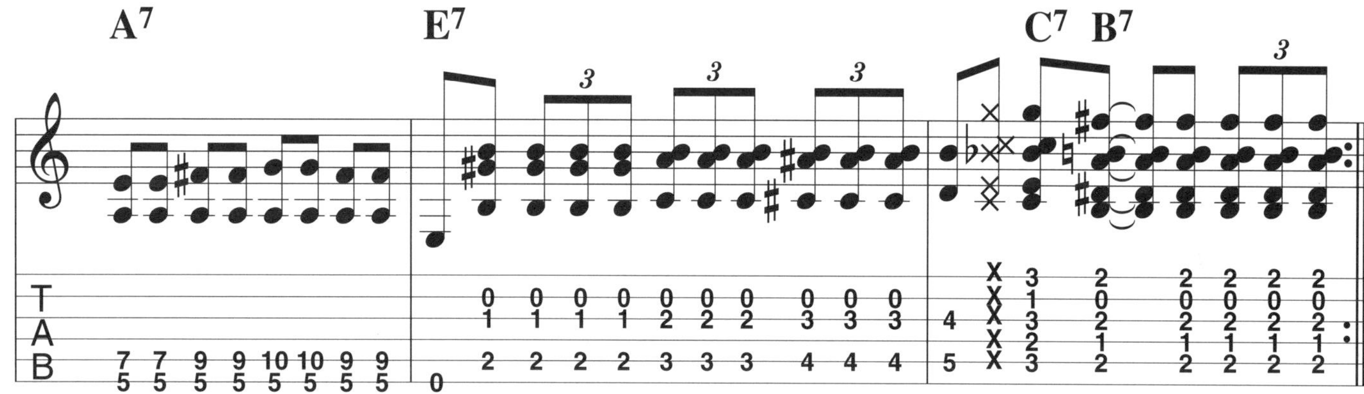

SECTION 3

More About Riffs, Extended Chords, Advanced Rhythm Playing

LESSON THIRTY SIX

CREATING RIFFS FROM SCALES

In lesson 28 you learnt about **riffs** (repeating rhythmic patterns of notes applied to chord progressions). Most riffs are created either from a scale or a combination of scales and arpeggios. The most common scale for creating riffs is the **minor pentatonic** scale. Pentatonic means five notes. In the **A minor pentatonic** scale these notes would be **A C D E** and **G.**

A Minor Pentatonic Scale

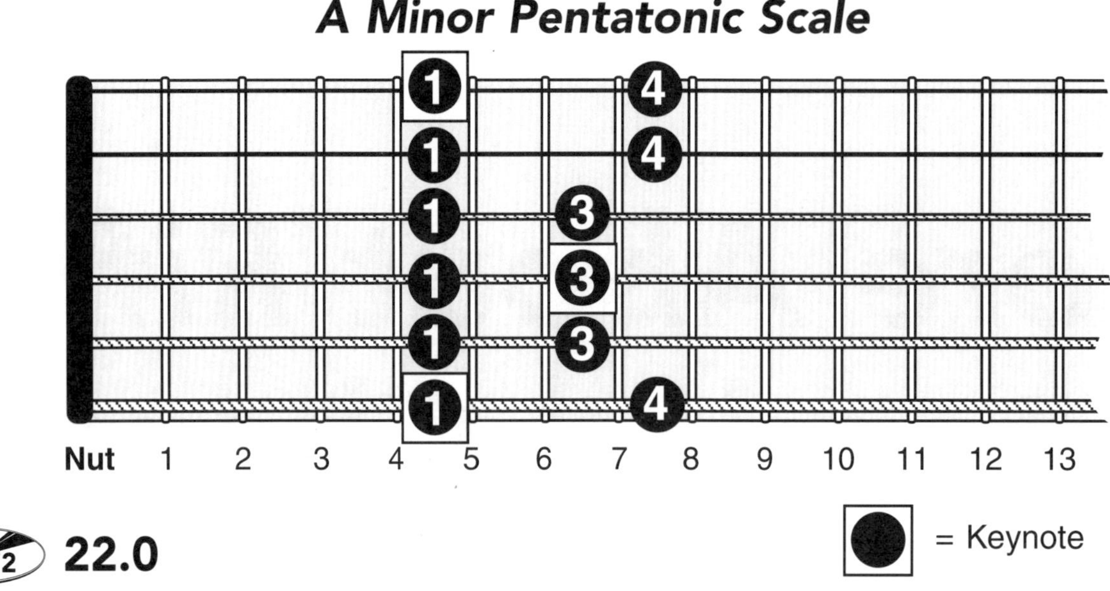

22.0

Play the scale ascending and descending as shown here. Try to get a smooth, even sound.

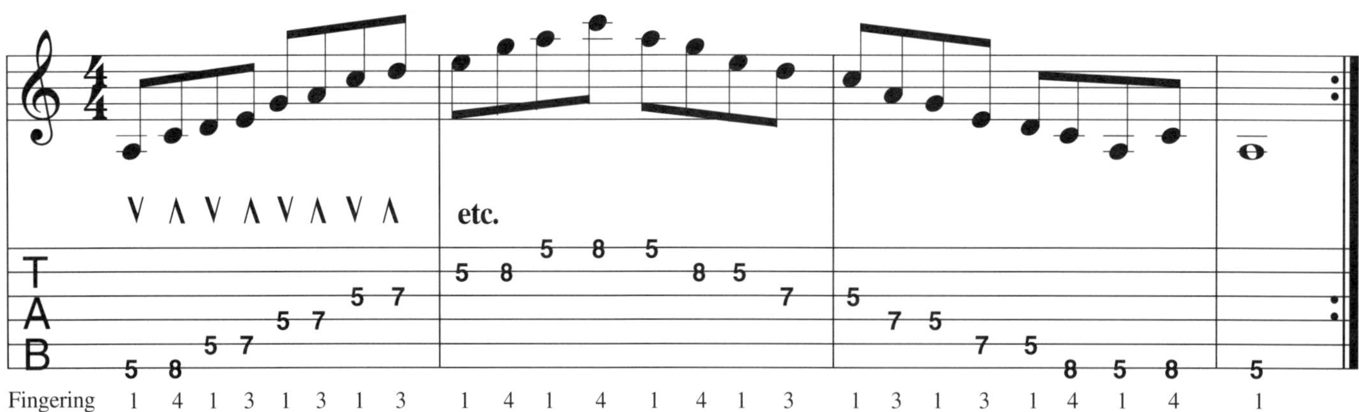

22.1

To help develop your picking it is a good idea to practice playing each note twice.

Here are some riffs derived from the A minor pentatonic scale. Memorize them and then try making up some of your own. The better you know the sound of the scale and the fingering, the easier this will be.

23.0

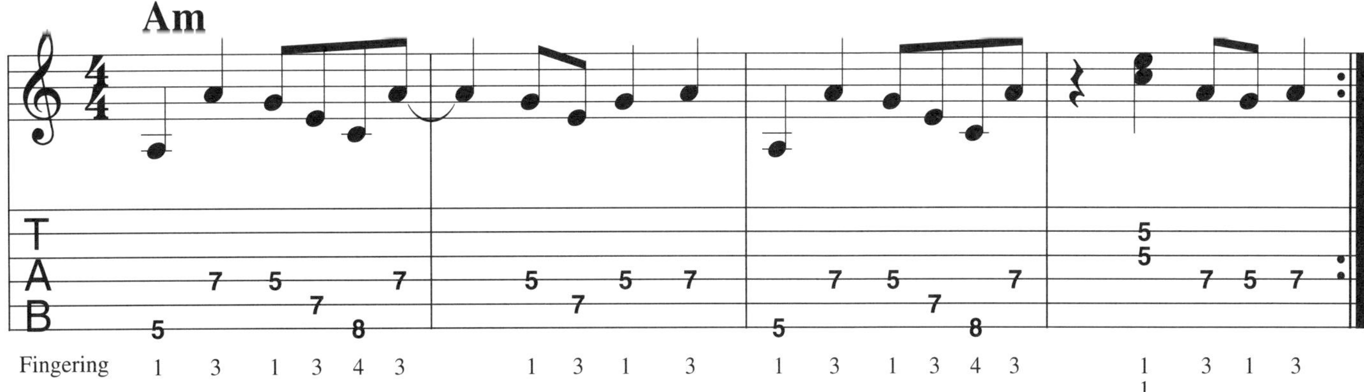

23.1

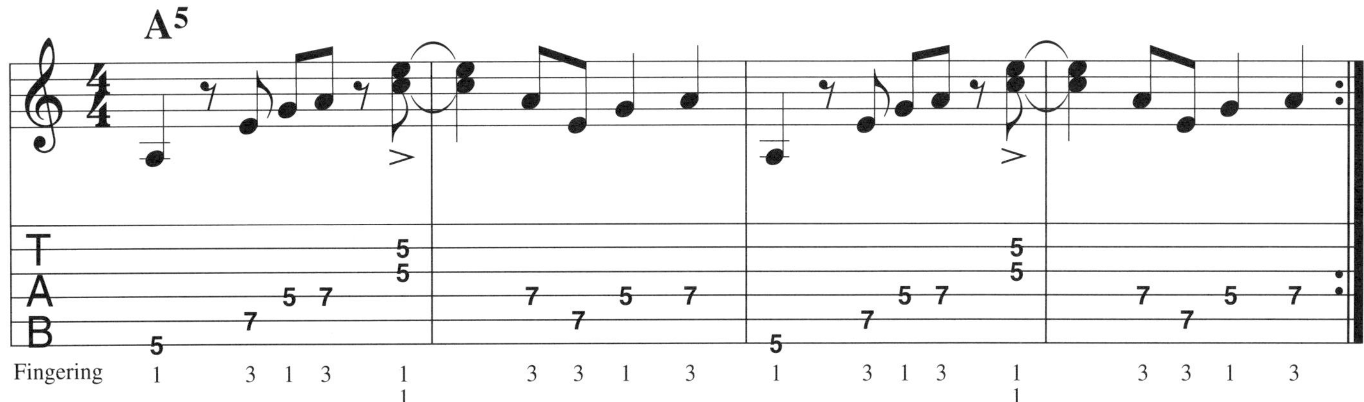

23.2

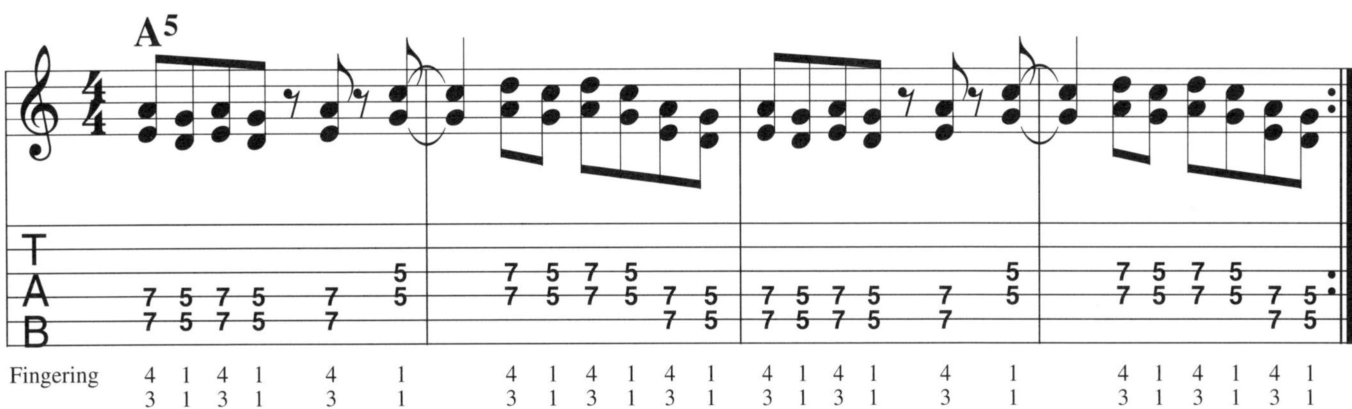

24. Chicago Shuffle 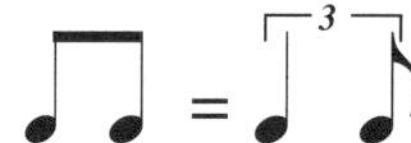

This 12 bar Blues shuffle riff in the key of **A** is also derived from the minor pentatonic scale. In the final bar, there is an extra note which comes from the Blues scale, which is discussed in later lessons. Notice the fingering in the second bar of this example. The second note of beat 3 and the first note of the triplet on beat 4 are both played with the 3rd finger. The first note is played with the tip of the finger and the finger is then flattened across towards the D string, so the second note can be played. This is a common technique, so it is worth spending some time practicing it.

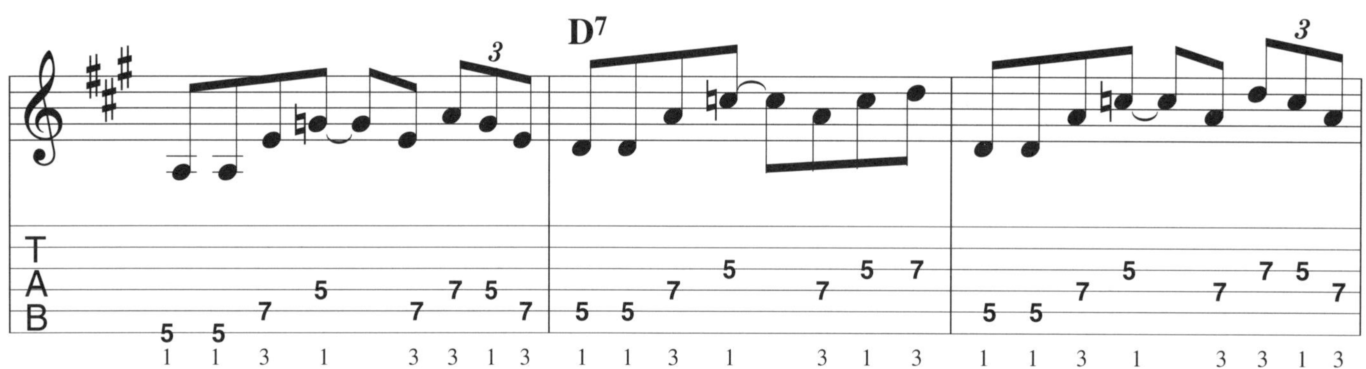

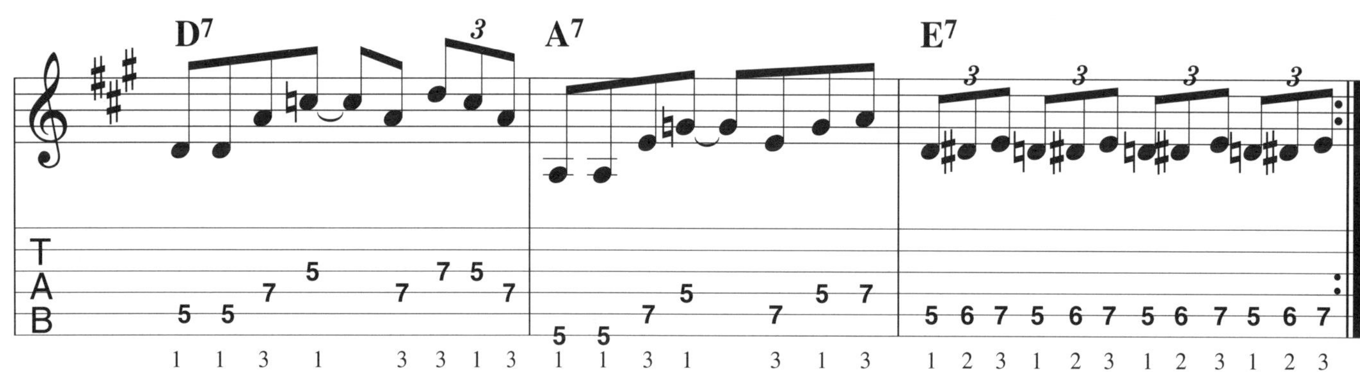

LESSON THIRTY SEVEN

OPEN POSITION MINOR PENTATONIC SCALE

It is always possible to play a scale or chord in more than one position on the fretboard. Here is the fingering for the **A minor pentatonic** scale in the open position. You already know all these notes, so it should be easy to memorize.

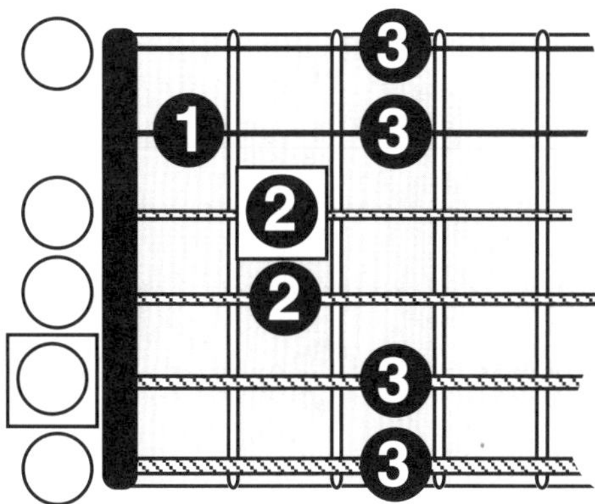

The following examples are derived from this scale. Notice that the notes are the same as those contained in the A minor pentatonic scale in the 5th position. Playing in the open position also gives you access to the low **E** and **G** notes on the **6th string**.

25.0

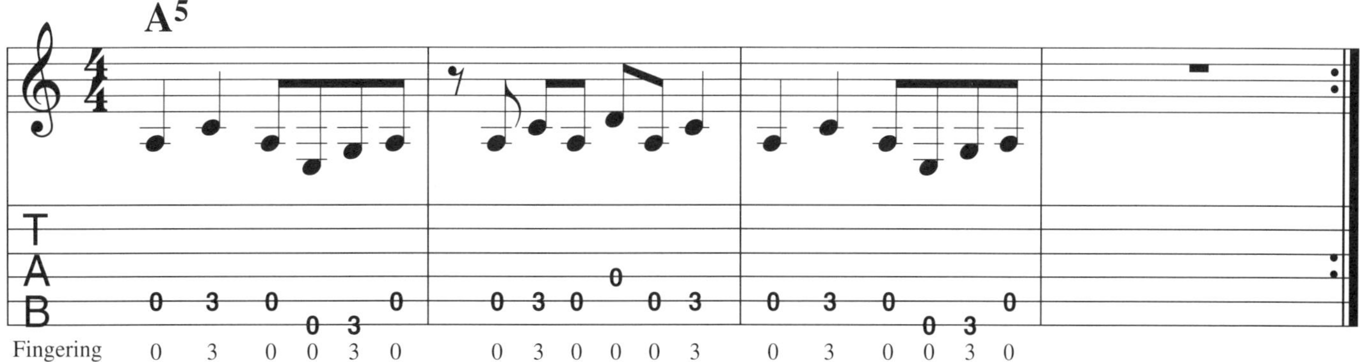

25.1

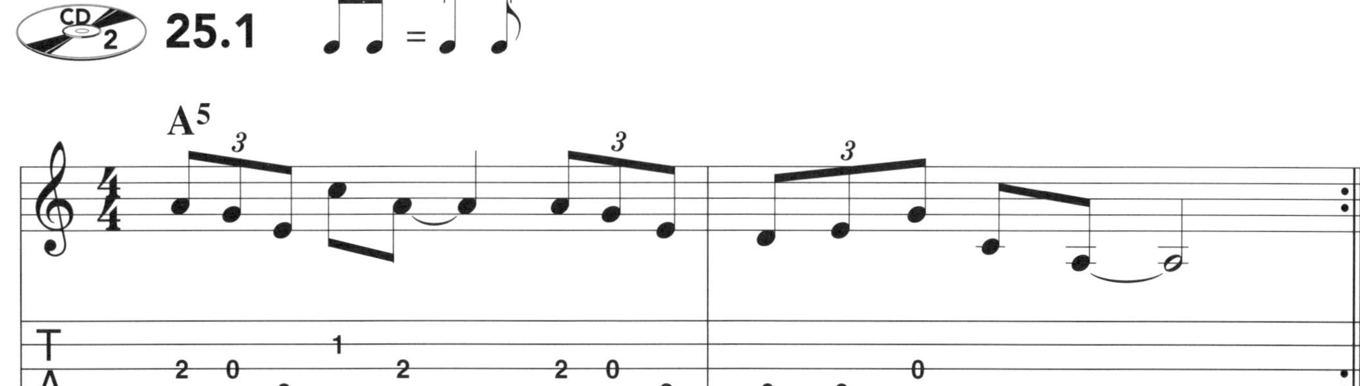

E MINOR PENTATONIC SCALE

The minor pentatonic scale can be played in any key. Shown below is the open position fingering for the **E minor pentatonic**. Notice that this is the same as the A minor pentatonic from the 5th fret, moved down so that the nut replaces the first finger. This results in open string notes being used on all six strings.

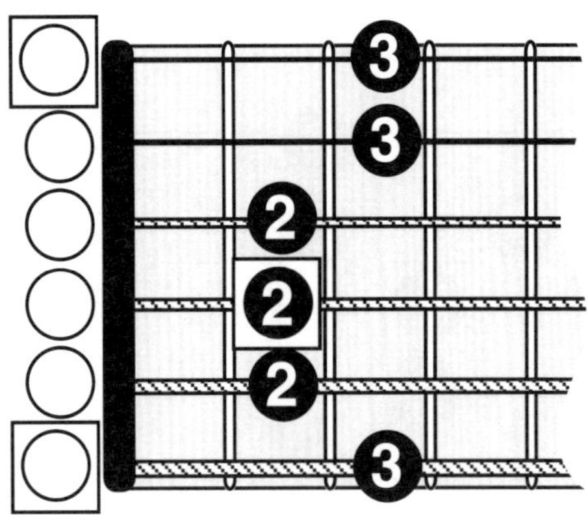

Here are some riffs derived from the E minor pentatonic scale. Learn them from memory and then use the ideas to invent some of your own licks. Good players often improvise riffs when they are playing live, so the more practice you have at this, the better.

 **26.0**

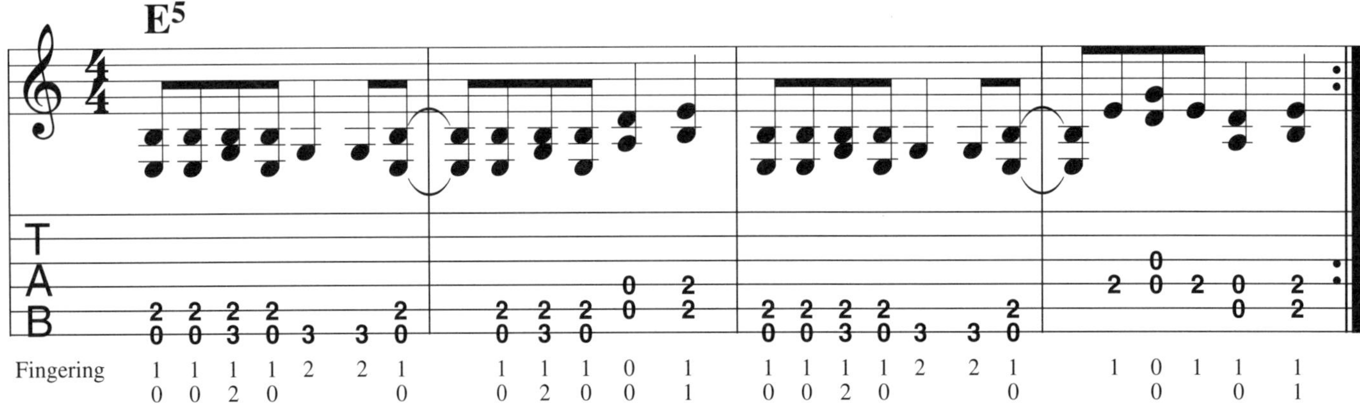

26.1

LESSON THIRTY EIGHT

THE BLUES SCALE

As shown in **Chicago Shuffle**, which you learned in lesson 36, it is possible to add extra notes to the minor pentatonic scale. The most common addition is the flattened 5th degree. Once this note is added, it becomes what is known as the **Blues Scale**.

A minor pentatonic	A	C	D	E	G	
	1	♭3	4	5	♭7	
A Blues scale	A	C	D	E♭	E	G
	1	♭3	4	♭5	5	♭7

Here is a common moveable fingering of the Blues scale in the key of A.

A BLUES SCALE

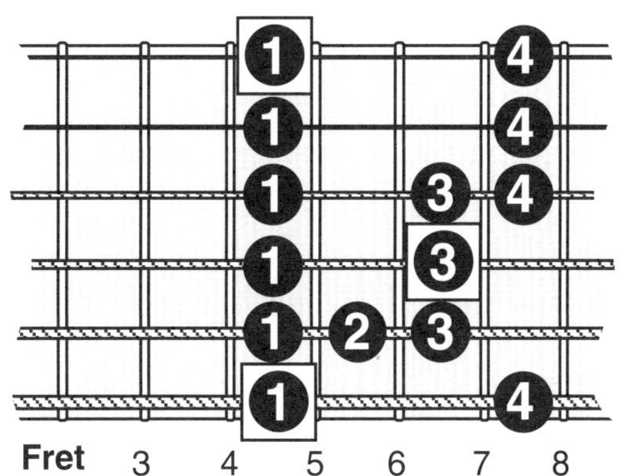

27.

Run through the fingering until you are comfortable with it and can play it from memory.

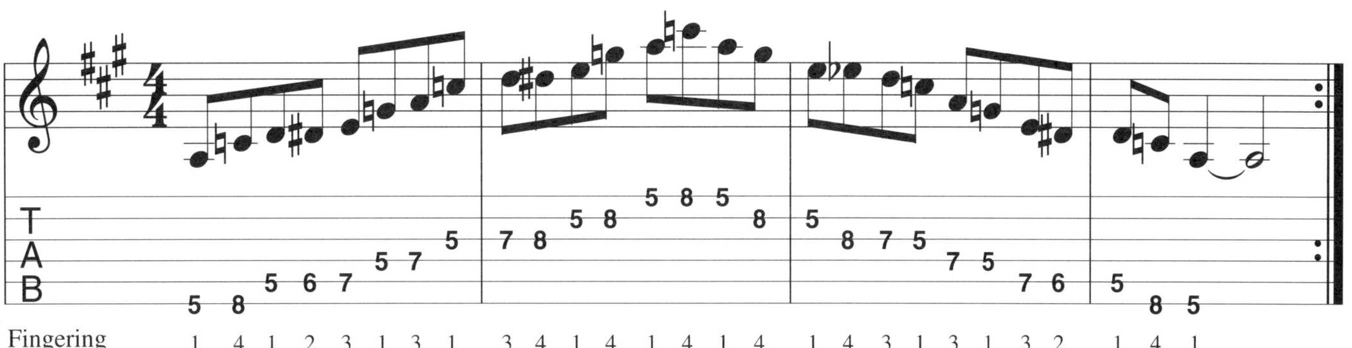

Once you have memorized the fingering, try these riffs which are derived from the Blues scale. As with the minor pentatonic scale, use the ideas presented here to create some of your own Blues scale riffs.

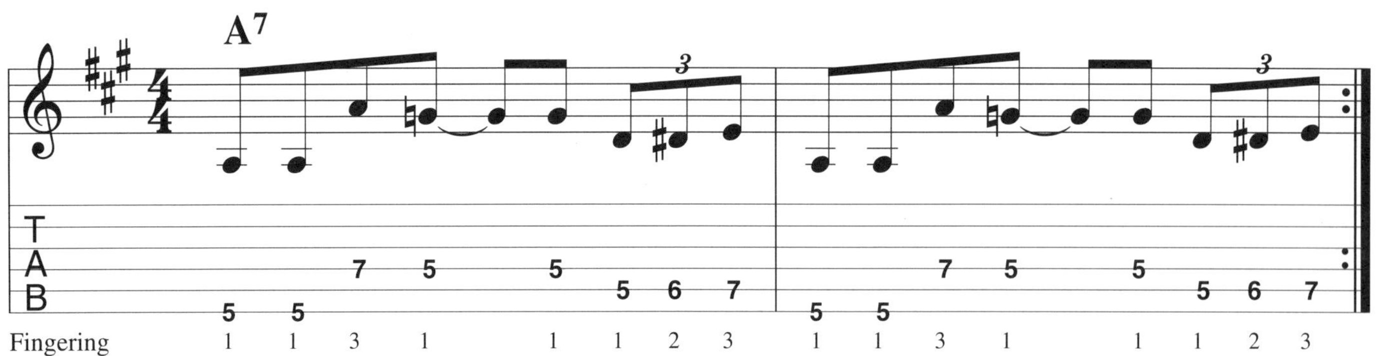

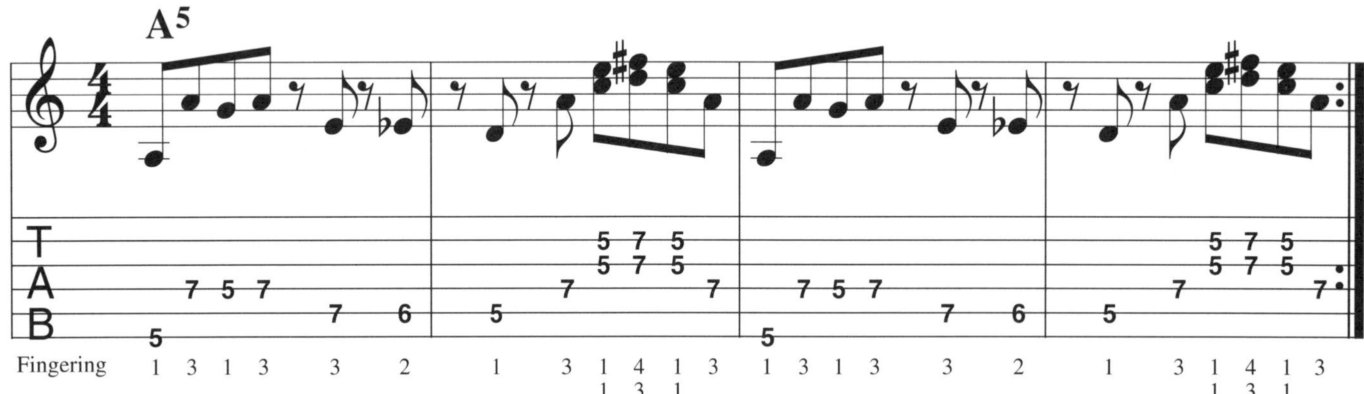

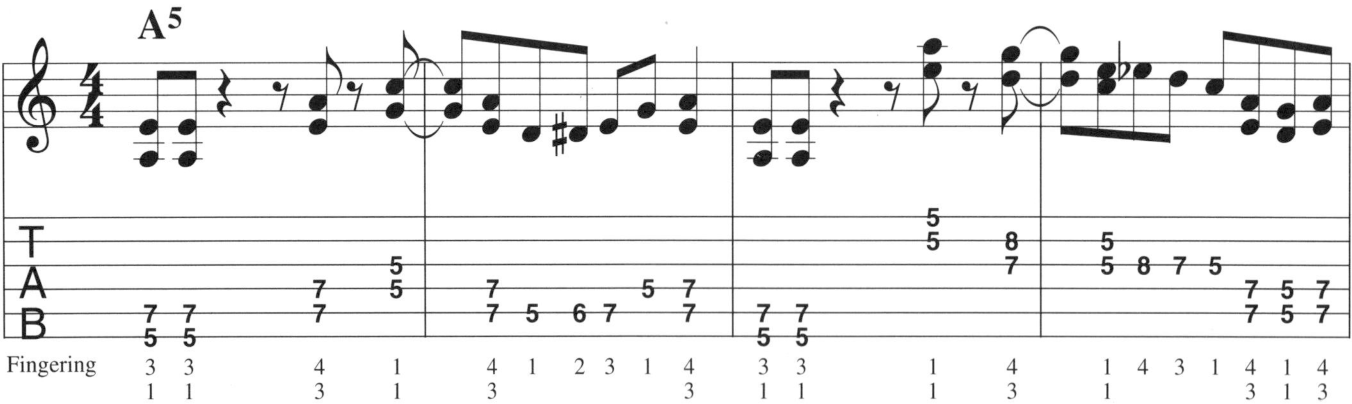

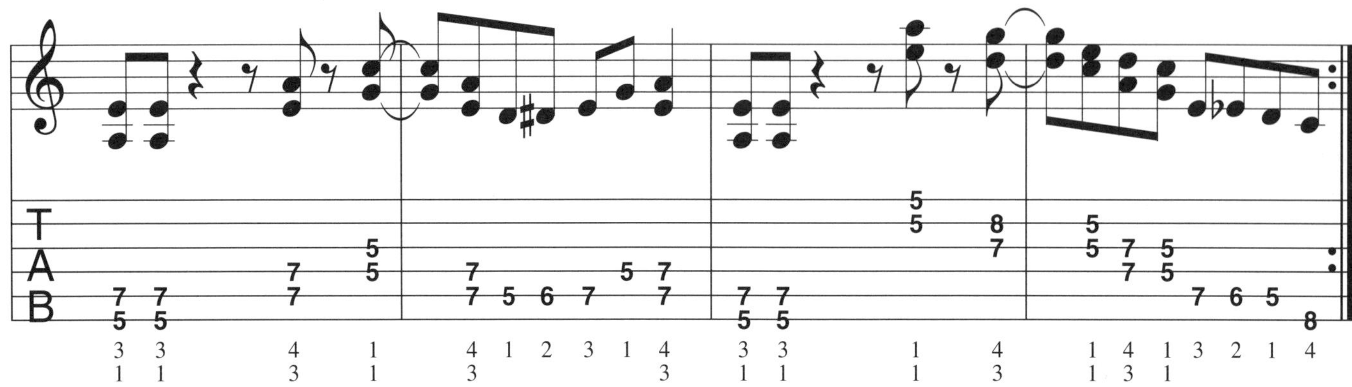

OPEN POSITION A BLUES SCALE

Shown below is the fingering for the **A Blues scale** in the open position. Remember that there is only one new note (E or D). All the other notes are the same as the A minor pentatonic scale.

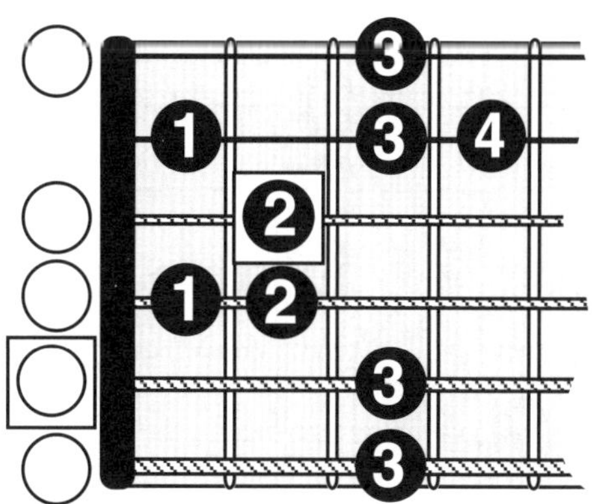

Here are a couple of riffs derived from the **A** Blues scale fingering shown above. Learn them and then use the ideas to create your own Blues scale licks.

29.0

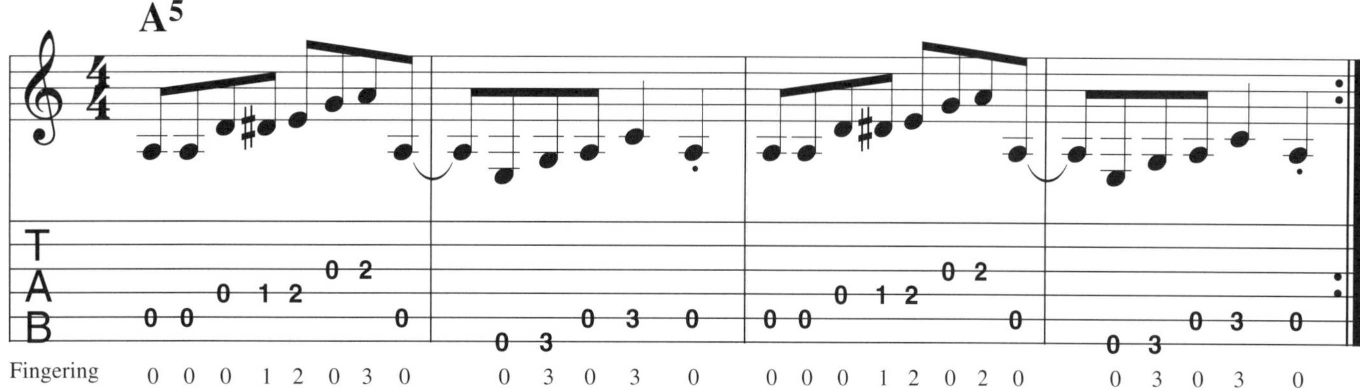

29.1

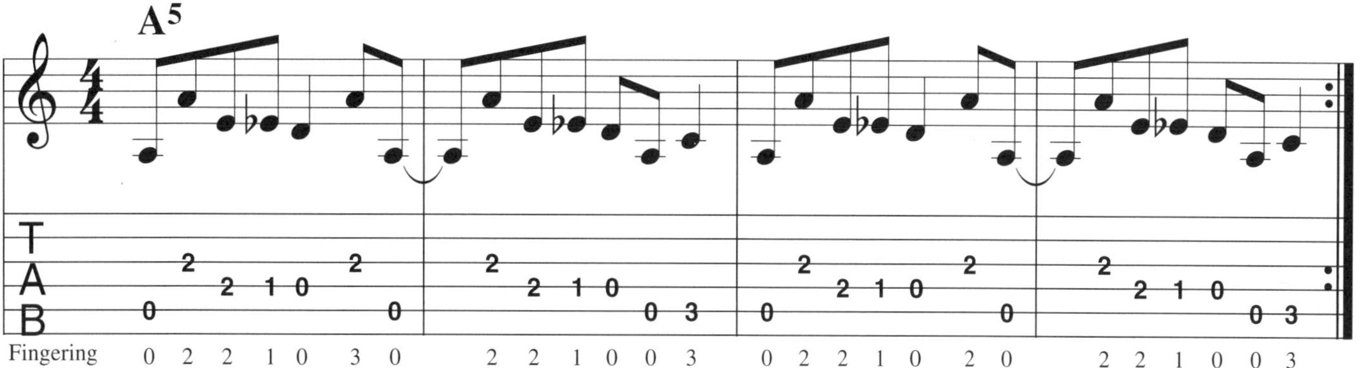

OPEN POSITION E BLUES SCALE

Shown below is the open position fingering for the **E Blues scale**. Remember that this is the same as the A Blues scale from the 5th fret moved down so that the nut replaces the first finger, resulting in open strings.

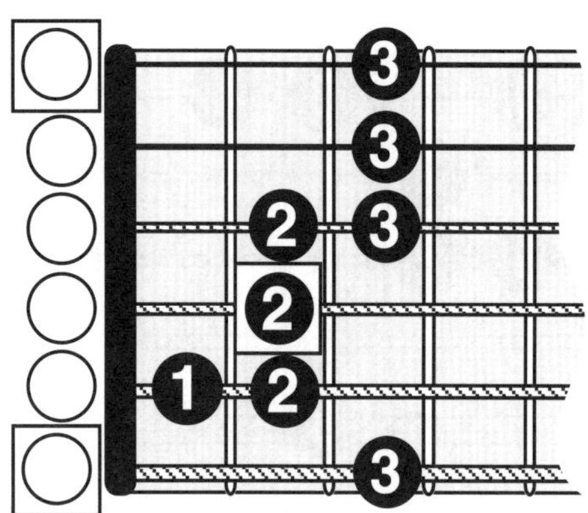

Here are some riffs derived from the **E** Blues scale. As always, learn them from memory and then use the ideas to invent your own licks.

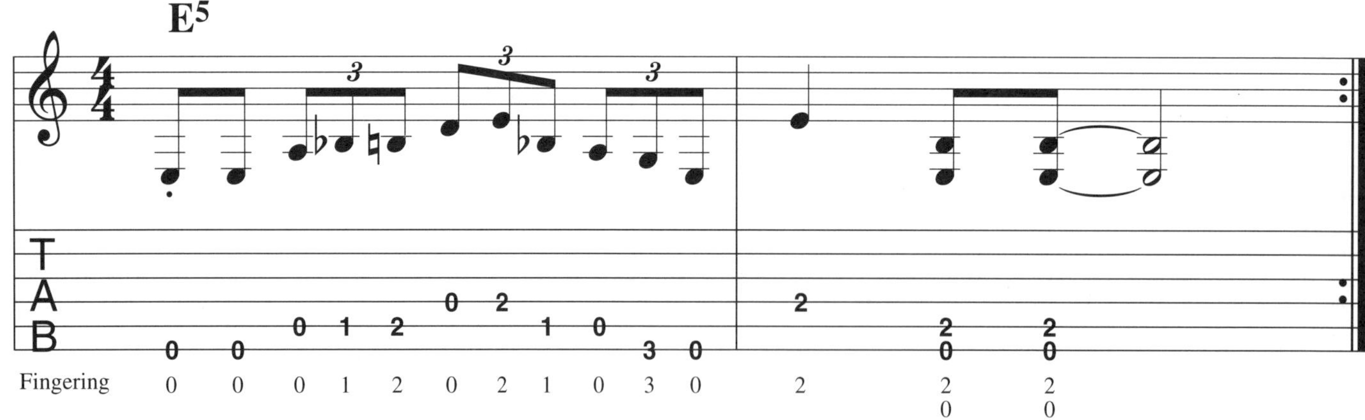

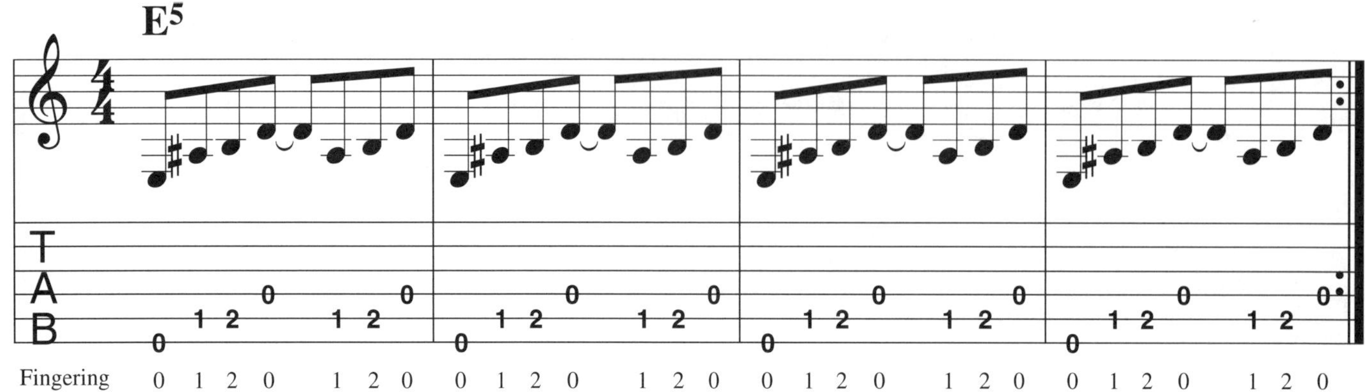

LESSON THIRTY NINE

BOOGIE RHYTHMS

A Boogie is a particular type of shuffle which makes use of rests and percussive strumming on the beat to help drive the rhythm along. Boogie songs often stay on one chord rather than following a 12 bar pattern. The artists best known for this style are John Lee Hooker and ZZ Top. The following example is a basic boogie rhythm.

31.0

Fingering 0 1 1 0 | 1 1 0 | 1 1 0 | 1 1 0 | 1 1 0 | 1 1 0 | 2 | 3

Here is a slight variation, this time using **percussive strums** in place of the rests.

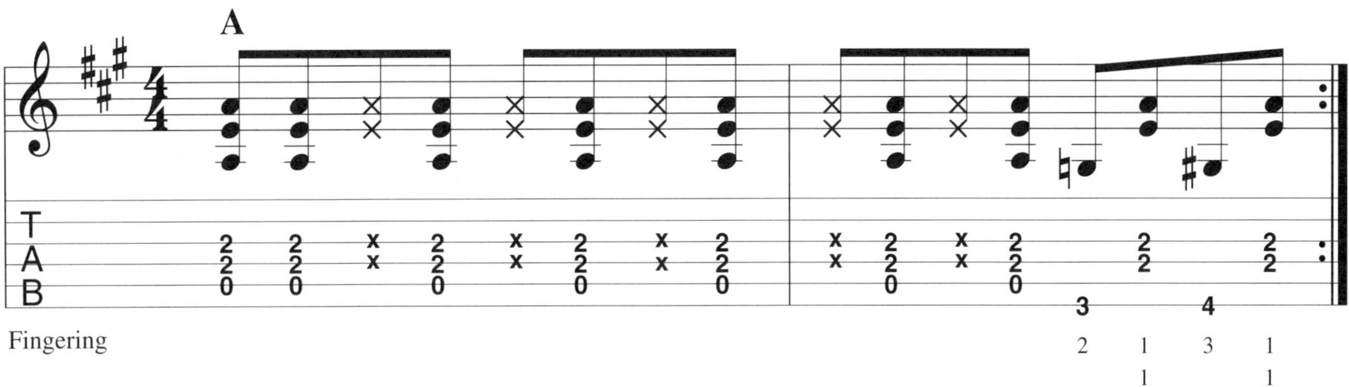

31.2

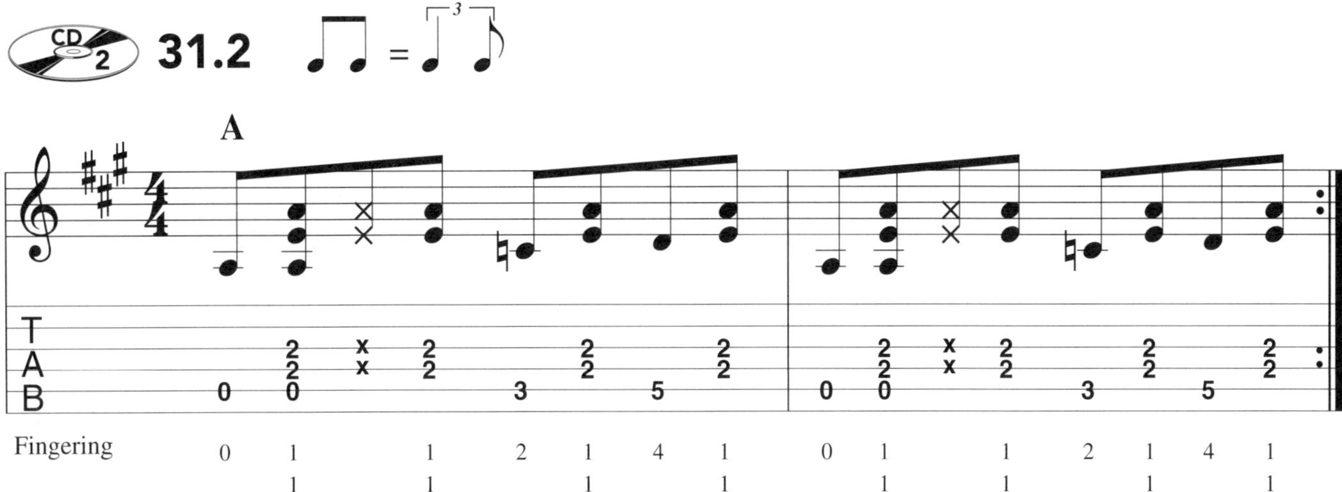

Here are two more variations, followed by an eight bar boogie solo.

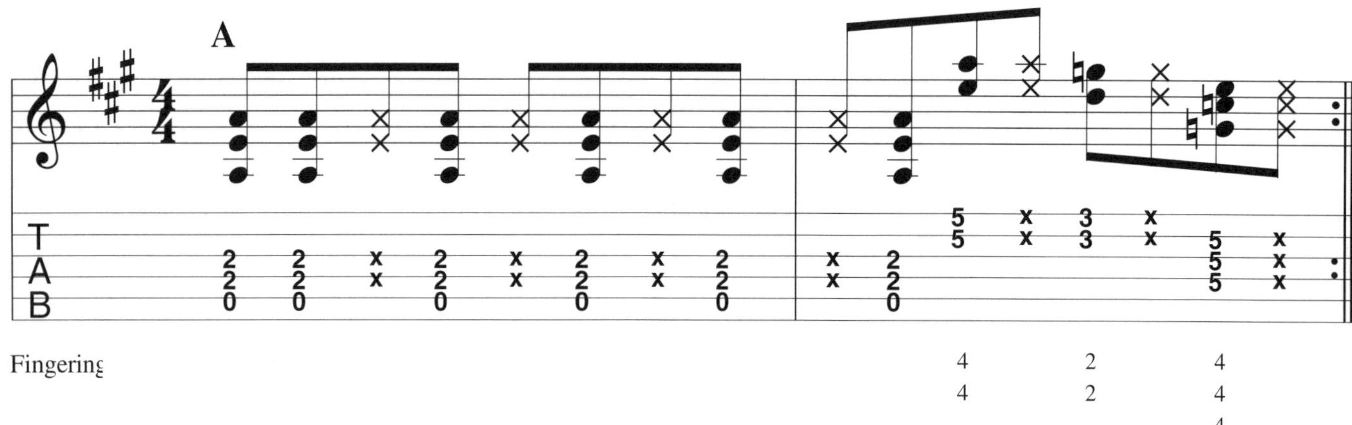

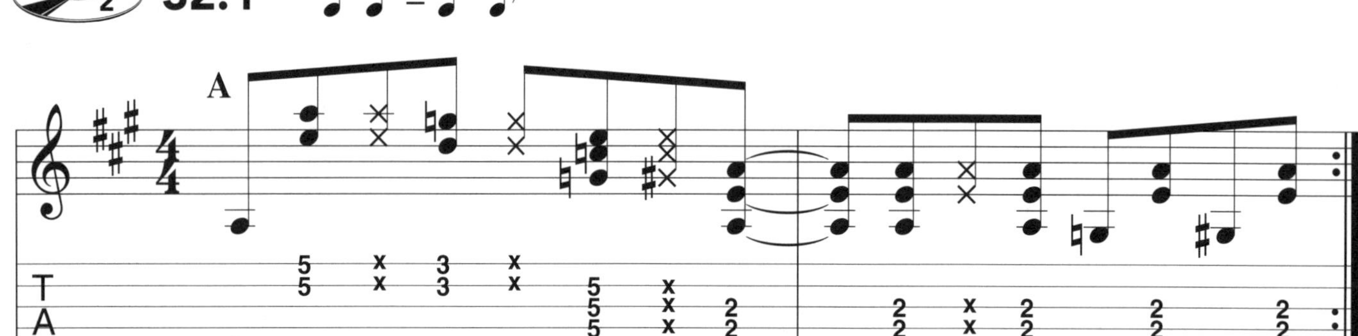

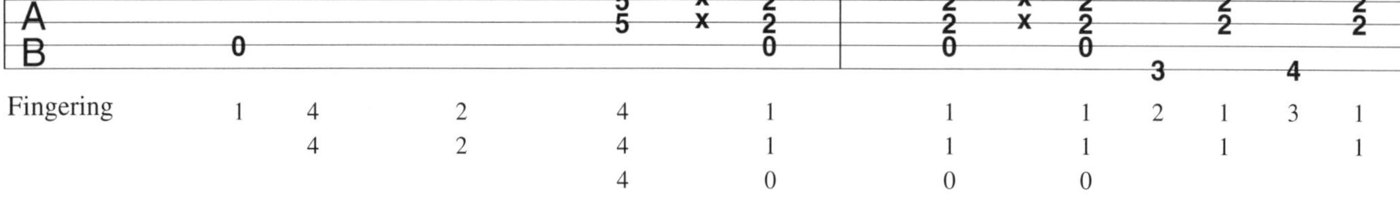

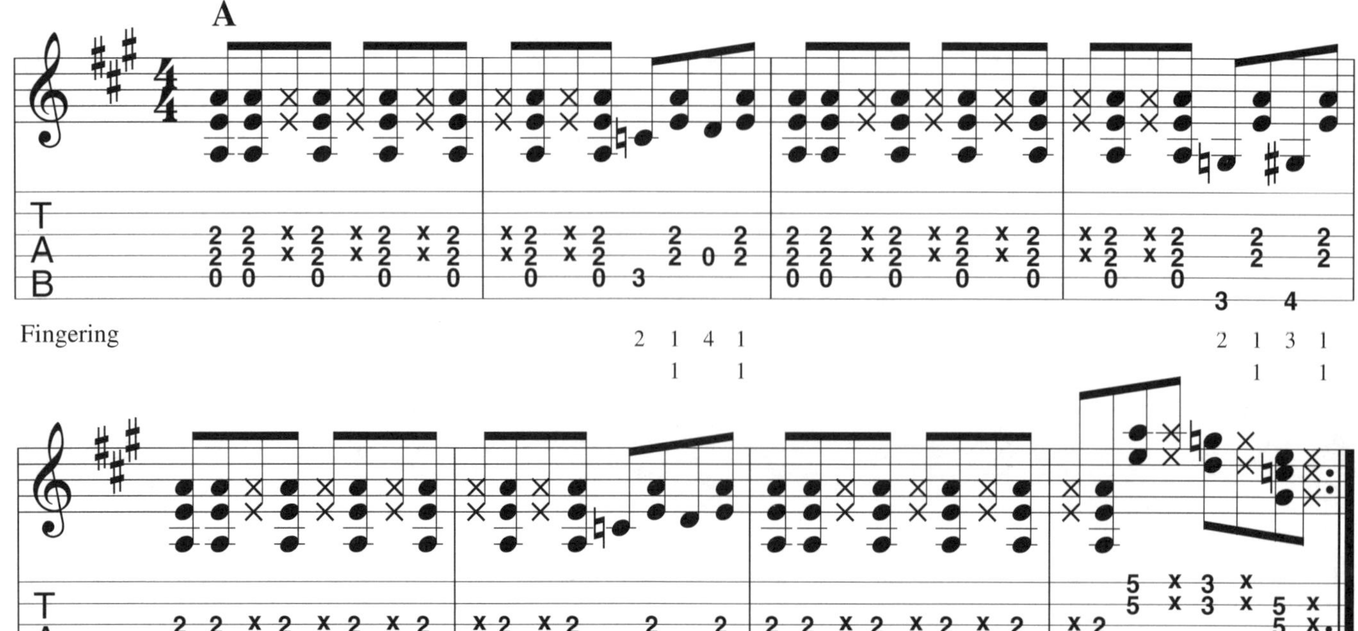

EXPERIMENTING WITH SOUNDS

Many riffs and licks are created from a variety of sources rather than just one scale. Usually, a person finds a combination of notes that **sound good** rather than thinking of right or wrong notes and particular scales. The following examples are riffs which contain notes from all the scales you have learnt, including the **chromatic scale** which contains all possible notes. Experiment with combining different scales and concentrating purely on what you think sounds good.

33.0

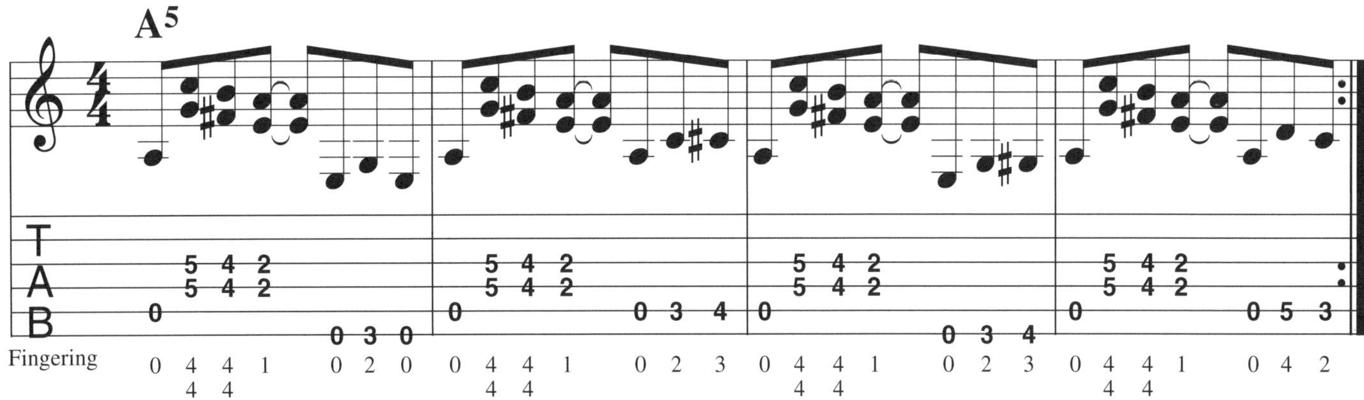

33.1

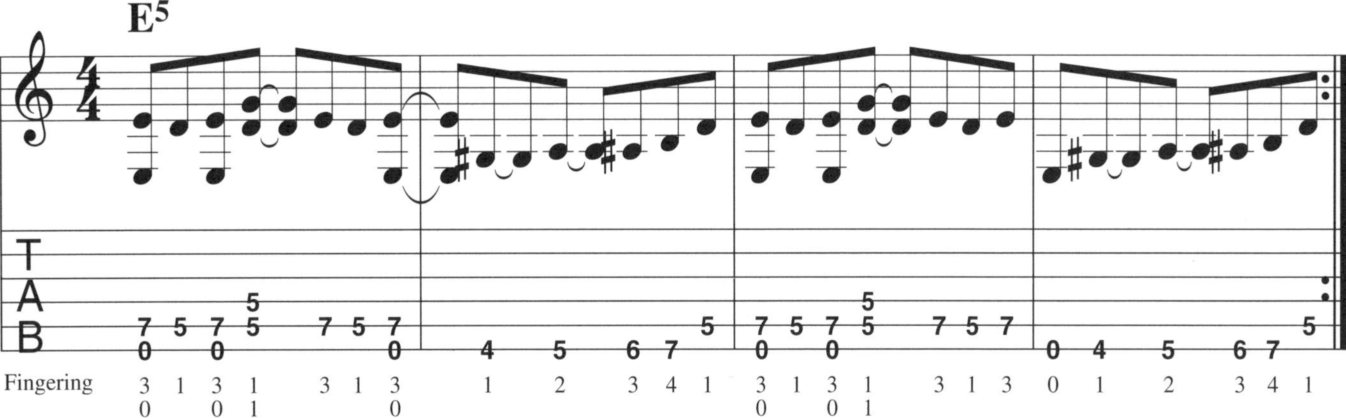

34. Stevie Ray Boogie

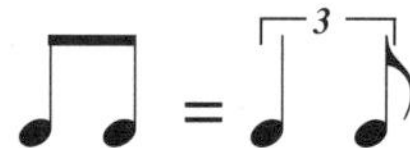

Here is a more complex rhythm part made up of a bass line and partial chords. Practice it slowly and make sure that only the notes you want to play are sounding and no extra unwanted open strings are ringing. Be patient if you find this difficult at first.

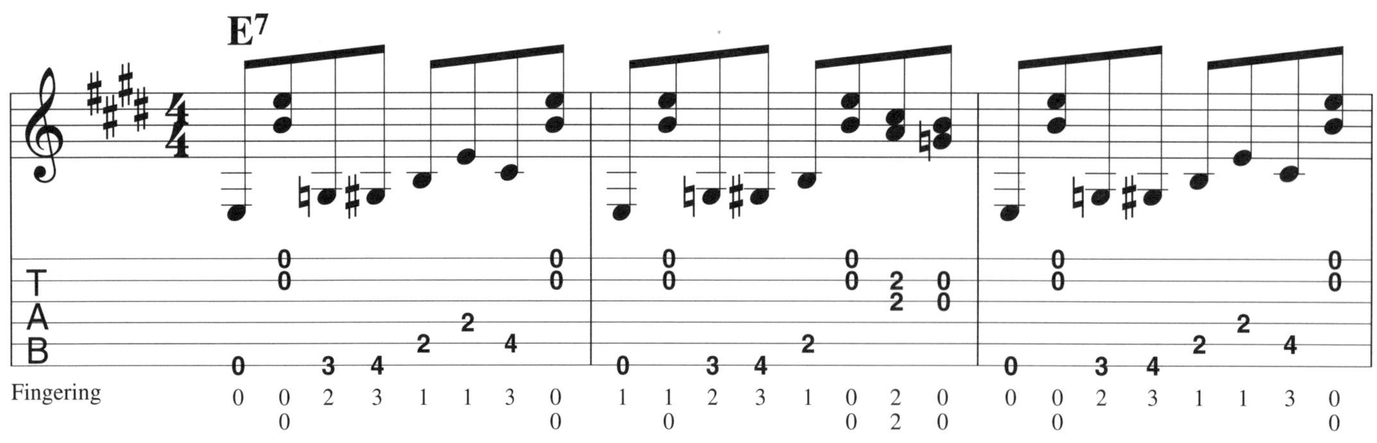

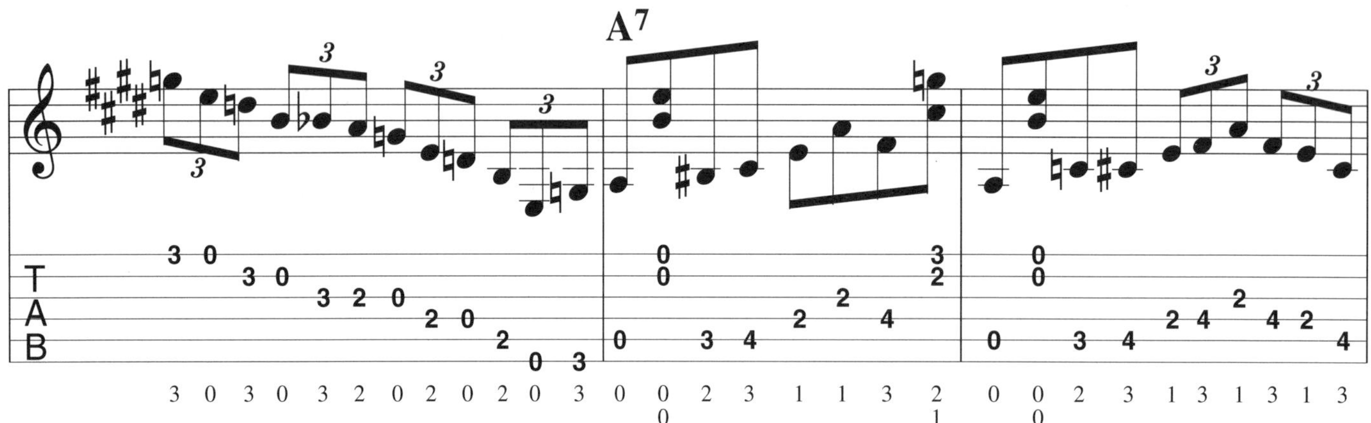

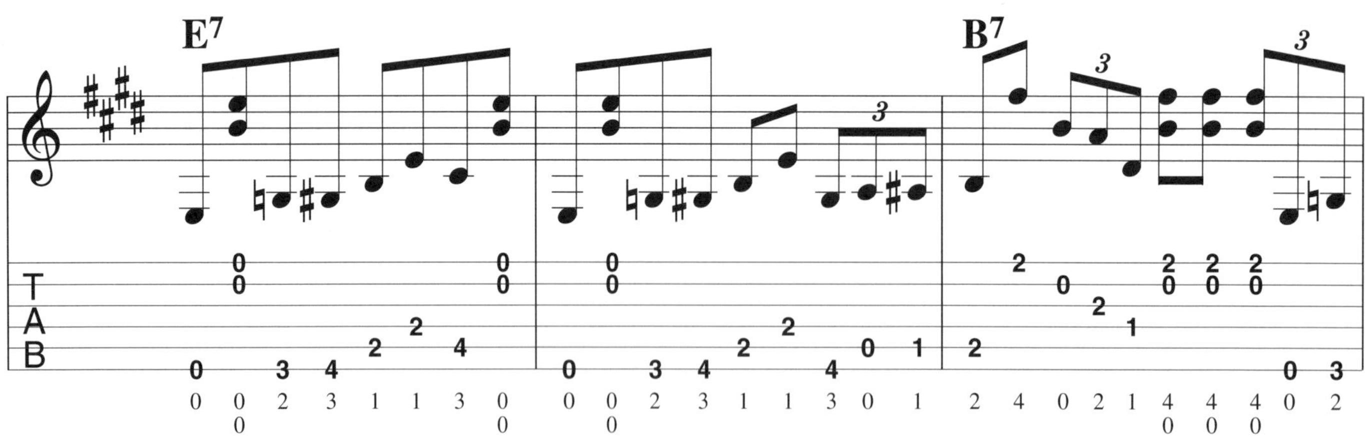

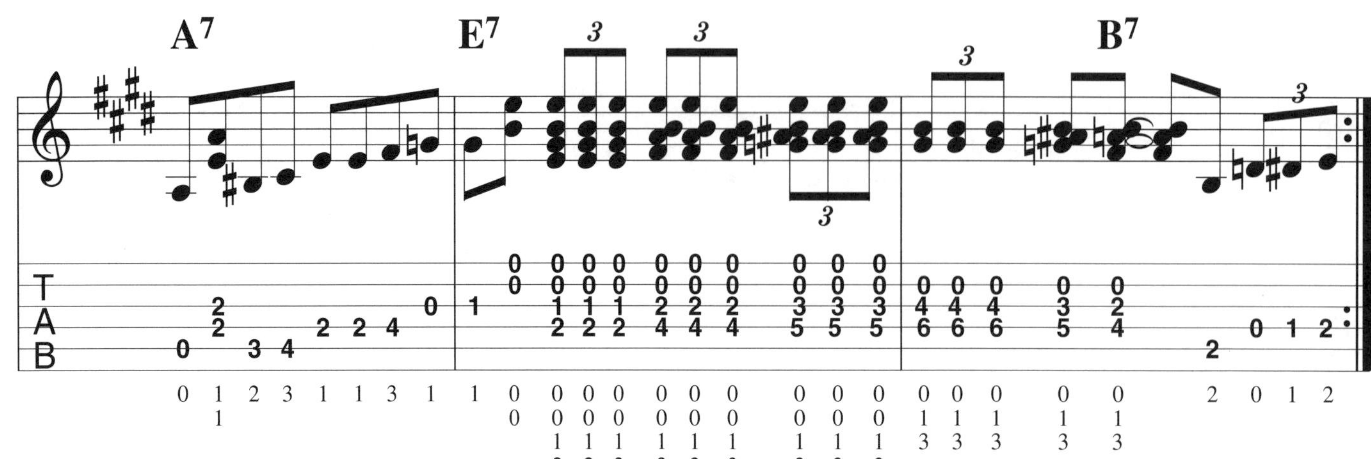

LESSON FORTY

SIXTEENTH NOTES

When playing more complex music, it is common to find beats subdivided into four. This is done by using **sixteenth notes**. Mastering sixteenth notes will enable you to play more sophisticated rhythms as well as being able to play faster.

A **sixteenth note** lasts for **one quarter** of a beat.
There are **four** sixteenth notes in one beat.
There are **16** sixteenth notes in one bar of $\frac{4}{4}$ time.

Two sixteenth notes joined together.

Four sixteenth notes joined together.

When counting 16th notes, notice the different sound for each part of the beat – **one ee and ah**, **two ee and ah**... etc (written **1 e + a**, **2 e + a**... etc).

35.0 How to Count Sixteenth Notes

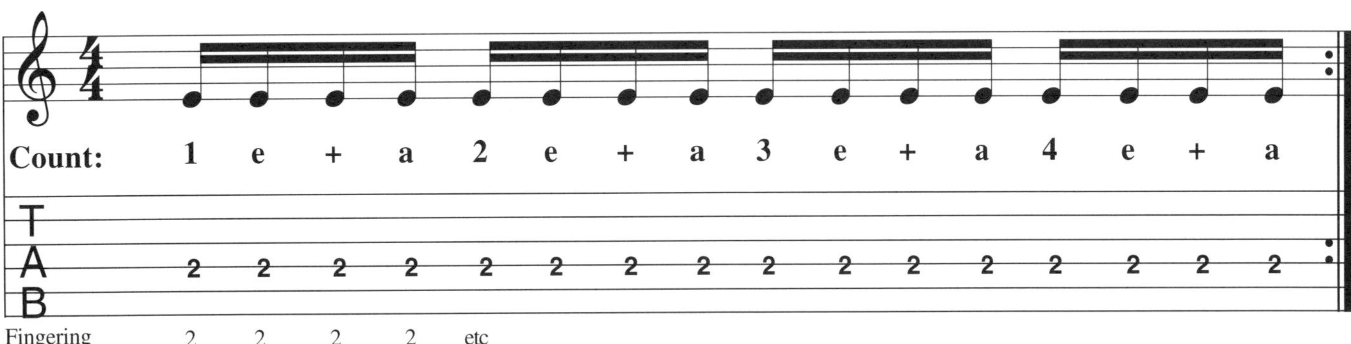

Once you are comfortable counting sixteenth notes on one note, apply them to the pentatonic scale, and then try the following pattern, which will help your picking technique.

35.1

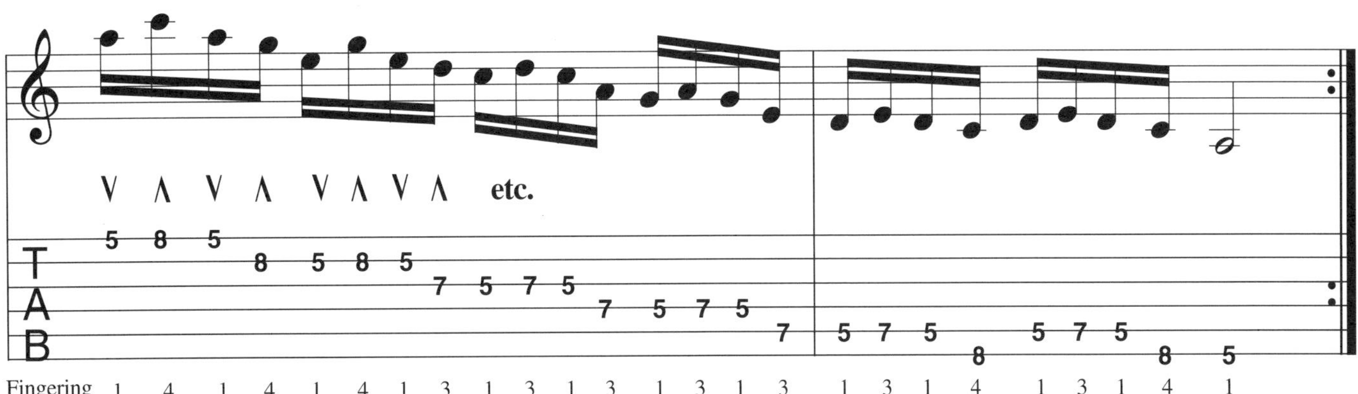

RIFFS USING SIXTEENTH NOTES

Here are some riffs using sixteenth notes. If you have trouble with the rhythms, practice them on one note until you are confident with them and then try the whole example. All the notes here are from the **A** minor pentatonic scale. Notice the use of staccato notes in example 36.1

36.0

36.1

Sixteenth notes are often used within a beat in conjunction with eighth notes or rests, as shown in the following example. Once again, practice the rhythms on one note at first if you need to.

36.2

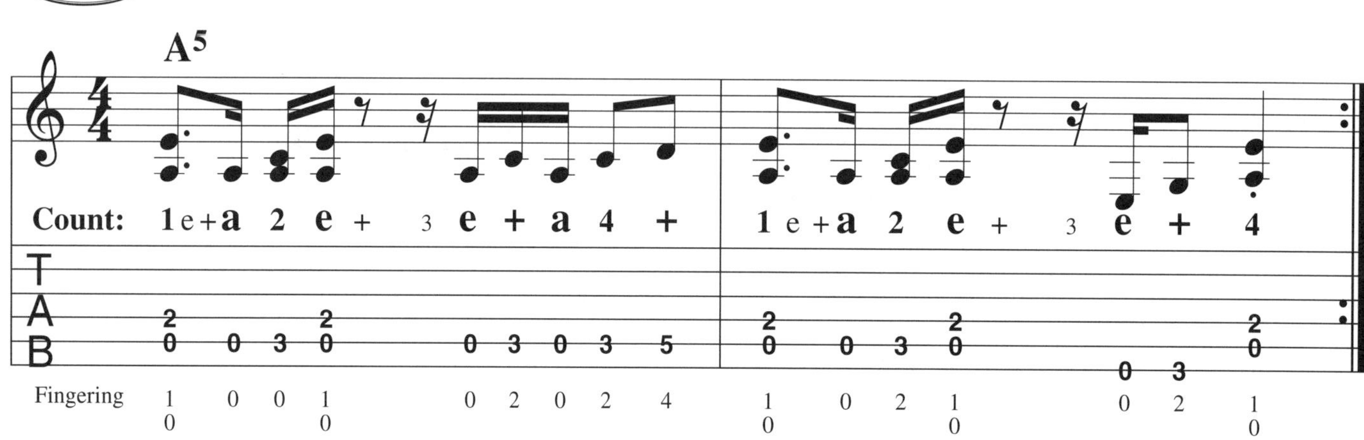

COMMON 16TH NOTE FIGURES

Here are some rhythmic figures which combine sixteenth notes and eighth notes within one beat. These figures are very common, so you will need to know them well. Practice each one carefully and be sure to tap your foot and count.

37.

Count: 1 e + a 2 e + a 3 e + a 4 e + a

Count: 1 e + a 2 e + a 3 e + a 4 e + a

Count: 1 e + a 2 e + a 3 e + a 4 e + a

Count: 1 e + a 2 e + a 3 e + a 4 e + a

Count: 1 e + a 2 e + a 3 e + a 4 e + a 1 e + a 2 e + a 3 e + a 4 e + a

Once you have learnt these rhythms on a single note, try using them with the minor pentatonic scale as shown here. The more familiar you are with these rhythms, the easier you will find it to play parts containing 16th notes as well as improvising with them.

38.

As soon as you start to feel comfortable with 16th note rhythms, try using them to create riffs. Here are some examples using the notes of the A minor pentatonic scale.

39.0

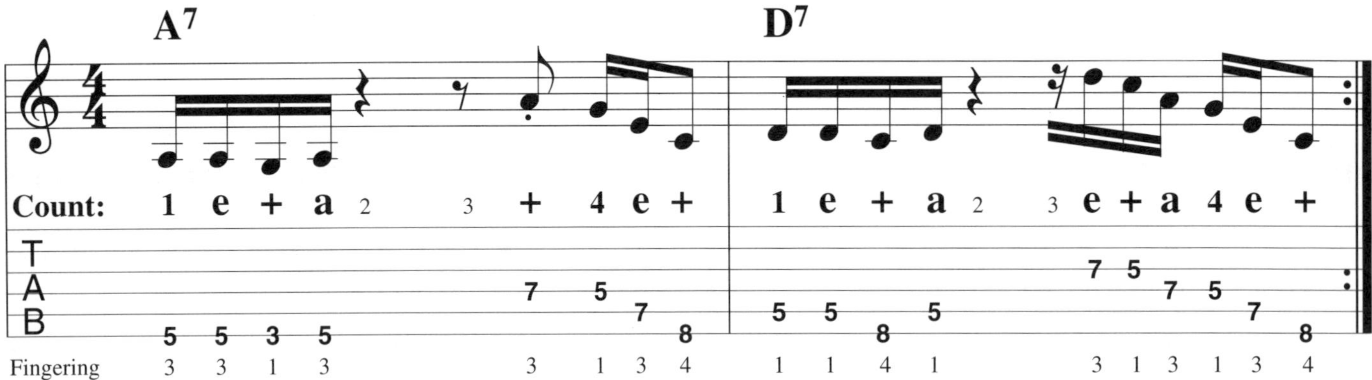

39.1

This one combines three note power chords with 4th intervals.

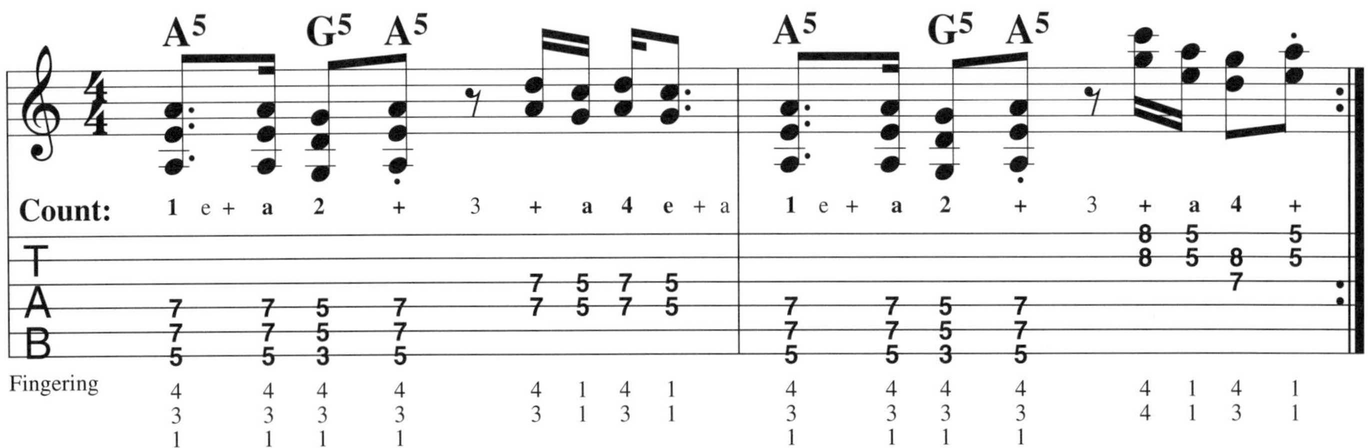

39.2

Here is another one with a more complex rhythm. Count carefully with this one.

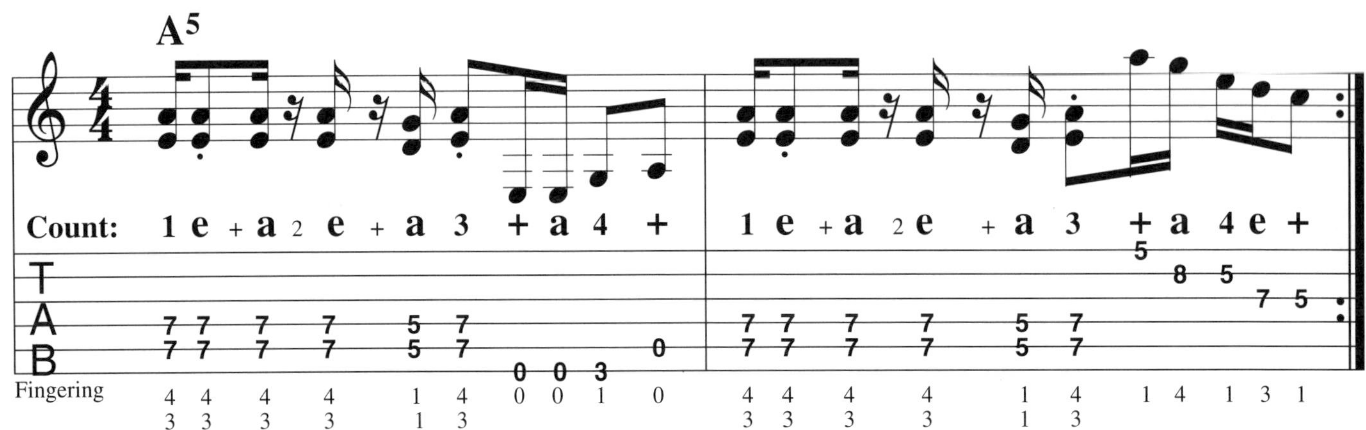

GAINING CONTROL OF SIXTEENTH NOTES

In a bar of sixteenth notes in $\frac{4}{4}$ time, there are **16** different positions for notes within the bar. The first beat is **1**, the second note of the first group of four is called the "**e of one**" the third note of the first group is called the "**and of one**", and the fourth note of the first group is called the "**a of one**". As with other subdivisions of the beat, the system then continues through the bar - **2**, **e of 2**, **and of 2**, **a of 2**, etc.

As with triplets and eighth notes, a good way to master the use of 16th notes is to strum constant 16ths with the right hand and select which part of the beat will sound by pressing down with the left hand. The other parts of each beat should be sounded as percussive strums. Here are some exercises using this technique. Be sure to use your metronome, count out loud and tap your foot on the beat without any hesitating or extra taps between beats.

40.

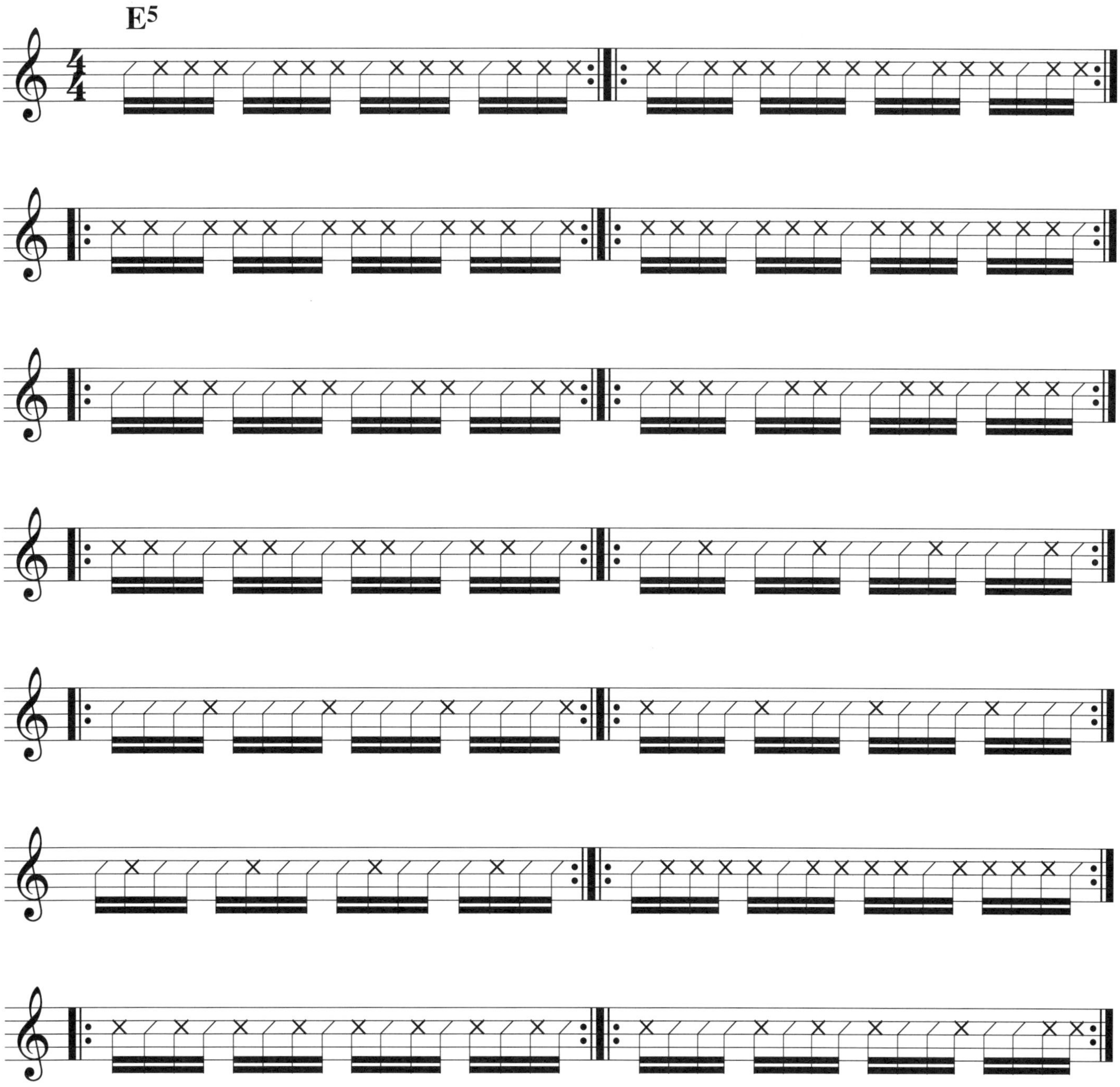

E5

POWER CHORD SIXTEENTH NOTE RHYTHM PARTS

Shown below are some common ways of using sixteenth notes with power chords. Notice the accents on each beat of the bar. Practice each pattern until you can play it easily at a slow tempo, and then try increasing the setting on your metronome two points at a time until you can play them along with the CD.

41.

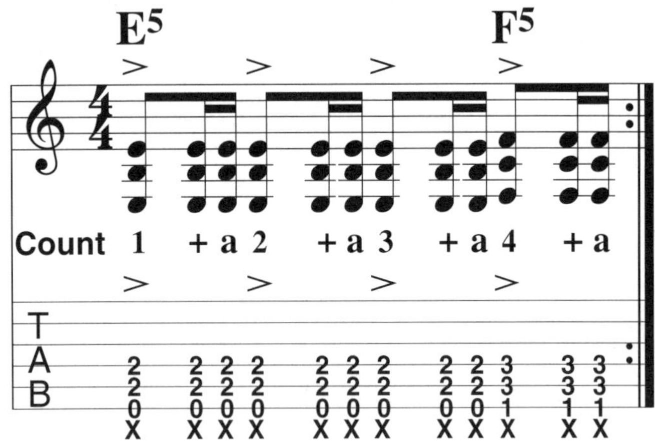

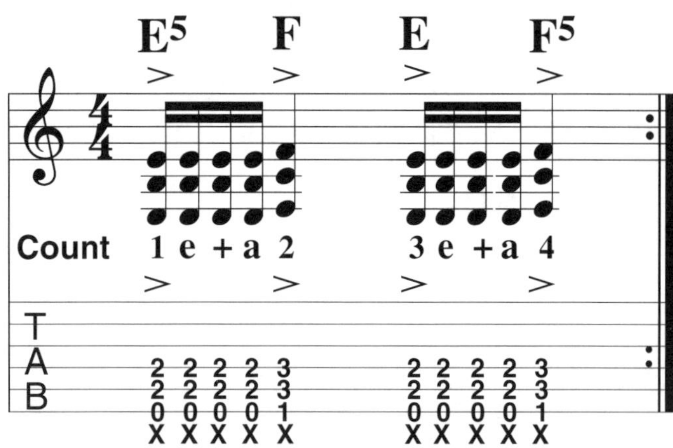

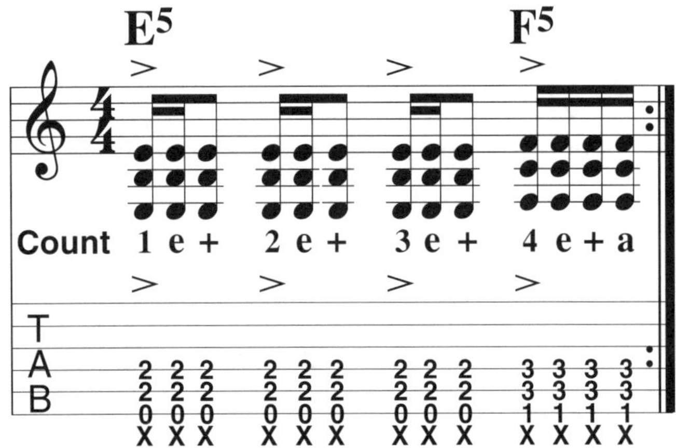

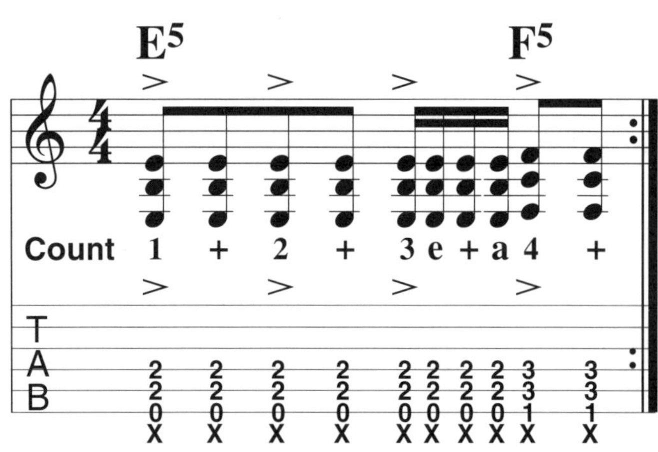

In order to produce a heavier more aggressive sound, try using downstrokes on every strum of a sixteenth note rhythms shown in the following example.

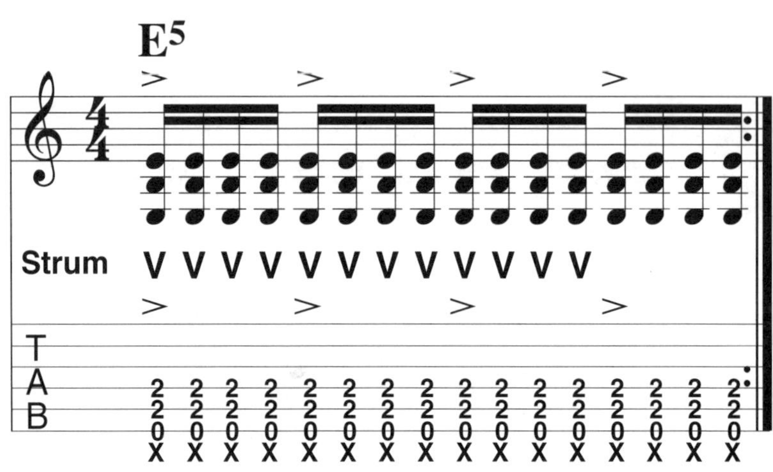

Here are some examples which use eighth and sixteenth notes in various combinations. Take each one slowly at first and count out loud until you are confident with the timing.

42.0

42.1

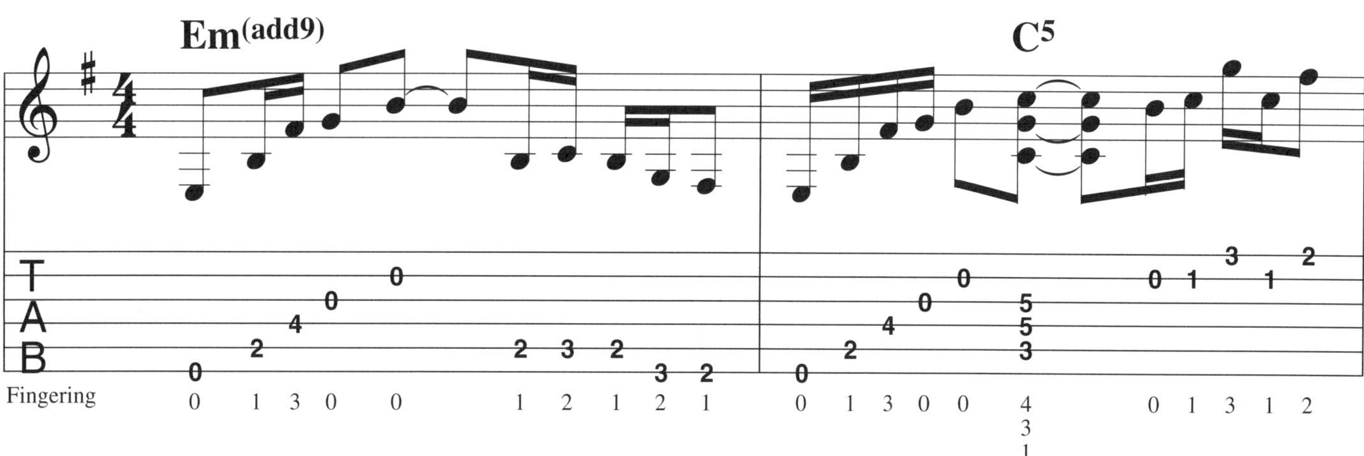

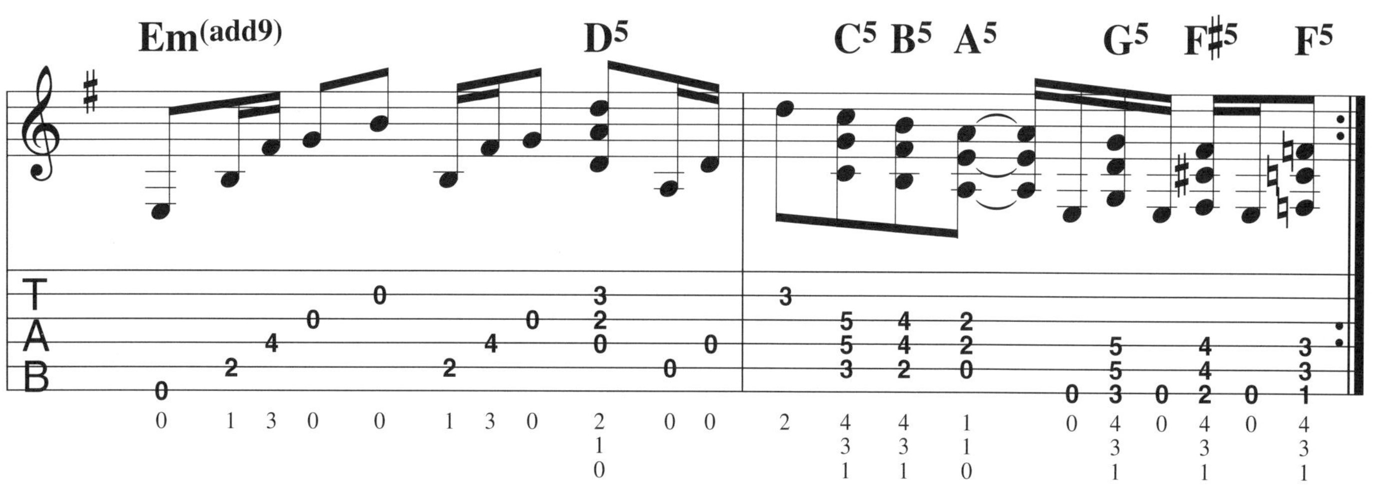

43. Hammerdrill

This Metal Rhythm part presents quite a challenge. Take it slowly until you have all the notes and rhythms under control. Then gradually increase the metronome speed until you are ready to play it along with the recording.

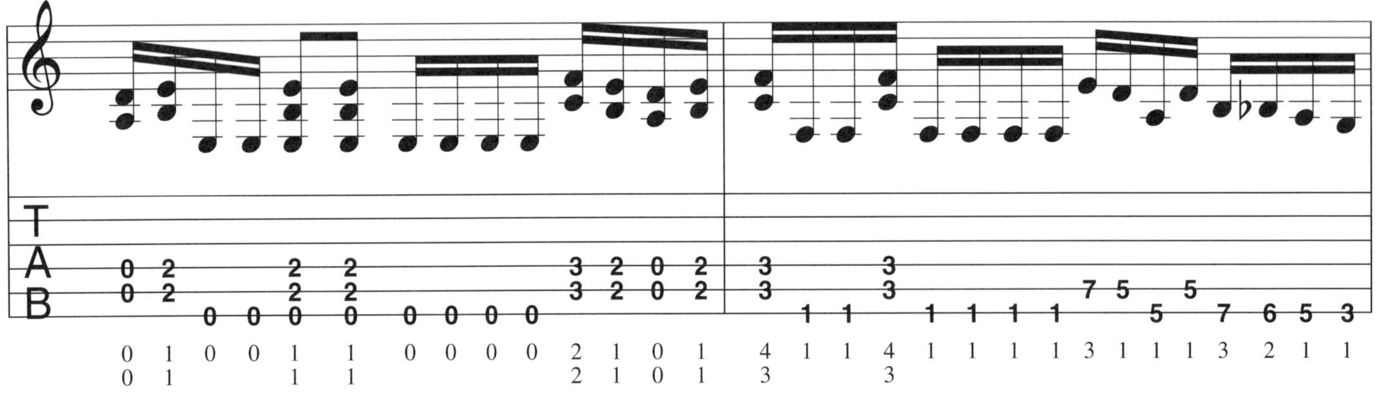

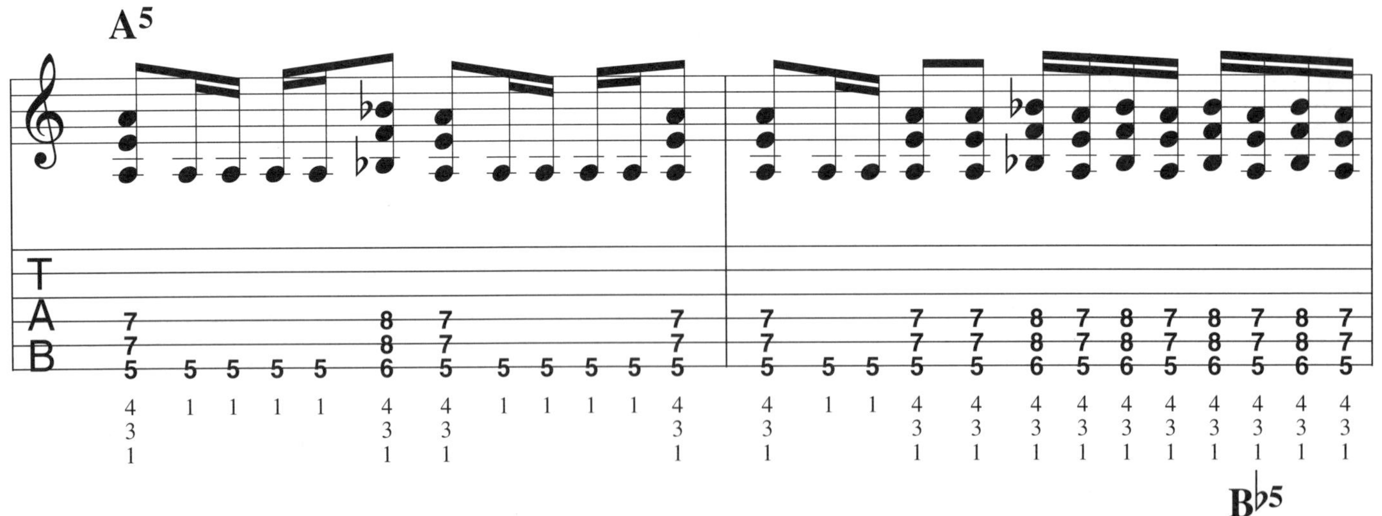

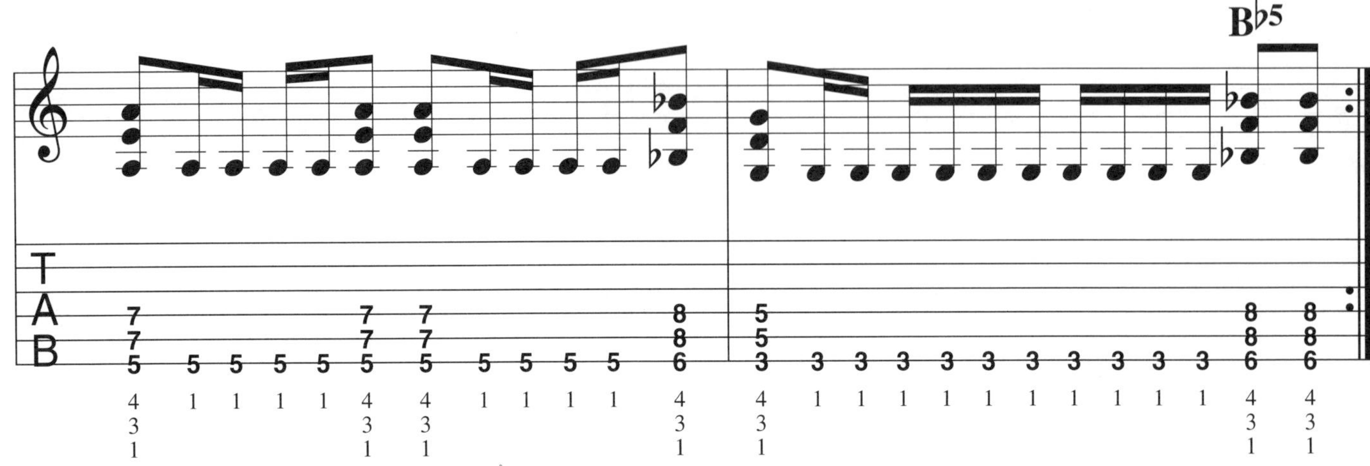

LESSON FORTY ONE

MAJOR 7TH CHORDS

Another important chord type is the **major 7th**. Some common voicings are shown below. Each one is played in example 44.0

Chord Symbol		*Chord Formula*
Maj7	**MAJOR SEVENTH CHORD FORMULA**	1 3 5 7

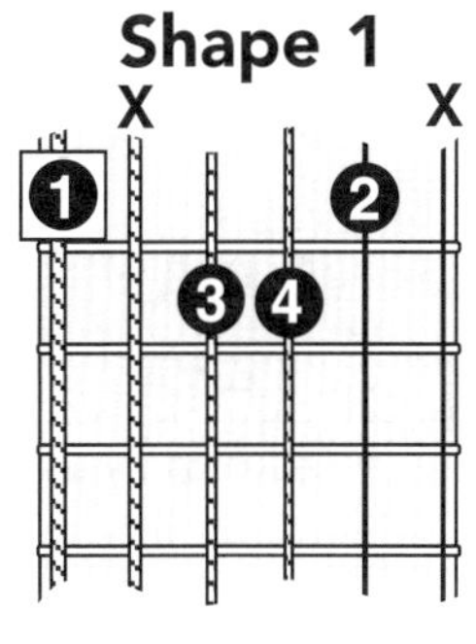

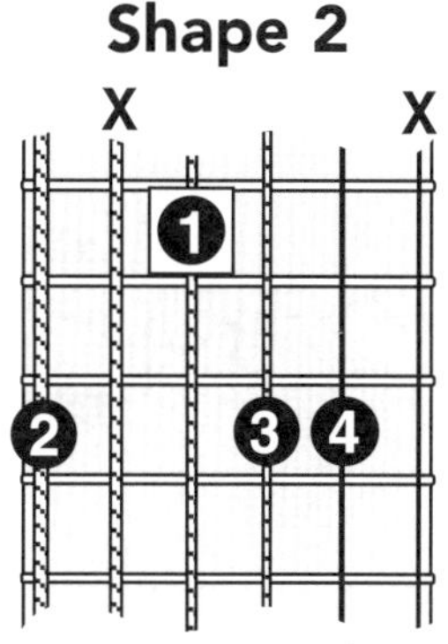

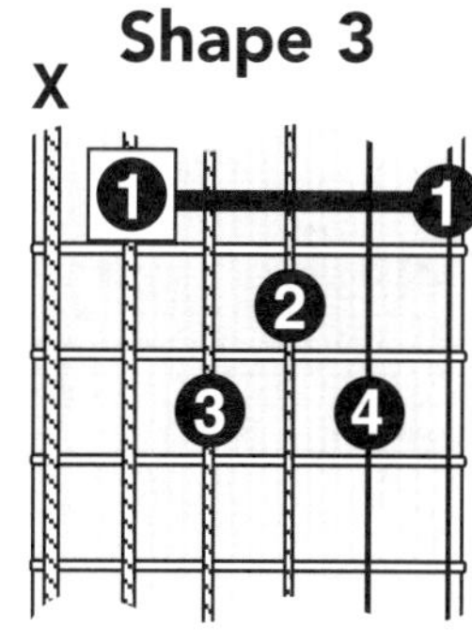

44.0

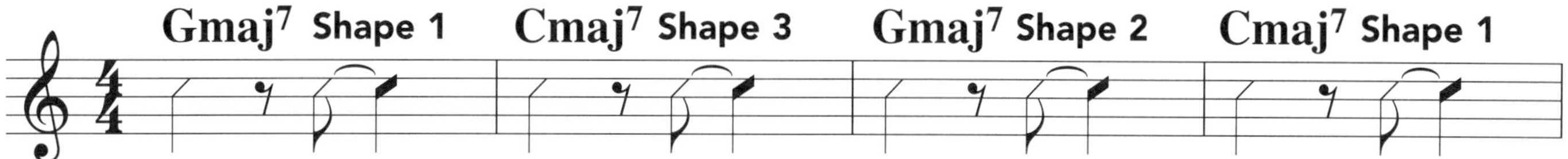

Here is an example which uses major 7th chords as arpeggios.

44.1

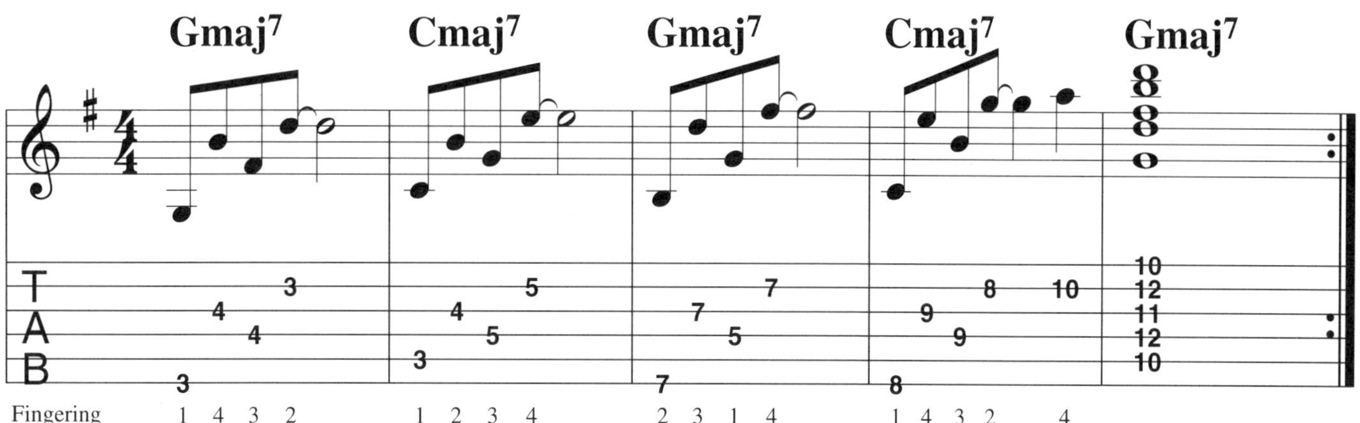

Here are some higher sounding major 7th shapes, followed by some examples demonstrating their use.

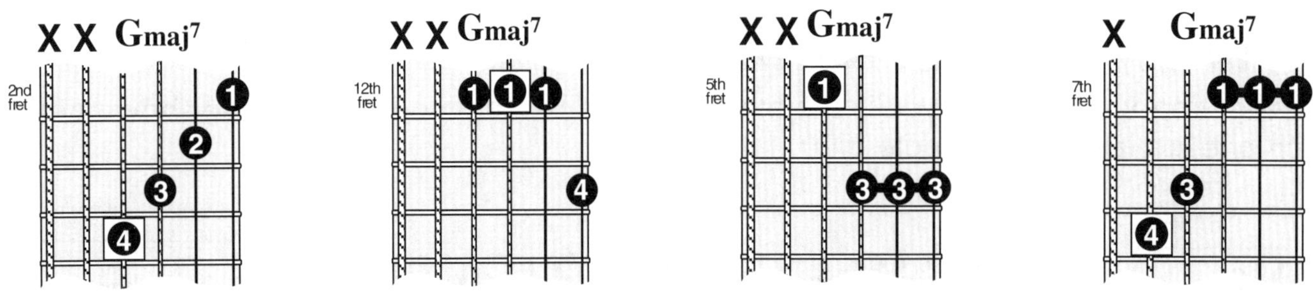

45.0

45.1

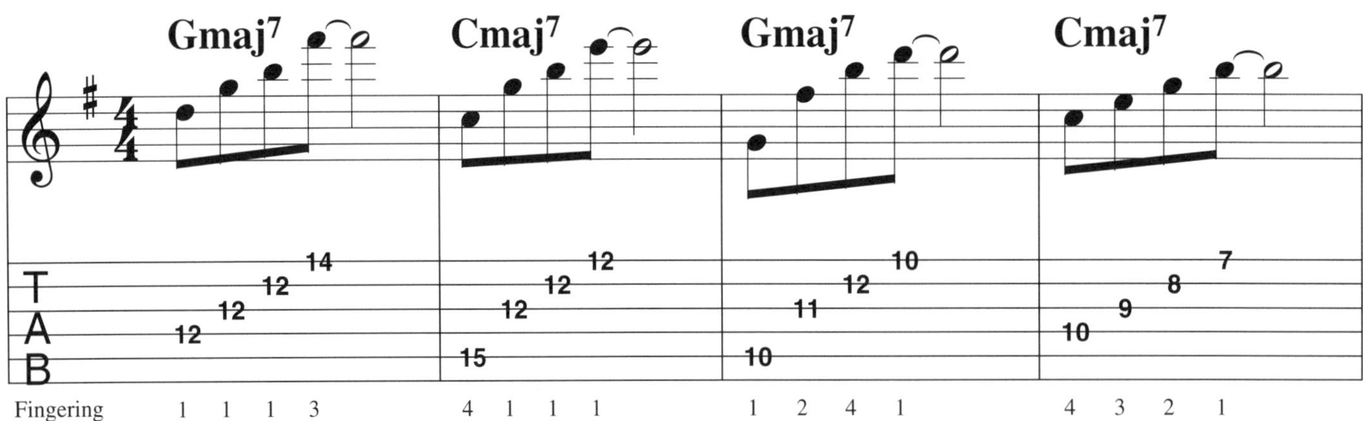

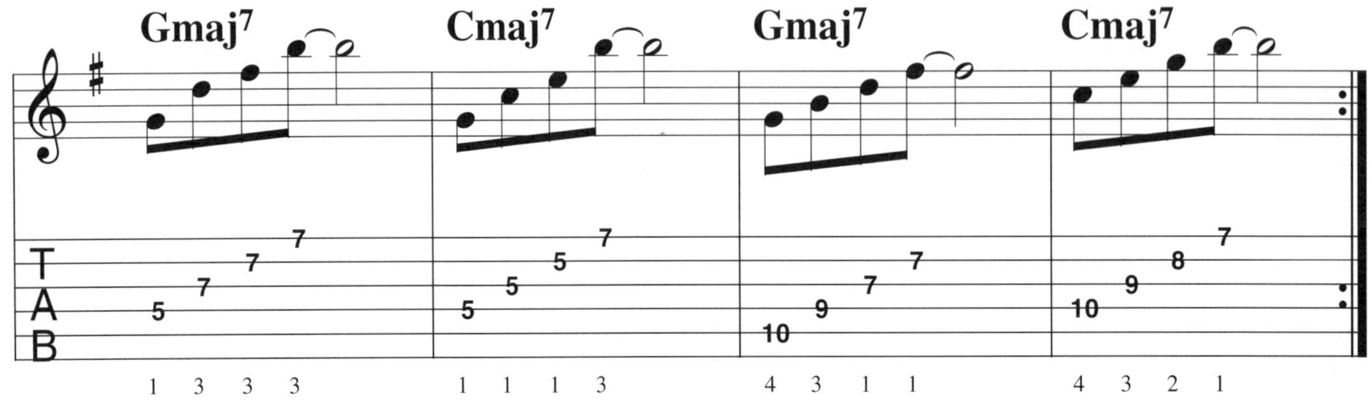

MINOR 7TH CHORDS

Minor 7th chords are also commonly used in Rock and all its related styles. The diagrams below show some commonly used minor 7th shapes. You can determine the forms by the positions of the root notes.

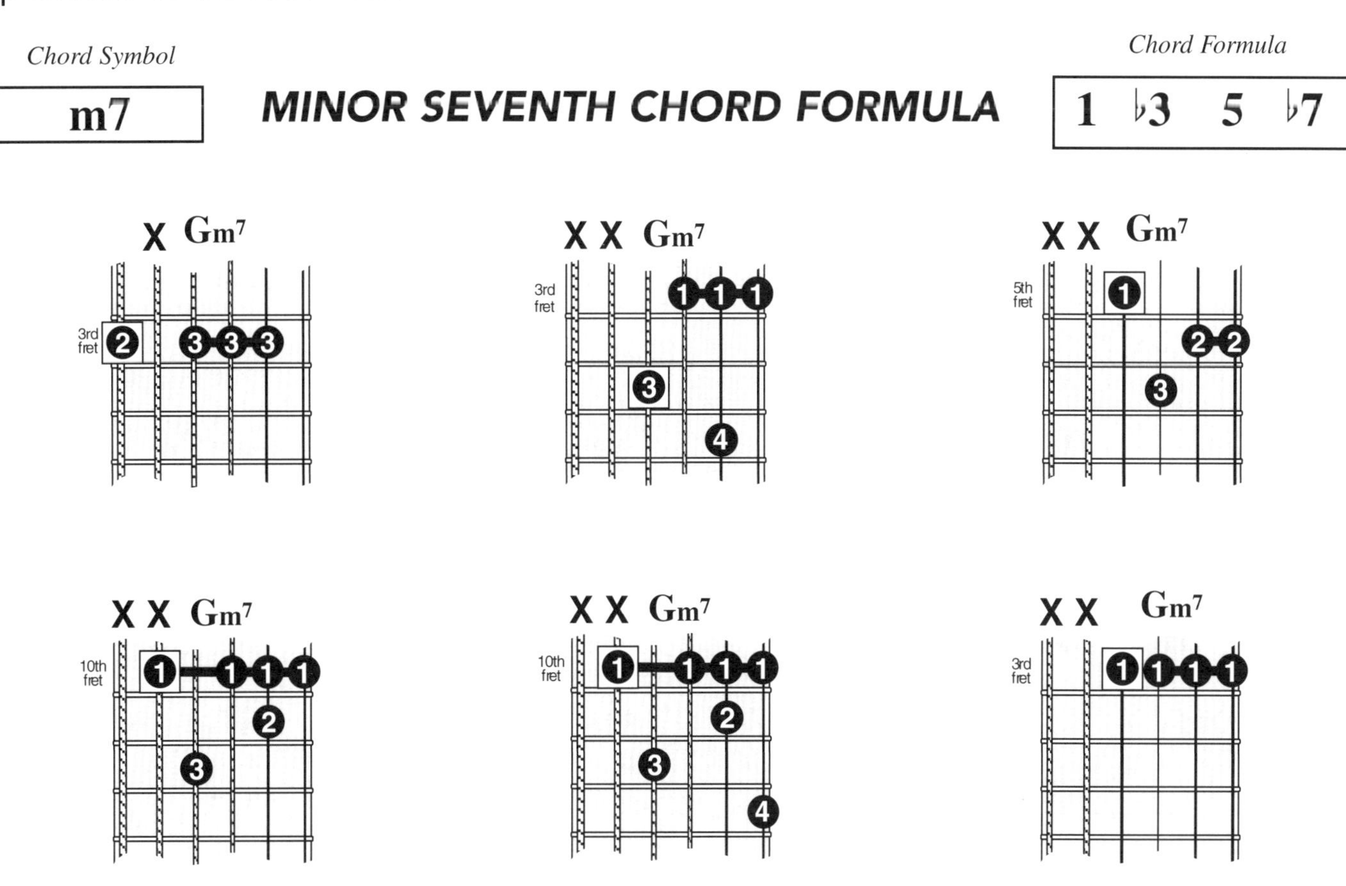

The following example is a 12 bar Blues which makes use of minor 7th chords. Try playing these chords as arpeggios, as well as experimenting with combinations of these and other chords you know.

46.

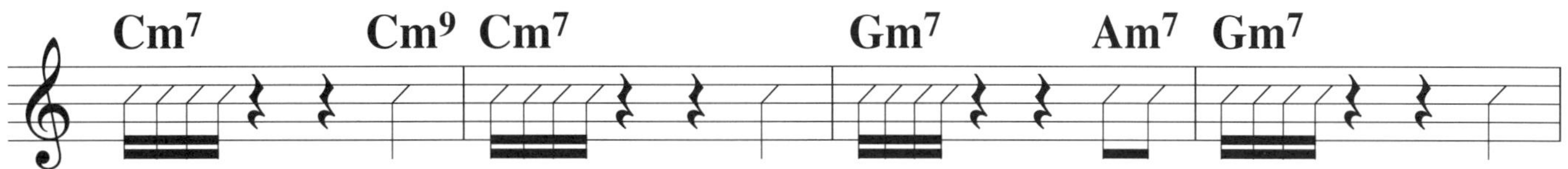

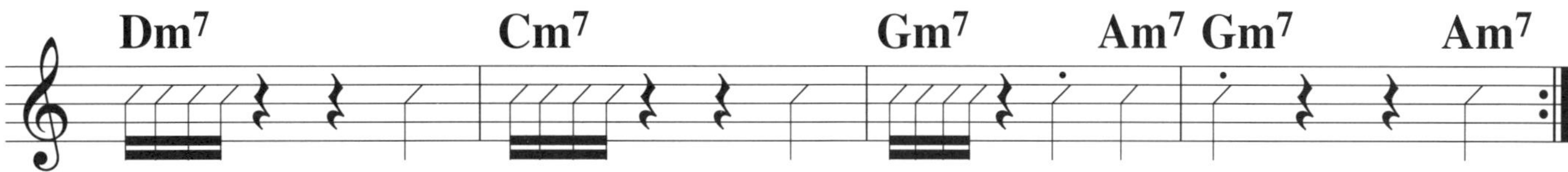

JAZZ PROGRESSIONS

Here are some Jazz progressions which use major, minor and dominant 7th chords. Learning Jazz tunes is a great way to expand your chord knowledge. There are no given chord shapes or rhythms for the following examples. There are many possibilities here. See if you can work some out from the recordings. Picking up chords, single note lines and rhythms by ear and improvising with them is essential in Jazz, as you need to be able to respond to what the other musicians are playing, and adapt your playing to a variety of situations instantly. Jazz musicians rarely play a tune the same way twice.

47.

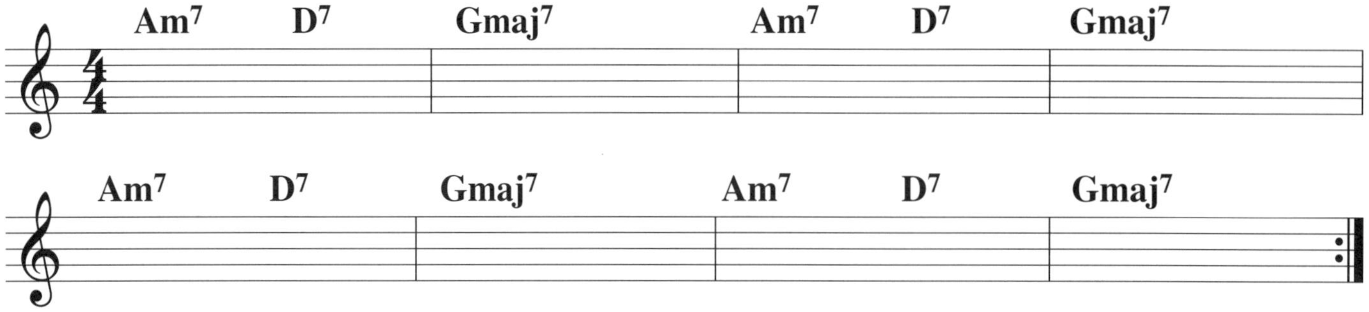

4/4

Am7 D7 | Gmaj7 | Am7 D7 | Gmaj7 |

Am7 D7 | Gmaj7 | Am7 D7 | Gmaj7 :||

48. Satin Swing

4/4

Dm7 G7 | Dm7 G7 | Em7 A7 | Em7 A7 |

Am7 D7 | A♭m7 D♭7 | Cmaj7 | :||

Gm7 C7 | Gm7 C7 | Fmaj7 | |

Am7 D7 | Am7 D7 | Dm7 G7 | Em7 A7 ||

Dm7 G7 | Dm7 G7 | Em7 A7 | Em7 A7 |

Am7 D7 | A♭m7 D♭7 | Cmaj7 | ||

LESSON FORTY TWO

NINTH CHORDS

So far we have dealt with major, minor and dominant 7th chords. Another popular sound used in many styles is the **Dominant 9th chord** (commonly called a 9th chord). A 9th chord is obtained by adding a major 3rd interval on top of a 7th chord. The chord will then contain the **1st, 3rd, 5th, ♭7th** and **9th** degrees of a major scale. Here is the most common voicing of the 9th chord. The third finger should clearly sound the 1st, 2nd and 3rd strings. The root note here is on the 5th string, under the second finger.

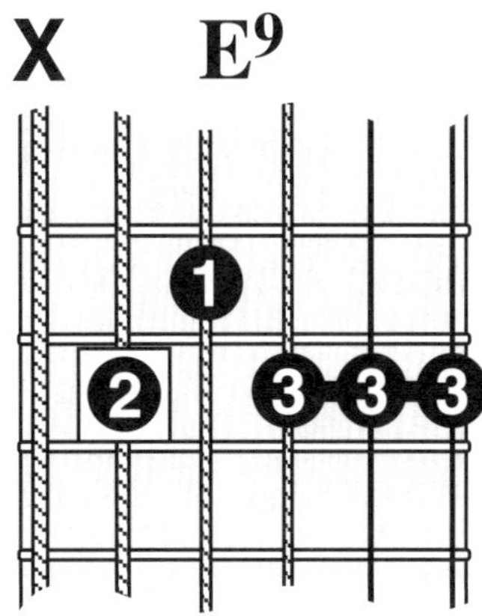

49.

Once you have the shape memorised, try this new 12 bar Blues which moves the 9th chord around the fretboard. In this exercise the shape is often moved briefly up or down one fret from chord I, IV or V. Listen to the effect it creates.

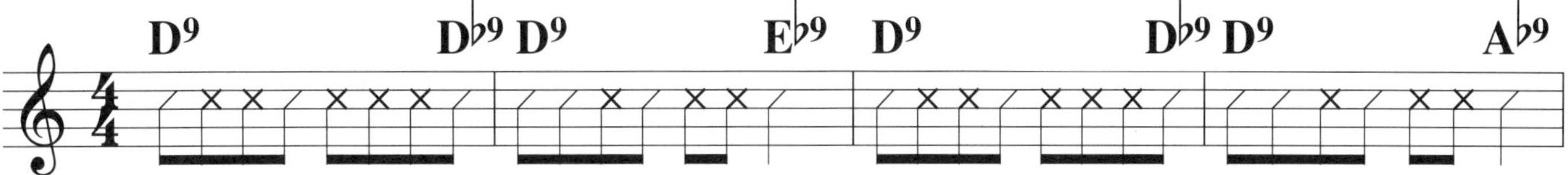

Here is another common **9th** chord shape. This one can be difficult to locate correctly, since it doesn't contain the root note, which is on the **6th string** at the same fret as the third finger.

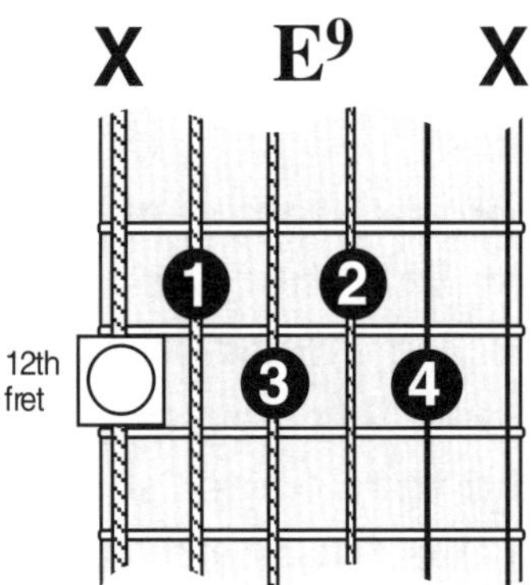

Once you are comfortable with each of the 9th chord shapes, try playing a 12 bar Blues alternating between the two, as shown here. This off-beat rhythm is also effective with 7th chords. Experiment with combining 7th and 9th chords in the one progression.

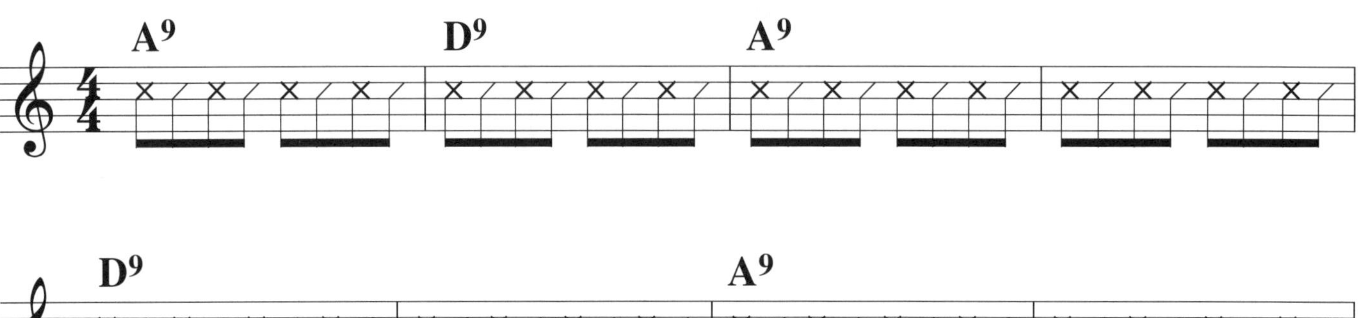

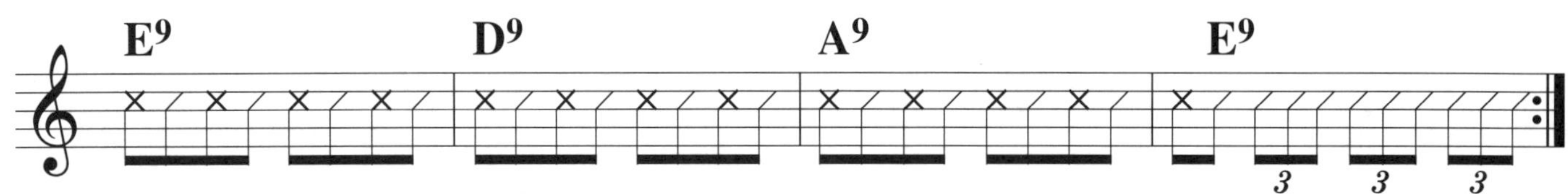

This one alternates between minor 7th and 9th chords.

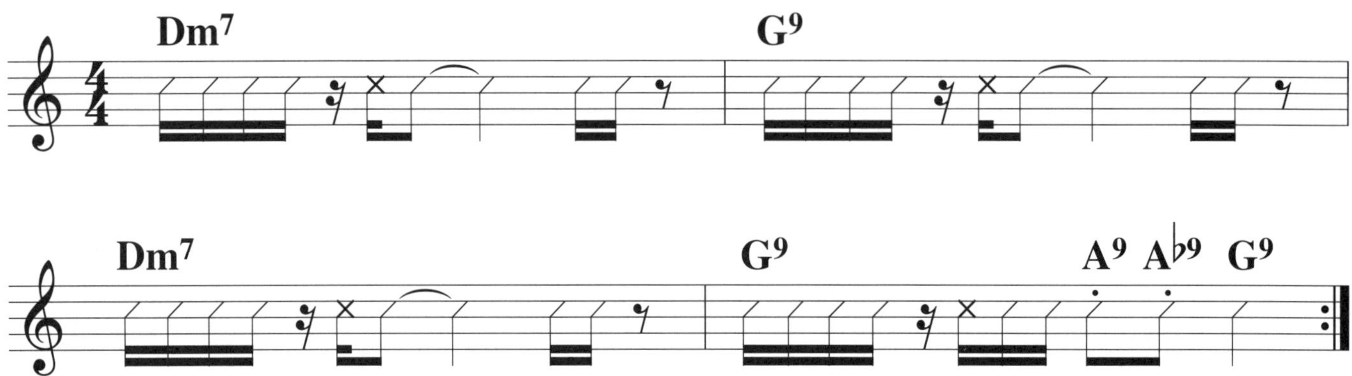

LESSON FORTY THREE

EXTENDED CHORDS

When you play Fusion, Funk, Jazz, Blues, Hip-Hop or R&B, you will often find chords which extend past the 7th, notably various types of **9th**, **11th** and **13th** chords. These higher numbers are formed by repeating the scale from which they are derived over two octaves. Thus, in the higher octave the 2nd becomes the 9th, the 4th becomes the 11th and the 6th becomes the 13th as shown below in the key of C.

C	D	E	F	G	A	B	C	D	E	F	G	A	B	C
1	2	3	4	5	6	7	8	9	10	11	12	13	14	15

Most chords are made up of various 3rd intervals stacked one on top of the other. By going through a scale in thirds (i.e. skipping every second note) it is easy to create chords up to a 13th. A **major triad** (3 note chord) contains the degrees **1**, **3** and **5** of the major scale. A **major 7th** chord is created by adding the **7th** degree on top of the major triad. This 7th degree is a 3rd above the 5th of the chord. By adding another 3rd on top of the major 7th chord, a **major 9th** chord is created. By adding another 3rd on top of the major 9th chord, a **major 11th chord** is created. If you add another 3rd on top of the major 11th chord, a **major 13th** chord is created. The 13th is as high as the chord can go, because if you add a 3rd on top of the major 13th chord, you end up with the root note of the chord again.

Depending on the nature of the 3rd and 7th degrees of the chord, 9ths 11ths and 13ths may be either major, minor or dominant in quality. E.g. if you add a **9th degree** on top of a **dominant 7th** chord, you end up with a **dominant 9th** chord (usually just called a 9th chord). If you add a 9th degree on top of a **minor 7th** chord, you end up with **a minor 9th** chord, etc. Written below are the formulas for some typical 9th, 11th and 13th chords.

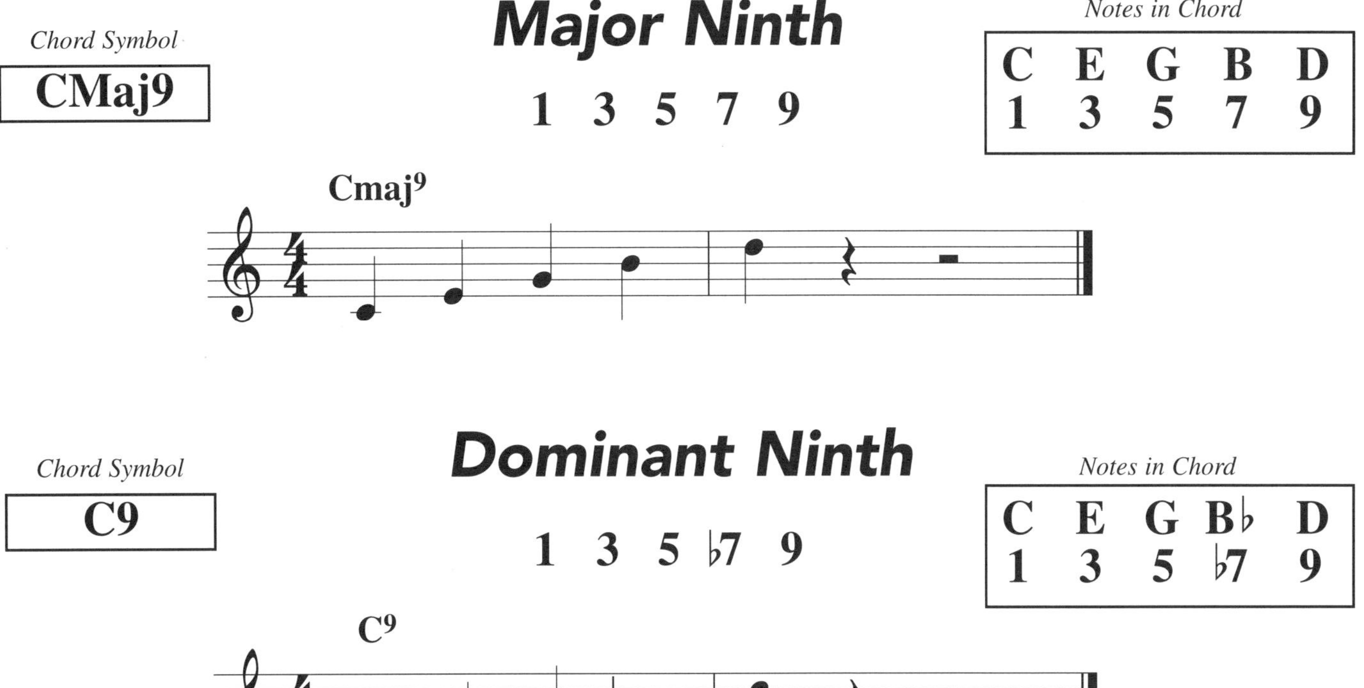

Minor Ninth

Chord Symbol

Cm9

1 ♭3 5 ♭7 9

Notes in Chord

C	E♭	G	B♭	D
1	♭3	5	♭7	9

ELEVENTH CHORDS

By adding another 3rd interval on top of a 9th chord, it is possible to create an **11th chord**. Depending on the 3rd and 7th of the chord, you can create major, minor and dominant 11th chords. The chord shown below is a C minor 11th (**Cm11**). By raising the 3rd of the chord from E♭ to E♮ it could be changed to a dominant 11th chord (**C11**). By raising the 3rd and the 7th it could be changed to a major 11th (**CMaj11**).

Minor Eleventh

Chord Symbol

Cm11

1 ♭3 5 ♭7 9 11

Notes in Chord

C	E♭	G	B♭	D	F
1	♭3	5	♭7	9	11

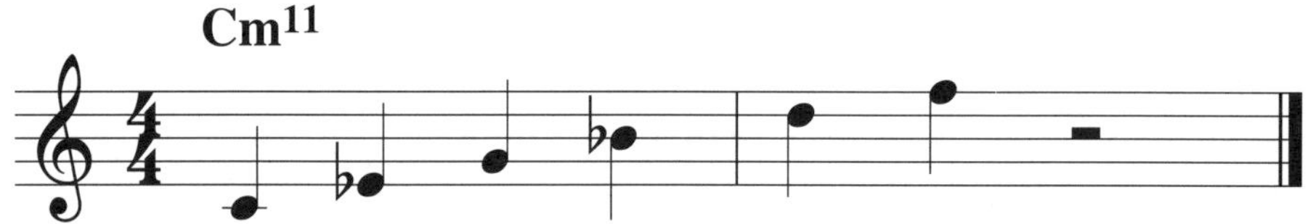

THIRTEENTH CHORDS

By adding another 3rd interval on top of an 11th chord, various types of 13th chords can be created. Once again depending on the 3rd and 7th of the chord, you can create major, minor and dominant 13th chords. The chord shown below is a C dominant 13th (**C13**). By flattening the 3rd of the chord it could be changed to a minor 13th chord (**Cm13**). By raising the 7th it could be changed to a major 13th (**CMaj13**).

Thirteenth

Chord Symbol

C13

1 3 5 ♭7 9 11 13

Notes in Chord

C	E	G	B♭	D	F	A
1	3	5	♭7	9	11	13

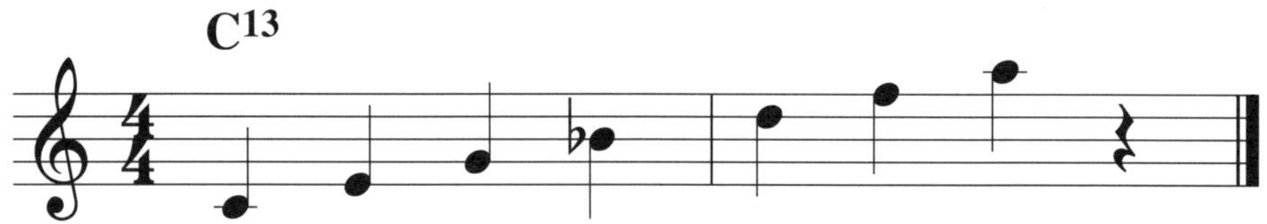

Since most chords are formed from notes of a major scale, you need to know the notes of all 12 major scales from memory in order to be able to create any chord in any key. This chart shows all existing major scales **up to the 13th** for reference in constructing chords. Try memorizing one scale per week until you know them all. You should also make a habit of choosing any starting note and building all chord types up to the 13th on that note.

Chord Construction Chart

Note's Position in Scale → / Scale ↓	1	2	3	4	5	6	7	8	9	10	11	12	13
A	A	B	C♯	D	E	F♯	G♯	A	B	C♯	D	E	F♯
A♭	A♭	B♭	C	D♭	E♭	F	G	A♭	B♭	C	D♭	E♭	F
B	B	C♯	D♯	E	F♯	G♯	A♯	B	C♯	D♯	E	F♯	G♯
B♭	B♭	C	D	E♭	F	G	A	B♭	C	D	E♭	F	G
C	C	D	E	F	G	A	B	C	D	E	F	G	A
C♯	C♯	D♯	E♯	F♯	G♯	A♯	B♯	C♯	D♯	E♯	F♯	G♯	A♯
D	D	E	F♯	G	A	B	C♯	D	E	F♯	G	A	B
D♭	D♭	E♭	F	G♭	A♭	B♭	C	D♭	E♭	F	G♭	A♭	B♭
E	E	F♯	G♯	A	B	C♯	D♯	E	F♯	G♯	A	B	C♯
E♭	E♭	F	G	A♭	B♭	C	D	E♭	F	G	A♭	B♭	C
F	F	G	A	B♭	C	D	E	F	G	A	B♭	C	D
F♯	F♯	G♯	A♯	B	C♯	D♯	E♯	F♯	G♯	A♯	B	C♯	D♯
G	G	A	B	C	D	E	F♯	G	A	B	C	D	E
G♭	G♭	A♭	B♭	C♭	D♭	E♭	F	G♭	A♭	B♭	C♭	D♭	E♭

OMITTING NOTES FROM CHORDS

The more notes you add to chords, the more difficult they are to play and the more muddy they can sound. For this reason it is common to omit notes from extended chords, keeping only the notes which most clearly indicate the quality (sound) of the chord. The most frequently omitted note is the **5th**, although sometimes the 3rd or the root can be omitted. Usually the bass will be playing the root note anyway. With a dominant 7th chord, as long as the ♭7 degree is in the chord you still get the effect of a 7th chord. With a dominant 9th chord, as long as you have the 3rd, ♭7th and 9th, you have the effect of a 9th chord, etc. Shown below are some common voicings of various 9th, 11th and 13th chords, along with some examples demonstrating their use. The first two are Major and Minor 9ths.

52.

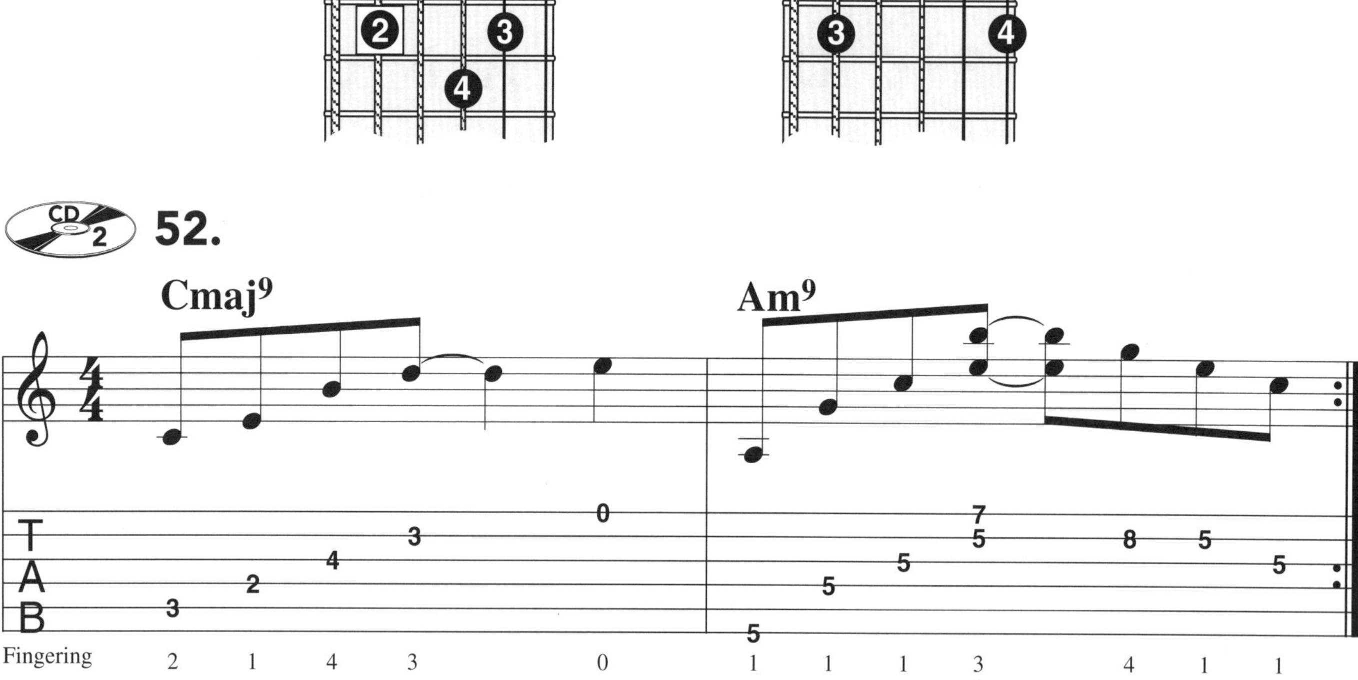

Here are two more commonly used dominant 9th chord shapes and an example making use of them. Both have the 5th omitted.

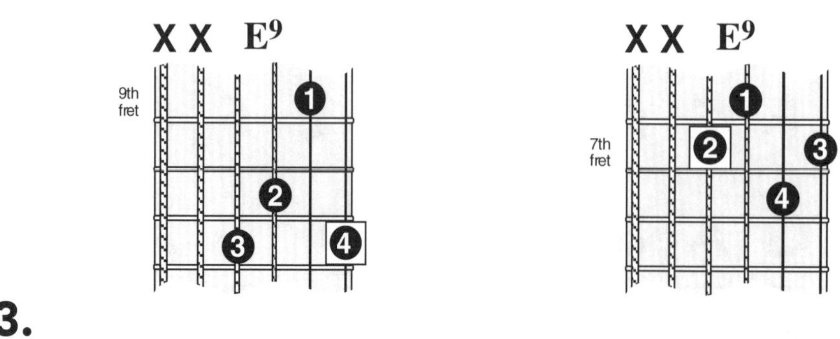

53.

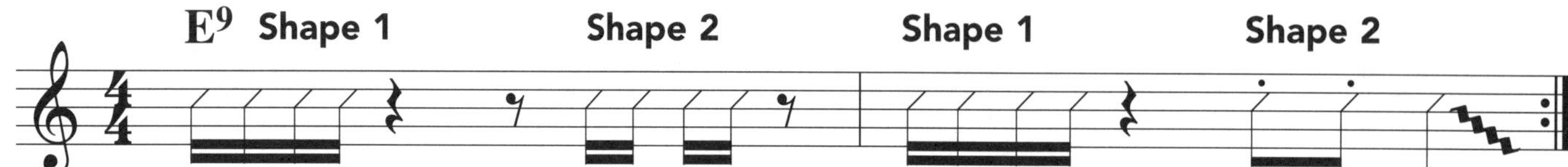

54.

This example uses **minor 11th** chords.

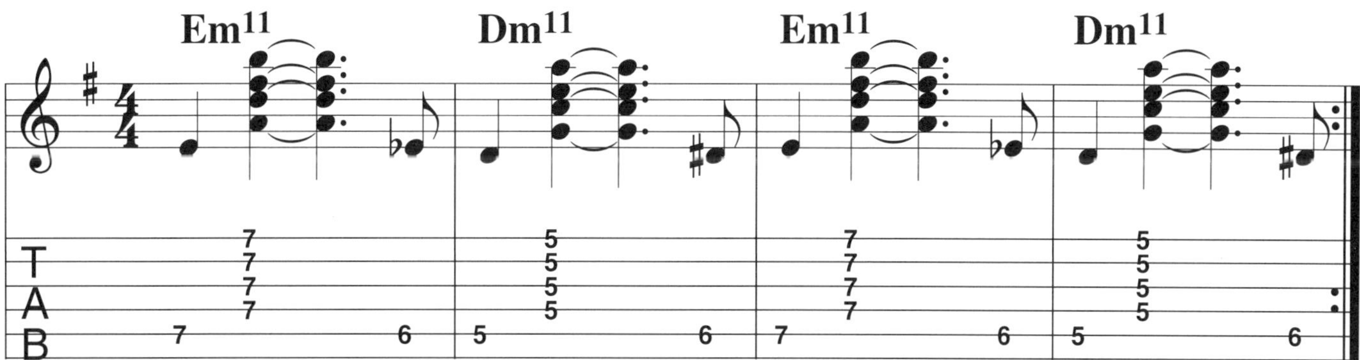

55. Kenny's Blues

This one is a Blues which uses **dominant 13th** Chords.

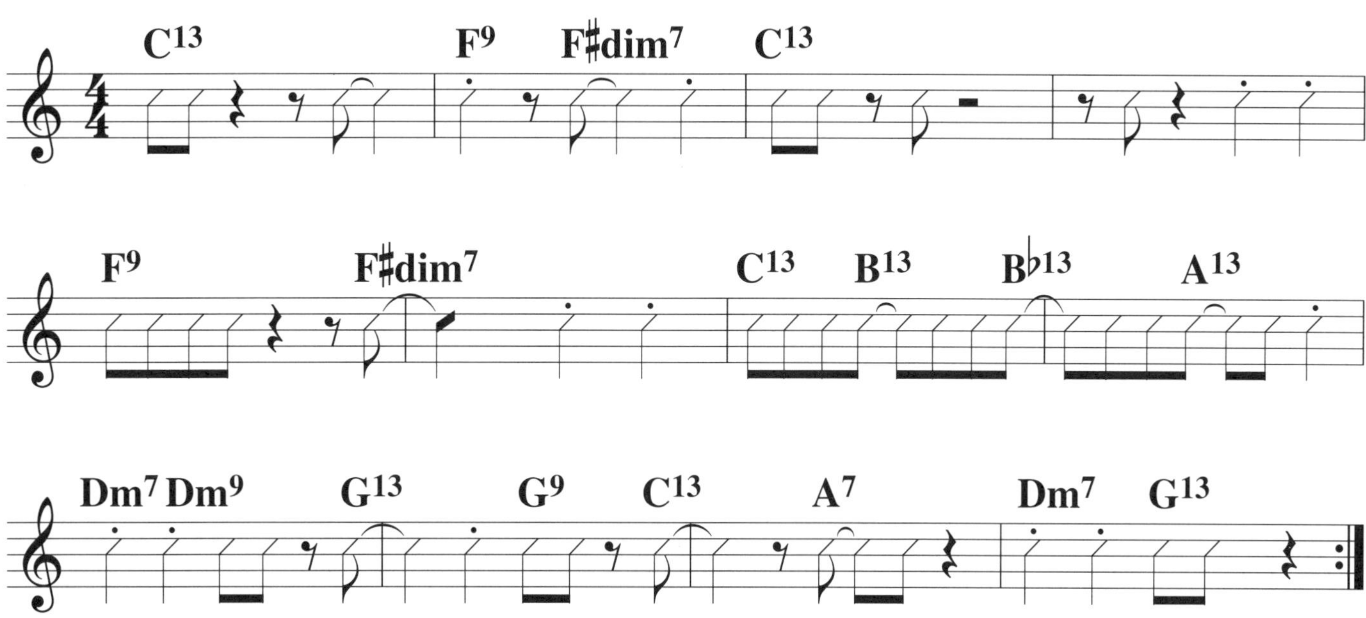

56. Rhythm Changes

Now try this progression which uses various types of 7ths, 9ths, 11ths and 13ths. It is based on the progression for George Gershwin's song "**I Got Rhythm**" and is commonly referred to as **Rhythm Changes**. To learn more about this style of playing, see *Progressive Complete Learn to Play Jazz Guitar Manual.*

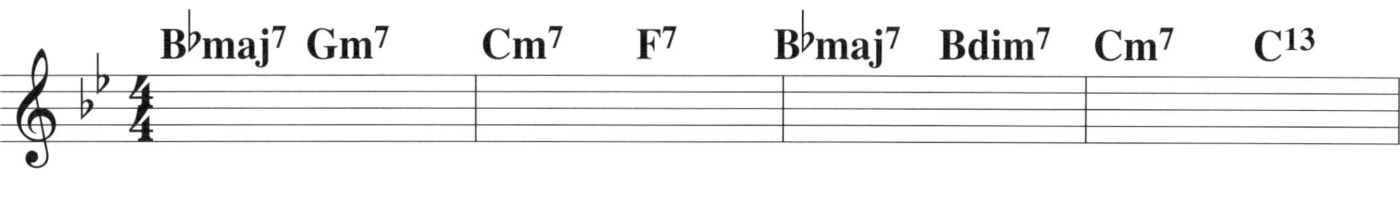

ALTERED CHORDS

All basic chord types can be varied to form **altered chords**. As shown in previous lessons, the raising and lowering of 3rds and 7ths is common, but other degrees of a chord may also be raised or lowered. When other degrees (e.g. the 5th, 9th, 11th or 13th) are altered, the chord becomes an **altered chord**. The most common altered chords involve changes to the **5th** and **9th** degrees. The name of the chord indicates the alterations, as in the examples below. Chord shapes for all these chords are shown on pages 226 to 228.

Seven Flat Five Chord Formula

Chord Symbol

C7♭5

1 3 ♭5 ♭7

Notes in Chord

C	E	G♭	B♭
1	3	♭5	♭7

57.0

Thirteenth Sharp Five, Flat Nine

Chord Symbol

C7 ♯5 ♭9

1 3 ♯5 ♭7 ♭9 11 13

Notes in Chord

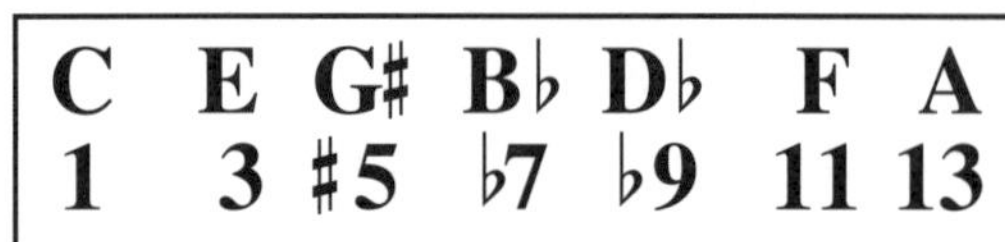

C	E	G♯	B♭	D♭	F	A
1	3	♯5	♭7	♭9	11	13

57.1

There are many more chord types and fingerings in addition to the ones demonstrated in this lesson. For a more in-depth study of extended and altered chords, see *Complete Learn to Play Jazz Guitar Manual.*

LESSON FORTY FOUR

SLIDING CHORDS

Sliding chords from one fret to another is a technique often used in rhythm guitar playing. The slide is indicated by a line between the chords accompanied by the letter **S**. Here is an example of this technique using a 9th chord and a 7th chord.

58.0

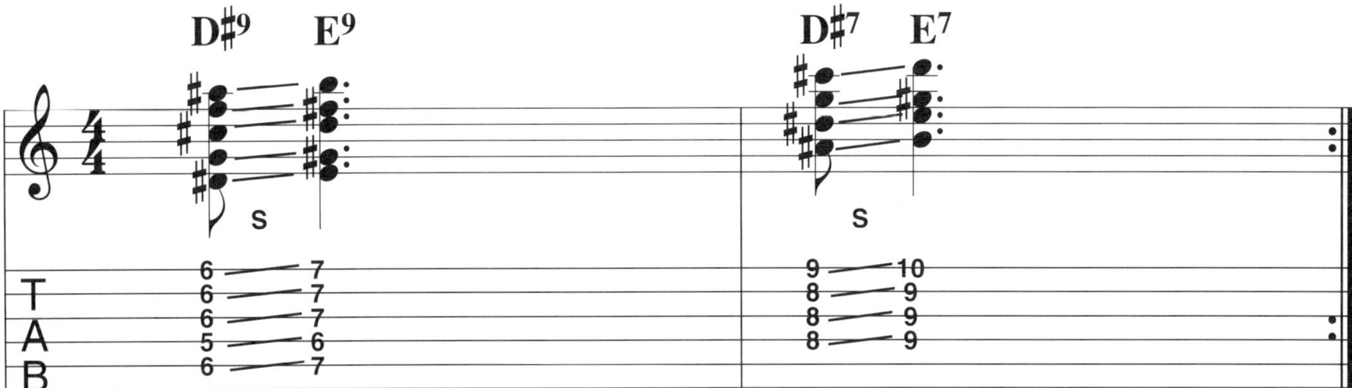

58.1

Here are two more examples using sliding chords. As you can hear, it's a very effective sound.

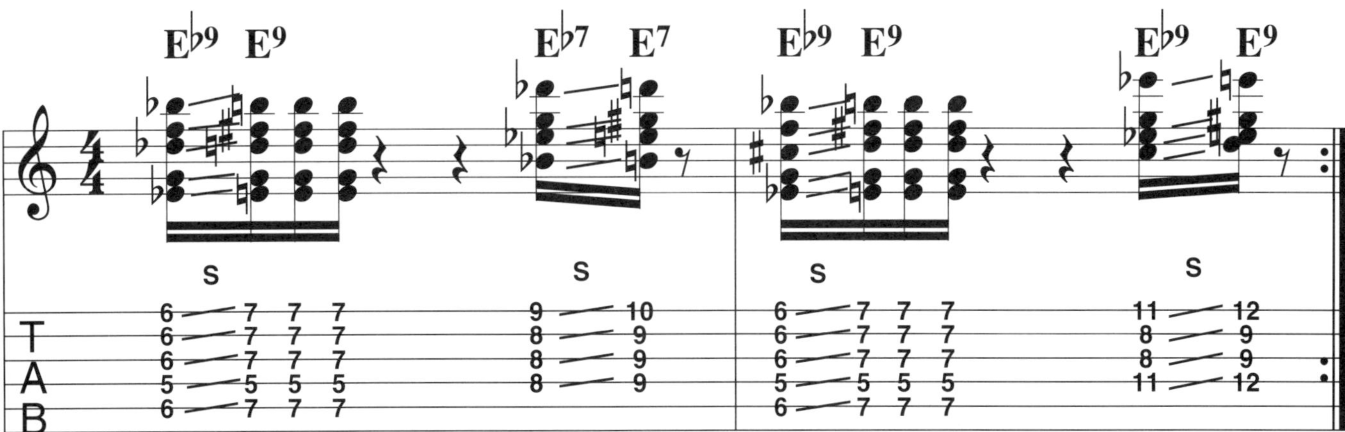

58.2

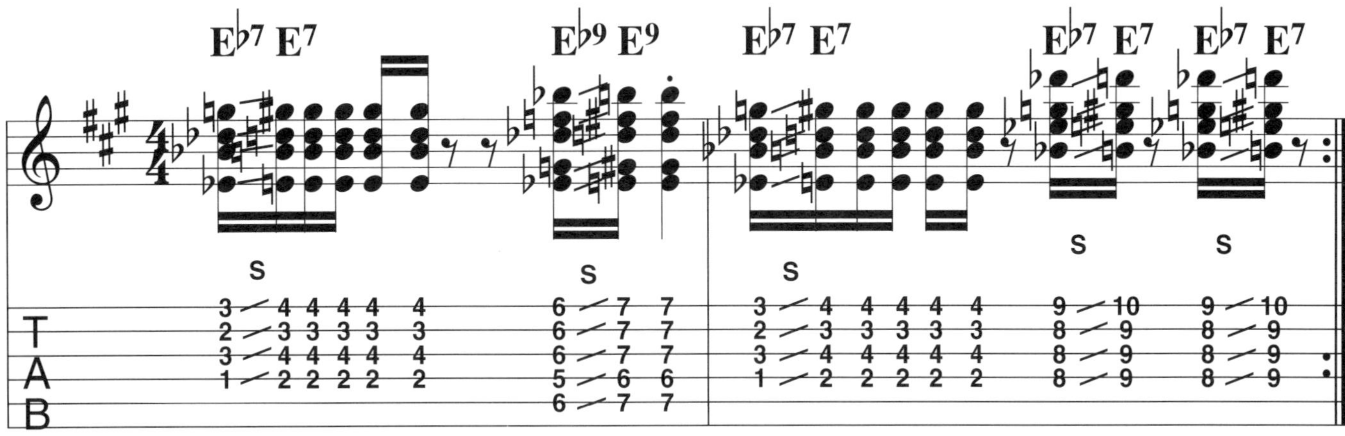

COMBINING RIFFS AND CHORDS

Many rhythm parts are combinations of single note riffs and chords. The following examples demonstrate Blues and Minor Pentatonic scale riffs combined with chords. Once you have learnt these, try creating some of your own.

59.0

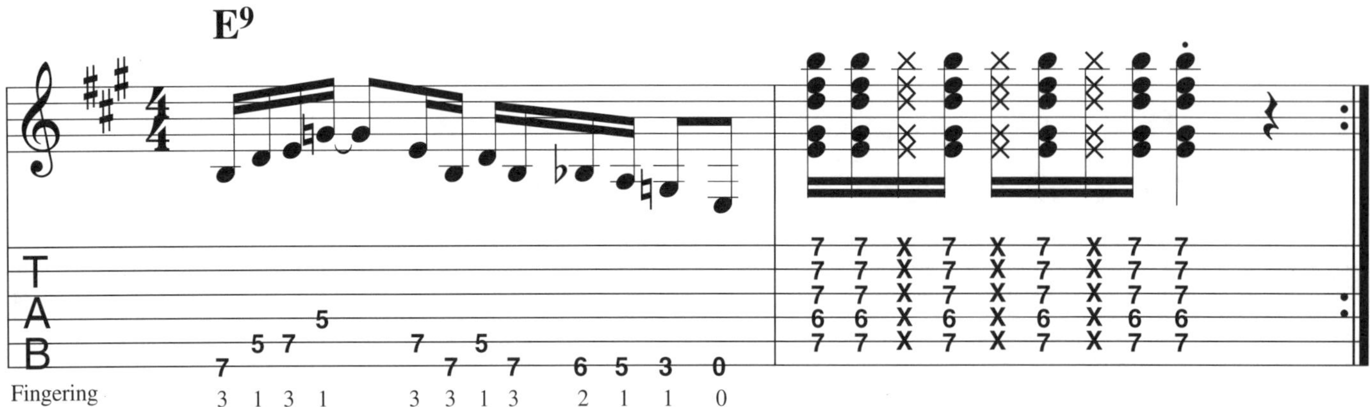

CD 2

59.1

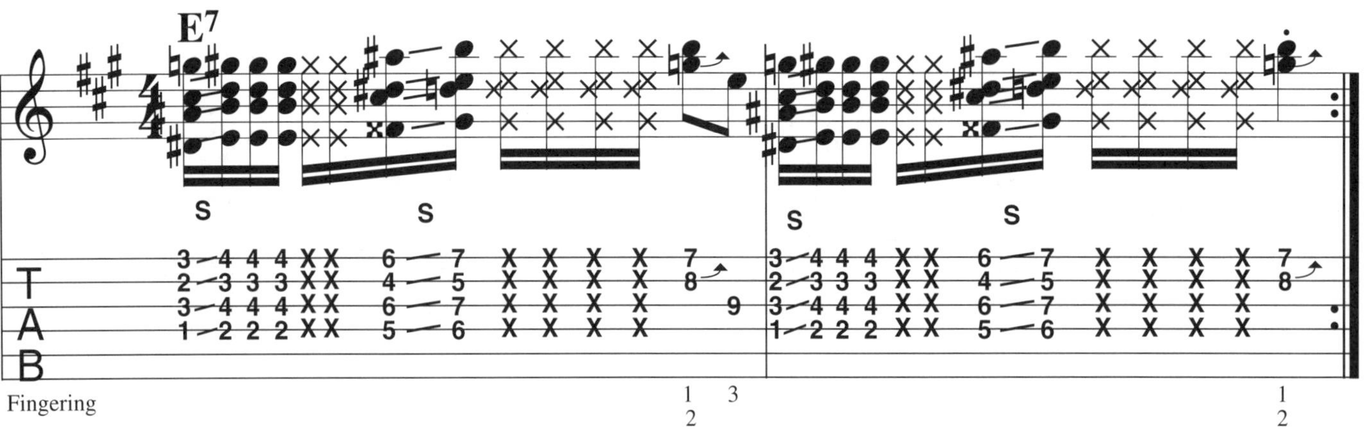

CD 2

59.2

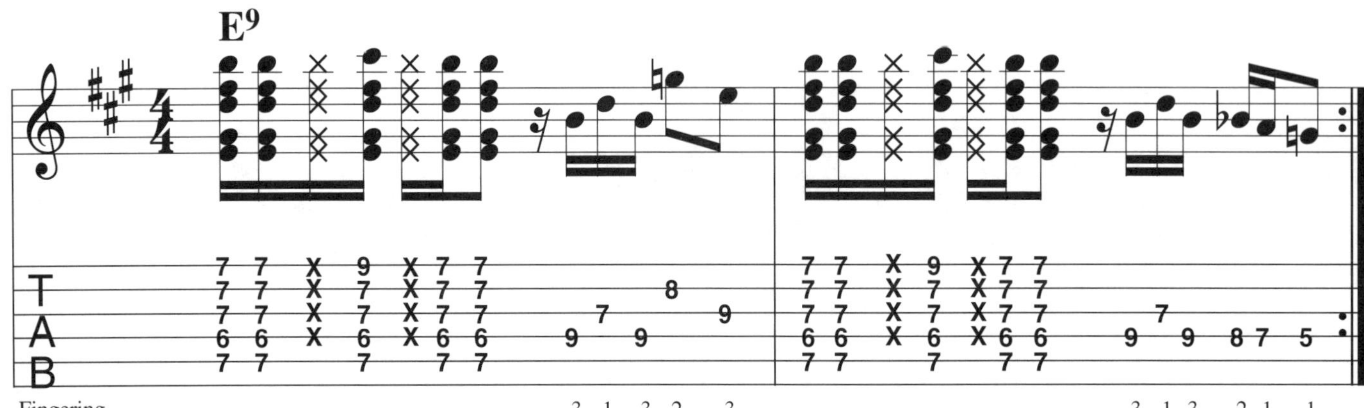

SIXTEENTH NOTE TRIPLETS.

Another important grouping is the **16th note triplet**. These are usually fairly quick, being three 16th notes played in the time of two. Here is an example.

60.

Like eighth notes, it is possible to swing 16th notes by tying together the first two notes of a 16th note triplet. Here are some examples.

61.0

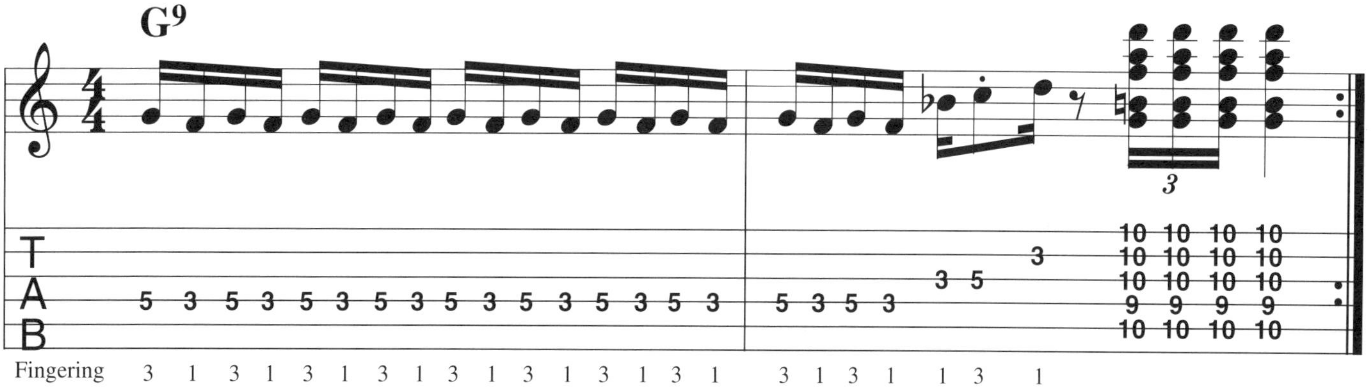

G9

61.1

E9

LESSON FORTY FIVE

SLURS

Although it is possible to make a good sound picking every note, it is more common to use a variety of left hand techniques to add expression to some of the notes. These techniques are essential in all styles of guitar playing and should definitely be mastered. Be sure to play right on the tips of the fingers when practicing these techniques.

When two notes or more are played in succession and only the first note is picked, the notes played by the left hand only are said to be "slurred". A **slur** is a way of connecting notes more smoothly than when articulating every note with the right hand. A slur is indicated by a curved line above or below two or more **different** notes.

THE HAMMER-ON

The **hammer-on** is executed by picking a note and then hammering a left hand finger onto the string. The hammer-on is indicated by a curved line and the letter "**H**".

62.0

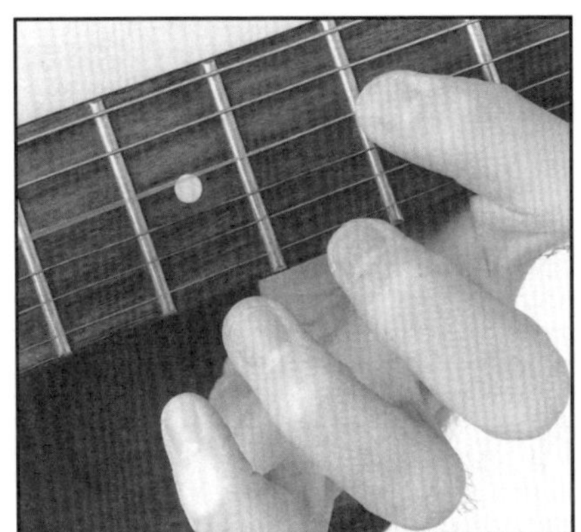

Begin by playing the note on the 5th fret, fourth string.

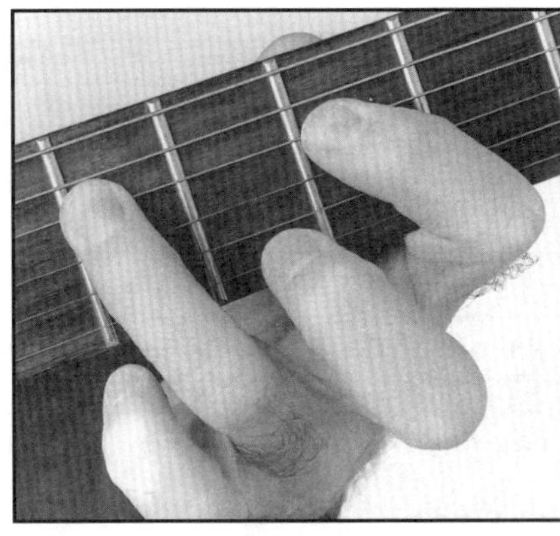

Hammer third finger onto 7th fret of fourth string.

62.1

Here is an exercise to help you develop the use of hammer-ons.

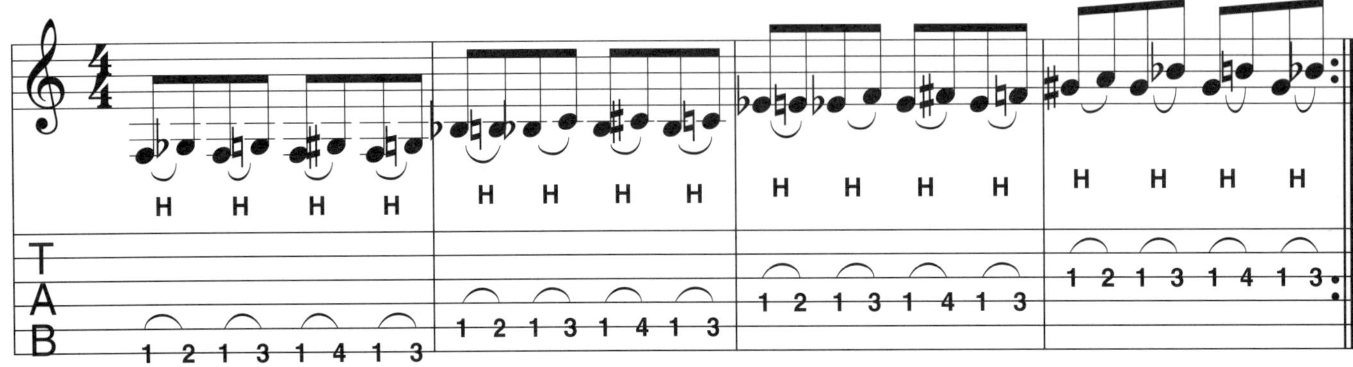

THE PULL-OFF

The pull-off is executed by playing a note and then pulling the left hand finger off the string towards the floor. This causes a new note to sound. The pull-off is indicated by a curved line and the symbol "**P**".

63.0

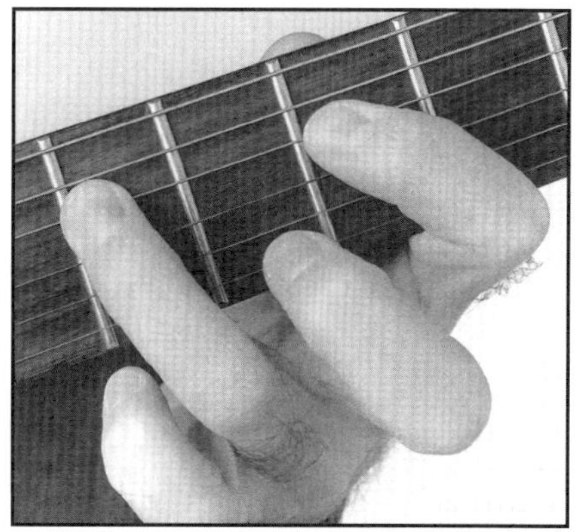

Begin by playing the note on the 7th fret, fourth string.

63.1

Here is an exercise for developing control of pull-offs.

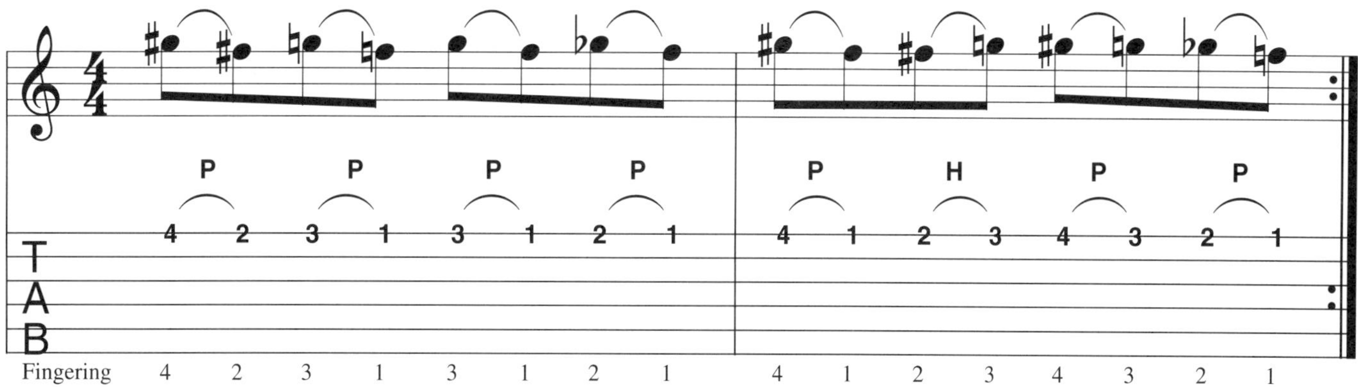

64.

The following example uses both hammer-ons and pull-offs. Make sure all the notes sound clearly and evenly.

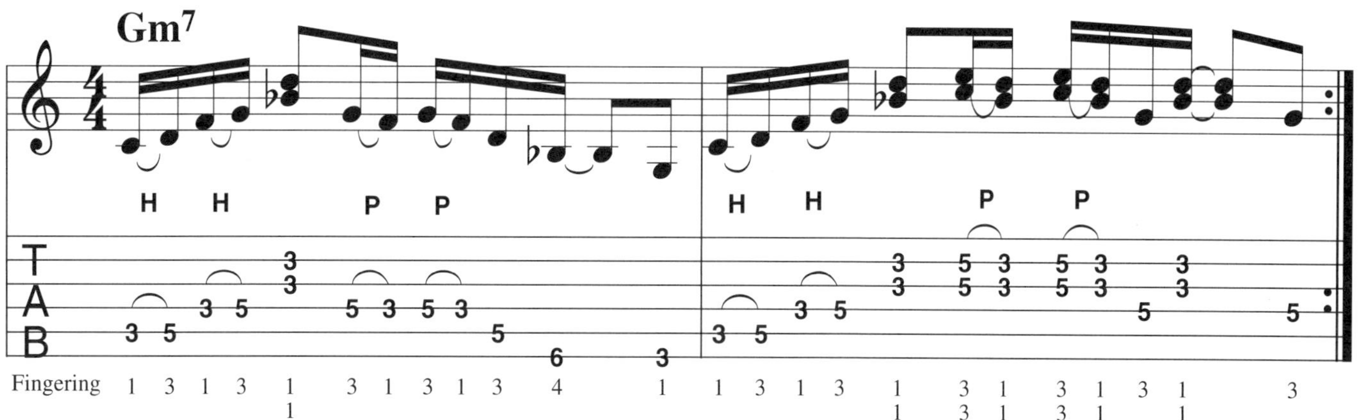

SLURS USING OPEN STRINGS

The examples below demonstrate the use of slurs involving open strings along with other slurs. These examples contain groups of slurred notes where only the first note is picked, while the remaining notes are either hammered-on or pulled-off. Make sure all the notes sound clearly and evenly when you play these examples. If you have trouble with any of the hammer-on's and pull-off's, isolate each one and practice it repeatedly at a slow tempo until you have control of it. Then try the whole example again.

65.0

It is always possible to play a scale or chord in more than one place on the fretboard. These examples are derived from the A minor pentatonic scale in the open position. The notes are the same as those in the 5th position; Only the fingering is different.

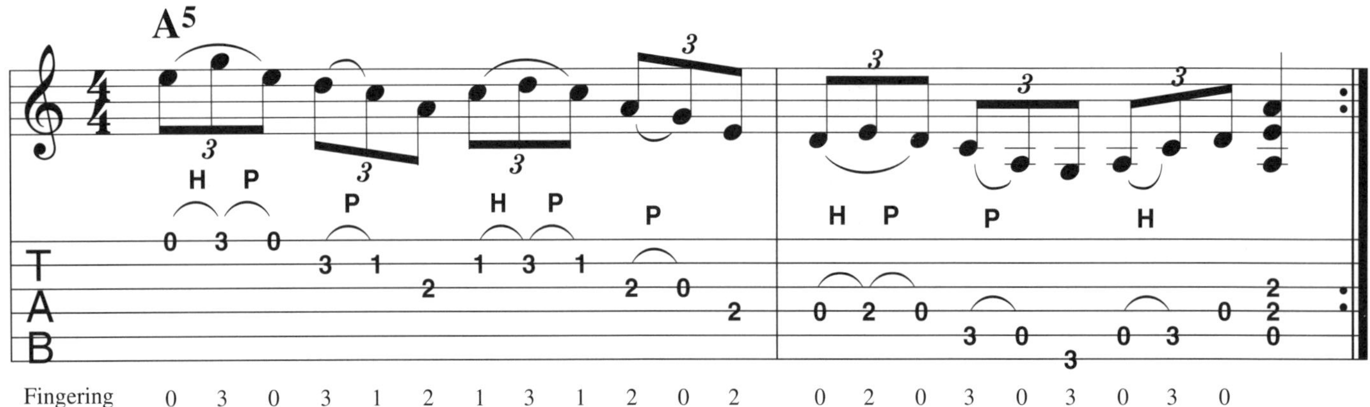

65.1

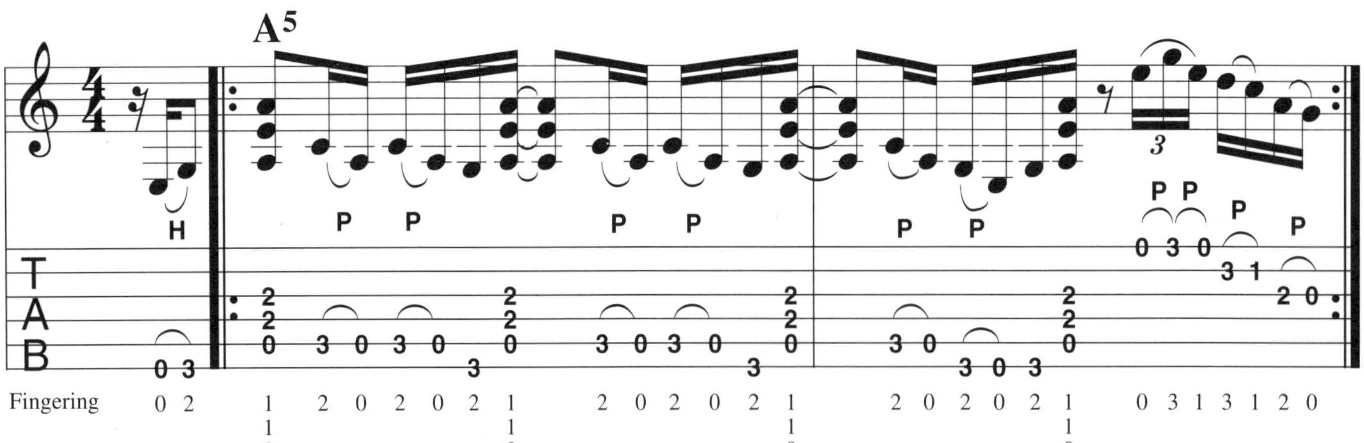

65.2

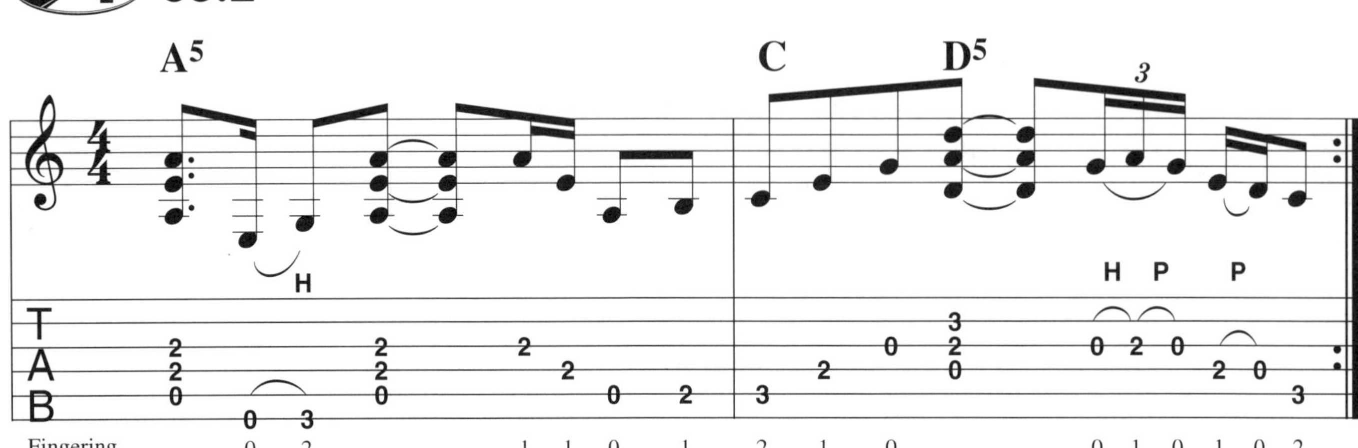

This Folk/Country style solo contains many slurs and uses most of the fretboard. Take your time with it, and be sure all the notes sound clearly. Be sure to damp out any extra unwanted notes, with either the right or left hand.

CD 2 66. Coming Home

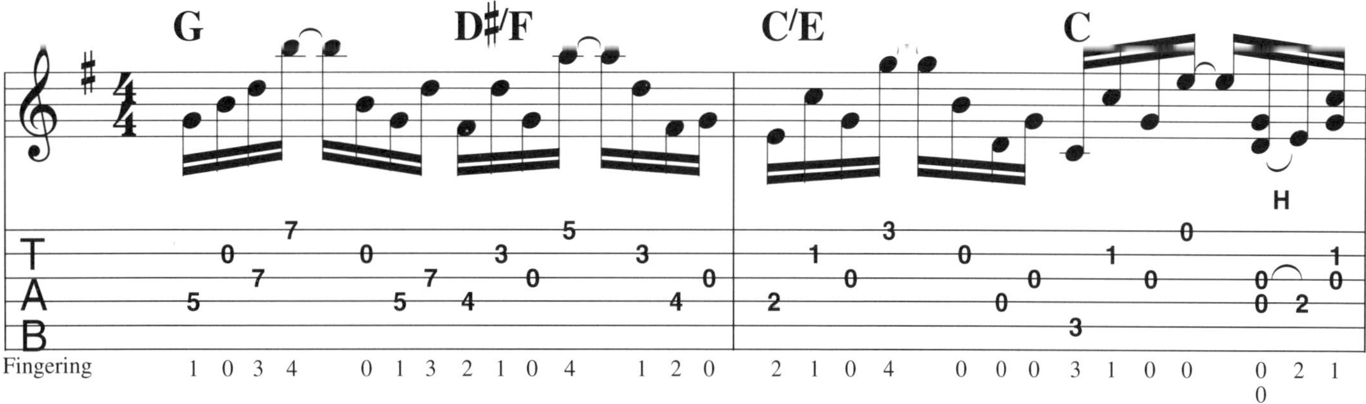

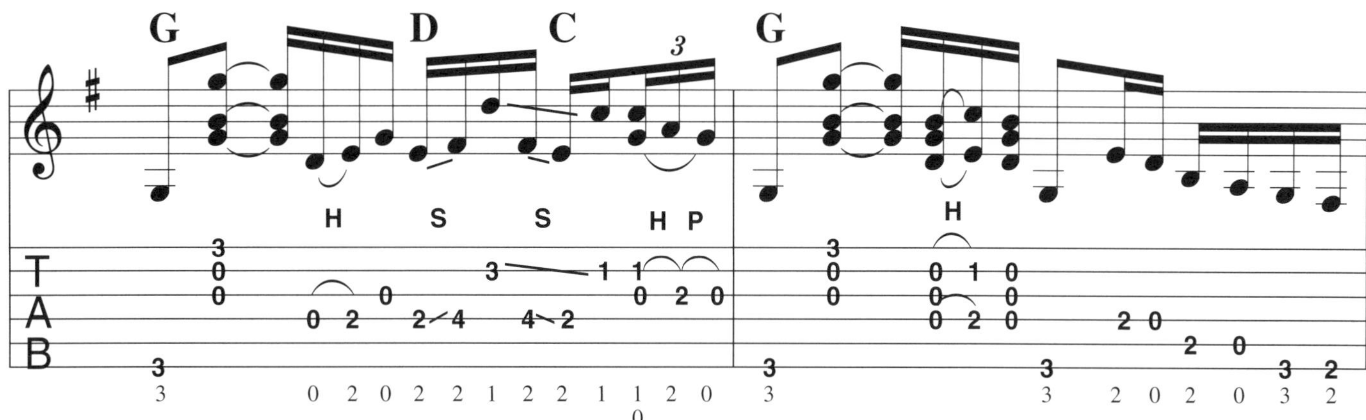

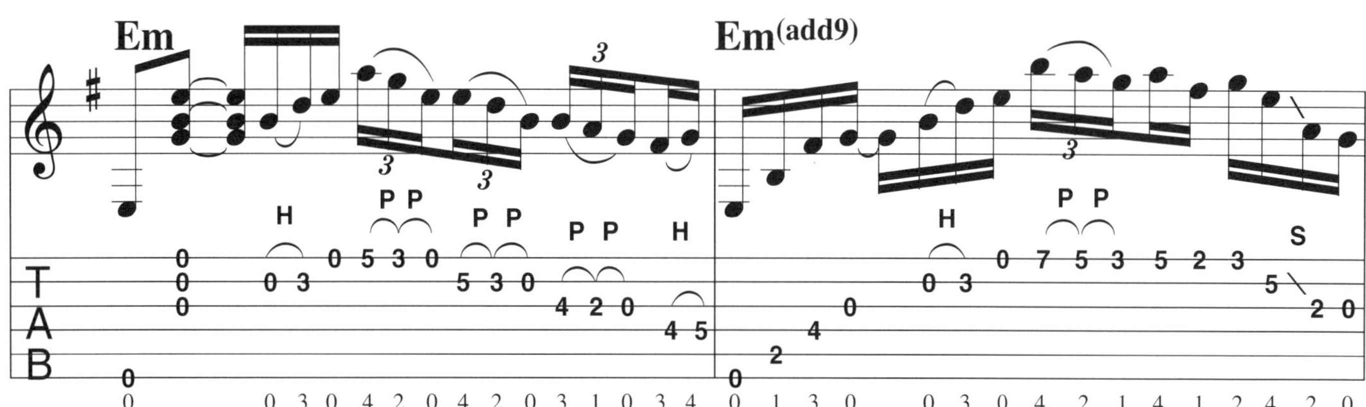

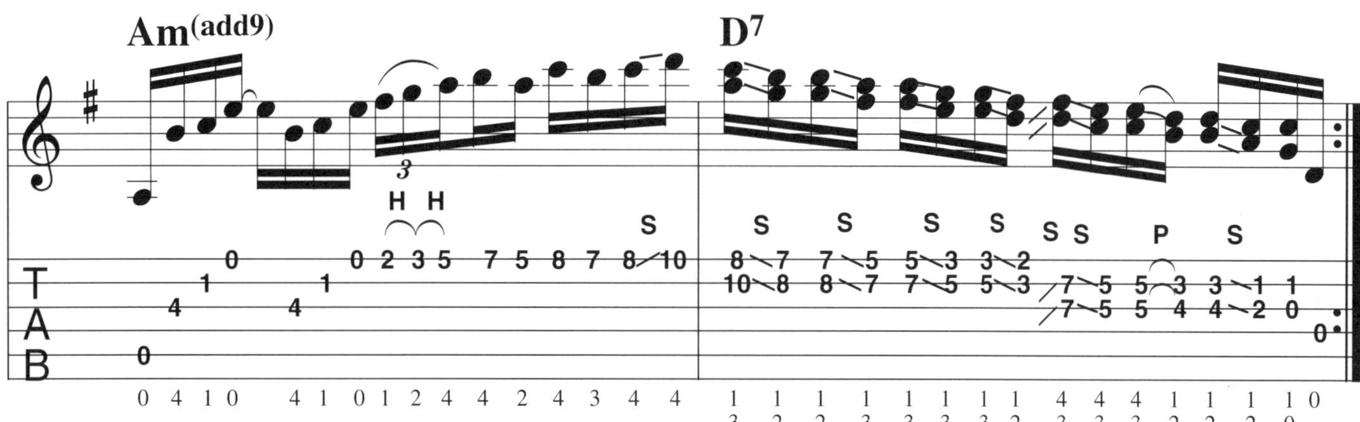

SWAMP SOUNDS

Another popular sound is the use of hammer-ons with 7th chords. It is particularly common in Southern R+B styles often referred to as Swamp Music. Here is the basic sound. Practice it slowly at first to be sure all the notes are sounding clearly.

67.0

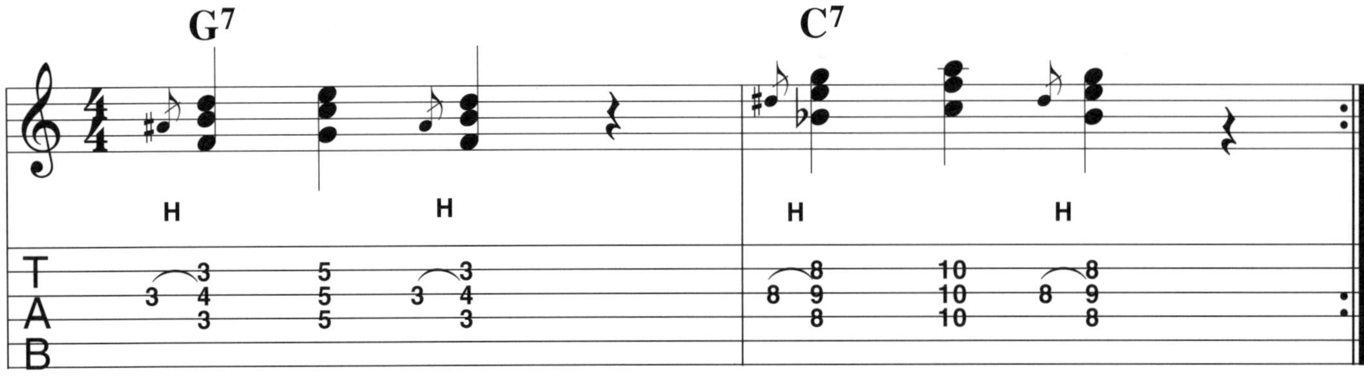

67.1

Here is the basic pattern again, this time with single note riffs added to it.

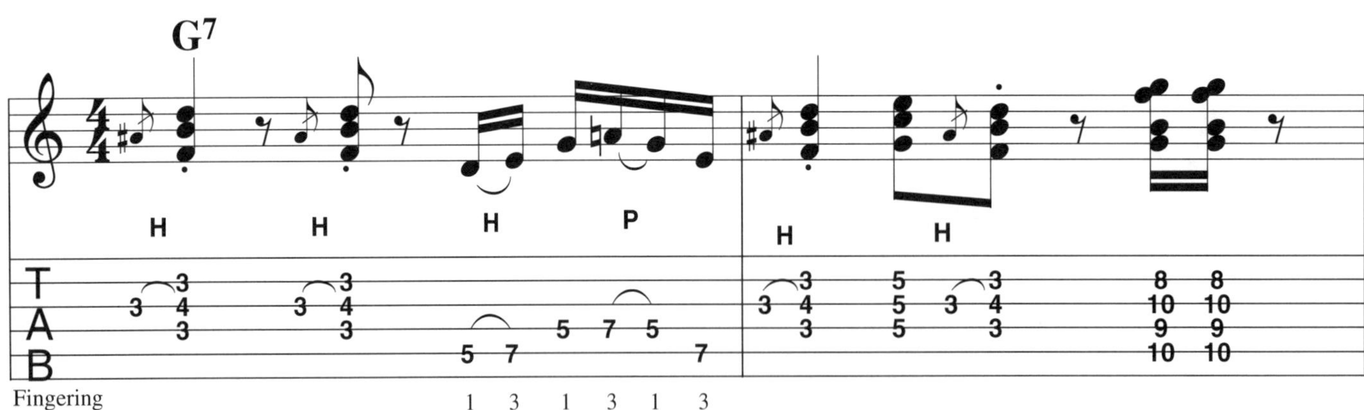

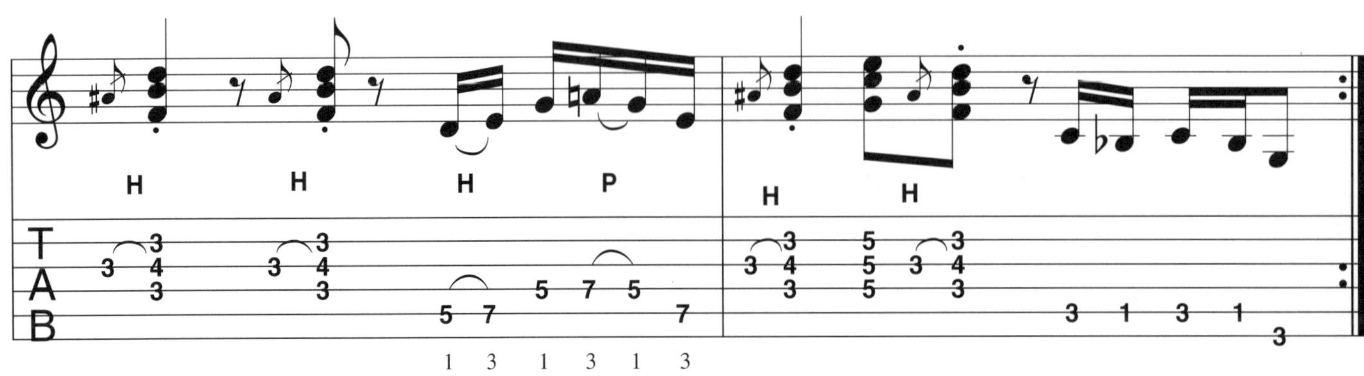

The following solo uses a new technique – the **trill**, which is a rapid succession of hammer-ons and pull-offs, with only the first note being picked. The trill is indicated by the symbol ***tr*** above or below the two notes concerned

68. Duck Soup

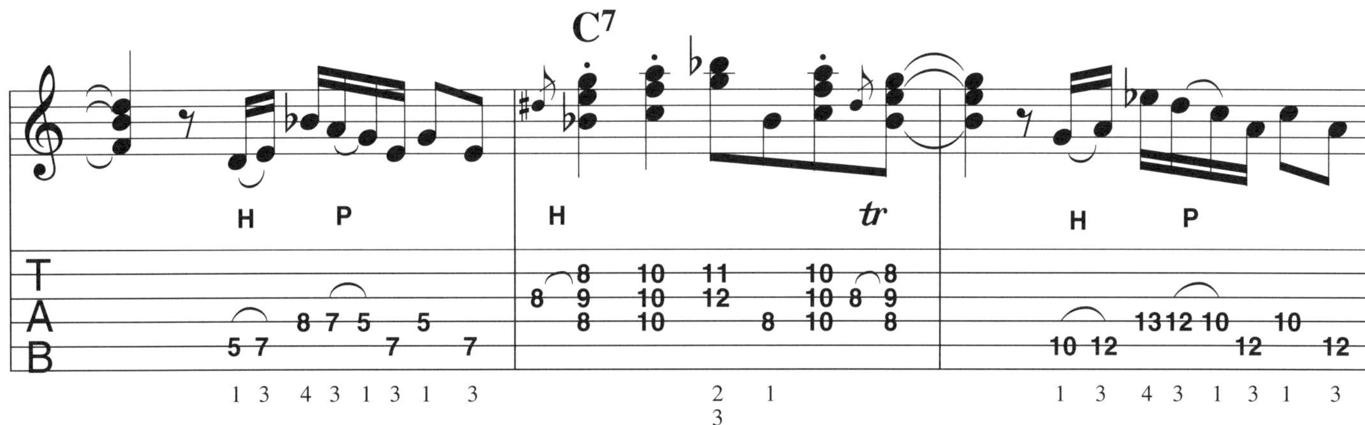

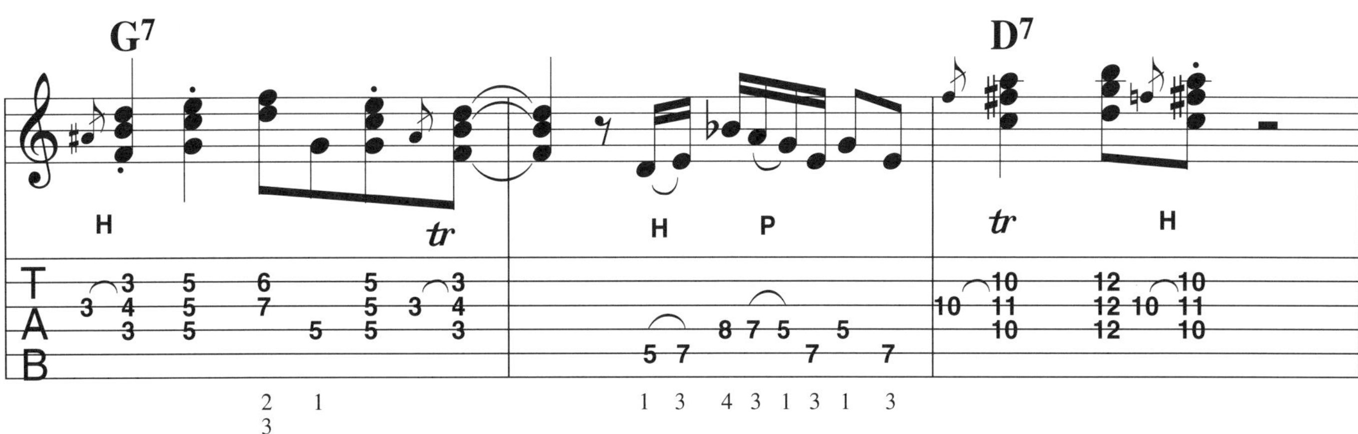

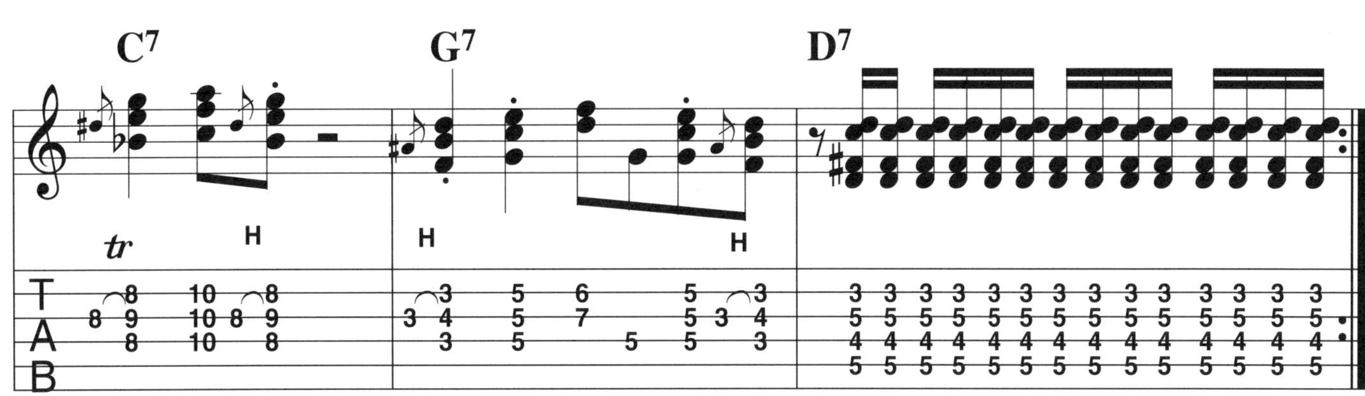

LESSON FORTY SIX

MODES

The term "**mode**" is another name for a scale. There are **seven** different modes which can be derived from the major scale by starting on each of the seven notes of the major scale. These modes were first used in ancient Greece and have been widely used throughout history in all types of music. Each of these modes can be played in **any key**. Just as there are twelve major keys, there are also twelve possible starting notes for each of the modes. Any note of the chromatic scale can be used as a starting note for any mode. This requires a knowledge of the formula for each mode. The names of the seven modes derived from the major scale are listed below along with their scale degrees.

MODE	*FORMULA*
Ionian =	**1 2 3 4 5 6 7**
Dorian =	**1 2 ♭3 4 5 6 ♭7**
Phrygian =	**1 ♭2 ♭3 4 5 ♭6 ♭7**
Lydian =	**1 2 3 ♯4 5 6 7**
Mixolydian =	**1 2 3 4 5 6 ♭7**
Aeolian =	**1 2 ♭3 4 5 ♭6 ♭7**
Locrian =	**1 ♭2 ♭3 4 ♭5 ♭6 ♭7**

Some of these modes are particularly useful for creating chord progressions which don't sound like a typical major or minor key. The Ionian mode is the major scale, so you already know what its possibilities are. The aeolian mode is the natural minor scale, which has also been dealt with earlier in the book. After these, the most commonly used modes are the mixolydian and the dorian, followed by the phrygian, lydian and lastly the locrian. The example below demonstrates a typical Mixolydian Rock riff. The three chords used here - G, D and A also occur in the key of D Major, but as you can hear, the tonality is clearly based around **A** rather than D. To learn more about modes in general, see ***Progressive Scales and Modes for Guitar***, or ***Progressive Complete Teach Yourself Jazz Guitar Manual***.

CD 2 **69.**

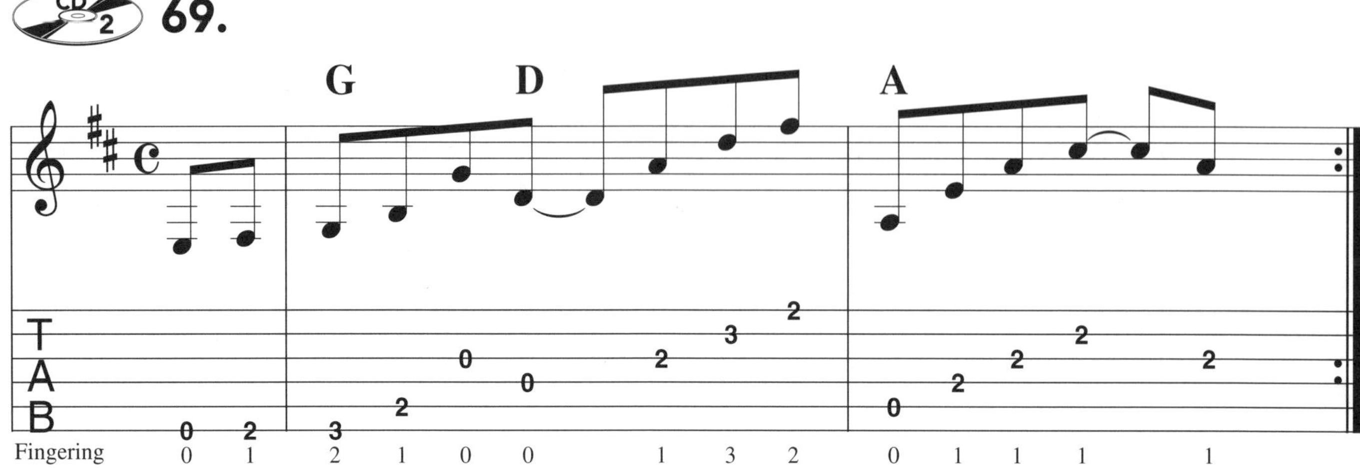

THE MIXOLYDIAN MODE

As mentioned on the previous page, one of the most commonly used modes is the **Mixolydian** mode. Its degrees are **1**, **2**, **3**, **4**, **5**, **6**, and **♭7**. Here it is in the key of **A**.

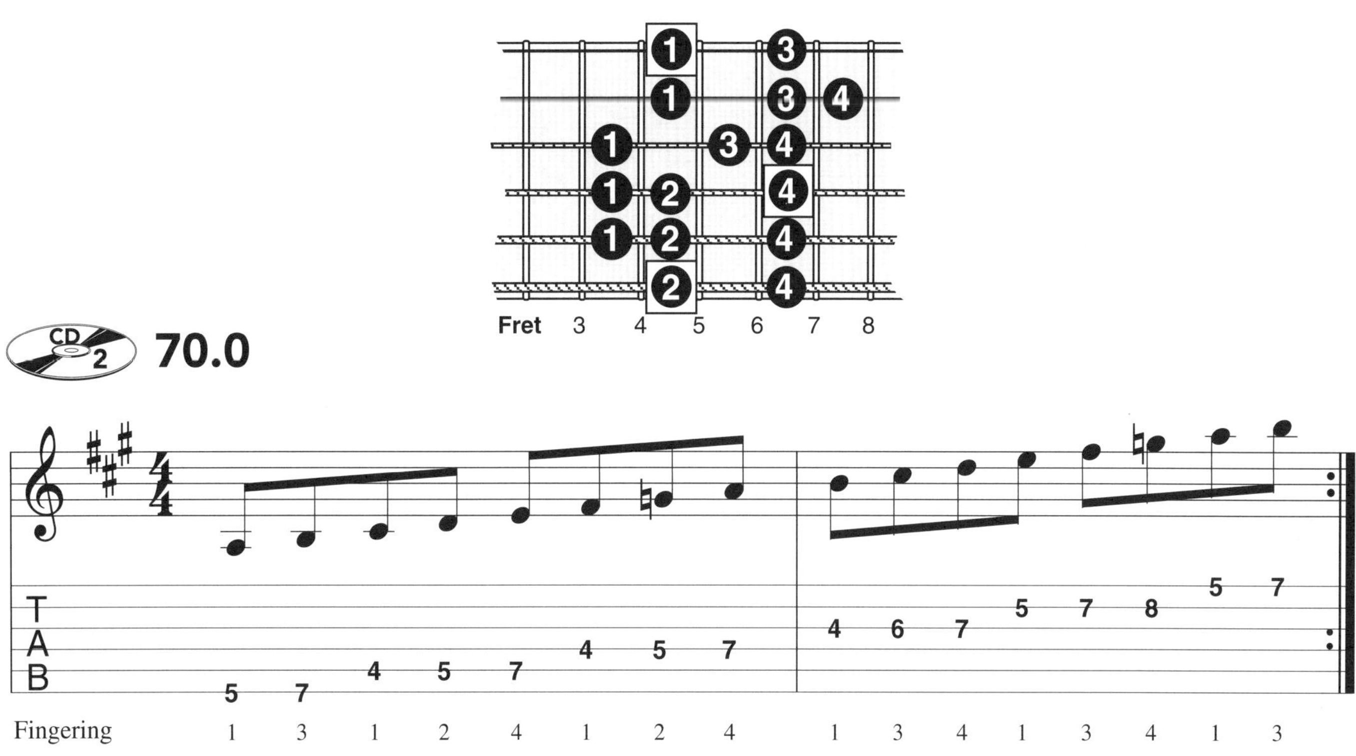

70.1

Here is a four bar riff derived from the **A** mixolydian mode.

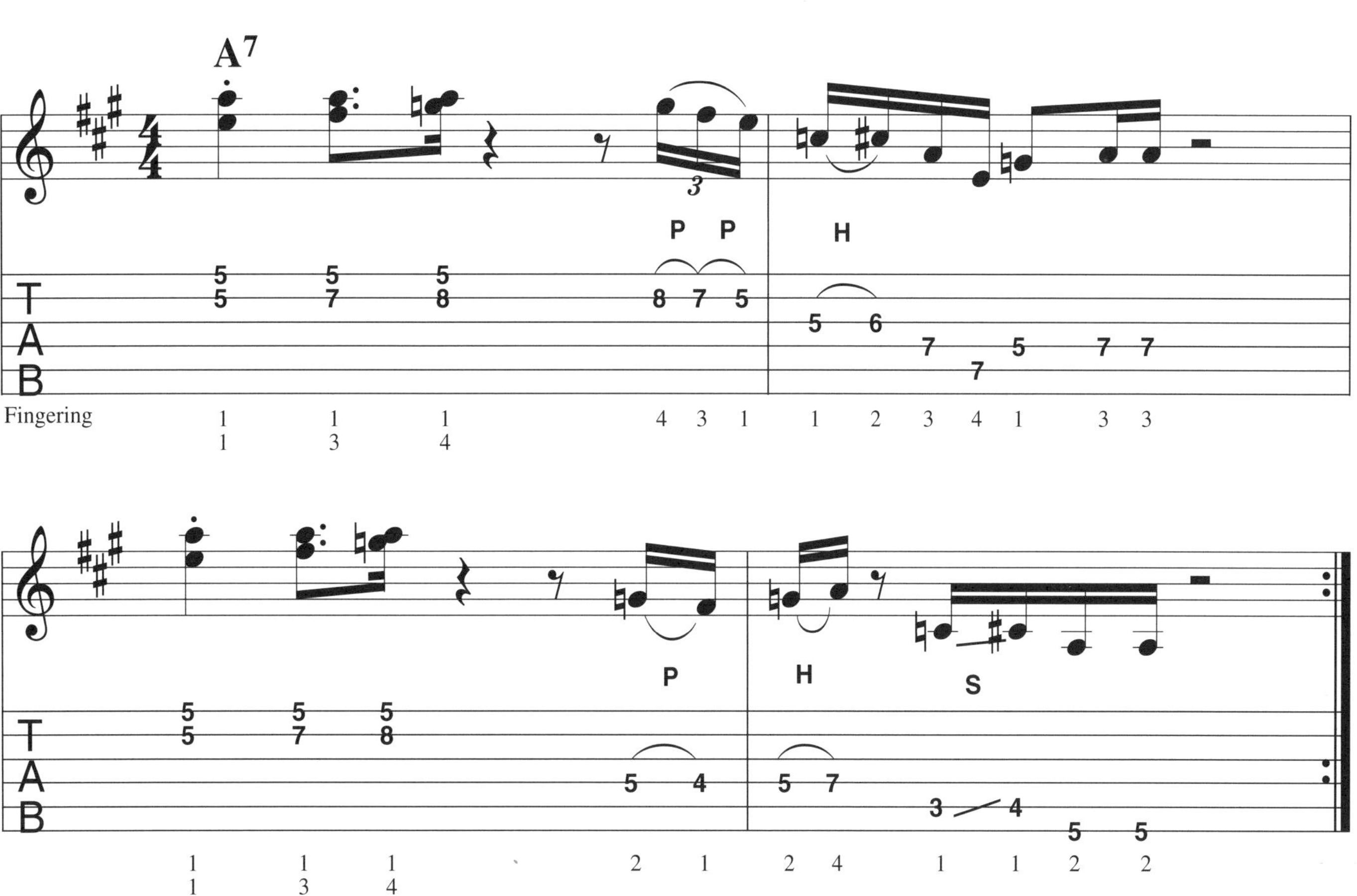

70.2

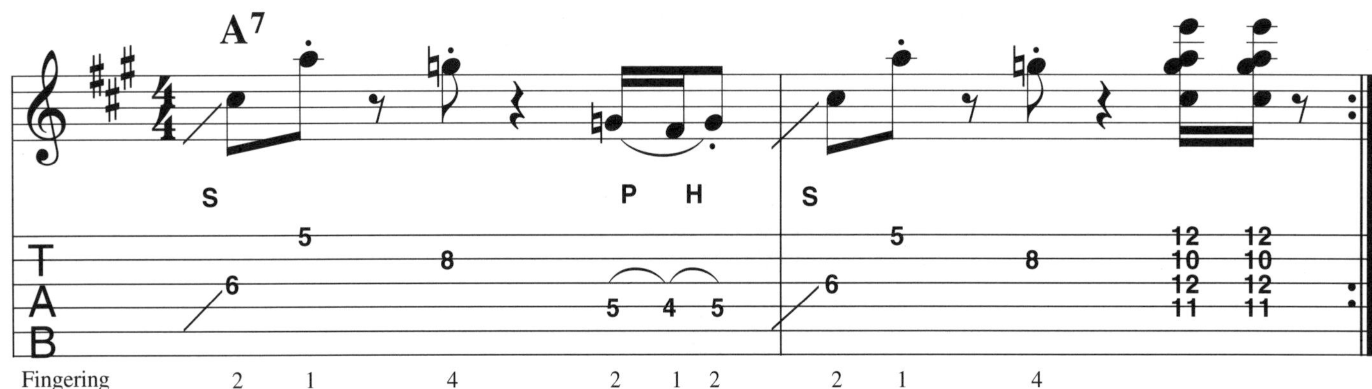

71. Walkin' to Texas

The Mixolydian mode is particularly common in Blues and Blues related styles. Observe the fingering carefully and pay special attention to the rhythm.

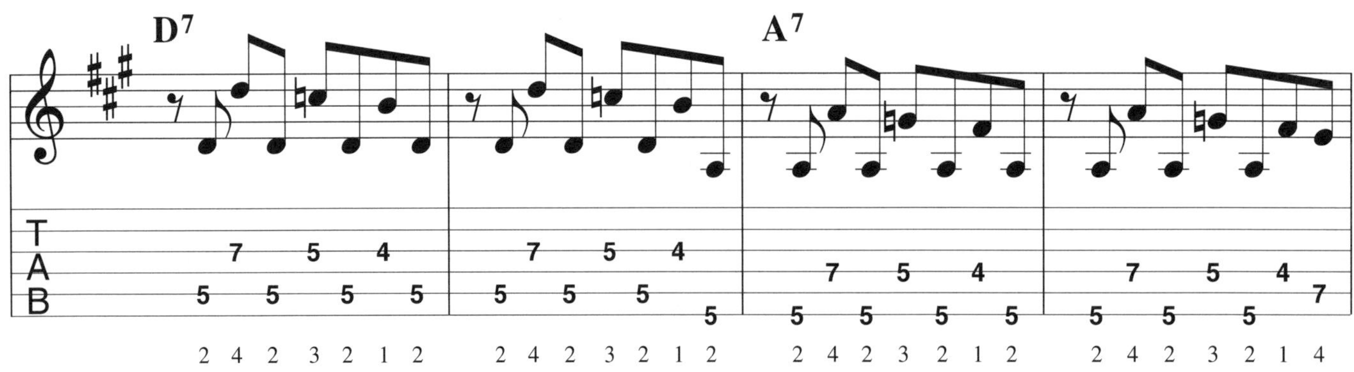

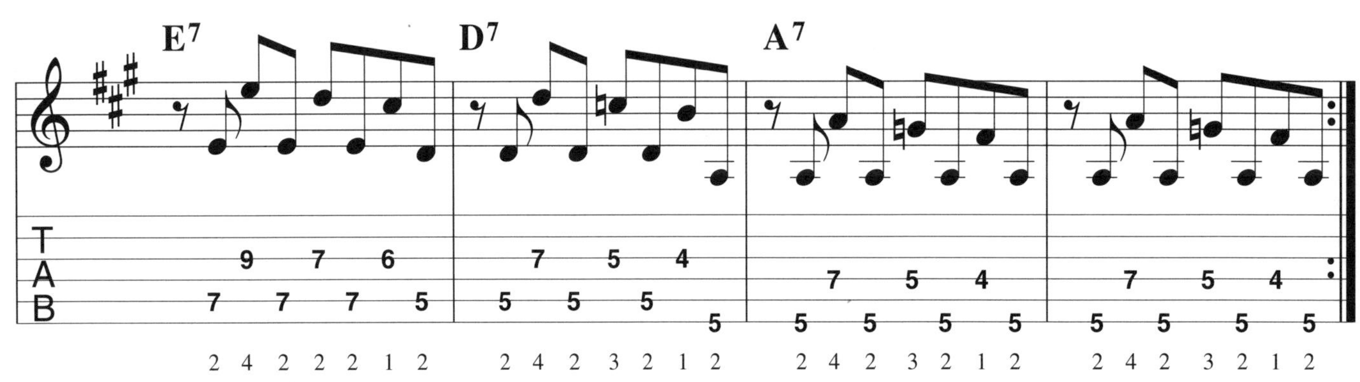

Here are some riffs using the mixolydian scale in various positions on the fretboard.

72.0

72.1

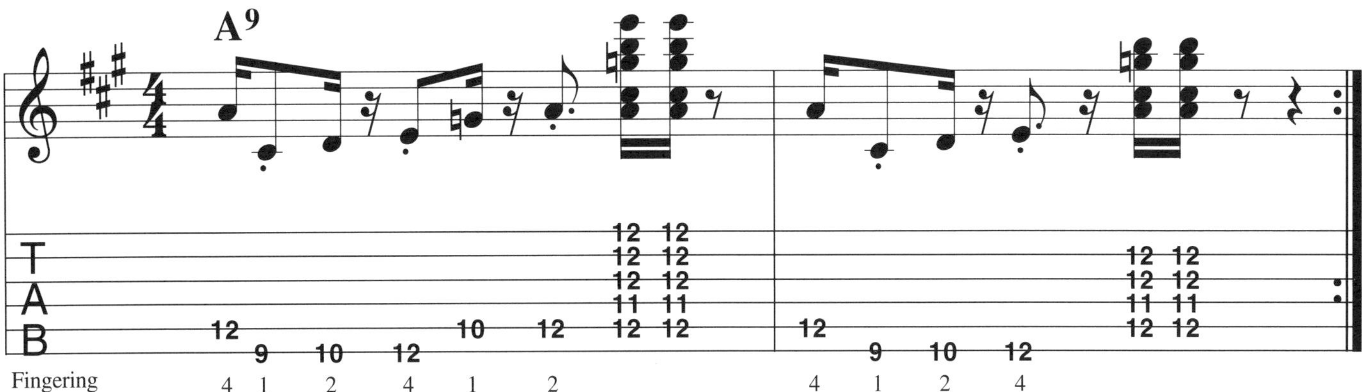

72.2

This one features swung sixteenth notes and staccato notes.

THE DORIAN MODE

Another common scale for creating riffs is the Dorian mode. Its degrees are **1 2 ♭3 4 5 6** and **♭7**. Here it is in the key of G, in the E form, followed by several riffs derived from it. Once you have learned them, try creating some of your own.

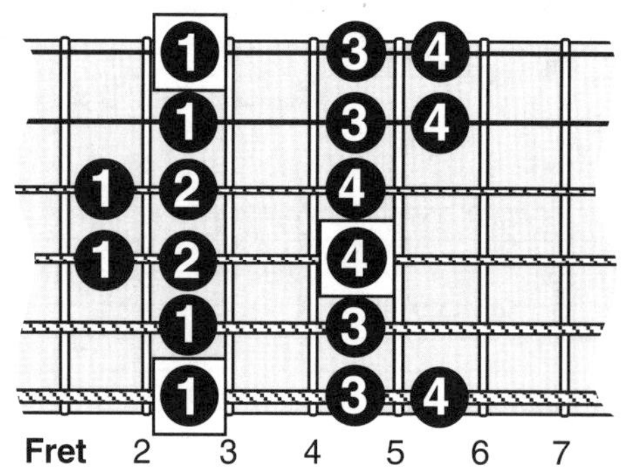

CD 2 **73.0**

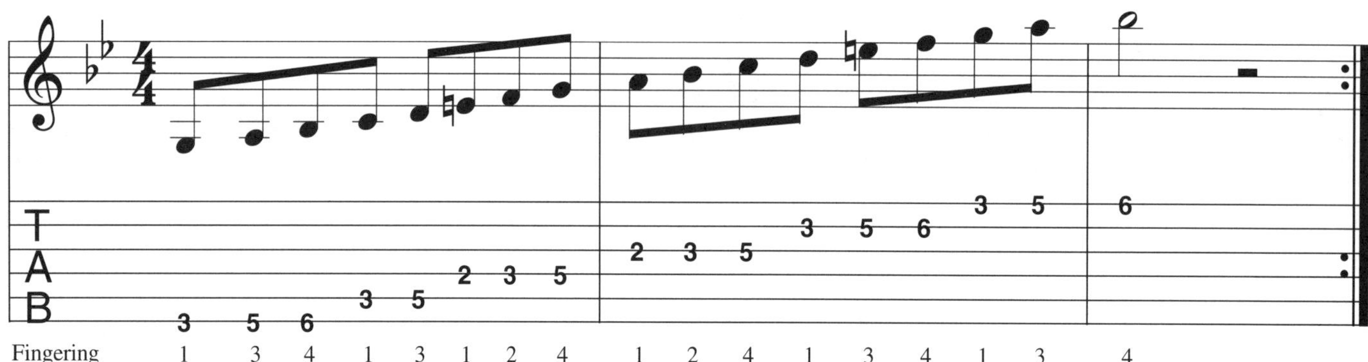

CD 2 **73.1**

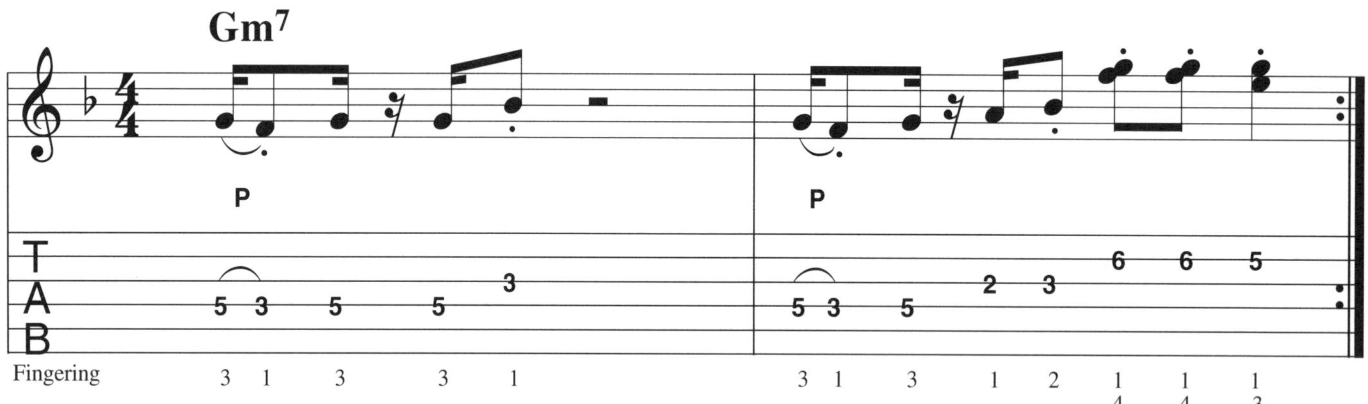

CD 2 **73.2**

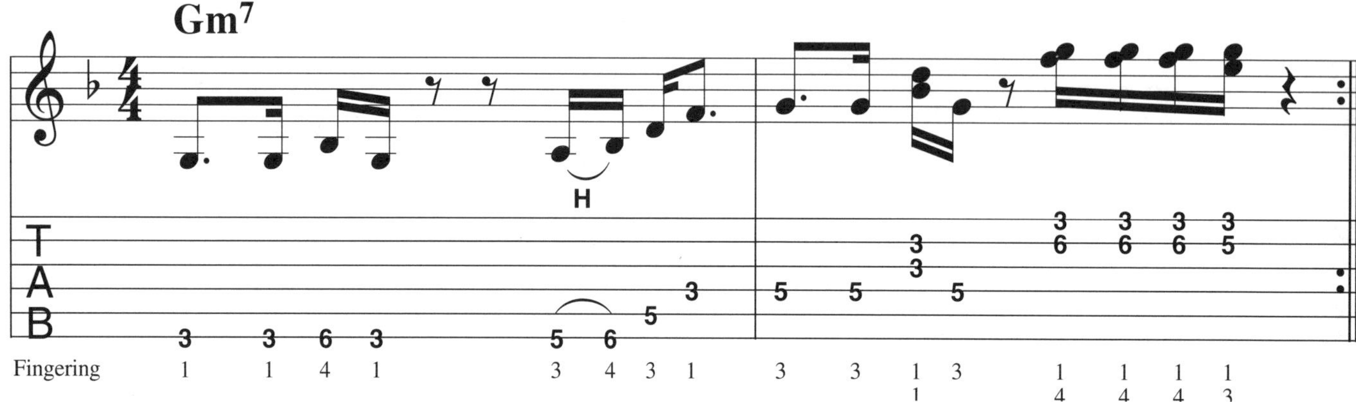

73.3

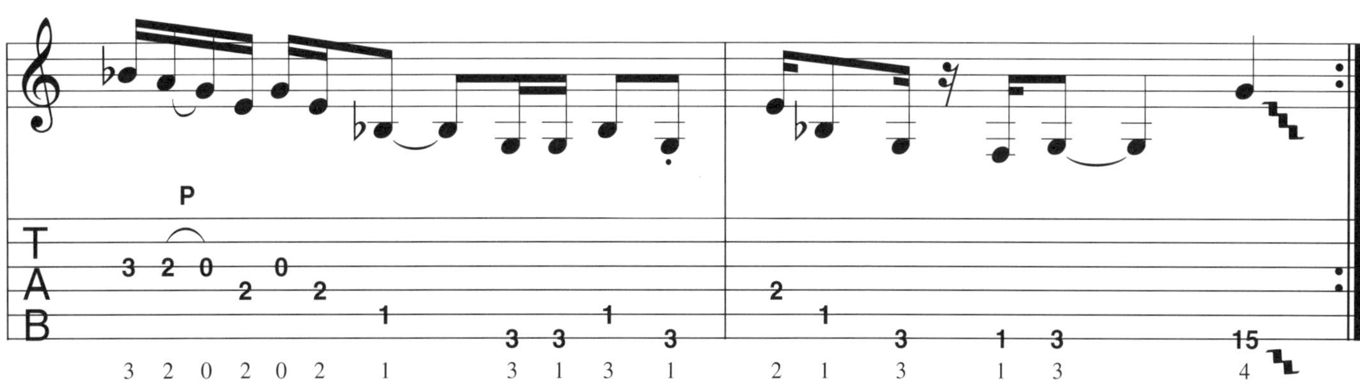

73.4

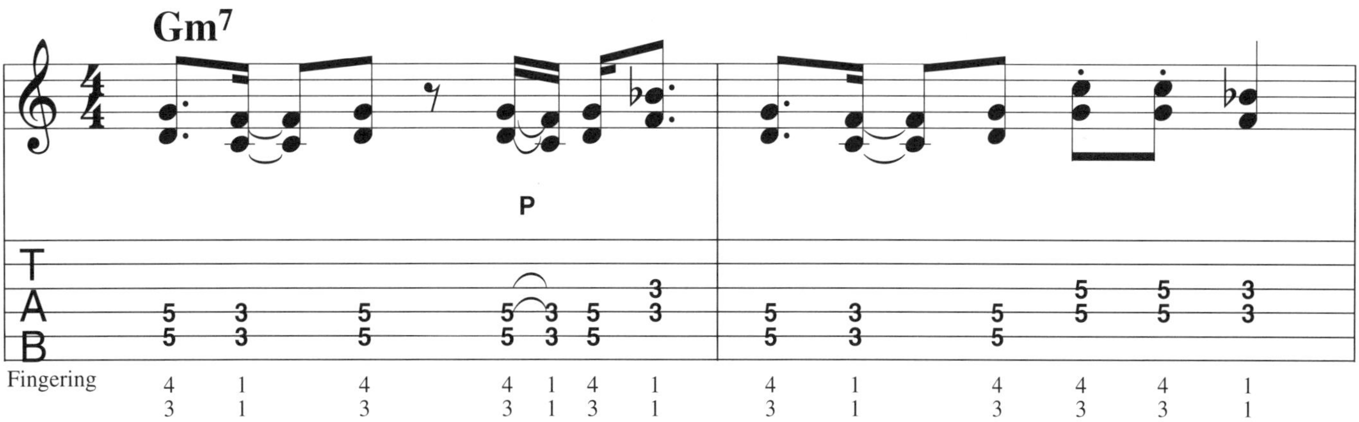

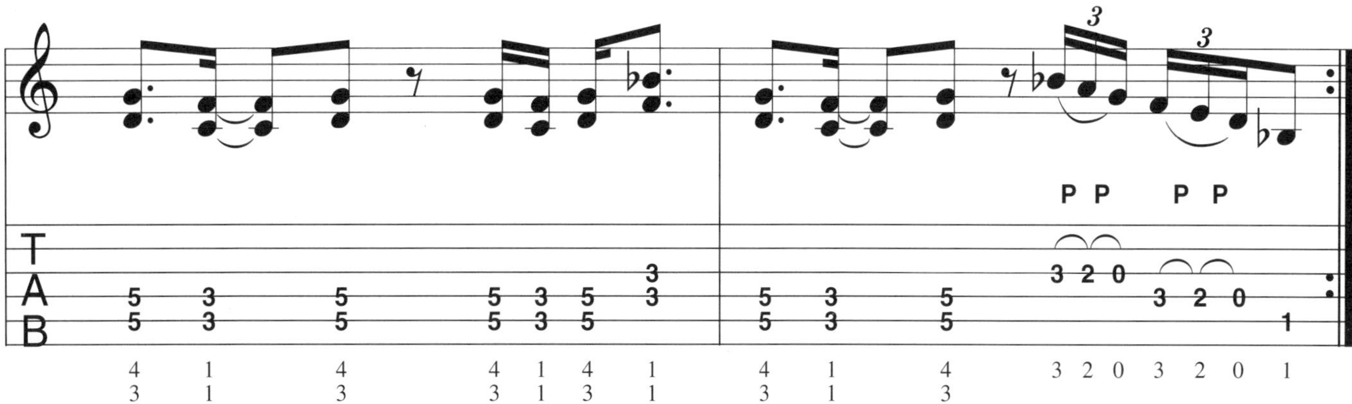

OTHER MODES

If you are serious about music, you should study **all** the modes in detail. Here are some parts derived from two slightly exotic sounding modes – the **Phrygian**, and the **Lydian**.

74.0 Phrygian

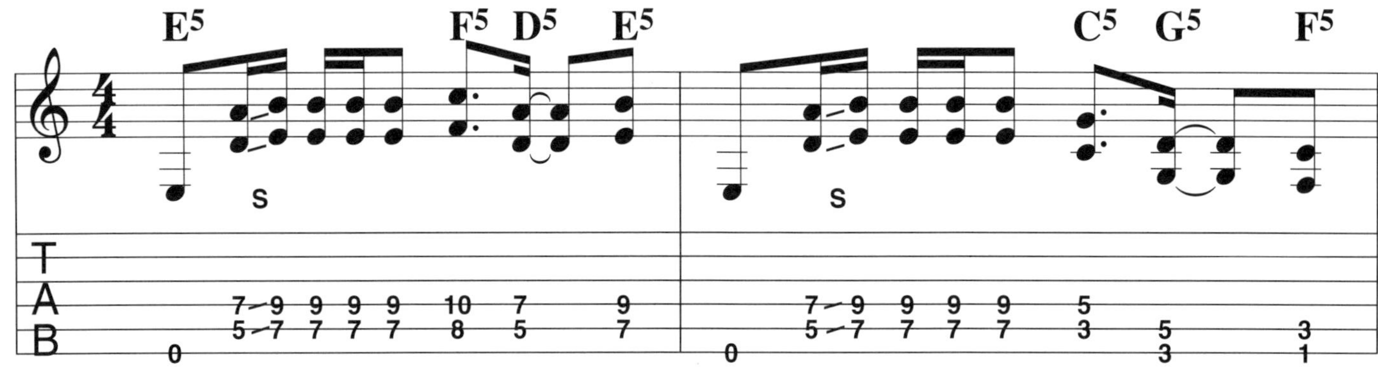

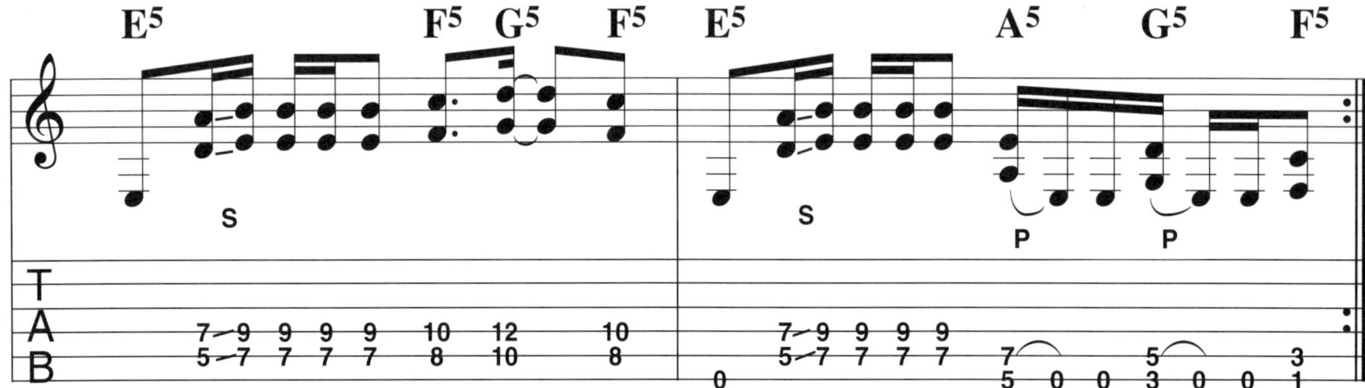

74.1 Lydian

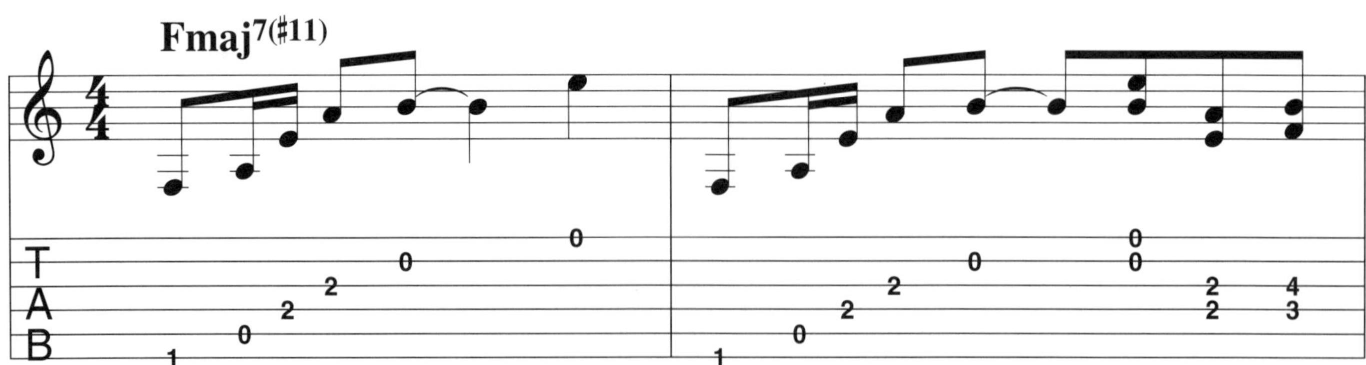

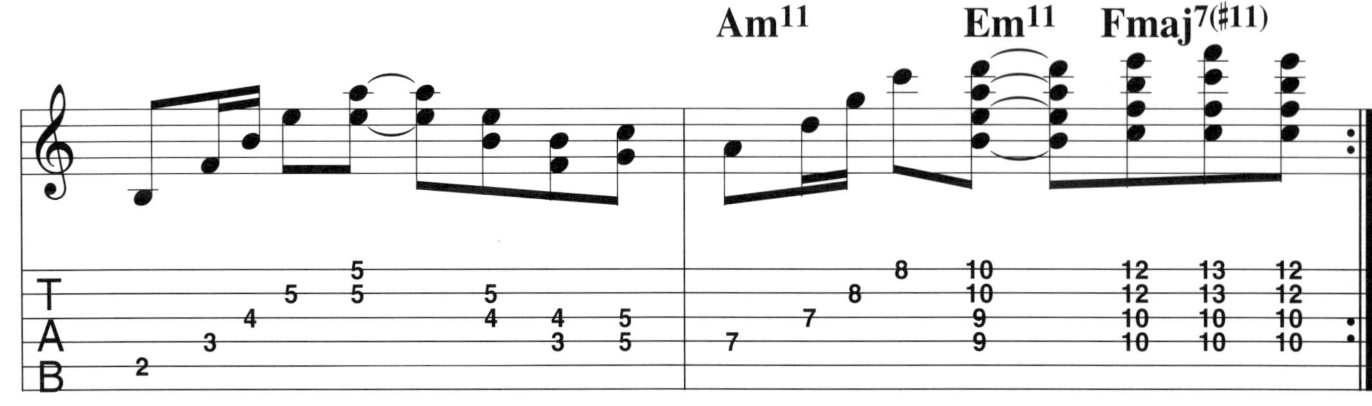

LESSON FORTY SEVEN

THE 7♯9 CHORD

One of the most common of all chords used in Rock, Jazz and Funk is the **7♯9** chord (often called the **Hendrix chord**). It is similar to a 9th, chord except that the actual 9th degree of the chord is raised. Here are three common fingerings for this chord.

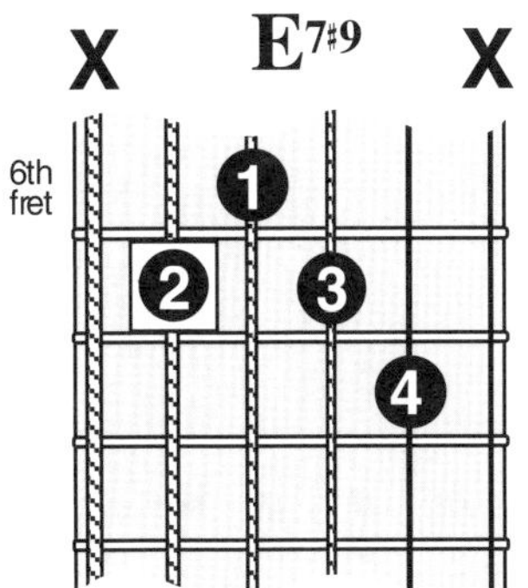

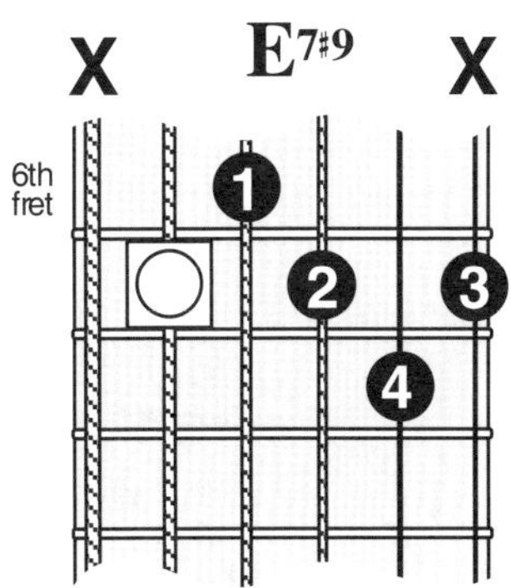

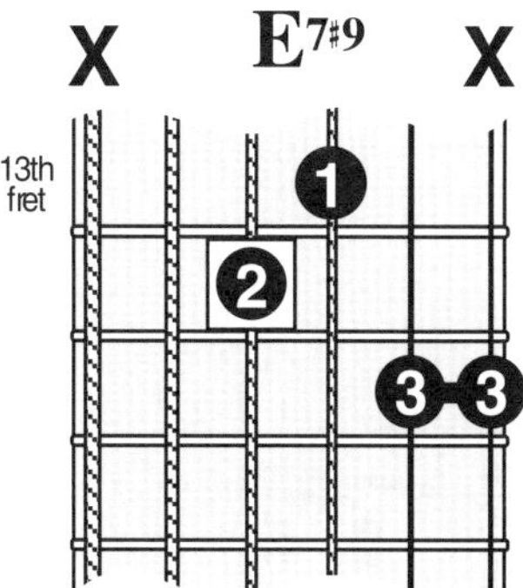

The following examples show some typical uses of **7♯9** chords.

75.0

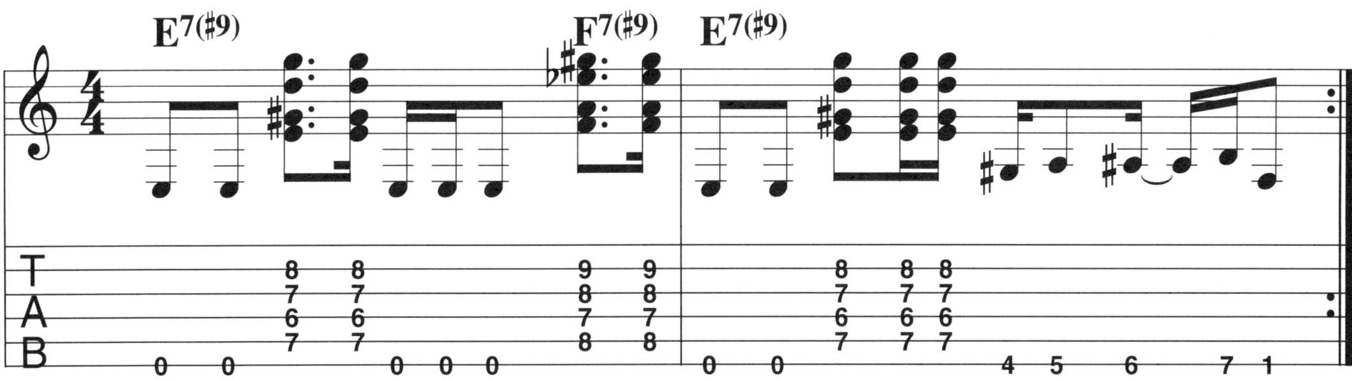

75.1

75.2

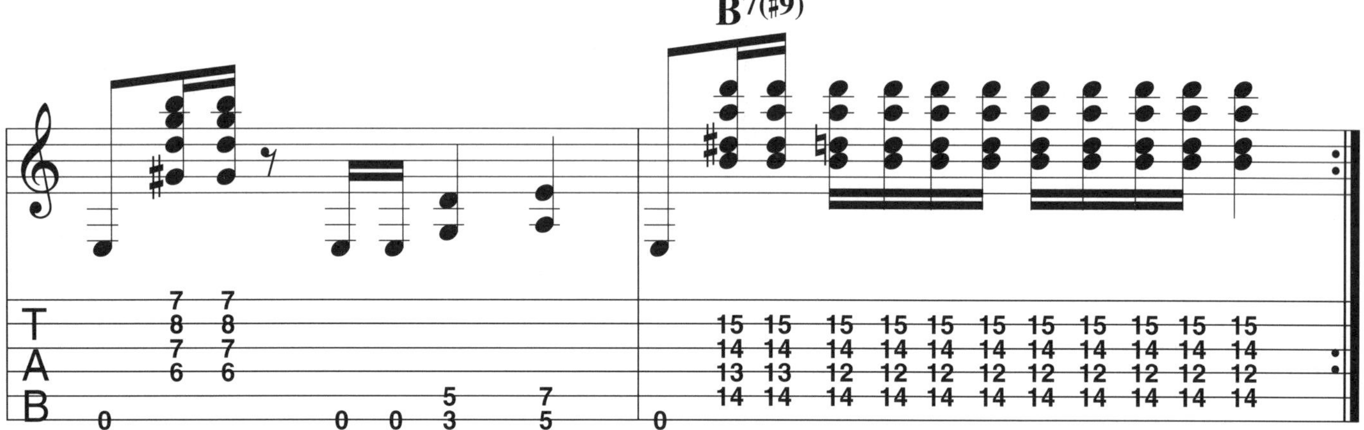

75.3

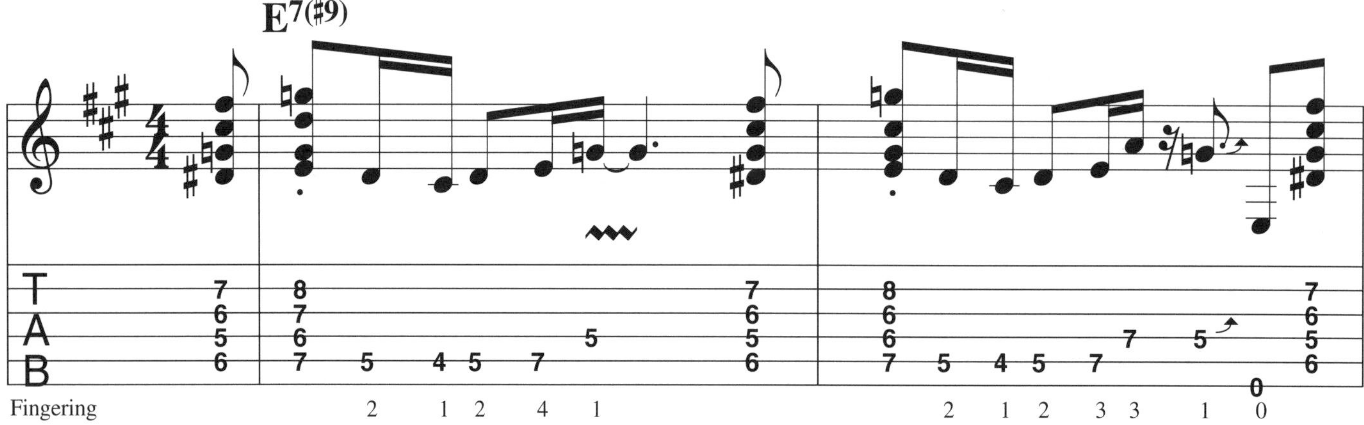

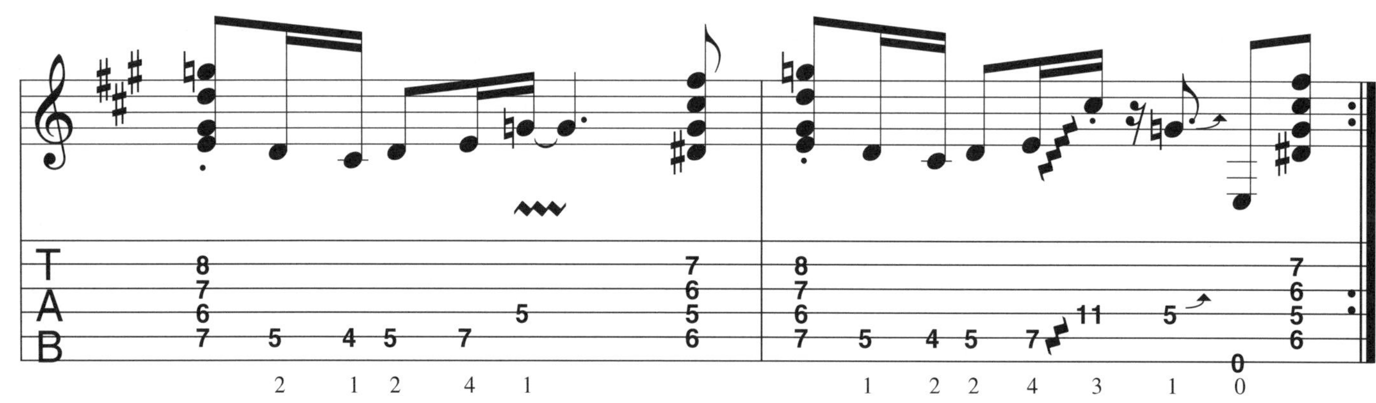

7SUS CHORDS

Another popular sound is the **7sus** chord. It is similar to a dominant 7th chord, except that the 3rd of the chord is replaced by the 4th. Here are some fingerings for it and some examples demonstrating its use.

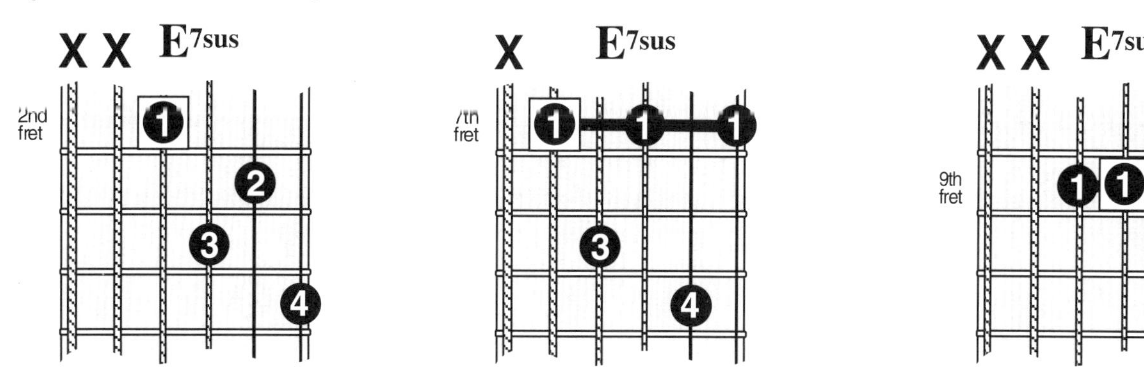

76.0

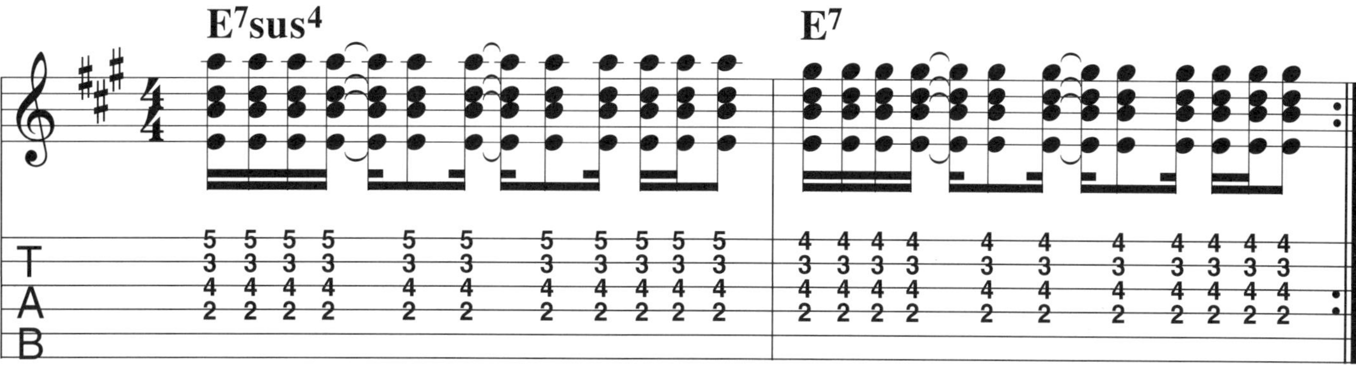

76.1

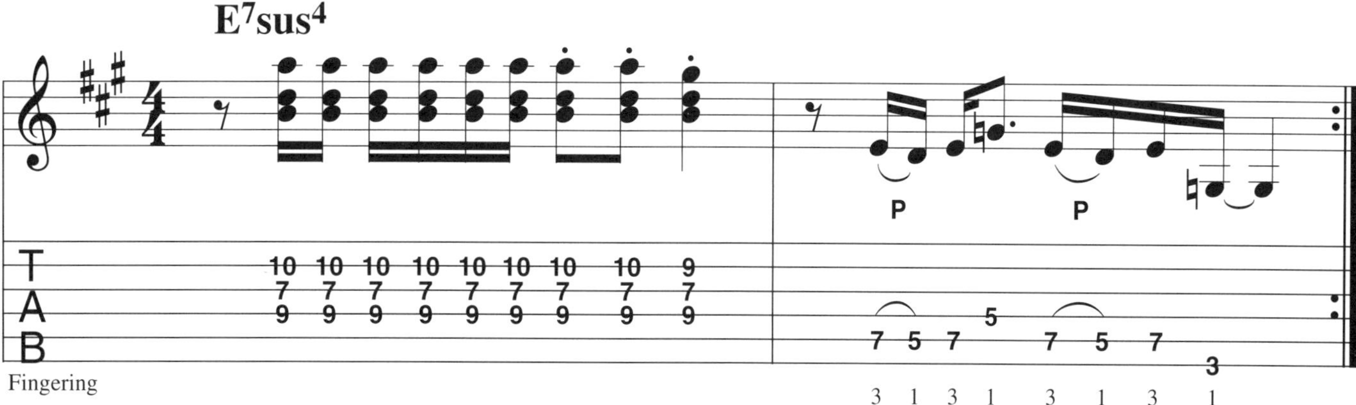

76.2

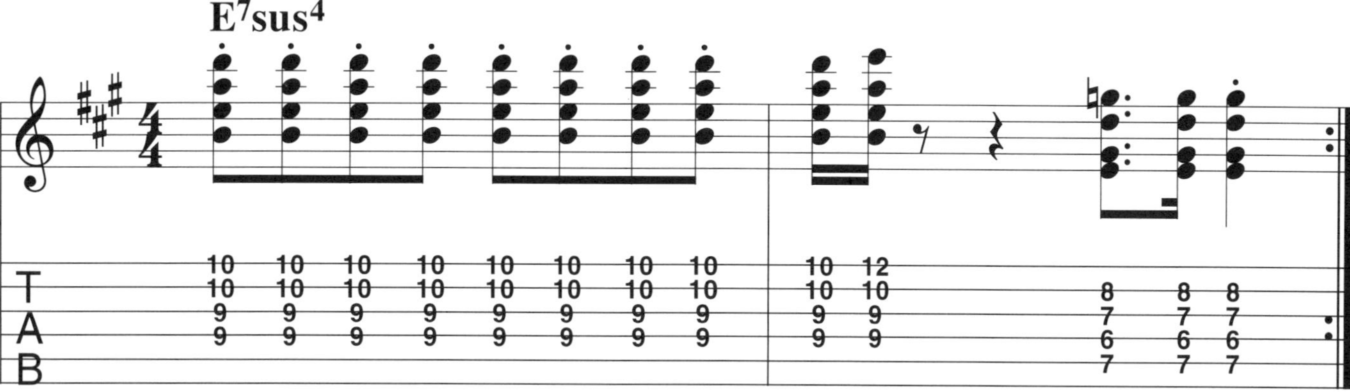

Here are a couple more chords you may find useful. They are slightly unusual, but are very colourful sounds. The minor 13th shape does not contain the root note. The second is called a ♭**5** chord even though it contains both flat 5 and natural 5. You may have heard this chord used by Prince. Listen to the examples below for ideas on how to use them.

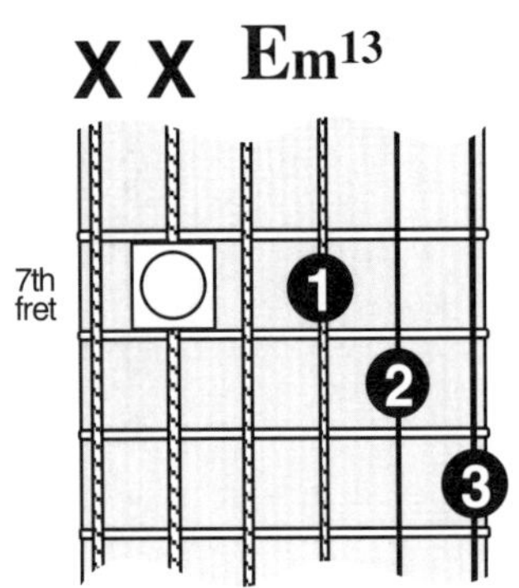

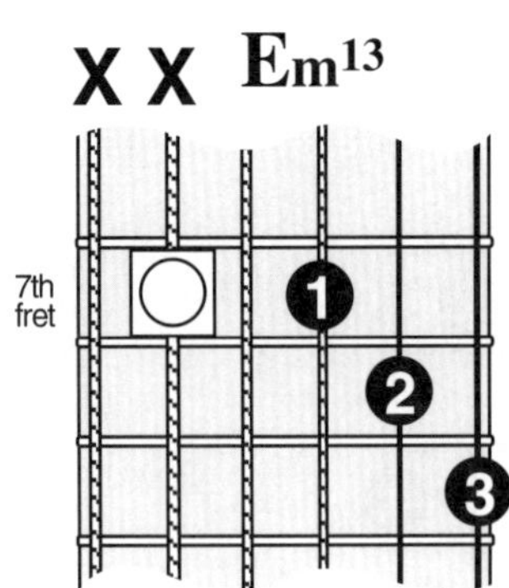

77.0

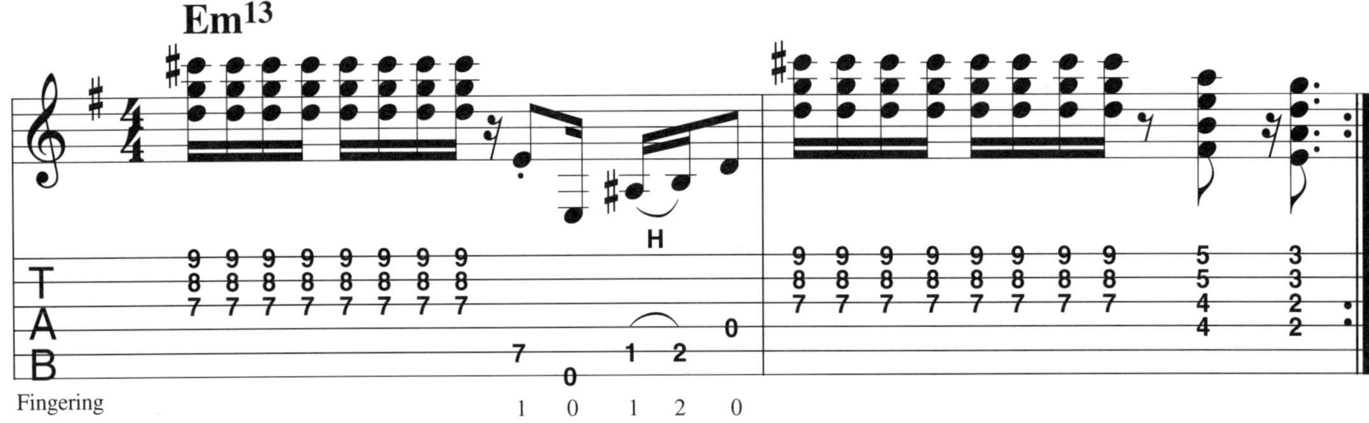

77.1

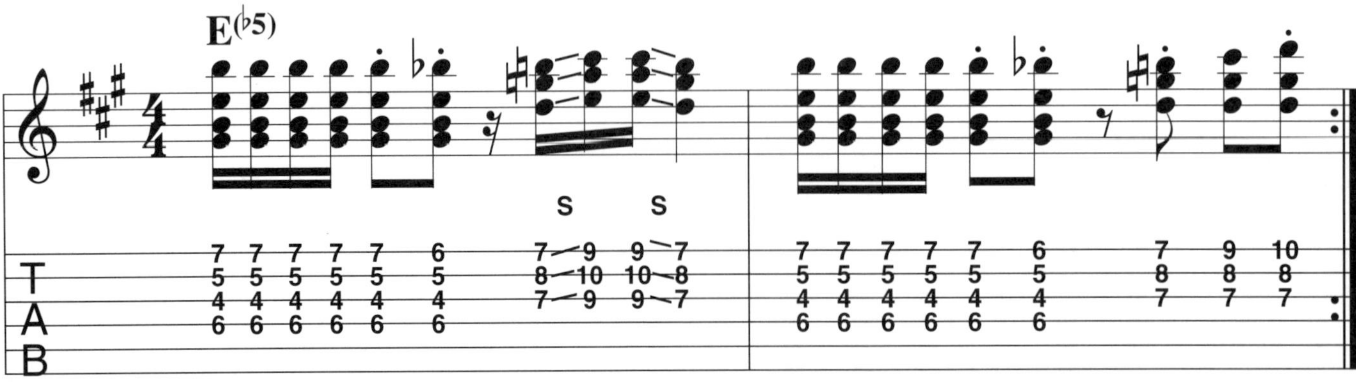

Here are some rhythm parts using a mixture of chords and single notes with slurs.

77.2

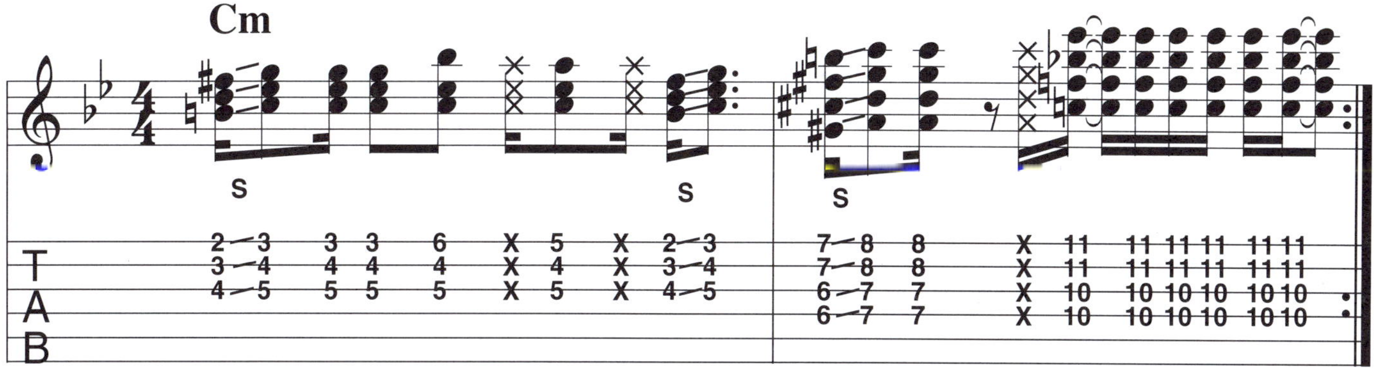

77.3

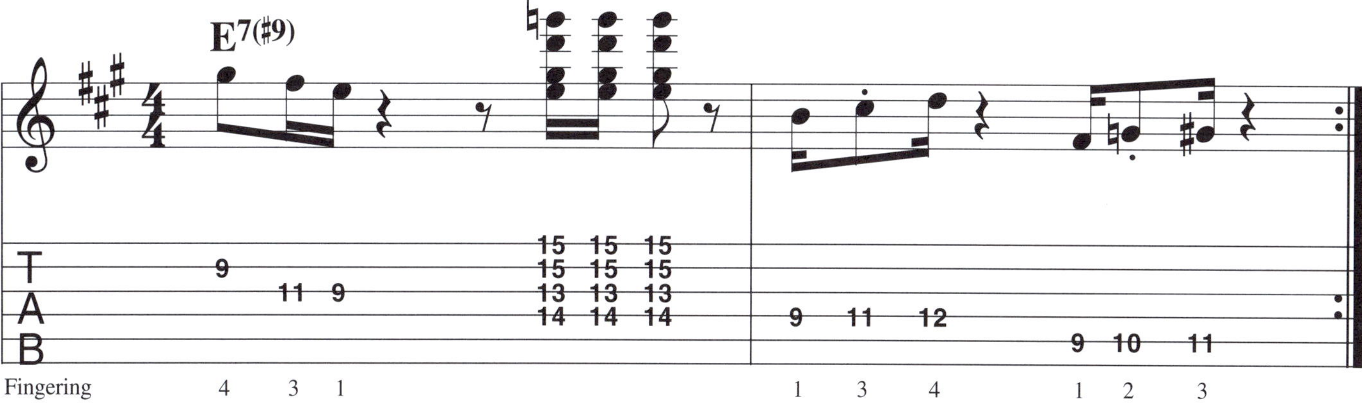

77.4

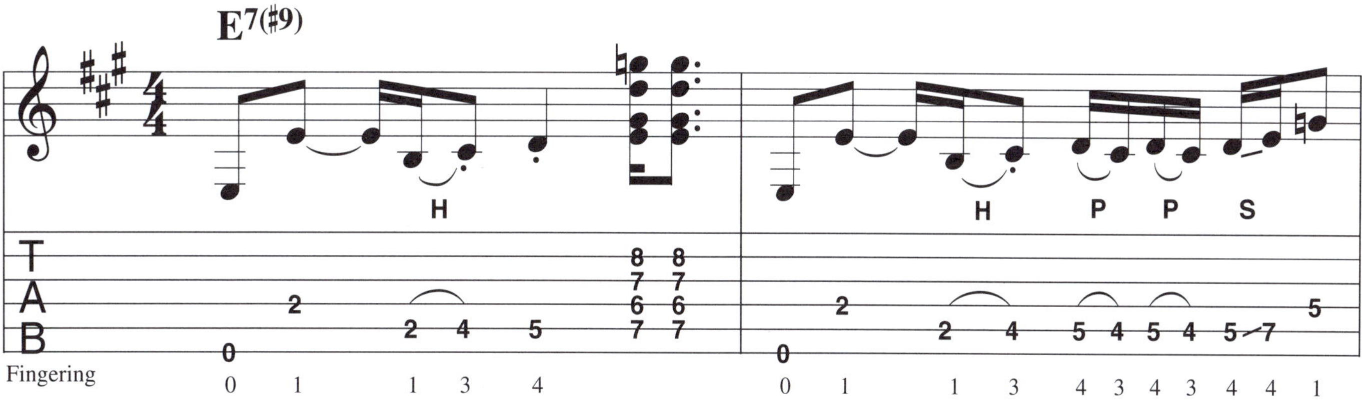

LESSON FORTY EIGHT

TRITONES

It is not always necessary to play a whole chord to get the effect of a chord. It often works well to use only the most essential notes of the chord, leaving the other notes to the bass player and whoever is playing the melody. Here is a **C7** chord. Its notes are **C E G B♭**. Beside it is a **tritone** interval consisting of the **3rd** (**E**) and **7th** (**B♭**). Listen to the effect it produces.

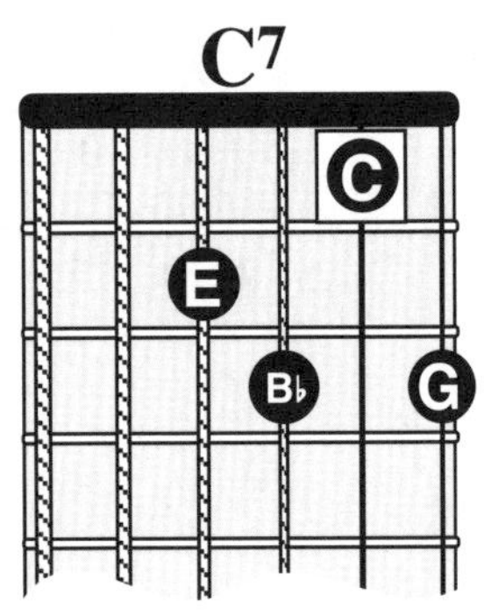

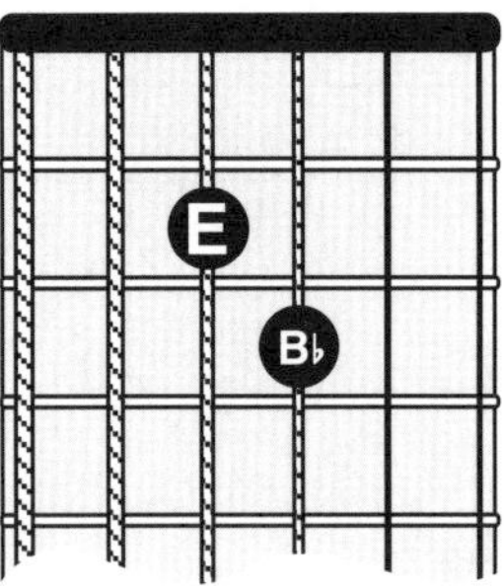

78.0

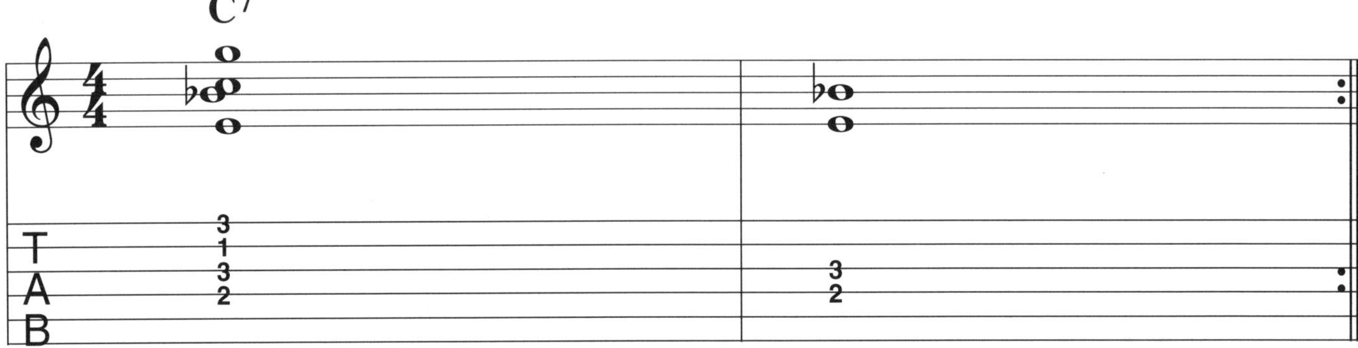

The root note (C) can be left to the bass player. The 5th (G) is not an essential note, so it can also be left out. It is the **3rd** (**E**) and the **flattened 7th** (**B♭**) which are essential to the sound of the dominant 7th chord. These are the notes which form the **tritone**.The tritone is so named because the two notes are exactly three whole tones apart. The tritone interval is exactly half an octave, which means if you invert it (turn it upside down), the two notes are still three whole tones apart. This means the tritone will work regardless of which note is on the top, making it possible to find tritones in many places on the fretboard. Here is an example of the way tritones may be used. As you can hear, it's a great sound.

78.1

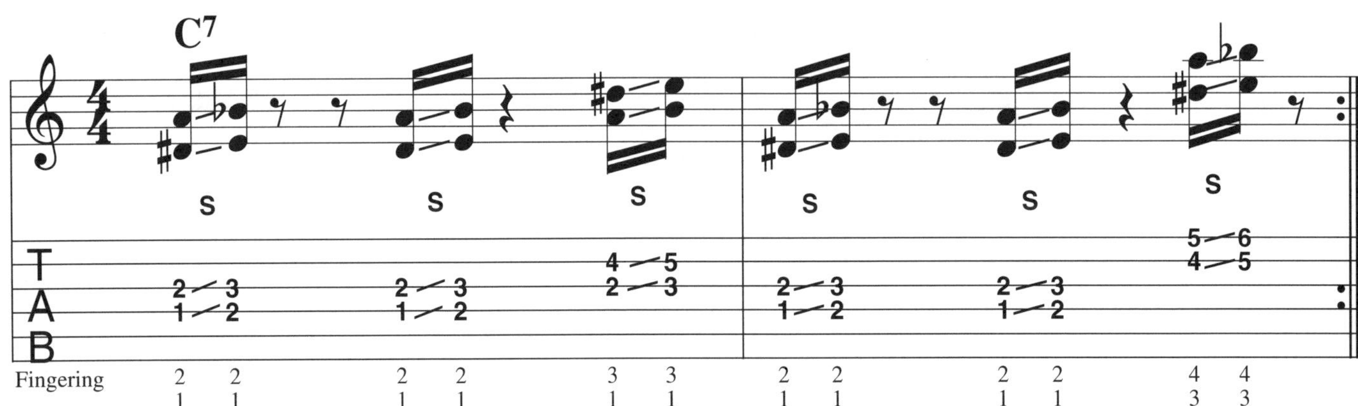

Here are two diagrams showing the patterns formed by tritones across the fretboard. Memorize the patterns and learn them in all keys.

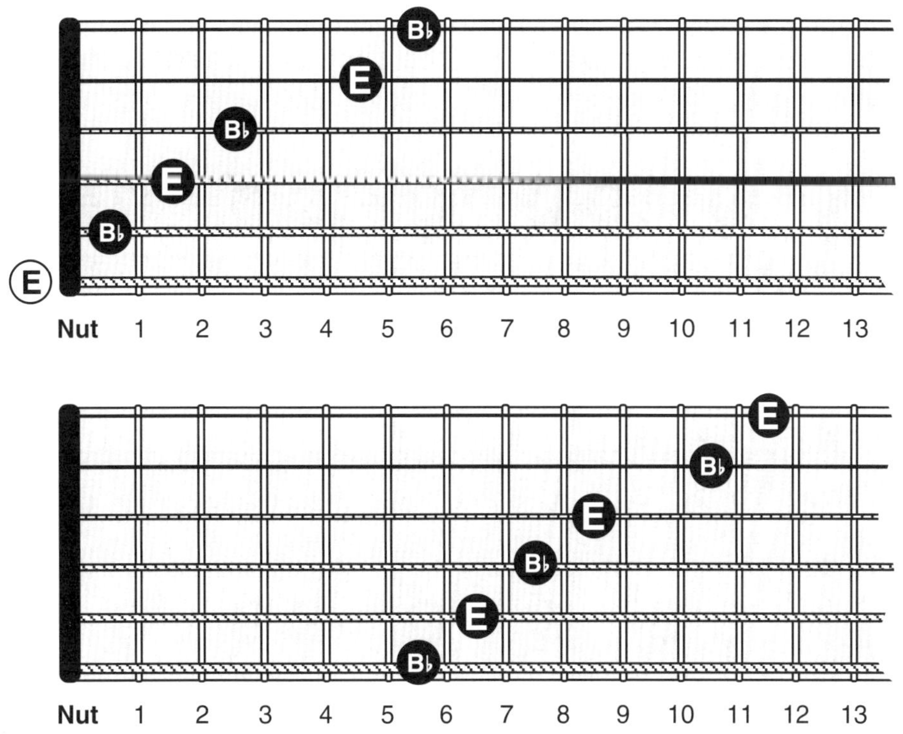

Here are some examples demonstrating typical uses of tritones.

79.0

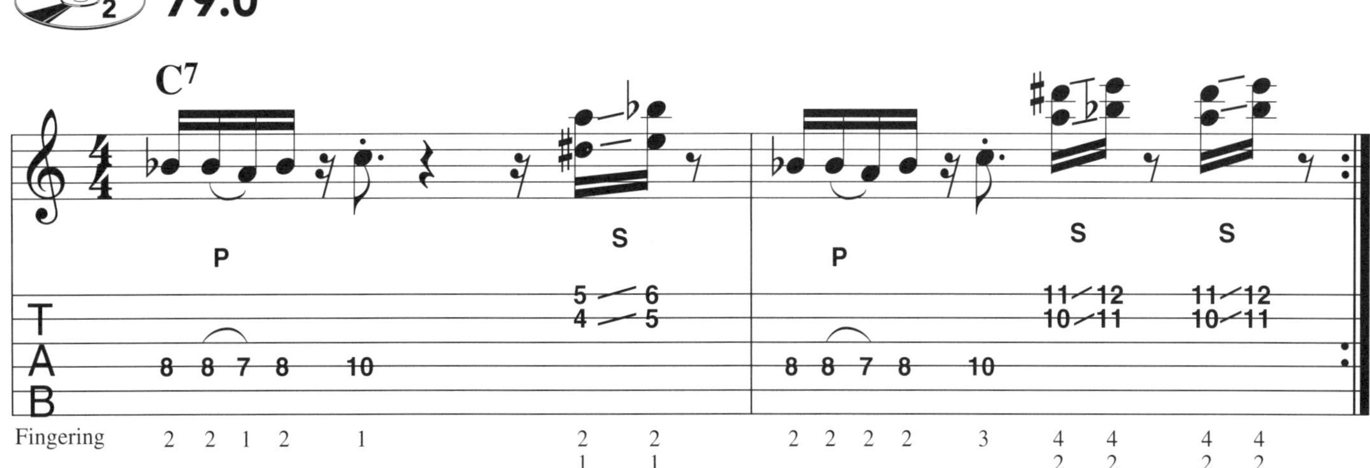

79.1

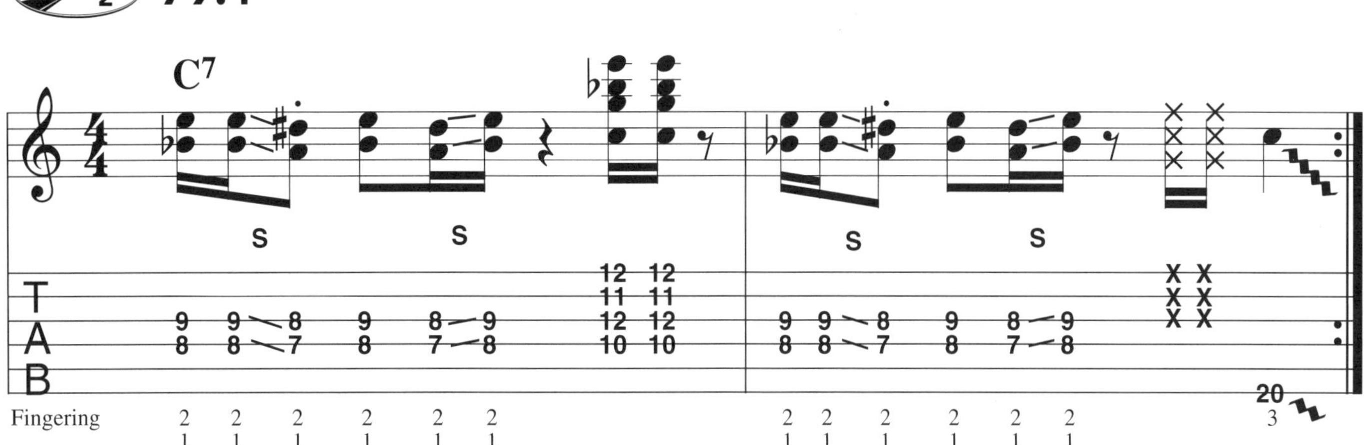

6THS

Technically, it is possible to use any interval to harmonise any scale or melody, although some sound better than others. 6ths and 3rds work particularly well. Here is the **E Mixolydian** mode harmonized in **6ths**, on the first and third strings and then on the second and fourth strings.

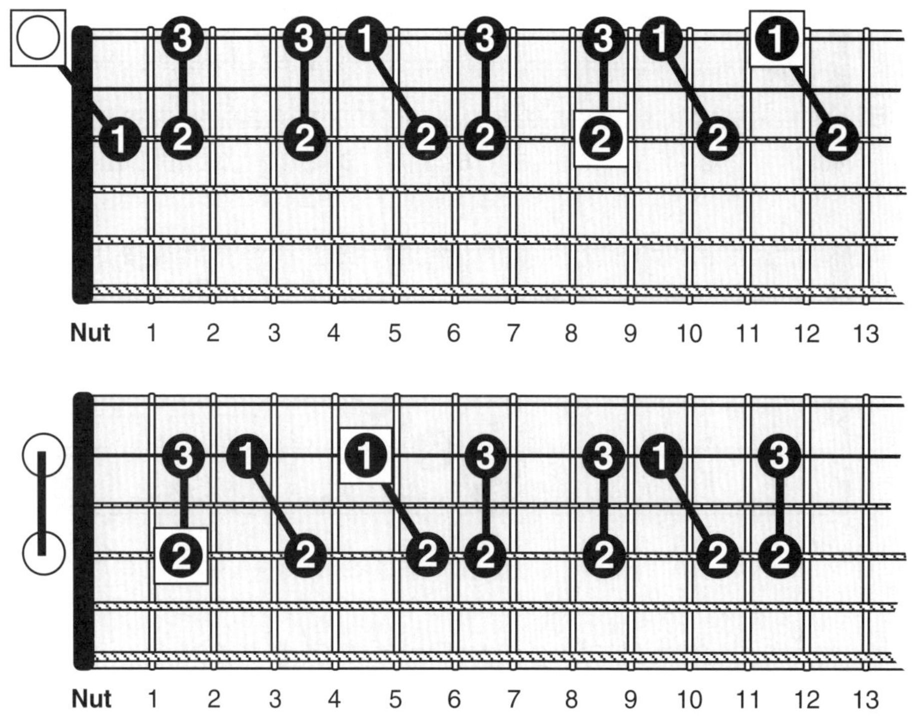

80.

Here is a rhythm part which demonstrates the use of 6th intervals.

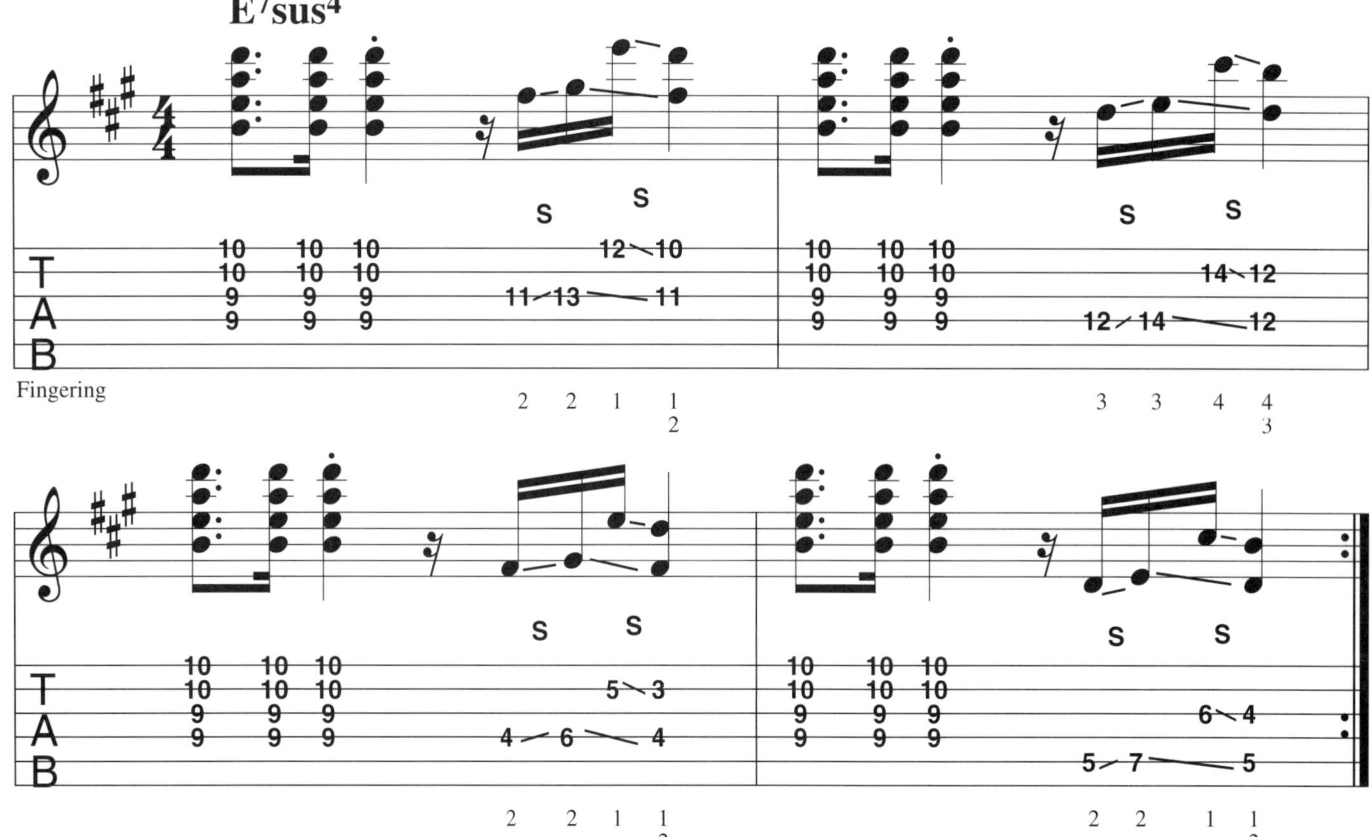

3RDS

Another useful interval for harmonizing melodies is the **3rd**. Here is the **E Dorian** mode harmonized in 3rds, along with an example using 3rds.

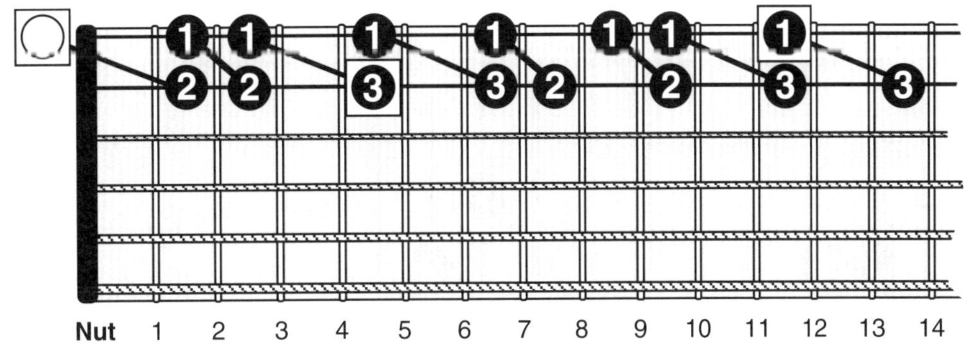

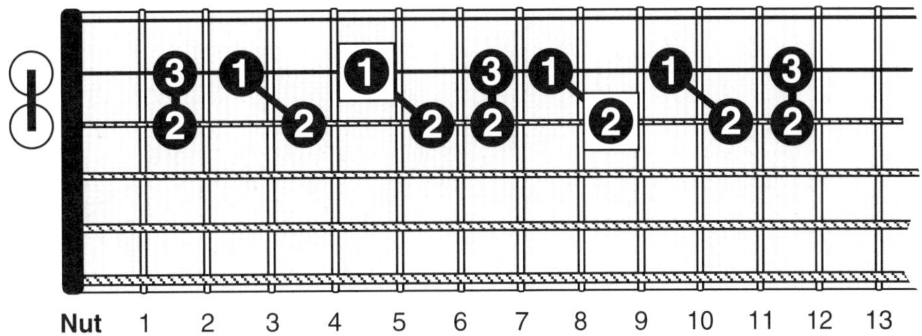

81.

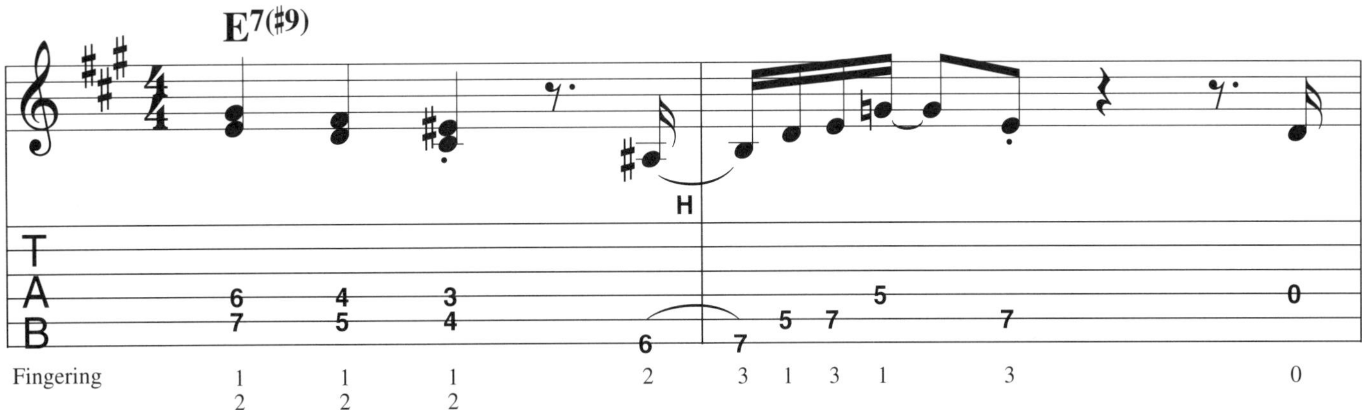

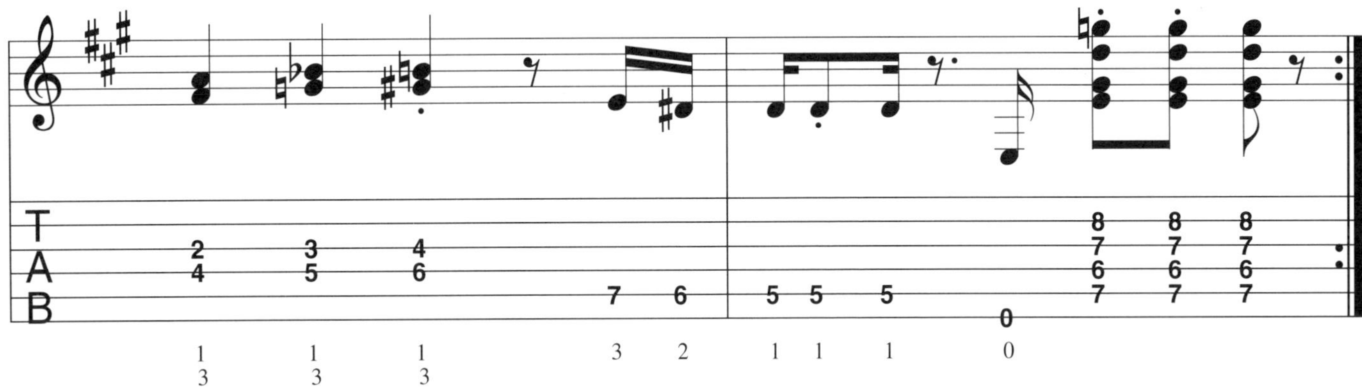

4THS

It is also possible to harmonize scales and melodies in 4ths or to use them as embellishments to a melody or chord progression. Here are the fingerings for 4ths across each pair of strings, along with an example of the way they sound.

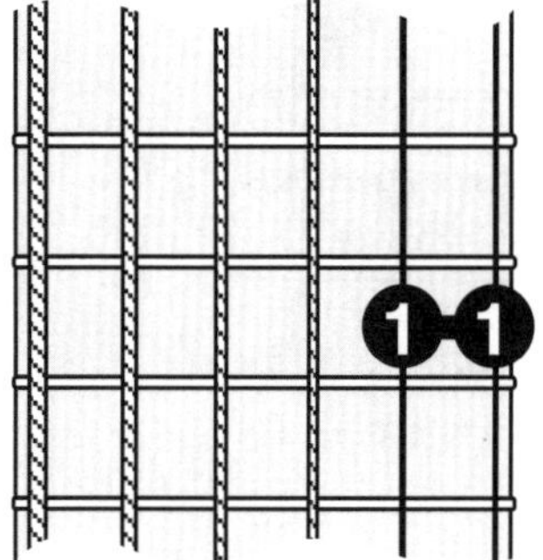

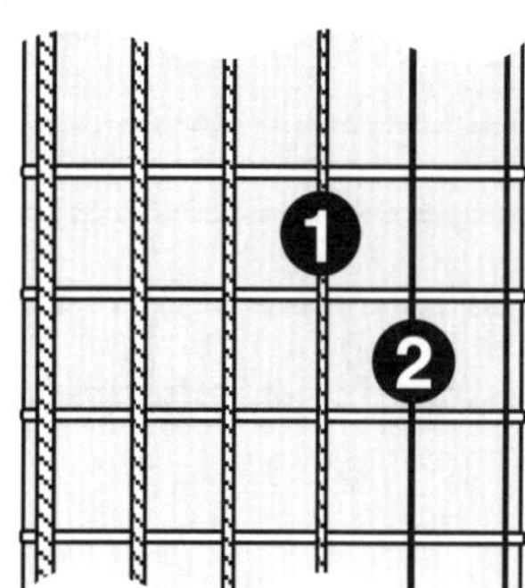

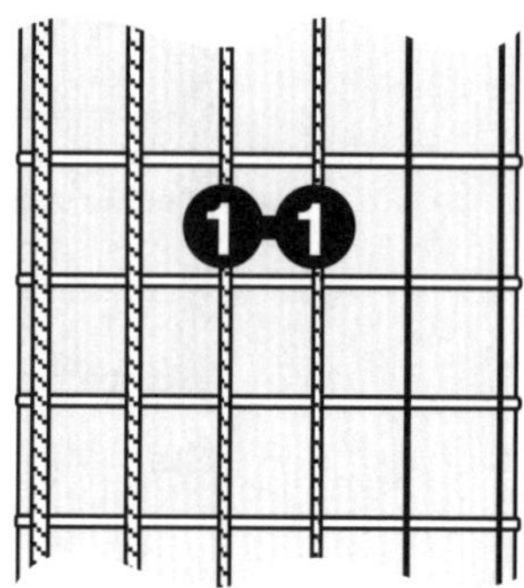

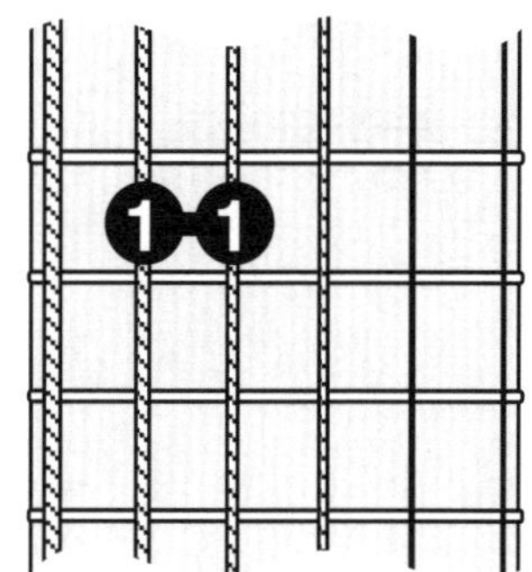

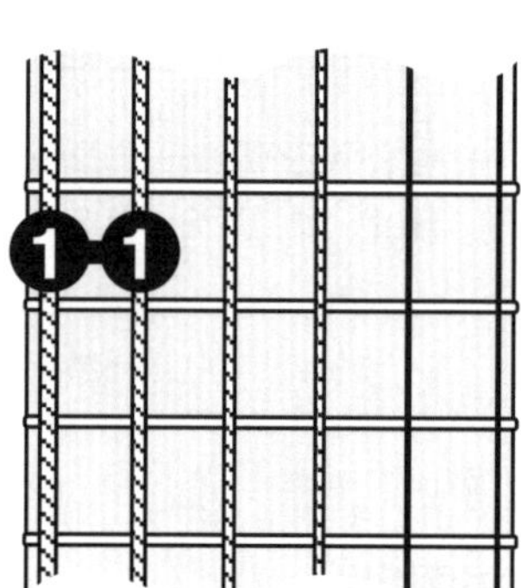

82.

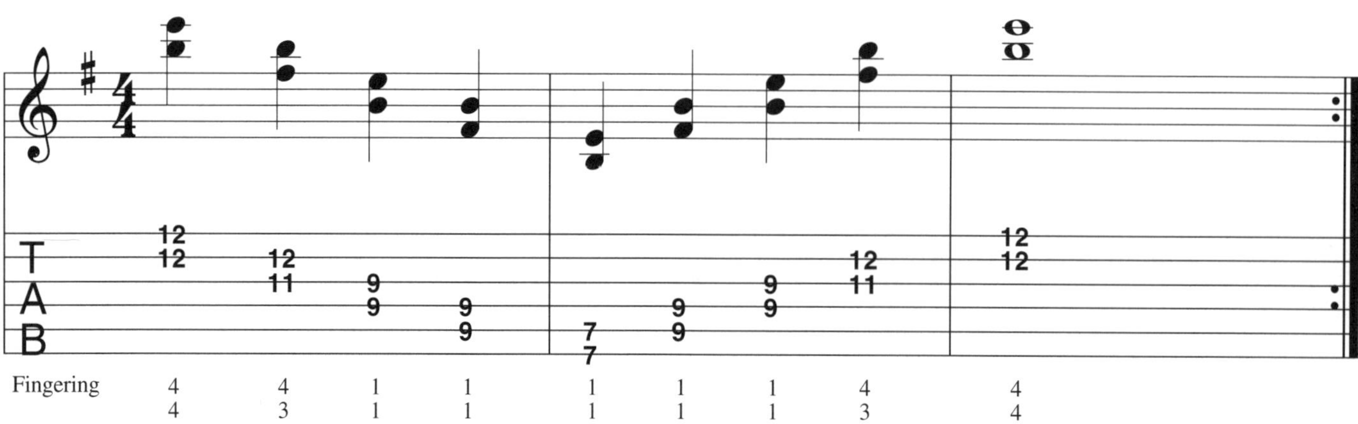

Here are some of the ways 4ths might be used in a song.

83.0

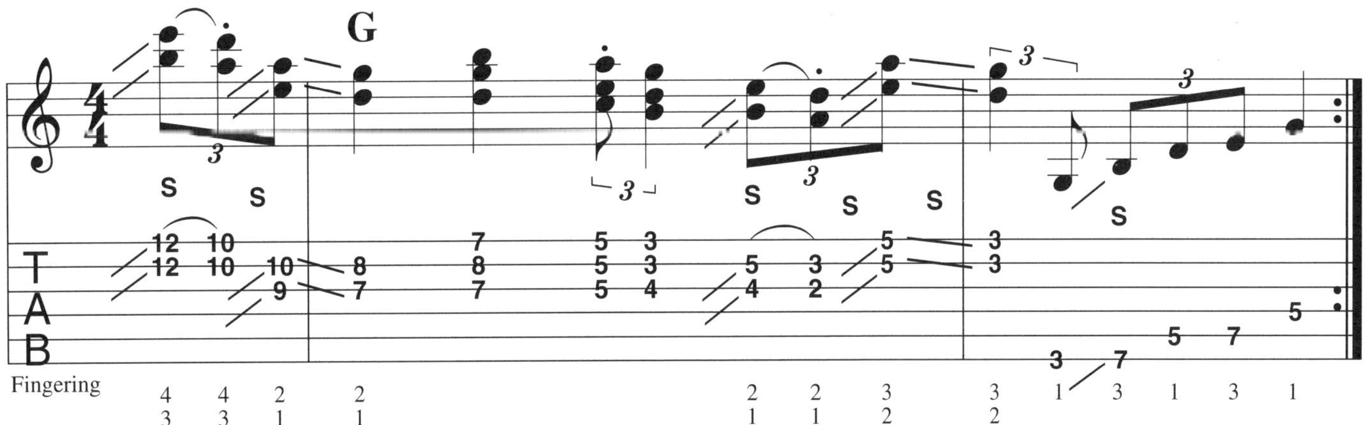

83.1

83.2

This one uses both 4ths and 6ths

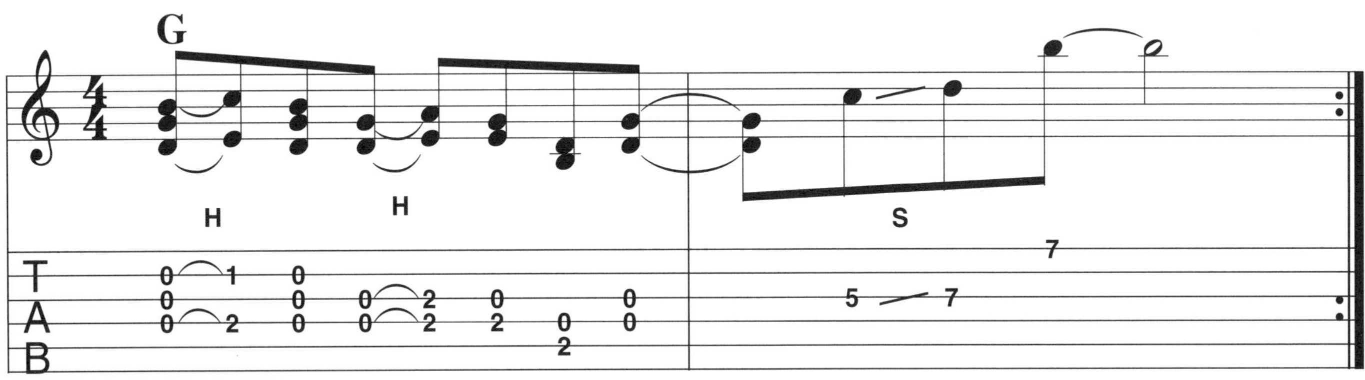

Another colourful sound used in Jazz and Funk is **chords made up entirely of 4ths** instead of 3rds. In the chords shown below, one basic shape is used but the name of the chord can change, depending on the position of the root note.

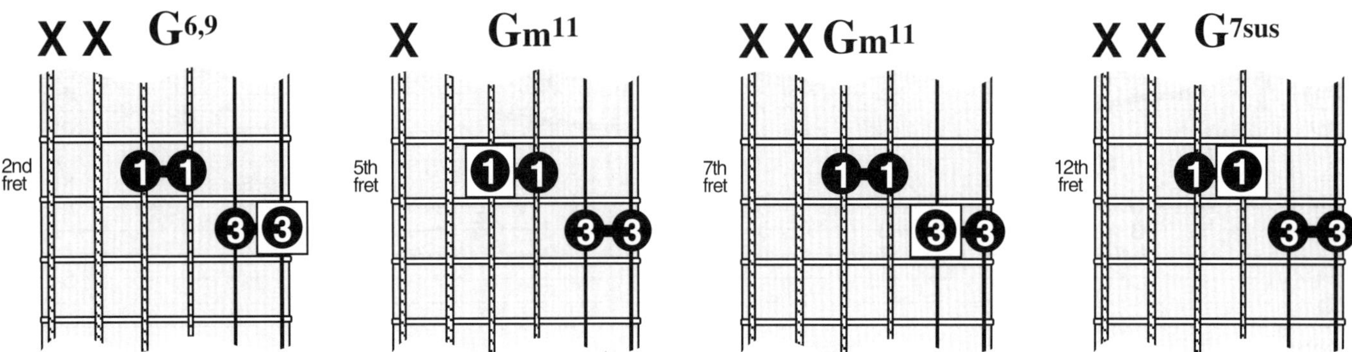

84.

It is possible to harmonize an entire scale with these chords. The example below shows the G Blues scale harmonized from below with chords voiced in 4ths.

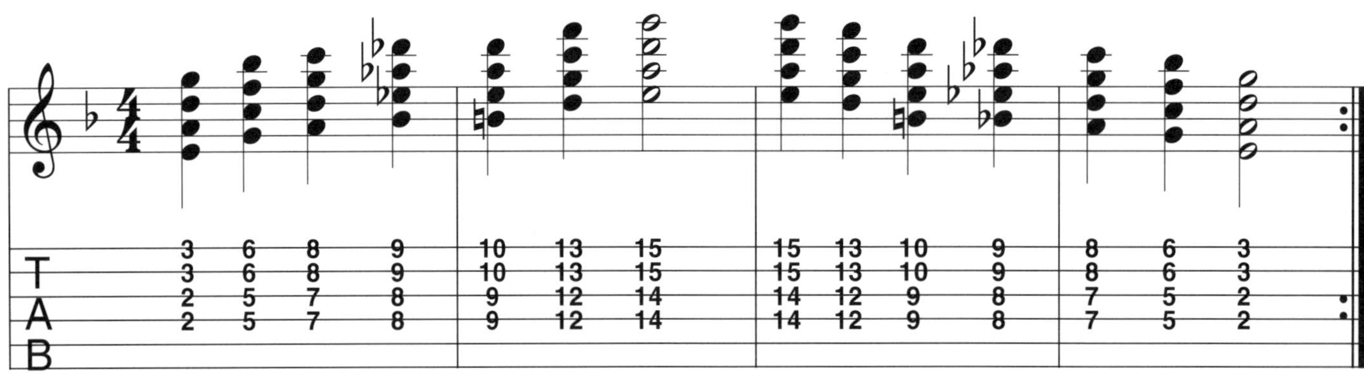

The following examples demonstrate some of the ways these chords can be used.

85.0

85.1

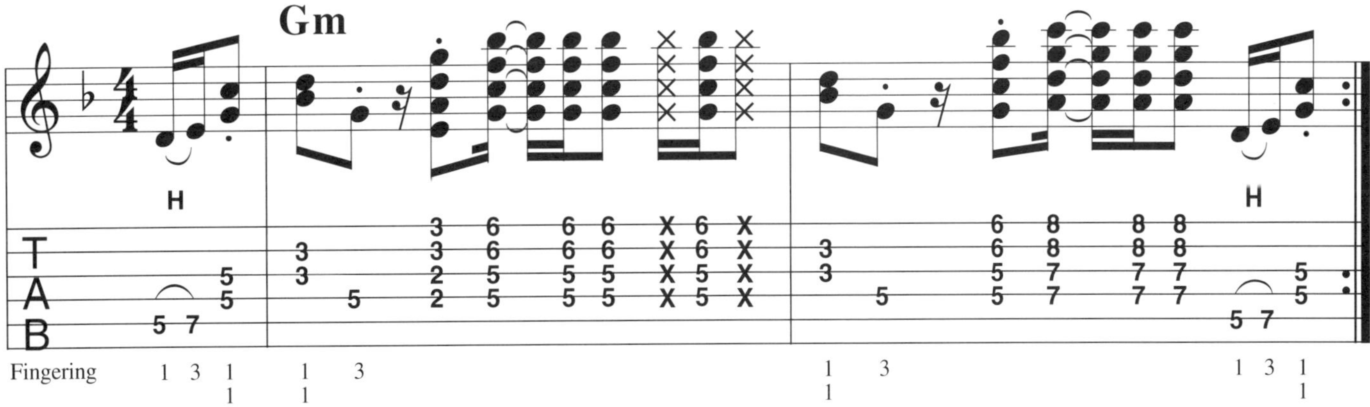

85.2

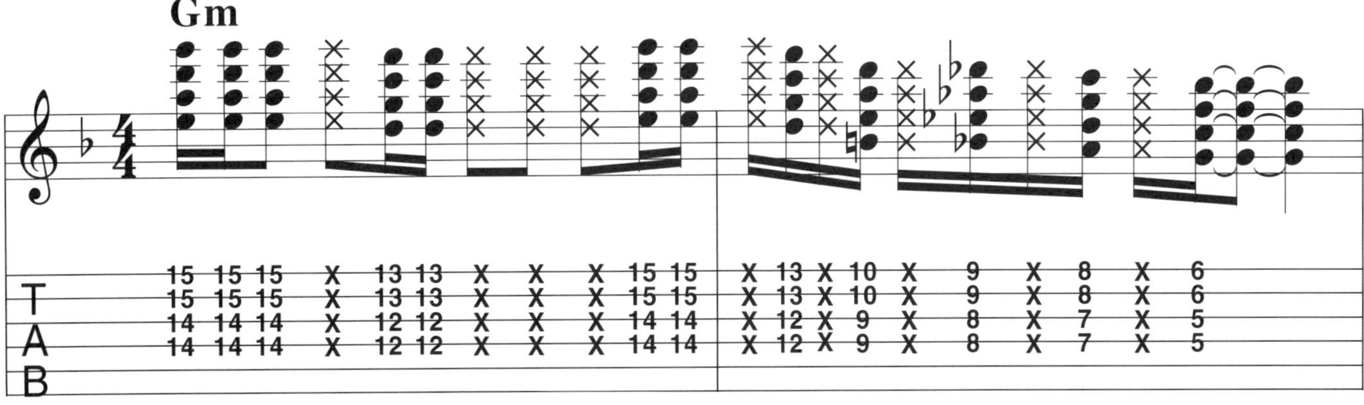

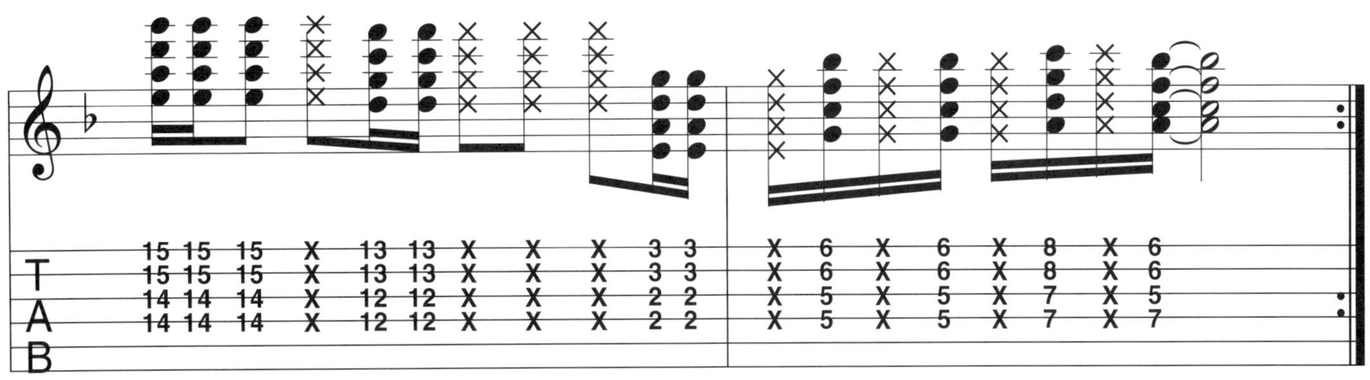

MAJOR 7THS

Major 7th intervals can be used to suggest a major 7th chord and also to create tension. Shown here are some common formations for major 7ths and an example demonstrating their use.

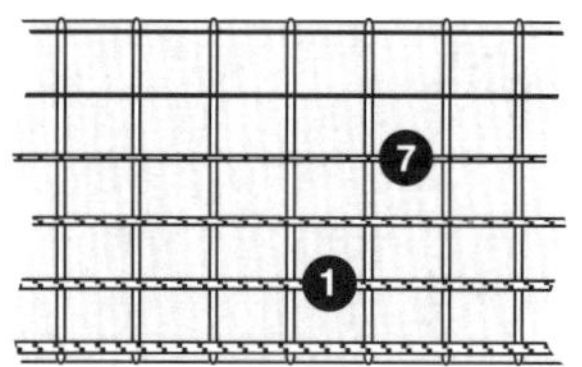

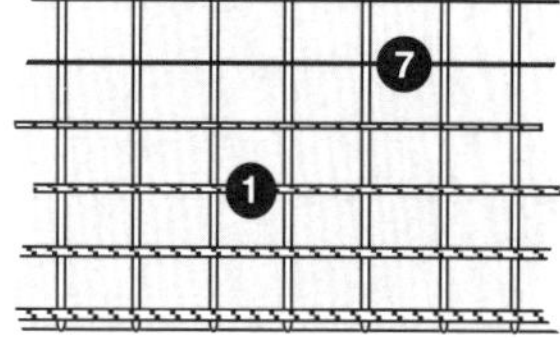

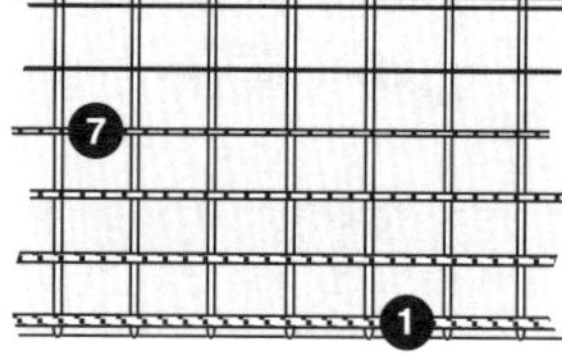

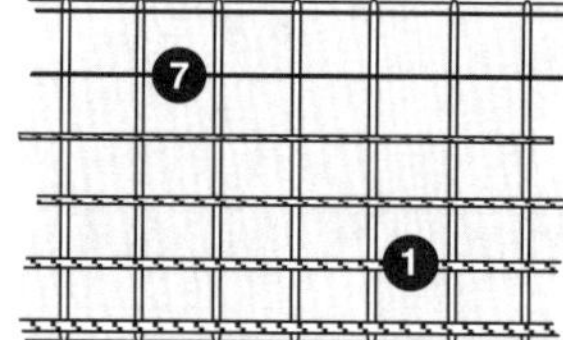

86.0

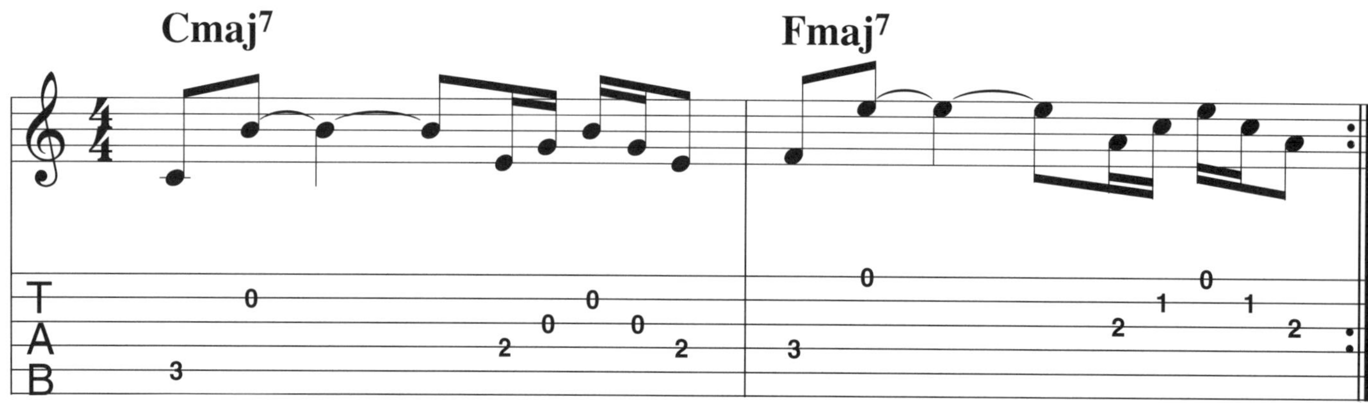

MINOR 7THS

The minor 7th interval can be used anywhere a dominant 7th or minor 7th chord occurs. Once again, some common formations are given, along with a musical example using them.

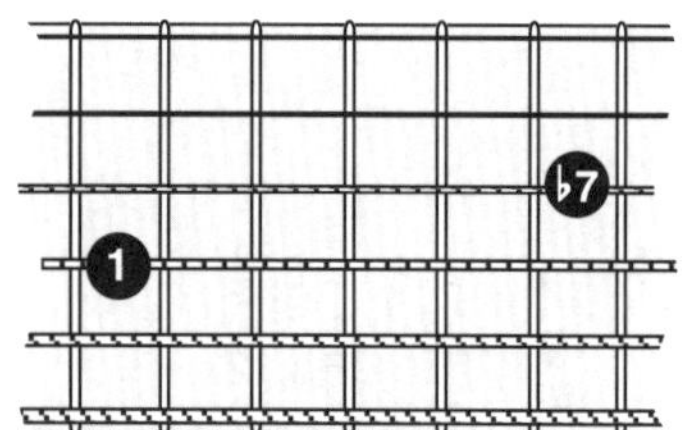

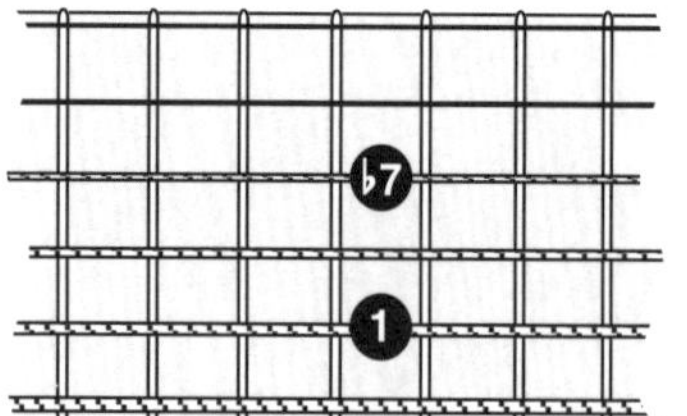

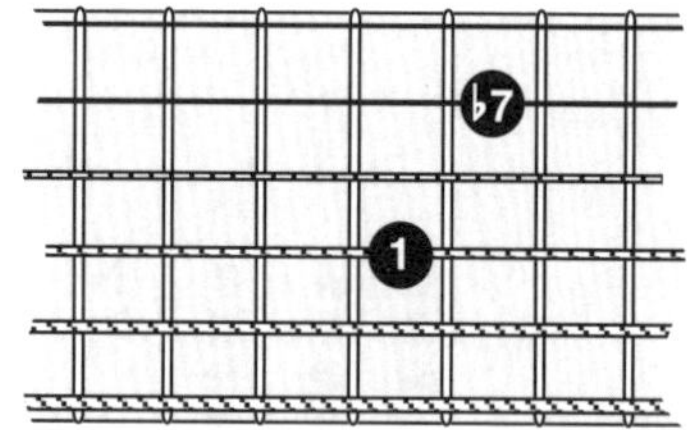

86.1

2NDS AND 5THS

Here is a rhythm part which uses a combination of power chords and intervals, notably **2nds** and **5ths**. Notice that a two note power chord is simply a 5th interval. If you invert it (reverse the order of notes) it becomes a 4th, as in bar 2. This is something useful to experiment with.

87. Trouble in Sin City

LESSON FORTY NINE

CHORD EMBELLISHMENT

Chord embellishment is the art of playing around the chords by adding notes to them and using runs to connect chords together. Hammer-ons and pull-offs are often used. Two players who frequently use chord embellishment are Curtis Mayfield and Jimi Hendrix.

88.0

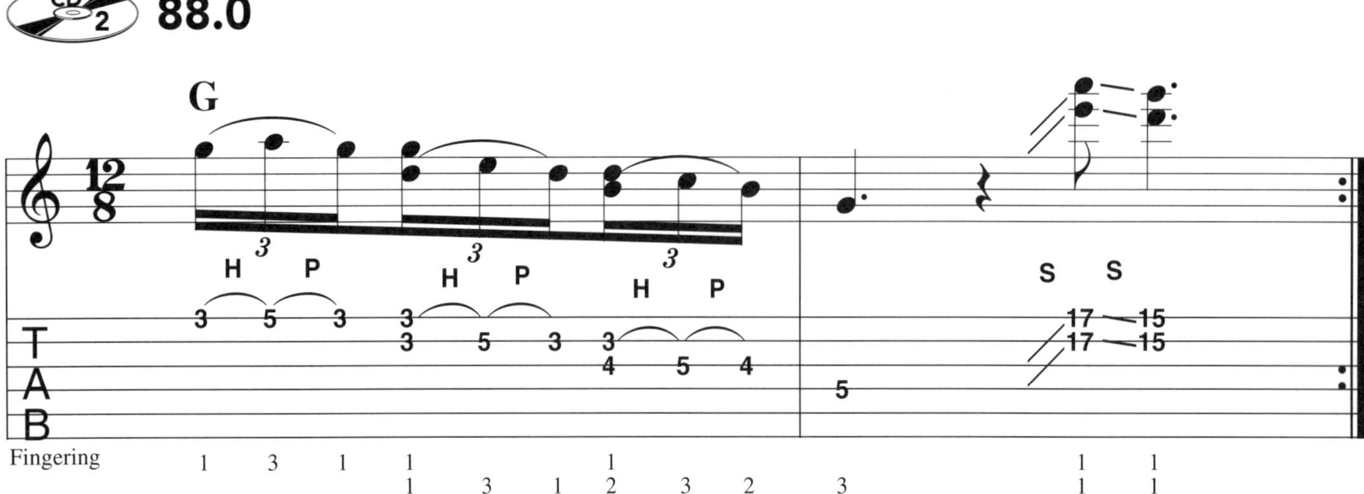

The next one is based around this minor 7th bar chord shape.

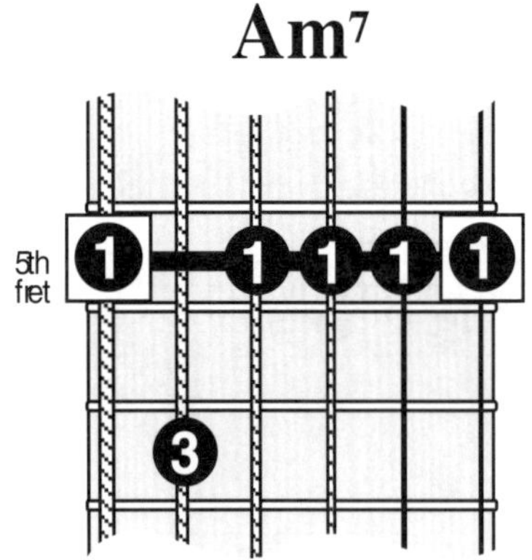

88.1

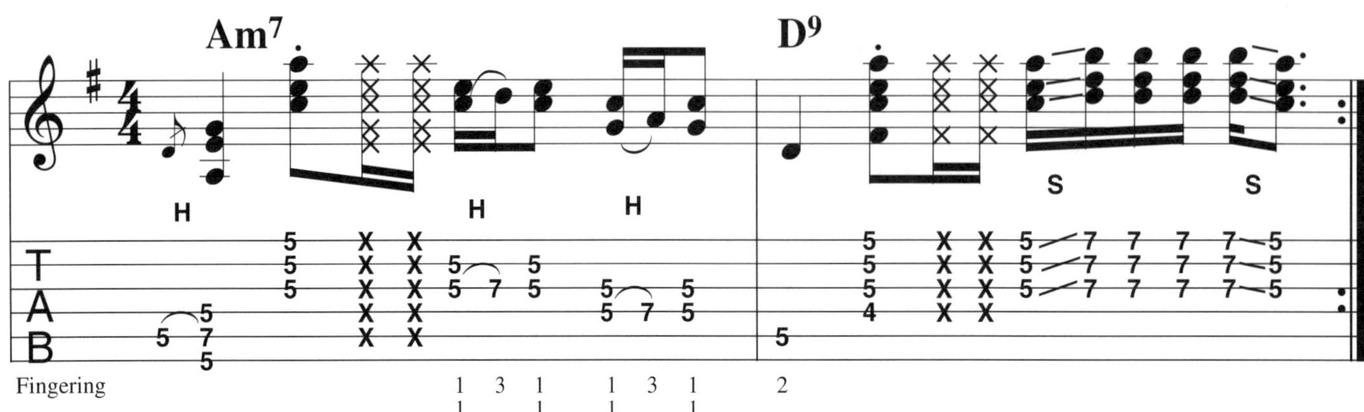

88.2

This example alternates between **G** and **C** chords.

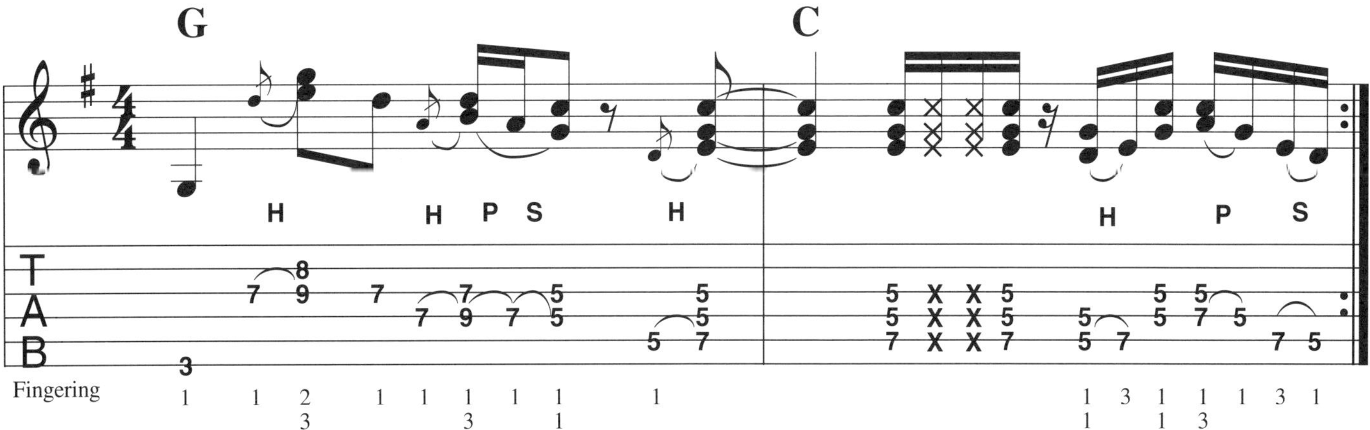

88.3

This one starts on **C** and changes to **G**.

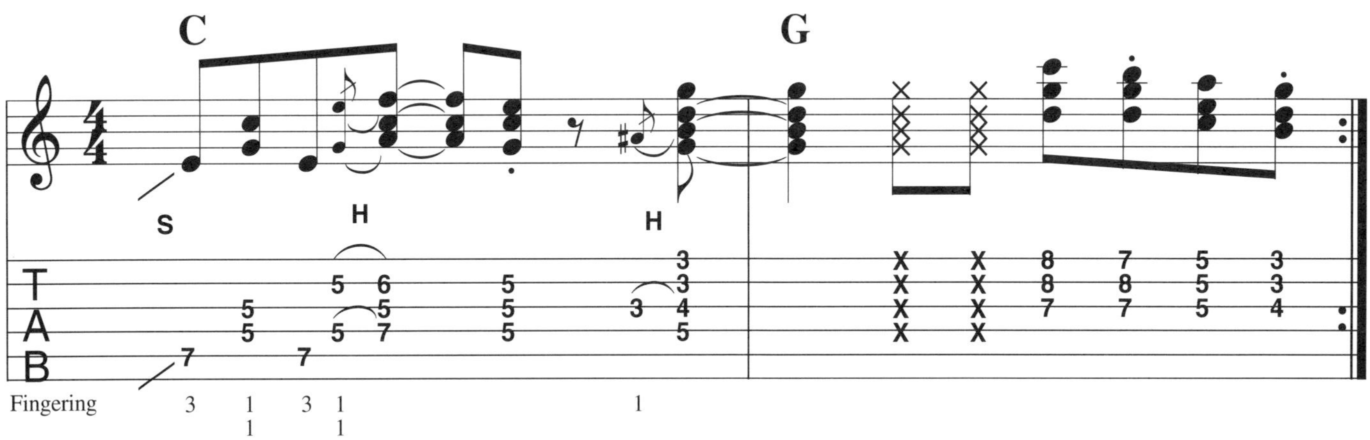

88.4

Here's one in a minor key.

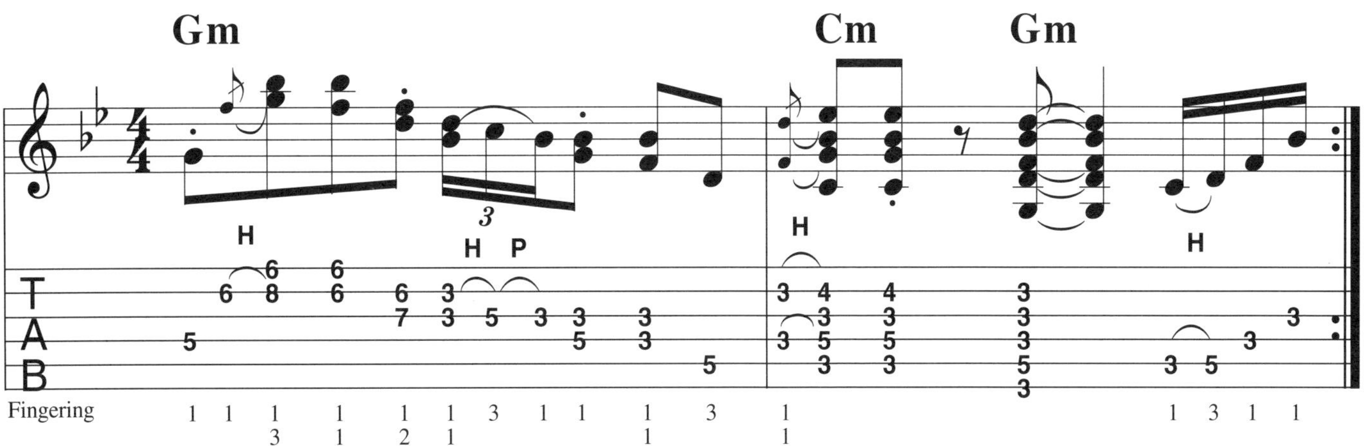

ODD TIME SIGNATURES

The majority of songs in most popular music styles are in 4/4 time. After this, 3/4 and 6/8 are the most common. However, occasionally you will encounter odd time signatures such as 7/4 (Pink Floyd's "Money" is a good example of this), 5/4, 5/8 or 7/8. In Jazz and Fusion, odd time signatures are common, and are becoming increasingly more popular in modern Rock and Metal styles as well, so regardless of the style you play, it is worth learning them. Playing in odd time signatures will also help your timing generally. Shown below is a four bar riff in 5/4 time. As the time signature suggests, there are five quarter notes per bar.

CD 2 89.0 5/4 Time

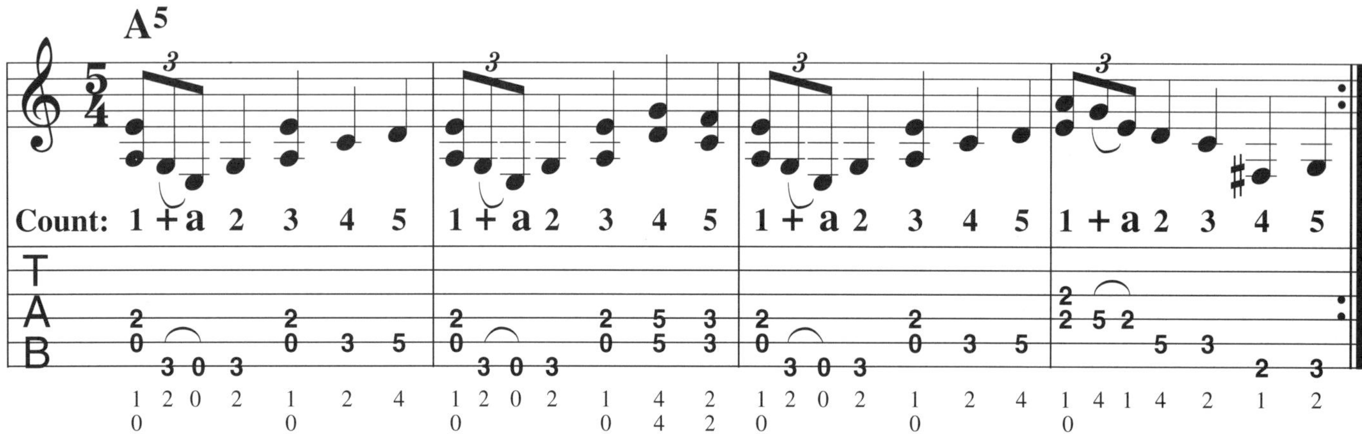

The following example is in 7/8 time. As the time signature suggests, each eighth note is one beat, so the 16ths are counted as the + (and) part of the beat. E.g. the first four 16th notes in each bar are counted "**1 + 2 +**" instead of **1e+a**.

CD 2 89.1 7/8 Time

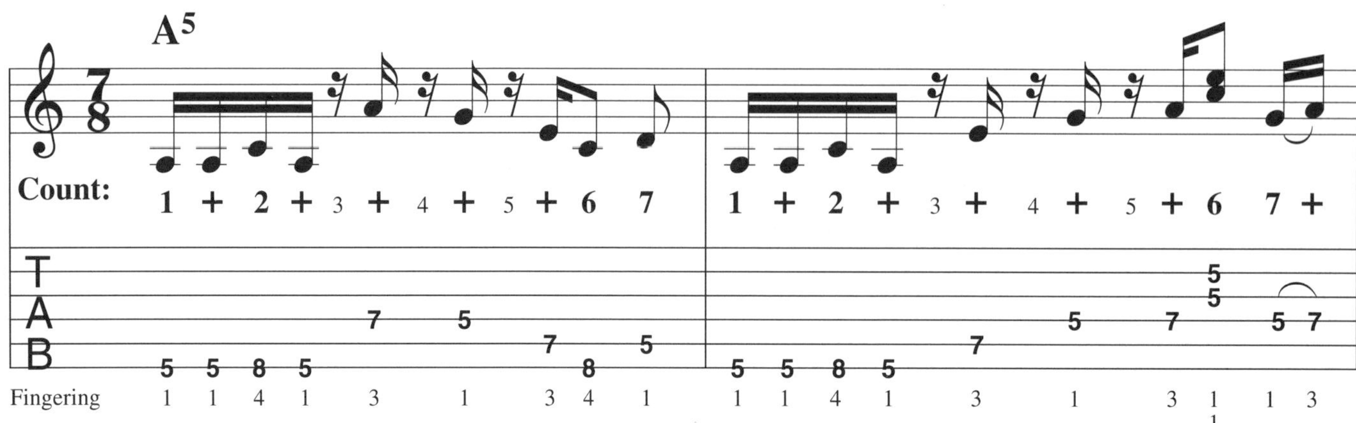

Some odd time grooves are made up of a combination of two different time signatures. E.g. some 7/4 grooves can be thought of as a bar of 4/4 and a bar of 3/4. Another time variation is to have a basic time signature such as 4/4 with an occasional odd time bar as part of the form. The odd time bar often happens at the end of the progression just before the whole pattern repeats. The following example uses three different time signatures. Take your time with it, and count until you are comfortable with the whole part, then try to just feel it as you play. You need to get to the point where an odd time groove feels as comfortable as a 4/4 groove.

90.

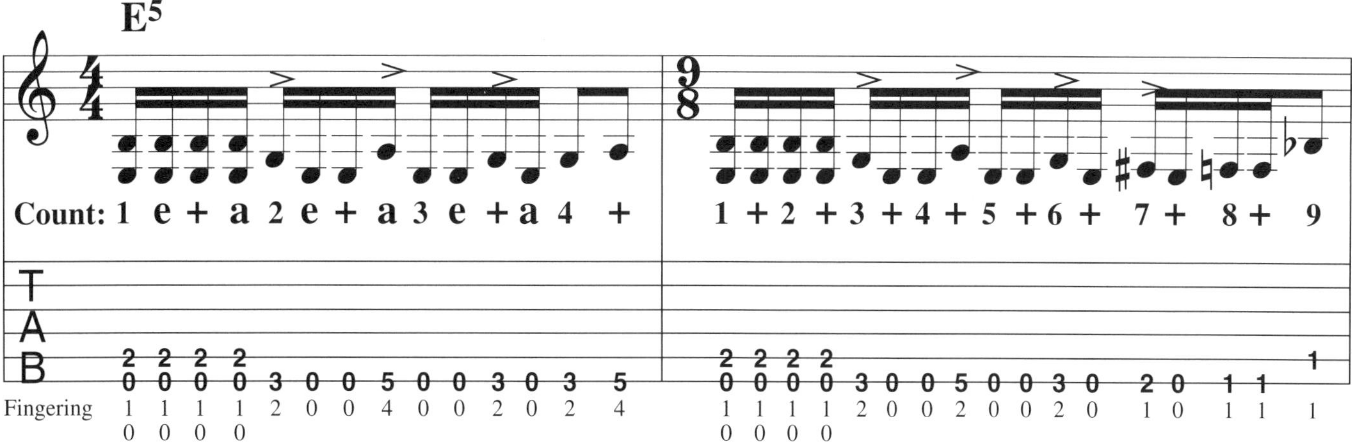

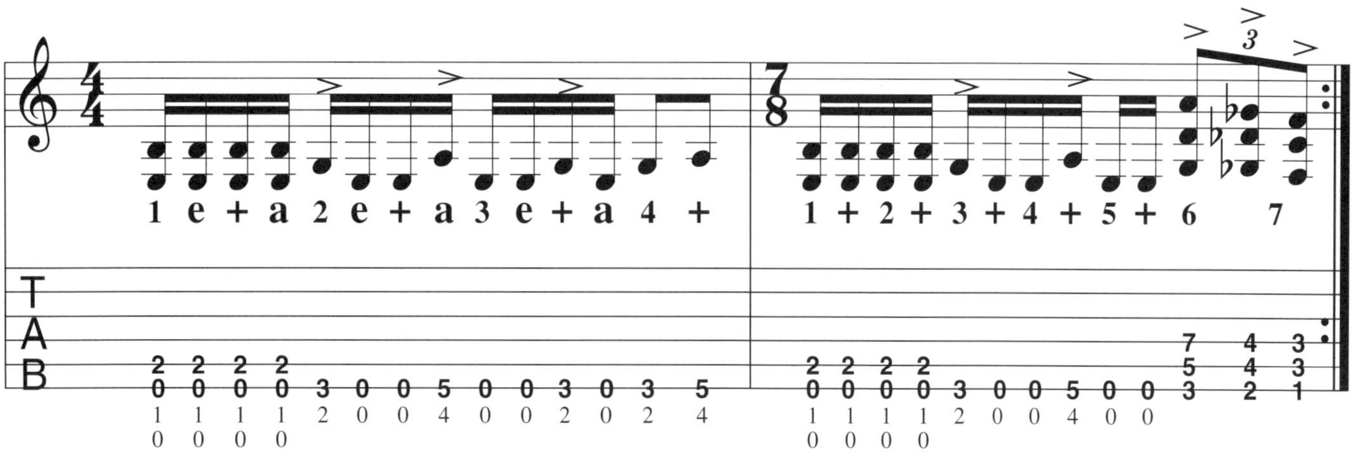

LESSON FIFTY ONE

PLAYING WITH A BAND

After you've worked on all the chords, scales, techniques and rhythms, the most important thing is knowing where and when to use them. This will usually depend on what the other instruments are playing. If you are not sure what to play, you can always get ideas from what the bass and drums are doing. When you are playing with other musicians, the most important thing is to listen to each other and try to respond to each other.

THE BASS

The bass helps to keep solid time and provide the basic feel and drive along with the drummer. The bass and bass drum parts are often closely linked. The bass also spells out the chords and lays the foundation for the harmony of the song. Together, the bass and drums are called the **rhythm section**. While a singer or horn player has time to breathe between phrases and a guitarist or keyboard player leaves space between lines or chords, the drummer and bass player have to play consistently to keep the groove going and feeling good. It is the job of the rhythm guitarist to "lock in" with the rhythm section to keep the feel tight and drive the song forward.

Most electric basses have four strings which correspond to the bottom four strings of the guitar (**E**, **A**, **D** and **G**). The difference is that they are tuned one octave lower than the guitar. The strings are much thicker than guitar strings and the lower frets are wider apart. Like the electric guitar, the bass has pickups (usually two) and is played through an amplifier. The bass is usually played with the index and middle fingers of the right hand, or "slap" style with the thumb and index finger, but it can also be played with a pick. The photo below shows a typical electric bass.

BASS MUSIC NOTATION

Bass music is written on the lines and spaces of the **bass staff**, which is similar to the treble staff, except that it uses a **bass clef** (shown below).

The Bass Clef

There is a bass clef at the beginning of every line of bass music.

The Bass Staff

A staff with a bass clef written on it is called a **bass staff**.

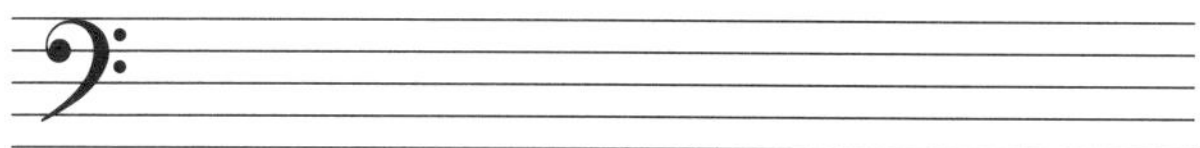

Notes on the bass staff are lower than those on the treble staff and the notes appear in different places. Every note is **one line or space down** from where it would be on the treble staff. The notes on the lines and spaces of the bass staff are shown below.

NOTES ON THE BASS STAFF

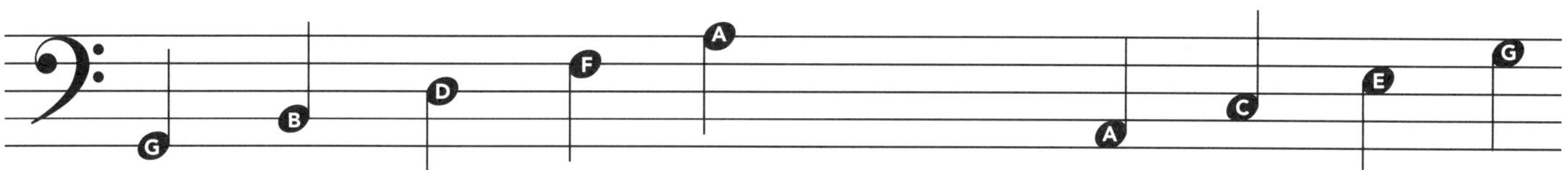

To remember the notes on the lines of the bass staff, say:
Good **B**oys **D**eserve **F**ruit **A**lways.

To remember the notes in the spaces of the bass staff, say:
All **C**ows **E**at **G**rass.

The following example demonstrates a riff played by the guitar and bass together (an octave apart). Listen to the recording to hear the effect this produces. The fingering is the same on both instruments as shown in the tablature.

CD 2 91. Guitar and Bass Together

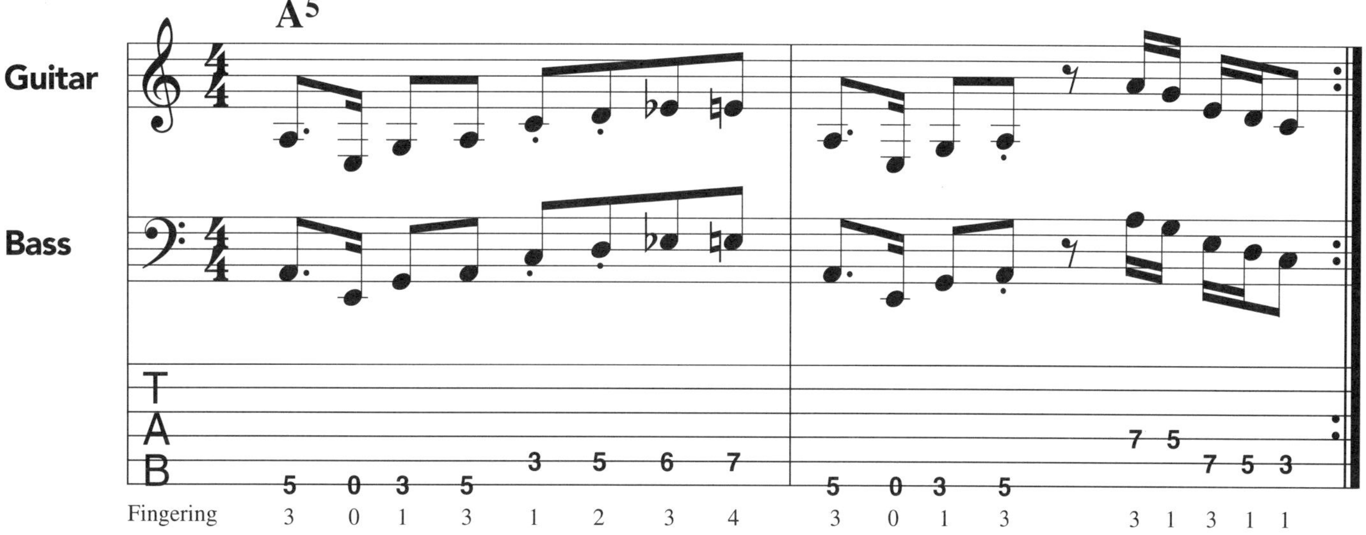

THE DRUMS

The drums set up and keep the basic feel of a song. They also drive the rhythm forward and provide endless rhythmic ideas for the other instruments through the use of accents, fills, and rhythmic patterns. The great thing about listening to the drummer is that you have three or four different parts that you can play around or lock in with. Many musicians (especially guitarists) rely on the drummer to keep time for them, but in a good band everybody has a strong sense of time and no-one relies on anyone else. If you are not confident keeping time for yourself, work with a metronome or drum machine every day until you are confident. The photo below shows all the basic parts of a drumkit.

This kit contains three tom toms, but many drummers use only two, as these are probably the least necessary part of the kit. In fact, most drum parts can be played using only the snare drum, the bass drum and the hi hat cymbals. The **bass drum** is played with the right foot and produces what is often called the "bottom end" sound of the drums. The **snare drum** is usually played with the left hand, but the right hand is also used for certain beats as well as playing fills. The **hi-hat and ride cymbals** are generally played with the right hand, but once again the left hand may be used in certain situations. The **crash cymbal** is played with either hand, depending on which one is most practical for each musical situation. The **tom toms** (toms for short) can also be played by either hand. **The hi-hat cymbals** can also be played by the left foot and the most common sounds using the open hi hats are achieved by using a combination of the right hand and the left foot.

DRUM NOTATION

Drum music is usually written in the spaces of the **bass staff**, including the space above the staff; to represent different parts of the drum kit. The most commonly used system is shown below. Notice that cymbals are notated with an **X** instead of a notehead.

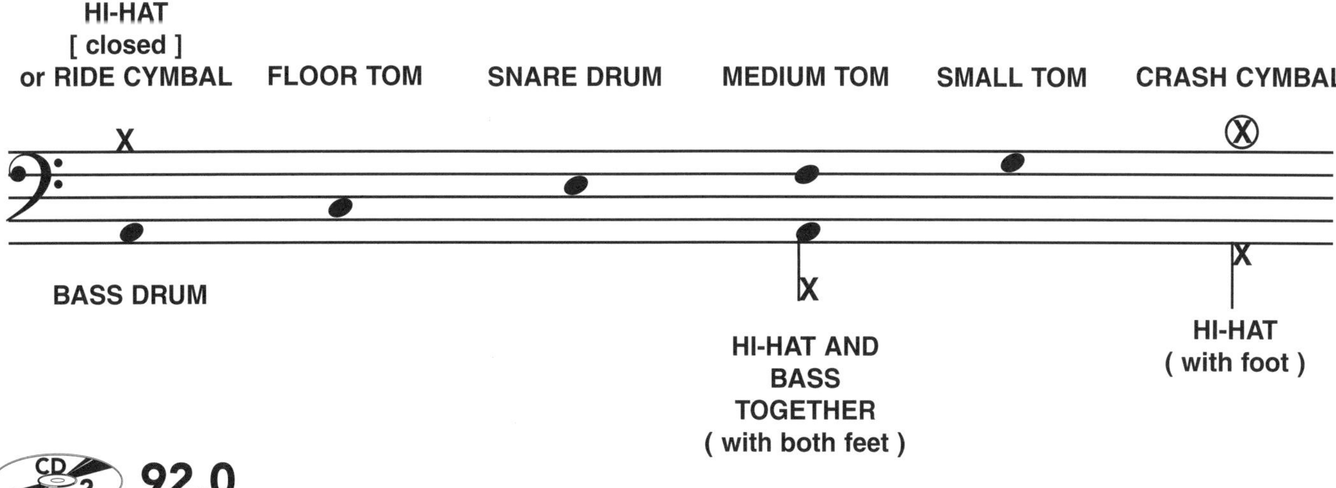

92.0

The following example demonstrates a simple Rock beat on the drums. Follow the notation as you listen to the recording and then try reading the notation without the recording and imagining the sounds of the drums as you follow the notes.

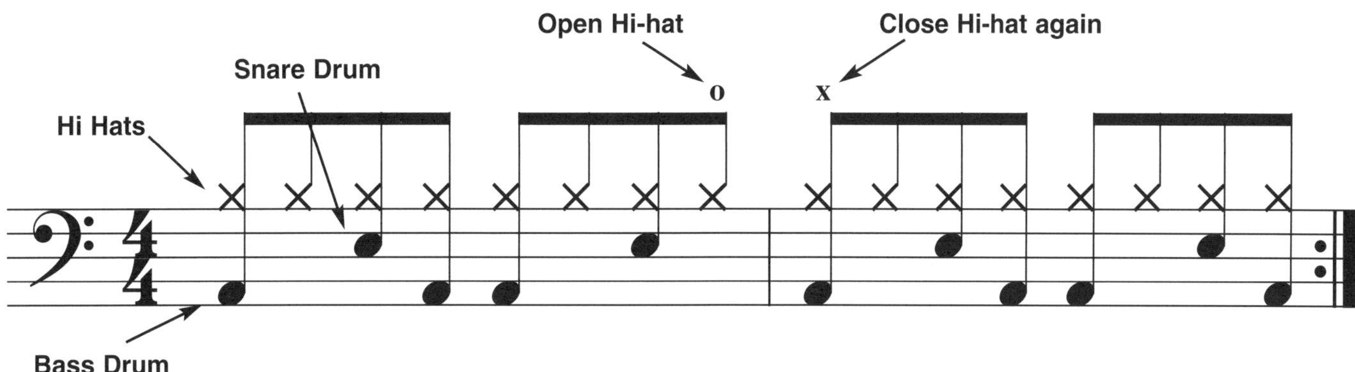

When a bass player is working out what to play with a drum part, the first thing they usually look at is where the bass drum falls. It is common for the bass and bass drum to play together, as demonstrated in the next example.

92.1

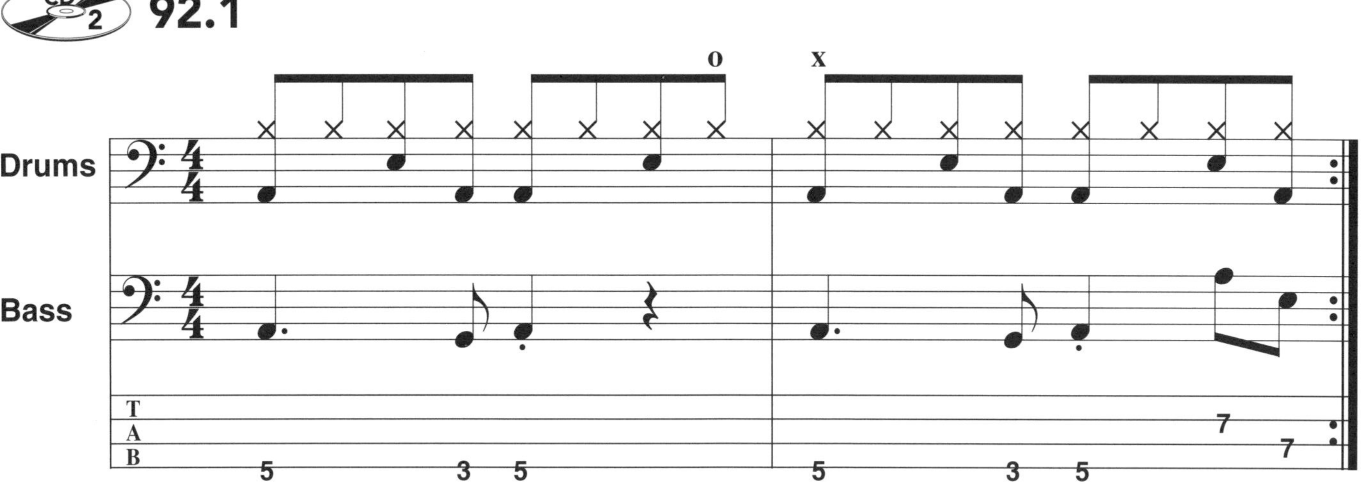

LESSON FIFTY TWO

PLAYING WITH A RHYTHM SECTION

If you were going to add a guitar part to the bass and drum parts shown in the previous example, there are several things you could do. The first thing is to play a constant eighth note rhythm along with the hi-hat part as demonstrated in the following example. When playing this type of part, listen carefully to the drums and make sure your playing is exactly in time with them. Because the hi-hats create a short, crisp sound, it is a good idea to use right hand damping when playing along with them. This helps the band to sound tight.

CD 2 93.0

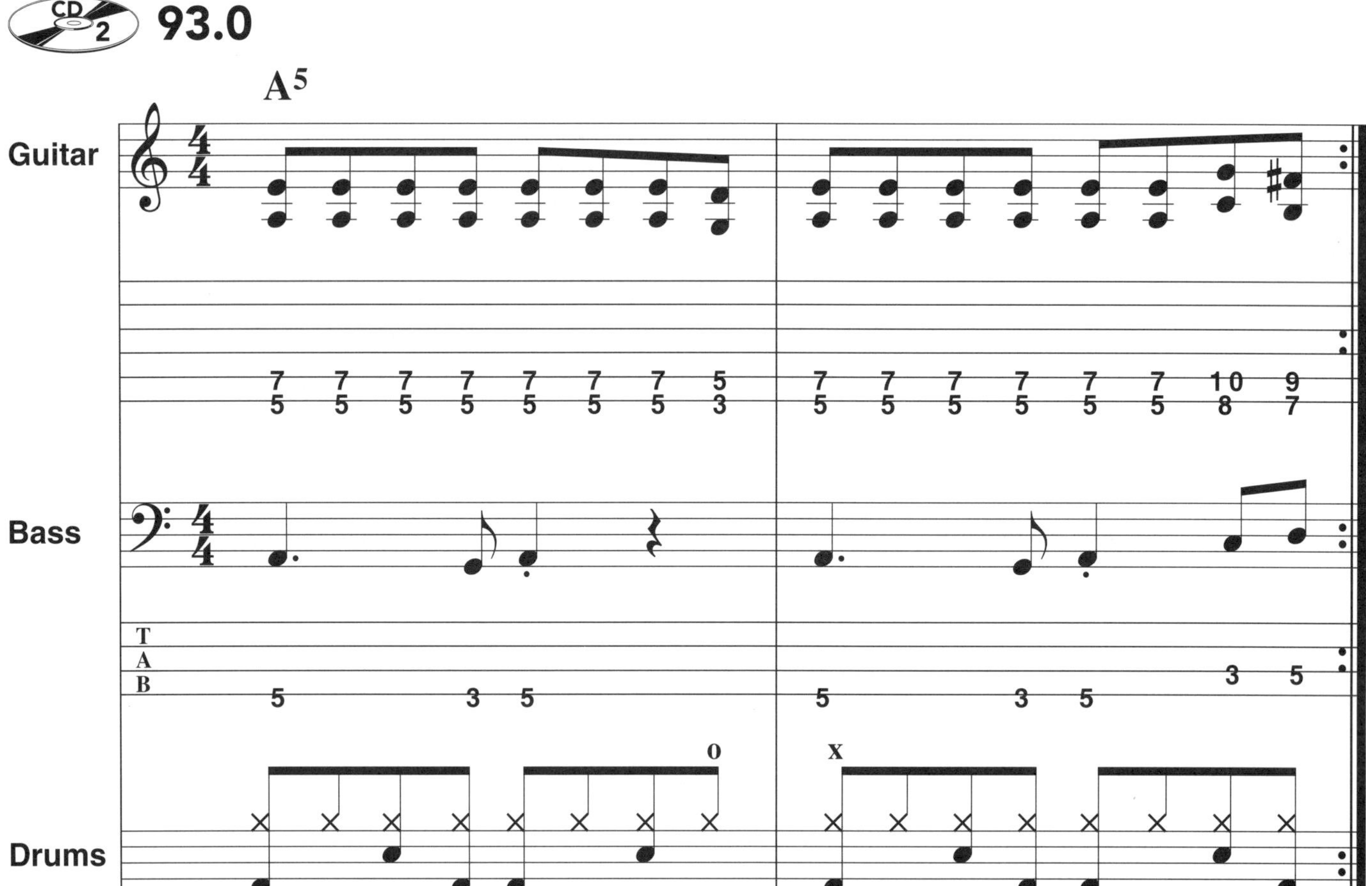

CD 2 93.1

Another approach is to play with some parts of the bass line and some part of the drum part, but leave space in between for the other instruments to be heard. This is demonstrated in the following example, which uses exactly the same bass and drum parts as the previous example.

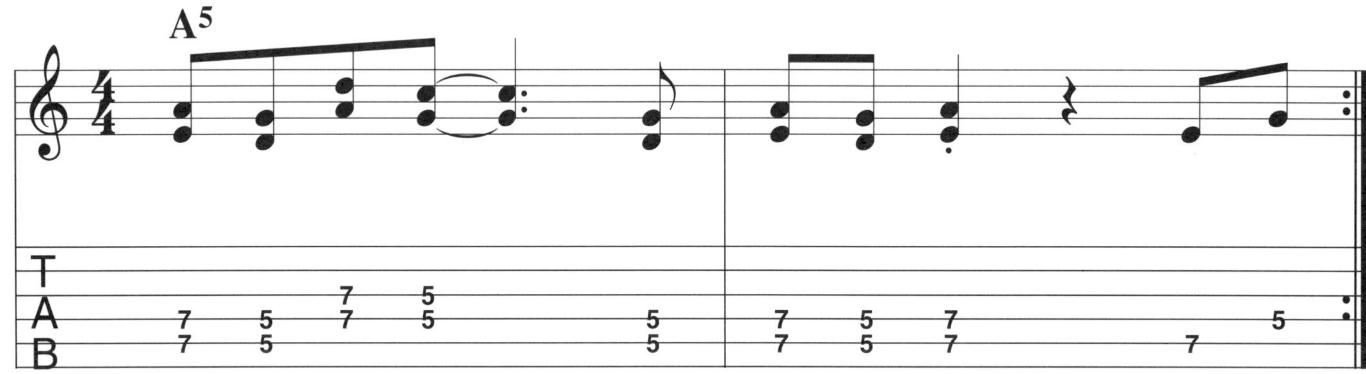

The following pages contain examples of guitar, bass and drums working together. Analyze them and notice where notes are played together and where one instrument leaves space for the others. A good general principle to use is: if one part is busy, it is best to have something simple played with it, rather than all the parts being busy. Interplay, communication and "locking in" together are the most important aspects of playing as a band. Always learn your own part well enough that you can listen to what everyone is playing rather than just hearing yourself.

94.0

94.1

Here is an alternative guitar part to go with the bass and drums from the previous example. There is always more than one part which will work with the rhythm section. The most suitable part for any instrument depends on the style of music. The best way to broaden your knowledge of what to play is to listen to a lot of different music and pay attention to how the instruments work together. Ask your teacher or guitar-playing staff in a music store to recommend some albums in different styles until you know what to listen for.

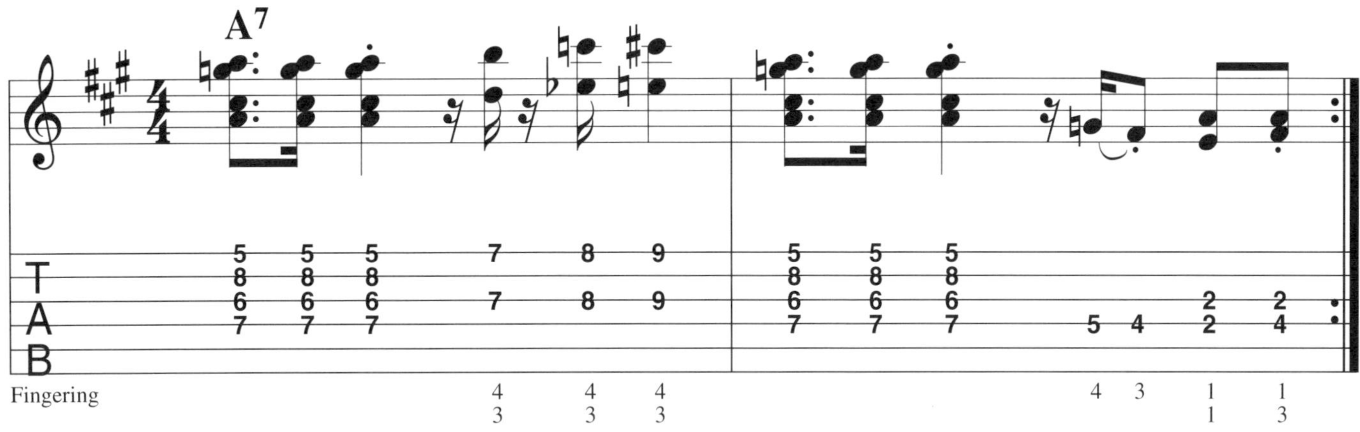

The next two examples are shuffles, as indicated by the swing symbol next to the CD number. Use the ideas presented here to create some parts of your own.

WORKING WITH ANOTHER GUITARIST

The following example features two guitar parts. Listen to how one leaves space for the other and how they connect at certain points to keep the sound tight. When you have two guitarists in a band, it is important to work out clearly defined parts so that they complement each other, rather than clashing. Careful listening, discipline and lots of rehearsal is the key. Listen to bands like ACDC, Lynyrd Skynyrd, and Metallica to hear great examples of two guitarists working together.

96. 2 Guitars

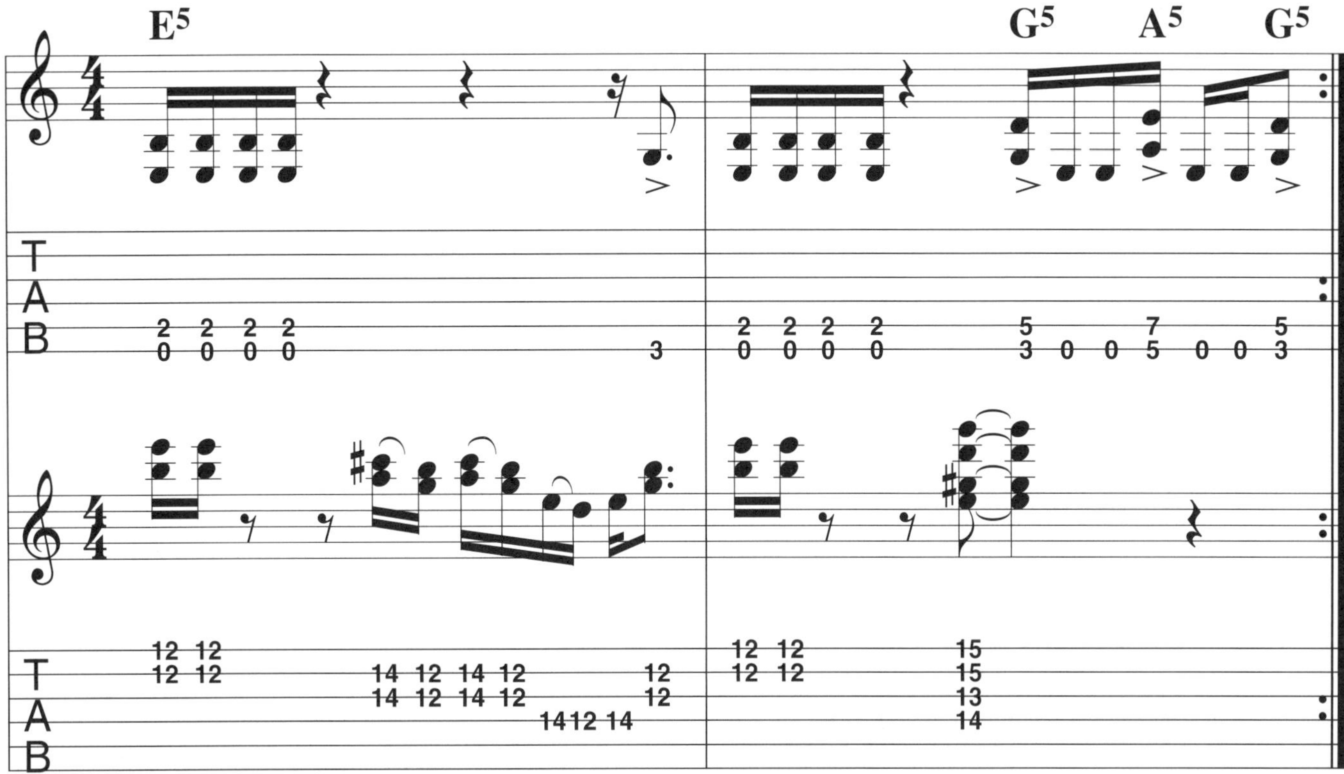

97. Guitar and Keyboards

Here is an example which features guitar and keyboards. When working with a keyboard player, the same principles apply as when working with another guitarist. In this example, the keyboard locks in with the drums and the guitar plays a complementary rhythm and then leaves space for the keyboard to be heard, before doubling the keyboard part just before it repeats.

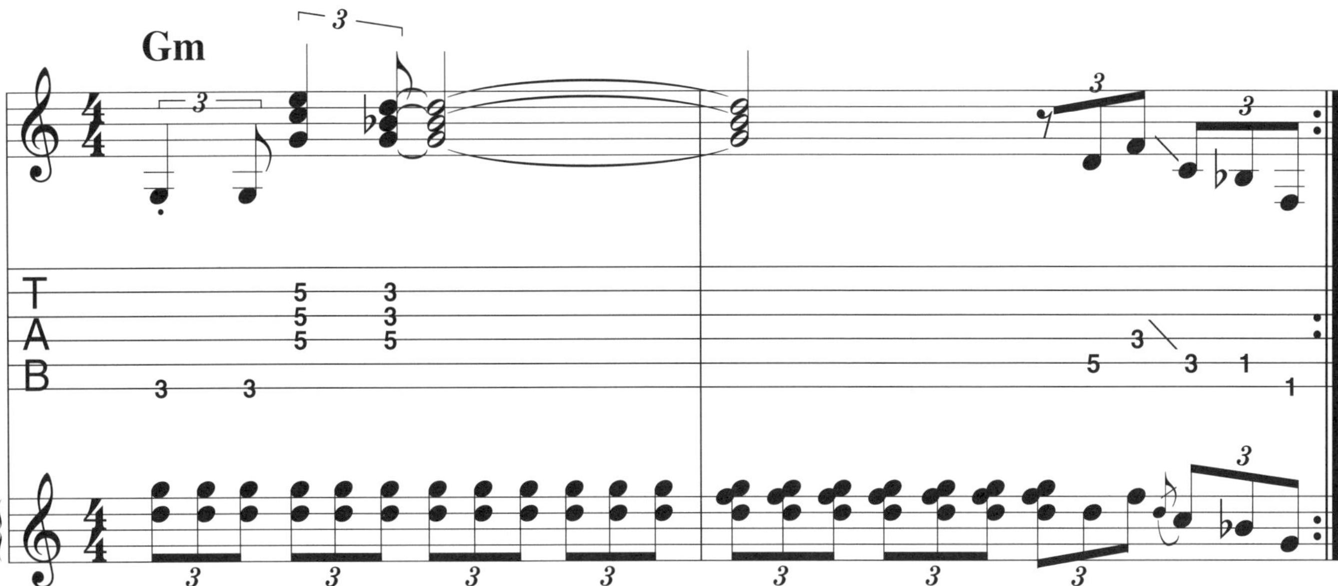

LESSON FIFTY THREE

PUTTING IT ALL TOGETHER

Well, if you've got this far, you are well on the way to becoming an excellent rhythm guitarist. To sum things up, here are a couple of chord solos which use almost everything covered in the book. The first one is a funky Blues which includes 7th and 9th chords, percussive strumming, 6th intervals, single note runs and various slur techniques.

98. Silver Shades

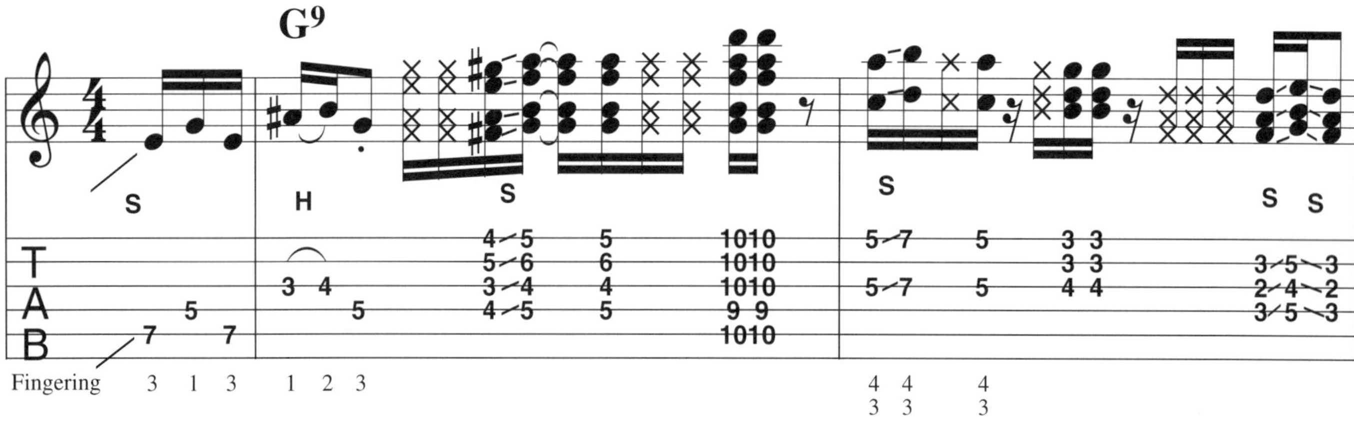

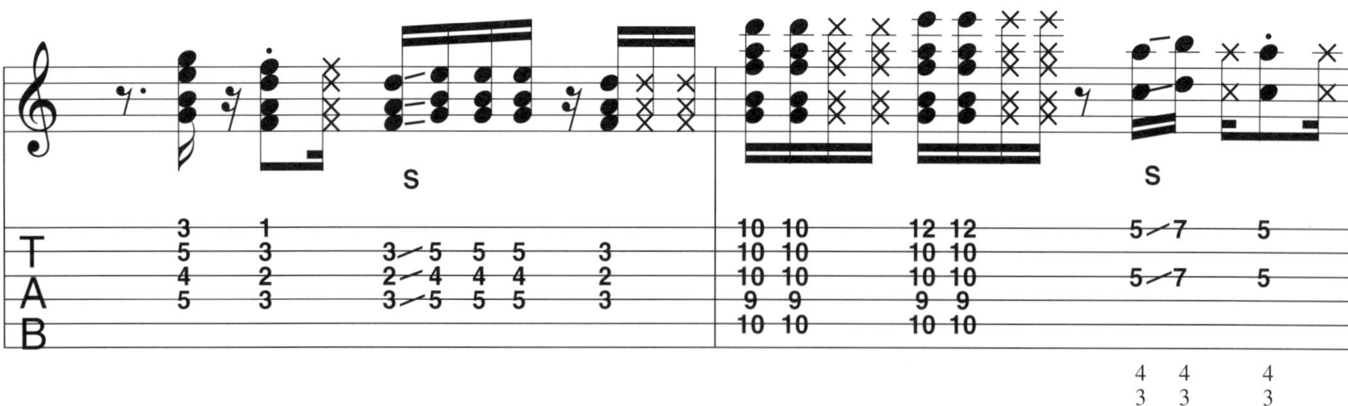

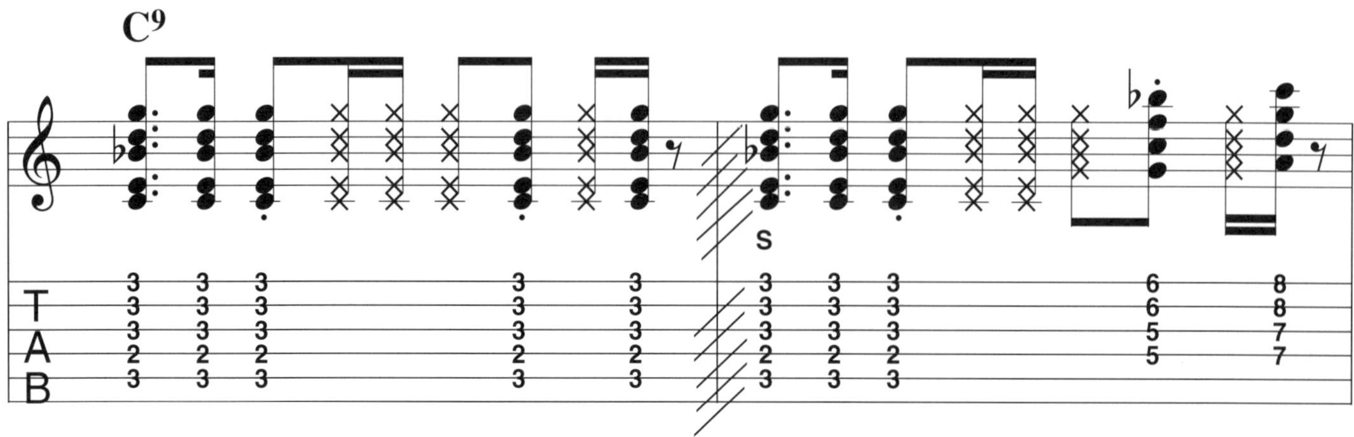

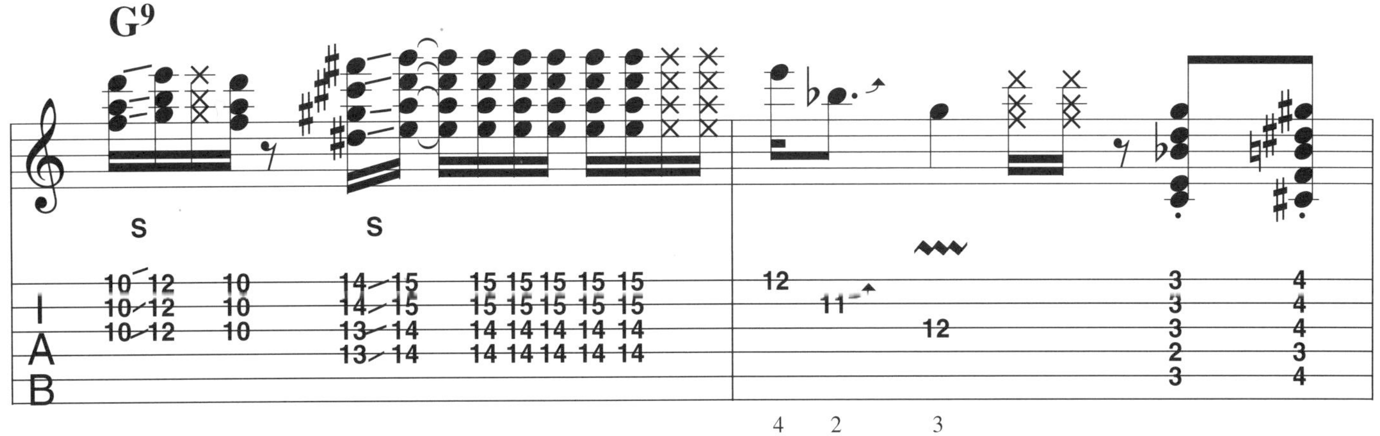

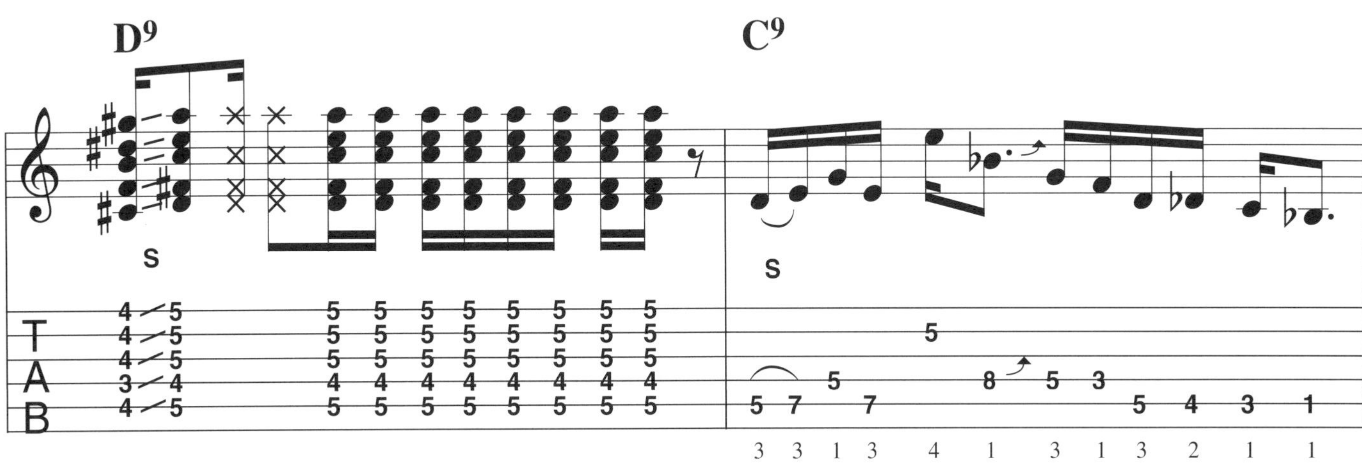

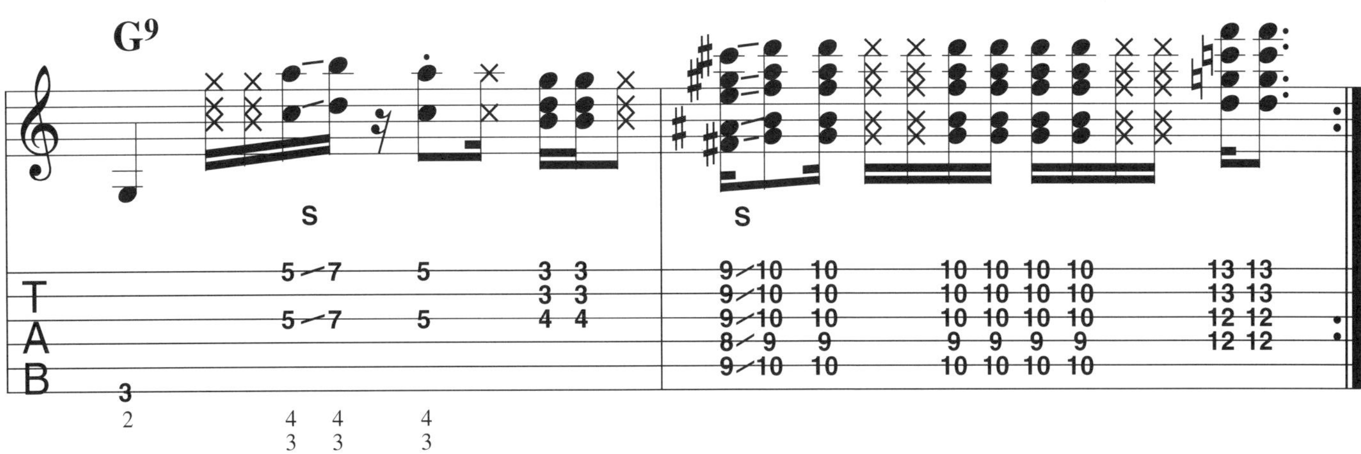

For more books and recordings by the author, check out **www.bentnotes.com**

This final piece has two distinct sections. The first contains moody minor key arpeggios and the use of swung 16th notes, while the second consists of power chords played with a double time triplet rhythm. Play the triplets using **all downstrokes**. As with everything you learn, memorize the parts, analyze them, and then create your own parts based on what you have learnt. Keep practicing, keep playing, and good luck.

99. Split Shift

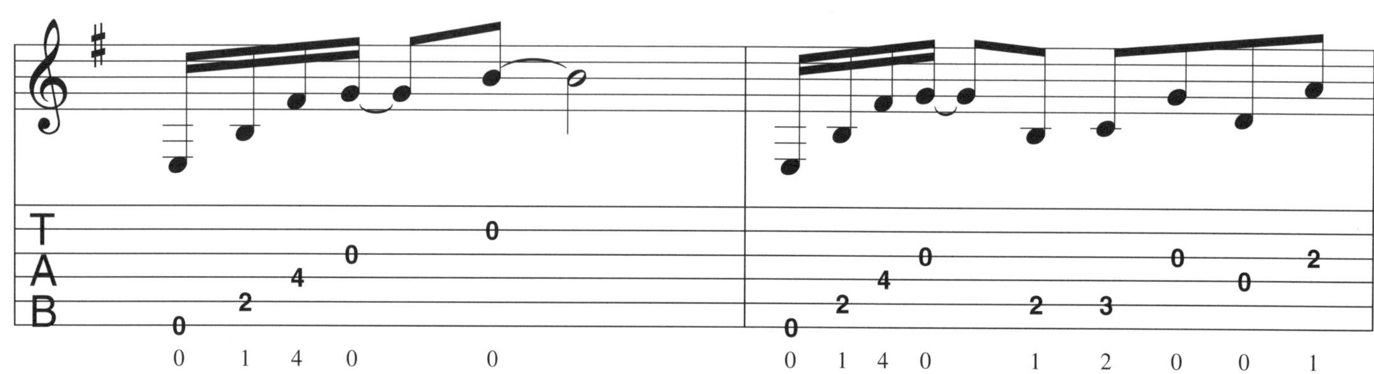

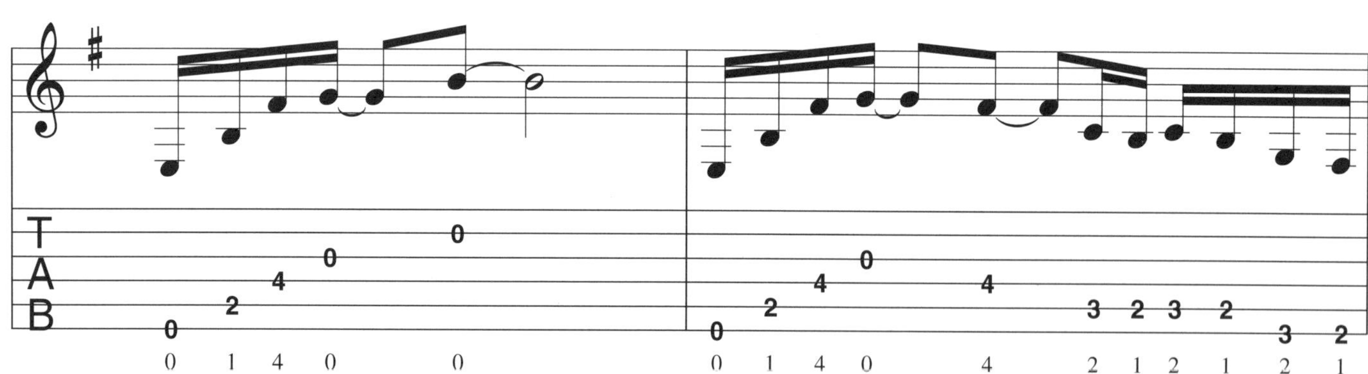

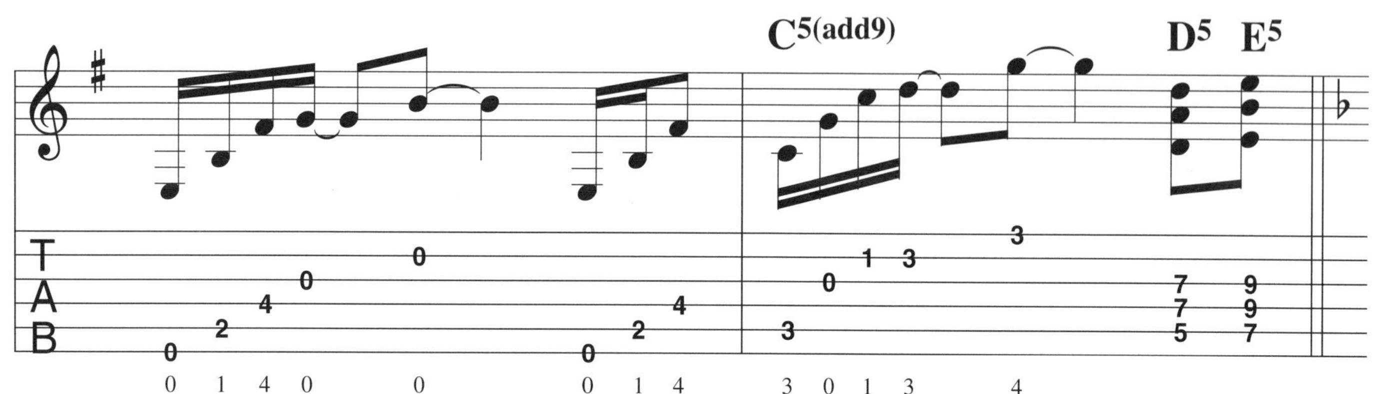

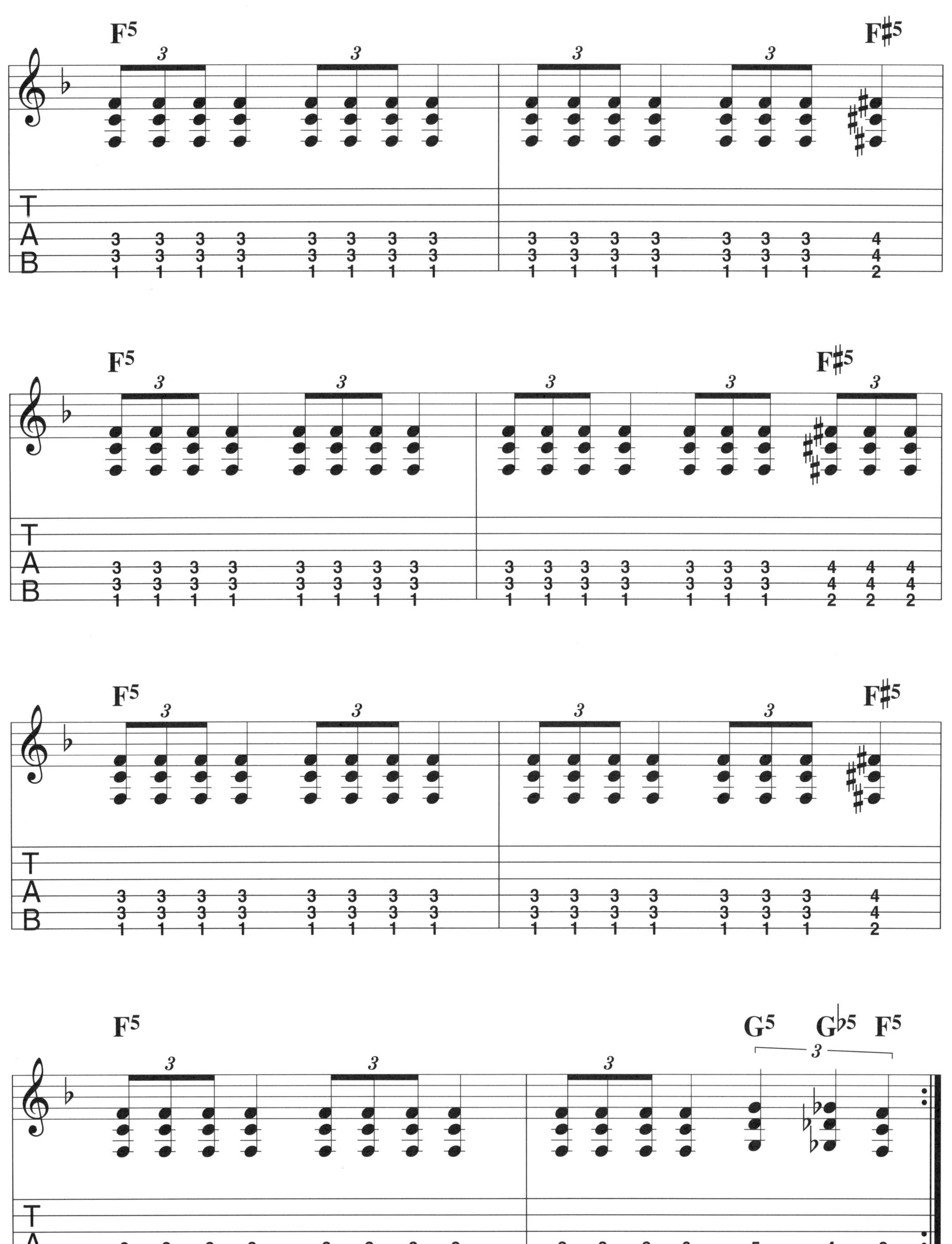
F5
F♯5
F5
F♯5
F5
F♯5
F5
G5
G♭5
F5

MOVEABLE CHORD SHAPES

Here are some commonly used moveable chord shapes which can be played in any key . Most chord types are covered here, but there are others. For a comprehensive dictionary of chord shapes, see ***Progressive Complete Learn to Play Guitar Chords Manual***.

Major

Chord Symbol

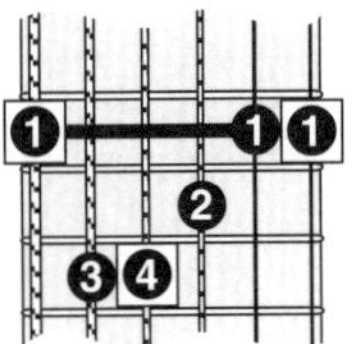
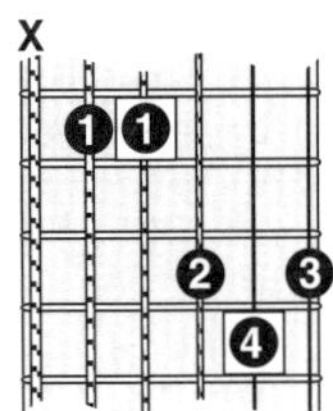
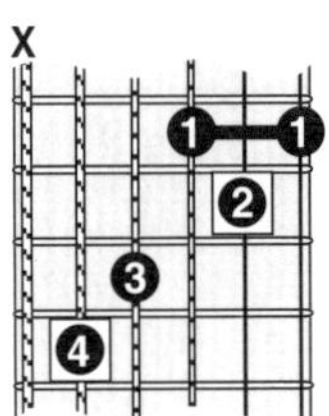
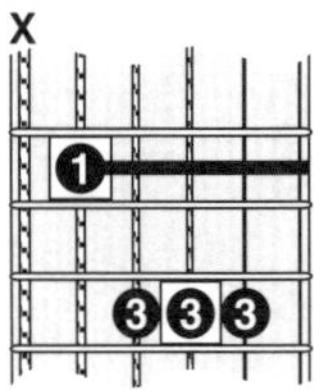
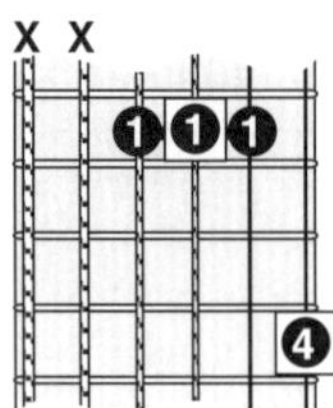
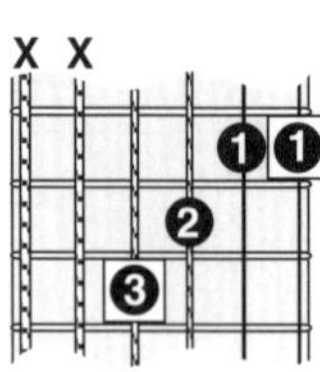

Minor

Chord Symbol

m

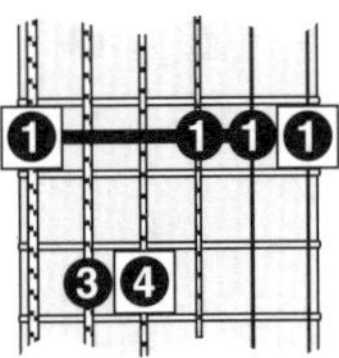
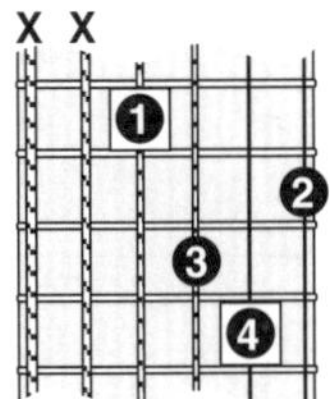
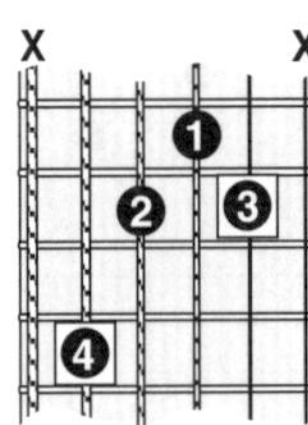
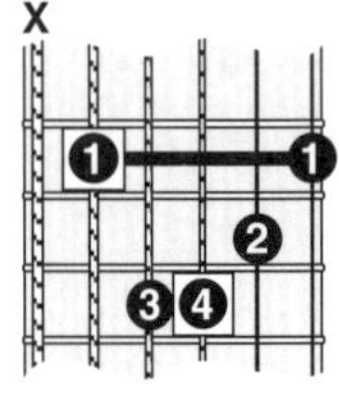
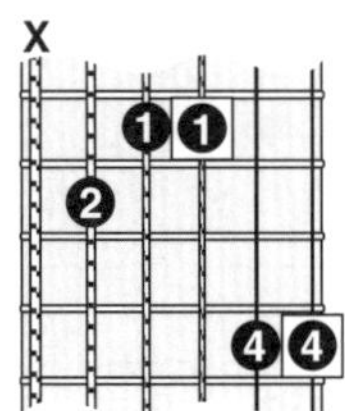
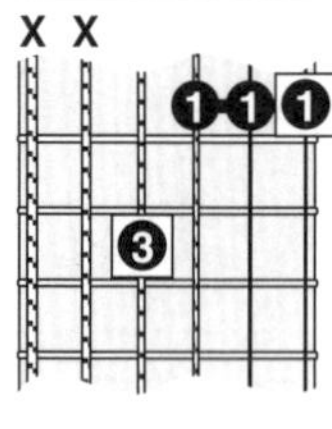

Suspended

Chord Symbol

sus

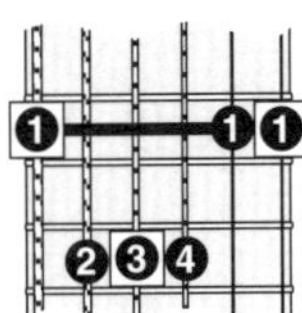
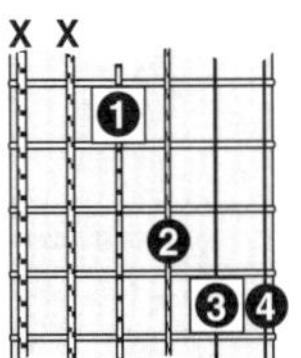
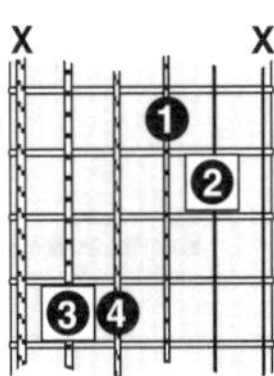
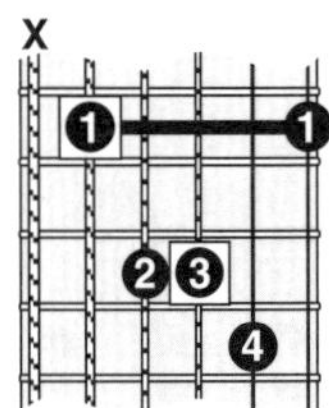
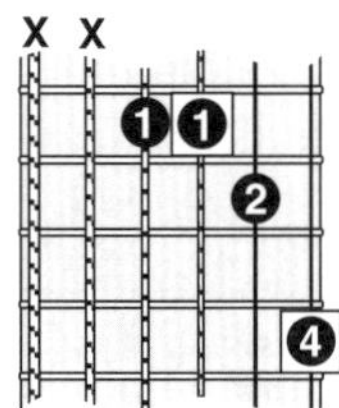
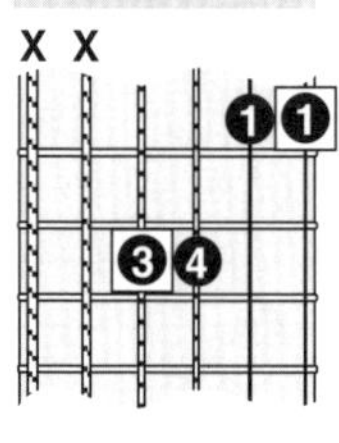

Major Add Nine

Chord Symbol

add9

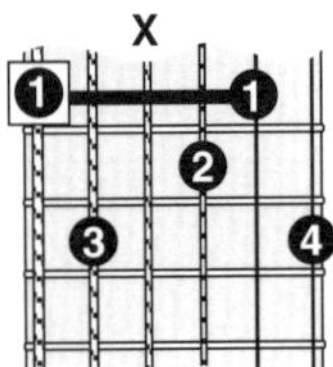
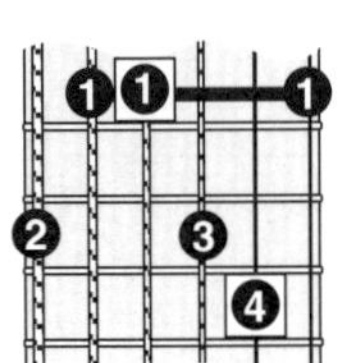
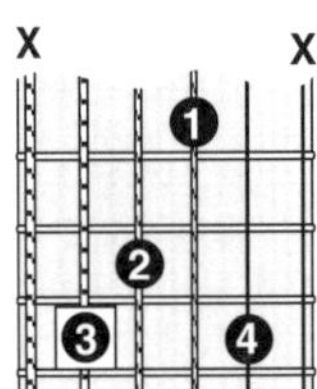
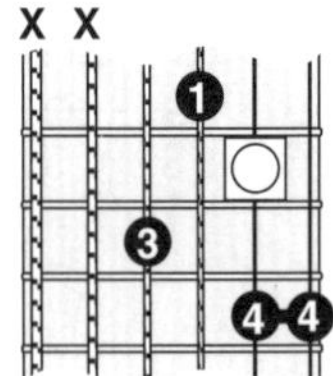
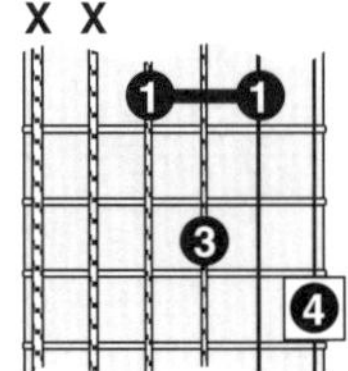
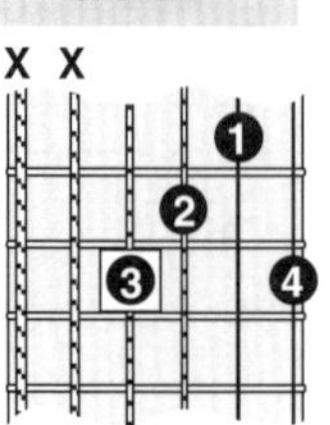

Minor Add Nine

Chord Symbol

m$^{\text{add9}}$

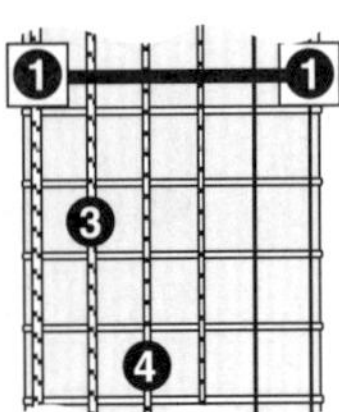
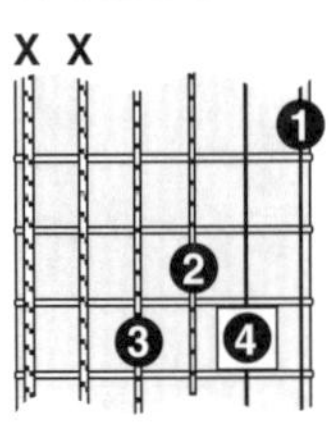
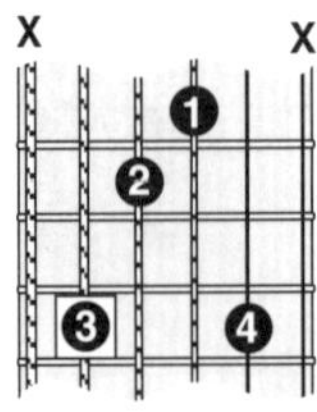
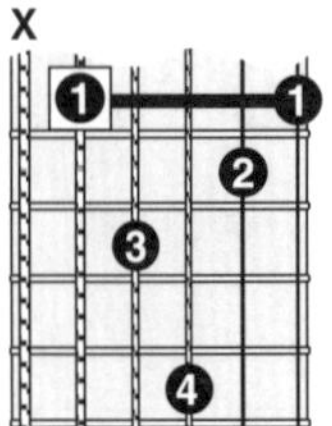
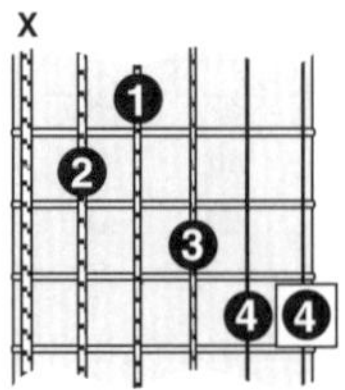
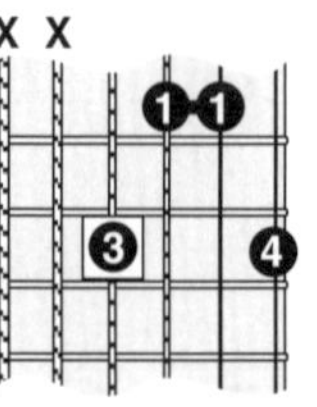

Augmented

Chord Symbol

+

Any note of an augmented chord can be the root.

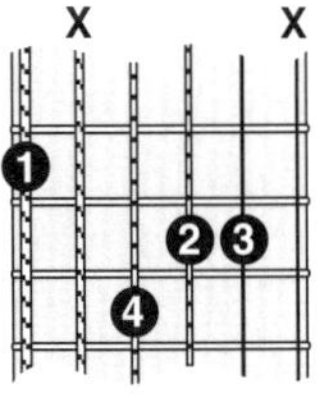
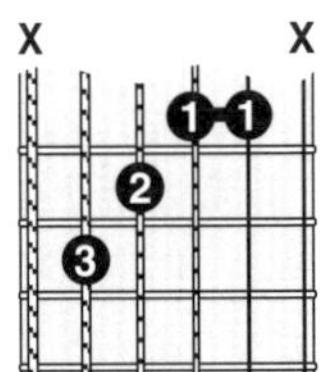
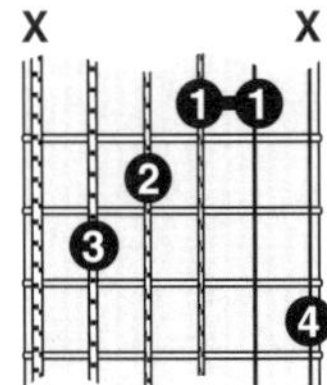
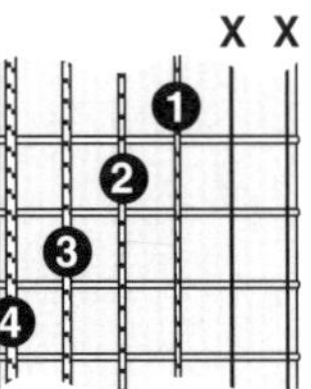
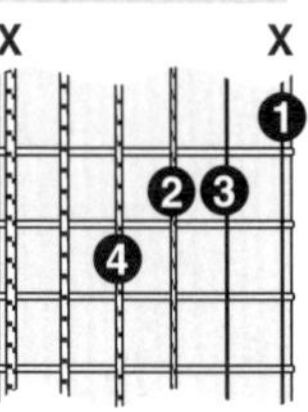

Major Seventh

Chord Symbol
Maj7

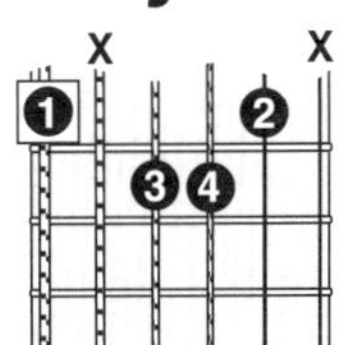
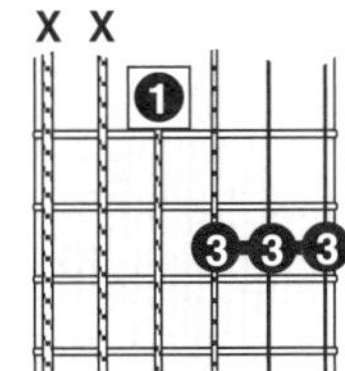
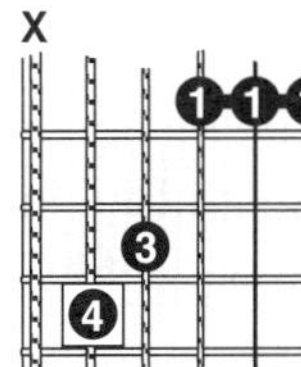
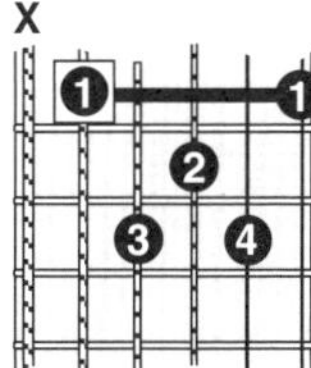
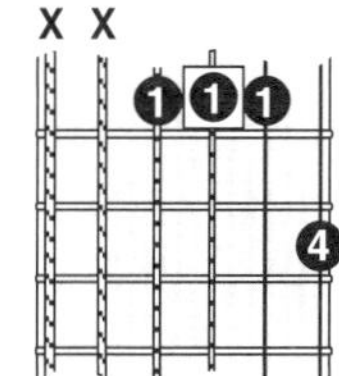
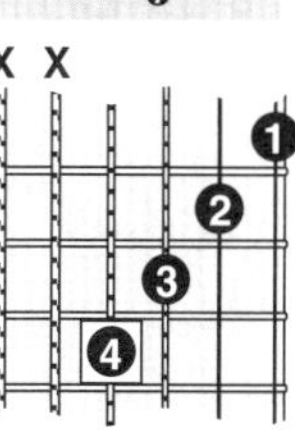

Dominant Seventh

Chord Symbol
7

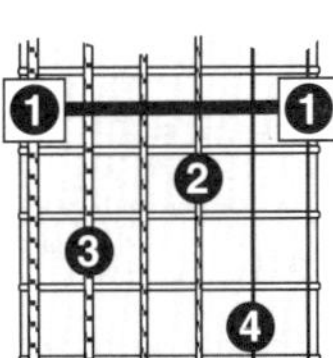
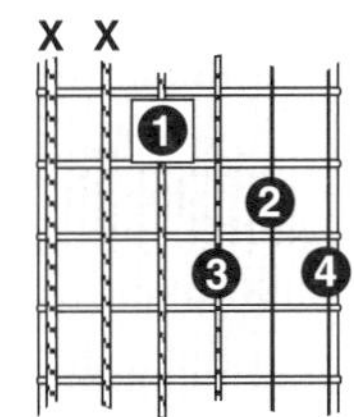
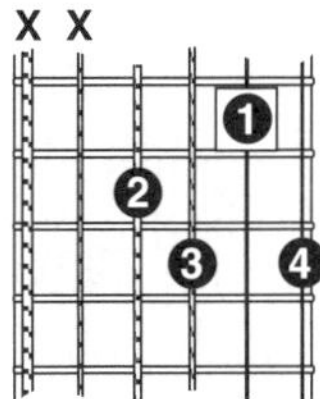
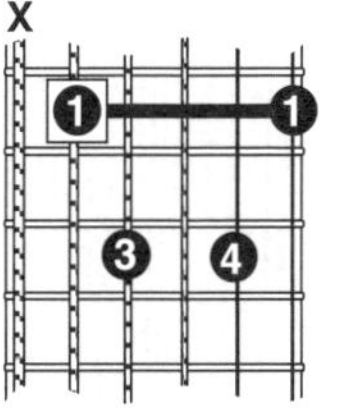
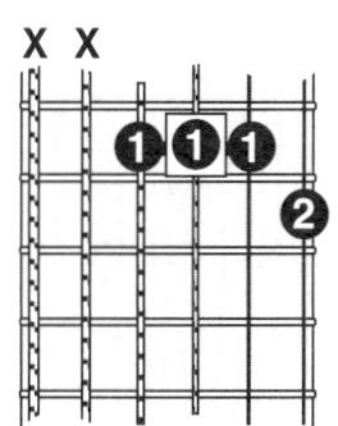

Minor Seventh

Chord Symbol
m7

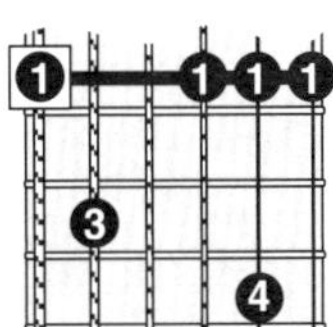
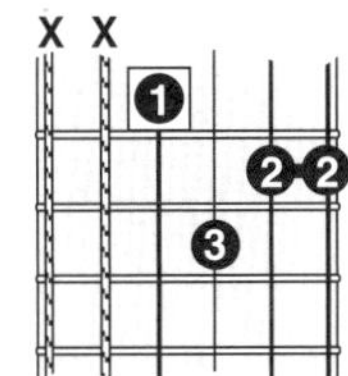
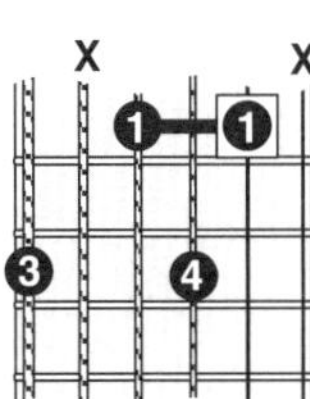

Minor Seven Flat Five

Chord Symbol
m7♭5

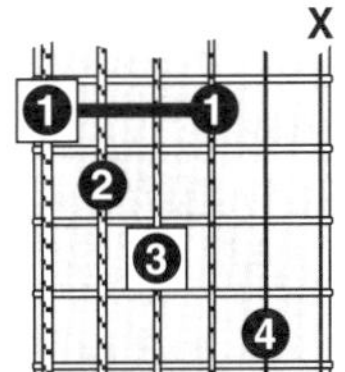
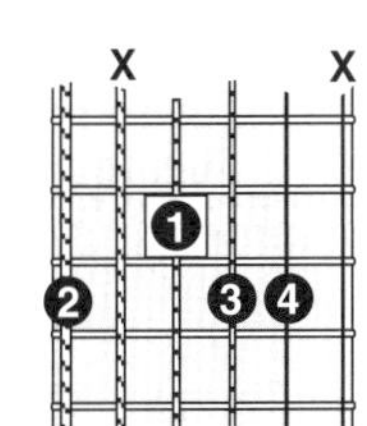
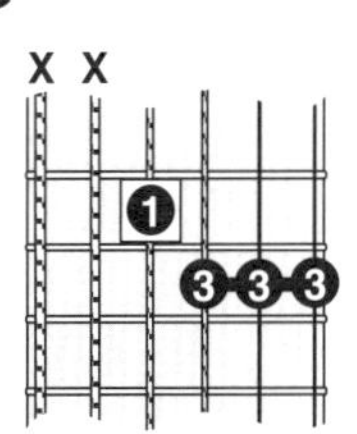
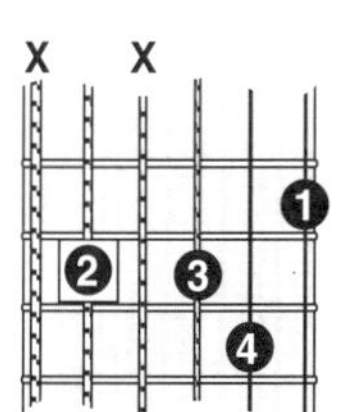

Diminished 7th

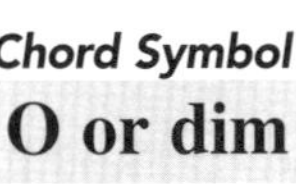
Chord Symbol
O or dim

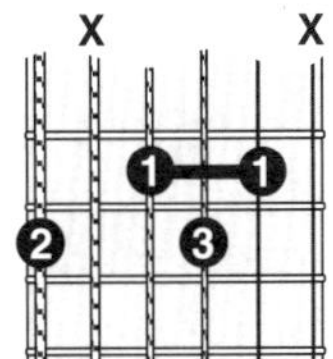
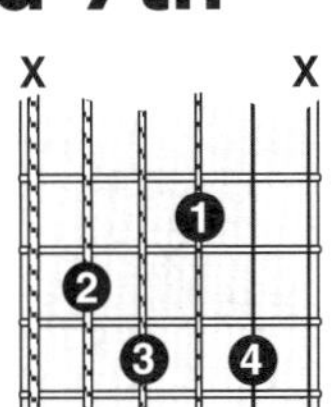
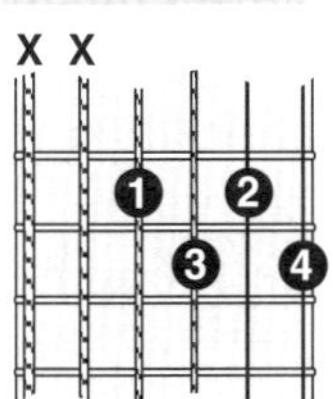

Seven Suspended

Chord Symbol
7sus

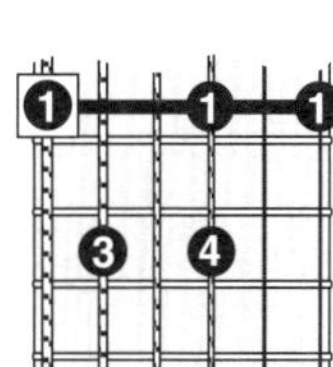
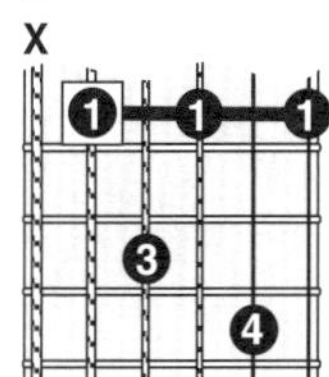

Seven Sharp Five

Chord Symbol
7♭5

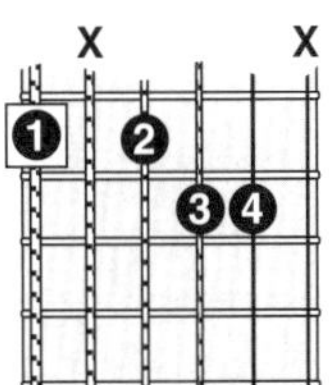
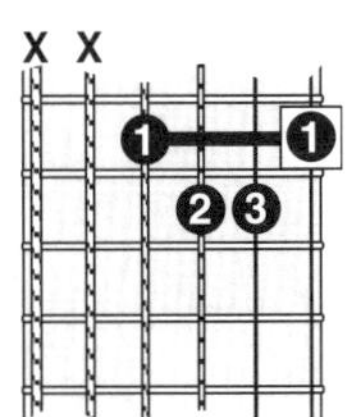
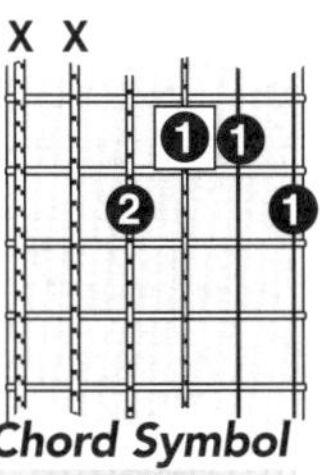

Seven Flat Five

Chord Symbol
7♭5

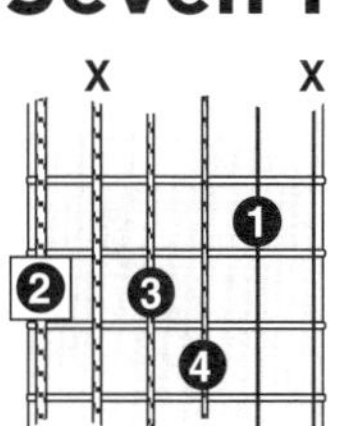
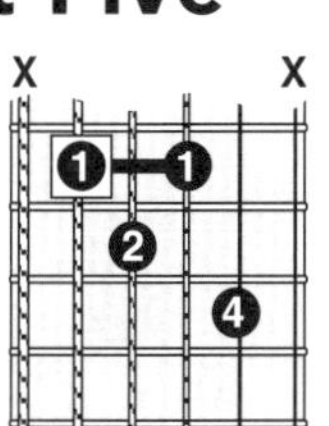
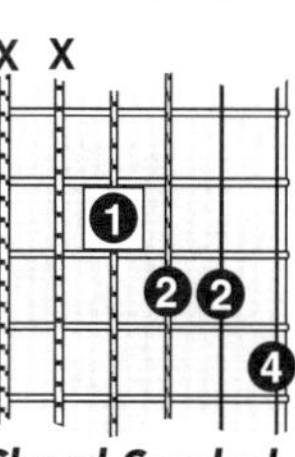

Major Sixth

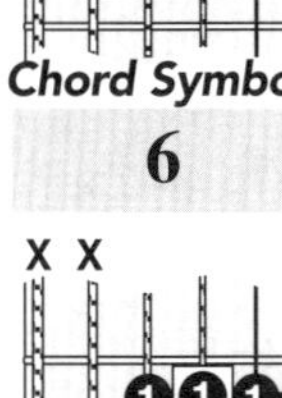
Chord Symbol
6

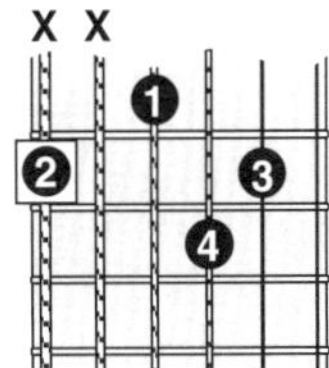
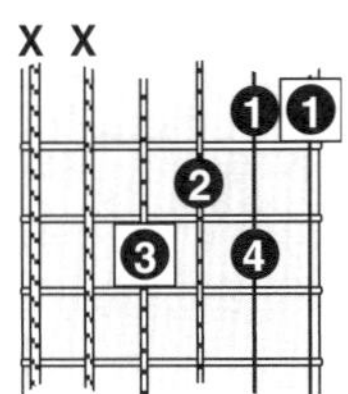

Minor Sixth

Chord Symbol
m6

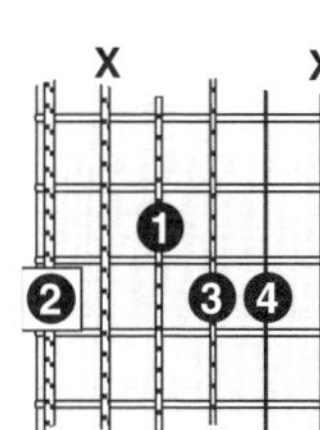
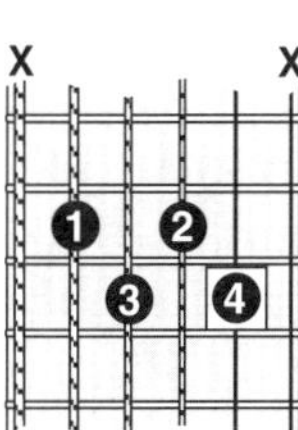
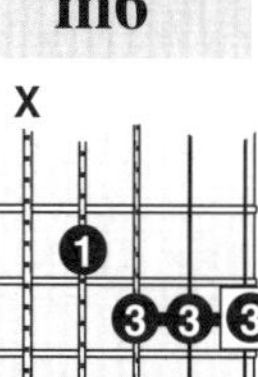

Major Ninth

Chord Symbol **Maj9**

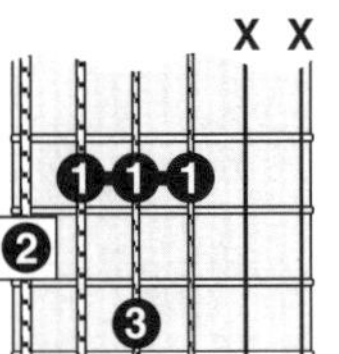
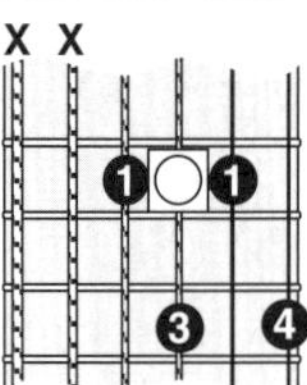

Ninth

Chord Symbol **9**

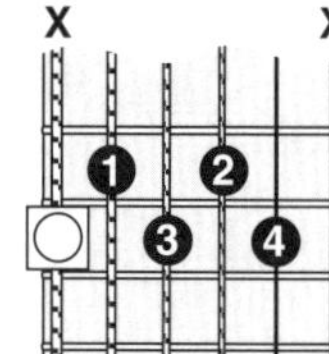
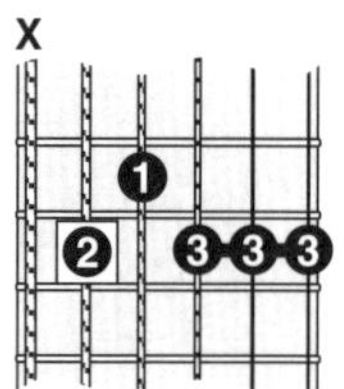
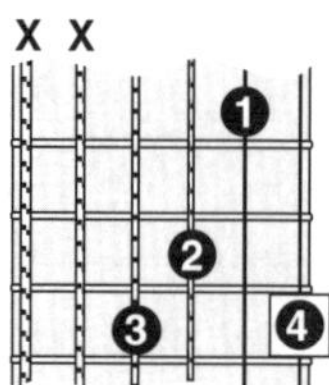

Minor Ninth

Chord Symbol **m9**

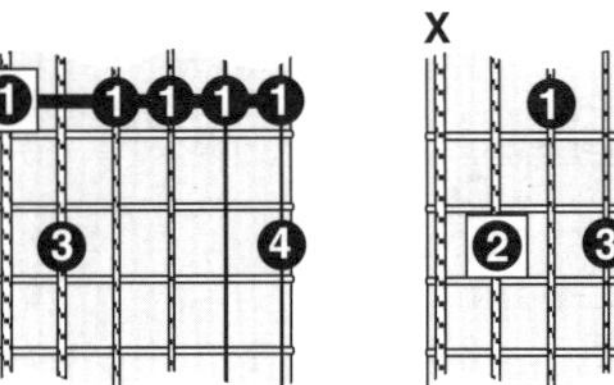
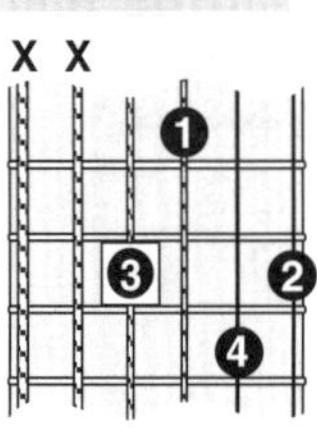

Seven Sharp Nine

Chord Symbol **♯**

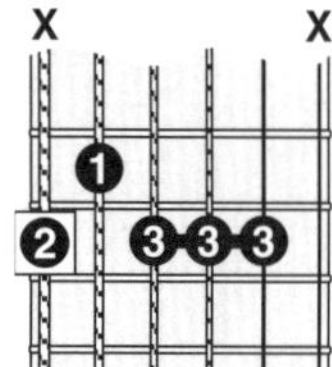
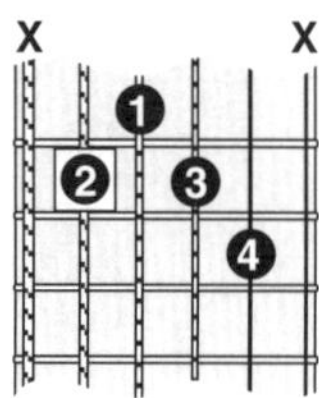

Seven Flat Nine

Chord Symbol **$7^{\flat 9}$**

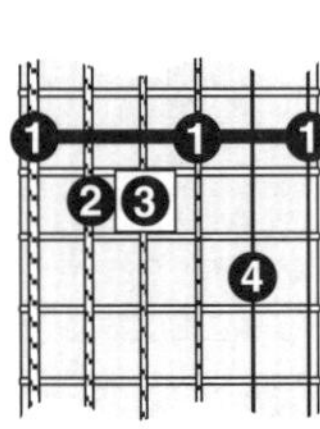
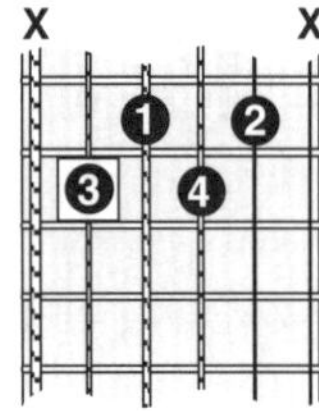
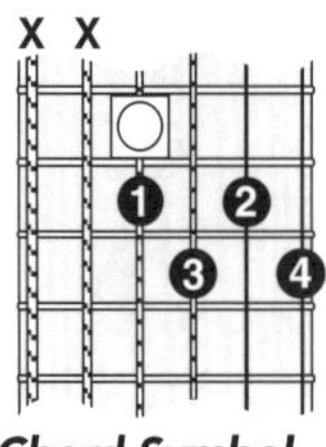

Six Nine

Chord Symbol **6/9**

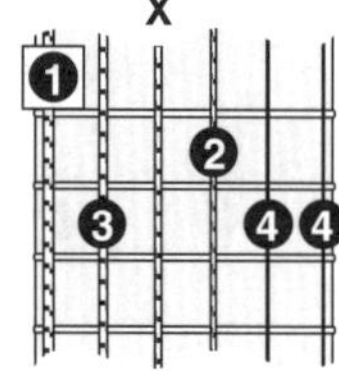
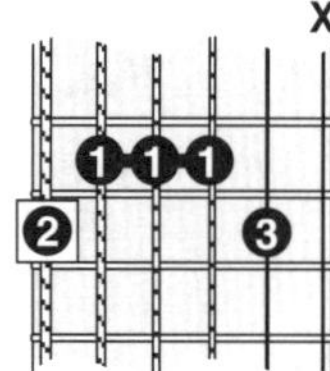
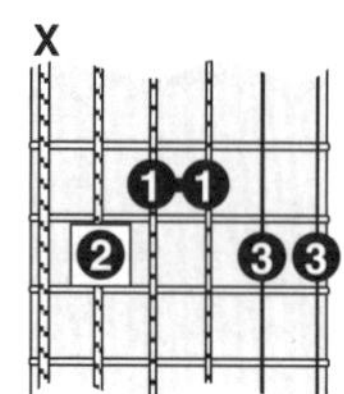

Eleventh

Chord Symbol **11**

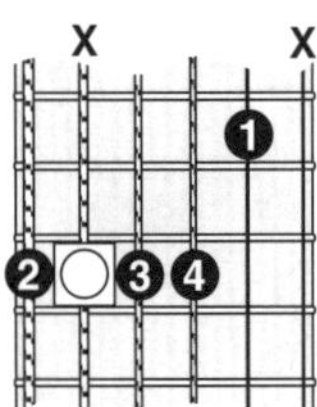
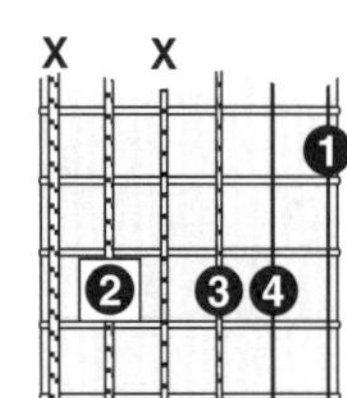

Minor Eleventh

Chord Symbol **m11**

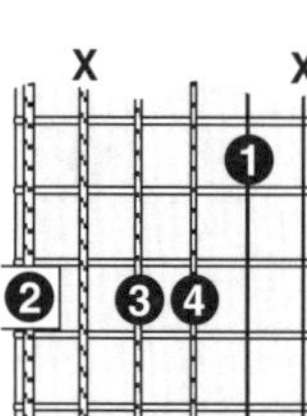
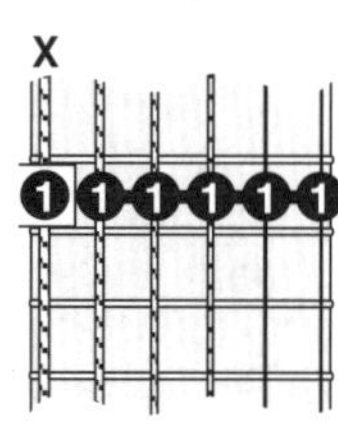

Maj7 Sharp Eleven

Chord Symbol **$Maj7^{\sharp 11}$**

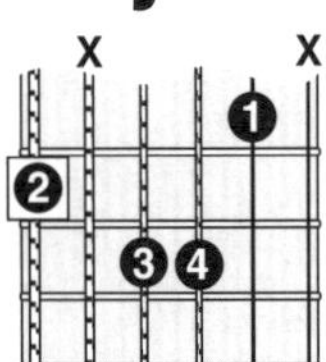
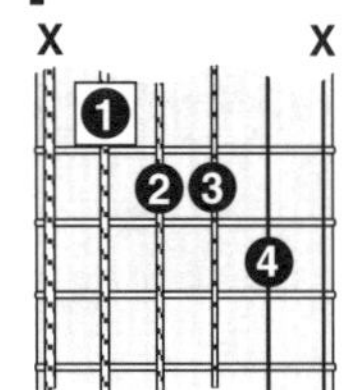
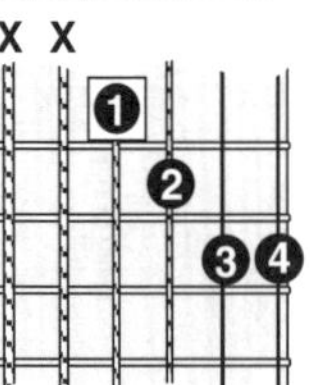

7 Sharp Eleven

Chord Symbol **♯**

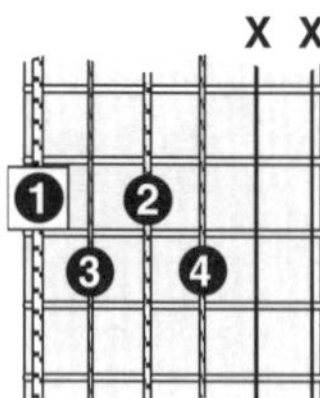
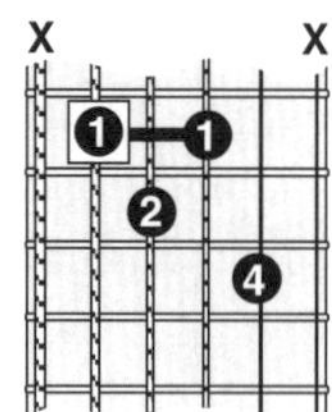
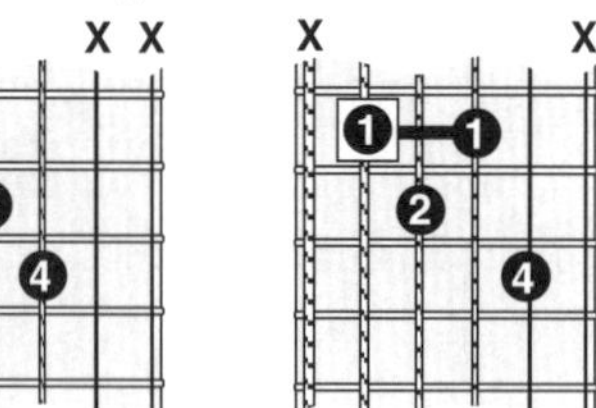
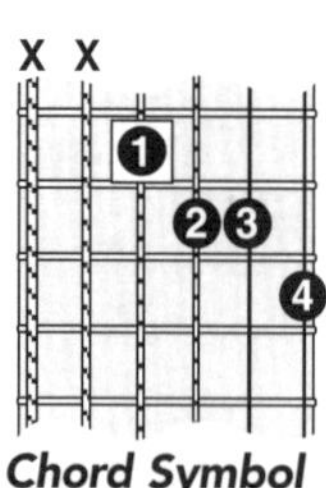

Maj Thirteenth

Chord Symbol **Maj13**

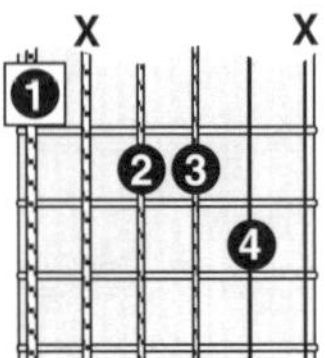
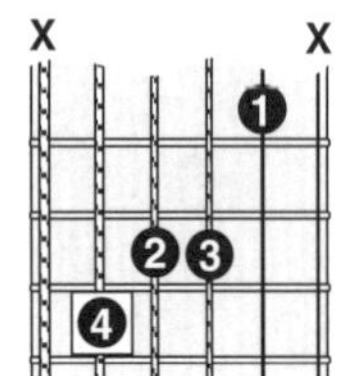
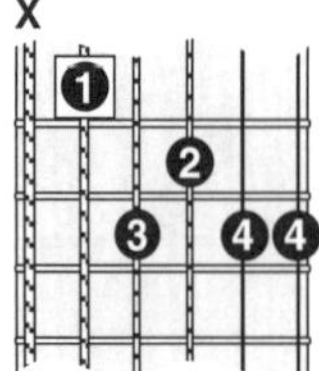

Thirteenth

Chord Symbol **13**

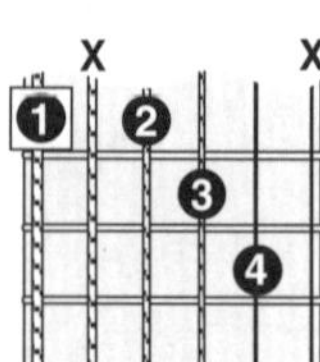
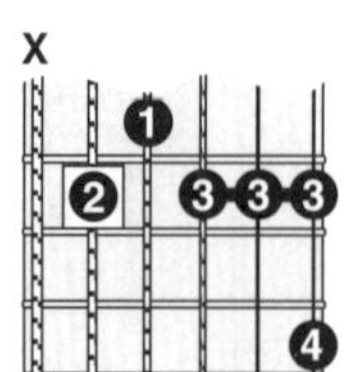

Minor Thirteenth

Chord Symbol **m13**

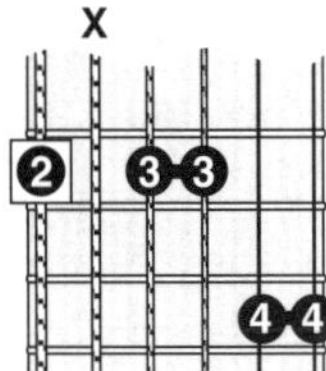
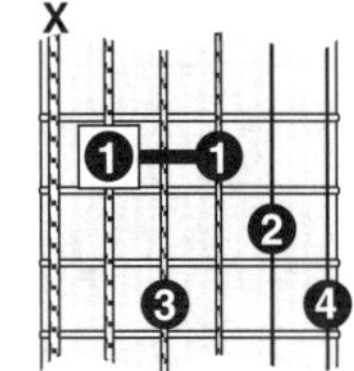
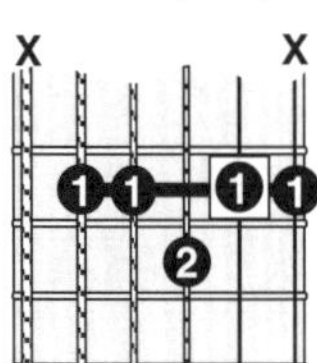

13 Flat Nine

Chord Symbol **$13^{\flat 9}$**

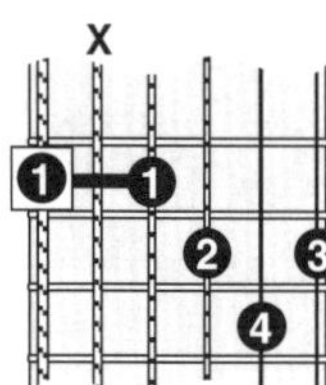
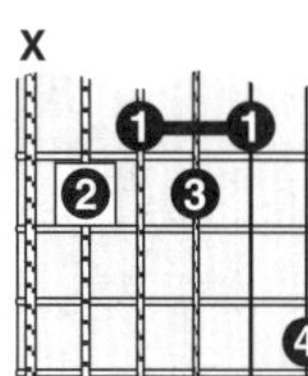
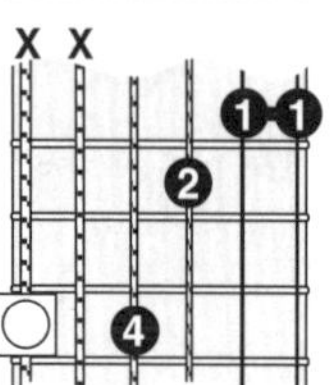

CHORD FORMULA CHART

The following chart gives a comprehensive list of chord formulas, together with an example based on the **C Scale**:

CHORD NAME	CHORD FORMULA	EXAMPLE	
Major	1 3 5	C:	C E G
Suspended	1 4 5	Csus:	C F G
Major add Ninth	1 3 5 9	Cadd9:	C E G D
Minor	1 ♭3 5	Cm:	C E♭ G
Augmented	1 3 ♯5	Caug:	C E G♯
Major Sixth	1 3 5 6	C6:	C E G A
Major Sixth add Ninth	1 3 5 6 9	C6/9:	C E G A D
Minor Sixth	1 ♭3 5 6	Cm6:	C E♭ G A
Minor Sixth add Ninth	1 ♭3 5 6 9	Cm6/9:	C E♭ G A D
Seventh	1 3 5 ♭7	C7:	C E G B♭
Seventh Suspended	1 4 5 ♭7	C7sus:	C F G B♭
Minor Seventh	1 ♭3 5 ♭7	Cm7:	C E♭ G B♭
Diminished Seventh	1 ♭3 ♭5 𝄫7	Cdim:	C E♭ G♭ B𝄫 (A)
Major Seventh	1 3 5 7	Cmaj7:	C E G B
Minor Major Seventh	1 ♭3 5 7	Cm(maj7):	C E♭ G B
Ninth	1 3 5 ♭7 9	C9:	C E G B♭ D
Minor Ninth	1 ♭3 5 ♭7 9	Cm9:	C E♭ G B♭ D
Major Ninth	1 3 5 7 9	Cmaj9:	C E G B D
Eleventh	1 3* 5 ♭7 9 11	C11:	C E* G B♭ D F
Minor Eleventh	1 ♭3 5 ♭7 9 11	Cm11:	C E♭ G B♭ D F
Thirteenth	1 3 5 ♭7 9 11* 13	C13:	C E G B♭ D F* A
Minor Thirteenth	1 ♭3 5 ♭7 9 11* 13	Cm13:	C E♭ G B♭ D F* A

*indicates that a note is optional.

A **double flat** 𝄫, lowers the note's pitch by **one tone**.
A **double sharp** 𝄪, raises the note's pitch by **one tone**.

SCALE TONE SEVENTH CHORD CONSTRUCTION

Scale tone seventh chords by adding another note of a third interval above scale tone triads, as illustrated in the following table:

7	B	C	D	E	F	G	A	B	*Third Interval*
5	G	A	B	C	D	E	F	G	*Third Interval*
3	E	F	G	A	B	C	D	E	*Third Interval*
C Scale: 1	C	D	E	F	G	A	B	C	
Chord Constructed:	Cmaj7	Dm7	Em7	Fmaj7	G7	Am7	Bm7♭5*	Cmaj7	
Chord Numeral:	Imaj7	IIm7	IIIm7	IVmaj7	V7	VIm7	VIIm7♭5	Imaj7	

*Another name for a minor seven flat five chord is half-diminished, indicated thus ∅.

From this example, the scale tone chords for any key will be:

I	II	III	IV	V	VI	VII	VIII
major7	m7	m7	maj7	7	m7	m7♭5 or (∅7)	maj7

SCALE TONE SEVENTH CHORDS IN ALL MAJOR KEYS

I	**II**	**III**	**IV**	**V**	**VI**	**VII**	**VIII**
Major7	**Minor7**	**Minor7**	**Major7**	**7**	**Minor7**	**Minor7♭5**	**Major7**
Cmaj7	Dm7	Em7	Fmaj7	G7	Am7	Bm7♭5	Cmaj7
Gmaj7	Am7	Bm7	Cmaj7	D7	Em7	F♯m7♭5	Gmaj7
Dmaj7	Em7	F♯m7	Gmaj7	A7	Bm7	C♯m7♭5	Dmaj7
Amaj7	Bm7	C♯m7	Dmaj7	E7	F♯m7	G♯m7♭5	Amaj7
Emaj7	F♯m7	G♯m7	Amaj7	B7	C♯m7	D♯m7♭5	Emaj7
Bmaj7	C♯m7	D♯m7	Emaj7	F♯7	G♯m7	A♯m7♭5	Bmaj7
F♯maj7	G♯m7	A♯m7	Bmaj7	C♯7	D♯m7	E♯(F)m7♭5	F♯maj7
Fmaj7	Gm7	Am7	B♭maj7	C7	Dm7	Em7♭5	Fmaj7
B♭maj7	Cm7	Dm7	E♭maj7	F7	Gm7	Am7♭5	B♭maj7
E♭maj7	Fm7	Gm7	A♭maj7	B♭7	Cm7	Dm7♭5	E♭maj7
A♭maj7	B♭m7	Cm7	D♭maj7	E♭7	Fm7	Gm7♭5	A♭maj7
D♭maj7	E♭m7	Fm7	G♭maj7	A♭7	B♭m7	Cm7♭5	D♭maj7
G♭maj7	A♭m7	B♭m7	C♭(B) maj7	D♭7	E♭m7	Fm7♭5	G♭maj7

ALTERED CHORDS

This next chord chart features chords which have a slight alteration to one of the given formulas, and are therefore called **altered chords**.

CHORD NAME	CHORD FORMULA	EXAMPLE	
Major Flat Fifth	1 3 ♭5	C♭5:	C E G♭
Minor Seventh Flat Fifth	1 ♭3 ♭5 ♭7	Cm7♭5:	C E♭ G♭ B♭
Seventh Sharp Fifth	1 3 ♯5 ♭7	C7♯5:	C E G♯ B♭
Seventh Flat Fifth	1 3 ♭5 ♭7	C7♭5:	C E G♭ B♭
Seventh Sharp Ninth	1 3 5 ♭7 ♯9	C7♯9:	C E G B♭ D♯
Seventh Flat Ninth	1 3 5 ♭7 ♭9	C7♭9:	C E G B♭ D♭
Seventh Sharp Fifth Flat Ninth	1 3 ♯5 ♭7 ♭9	C7♯5♭9:	C E G♯ B♭ D♭
Ninth Sharp Fifth	1 3 ♯5 ♭7 9	C9♯5:	C E G♯ B♭ D
Ninth Flat Fifth	1 3 ♭5 ♭7 9	C9♭5:	C E G♭ B♭ D
Ninth Sharp Eleventh	1 3 5 ♭7 9 ♯11	C9♯11:	C E G B♭ D F♯
Minor Ninth Major Seventh	1 ♭3 5 7 9	Cm9(maj7):	C E♭ G B D
Thirteenth Flat Ninth	1 3 5 ♭7 ♭9 11* 13	C13:	C E G B♭ D♭ F* A
Thirteenth Flat Five Flat Ninth	1 3 ♭5 ♭7 ♭9 11* 13	C13♭5♭9:	C E G♭ B♭ D♭ F* A

In altered chords, the notes to be altered are always written as part of the chord name, enabling you to construct the chord. For example, a **Cm7♯5♭9** (not listed above) is a **Cm7** chord with the fifth sharpened (**♯5**) and the ninth flattened (**♭9**). When you are working out a suitable shape for this chord, remember that the root note and/or the fifth note may be omitted.

Another type of alteration occurs when chord symbols are written thus:

Example 1: **G/F♯** bass
This indicates that a **G** chord is played, but using an F♯ note in the bass.

Example 2: **C/G** bass
This indicates a **C** chord with a **G** bass note.

Sometimes the word 'bass' will not be written (i.e. the symbol will be just G/F♯), but the same meaning is implied. These chords are often referred to as **slash chords**.

TUNING

TUNING TO ANOTHER INSTRUMENT

If you are playing along with another instrument, it is essential that your guitar be in tune with that instrument. Tune the open strings of your guitar to the corresponding notes of the accompanying instrument. E.g., To tune to a piano, tune the open 6th string to the **E** note on the piano, as shown on the keyboard diagram. Then tune your guitar to itself from this note, using the method outlined below, or tune each string of your guitar to those notes of the piano shown on the keyboard diagram.

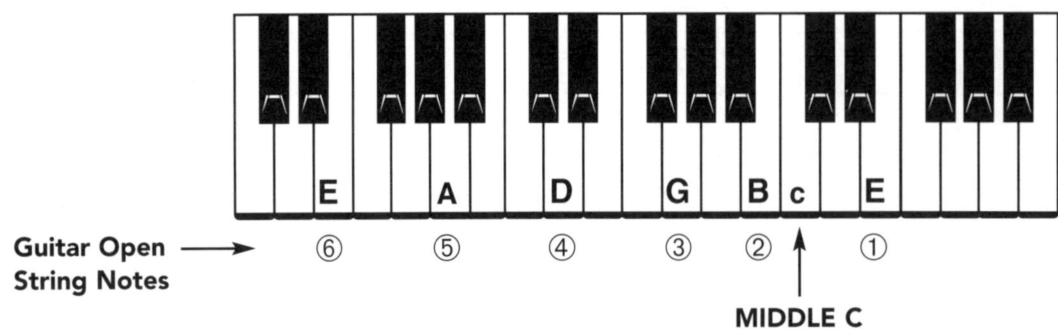

TUNING THE GUITAR TO ITSELF

If you do not have another instrument to tune to, you can tune the guitar to itself by using the following method. However, this usually requires many months of practice. You will probably need your music teacher or musician friend to help you tune when you are learning.

1. Place a left finger on the **6th** string (thickest string) at the **fifth** fret, and play the string.
2. Play the **open 5th string** (an **A** note). If this note sounds the same as the note you played on the **6th** string at the **fifth** fret, the **A** string is in tune.
3. If the open A string sounds **higher**, it means that it is **sharp**. Turn the tuning key slowly in a clockwise direction. This will lower the pitch of the string. Play the two strings again and compare the notes. Keep doing this until the open A string sounds the same as the E string at the fifth fret.
4. If the open A string sounds **lower**, it means that it is flat. Turn the tuning key slowly in a counter-clockwise direction. This will raise the pitch of the string. Play the two strings again and compare the notes. Keep doing this until the open A string sounds the same as the E string at the fifth fret.
5. Tune the **open 4th string** (a **D** note), to the note on the **fifth** fret of the **5th** string, using the method outlined above.
6. Tune all the other strings in the same way, except for the **open 2nd string** (a **B** note), which is tuned to the note produced on the **fourth** fret of the **3rd** string (see diagram).

E A D G B E

B

A D G E

5th Fret

6 5 4 3 2 1